ANGLO-BOER WAR

(South African War) 1899 - 1902

Historical Guide to Memorials
and Sites in South Africa

ANGLO-BOER WAR

(South African War) 1899 - 1902

Historical Guide to Memorials and Sites in South Africa

Jackie Grobler

Published in 2018 by

30° South Publishers (Pty) Ltd
16 Ivy Road
Pinetown 3610
South Africa
website: www.30degreessouth.co.za

Copyright © Jackie Grobler

Cover design and concept by Anthony Cuerden
Email: ant@flyingant.co.za
Page layout by Blair Couper

Copy-editing and proofreading by Idette Noomé,
Department of English, University of Pretoria

Printed by PINETOWN Printers (Pty) Ltd; Pinetown, KwaZulu-Natal

ISBN 978-1-928211-29-7

All rights reserved. No part of this publication may be reproduced, stored, manipulated in any retrieval system, or transmitted in any mechanical, electronic form or by any other means, without the prior written authority of the publishers, except for short extracts in media reviews. Any person who engages in any unauthorized activity in relation to this publication shall be liable to criminal prosecution and claims for civil and criminal damages.

Dedicated to the memory of my grandparents –
Gerhardus Grobler, who fought to the bitter end, and
Hester Grobler (born Van Zyl), who survived the Mafeking Concentration Camp

They are buried in a family cemetery on the farm Rhenosterfontein in the Klein Marico
▶ *About 20 km south of Zeerust, North West.*
◉ *About 150 m north of S25° 43.067, E26° 08.165.*

Contents

Preface 9

Acknowledgements 10

Abbreviations 11

Notes on terminology 11

Map of South Africa at the time of the Anglo-Boer War 12

1. Introduction 13
   1.1 Types of monuments, memorials and other forms of commemorative places 13
   1.2 The nature of Anglo-Boer War commemoration in South Africa 17

2. Prelude to the war 25
   2.1 How the war started 25
   2.2 The objectives of the war pursued by the opposing forces 27
   2.3 Some statistics on the war 28
   2.4 How the opposing sides prepared for the war 29

3. The military history of the war: the first year (11 October 1899–10 October 1900) 32
   3.1 Early encounters, 12 October–22 November 1899 32
   3.2 The sieges of Mafeking, Kimberley and Ladysmith 40
       3.2.1 Mafeking 40
       3.2.2 Kimberley 45
       3.2.3 Ladysmith 47
   3.3 The first British offensive up to Black Week, 23 November–15 December 1899 55
   3.4 The struggle continues, 16 December 1899–10 February 1900 63
   3.5 The second British offensive, 11 February–12 March 1900 69
       3.5.1 Western front 70
       3.5.2 Natal front 74
       3.5.3 Southern and south-eastern fronts 75
       3.5.4 British advance on Bloemfontein 78
   3.6 Occupation of the Boer capitals, 13 March–5 June 1900 79
   3.7 Persistent fighting, 6 June–10 October 1900 92

4. The guerrilla phase of the war (11 October 1900–31 May 1902) 114
   4.1 The guerrilla war in the ZAR 114
       4.1.1 11 October–31 December 1900 115
       4.1.2 ZAR January–June 1901 124
       4.1.3 ZAR July–December 1901 143
       4.1.4 The controversial history of the Bushveldt Carbineers 152
       4.1.5 ZAR January–May 1902 156

	4.2	The guerrilla war in Natal	166
	4.3	The guerrilla war in the Orange Free State	167
	4.4	The guerrilla war in the Cape Colony	187

5. The war of attrition 212

	5.1	Black South Africans and the war	212
		5.1.1 Concentration camps for black civilians	217
	5.2	The scorched earth policy	218
	5.3	Concentration camps for white civilians	221
		5.3.1 Gauteng	225
		5.3.2 Mpumalanga	226
		5.3.3 Limpopo	228
		5.3.4 North-West	228
		5.3.5 Free State	230
		5.3.6 KwaZulu-Natal	234
		5.3.7 Northern Cape	235
		5.3.8 Eastern Cape	236
		5.3.9 Other concentration camp places of remembrance	237
	5.4	Boer women and children who eluded internment in the camps	240
	5.5	The British blockhouse system	241
		5.5.1 Blockhouses and fortifications in the ZAR	242
		5.5.2 Blockhouses in the Orange Free State	243
		5.5.3 Blockhouses and fortifications in the Cape Colony	244
		5.5.4 Blockhouses in Natal	248
	5.6	Prisoners of war	248
		5.6.1 Prisoner-of-war sites for British soldiers	248
		5.6.2 Prisoner-of-war sites for Republican burghers	250
	5.7	The treatment of civilian opposition, perceived traitors and collaborators by both sides	253
		5.7.1 A well-known civilian death	253
		5.7.2 Those accused of treason, collaboration with the enemy and committing foul deeds	253
	5.8	Medical support and the war	262
		5.8.1 Hospitals and ambulances	263
		5.8.2 Medical personnel who died in battles/skirmishes or of wounds	268
		5.8.3 Medical personnel who died of disease	269
		5.8.4 Medical personnel who survived the war, but for whom there are memorial sites	271

6. Peace 273

6.1	Preliminary meetings	273
6.2	Vereeniging and Melrose House	274
6.3	The reasons for which the Boers surrendered	275

7. The legacy of the war 278

	7.1	The "age of the generals"	278
	7.2	Burgher monuments	280
		7.2.1 Gauteng	281
		7.2.2 North West	282

	7.2.3	Limpopo	283
	7.2.4	Mpumalanga	284
	7.2.5	Free State	287
	7.2.6	KwaZulu-Natal	294
	7.2.7	Eastern Cape	295
	7.2.8	Western Cape	296
	7.2.9	Northern Cape	296
7.3	Other Boer commemorative places	305
	7.3.1	Historical buildings closely associated with the war	305
	7.3.2	Sites associated with participants in the war	306
7.4	British memorials and gardens of remembrance	315
	7.4.1	Gauteng	315
	7.4.2	North West	318
	7.4.3	Limpopo	320
	7.4.4	Mpumalanga	321
	7.4.5	Free State	324
	7.4.6	KwaZulu-Natal	334
	7.4.7	Eastern Cape	339
	7.4.8	Northern Cape	342
	7.4.9	Western Cape	346
	7.4.10	British graffiti	348

8. Sources 351

Index 359

Preface

My passion for the history of the Anglo-Boer War was firmly implanted when, as a young boy, I regularly visited the Turffontein Concentration Camp Memorial in Johannesburg, which was close to where I grew up. It is therefore an honour and a pleasure to introduce this comprehensive field guide and reference work, not only to the general public, but also to established Anglo-Boer War scholars.

Jackie Grobler is well known for a wide range of publications on aspects of South African history and on the South African commemorative landscape. A wonderful example of his innovative style can be found in *The War Reporter: The Anglo-Boer War Through the Eyes of the Burghers*, which offers a fresh way of portraying almost a virtual history.

This extremely well-researched field guide and reference book provides both scholars and lay readers with the first detailed overview ever published of the war as seen through its memorials in South Africa. The book offers concise factual background information, and information pertinent to all those who are interested in the memorials of the war. The practical approach of the book is supported by the inclusion of GPS coordinates, providing added value to local and international tourists. The extensive references and source list testify to the exceptional scholarly merit of this work. The 1 200 photographs are the result of thorough field work, and the index is a handy quick reference.

Information is provided on well-known places of remembrance, and on obscure graves and monuments to now forgotten generals and soldiers. The author has included an important and detailed section on memorials dedicated to black people's participation in the war, and provides information on the location of black concentration camps, and on civilian casualties.

It is hard to believe that it took more than a century for the first comprehensive publication of this nature to appear. It is appropriate that it coincides with the 118th anniversary of the outbreak of the Anglo-Boer War.

This book makes a valuable contribution to South African historiography as a whole and to our knowledge of the Anglo-Boer War in particular. It is thus with confidence that I recommend the book, not only to serious researchers and scholars, but also to armchair enthusiasts. Hopefully it will encourage younger readers of all races to learn more about this very important conflict, which changed the face of South Africa. It is my hope that it will serve as an inspiration to all to contribute to South Africa's heritage in future.

Dr Arnold van Dyk
Bloemfontein

Acknowledgements

I would like to acknowledge with great gratitude the assistance of a large number of people whose support enabled me to complete this book. These include my wife, Elize Grobler, who visited many sites with me and whose excellent navigational skills helped me to find those sites; colleagues at the University of Pretoria, especially Fransjohan Pretorius, whose phenomenal knowledge of the war enriched my quest; former students at the University of Pretoria, such as Vicky Heunis, Louis Eksteen and Richard Wylie; Arnold van Dyk and Johan Looch of Bloemfontein, who provided me with valuable information on specific sites all over South Africa; Dirk Schellingerhout, who took me through Hankey, Port Elizabeth and Uitenhage, and helped me to locate a number of sites there and elsewhere; Stephan Botha, who assisted me in a similar way in Klerksdorp; Hannes and Marie van Zyl, who introduced me to the Stormberg Battlefield in the Eastern Cape; Vincent Horn, who guided me in Ladysmith; Jan Fourie and Willie Young, who took me to Moedwil; Ludi Schultze, who guided me at Mahikeng; Kees Els, who took me around Dordrecht; Dave Sutcliffe, who took me around the Majuba area and through the old Laings Nek tunnel; Arend Posthuma, Pierre Edwards and Chris van Wyk, who toured with me through parts of Mpumalanga; Paul Greyling, who introduced me to the Old Church Street Cemetery and the Rebecca Street Cemetery in Pretoria; Ludwig Ankiewics, who enlightened me on the Barnardskoppe area of Mpumalanga; Louis Changuion and Poog Henning, who led me on the trail of the Bushveldt Carbineers; Attie Meintjies, who showed me around Reitz and Graspan; Daniel Jacobs, who regularly sent me information about the location of sites that I was not yet aware of; my friends at the *Erfenisstigting* in Pretoria, especially Cecilia Kruger; Johan van Zyl and Dané van Wyk of the War Museum of the Boer Republics; and the numerous authors whose books, articles and other reports on struggle sites broadened my knowledge.

I provide GPS coordinates of places associated with the war as far as possible. However, I did not always have the facilities to take GPS readings when I visited sites, so I have sometimes had to rely on coordinates provided by others or as indicated on *Google Maps*. My thanks are hereby extended to friends who supplied coordinates.

To all those named above and to many others who helped me in various ways – I am grateful beyond words.

Photo acknowledgements

I took the vast majority of the photographs in this book, but a number of people made photographs available to me. In some cases, they took the initiative to send photographs to me for inclusion in the book. These contributors include Arnold van Dyk, Sonja Myburgh, Dirk Schellingerhout, Stephan Botha, Bert Gaffen, Claudia Gouws, Willie Engelbrecht, Emile Coetzee, Arthur Hall, Nico Jacobs, Robin Binckes, Daneel van Dyk and Karien Muller. In addition, I thank the Genealogical Society of South Africa, which, through Petro Coreejes-Brink, gave me permission to use photographs published on the Society's website. The generosity of all these photographers is gratefully acknowledged.

Abbreviations

General abbreviations used in the text and in photo captions

&	-	and
Ave	-	Avenue
CBD	-	central business district
c/o	-	corner of
CP	-	colour photograph
Dr	-	Drive
GPS	-	Global Positioning System
km	-	kilometre/kilometres
m	-	metre/metres
mm	-	millimetre/milllimetres
P	-	photograph
p.	-	page
pp.	-	pages
Rd	-	Road
St	-	Street
ZAR	-	*Zuid-Afrikaansche Republiek* (South African Republic)

Abbreviations used in the endnotes

ca	-	*circa* (about)
ed./eds	-	editor/editors
et al.	-	*et alii* (and others)
s.a.	-	*sine anno* (date of publication not indicated)
s.l.	-	*sine loco* (no place of publication given)
s.p.	-	*sine pagina* (no page number in the source referred to)

A note on terminology

Across the world, there are many wars that are known by more than one name, and names tend to change over time. Thus, for example, initially, to the Western Allies, what we now call the First World War (1914–1918) was known as the Great War but, after 1939, this name was replaced. The Second World War (1939–1945), as it is known to the Western Allies and to Germans, was officially known as the Great Fatherland War in the former Soviet Union.

From the start of the Anglo-Boer War (which is the preferred name in this book) in October 1899, the war has been referred to by a number of names. The Great Boer War and the South African War were amongst the first designations. Since it was primarily a war between the Boer Republics and the British Empire, and since the Boer and British authorities played the leading roles in both the course and the resolution of the conflict, the name Anglo-Boer War is preferred here.

South Africa is currently going through a phase of sweeping geographic name changes – especially in the four northernmost provinces. The new official place and street names are indicated in the text, but in descriptions of events associated with the war, the names that were in use at the time of the war are preferred.

ANGLO-BOER WAR   Historical Guide to Memorials and Sites in South Africa

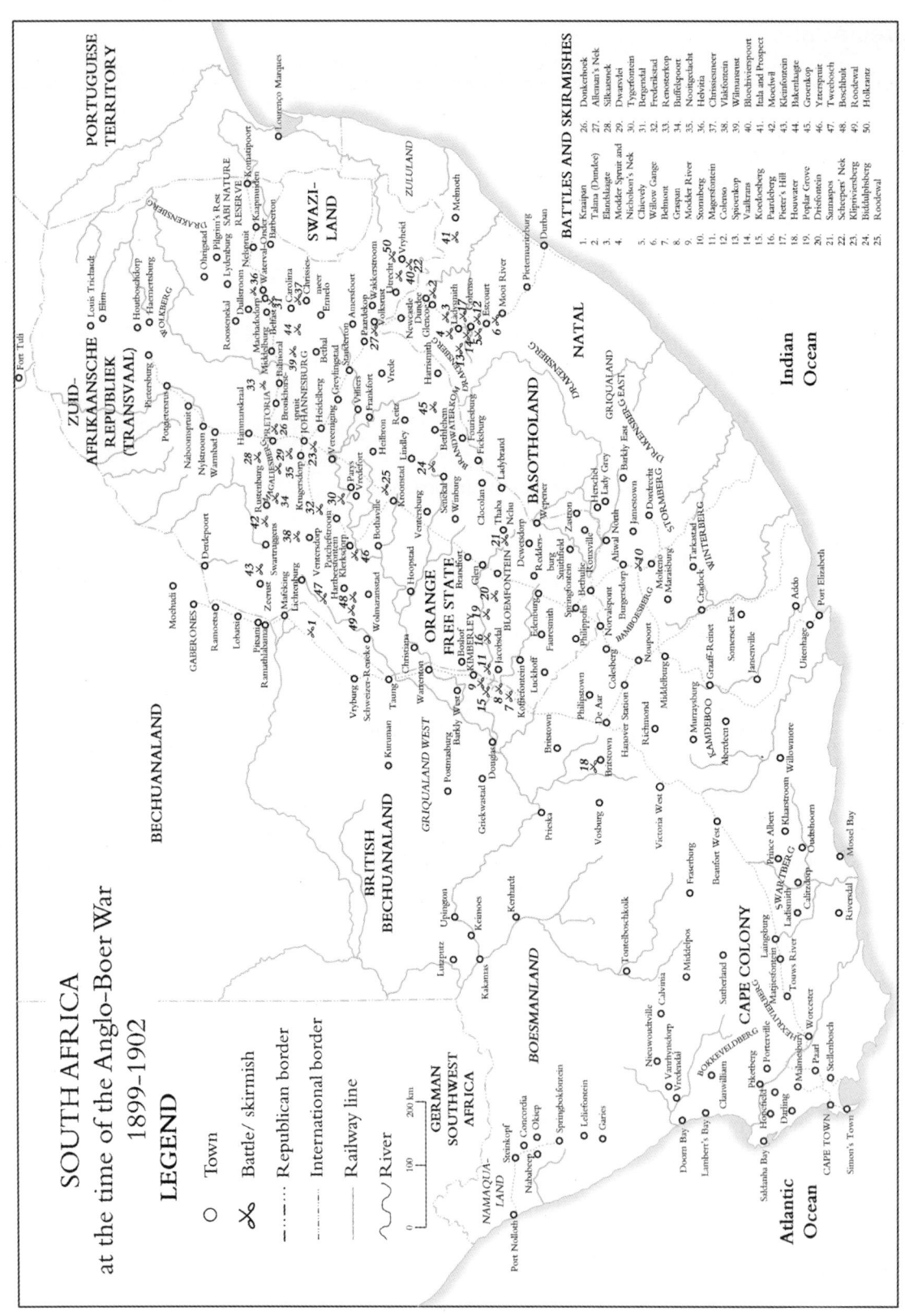

Part 1

Introduction

One of the most important legacies of any war is the memory that it leaves behind. That memory is not only kept alive, but is constantly constructed, reconstructed and redefined by places of remembrance of the war and by memorials erected to commemorate leaders, heroes, victims, victories and disasters associated with the war.

Although several wars, including the *difaqane* and the Struggle, have had a significant impact on South Africa's history and its future, no war in the history of South Africa has thus far left a more significant mark on the country's commemorative landscape than the Anglo-Boer War of 1899–1902. In addition to numerous battlefields, there are thousands of graves of victims of the war across the length and the breadth of the country. Furthermore, there are hundreds of monuments, memorial plaques, statues of participants in the war and other commemorative structures. These include more than a hundred memorials that commemorate women and children. Indeed, it seems as if there are more memorials for women in South Africa than in any other country in the world. An analysis of these sites of remembrance not only points to the broad range and variety of such places, but also to their distribution across the entire country.

1.1 Types of monuments, memorials and other forms of commemorative places

The places of remembrance relating to the Anglo-Boer War take various forms and can be classified as follows:

- **Historical landscapes and terrains**

Historical landscapes and terrains are large areas in which particular historical events occurred. One such landscape would be Tugela Heights – the area immediately north of the Thukela River, both above and below Colenso in KwaZulu-Natal. It is generally regarded as a particularly important terrain in the history of the Anglo-Boer War. The same can be said about the green, mountainous landscape of the eastern Free State and the arid Karoo landscape in the vicinity of Colesberg in the Northern Cape, where many a battle and skirmish were fought.

P1.1 Karoo landscape at Agtertang, east of Colesberg, Northern Cape.
◉ S30 40.515, E25° 19.139.

- **Monuments and memorials**

For the purposes of this book, monuments are regarded as structures specifically erected to commemorate people involved in or events of the war. This broad definition implies that monuments include memorials, which are generally regarded as objects created in memory of a person or event.

P1.1

P1.2

ANGLO-BOER WAR   Historical Guide to Memorials and Sites in South Africa

- **Statues and busts**

Statues and busts of the Anglo-Boer War represent two categories:

- Statues and busts of individual well-known participants
P1.2 Bronze bust (880 mm high) of a famous Boer commander, Christiaan de Wet, by sculptor Anton van Wouw.[1]
▶ War Museum of the Boer Republics, Monument Rd, Bloemfontein, Free State.
◉ *S29° 08.397, E26° 12.569.*

- Statues and busts of participants/victims in general
P1.3 Statue of a Boer mother and child in the Mafeking Concentration Camp, unveiled 1935.[2]
▶ *Martin St, Golf View, between Connaught St & N18 Nelson Mandela Dr, Mahikeng, North West.*
◉ *S25° 51.732, E25° 38.742.*

- **Memorial plaques**

British participants in the war – both individuals and military units such as regiments – were often commemorated on plaques attached to or built into the walls of churches, especially Anglican churches.

On the Boer side, memorial plaques related to the war were also affixed to the walls of churches. Most of these plaques commemorate the deaths in the war of burghers, women and children.

However, plaques are not limited to churches, and they can be found all over the South African commemorative landscape.

P1.4 Plaque: "To the glory of God and in memory of the Officers, NCOs [non-commissioned officers] and men, 1st Battn [Battalion] Gloucestershire Regiment, who were killed, or died during the Boer War, 1899-1900."
▶ *Municipal cemetery, on the southern side of Cemetery Rd, between Illings St & Mandela St, Ladysmith, KwaZulu-Natal.*
◉ *S28° 33.322, E29° 47.687.*

- **Historical markers**

Such markers often merely point out where specific events took place, sometimes adding a few details.

P1.5 Historical marker of polished granite at Fort Edward, "The base from where the Bushveldt Carbineers (Breaker Morant) launched their attacks on the Boer commandos in 1901."
▶ *Fort Edward is signposted, about 50 m south of the tarred road between Elim and Bandelierkop, less than 6 km west of Elim, Limpopo, on the crest of a low hill.*
◉ *S23° 11.331, E30° 00.013.*

 P1.3
 P1.4
 P1.5

---

1 Van Schoor 1989a, 97; Duffey 2008, 126 & 140.
2 Westby-Nunn 2000, 155.

Part 1 – Introduction

- **Historical buildings**

Buildings associated with specific events, important individuals or circumstances regarding the war can be found throughout South Africa.

> *P1.6 The Mount Nelson Hotel, a popular retreat during the war for British officers and prominent visitors, including the writer Rudyard Kipling and journalist Winston Churchill. The hotel even earned a nickname, "the Helot's Rest", due the presence of refugee mining magnates from Kimberley and Johannesburg. The Mount Nelson Hotel served as the headquarters of the British forces in South Africa for a while.[3] It is still in operation.*
> ▶ *76 Orange St, Cape Town, Western Cape.*
> ◉ *S33° 55.542, E18° 24.428 (Google Maps).*

- **Commemorative buildings**

Some buildings were erected specifically to commemorate participants or victims of the war.

> *P1.7 The church built in Middelburg, Mpumalanga, in 1906, specifically to commemorate the approximately 1 370 men, women and children who died in the concentration camps in Middelburg.[4]*
> ▶ *South St; on the premises of the Technical High School, Middelburg.*
> ◉ *S25° 46.572, E29° 27.615.*

- **Historical sites**

Across South Africa, there are sites with historical importance connected with the war, including battlefields, the sites of massacres, sites where negotiations took place, or where specific individuals were killed, wounded or captured.

> *P1.8 The Magersfontein battlefield, seen from Magersfontein Ridge, behind the site museum, looking towards the south. The British forces approached the Boer position across the plain, which provided no cover (see Part 3.3).*
> ▶ *Eastern side of an unnamed road between the S1320 and the S574, Northern Cape.*
> ◉ *Near S28° 57.201, E24° 44.071.*

- **Museums and museum exhibits**

There are several museums that contain or feature Anglo-Boer War exhibits in South Africa. The most important of these is the War Museum of the Boer Republics in Bloemfontein, which features numerous exhibits specifically on this war.

P1.6

P1.7

P1.8

---

3   Durbach 1988, 42; Westby-Nunn 2000, 36-38; Bossenbroek 2014, 244-245.
4   Van der Westhuizen & Van der Westhuizen 2000, 187; Richardson 2001, 255.

P1.9 War Museum of the Boer Republics, opened in 1931 by the then Prime Minister and former Boer leader, General J.B.M. Hertzog.[5]
▶ *Monument Rd, Bloemfontein, Free State.*
◙ *S29° 08.397, E26° 12.569.*

P1.10 The South African National Museum of Military History in Johannesburg. This museum focuses on the two World Wars, the War in Korea (1950-53) and the Border War in Angola, but does contain exhibits on the Anglo-Boer War.[6]
▶ *Entry from the western end of Eastwold Way, Saxonwold, Johannesburg, Gauteng.*
◙ *S26° 09.854, E28° 02.563 (Google Maps).*

- **Historical works of art**

It is not surprising that an event as historically important as this war inspired numerous works of art, including literature, music, painting and sculpture. Many art lovers regard sculptor Anton van Wouw's table sculpture entitled "Bad news" as a sculptural masterpiece inspired by the war.

P1.11 "Bad news".[7]
▶ *Art collection of the University of Pretoria, c/o Lynnwood Rd & Roper St, Pretoria, Gauteng.*
◙ *S25° 45.362, E28° 13.863 (Google Maps).*

- **Cemeteries and burial sites**

There are numerous types of burial sites.
- In most cases, the dead were buried in local cemeteries, and there is a wide variety of these:
  - There are municipal cemeteries in almost every city, town or township in South Africa. Most war victims were probably buried in such cemeteries. Many cemeteries contain a separate section with a British Garden of Remembrance or a Concentration Camp burial site. In some cemeteries, both are present, for example, in Klerksdorp in North West, and Harrismith in the Free State.
  - Cemeteries can also be found in the grounds of some churches, where war dead were often buried. An example is the grave of Major-General Penn-Symons in Dundee in KwaZulu-Natal (see P3.1.5). Sometimes, war dead were reinterred in mass graves on church grounds, for example, in the burghers' mass grave at the Dutch Reformed Church in Dundee (see P3.1.9).
  - Some of those who fell in the war were buried in private or family cemeteries, often on farms. An example is the graves of burghers who fell in the Battle of Silkaatsnek in North West (see P3.7.22-23)
  - There are military cemeteries, often on or near former battlefields. Some examples are the cemeteries at Elandslaagte in KwaZulu-Natal (P3.1.15), Sannaspos in the Free State (P3.6.7), Nooitgedacht in North West (P4.1.1.23) and many others.

P1.9

P1.10

P1.11

---

5   Van der Bank 2001, 90.
6   National Museum of Military History 2015.
7   Duffey 2008, 53-55.

- Concentration camp cemeteries were used. In some cases, the original cemeteries and graves are still there. Examples can be seen at Vredefort in the Free State (P5.3.5.10) and at Doornbult in the Northern Cape (P5.3.7.4). Sometimes, the dead were reinterred in mass graves on the site of the original cemetery, for example, at Irene in Gauteng (P5.3.1.3) and at Merebank in KwaZulu-Natal (P5.3.6.3). In some cases, the concentration camp dead were (for a variety of reasons) reinterred in new sites close to the original cemeteries, for example, at Aliwal North in the Eastern Cape (P5.3.8.1) and at Bethulie in the Free State (P5.3.5.1).
- There are a few war cemeteries where the concentration camp dead and the British dead were buried next to each other, with little or no attempt to separate the graves, for example, at Springfontein in the Free State (P5.3.5.12) and at Winburg in the Free State (P5.3.5.14).
- Both British soldiers and burghers who were killed in action or executed were often buried where they fell, and their graves are still there. Examples are the graves of Lieutenant S.R. Theobald, south of Middelburg in the Eastern Cape (P4.4.32) and of the joiners Pieter Bouwer and Adolf van Emmenis, south of Greylingstad in Mpumalanga (P5.7.8).
- In the course of time, interested parties have deemed it necessary to rebury the dead whose graves were threatened by urban growth or industrial expansion, such as mining activity. In such cases, the remains were sometimes buried in communal graves in public spaces where memorials were then erected, for example, the remains of people who died in the Turffontein Concentration Camp in Johannesburg in Gauteng (P5.3.1.4).

- **Historical names/place names**

Several prominent figures in the war have been honoured by having places named or renamed after them. In Pretoria, Roberts Heights (subsequently renamed Voortrekkerhoogte and recently renamed Thaba Tshwane) was named after the British Commander-in-Chief, Lord Roberts. Delareyville in North West was named after the Boer general, J.H. (Koos) de la Rey. Towns as far afield as Hartenbos on the south coast of the Western Cape, and Potchefstroom in North West have streets named after battles in which the Boers were victorious, such as the battles at Spioenkop and Colenso.

1.2 The nature of Anglo-Boer War commemoration in South Africa

It has been said that warfare "constructs the nation as a sacred community of sacrifice".[8] In the Anglo-Boer War, three "nations" were called upon to make enormous sacrifices, namely the Boers, the British and black South Africans. The Boers and British participants, and their descendants, have constructed themselves as communities of sacrifice in the places of remembrance they erected, especially in the form of monuments/memorials which were intended to pay fitting tribute in a lasting way[9] to the dead, to outstanding leaders and noteworthy martyrs. Black South Africans, however, did not construct themselves as communities of sacrifice by erecting monuments/memorials to those who died in this war, and to outstanding leaders and noteworthy martyrs, except in the case of Abraham Esau.[10]

The message conveyed by British places of remembrance is that the Imperial soldiers died while loyally serving the Empire – in other words, they were seen as having given their lives for the sake of their country. According to its inscription, the Imperial Light Horse Memorial at Mareetsane in North West was erected in memory of the non-commissioned officers and troopers killed in action at Mareetsane on 13 May 1900, and it exhorts those who gaze upon it to "[t]ell England, ye who pass this monument, we, who died serving her, rest here content".

CP on p. 302 Inscription on the Imperial Light Horse Memorial, Mareetsane, North West.
▶ On a low hill, eastern side of the N18 linking Vryburg and Mahikeng, 56.4 km from Mahikeng, 100 m from the road, signposted.
◙ S26° 11.122, E25° 13.802.

The Afrikaner community, as direct or spiritual descendants of the Boers of the two Republics, have gone through four stages of memorialisation of the Anglo-Boer War:

---

8 Hutchinson 2009, 1.
9 Casey 1987, 226.
10 Nasson 2003.

- The first stage began almost immediately after peace was declared. It lasted into the early 1930s. In this stage, it was often survivors of the war who took the initiative. Their aim was usually to honour the victims of the war – both the burghers who sacrificed their lives on the battlefield and the women and children who died in the concentration camps. Most burgher monuments and the first concentration camp memorials date from this period. It is noticeable that the majority of the early burgher monuments were erected on church grounds – in most cases, Dutch Reformed Churches. One reason is probably that these grounds belonged to local church congregations and did not fall under local government, which was under British control in the immediate post-war years.
- The second stage was related to the Great Trek centenary in 1938, when a number of memorials were erected. Examples include the Burgher Monument in the municipal cemetery in Rustenburg in North West (see P7.2.2.4) and the *Oudstryders* (Veterans') Memorial at Cottesloe in Johannesburg in Gauteng (see P7.2.1.4).
- The third stage began after 1948 and reached its height in the 1970s. During this period, the National Party government controlled Afrikaner commemoration. The era was characterised by serious attempts at the conservation of threatened sites and by the erection of vast commemorative structures such as the Burgher Monuments at Magersfontein in the Northern Cape (see P3.3.14), at Platrand, near Ladysmith in KwaZulu-Natal (see P3.2.3.19) and at Bergendal in Mpumalanga.

P1.13 Bergendal Burgher Monument. Unveiled in 1970, this tall memorial contains a mass grave as well as a list of the names of burghers who died in action in that part of the eastern Transvaal and were reinterred there.[11]
▶ *Signposted, clearly visible from the N4 national road between Belfast and Machadodorp, Mpumalanga, on the southern side of the road.*
◉ *S25° 44.072, E30° 06.198.*

Some of the new burgher monuments were erected on the civic squares of prominent towns, especially in the former Transvaal province, for example, in Bethal (see P7.2.4.3) and Delareyville (see P7.2.2.1). In Ermelo, the burgher monument originally unveiled by General Jan Smuts in front of the Dutch Reformed Church (see P7.2.4.6) was moved to the civic square in the centre of town and unveiled by Lieutenant-General Constand Viljoen (then Chief of the Army) in 1977.[12] However, after the African National Congress (ANC) took control of the municipal district in 1994, the burgher monument was moved back to the church grounds.
- The fourth stage was stimulated by the centenary of the Anglo-Boer War in 1999–2002. During this stage, private initiatives became the sole agents of commemoration, because, for political reasons, the ANC-led government was reluctant to involve itself in historical activities that seemed to be of little consequence to the black majority of the population. Nevertheless, a number of noteworthy memorials were constructed in this period. Examples are the Concentration Camp Memorial at Belfast in Mpumalanga (see P5.3.2.3) and the Burgher Memorial at Laborie, near Paarl in the Western Cape (see P7.2.8.1). As is often the case in Afrikaner history, those who participated in the commemorative activities were divided, with the Volkskomitee (People's Committee) of the Boer Republics representing the right wing and a variety of other movements representing the remainder of Afrikaner civil society.

P1.13

P1.14

---

11   Lombard 1989, 222-223.
12   Van der Westhuizen & Van der Westhuizen 2000, 103.

Part 1 – Introduction

The division in Afrikaner ranks seems to have dissipated as time went by, but there is still an urge to erect monuments or memorial plaques. Since the beginning of the second decade of this millennium, a few new memorials have been unveiled, including three on the grounds of the War Museum of the Boer Republics in Bloemfontein in the Free State; one in and one near the Concentration Camp Cemetery in Irene in Gauteng; one in the Eastern Cape one at Fort Amiel in Newcastle in KwaZulu-Natal; and one on Platrand, near Ladysmith in KwaZulu-Natal. It is of particular interest that one of the Irene monuments commemorates Lieutenant Bruce, the British officer in charge of the Irene Concentration Camp in the last phase of the war, who was known to be exceptionally sympathetic towards the fate of the Boer women and children in the camp.[13] This monument was erected by members of the Afrikaans community. Clearly, the crude stereotyping at the height of Afrikaner nationalism of all members of the British forces as cruel and vindictive individuals is now being redressed.

P1.14 Monument in honour of Lieutenant Bruce.
▶ *C/o Hamilton Rd & The Oval Circle, Irene, Gauteng.*
◉ *S25° 52.147, E28° 13.201 (Google Maps).*

It can be argued that the Afrikaner community initially constructed memorials as a means to come to terms with their defeat and loss in the Anglo-Boer War. It has been said that memorials are erected to assist communities on the losing side in conflicts to come to terms with their defeat, as happened in the American South after the Civil War of 1861–1865.[14] Hutchinson writes:

> Arguably, the trauma of defeat generates more radical energies. In the words of Nietzsche: 'If something is to be held in the memory it must be branded there: only that which never stops hurting stays in the memory.' Shattering defeats and conquests can inspire programmes of regeneration and irredentist campaigns for lost territories that can last for generations.[15]

Hutchinson suggests another perspective:

> [W]ar myths serve multiple functions including the creation of meaning out of suffering. Traumatic memories generally have a very long life, affecting not just the survivors but also their children and grandchildren, through identification of the latter with the suffering of their parents.[16]

This argument also applies to the concentration camp memorials in South Africa. Hutchinson takes John Gillis to task for taking too narrow a view:

> Gillis argues that what was publicly memorialised was selected by those with power, which reflected the interests of the official elites, of men rather than women and dominant rather than minority groups. ... [T]his perspective is too narrow. Instrumental interpretations of national myths as inventions of official elites fail to recognise the spontaneity and plurality of myth production, their different purposes, and neglect the question of popular resonance. The initiative in commemorating military sacrifice in national terms was often taken from below by a variety of social groups.[17]

This is what happened in the case of Anglo-Boer War memorialisation.

It is important to consider the role of places of remembrance in the construction of nationalistic communities. This certainly happened in South Africa, especially at the time of the Great Trek centennial, and also in the era of National Party rule from 1948 to about 1980. However, it would be incorrect to allege that a nationalistic agenda was predominant or even present in Afrikaner commemoration of the war throughout the 115 years since peace was declared. Clearly, in the first two decades, the main objective was to pay tribute to or to honour friends and family members who had died in the war. In the period since then, attempts to salvage Afrikaner history on the one hand, and on the other to foster nostalgia about the terrible ordeal of the burghers and civilians, and identify with the suffering of their forebears seemed to play the determining role.

Most of the memorials for members of the British Imperial forces were erected within the first decade after the end of the war. The First World War dwarfed the Anglo-Boer War by its magnitude and the high number of casualties. Since then, commemoration of the Anglo-Boer War has played insignificant second fiddle. The large Anglo-Boer War memorials in Cape Town (see P7.4.9.2), Durban (see P7.4.6.3), Kimberley (see P3.2.2.7), Grahamstown (see P7.4.7.8) and other towns across South Africa were all erected before 1914. The same applies for the Horse Memorial in Port Elizabeth (P2.3.3) and the colossal war memorial in Johannesburg. The Johannesburg memorial was originally

---

13   Brandt 2007, 454-455.
14   Grobler 2006, 199-225.
15   Hutchinson 2009, 7.
16   Hutchinson 2009, 15.
17   Hutchinson 2009, 11-12, citing J. Gillis, 'Introduction', in Gillis, J. (ed.) 1994. *Commemorations*. Princeton, NJ: Princeton University Press.

called the Rand Regiments War Memorial, and it was designed by British architect Sir Edwin Lutyens. The memorial features an ornate Angel atop a dome; the pillars inside list the Rand Regiments and soldiers from these regiments who died in the conflict. In 2002, the memorial was rededicated as the Anglo-Boer War Memorial in recognition of the men, women and children of all races and nations that lost their lives in the Anglo-Boer War.[18]

> P1.15 The Anglo-Boer War Memorial (formerly Rand Regiments War Memorial).
> ▶ Grounds of the South African National Museum of Military History, entry from the western end of Eastwold Way, Saxonwold, Johannesburg, Gauteng.
> ◉ Near S26° 09.854, E28° 02.563 (Google Maps).

Casey points out that
> ...many memorials are constructed of stone, the most durable natural substance available in large quantities. The very hardness and hardiness of granite or marble concretize the wish to continue honouring into the quite indefinite future – and thus, by warding off the ravages of time, to make commemoration possible at any (at least foreseeable) time. At the same time, a memorial in stone ... is a public presence and hence accessible to many potential viewers. *The distension in time is matched by a comparable extendedness in space.*[19]

This observation certainly holds true for the Anglo-Boer War memorials in South Africa. Most of them were built of stone – sandstone and granite were popular. Most of the statues are made of steel or bronze.

In Anglo-Boer War places of remembrance, the dead are often described as martyrs and are held up as role models.[20] Memorials usually underline superior moral qualities attributed to the dead, who are depicted less as examples of military excellence than as possessing ethical qualities of the highest order. They are held up as the embodiment of supreme human values. The moral qualities of the dead are also regarded as qualities that the living should emulate if the living are genuinely to honour those who died.[21] Thus the first South Australian officer who fell in the war is lauded on his gravestone as "A Loving Son, A Loyal Churchman, A Gallant Soldier" – a true embodiment of supreme human values.

> P1.16 Gravestone paying tribute to Lieutenant J.W. Powell.
> ▶ British Garden of Remembrance, western side of Station Rd, near the northern edge of town, Colesberg, Northern Cape.
> ◉ S30° 42.730, E25° 06.086 (Google Maps).

South African memorials to the white concentration camps proclaim four different messages:
• The memorials commemorate the women and children who were interned in such camps as heroines and child heroes, for example, in the inscription on the National Women's Monument in Bloemfontein.

> P1.17 Inscription on the National Women's Monument. It can be translated as "To our heroines and beloved children."
> ▶ Monument Rd, Bloemfontein, Free State.
> ◉ S29° 08.397, E26° 12.569.

P1.15

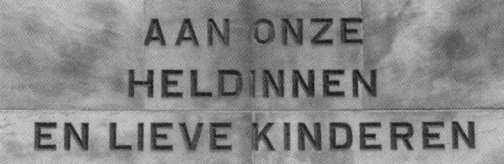
P1.17

P1.16

---

18   Walker s.a.(a).
19   Casey 1987, 226-227.
20   Hutchinson 2009, 6, citing Mosse, G. 1991. *Fallen soldiers*. Oxford: Oxford University Press.
21   King 1998, 15-16.

Part 1 – Introduction

- They are portrayed as innocent victims and/or casualties of a war over which they had no control whatsoever.

  P1.18 Statue by sculptor Jo Roos of a typical camp victim – an emaciated young girl staring with hopeless eyes at the rows of graves in the cemetery of the Pietersburg Concentration Camp (see also CP37 on p. 304).
  ▶ *Agaat St, Nirvana (Superbia – the industrial area), Polokwane, Limpopo Province.*
  ◉ *Entrance at S23° 54.568, E29° 26.254.*

  P1.19 Gravestone of Louis Hoffmann, who died in the Bethulie Concentration Camp on his fourth birthday. He is described as an "onskuldige slagoffer" (innocent victim).
  ▶ *Bethulie Concentration Camp Cemetery, to the east of Bethulie, Free State.*
  ◉ *S30° 29.089, E25° 59.954.*

- They are honoured as heroes and heroines who gave their lives for a universal cause, namely freedom and justice.

  P1.20 Entrance gate to the Springfontein Concentration Camp Cemetery, with graves visible in the background. This is a cemetery for babies and children who died in the Springfontein Concentration Camp before they could be baptized. The inscription is "Vir Vryheid en vir Reg" ("For Freedom and Justice").
  ▶ *Next to the S538 (road to Jagersfontein) in the north-western part of Springfontein, Free State.*
  ◉ *S30° 15.450, E25° 42.076.*

- They are also portrayed as citizens who had no option but to give their lives for a higher cause, namely the future of the nation – in this case, of the Afrikaner *volk*.

  P1.21 Memorial plaque unveiled at the Johannesburg Concentration Camp in 1941. The plaque states: "Opgerig ter nagedagtenis aan hulle wat die hoogste offer van liefde vir land en volk gebring het …" ("Erected in memory of those who made the highest sacrifice for love of [their] country and people …")
  ▶ *Maluti St, between Magaliesberg St and Endymion St, Suideroord, Johannesburg, Gauteng.*
  ◉ *S26° 16.322, E28° 01.412.*

Grave sites are an important category of Anglo-Boer War places of remembrance. Since more than 70 000 participants died in the war, of whom about two thirds were civilians, graves make up more than half of the places of remembrance. Of the approximately 70 000 who died, only a small number have marked graves that can be visited. These include the graves of some concentration camp victims, of burghers of the two Boer Republics, and of members of the British Imperial forces. The graves of members of the British forces make up the majority of marked graves. Very few marked graves of black victims have survived.

The gravestones of soldiers often have touching stories to tell which are not reflected in history books, which supply only cold and impersonal statistics. The municipal cemetery in Ladysmith in KwaZulu-Natal has a large British Garden of Remembrance. It contains, amongst many others, the grave of W.S. Smith, who died at the age of 24. In his *The Anglo-Boer War: A chronology*, P.G. Cloete notes that on 18 December 1899, "[f]our sentries of the Natal Carbineers as well as a number of blacks who were employed as trench diggers on Caesar's Camp, Platrand, [were]

P1.18

P1.19

P1.20

killed by Republican shelling".[22] Smith was one of those sentries. He is also listed on a plaque at Maritzburg College in Pietermaritzburg, where he went to school.

> P1.22 Memorial plaque in Victoria Hall at Maritzburg College for former pupils of the College who died serving the British forces in the Anglo-Boer War. Smith's name is fifth from the top.
> ► College Rd, Pietermaritzburg, KwaZulu-Natal.
> ◉ S29° 36.995, E30° 22.873 (Google Maps).

The inscription on his gravestone has a more touching message: "Erected by his loving parents in sacred memory of William Craighead Smith ("Craig"), Natal Carbineers, eldest and dearly beloved son of William Craighead and Janet Smith, who was killed by a Boer shell ...

> A light has from our household gone,
>   A voice we loved is stilled;
> A place is vacant at our hearth,
>   That never can be filled."

> P1.23 The gravestone of W.C. Smith of the Natal Carbineers, who was killed on 18 December 1899, aged 24 years.
> ► British Garden of Remembrance, Municipal Cemetery, southern side of Cemetery Rd, between Illings St & Mandela St, Ladysmith, KwaZulu-Natal.
> ◉ S28° 33.322, E29° 47.687.

Sadly, the names of the unknown number of black trench diggers who were also killed by that deadly Boer shell have disappeared from history and from memory.

Some cases stand in stark contrast to the melancholy inscription on Smith's gravestone, as a sense of humour seems to have accompanied the erection of some gravestones. The Commonwealth War Graves section of the Maitland Cemetery in Cape Town contains a British Anglo-Boer War Garden of Remembrance. Here, the epitaph on the grave of a soldier who died by falling from a train near Worcester in the south-western Cape en route to the front simply reads: "Hard Luck".

> P1.24 The gravestone of Private E. Millen, Argyle & Sutherland Highlanders, who died when he fell from a train near Worcester on 17 November 1899.
> ► Anglo-Boer War Garden of Remembrance, Commonwealth War Graves section, Maitland Cemetery, Voortrekker Rd, Cape Town, Western Cape.
> ◉ S33° 55.022, E18° 32.280 (Google Maps).

The messages in the inscriptions on some graves call on visitors to engage with the deceased and become involved. A plaque on a grave in Kimberley requests visitors to act as links between the soldier buried there and his grieving mother: "Those who may visit this dear grave, please send a blade of grass or a green leaf from beside it to his poor mother."

P1.21

P1.22

P1.23

P1.24

---
22   Cloete 2000, 75.

P1.25 Plaque on the grave of a British soldier.
▶ *West End Cemetery, c/o Green St & Reserve Rd, Kimberley, Northern Cape.*
◉ *S28° 44.078, E24° 44.170 (Google Maps).*

Gravestones of participants in war, including the Anglo-Boer War, sometimes carry messages that not everybody would agree with. H.W. Howard, the Superintendent of the "Burgher Camp" in Klerksdorp – one of the most notorious concentration camps of the war – passed away on 29 December 1901. The inscription claims that his gravestone was "Erected in affectionate memory by the Staff of the Burgher Camp".

P1.26 Grave of Civilian Superintendent H.W. Howard (42), Superintendent Burgher Camp, Klerksdorp, who died on 29 December 1901.
▶ *British Garden of Remembrance, municipal cemetery, Klerksdorp, North West, near Margaretha Prinsloo St, between O.R. Tambo St & Kadria St.*
◉ *S26° 52.576, E26° 40.130.*

While it may perhaps be argued that the staff liked him, it seems that only a few (if any) of the Boer women who struggled to survive in the Klerksdorp concentration camp would have held fond memories of Howard. Mrs Alida Badenhorst recorded in her diary on Christmas Day 1901, when it became known that the Superintendent was very ill, that one woman said: "I want to see him perish like the beasts." Four days later, when they heard that Howard had died, Mrs Badenhorst wrote: "The women clamoured for his death and he is dead … So our hard, stern Baas himself will be amongst the many who have perished this month."[23]

Some gravestones contain specific messages, including blunt accusations. The grave of G.B. Mousley is in the municipal cemetery in Ficksburg in the eastern Free State. He was an English-speaking citizen of the Republic of the Orange Free State who was shot by the Boers on a charge of having assisted the British forces in their war effort. His grave is adorned with an impressive grave monument depicting a woman kneeling next to a cross and staring despondently into the distance. Mousley's wife insisted that an indictment be expressed on his gravestone.[24]

P1.27 Grave of G.B. Mousley. The inscription on the gravestone reads: "Erected by Susan Mousley (née Ballot), the beloved wife of G.B. Mousley of 'Madrid' Dist. Bethlehem who was shot in cold blood near Ficksburg Nov 17th 1900, aged 37. 'Vengeance is mine, I will repay saith the Lord'."
▶ *Old town cemetery, Ficksburg, Free State. Entry from Veld St, near c/o Veld St & Piet Retief St.*
◉ *S28° 52.027, E27° 52.637.*

How important are such places of remembrance as sources on the war? Memorials and monuments are by their very nature primary sources on the past. They provide information on a specific person or persons and/or events and incidents, and convey some information on the people who decided to build these monuments or to declare a place a monument or heritage site, on how they approached this task, and on their objectives and views. Monuments reflect the *Zeitgeist* of the time of their erection.

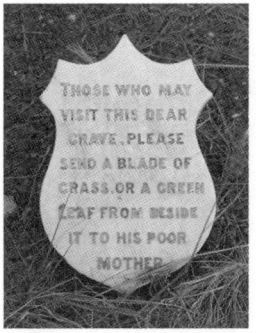  

P1.25   P1.26   P1.27

---

23   Badenhorst 1923, 279.
24   Blake 2010, 220-229.

An inscription on the concentration camp monument erected in 1908 in the Mineralia Cemetery in Middelburg, Mpumalanga, calls on all those who visit the camp graves to remain loyal to their people and their history, and to tell their descendants about it. This clearly reflects a patriotism undimmed by the horrors of the camps or by the Boer Republics' defeat.

P1.28 Plaque on the Concentration Camp memorial in the Mineralia Cemetery, Middelburg, Mpumalanga, unveiled in 1908. The wording can be translated thus: "Love the Fatherland. People of the Transvaal, cherish your history as a treasure and retell from generation to generation how many loved ones rest in the earth for love of fatherland and nation."
▶ *Oranje St, Middelburg, Mpumalanga.*
◙ *S25° 47.367, E29° 27.793.*

There are a large number of commemorative places of the Anglo-Boer War – memorials, plaques, gravestones, and works of art. Each reflects some aspect of the war and its impact. Taken together, they assist the visitors who gaze upon them to gain some understanding of what happened in the war, thus contributing to knowledge about the war.

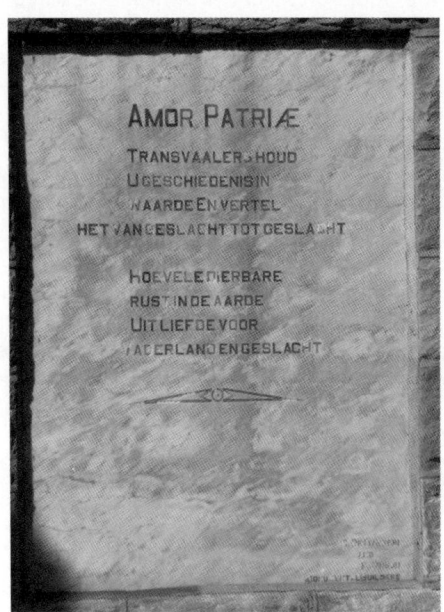

P1.28

Part 2

Prelude to the war

The fighting of the (Second) Anglo-Boer War was mainly restricted to the borders of what is today the Republic of South Africa, with the exception of some minor confrontations in what is now Botswana and Zimbabwe, but the war's significance extends beyond South Africa itself. From a British perspective, it was the biggest war since the Napoleonic Wars, which were fought in Europe at the beginning of the 19th century. Furthermore, soldiers from various parts of the British Empire, including Australia, New Zealand and Canada, were shipped to South Africa. For the Australians, it was the biggest war in which they were involved until the First World War. Moreover, volunteers from various countries in Europe, from Russia and from the United States of America joined the Boer forces. Boer prisoners of war were sent to camps in Bermuda and St Helena Island, as well as to India and Ceylon (now Sri Lanka). In view of all these circumstances, one may argue that the Anglo-Boer War was the first truly international conflict of the 19th century.

2.1 How the war started

Politically speaking, in the 1890s, the area now known as South Africa consisted of two Boer Republics and two British colonies. The sovereignty of both Boer Republics, namely the *Zuid-Afrikaansche Republiek* (the ZAR, or the Transvaal) and the Orange Free State, was already recognised by Britain in the 1850s. The causes of the war may be traced to a change in British colonial policy towards southern Africa in the 1890s. The discovery of the rich gold reef on the Witwatersrand in the Transvaal in 1886 was the decisive factor in this change. The reef turned out to be the richest single source of gold in the world, which made the Transvaal the economic hub of South Africa. As mining activity increased in the 1890s, Britain became determined to gain control of this gold-producing area, but it could not do so unless the Transvaal government could be removed. The only way to achieve this objective seemed to be through war. Moreover, the Transvaal posed a challenge to British supremacy in South Africa. From Britain's perspective, this obstacle could be removed by forcing the Transvaal government to concede that Britain had a right to intervene in the domestic affairs of the Republic.[25]

War clouds began to gather from the time of Sir Alfred Milner's arrival in South Africa in 1897 as Governor of the Cape Colony and British High Commissioner for South Africa. Milner regarded it as his mission and destiny to gain political control of the Transvaal for Britain. By the winter of 1899, as tensions approached breaking point, President M.T. (Theunis) Steyn of the Orange Free State invited President S.J.P. (Paul) Kruger of the Transvaal and Milner to Bloemfontein to discuss a solution to the issue of voting rights for foreign miners on the Witwatersrand, whom the Kruger government regarded as *Uitlanders* (Outlanders). The conference at the Railway Bureau in Bloemfontein lasted from 31 May to 5 June. A solution was not found, and Milner decided to break off the negotiations. It was reported that when Kruger left the meeting, he flung an accusation at Milner – he said: "It is our country you want!"[26]

P2.1.1 The Railway Bureau building, designed by architect D.E. Wentink and built in 1898–1899.[27]
▶ *South western c/o Harvey Rd & Charlotte Maxeke St, Bloemfontein, Free State.*
◉ *S29° 07.136, E26° 13.546 (Google Maps).*

P2.1.1

---

25   Porter 1980, Chapters 3-8; Smith 1996; Du Pisani 1999, 205-215.
26   Pakenham 1982, 68; Van Schoor 2009, 106-107.
27   Richardson 2001, 173; Van der Bank 2001, 17.

P2.1.2 There are a number of statues and busts of Paul Kruger in South Africa. The best-known statue (shown here) portrays him in formal dress as president of the ZAR. It is the centre-piece of the Kruger Monument designed by Anton van Wouw.[28]
▶ *Church Square, in the centre of Pretoria, Gauteng.*
◉ *S25° 44.788, E28° 11.284 (Google Maps).*

P2.1.3 The best-known full-figure statue of Steyn was designed by Anton van Wouw. It portrays Steyn in formal attire as president of the Orange Free State. It was unveiled in 1929.[29]
▶ *In front of the Old Administration Building, University of the Free State; entrance at c/o Nelson Mandela Ave & University Rd, Bloemfontein, Free State.*
◉ *S29° 06.392, E26° 11.556 (Google Maps).*

P2.1.4 There is no statue of Milner in South Africa. He is commemorated on a plaque in St George's Cathedral, in Cape Town. This cathedral contains numerous Anglo-Boer War commemorations.
▶ *C/o Wale St & Queen Victoria St, Cape Town, Western Cape.*
◉ *S33° 55.461, E18° 25.139 (Google Maps).*

On 22 September 1899, the British Cabinet unanimously decided on the wording of an ultimatum which was to be handed to the ZAR about four weeks later, but the existence of the ultimatum was kept secret. In the same month, the British War Office began to dispatch thousands of troops to South Africa. The government of the ZAR reacted to these developments by calling up its burgher force on 27 September. The government of the Orange Free State called up its own Republican burgher force on 2 October 1899.[30] The burgher commandos immediately began to congregate on the borders of the Republics, but remained inside the Republics.

P2.1.5 Statue by sculptor Danie de Jager of a burgher leaving for the front, greeting beloved family members – a wife and child[31] (see CP1 on p. 129).
▶ *Garden of the War Museum of the Boer Republics, Monument Rd, Bloemfontein, Free State.*
◉ *S29° 08.397, E26° 12.569.*

P2.1.6 In the western Orange Free State, the burghers of Jacobsdal congregated on a low hill on the outskirts of the town, where each of them placed a stone with his name carved into it on a cairn.[32] This memorial, which was erected in 1999, contains four of the original stones.
▶ *Municipal cemetery, De Villiers St, Jacobsdal, Free State.*
◉ *S29° 08.091, E24° 46.510.*

P2.1.7 The Jacobsdal cairn was repaired and re-dedicated in 1999, on the same spot and exactly 100 years after the original stones were stacked in this place.

P2.1.2 P2.1.3 P2.1.4 P2.1.5

28   Breytenbach 1954.
29   Van Schoor 1989b, 95-96.
30   Cloete 2000, 27-31.
31   Van Schoor 1989c, 106-107.
32   Oosthuizen ca 2000, 16-17.

▶ *Saunders Heights, on the grounds of the Jacobsdal Agricultural High School, on the outskirts of Jacobsdal, Free State. The area around the cairn is surrounded by a security fence. The gate keys are available from the school office.*
◉ *S29° 07.376, E24° 44.994.*

Once he had the assurance of the Republic of the Orange Free State that it would support him, President Kruger handed his own ultimatum to the British representative in Pretoria on 9 October. He did not want to give Britain an opportunity to gather more troops on the Transvaal's borders. The ultimatum demanded that British troops withdraw from the borders of the Boer Republics and that reinforcements which had disembarked since the start of June return to Britain. However, Britain rejected the ultimatum on the afternoon of 11 October, which served as the official declaration of war with the Transvaal. The Republic of the Orange Free State immediately joined the war on the ZAR's side.[33] The fact that it was the ZAR, and not Britain, that actually issued an ultimatum subsequently allowed Britain to portray the Republics as aggressors that threatened British interests.[34]

P2.1.8 This granite marker indicates the place where the ultimatum was handed to the British agent at his residence in Sunnyside, Pretoria (the house no longer stands).[35]
▶ *North-western c/o Rissik St & Steve Biko St, Sunnyside, on the grounds of the Tempo Residence of the Tshwane University of Technology; entry through the security gate next to Rissik St. Memorial on the edge of a lawn between the buildings.*
◉ *S25° 45.348, E28° 12.022.*

2.2　The objectives of the war pursued by the opposing forces

Britain's objective was simple. It wanted to force the Republics into submission and to incorporate both into a unified British South Africa. This objective could be accomplished by invading the Republics, occupying their capital cities, destroying the armed forces of both, and then imposing Britain's will on the governments of the Republics.

The British faced a problem that was to influence on their strategy at the start of the war considerably: in this last major war before the advent of the age of the automobile, the British forces were, especially in the initial phases of the war, almost wholly dependent on railway lines for transporting their war supplies. As a result, during the first ten months of the war, the location of the railway lines in South Africa largely determined the course of events.

The main railway line from Natal to the Transvaal played an important role. The border between Natal and the Boer Republics ran along the Drakensberg, a mountain range that could only be traversed via a limited number of mountain passes. The railway line crossed this mountain range at Majuba Hill. The British decided to concentrate their main force along this railway line. They planned to follow the railway line across the mountains into the Republics, and in the process they would achieve a secondary goal – to avenge the defeat they had suffered at the hands of the Boers at Majuba in 1881, in the First Anglo-Boer War.

The main Boer objective was equally clear, namely to safeguard their freedom and independence. The campaign plan was to invade Natal from the north and the west, to overwhelm the British garrisons in Newcastle,

P2.1.6

P2.1.7

P2.1.8

33　Amery I 1900, 373; Cloete 2000, 31-32; Grobler 2004, 1-2.
34　Creswicke I ca 1902, 185.
35　Greyling 2000, 76-77.

Dundee and Ladysmith, and then move on to Durban and occupy the port. Other Republican forces were to cross the western borders of the two Republics, to occupy Mafeking, Vryburg and Kimberley along the railway line from the Cape to Bechuanaland and then move south to support an expected pro-Republican uprising of Cape Afrikaners. The Boers believed that the British government would soon negotiate for peace, as it had done in 1881, since the war would be prohibitively expensive, and the British public would not be prepared to keep on paying for it. Lastly, the Boers hoped to call on friendly nations in Europe with which they had diplomatic ties, such as Germany, France and Russia, as well as the United States of America, to put pressure on Britain to end the war. The plan looked good on paper, but the commander of the Transvaal forces, the elderly and cautious Commandant-General Piet Joubert, was not convinced that it was realistic, and failed to implement the plan with any urgency.[36]

P2.2.1 This statue of Joubert and his wife Hendrina portrays them at Majuba in 1881.[37]
▶ *On the civic square, south-western c/o Thabo Mbeki St & Landdros Maré St, Polokwane, Limpopo.*
◉ *S23° 54.720, E29° 27.105.*

P2.2.2 Bust of Piet Joubert, portraying him in his uniform as Commandant-General.[38]
▶ *At Fort Schanskop, grounds of the Voortrekker Monument, Eeufees St, Pretoria, Gauteng.*
◉ *S25° 46.628, E28° 11.035.*

2.3 Some statistics on the war

The combined white population of the two Boer republics probably did not exceed 300 000 people. Of those, a maximum of 57 000 were able men between the ages of 16 and 60. In addition, about 13 000 Afrikaners from the Cape Colony and Natal joined the Republican cause. There were also a small number of foreign volunteers, mainly from Continental Europe, as well as a sprinkling of Americans – altogether about 2 000 men.[39] Like the burghers, they received no pay for their services while on commando.

P2.3.1 Memorial for the foreign volunteers who fought on the side of the Republics.
▶ *In the garden of the Old Dutch Reformed Church Parsonage (now the Utrecht Museum), Church St, Utrecht, KwaZulu-Natal.*
◉ *S27° 39.342, E30° 19.128.*

P2.3.2 Irish Monument. This memorial, which was designed by Jan van Wijk and was unveiled by Mrs Betsie Verwoerd in 1975, was moved from Johannesburg to Orania in 2002. It commemorates the Irish volunteers who fought on the Republican side.[40]
▶ *R369, Orania, Northern Cape*
◉ *S29° 48.715, E24° 25.174.*

P2.2.1

P2.2.2

P2.3.1

36	Mouton 1957, 232; Judd & Surridge 2003, 106.
37	Grobler 2012, 3.
38	Malan 1989, 188.
39	Pretorius 2001b, 21.
40	Van Wijk 1989, 138.

Part 2 – Prelude to the war

On the eve of the war, Britain had a population of approximately 30 million people. Its self-governing colonies, which contributed soldiers to fight on the British side, had a combined population of several million people. This number excludes British India, since the British Prime Minister, Lord Salisbury, announced even before the outbreak of the war that only white soldiers would be used in South Africa.[41] Even so, the British War Office had a vast reservoir of manpower from which soldiers could be drawn.

When the war broke out, there were already about 30 000 British soldiers in South Africa. This number steadily grew, reaching 250 000 by mid-1900. This excludes men recruited in South Africa itself, especially in Natal and the Cape Colony, to fight for "queen/king and country". By the end of the war, a total of about 450 000 men had fought on the British side. Thus the number of soldiers fighting on the British side was considerably larger than the combined total Republican population of both Boer Republics.[42]

In addition to men, the British authorities brought in tens of thousands of horses – eventually a total of about a quarter of a million – to South Africa for the use of the soldiers. The horses came chiefly from Britain, North America, Hungary and Australasia. It is estimated that over the duration of the war the British Army Remount Department provided about 520 000 horses, of which about 350 000 were killed in action or died. In addition, the Remount Department provided 150 000 mules, of which 50 000 perished.[43]

P2.3.3 The famous horse memorial erected in 1905. It commemorates the importance and use of horses by the British forces in the war (see also CP22 on p. 299).
▶ *C/o Russell Rd & Cape Rd, Port Elizabeth, Eastern Cape.*
◉ *S33° 57.728, E25° 36.528 (Google Maps).*

P2.3.4 A monument in memory of the more than 500 000 horses that died in the Anglo-Boer War.
▶ *In the garden in front of the Lalapanzi Hotel. On the eastern side of the N1, about 28 km south of Makhado (formerly Louis Trichardt).*
◉ *S23° 16.630, E29° 49.735.*

A large percentage of the British soldiers were professionally trained, but those from Canada, Australia and New Zealand, and from the British colonies in South Africa, were often civilian volunteer conscripts.

As for the Boers, neither the officers nor the ordinary soldiers, called burghers, had received any formal military training whatsoever, with the exception of fewer than a thousand artillerists. The Boer military units, known as commandos, were true citizen armies – often grandfather, father and son fought side by side – and officers were elected by the burghers themselves. Many of the Boers had grown up on farms, so they knew the veld and had learned how to use rifles from an early age. Generally speaking, they were excellent marksmen and they had an inborn knowledge of the terrain on which the war was fought. This knowledge gave them a tremendous advantage over the British.

2.4 How the opposing sides prepared for the war

The Boers were more or less ready for war when negotiations finally broke down in 1899. Ever since 1896, when the Outlanders and the mine owners had failed in their attempt to topple President Kruger's government in an uprising

P2.3.2

P2.3.3

P2.3.4

---
41 Cloete 2010, 24.
42 Pretorius 2001b, 21.
43 Holt 1958, 126.

in Johannesburg, supported by an invasion from the Cape Colony (the infamous Jameson Raid), the Transvaal government had bought modern arms. The Republic of the Orange Free State had done likewise. Hence, by the start of the war, about 100 000 of the most modern rifles available had been purchased in Europe, together with about 50 million rounds of ammunition.[44]

Most of these rifles were German 7 mm Mauser magazine rifles, the best rifles in the world at that time. As the war dragged on, the Boers ran out of ammunition and their Mausers became useless. As a result, by the end of the war, virtually all the Boers used standard British army rifles which they had seized from the British forces.

In addition to rifles, the Boers (especially the Transvaal military authorities under Commandant-General Piet Joubert) bought a number of field and siege guns in the last few years before the war. Several of these were placed in the formidable stone fortresses that were constructed between 1896 and 1899 on low hills around the capital city, Pretoria.

> P2.4.1 The four forts constructed around Pretoria are Fort Schanskop, Fort Klapperkop, Fort Wonderboompoort and Fort Daspoortrand. In the end, the Boers did not use these forts to defend Pretoria during the war, but the British stationed military units in them for defensive purposes after occupying Pretoria in June 1900.[45]
> ▶ Fort Schanskop is on the grounds of the Voortrekker Monument, Eeufees St, Pretoria, Gauteng. There are a number of Anglo-Boer War-related exhibits at the Fort, including a small museum and busts, as well as paintings of prominent role-players on the Boers' side.
> ◉ S25° 46.628, E28° 11.035.

The Transvaal government also constructed a fort in Johannesburg, around the existing prison buildings on Hospital Hill on the northern side of the city. This fort was also not employed for military purposes by the Boers, but the British used it after their occupation of Johannesburg in May 1900, *inter alia* as a holding camp for prisoners of war.[46]

> P2.4.2 Interior of the Johannesburg Fort which now forms part of the Constitution Hill site.
> ▶ C/o Kotze St & Joubert Street, Johannesburg, Gauteng.
> ◉ S26° 11.385, E28° 02.549 (Google Maps).

The most famous of the Boer guns were their four Creusot siege guns, nicknamed "Long Toms". These French-made canons had a calibre of 155 mm and could launch a projectile weighing about 40 kg at targets as far as 10 km away. They were the most formidable canons of their time. Although they were designed for use as siege or fortress guns, the Boers used them as field guns in the war and achieved considerable success with them.[47]

> P2.4.3 Replica of the Long Tom gun on the grounds of the War Museum of the Boer Republics. The museum displays examples of many types of weapons acquired on the eve of the war, including various types of rifles, as well as several other relics of the war.
> ▶ Monument Rd, Bloemfontein, Free State.
> ◉ S29° 08.397, E26° 12.569.

P2.4.1

P2.4.2

---

44   Breytenbach I 1969, 85.
45   Ploeger 1968; Oberholster 1972, 305; Van Vollenhoven 1995; Greyling 2000, 86-88; Richardson 2001, 212.
46   Oberholster 1972, 290-292; Richardson 2001, 195.
47   Changuion 2001.

Part 2 – Prelude to the war

In addition to constructing fortresses and procuring arms and ammunition, the Boers also procured other war supplies such as tents, pack saddles, preserved food and clothing.

P2.4.4 Pack saddle used by the Boers in the early part of the war to transport ammunition on the battlefield. This specific type was made by the Lyle Brothers in Natal before the war.
▶ *Rhode House Museum, Athlone St, Mooi River, KwaZulu-Natal.*
◉ *S29° 12.548, E29° 59.760.*

The British military authorities made extensive war preparations too. They had learned a number of valuable lessons in the Anglo-Transvaal War of 1880–1881. The first of these was that it was an act of madness to enter the field of battle wearing bright red, blue or green coats and white helmets when they were facing efficient marksmen who aimed at individual targets. As a result, the British army introduced khaki uniforms that would make soldiers much less conspicuous.

Secondly, the British had learned to appreciate the value of marksmanship. In the war of 1880–1881, few British soldiers were accomplished marksmen. They had been trained to fire volleys in the direction of the enemy, rather than to aim at the enemy with the objective of eliminating specific targets. After that war, soldiers were taught marksmanship during a period of reform undertaken by the British army. Furthermore, the British high command had come to recognise the value of high mobility. This led to the introduction on a massive scale of a new type of soldier, the mounted infantryman. The tactical shift in the training of British soldiers resulted in a new breed of men, much better equipped to fight the Boers than their predecessors had been in 1880.

The British army also acquired modern artillery, such as Armstrong field guns that were easy to handle and highly mobile. Since the British had nothing to equal the Boer Long Tom guns, they transformed heavy naval weaponry into field guns.

P2.4.5 Replica of a British 5-inch Armstrong field gun.
▶ *Grounds of the War Museum of the Boer Republics, Monument Rd, Bloemfontein, Free State.*
◉ *S29° 08.397, E26° 12.569.*

P2.4.3

P2.4.4

P2.4.5

Part 3

The military history of the war: the first year (11 October 1899–10 October 1900)

3.1 Early encounters, 12 October–23 November 1899

During the night of 12 to 13 October, the first engagement took place. General Koos de la Rey's burghers derailed and captured a British armoured train at Kraaipan station, south of Mafeking, on the western front. It is claimed that the first shot was fired at 22:45 on 12 October, less than 30 hours after the outbreak of the war. The Boers suffered no casualties, and seized a number of light field guns. On the British side, nine men were wounded.[48]

> *P3.1.1 Memorial at Kraaipan, North West, that commemorates this skirmish. There is also a small museum nearby, as well as markers to indicate where the train was derailed and a small cemetery that contains the graves of two members of the British forces who died in the war.[49]*
> ▶ *At the Kraaipan railway halt, next to the railway line linking Vryburg and Mahikeng, North West.*
> ◙ *S26° 17.840, E25° 18.305 (Google Maps).*

On the eastern side of the Republics, Boer commandos lead by Commandant-General Piet Joubert of the Transvaal and Chief Commandant Marthinus Prinsloo of the Free State crossed the Drakensberg mountain range into Natal. After serious delays due to wet weather and muddy roads, the Transvaal forces reached and occupied Newcastle on 16 October 1899.[50]

> *P3.1.2 The house used by Commandant-General Joubert as his temporary headquarters in Newcastle. Today it has been converted to commercial premises.[51]*
> ▶ *42 Ayliff St, Newcastle, KwaZulu-Natal.*
> ◙ *S27° 45.379, E29° 56.313 (Google Maps).*

> *P3.1.3 The Newcastle Town Hall. The Boers summarily hoisted the Vierkleur (the flag of the ZAR) on the clock tower. Numerous burghers posed in front of this building for photographs after their occupation of the town.[52]*
> ▶ *Scott Street, between Sutherland St & Voortrekker St, Newcastle, KwaZulu-Natal.*
> ◙ *S27° 45.455, E29° 55.906.*

The first engagement in Natal took place on 18 October 1899, when Free State forces under Commandant C.J. de Villiers drove a force of about 600 Natal Carbineers and colonial volunteers away from Bester Station.[53]

P3.1.1

P3.1.2

P3.1.3

---

48   Oosthuizen 1942, 68-86; Pretorius 2010, 222.
49   Watt 2000, 471.
50   Meintjes 1971, 172-173; Cloete 2000, 49.
51   Van der Westhuizen & Van der Westhuizen 2000, 28.
52   Eksteen 2008, 7-8.
53   Breytenbach I 1969, 196; Cloete 2000, 50.

Part 3 – The military history of the war: the first year (11 October 1899–10 October 1900)

P3.1.4 Memorial for the first Free State burgher killed in action in the war, Fred Johnson of the Harrismith Commando, who fell in this engagement.[54] Johnson's name also appears on the Burgher Memorial at Platrand, Ladysmith (see P3.2.3.19).
▶ *At Bester Station, north of Ladysmith, KwaZulu-Natal.*
◉ *Near S28° 26.261, E29° 38.573 (Google Maps).*

The first major battle of the war took place on the Natal front on 20 October 1899 on the outskirts of Dundee – the Battle of Talana. The British forces under Major-General Sir W. Penn-Symons warded off an attack by the Boers under General Lukas Meyer. Since the British remained in occupation of the battlefield, they could claim victory, but at a high price. The British suffered a loss of 446 men in total, of whom 41 (including Penn-Symons) were killed or died of wounds, 185 were wounded and 220 were taken prisoner. On the Boer side, about 53 were killed or died of their wounds and 82 others were wounded. The British forces abandoned Dundee and retreated to Ladysmith two days after the battle.[55]

P3.1.5 Major-General Penn-Symons's grave.
▶ *Grounds of St James Church, Boundary St, between Gladstone St & Gray St, Dundee, KwaZulu-Natal.*
◉ *S28° 09.681, E30° 14.044.*

P3.1.6 The Talana Museum, Battlefield and Heritage Park contain numerous relics of this battle.
▶ *Outskirts of Dundee, KwaZulu-Natal; entry from Victoria St, between Hajee Jamal and the R33.*
◉ *S28° 09.346, E30° 15.617.*

The spot where Penn-Symons was killed is indicated by a white-washed cairn at the edge of the Talana Museum Grounds.

There is a Royal Dublin Fusiliers marker next to a footpath leading from the Talana Museum to the summit of Talana Hill.

P3.1.7 Some of the British soldiers killed in the Battle of Talana were buried in the Smith family cemetery on the Talana Museum grounds (see also CP2 on p. 130).
▶ *Outskirts of Dundee, KwaZulu-Natal, entry from Victoria St, between Hajee Jamal and the R33.*
◉ *S28° 09.346, E30° 15.617.*

P3.1.8 Some British soldiers who died in the battle were buried in the cemetery of the Wesleyan Church in Dundee.

British soldiers who died of their wounds at the Swedish Mission were buried in the Betania Mission Church grounds.

P3.1.9 The Boer memorial of the battle, including the crypt that contains the remains of burghers who fell in the battle and who were reinterred here, and a roll of honour on the lid of the crypt (see also CP6 on p. 132).

P3.1.4

P3.1.5

P3.1.6

---

54 Hopkins 1963, 55.
55 Preller 1942b; Breytenbach I 1969, 214-236; McFadden 1999a; Pretorius 2010, 450-452.

P3.1.7   P3.1.8   P3.1.9

▶ Against the outer wall of the Dutch Reformed Church, Wilson St, between Beaconsfield St & Gray St, Dundee, KwaZulu-Natal.
◉ S28° 09.629, E30° 14.148.

A memorial plaque containing the names of 48 burghers who were killed in action in this battle and five who died of wounds is affixed to the Burgher Monument, Platrand (Wagon Hill), Ladysmith, KwaZulu-Natal (see P3.2.3.19).

P3.1.10 Gravestone of P.L. Uys, who was killed in action in the Battle of Talana.
▶ Affixed to the outer wall of the Burgher Monument, Platrand (Wagon Hill), Ladysmith, KwaZulu-Natal. The gravestone of J.N. Boshoff, who was also killed in action in the Battle of Talana, is also attached to this wall.
◉ S28° 35.278, E29° 46.357.

The very next day, on 21 October 1899, Republican forces under the command of the over-confident General Jan Kock, including a German Corps and a *Hollander* (Dutch) Corps of volunteers – were routed by a British force commanded by Major-General John French at the Elandslaagte railway station on the main railway line in Natal, north of Ladysmith. It was the first time that the Boers encountered a British lancer charge. A total of 46 Boers (of whom eight died of their wounds after the battle) and about 50 British soldiers were killed in this battle. This included the commander of the Imperial Light Horse regiment, Colonel J.J. Scott-Chisholme. The heavily wounded General Kock fell into British hands, and died a few days later in captivity. Both the German Corps and the Dutch Corps were disbanded after the battle.[56]

P3.1.11 Natal Field Artillery at Elandslaagte.
▶ Relief sculpture on the pedestal of the Anglo-Boer War memorial, Francis Farewell Square, c/o Anton Lembede St & Dorothy Nyembe St, Durban, KwaZulu-Natal.
◉ S29° 51.525, E31° 01.514 (Google Maps).

A memorial plaque containing the names of 42 burghers who were killed in action in this battle and eight who died of their wounds is affixed to the Burgher Monument, Platrand (Wagon Hill), Ladysmith, KwaZulu-Natal (see P3.2.3.19).

P3.1.10   P3.1.11   P3.1.12   P3.1.13

56   Amery II 1902, 175-196; Breytenbach I 1969, 237-263; McFadden 1999b; Pretorius 2010, 137-138 & 187.

Part 3 – The military history of the war: the first year (11 October 1899–10 October 1900)

There are a number of memorials spread out across the Elandslaagte battlefield, including the following:

P3.1.12 Memorial commissioned by citizens of the Netherlands and designed by Pretoria architect Gerard Moerdijk in memory of members of the Dutch Corps who fell in this battle.[57]
▶ *On a hillock on the northern side of the D771, east of the Elandslaagte railway station.*
◉ *S28° 25.437, E29° 58.748.*

P3.1.13 Burgher memorial containing the names of Boers who fell in the Battle of Elandslaagte. Boers buried on the battlefield were later exhumed and reinterred at the Burgher Memorial on Platrand at Ladysmith, KwaZulu-Natal.
▶ *Next to the D771, on the northern side of the road, east of the Elandslaagte railway station.*
◉ *S28° 25.437, E29° 58.748.*

The gravestone of J.A.P. Grobler, who died of wounds sustained in the Battle of Elandslaagte.
▶ *Affixed to the outer wall of the Burgher Monument, Platrand (Wagon Hill), Ladysmith, KwaZulu-Natal.*
◉ *S28° 35.278, E29° 46.357.*

P3.1.14 Imperial Light Horse Memorial (left) and a large obelisk (right) commemorating Colonel Scott-Chisholme, close to the spot where he was killed in action. He was initially buried on the battlefield, but he was exhumed four days later and reinterred in the Ladysmith municipal cemetery, where his grave can still be seen in the British Garden of Remembrance.[58]
▶ *On a hillock on the southern side of the D771, east of the Elandslaagte railway station.*
◉ *S28° 25.437, E29° 58.748.*

P3.1.15 Memorial for members of the 2nd Battalion Gordon Highlanders Regiment who fell at Elandslaagte and are buried in a cemetery at the foot of the ridge, called Battleridge, on the battle terrain. There are also memorials for members of the 1st Battalion Manchester Regiment and the Imperial Light Horse who fell in the battle, and who were also buried in this cemetery.
▶ *On the southern side of the D771, east of the Elandslaagte railway station, KwaZulu-Natal, about 40 m from the entrance to a game farm.*
◉ *S28° 25.463, E29° 58.949 (Google Maps).*

P3.1.16 British military cemetery near the Elandslaagte railway station for soldiers killed in this battle.
▶ *Turn into the R602 from the N11 between Ladysmith and Newcastle, turn right on small road (the P555) after about 2 km, before crossing the railway line; drive across the railway line on this gravel road; the cemetery is immediately south of the railway line and east of this road.*
◉ *S28° 24.805, E29° 56.866.*

P3.1.14   P3.1.15   P3.1.16

---

57 Richardson 2001, 225.
58 Watt 2000, 371.

P3.1.17 Grave of General J.H.M. (Jan) Kock. His body was handed over to the Republican forces and he was buried with full military honours in the Old Church Street West Cemetery, Pretoria, on 2 November 1899.[59] Dr H.J. Coster of the Dutch Corps was also originally buried near the Elandslaagte railway station but was reinterred in the same cemetery in 1961.[60]
▶ *Entry to cemetery from Es'kia Mphahlele St (previously D.F. Malan Dr), north of W.F. Nkomo Dr (previously Church St West).*
◉ *Near S25° 44.777, E28° 10.549 (Google Maps).*

P3.1.18 Grave of Harra von Zeppelin, a Baron of German origin, who fought on the Boer side, was wounded at Elandslaagte on 21 October and died of his wounds on 23 October 1899.[61]
▶ *Kloof Cemetery, on the banks of the Kloof Spruit, northern side of extension of Fenter St, Heidelberg, Gauteng.*
◉ *S 26° 29.717, E 28° 20.770.*

In spite of their victory at Elandslaagte, the British were pushed back to Ladysmith when Republican forces occupied the Rietfontein-Tintinyoni area, east and north of the Modderspruit railway station, about 11 km from Ladysmith. The British commander in Ladysmith, Lieutenant-General Sir George White, launched a failed attack on the Republican commandos on 24 October. Both sides suffered losses: the British casualties were 12 killed, 103 wounded and two missing, and on the Boer side, nine were killed and 21 were wounded.[62]

There are a number of commemorative structures at Rietfontein.
▶ *Cemetery near farmhouse on privately owned land, north-east of Ladysmith, KwaZulu-Natal. Take Rietfontein Rd from the N11 towards the north. Continue on this gravel road after crossing the railway line. Turn right where the road forks.*

P3.1.19 British military cemetery at Rietfontein. There are also the graves of nine British soldiers of the Gloucester Regiment on the battlefield and a cairn that marks a spot where two members of the Natal Volunteers were killed.

P3.1.20 Some of the burghers who were killed in action at Rietfontein, as well as burghers who died fighting around Ladysmith on 30 October, and who were originally buried in a cemetery near the Rietfontein farmhouse, were later reinterred at the Burgher Monument on Platrand. This photograph is of the memorial stone at Rietfontein for 20 burghers who were originally buried at Rietfontein but were reinterred at the Burgher Monument, Platrand, in 1979. A memorial plaque with the names of 10 burghers killed in action at Rietfontein on 24 October, and four burghers who died there of other causes, is attached to the Burgher Monument, Platrand (Wagon Hill), Ladysmith, KwaZulu-Natal (see P3.2.3.19). There is also a memorial tablet for 12 known and 26 unknown burghers who died in the course of duty in the Rietfontein area, 1899 to 1900.

P3.1.17   P3.1.18   P3.1.19

---

59 Schoeman 1972, 378-379; Grobler 2004, 10.
60 Ploeger 1972, 148.
61 Van der Westhuizen & Van der Westhuizen 2000, 170.
62 Breytenbach I 1969, 291-300; Pretorius 2010, 384; Von der Heyde 2012, 168-169.

Part 3 – The military history of the war: the first year (11 October 1899–10 October 1900)

P3.1.21 Gravestone of Colonel E.P. Wilford (53) of the 28th Gloucestershire Regiment, who fell at the head of his regiment at Rietfontein on 24 October 1899. British Garden of Remembrance, municipal cemetery, Ladysmith, KwaZulu-Natal. The graves of Sergeant A.E. Colville (39) and of Trooper W. Cleaver of the Natal Carbineers, who also fell in this engagement, are in the same cemetery. So is the grave of Trooper S. Brown (30) of the Border Mounted Rifles who was killed in action at Tintinyoni on 24 October 1899. [63]
▶ *Southern side of Cemetery Rd, between Illings St and Mandela St.*
◉ *S28° 33.322, E29° 47.687.*

More Republican commandos gathered around Ladysmith within the next few days, and Lieutenant-General White decided to attack again on 30 October – a date that became known in British military history as Mournful Monday. The British forces suffered a humiliating defeat when General Louis Botha, the future commandant-general of the Transvaal, scored his first victory as a commander in this battle. The famous future general, Christiaan de Wet, who was at that time a provisional commandant, was also victorious when he forced a British unit to capitulate at Nicholson's Nek (also known as Tchrengula), north of Ladysmith. The British subsequently called the clash as a whole the Battle of Ladysmith, but the Boers referred to the Battle of Modder Spruit and the Battle of Nicholson's Nek. The total British losses on Mournful Monday amounted to about 106 killed, 374 wounded and 1 284 taken prisoner. The Republican loss was 16 killed and 75 wounded.[64]

The 52 British soldiers killed at Tchrengula are buried in two mass graves on the summit of this low hill. To the south, the mass grave of the Gloucester Regiment is identified by a stone obelisk. The burial place of the Royal Irish Fusiliers nearby is marked by a marble cross and that of the Mountain Battery by a metal cross.
▶ *These memorials are situated on privately owned land, which can be accessed through the Trenchgula Lodge.*[65] *Exit Ladysmith to the north via Hyde Rd and follow signs to the lodge, about 7 km from the Ladysmith CBD.*
◉ *S28° 30.088, E29° 46.404.*

Most of the soldiers who fell near the Modder Spruit were buried in Ladysmith. Thus the grave of Lieutenant J.T. MacDougall (28) of the 42nd Battery Royal Field Artillery, who was killed in action at Lombard's Kop on 30 October 1899, is in the British Garden of Remembrance, Ladysmith municipal cemetery.[66]
▶ *Southern side of Cemetery Rd, between Illings St and Mandela St.*
◉ *S28° 33.322, E29° 47.687.*

Some of the soldiers who fell in this battle were buried elsewhere:

P3.1.22 Grave of Lieutenant W.M.J. Clapham (29), Natal Mounted Rifles, killed in action at Lombard's Kop on 30 October 1899.[67]
▶ *Old town cemetery, eastern side of Chief Albert Luthuli St, near corner with Geere St, Pietermaritzburg, KwaZulu-Natal.*
◉ *S29° 36.537, E30° 23.147 (Google Maps).*

P3.1.20

P3.1.21

P3.1.22

---

63 Watt 2000, 50, 78, 83 & 451.
64 Breytenbach I 1969, 303-341; Scholtz 2003, 19-21; Pretorius 2010, 231-236; Watt 2014.
65 Von der Heyde 2012, 167.
66 Watt 2000, 259.
67 Watt 2000, 74.

A memorial plaque containing the names of 25 burghers who were killed in action at Modder Spruit and Nicholson's Nek on 30 October, as well as three burghers who died of wounds sustained there is affixed to the Burgher Monument, Platrand (Wagon Hill), Ladysmith, KwaZulu-Natal (see P3.2.3.19).

After the Boer success at Ladysmith at the end of October 1899, Commandant-General Joubert led a relatively small Boer commando further into Natal, advancing along the railway line. On 15 November, burghers of this commando, led by General Louis Botha, derailed a British armoured train at Chieveley, taking prisoner a British war correspondent who later became a famous international statesman – Winston Churchill. Four British soldiers were killed in this incident.[68]

P3.1.23 The armoured train incident of 15 Nov.
▶ *Relief sculpture on the pedestal of the Anglo-Boer War memorial, Francis Farewell Square, c/o Anton Lembede St & Dorothy Nyembe St, Durban, KwaZulu-Natal.*
◉ *S29° 51.525, E31° 01.514 (Google Maps).*

P3.1.24 This small monument next to the railway line marks the place where Churchill was taken prisoner.
▶ *Immediately north of the junction of the R74 and the R103, near Chieveley, KwaZulu-Natal.*
◉ *S28° 52.410, E29° 46.068.*

P3.1.25 The soldiers who were killed in the action are buried in a cemetery close by, on the eastern side of the railway line.
▶ *Either walk directly east across the railway line from the monument, or use the underpass about 200 m to the north of the monument.*

After capturing Churchill, the Republican task force moved further south into Natal in the direction of Pietermaritzburg. A few kilometres south of the town today known as Estcourt, they engaged with British forces at Brynbella, in what was subsequently called the Battle of Willow Grange on 22 and 23 November. The result of this encounter was inconclusive; British losses amounted to 11 killed and 67 wounded, while Boer losses were two killed and two wounded. The Republican forces returned to the north bank of the Thukela River, where they dug themselves in.[69]

The names of four burghers who were killed in action during this Boer incursion into Natal in the second half of November 1899, as well as two who died of other causes, are listed on the Burgher Monument at Platrand, Ladysmith, KwaZulu-Natal (see P3.2.3.19).

One of the British soldiers killed in this battle was Trooper George J. Fitzpatrick, the brother of the famous author Sir Percy Fitzpatrick. His grave is in the municipal cemetery in Estcourt, KwaZulu-Natal.[70]

P3.1.23

P3.1.24

P3.1.25

68 Breytenbach I 1969, 367-371; Churchill 1972, 250-259; Grobler 2004, 13; Pretorius 2010, 86.
69 Breytenbach I 1969, 374-382; Grobler 2004, 15.
70 Von der Heyde 2013, 61.

Part 3 – The military history of the war: the first year (11 October 1899–10 October 1900)

P3.1.26 Willow Grange battlefield, looking to the north from the gravel road that crosses the centre of the field. The stone wall which featured prominently in the battle is still there.
▶ *Next to the P173-1, Lowlands, KwaZulu-Natal, between the P170 and the P173-2.*
◉ *S29° 05.933, E29° 55.332.*

P3.1.27 This military cemetery containing mostly British graves is next to the Willow Grange battlefield on the southern side of the gravel road. The stone wall is visible in the background.
▶ *Next to the P173-1, Lowlands, KwaZulu-Natal, between the P170 and the P173-2.*
◉ *S29° 05.933, E29° 55.332.*

The northern Boer forces were singularly unsuccessful in their attempts to subdue a small British detachment in what is today the eastern tip of Botswana.[71] In the south, General J.H. Olivier of the Orange Free State crossed the bridge across the Orange River at Aliwal North with a large commando on 13 November 1899. He announced that Aliwal North's name would become Oliviersfontein and that he was annexing the whole district to become part of the Republic of the Orange Free State.[72] The magistrate's office in Aliwal North became the headquarters of the Republican forces for the duration of this annexation (about four months).[73]

P3.1.28 The Old Magistrate's Office in Aliwal North is today used for commercial purposes.
▶ *C/o Somerset St & Grey St, Aliwal North, Eastern Cape.*
◉ *S30° 41.407, E26° 42.531 (Google Maps).*

The Republican forces, assisted by large numbers of what the British called Cape Rebels (Afrikaners from the Cape Colony who were sympathetic to the Republican cause), subsequently invaded a number of border districts, which they promptly proclaimed part of the Republic of the Orange Free State.[74]

P3.1.29 Agtertang railway halt, east of Colesberg in the Cape Colony. On 5 November 1899, the Boers blew up the railway bridge across the Oorlogspoort River near this spot to make the line inoperable by the British forces.[75]
▶ *On the southern side of a gravel road that runs parallel to the R58 between Colesberg and Norvalspont, Northern Cape.*
◉ *S30° 40.515, E25° 19.139 (Google Maps).*

On the south-western border of the Orange Free State, there was a steady build-up of British troops. On 9 November 1899, Colonel B. Gough crossed the Orange River with a combined force of about 700 men. They advanced in a northerly direction towards Belmont railway halt, but were confronted by about 350 burghers on 10 November. The confrontation took place at Luiperdskop, about 15 km west of Belmont. The Republicans managed to hold off the British advance and to force Gough to retire.[76]

P3.1.26

P3.1.27

P3.1.28

---

71 Breytenbach I 1969, 408-436; Grobler 2004, 10 & 14.
72 Breytenbach I 1969, 444-447.
73 Oosthuizen 1998, 32.
74 Grobler 2004, 14.
75 Amery II 1902, 291; Breytenbach I 1969, 443.
76 Amery II 1902, 290-291; Cloete 2000, 61-62.

P3.1.30 Memorial to Lieutenant-Colonel C.E. Keith-Falconer (39), 1st Battalion 5th Northumberland Fusiliers, killed in action at Luiperdskop near Belmont on 10 November 1899. His brother, Lieutenant V.F.A. Keith-Falconer, was killed in action in Natal on 21 February 1900.[77]
▶ *West End Cemetery, c/o Green St & Reserve Rd, Kimberley, Northern Cape. In the same cemetary, there are two memorial stones for Lieutenant C.C. Wood (23), Loyal North Lancashire Regiment, who was wounded in the fighting on 10 November 1899, and died of his wounds on 15 December 1899. Wood was a great-grandson of the United States' 12th president, Zachary Taylor (d. 1850).[78]*
◉ *S28° 44.078, E24° 44.170 (Google Maps).*

3.2 The Sieges of Mafeking, Kimberley and Ladysmith

3.2.1 Mafeking

The Republican forces on the western front, which were commanded by General Piet Cronjé, began their siege of the British garrison in Mafeking (now called Mahikeng) on 13 October 1899.[79] The British commander in Mafeking was Colonel Baden-Powell, whose endurance earned him lasting fame and who became one of the first British heroes of the Anglo-Boer War.[80] Sol Plaatje, who in later life became a well-known public figure and author, also gained prominence as a result of the siege of Mafeking. He served as court interpreter for the British forces. His personal diary of the siege is a valuable source on these events.[81]

P3.2.1.1 Maratiwa House, built by Silas Molema, son of the founder of Mahikeng. This is where Sol Plaatje stayed during the siege.
▶ *Montshioa Stad, on an unnamed road off Prince of Wales Way.*
◉ *S25° 52.482, E25° 37.840.*

A skirmish on 14 October 1899 on the northern side of the town resulted in casualties on both sides. On the Republican side, Ockert Oosthuizen became the first burgher to be killed in action in the war as a whole.[82]

P3.2.1.2 Oosthuizen was originally buried near Mafeking, but was subsequently reinterred at the Burgher Memorial in Zeerust, North West, where his gravestone was mounted on a wall.
▶ *In a memorial garden, c/o Hendrik Potgieter St & Forsman St.*
◉ *S25° 32.501, E26° 04.540.*

The Republican forces launched three significant attacks on the garrison in Mafeking, which all failed. The first was on 25 October 1899, when the Boers attacked from all sides. The Potchefstroom Commando and the Scandinavian volunteers on the Republican side made significant inroads into the defences on the western side of the town, but

P3.1.29

P3.1.30

P3.2.1.1

---

77 Amery II 1902, 291; Watt 2000, 228.
78 Watt 2000, 460; Cloete 2010, 62.
79 Breytenbach VI 1996, 7; Grobler 2004, 5.
80 Gardner 1966.
81 Plaatjie 1973 (his diary was edited and published in 1973 by Jean Comaroff).
82 Stafleu 1985, 51; Breytenbach VI 1996, 8.

were eventually forced back. Some sources claim that armed Barolong warriors on the British side should actually be credited with saving the town from the Boers on that day.[83]

> *P3.2.1.3 The "Battle of Molopo (25 Oct 1899) memorial" pays tribute to the black defenders of war-time Mafeking in general.*
> ▶ *Montshioa Stad, on unnamed road between Prince of Wales Way and Doctor James Moroka Dr.*
> ◉ *S25° 52.579, E25° 37.752.*

The second Republican assault on Mafeking took place on 31 October and was aimed at the British gun emplacement on Kanon Kopje. The defenders held back the attacking forces, but suffered casualties.[84]

> *P3.2.1.4 The Kanon Kopje gun emplacement (see also CP4 on p. 131).*
> ▶ *Next to the Bophelong Hospital, between Link St & Twist St.*
> ◉ *S25° 52.936, E25° 39.154.*

> *P3.2.1.5 Grave of Captain D.H. Marsham (28), British South Africa Police, killed in action at Kanon Kopje, 31 October 1899.[85]*
> ▶ *Cemetery, Carrington St, between Carney St & 1st Lane, Mahikeng, North West.*
> ◉ *S25° 51.448, E25° 38.202.*

British patrols launched several attacks on the Boer positions around the town. On 26 December, they attacked the Boer defenders of Platboomfort (which the British called Game Tree Hill Fort). The attack failed and resulted in 51 British casualties. Only two burghers were killed and seven were wounded.[86]

> *P3.2.1.6 Grave of Captain H.C. Sandford (30), Indian Staff Corps, killed in action on 26 December 1899 in the attack on Game Tree Hill Fort.[87] The grave of Captain R.J. Vernon (33), 60th Rifles, who was also killed in action on 26 December 1899 in the same attack, is in the same cemetery.[88] So are the graves of two members of the British South Africa Police, Trooper D. Francis (40), who on 3 February 1900 died of wounds received at Kanon Kopje on 1 December 1899, and his brother Trooper W. Francis (23), killed in action at Kanon Kopje, 6 May 1900.[89]*
> ▶ *Cemetery, Carrington St, between Carney St & 1st Lane, Mahikeng, North West.*
> ◉ *S25° 51.448, E25° 38.202.*

The burghers launched sporadic attacks on Mafeking, and Republican artillery intermittently shelled the town. At one stage, they pounded Mafeking with a Long Tom gun, albeit not very effectively. The extensive earthworks

P3.2.1.2

P3.2.1.3

P3.2.1.4

---

83 Cloete 2010, 55.
84 Botha 1967, 126-134; Ross 1980, 36-37; Stafleu 1985, 94-96.
85 Watt 2000, 267.
86 Ross 1980, 77-79; Stafleu 1985, 171-175; Cloete 2010, 83.
87 Watt 2000, 367.
88 Watt 2000, 429.
89 Watt 2000, 144-145.

erected by the defenders minimized the danger. Some damage was done to various buildings, and there were some casualties, both military and civilian, but the town held out.[90]

> P3.2.1.7 There are several graves of siege victims in the municipal cemetery, including that of 9-year-old Frankie Brown, who died from the effects of a shell wound, 17 January 1900, that of Corporal W. Frankish (26), Protectorate Regiment, killed by a shell on 7 December 1899[91] and that of Private James Dall (41), Mafeking Town Guard, killed by a shell on 10 February 1900.[92]
> ▶ Cemetery, Carrington St, between Carney St & 1st Lane, Mahikeng, North West.
> ◉ S25° 51.448, E25° 38.202.

By the end of March 1900, the relief of Mafeking was high on the agenda of the British forces in South Africa. Colonel H.C.O. Plumer approached the town from the north with a Rhodesian force that included about 270 mounted troops. When they reached Ramatlhabama, he launched an attack on the burghers who besieged the town. The attack failed, with Plumer suffering the loss of nine men killed, 30 wounded and 14 missing. Republican losses were one man killed and two wounded.[93]

> P3.2.1.8 Grave of Captain F.H. Crewe (31), Crewe's Scouts, Rhodesian Forces, who died on 2 April 1900, after being taken prisoner by the burghers, of wounds received on 31 March 1900 outside Mafeking.[94]
> ▶ Cemetery, Carrington St, between Carney St & 1st Lane, Mahikeng, North West.
> ◉ S25° 51.448, E25° 38.202.

On 12 May 1900, the adventurous Commandant Sarel Eloff, one of President Kruger's grandsons, persuaded the Boer commander besieging Mafeking, General Kooitjie Snyman, to launch an attack on Mafeking. Eloff and his men were initially successful and occupied a part of the town, capturing 35 soldiers in the process, but they were pinned down in the British South African Police Fort when Baden-Powell launched a counter-attack that forced Eloff to surrender.[95] Boer losses amounted to 10 burghers killed, 19 wounded and 108 taken prisoner. The besieged lost 12 men killed and 20 men were wounded.[96]

> P3.2.1.9 Gravestone of J.P. Eksteen, killed in action on 12 May 1900 in the assault on Mafeking.
> ▶ At the burgher memorial, c/o Hendrik Potgieter St & Forsman St, Zeerust, North West, where he was reinterred.
> ◉ S25° 32.501, E26° 04.540.

> P3.2.1.10 The British South Africa Police Fort, also known as Warren's Fort.
> ▶ Old Imperial Reserve, on the grounds of the police station, Montshioa Stad, between the N18/R49 and 1st Lane.
> ◉ S25° 52.175, E25° 38.095.

P3.2.1.5   P3.2.1.6    P3.2.1.7    P3.2.1.8

---

90 Changuion 2001, 37-43.
91 Watt 2000, 145.
92 Watt 2000, 100.
93 Breytenbach VI 1996, 41-42; Cloete 2010, 131.
94 Watt 200, 94.
95 Van Dyk 1977, 277-278; Breytenbach VI 1996, 48-53; Pretorius 2010, 141-142.
96 Cloete 2010, 146.

Part 3 – The military history of the war: the first year (11 October 1899–10 October 1900)

P3.2.1.9

P3.2.1.10

P3.2.1.11

P3.2.1.11 The Masonic Lodge, built in 1894. It was used for concerts during the siege. After the failure of their assault on 12 May 1900, Commandant Sarel Eloff and some of his burghers were imprisoned here before being despatched to St Helena as prisoners of war. The others were held in the town prison.[97]
▶ *Tillard St, between Robinson St & Warren St.*
◉ *S25° 51.741, E25° 38.587.*

A British soldier, Staff Orderly Arthur Hazlerigg (27) of the Cape Mounted Police, was seriously wounded while carrying messages from Baden-Powell to beleaguered parts of the British garrison during Eloff's attack. It was reported afterwards by Lady Wilson, who comforted Hazlerigg on the night he died, that his last words to her were: "Tell the Colonel, Lady Sarah, I did my best to give the message, but they got me first."[98]

P3.2.1.12 Hazlerigg's grave.
▶ *Cemetery, Carrington St, between Carney St & 1st Lane, Mahikeng, North West.*
◉ *S25° 51.448, E25° 38.202.*

On 13 May 1900, realizing that British forces were approaching to relieve Mafeking, Boer commandos attempted to push them back. The commando, led by General P.J. Liebenberg, attacked the relief force marching to Mafeking, and there was a skirmish at Koedoesrand near Mareetsane, about 55 km south of the besieged town. The burghers' attack failed.[99]

P3.2.1.13 Imperial Light Horse memorial at Koedoesrand (Mareetsane) where the skirmish occurred.
▶ *On a low hill, eastern side of the N18 linking Vryburg and Mahikeng, North West, 56.4 km from Mahikeng, 100 m from the road, signposted.*
◉ *S26° 11.122, E25° 13.802.*

P3.2.1.12

P3.2.1.13

P3.2.1.14

---

97   Cloete 2010, 147.
98   Flower-Smith & Yorke 2000, 144. According to Watt (2000, 187), his surname was spelled Hazelrigg.
99   Breytenbach VI 1996, 55; Cloete 2010, 147.

P3.2.1.15   P3.2.1.16   P3.2.1.17   P3.2.1.18

P3.2.1.14 Grave of Commandant P.J. Lemmer, who was wounded in this engagement and died of his wounds on 5 July 1900. At his widow's request, his gravestone states that he was a courageous hero in the war for freedom and that his last words were: "Fight for freedom and justice!" [100]
▶ Municipal cemetery, Lichtenburg, North West, near Christa St, between Lang St & Burgers St (entry from Thabo Mbeki St).
◉ S26° 08.461, E26° 09.228.

On 16 May, burghers led by General de la Rey engaged in battle with two British brigades attempting to fight their way through to the besieged town. The burghers initially held the attack at bay, but heavy bombardment eventually drove them out of their fortifications, and by nightfall the way to Mafeking had been cleared by the Imperial forces. Both sides suffered casualties.[101]

P3.2.1.15 Grave of Sergeant T.St.W.L. Gates (29), Crewe's Scouts, Rhodesia Regiment, killed in action at the relief of Mafeking on 16 May 1900.[102]
▶ Cemetery, Carrington St, between Carney St & 1st Lane, Mahikeng, North West.
◉ S25° 51.448, E25° 38.202.

The siege of Mafeking dragged on for more than 216 days before Colonel Herbert Plumer, approaching from the north, and Colonel B.T. Mahon, coming up from the south, joined forces to overcome General Koos de la Rey's final attempt to stop them. British forces relieved Mafeking on 17 May 1900, to the immense joy of the Empire.[103]

P3.2.1.16 The British siege memorial in front of the Mahikeng Museum.
▶ C/o Robinson St & Martin St, Mahikeng, North West.
◉ S26° 08.461, E26° 09.228 (Google Maps).

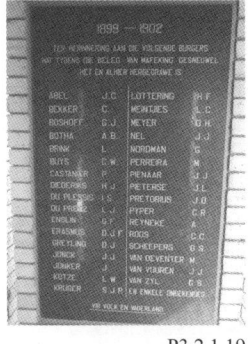  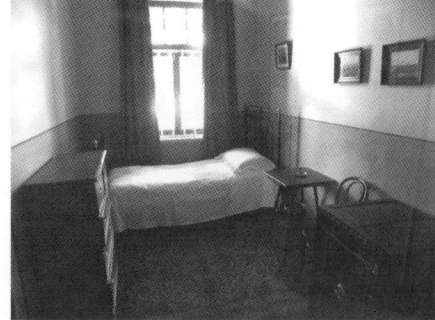

P3.2.1.19   P3.2.2.1   P3.2.2.2

100   Lemmer 2000, 84.
101   Grobler 2004, 68; Cloete 2010, 147-148.
102   Watt 2000, 152.
103   Breytenbach VI 1996, 58; Cloete 2010, 148.

Part 3 – The military history of the war: the first year (11 October 1899–10 October 1900)

P3.2.1.17 The Mahikeng Museum contains several exhibits on the siege.
▶ C/o Robinson St & Martin St, Mahikeng, North West.
◉ S26° 08.461, E26° 09.228 (Google Maps).

P3.2.1.18 St John's Anglican Church, designed by architect (Sir) Herbert Baker, and built in commemoration of the siege. The inscription on the foundation stone reads: "To the glory of God and in memory of those who died during the Siege of Mafeking, and as an act of thanksgiving for the Relief of the Town."
▶ C/o Robinson St & Martin St (across the street from the Mahikeng Museum).
◉ S25° 51.837, E25° 38.583.

P3.2.1.19 The names of the burghers who fell during the siege of Mafeking are inscribed on a memorial plaque at the Concentration Camp Cemetery.
▶ On the outskirts of Mahikeng, North West, next to the N18/R49 main road going southwards to Vryburg.
◉ S25° 52.865, E25° 36.490 (Google Maps).

3.2.2 Kimberley

The siege of Kimberley by the Republican forces began on 15 October 1899 when Boer commandos surrounded the town. The British garrison in Kimberley consisted of more than 4 000 men, equipped with 14 light field-guns, 11 machine guns and a vast supply of ammunition. The garrison was commanded by Lieutenant-Colonel R.G. Kekewich. Mining magnate Cecil John Rhodes, who had served as Prime Minister of the Cape Colony from 1890 to 1896, was trapped in Kimberley for the four-month siege.[104]

P3.2.2.1 This enormous equestrian statue of Rhodes, sculpted by Hamo Thornycroft, was unveiled in 1907.[105]
▶ C/o Du Toitspan Rd & Regiment Way, Kimberley, Northern Cape.
◉ S28° 44.502, E24° 46.142 (Google Maps).

P3.2.2.2 The bedroom where Rhodes was lodged for the duration of the siege.
▶ In the Alexander McGregor Memorial Museum, c/o Du Toitspan Rd & Chapel St, Kimberley, Northern Cape.
◉ S28° 44.404, E24° 45.911 (Google Maps).

P3.2.2.3 Siege of Kimberley exhibit.
▶ Alexander McGregor Memorial Museum, c/o Du Toitspan Rd & Chapel St, Kimberley, Northern Cape.
◉ S28° 44.404, E24° 45.911 (Google Maps).

P3.2.2.4 Memorial designed by William T. Timlin for Lieutenant-Colonel Sir David Harris, who was the commander of the Kimberley Town Guard at the time of the siege.[106]

P3.2.2.3

P3.2.2.4

P3.2.2.5

P3.2.2.6

---

104 Roberts 1984, 313-332; Cloete 2010, 48-49.
105 Roberts 1984, 338-339.
106 Harris 1931.

▶ *C/o Park Rd & Regiment Way, Kimberley, Northern Cape.*
◉ *S28° 44.518, E24° 46.280 (Google Maps).*

Initially, only burgher commandos from the Orange Free State participated in the siege of the British garrison in Kimberley. The burghers took up position in an irregular circle around the large mining town. At first, the burghers did very little to disrupt the defensive measures instituted by Kekewich, and Kekewich hardly attempted to harass the Boers, but on 24 October, there was a skirmish at Dronfield, north of Kimberley, when a commando of 600 burghers attacked a British patrol escorting an armoured train. British losses amounted to three killed and 21 wounded, while the Boers lost two men and had seven wounded.[107]

P3.2.2.5 Gravestone of Field Cornet Petrus Johannes Botha, killed in action at Dronfield, Kimberley, on 24 October 1899.
▶ *On the wall of the entrance to the Burgher Memorial, Magersfontein, Northern Cape.*
The gravestone of N.J. Botha, a burgher who was killed in action in an engagement with British forces at Kopje Enkel, Kimberley, on 3 November 1899, is also attached to the wall of the entrance to the Burgher Memorial at Magersfontein.
◉ *S28° 57.201, E24° 44.071.*

By November 1899, Kimberley was completely surrounded by the Republicans, whose numbers had by then grown to about 7 000 burghers. Of those, more than 2 000 were from the Transvaal, under the command of General Koos de la Rey. However, the majority of the Boer forces, including De la Rey, left the Kimberley area by the beginning of December to face a new British offensive from south of the Orange River. By the end of 1899, there were only about 1 500 burghers left to besiege the town.[108]

The Republican forces had a number of field guns which they periodically used to shell Kimberley. The population of the town had risen to 50 000 by the height of the siege. The burghers managed to capture horses and cattle belonging to people in the besieged town, aggravating food shortages in the town.[109] Shots were regularly exchanged and numerous casualties resulted from these encounters, but the numbers of those who were killed or wounded remained relatively low throughout the siege.

P3.2.2.6 Grave of Corporal T. Muir (24), Scotts Railway Guards, who died on 21 December 1899 of wounds received at Bakenkop (Beacon Kop) near Kimberley earlier that same day.[110]
▶ *West End Cemetery, c/o Green St & Reserve Rd, Kimberley, Northern Cape.*
◉ *S28° 44.078, E24° 44.170 (Google Maps).*

George Labram, an American mining engineer, assisted by the draughtsman Edward Goffe, designed and manufactured a large field gun in the De Beers Consolidated Mines workshop to counter Boer artillery shelling of the besieged town. The barrel had a length of 3 m and it was mounted on a steel carriage. The gun was nicknamed "Long

P3.2.2.7

P3.2.2.8

P3.2.2.9

P3.2.2.10

---

107 Breytenbach II 1971, 366-368; Cloete 2010, 54.
108 Breytenbach II 1971, 395.
109 Breytenbach II 1971, 394-408.
110 Watt 2000, 300.

Part 3 – The military history of the war: the first year (11 October 1899–10 October 1900)

Cecil", in honour of Cecil John Rhodes. The 104 mm calibre gun could fire a shell weighing about 13 kg a distance of more than 7 km. The Royal Artillery used it during the last 28 days of the siege to help defend the town against the Boers. Labram himself was killed by a Boer artillery shell during the siege.[111]

P3.2.2.7 The impressive Kimberley Siege Monument was designed by the well-known architect Sir Herbert Baker.[112] Long Cecil, the field gun designed by Labram, is part of the monument. Towards the end of the war, this gun was used as a gun carriage at Rhodes's funeral in Cape Town, and also in the Matobo Hills in present-day Zimbabwe, where Rhodes was buried. There is a memorial plaque paying tribute to Labram on one side of the memorial, and a plaque paying tribute to soldiers who fell defending Kimberley during the siege.
▶ *On traffic circle in Memorial Rd, c/o Oliver Rd, Kimberley, Northern Cape.*
◉ *S28° 45.080, E24° 46.163 (Google Maps).*

The Republican siege of Kimberley ended on 15 February 1900, when the town was relieved by a British task force. However, the last major action at Kimberley only occurred the next day, when the British forces had to fight hard to drive the last burghers from the outskirts of town. The northern side of the town at Riverton, Dronfield and Macfarlane saw the most action, as the Boers put up tough resistance for more than 12 hours before finally retreating with their Long Tom gun under cover of a dust storm. The British forces suffered 28 casualties, and Republican losses amounted to 19 burghers killed, wounded or taken prisoner, and the loss of one old Armstrong gun, which they left behind.[113]

P3.2.2.8 Grave of Trooper J. Sutton (23), Kimberley Light Horse, who died on 19 February 1900 of wounds received in action at Dronfield, Kimberley, on 16 February 1900.[114]
▶ *Gladstone Cemetery, eastern side of Kenilworth Rd, opposite the junction with Gulab Ave (immediately to the north of the De Beers Stadium), Kimberley, Northern Cape.*
◉ *S28° 43.357, E24° 46.601 (Google Maps).*

P3.2.2.9 Grave of Private H. Lynn, Royal Scots Greys, killed in action at Dronfield, Kimberley, on 16 February 1900. The graves of two other soldiers killed in action in that engagement are close by.[115]
▶ *Kenilworth Cemetery, eastern side of Tienie Louw St, Kimindustria, Kimberley, Northern Cape.*
◉ *S28° 41.909, E24° 47.481 (Google Maps).*

The grave of Second Lieutenant P.F. Brassey (23), 9th Lancers, who was also killed in action in Kimberley on 16 February 1900,[116] is in Kimberley's West End Cemetery.
▶ *West End Cemetery, c/o Green St & Reserve Rd, Kimberley, Northern Cape.*
◉ *S28° 44.078, E24° 44.170 (Google Maps).*

P3.2.2.10 Cape Police Memorial, unveiled in 1904. At its base is the Armstrong gun captured from the Boers at Dronfield in 1900.
▶ *Lodge St, between Rendlesham Rd & McInnes St, Kimberley, Northern Cape.*
◉ *S28° 44.764, E24° 46.652 (Google Maps).*

3.2.3 Ladysmith

The Siege of Ladysmith began three days after the Republican victory at Modder Spruit and Nicholson's Nek on 30 October 1899. The British forces, commanded by Lieutenant-General Sir George White, garrisoned themselves in the town. Instead of pressing on to Durban, the Boers under Commandant-General Joubert besieged the British forces in Ladysmith for the next four months. However, even though the Boers constructed gun-placements on all the hills around the town and continually shelled the British, they failed to force the British to surrender.[117]

---

111 Pretorius 2010, 247-248.
112 Greig 1970, 105, 109-111.
113 Breytenbach IV 1977, 226-229; Cloete 2010, 107.
114 Watt 2000, 405.
115 Watt 2000, 258.
116 Watt 2000, 43.
117 Macdonald 1900; Watt 1999a.

P3.2.3.1   P3.2.3.2   P3.2.3.3

In Ladysmith itself, there are a number of places that serve as memorials of the siege:

P3.2.3.1 The house that served as General White's headquarters for most of the siege.
▶ *Signposted, eastern side of Poort St (Harrismith Rd).*
◉ *S28° 33.534, E29° 46.515 (Google Maps).*

P3.2.3.2 The Siege Museum.
▶ *Murchison St, on the eastern side of the Town Hall, Ladysmith, KwaZulu-Natal.*
◉ *S28° 33.547, E29° 46.847 (Google Maps).*

P3.2.3.3 Two British guns, nicknamed Castor and Pollux, which were used by the defenders.
▶ *In front of the Ladysmith Town Hall, c/o Murchison St & Queen St, Ladysmith, KwaZulu-Natal.*
◉ *S28° 33.565, E29° 46.854 (Google Maps).*

P3.2.3.4 Plaque on wall of the All Saints Anglican Church with 54 names on it, "In memory of those civilians who died during the Siege of Ladysmith". This Church is to a large extent a memorial to the British soldiers who gave their lives in the battles in and around Ladysmith. There is a roll of honour for those who fell on the interior walls of the church, as well as a number of commemorative plaques that honour the victims of the siege.[118]
▶ *Murchison St, north-east of the corner with Princess St, Ladysmith, KwaZulu-Natal.*
◉ *S28° 33.840, E29° 46.649 (Google Maps).*

P3.2.3.5 The Fly Kraal cairn indicating the spot where the camp of the 2nd Gordon Highlanders was situated in 1899-1900.
▶ *South-western c/o Christy Rd & Zia Rd, Ladysmith, KwaZulu-Natal.*
◉ *S28° 34.968, E29° 46.572.*

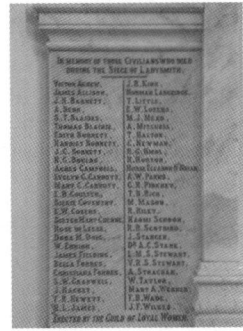  

P3.2.3.4   P3.2.3.5   P3.2.3.6

---

118   Christopher & Christopher 1982, 4-9.

Part 3 – The military history of the war: the first year (11 October 1899–10 October 1900)

P3.2.3.6 Memorial in the Intombi Cemetery "In Memory of NCO's [non-commissioned officers] and Riflemen, 1st & 2nd King's Royal Rifles, who died of wounds or disease during the siege of Ladysmith between 2 November 1899 & 28 February 1900".
▶ Between the Klip River and the railway line, 7.2 km south of the Siege Museum, near the L1298, Ladysmith, KwaZulu-Natal.
◉ S28° 35.748, E29° 49.313.

P3.2.3.7 The Leicestershire Regiment Memorial on Observation Hill, at the point from which this Regiment provided a picket for the duration of the siege.
▶ Observation Hill, near Ruby Gailey Dr.
◉ S28° 31.973, E29° 46.045.

To break the monotony of the siege, a number of war correspondents trapped in Ladysmith produced an irregular newspaper called *The Ladysmith Lyre*. Its editor was George Steevens. Four issues appeared, the final one soon after the death of Steevens in January 1900 of typhoid fever.[119]

P3.2.3.8 Gravestone of George Steevens (31).
▶ British Garden of Remembrance, municipal cemetery, southern side of Cemetery Rd, between Illings St & Mandela St, Ladysmith, KwaZulu-Natal.
◉ S28° 33.322, E29° 47.687.

Several engagements between the besieging Republican forces and the besieged British forces occurred in the course of the four months of the siege. On 3 November 1899, a mounted British force attacked the Free State commandos outside Ladysmith, but were held off. The attackers suffered five casualties, including Captain J.C. Knapp (43) and Lieutenant A.E. Brabant (33), the son of Major-General Y.E. Brabant, plus 28 wounded and one missing.[120]

P3.2.3.9 The Imperial Light Horse memorial on which both Captain Knapp and Lieutenant Brabant are commemorated.
▶ British Garden of Remembrance, municipal cemetery, Ladysmith, southern side of Cemetery Rd, between Illings St & Mandela St, Ladysmith, KwaZulu-Natal. The graves of Captain Knapp and Lieutenant Brabant, who both served in the Imperial Light Horse Regiment, are also in this cemetery.
◉ S28° 33.322, E29° 47.687.

On 18 November, Dr A.C. Stark was killed by a Boer shell while walking on the pavement in front of the Royal Hotel in the central part of the town.[121]

P3.2.3.10 The spot where Stark was killed is marked by a plaque on the pavement.
▶ In front of the Royal Hotel, Murchison St, south of corner with Queen St, Ladysmith, KwaZulu-Natal.
◉ S28° 33.626, E29° 46.822 (Google Maps).

P3.2.3.7   P3.2.3.8   P3.2.3.9   P3.2.3.10

---

119 Watt 2000, 397; Pretorius 2010, 431.
120 Breytenbach I 1969, 353-355; Watt 2000, 41 & 237; Cloete 2010, 59.
121 Craw 1972, 18-19; Cloete 2010, 65.

On 20 November, the All-Saints Church was hit by a shell which the Republican artillery fired from Pepworth Hill; the porch and south-east corner of the church were destroyed.

> P3.2.3.11 The shell, which did not explode, was recovered. After the war, when the church building was repaired, the shell was mounted in a memorial plaque on the church wall.[122]
> ▶ Murchison Street, north-east of the corner with Princess St, Ladysmith, KwaZulu-Natal.
> ◉ S28° 33.840, E29° 46.649 (Google Maps).

During the night of 7 December, a British force of 650 men under Lieutenant-General Sir Archibald Hunter moved out of Ladysmith under cover of darkness, and surprised the crew and a guard of 25 burghers at the Republican gun emplacement on Lombard's Kop (which the British called Gun Hill). They damaged the Long Tom gun and a howitzer in the emplacement with gun cotton, and carried off the gun's breech block with them on their return to Ladysmith. One British officer was killed in this incident.[123]

> P3.2.3.12 British troops climbing up Lombard's Kop (Gun Hill) on the evening of 7 December.
> ▶ Relief sculpted on pedestal of the Anglo-Boer War memorial, Francis Farewell Square, c/o Anton Lembede St & Dorothy Nyembe St, Durban, KwaZulu-Natal.
> ◉ S29° 51.525, E31° 01.514 (Google Maps).

> P3.2.3.13 The breech block is currently exhibited in the Siege Museum.
> ▶ Murchison St, on the eastern side of the Town Hall, Ladysmith, KwaZulu-Natal.
> ◉ S28° 33.547, E29° 46.847 (Google Maps).

> The gravestone of Trooper R.G. Nicol of the Imperial Light Horse, who was mortally wounded on Gun Hill on 8 December 1899.[124]
> ▶ British Garden of Remembrance, municipal cemetery, Ladysmith, southern side of Cemetery Rd, between Illings St & Mandela St, Ladysmith, KwaZulu-Natal.
> ◉ S28° 33.322, E29° 47.687.

On the night of 11 December, 12 British officers and 488 men from Ladysmith, led by Lieutenant-Colonel C. Metcalfe, again managed to occupy a Boer gun emplacement on Vaalkop, which was subsequently called Surprise Hill by the British forces. They managed to destroy a Boer howitzer and some ammunition with explosives, but the cost was high: at least 20 men were killed, 14 were wounded and six were taken prisoner in the operation. The Republican losses were four killed or died of wounds, five wounded and three missing.[125]

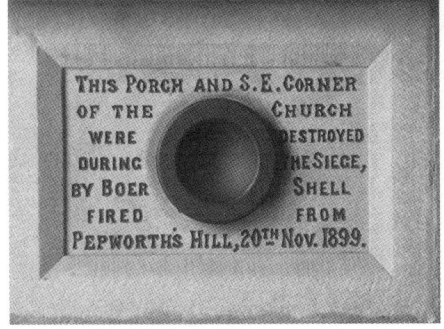

P3.2.3.11

P3.2.3.12

P3.2.3.13

---

122 Christopher & Christopher 1982, 4.
123 Amery III 1905, 167-168; Cloete 2010, 73-74.
124 Watt 2000, 309.
125 Pretorius 2010, 170-171.

Part 3 – The military history of the war: the first year (11 October 1899–10 October 1900)

P3.2.3.14 These memorials on Vaalkop (Surprise Hill) indicate where the attack took place.
▶ *A few kilometres north of Ladysmith, KwaZulu-Natal. Access to this site is restricted and permission has to be obtained from the landowner. The use of a guide is recommended.*
◙ *GPS co-ordinates not available.*

Lieutenant G.C.D. Fergusson (25), 2nd Battalion Rifle Brigade, was killed in action in the night attack on Surprise Hill.[126]
▶ *His grave is in the British Garden of Remembrance, municipal cemetery, Ladysmith, southern side of Cemetery Rd, between Illings St & Mandela St, Ladysmith, KwaZulu-Natal.*
◙ *S28° 33.322, E29° 47.687.*
The grave of Sergeant R. Patterson, 2nd Battalion Rifle Brigade, killed in action in the same engagement, is also in this cemetery.[127]

P3.2.3.15 The gravestone of D.T. (Désiré) de Villiers, a young burgher of the Pretoria Commando who was killed on Surprise Hill. He was initially buried in Natal, but was reinterred after the war in the Old Church Street West Cemetery, Pretoria. The grave statue of Carara marble was ordered from Italy by his father, Tielman de Villiers. It portrays a wounded young burgher, rifle in hand.[128] Two other members of the Pretoria Commando killed in the same engagement, John Niemeyer and Harry Spanier, were also reinterred in the same cemetery after the war.
▶ *Entry to cemetery from Es'kia Mphahlele St (previously D.F. Malan Dr), north of W.F. Nkomo Dr (previously Church St West).*
◙ *De Villiers's grave is at S25°44.473, E28°10.323, Niemeyer's among the burgher graves and Spanier's in the Jewish section, on the western side of the cemetery, near the entrance (S25°44.460, E28°10.236).*

Despite these setbacks, the Republican siege of Ladysmith continued. The town was constantly bombarded by artillery from gun emplacements on various hills. On 18 December, four sentries of the Natal Carbineers and a number of black trench diggers at Caesar's Camp, Platrand, were killed by Republican shelling.[129]

The gravestone of Trooper R.M. Milne-Miller (25) of the Natal Carbineers, who was killed by the Boer shell on 18 December 1899. The gravestones of Troopers T. Elliot (17), W. Buxton (47) and W.S. Smith who were killed in action in the same incident are close to that of Milne-Milner.[130] (P1.23 shows Smith's gravestone.)
▶ *British Garden of Remembrance, municipal cemetery, Ladysmith, southern side of Cemetery Rd, between Illings St & Mandela St, Ladysmith, KwaZulu-Natal.*
◙ *S28° 33.322, E29° 47.687.*

P3.2.3.14

P3.2.3.15

P3.2.3.16

---

126   Watt 2000, 135.
127   Watt 2000, 324.
128   Van Bart & Scholtz 2003, 53.
129   Cloete 2000, 73.
130   Watt 2000, 60, 127 & 289.

On 20 December 1899, the Republican Long Tom gun firing from Bulwana hit and damaged the clock tower of the Ladysmith Town Hall. Nobody was injured.[131]

P3.2.3.16 The Ladysmith Town Hall – repaired after the war.
▶ *C/o Murchison St & Queen St, Ladysmith, KwaZulu-Natal.*
◉ *S28° 33.565, E29° 46.854 (Google Maps).*

Several officers of the 1st Devonshire Regiment were killed by a Republican shell while they were having breakfast on 27 December 1899.[132]

The gravestone of Lieutenant A.F. Dalzel of the 1st Devonshire Regiment, one of the officers killed by a Republican shell on 27 December 1899.[133]
▶ *British Garden of Remembrance, municipal cemetery, Ladysmith, southern side of Cemetery Rd, between Illings St & Mandela St, Ladysmith, KwaZulu-Natal.*
◉ *S28° 33.322, E29° 47.687.*

The Boer besiegers of Ladysmith attempted to capture the British defensive positions on Platrand, south-east of the town, on 6 January 1900. Transvaal burghers led by General Schalk Burger stormed the British at Caesar's Camp, and Free State burghers led by Chief Commandant Marthinus Prinsloo attacked the defenders of Wagon Hill. Commandant C.J. de Villiers of Harrismith led the Free State assault. Both Republican attacks stalled early on, but fighting continued the whole day. A heavy thunderstorm in the late afternoon worsened the conditions. The Boer retreat began soon after the rain ended; De Villiers was reportedly the last to leave. Casualties on both sides were high: the British lost about 150 men killed, and 275 were wounded. Boer losses amounted to 65 killed and 130 wounded.[134]

Numerous memorials and grave sites are scattered across the summit and slopes of Platrand/Wagon Hill.
▶ *Turn south on the gravel road from the N11 between Ladysmith and the N3 highway.*
◉ *S28° 35.458 E29° 45.575.*

The memorials include the following on the Republican side:

P3.2.3.17 Monument honouring Commandant de Villiers.

P3.2.3.18 Kestell memorial, with the following inscription: "It was here that during the battle on 6th January 1900 the Reverend John Daniel Kestell Minister of the Harrismith Commando in great danger and under heavy fire brought succor to wounded friend and foe alike. A grievously wounded British sergeant said to him: 'You are preaching a good sermon to-day'."

P3.2.3.17

P3.2.3.18

P3.2.3.19

---

131 Cloete 2010, 82.
132 Craw 1972, 42; Cloete 2010, 84.
133 Watt 2000, 101.
134 Kestell ca 1903, 35-42; Pretorius 2010, 332-335a.

Part 3 – The military history of the war: the first year (11 October 1899–10 October 1900)

P3.2.3.19 The enormous Burgher Monument commemorates the 781 burghers who died in Natal in the Anglo-Boer War, including the burghers killed in action in the assault on Platrand on 6 January 1900. The crypt at the memorial contains the remains of 310 burghers, as well as two little Boer girls who were reburied here – one died in the Ladysmith concentration camp and the other in the prisoner-of-war camp[135] (see also CP9 on p. 132).
▶ *On the eastern side of the summit of Platrand.*
◉ *S28° 35.278, E29° 46.357.*

A number of original Boer gravestones are mounted on the exterior wall of the memorial. These include the gravestones of four burghers killed in action in the assault on Platrand, namely H.N.W. Wessels (47), J. de Kock (23), G.G. Jacobs (23) and A.W. Raath (20).

Sites on Platrand/Wagon Hill commemorating British participants in the battle of 6 January 1900 include the following:

P3.2.3.20 Memorial for the Duke of Ava who died of wounds received in this battle.

P3.2.3.21 The Royal Engineers Cairn with the following inscription: "On this spot fell on Jan. 6th 1900 Lieut. R.J.T. Digby Jones. VC [Victoria Cross] and near him, 2nd Lieut. G.B.B. Denniss, Sergeant C. Jackson, 2nd Corporal E. Hunt, Lance Corporal H. Bailey, [and] Sapper[s] W. Bland, W. Simmonds [&] T. Cox, Royal Engineers." Lieutenant Digby-Jones's grave is in the municipal cemetery, Ladysmith.[136]

P3.2.3.22 Imperial Light Horse Monument listing the names of 12 members of that unit who were killed in action on 6 January 1900 and six who died of their wounds.

P3.2.3.23 Memorial with the names of 22 members of the 1st Battalion Devonshire Regiment killed in action on 6 January 1900.

P3.2.3.24 Graves of 13 Devonshire Regiment soldiers, on the lower slopes of Platrand/Wagon Hill.

P3.2.3.25 Hussars' Memorial near the Burgher Monument. The inscription reads: "This post and the outlying works were held by the 18th Hussars, from January 1900, to the end of the siege of Ladysmith."

P3.2.3.26 Rock in the Hussars' memorial with the inscription: "Manchesters Fort built by F & H Coys [Companies]1st Bn Manchester Regiment. Garrisoned during the siege of Ladysmith 1899 as follows. H Coy [Company] Capt A. Menzies 2nd Lt W. Baldowes 80 NCO's & men. F Coy [Company] Lt H.V. Roe 76 NCO's & men."

P3.2.3.27 British military cemetery on the lower slopes of Platrand/Wagon Hill (see also CP5 on p. 131).

 P3.2.3.20
 P3.2.3.21
 P3.2.3.22
 P3.2.3.23

---

135 Bakkes 1989a, 231-233.
136 Uys 2000, 32-34; Watt 2000, 112.

P3.2.3.24   P3.2.3.25   P3.2.3.26

P3.2.3.28 King's Royal Rifles Memorial in memory of the 1st & 2nd Battalion King's Royal Rifles killed in action on Platrand/Wagon Hill.

P3.2.3.29 Gordon Highlanders memorial on the mass grave of 14 members of the 2nd Battalion of that regiment killed in action on Platrand at Caesars Camp.

P3.2.3.30 Cairn indicating the spot where Lieutenant-Colonel W.H. Dick-Cunyngham (awarded the Victoria Cross), commanding the 2nd Battalion Gordon Highlanders, was mortally wounded. Dick-Cunyngham's grave is in the municipal cemetery, Ladysmith.[137]
▶ *About 300 m from Dry Rd, across from the Indoor Sports Centre, Ladysmith, KwaZulu-Natal.*
◉ *S28° 34.153, E29° 46.144.*

Some of the burghers who were killed in the Battle of Platrand were buried elsewhere:

P3.2.3.31 Grave of Herman Nienhuis, born in Holland, who lived in the ZAR from 1884.
▶ *Kloof Cemetery, next to the Kloof Spruit on the northern side of the extension of Fenter St, Heidelberg, Gauteng.*
◉ *S26° 29.717, E28° 20.770.*

P3.2.3.32 Grave of C.J. de Jager (47), killed in action on 6 January 1900 at Platrand, Ladysmith. The graves of the burghers F.J. Roos (30) and F.W. Wagner (18), who were also killed in action at Platrand on 6 January 1900, are also in this cemetery.
▶ *Old Church Street West Cemetery, Pretoria, Gauteng, entry from Es'kia Mphahlele St (previously D.F. Malan Dr), north of W.F. Nkomo Dr (previously Church St West).*
◉ *Close to S25° 44.473, E28° 10.323.*

P3.2.3.27   P3.2.3.28   P3.2.3.29   P3.2.3.30

---

137   Watt 2000, 111.

Part 3 – The military history of the war: the first year (11 October 1899–10 October 1900)

Some of the British soldiers who died from wounds received in the battle were also buried elsewhere:

The gravestone of Lieutenant Archibald, Earl of Ava (36), mortally wounded on 6 January 1900,[138] is in the British Garden of Remembrance in the municipal cemetery in Ladysmith, as is the grave of Major D.E. Doveton (54), Imperial Light Horse, who died from his wounds on 14 February1900.[139]
▶ *British Garden of Remembrance, municipal cemetery, Ladysmith, southern side of Cemetery Rd, between Illings St & Mandela St, Ladysmith, KwaZulu-Natal.*
◉ *S28° 33.322, E29° 47.687.*

P3.2.3.33 Captain S. Mills (23), 2nd Battalion Rifle Brigade, died of wounds in Intombi Camp on 2 February 1900.[140]
▶ *Intombi Garden of Remembrance, between the Klip River and the railway line, 7.2 km south of the Siege Museum, near the L1298, Ladysmith, KwaZulu-Natal.*
◉ *S28° 35.748, E29° 49.313.*

The grave of A.W. Mance (29), of Cape Town, killed in action near Ladysmith, 6 January 1900,[141] is also in the Old Church Street West Cemetery.
▶ *Old Church Street West Cemetery, Pretoria, Gauteng, entry from Es'kia Mphahlele St (previously D.F. Malan Dr), north of W.F. Nkomo Dr (previously Church St West).*
◉ *Close to S25° 44.473, E28° 10.323.*

The siege of Ladysmith ended on 28 February 1900 when the British forces in Natal finally broke through the Republican defensive lines on the northern side of the Thukela River.[142] This joyous event, from a British perspective, led to the formation of a new unit, the Irish Guards, in April 1900.

P3.2.3.34 Irish Guards memorial. The inscription reads: "Dedicated to those whom Queen Victoria called 'My brave Irish soldiers' whose courage and sacrifice in the fighting that led to the relief of Ladysmith on 28 February 1900 inspired the formation of the Irish Guards by Royal Command on 1 April 1900 'Quis Separabit'."
▶ *In front of the Siege Museum, Murchison Street, Ladysmith, KwaZulu-Natal.*
◉ *S28° 33.547, E29° 46.847 (Google Maps).*

3.3 The first British offensive up to Black Week, 23 November–15 December 1899

The first British offensive got underway towards the end of November and began with the approach of a British force from the Cape Colony. The commander was Lieutenant-General Lord Methuen, who was destined to be involved in the war right up to the end. He and his forces came by way of the railway line from Cape Town, passing through towns such as Wellington, Worcester, Matjiesfontein, Beaufort West and De Aar up to the Orange River (now Gariep

P3.2.3.31

P3.2.3.32

P3.2.3.33

P3.2.3.34

---

138 Watt 2000, 13.
139 Watt 2000, 117.
140 Watt 2000, 289.
141 Watt 2000, 263.
142 Creswicke II ca 1902, 86-92; Grobler 2004, 46; Cloete 2010, 117.

River) at Hopetown. From there, the railway line ran parallel to the western border of the Orange Free State through Kimberley, onwards along the western border of the Transvaal through Mafeking (now Mahikeng) and then into Bechuanaland (now Botswana) on its way to Rhodesia (now Zimbabwe).

Methuen crossed the Orange River with the First Division, consisting of 10 500 men, before the Boers had the opportunity to blow up the railway bridge. They did, however, attempt to halt his approach north of that river, but Methuen repulsed them. The first battle took place on 23 November near the Belmont railway station, when General Jacobus Prinsloo's 1 500 Free State burghers were driven back. The Boer losses appear to have been 15 killed and 30 wounded, while the British casualties amounted to 54 killed and 243 wounded.[143]

> P3.3.1 Small cemetery where several burghers killed in action in the Battle of Belmont were buried.
> ▶ South-east of and close to the Belmont railway station, next to the S653 gravel road linking the N12 with the S892, Free State.
> ◉ Near S29° 24.978, E24° 22.142 (Google Maps).
>
> P3.3.2 The Republican Battle of Belmont memorial (see also CP10 on p. 133).
> ▶ On a low hill east of the Belmont railway station, on the northern side of the S653 gravel road (the same road that passes the small cemetery) linking the N12 with the S892, Free State. It is clearly visible from the road, and is fenced.
> ◉ GPS co-ordinates not available.
>
> The names of 25 burghers who fell in the Battle of Belmont are inscribed in a roll of honour on the Burgher Monument at Magersfontein (see P3.3.14).
> ▶ On the western side of an unnamed gravel road linking the S1320 and the S574, Northern Cape.
> ◉ S28° 57.201, E24° 44.071.
>
> P3.3.3 Memorial to Captain E.B. Eager (39) and Lieutenant R.W.M. Brine (24), and 13 men of the 1st Battalion Fifth Fusiliers (Northumberland), killed in action at Belmont, 23 November 1899.[144]
> ▶ West End Cemetery, c/o Green St & Reserve Rd, Kimberley, Northern Cape. There is a memorial for five men of the Brigade of Guards. The graves of Lieutenants W.A.H. Blundell (28) and F.L. Fryer (26), both of the 3rd Battalion Grenadier Guards,[145] who all fell at Belmont on 23 November 1899, are in the same cemetery.
> ◉ S28° 44.078, E24° 44.170 (Google Maps).
>
> Two British soldiers, Privates J. Schultz and T. Lynn, who were wounded at Belmont and died while being evacuated by train to Cape Town, were buried at Fraserburg Road Station (now Leeu-Gamka, Western Cape), where their gravestone, with the touching inscription "And there was no more war", can still be seen in a small cemetery on the southern outskirts of the town.[146]
> ◉ GPS co-ordinates not available.

P3.3.1

P3.3.2

P3.3.3

---

143 Pretorius 2010, 32.
144 Watt 2000, 46 & 122.
145 Watt 2000, 36 & 148.
146 Watt 2000, 258 & 370 gives their names as H. Schultze and H. Lynn; Marincowitz 2014, 43.

Part 3 – The military history of the war: the first year (11 October 1899–10 October 1900)

Two days after the Battle of Belmont, on 25 November, Methuen's First Division again attacked the Boers, who had retreated about 16 km northwards from Belmont and had taken up position in the low hills at Graspan, also referred to as Enslin or Rooilaagte. The combined Republican force of about 2 000 burghers included Free State burghers commanded by General Jacobus Prinsloo and Transvaal burghers commanded by General Koos de la Rey. The burghers were again forced to retreat northwards, but only after inflicting heavy casualties on Methuen's forces. British losses were 168 men killed and 143 wounded, and the Boers lost 19 killed and 41 wounded.[147]

P3.3.4 The British memorial near the Graspan railway station, Northern Cape, where the battle took place.
▶ *On high ground east of the N12 highway (clearly visible from the road) near the Enslin railway halt, Northern Cape. It is on a fenced-in farm. Access from the N12 can be obtained through a gate a few hundred metres north of the memorial – keys are kept at a farmhouse on the western side of the N12 immediately opposite the access gate.*
◉ *S29° 16.724, E24° 28.575.*

There is a memorial in honour of 12 members of the Royal Navy & Royal Marines who were killed in action or died of wounds received at Graspan on 25 November 1899 in Kimberley. The gravestone of Trooper W. Wilkins, 9th Lancers, killed in action at Honey Nest Kloof in the Battle of Graspan, is in the same cemetery. This gravestone also commemorates Trooper J.A.W. Robinson (24), Scotts Railway Guards, killed in action at Gannaputs, Orange Free State, 26 June 1901.[148]
▶ *West End Cemetery, c/o Green St & Reserve Rd, Kimberley, Northern Cape.*
◉ *S28° 44.078, E24° 44.170 (Google Maps).*

P3.3.5 The grave of M.C. Groenewald, a burgher who was wounded at Graspan and died of his wounds four days later.
▶ *Municipal Cemetery, Boshof, Free State.*
◉ *South-eastern side of the town, near S28° 32.530, E25° 14.708.*

A monument was erected by the Dutch Reformed Church congregation of Jacobsdal to commemorate the burghers who died in the Battle of Graspan near the Rooilaagte/Enslin Railway Halt,[149] but the author could not locate it.

On 28 November, a stronger Republican force of about 2 100 men, which included both Free State and Transvaal burghers, attempted to halt the progress of Methuen's First Division at the place where the railway line from the south to Kimberley crosses the Modder River. The result was the Battle of Modder River, also called the Battle of Twee Riviere (Two Rivers), because the battle was fought at the confluence of the Riet River and the Modder River. The outcome of the battle hung in the balance for hours until the British finally gained the upper hand and the Boers were forced to retire. Both Methuen and De la Rey were wounded in the battle. One of the 16 men on the Boer side

P3.3.4

P3.3.5

P3.3.6

P3.3.7

---

147   Creswicke II ca1902, 92-97; Pretorius 2010, 164.
148   Watt 2000, 357 & 452.
149   Van der Bank 1995, 43.

who were killed or died of wounds was Adaan de la Rey, General Koos de la Rey's eldest son. Altogether 66 burghers were wounded. The First Division casualties amounted to about 70 men killed and more than 400 wounded.[150]

P3.3.6 The heavily wounded Adriaan Johannes Gysbertus (Adaan) de la Rey was carried to the Boer military hospital in Jacobsdal by his father and friends, but died on arrival.[151] He was initially buried there, but was later reburied at the Burgher Monument at Magersfontein.
▶ *His gravestone is mounted on the wall of the entrance gate to the Burgher Monument, on the western side of an unnamed gravel road linking the S1320 and the S574, Northern Cape.*
◉ *S28° 57.201, E24° 44.071.*

P3.3.7 Memorial gravestone of N.F. van der Merwe (24), a burgher killed in action at Modder River on 28 November 1899; the same stone commemorates S.W. van der Merwe, a burgher killed in action at Witputs, on 7 November 1900.
▶ *Municipal cemetery, c/o Rabie St & Lombaard St, Luckhoff, Free State.*
◉ *S29° 44.969, E24° 46.945.*

P3.3.8 The Yorkshire Light Infantry Memorial at the Modder River displays a plaque commemorating British soldiers who died in that battle.
▶ *On the northern side of a gravel road that joins the N12 highway from the west, a short distance south of the Modder River, Northern Cape.*
◉ *S29° 02.713, E24° 36.405.*

Kimberley's West End Cemetery contains the graves of a number of members of the British forces who fell at Modder River on 28 November 1899, including those of Lieutenant-Colonel H.P. Northcott (43), Leinster Regiment, Lieutenant-Colonel H.S. Stopford (43), commanding the 2nd Battalion Coldstream Guards, and Captain S. Earle (34) of the same regiment.[152]
▶ *West End Cemetery, c/o Green St & Reserve Rd, Kimberley, Northern Cape.*
◉ *S28° 44.078, E24° 44.170 (Google Maps).*

In all three encounters undertaken during the first British offensive on the western border of the Orange Free State, the casualties suffered by the British were much higher than those of the Boers. More importantly, the Boers learned more about British tactics in each encounter and began working on plans to halt British successes.

Methuen was not the only British commander who attempted to take the offensive. In Natal, the main British force was gathering strength south of the Thukela River under the command of General Sir Redvers Buller, who was then the supreme commander of the British forces in South Africa. By the middle of December, he had a force far superior in numbers and in artillery than that of the two Republics put together.

In the eastern Cape Colony, a British force under Major-General William Gatacre was gathering near the important railway junction at Stormberg, which was occupied by the Boers, with the specific objective of scattering the burghers and gaining control of the junction.

P3.3.8

P3.3.9

P3.3.10

---

150   Creswicke II ca1902, 97-108; Pretorius 2010, 285-288.
151   D'Assonville 2001.
152   Watt 2000, 123, 311 & 401.

Part 3 – The military history of the war: the first year (11 October 1899–10 October 1900)

Towards the end of November, on the Natal front, Commandant-General Joubert was badly injured in a fall from his horse, and had to leave the front for treatment. On 25 November, he appointed the young General Louis Botha as acting supreme commander. The Boers were aware that the British were preparing a major offensive, and Botha energetically prepared a defensive line along the banks of the Thukela River to the southeast of Ladysmith.[153]

P3.3.9 Louis Botha is portrayed as a Republican commander on the Natal front in this bas relief.
▶ *On the pedestal of Botha's monumental statue, Gardens of the Union Buildings, northern side of Stanza Bopape St (formerly Church St), Pretoria.*
◉ *S25° 44.650, E28° 12.658.*

On the southern front, there were frequent skirmishes between Republican and British forces in the Colesberg area from the end of November 1899, into December. British military tactics on this front involved attempting to confuse the Republican forces by creating the impression that the Boers might be attacked by a large force at any time. Hence, the Republican forces remained largely passive. Only on 12 December did heavy fighting occur after an unsuccessful attempt by Boer commandos to cut off British troops stationed in the vicinity of the Arundel railway station from Noupoort in the south. However, neither side suffered heavy casualties.[154]

P3.3.10 Gravestone of Private W. Ross, 6th Dragoon Guards, killed in action at Jasfontein, near Arundel, on 12 December 1899.[155]
▶ *British Garden of Remembrance, western side of Station Rd, near the northern limit of the town, Colesberg, Northern Cape.*
◉ *S30° 42.730, E25° 06.086 (Google Maps).*

The first British offensive came to an abrupt and disastrous halt for the British in one terrible week, from 10 to 17 December 1899. On Sunday 10 December, Gatacre's intended onslaught on the Stormberg railway junction failed because his troops got lost in the dark and became easy targets for General J.H. Olivier's Boers on Kissieberg soon after daybreak. Moreover, in their confusion, British artillerists fired on their own men. After only 75 minutes of fighting, Gatacre ordered his men to retreat to Molteno. About 600 of his men never received the order and were eventually taken prisoner. This humiliating defeat cost the British 28 killed, 61 wounded and 634 taken prisoner. Three of their Armstrong guns were captured. The Boer losses were eight killed and 26 wounded.[156]

P3.3.11 There is no Republican memorial commemorating the Battle of Stormberg. On the battlefield itself, one can still see the fortifications built by the Boers on Kissieberg. There is also a British military cemetery on the battle field.[157]
▶ *The battlefield is on a privately owned farm on the northern side of the R56 between Molteno and Steynsburg, about 10 km west of Molteno, Eastern Cape.*
◉ *Near S31° 18.407, E26° 15.579 (Google Maps).*

P3.3.11   P3.3.12   P3.3.13

---

153   Meintjies 1971, 180-184; Grobler 2004, 19; Cloete 2010, 68.
154   Cloete 2010, 78.
155   Watt 2000, 361.
156   Meintjies 1969a, 81-103; Cloete 2010, 75.
157   Oosthuizen 1998, 18-19.

ANGLO-BOER WAR   Historical Guide to Memorials and Sites in South Africa

P3.3.12 Grave of Lieutenant-Colonel H.A. Eager (46), who commanded the 2nd Battalion Royal Irish Rifles, wounded in the Battle of Stormberg on 10 December 1899; died on 13 February 1900.[158]
▶ *British Garden of Remembrance, municipal cemetery, next to the R344/397, Sterkstroom, Eastern Cape.*
◉ *S31° 33.202, E26° 32.759.*

P3.3.13 There is an exhibit on the Battle of Stormberg in the Queenstown Museum.
▶ *13 Shepstone Street, Queenstown, Eastern Cape.*
◉ *Parking at S31° 53.673, E26° 52.386.*

The very next day, on Monday 11 December 1899, the Stormberg disaster was repeated when Methuen's First Division attacked the Boers on the western front at Magersfontein. His soldiers walked straight into heavy Boer fire. The burghers were waiting for the soldiers in well-concealed trenches, dug on the insistence of General Koos de la Rey, on the plains below the Magersfontein heights. Fighting began before daybreak and kept on until late afternoon.[159]

On the Republican side, the Scandinavian Corps came under severe pressure, but they fought bravely. Their commander, Captain Johannes Flygare, and all the other officers became casualties. Republican casualties were high: an estimated 87 were killed and 184 were wounded. Methuen's men suffered more than 1 000 casualties, of whom 210 were killed, including the commander of the Highland Brigade, Major-General Andy Wauchope. It is generally accepted that the position of the Boer trenches had a major impact on the outcome of the battle, since the British seemed to have no idea where the defensive line of the Boers was and assumed that the defenders would be closer to the Magersfontein heights.[160]

The Magersfontein battlefield site has been well developed for tourism. There are a number of things to see, including
- *a relief model of the battle-field;*
- *the battlefield itself (see P1.8 on p. 15 and also CP3 on p. 130);*
- *the remains of the Boer trenches below the Magersfontein ridge.*

P3.3.14 The new tall Burgher Monument, unveiled in 1969, straddles the original Burgher Monument unveiled by N.C. (Klasie) Havenga in 1931.[161]
▶ *North of the battlefield itself, on the eastern side of an unnamed gravel road linking the S1320 and the S574, Northern Cape.*
◉ *S28° 57.201, E24° 44.071.*

The gravestones of a number of Republican casualties of this battle are mounted on a wall of the entrance gate to the Burgher Monument. These include the gravestones of Jacobus Christoffel van Tonder (66), killed in action in the battle, J.M. de Wet (53) and I.S. van Rooyen (22).

P3.3.14

P3.3.15

P3.3.16

---

158   Watt 2000, 122.
159   Grobler 2004, 22.
160   Amery II 1902, 396-420; Lane 2001, 40-43; Pretorius 2010, 259-262, 404.
161   Cronjé 1989b, 77.

Part 3 – The military history of the war: the first year (11 October 1899–10 October 1900)

P3.3.15 Exhibit of a Boer trench in the battlefield museum.
▶ *On the western side of an unnamed gravel road linking the S1320 and the S574, Northern Cape. This battlefield site is signposted on the N12 highway. Ask for a map of the site at the entrance gate to the terrain.*

P3.3.16 Replica of a Krupp canon used by the Boer forces on a low hill overlooking the battlefield.

P3.3.17 Monument for the Scandinavian Corps, who fought on the Republican side. It was unveiled by General Louis Botha in 1908. Four obelisks stand at the corners of the monument; each represents a Scandinavian country – Sweden, Denmark, Norway and Finland. Each carries an inscription in the language of the country that it represents, and engravings representing Scandinavian folklore[162] (see also CP7 on p. 132).

P3.3.18 Mass graves of members of the Scandinavian Corps killed in action fighting on the Boer side.

There are a number of memorials for the British forces who participated in the Battle of Magersfontein, including the following:

P3.3.19 The Scottish Memorial near the museum.

P3.3.20 The Scottish memorial and roll of honour on a battlefield mass grave.

P3.3.21 Memorials with the names of specific officers who were originally buried on the battlefield, but have since been reinterred in the British Garden of Remembrance in the West End Cemetery, Kimberley, Northern Cape. This cemetery contains a memorial to Captains A.F. Lambton and J.R. Clarke, and Lieutenant W.R. Cowie and 18 men of the Highland Brigade killed in action at Magersfontein on 11 December 1899, as well as a number of other memorials and gravestones of members of the British forces who fell at Magersfontein on that fateful day.
◉ *S28° 44.078, E24° 44.170 (Google Maps).*

P3.3.22 Commemorative plaque at the Burgher Monument indicating the area where an unknown young Scottish soldier who died of his wounds was buried by the burghers. He has since been identified as Drummer William Milne, Seaforth Highlanders.[163]
◉ *S28° 57.201, E24° 44.071.*

P3.3.23 Grave of Major-General Andy Wauchope (53), Commander of the Highland Brigade, who was killed in action in the Battle of Magersfontein.[164]
▶ *Monument Cemetery, 10 km west of Matjiesfontein, Western Cape (towards Cape Town) – next to the railway line.*
◉ *S33° 14.307, E20° 28.402.*

P3.3.17　　　P3.3.18　　　P3.3.19　　　P3.3.20　　　P3.3.21　　　P3.3.22

162　Van Bart & Scholtz 2003, 65.
163　Watt 2000, 290.
164　Watt 2000, 441.

P3.3.24 Memorial in honour of Wauchope (see also CP8 on p. 132).
▶ *Same as P3.3.23, but above the cemetery.*

Two days after the Battle of Magersfontein, on 13 December, two British patrols crossed the border of the Orange Free State from the Cape Colony at Soutpansdrif, west of Luckhoff. Commandant Lourens Fourie and his burghers engaged in heavy fighting with them at Bloudraai. The British patrols were forced to retreat after suffering casualties. On the Free State side, Fourie himself was killed in action.[165]

P3.3.25 Gravestone of Captain W.E.J. Bradshaw (31), York & Lancaster Regiment, killed in action at Zoutpan (near Bloudraai) on 13 December 1899,[166] "Erected to the Memory of the Truest, Bravest, Kindest Son by his broken hearted mother, Mrs Shapland Tandy, Kingstown, Ireland."
▶ *West End Cemetery, corner of Green St & Reserve Rd, Kimberley, Northern Cape.*
◉ *S28° 44.078, E24° 44.170 (Google Maps).*

P3.3.26 Grave (vandalised) of Commandant L.H. Fourie, killed in action at Bloudraai on 13 December 1899.[167]
▶ *Municipal cemetery, c/o Rabie St & Lombaard St, Luckhoff, Free State.*
◉ *S29° 44.969, E24° 46.945.*

Four days after Magersfontein, on Friday 15 December 1899, the British forces suffered an even greater disaster when Buller's attempt to cross the Thukela River at Colenso and relieve the garrison in Ladysmith turned into a humiliating rout. General Louis Botha's Boer forces not only drove the attackers back but captured ten British 15-pounder Armstrong guns with their ammunition wagons. The Boers suffered the loss of 39 men. By contrast, Buller's casualties amounted to 1 139 men, of whom seven officers and 136 men were killed.[168]

The names of the eight burghers who were killed in action in the Battle of Colenso on 15 December, as well as those of two burghers who died of other causes, are engraved on a roll of honour on the Burgher Monument, Platrand, Ladysmith, KwaZulu-Natal (see P3.2.3.19).
◉ *S28° 35.278, E29° 46.357.*

P3.3.27 The diorama of the Battle of Colenso in the Stevenson Museum in the old toll house.
▶ *Sir George Street, where the street crosses the Thukela River at Colenso, KwaZulu-Natal.*
◉ *S28° 44.127, E29° 49.318.*

British commemorative places of the Battle of Colenso include the following:

P3.3.23 P3.3.24 P3.3.25 P3.3.26 P3.3.27

165	Cloete 2010, 78.
166	Watt 2000, 42.
167	Oosthuizen ca 2000, 18.
168	Hall 1999; Pretorius 2010, 90-92; Bourquin & Torlage 2014.

Part 3 – The military history of the war: the first year (11 October 1899–10 October 1900)

P3.3.28 Markers showing the position of the British field guns captured by the Boers in the Battle of Colenso.
▶ *Signposted, on the outskirts of Colenso, KwaZulu-Natal.*
◉ *S28° 44.313, E29° 49.585.*

P3.3.29 Graves of soldiers killed in action in the Clouston Memorial Garden.
▶ *Next to R74 south of Colenso at Nkankezi, between the L237 and the P294, KwaZulu-Natal.*
◉ *S28° 46.748, E29° 48.596.*

There are also graves in the Ambleside Cemetery, about 3.2 km west of Colenso, on the northern side of the road leading to Winterton, KwaZulu-Natal.[169]

P3.3.30 Lieutenant/Sergeant Francis Talbot, 2nd Battalion (Princess Victoria's) Royal Irish Fusiliers, was mortally wounded at Colenso on 15 December 1899, while defending the British guns. He was taken to the British military hospital in Rondebosch, Cape Town, where he died on 1 January 1900.[170]
▶ *His grave is in the Anglo-Boer War Garden of Remembrance, Commonwealth War Graves section, Maitland Cemetery, Voortrekker Rd, Cape Town, Western Cape.*
◉ *S33° 55.022, E18° 32.280 (Google Maps).*

One of the British officers killed in the Battle of Colenso was Lieutenant Freddy Roberts, only son of Field Marshal Lord Roberts, who became the British Commander-in-Chief in South Africa. Lieutenant Roberts was one of six British soldiers awarded a Victoria Cross for bravery in the battle – some posthumously.[171]

P3.3.31 Memorial gravestone of Lieutenant F.H.S. (Freddy) Roberts (awarded the Victoria Cross)(27).[172]
▶ *Garden of Remembrance, Chieveley, KwaZulu-Natal (signposted, off the R103 near Frere). Turn to the east from the R74 about 5 km south of the Clouston Memorial Garden. Cross the railway line on this gravel road and turn south. Keep to the right where the road forks. The cemetery is under trees between the railway line and the gravel road.*
◉ *S28° 50.013, E29° 48.410 (Google Maps).*

Colenso was the last battle of what was truly a *Black Week*, to use a term from British newspapers, for the British forces in South Africa. After the setbacks that they suffered, Gatacre, Methuen and Buller were not in a strong enough position to resume the offensive without difficulty.

3.4 The struggle continues, 16 December 1899–10 February 1900

After "Black Week", a month of reduced activity followed on all war fronts. That does not, however, mean that the war had come to an end. Indeed, it went on for more than 30 months. Throughout the war, there were occasional

P3.3.28   P3.3.29   P3.3.30

---

169   Von der Heyde, 2012, 152-153.
170   Watt 2000, 407.
171   Creswicke VI 1902, 191-192; Creswicke VII 1902, 212; Uys 2000, 19-25; Cloete 2010, 79-80.
172   Watt 2000, 355.

skirmishes between Boer and Brit, in addition to the well-known engagements and battles. The widespread presence of graves – of both burghers and British soldiers who fell in these engagements – serve as memorials to those clashes, and provide evidence of some incidents which are not well documented in books. Photographs of some of these graves and/or particulars about some of the victims are included throughout this book.

Thus there was intermittent fighting around Colesberg in the Northern Cape, which served as the headquarters of the Republican forces in this area for more than three months.

P3.4.1 Grave of Trooper Wilfred Moss Johnson (20), 32nd Company Imperial Yeomanry and Lieutenant 2nd Lancashire Volunteer Artillery, killed in action at Hamelfontein, near Colesberg, on 17 December 1899.[173]
▶ British Garden of Remembrance, western side of Station Rd, near the northern limit of the town, Colesberg, Northern Cape.
◉ S30° 42.730, E25° 06.086 (Google Maps).

The graves of other members of the Imperial forces who fell in this period and were buried in this cemetery include those of
- *Second Lieutenant A.V. West (23), Royal Berkshire Regiment, killed in action near Colesberg on 1 January 1900.[174]*
- *Major Charles Bateson Harvey (40), 10th Royal Hussars, killed in action at Suffolk Hill, near Rensburg, south of Colesberg, on 4 January 1900.[175]*

On New Year's Day 1900, General French's British forces attacked the Boer positions around Colesberg and made slight gains. One British officer was killed and 21 soldiers were wounded in comparison to Republican losses, which totalled nine burghers wounded.[176] Four days later, General Piet de Wet launched a counter-attack against the British forces who were threatening the Republican positions in Colesberg. His offensive failed, as the Boer losses amounted to five burghers killed, ten wounded and 21 taken prisoner. British casualties came to seven killed and 15 wounded.[177]

On 6 January, a force consisting of 305 soldiers of the Suffolk Regiment, under the command of Lieutenant-Colonel A.J. Watson, failed in their attack on a Republican position on Graskop (Grassy Hill, subsequently called Suffolk Hill by the British). In all, 37 men were killed (including Watson), 52 were wounded and 99 were taken prisoner (including 29 of the wounded).[178]

P3.4.2 Memorial for 33 members of the Suffolk Regiment and three unknown soldiers killed in action at Suffolk Hill, Colesberg, on 6 January (incorrectly indicated on the memorial as 9 January) 1900. The gravestone of

P3.3.31

P3.4.1

P3.4.2

P3.4.3

---

173 Watt 2000, 221.
174 Watt 2000, 444.
175 Watt 2000, 183.
176 Breytenbach IV 1977, 33-35; Cloete 2010, 87.
177 Grobler ca 1937, 39-43; Breytenbach IV 1977, 44; Cloete 2010, 88.
178 Breytenbach IV 1977, 50-55; Cloete 2010, 89.

Part 3 – The military history of the war: the first year (11 October 1899–10 October 1900)

Captain Arthur Wale Brown (32), 1st Suffolk Regiment, who died on 8 January 1900 of wounds received in action at Pink Hill (Suffolk Hill) on 6 January,[179] is also in this garden of remembrance.
▶ British Garden of Remembrance, western side of Station Rd, near the northern limit of the town, Colesberg, Northern Cape.
◉ S30° 42.730, E25° 06.086 (Google Maps).

On 11 January 1901, a British artillery unit managed to hoist a 15-pounder Armstrong gun to the top of the 250 m high Coleskop, from where they fired on the town and its surrounds.[180]

P3.4.3 Coleskop (Coles Hill), which towers almost 300 m above the surrounding landscape, is a very prominent landmark in that part of the Northern Cape.
▶ Photograph taken from the N9 south of Colesberg.
◉ S30° 42.543, E25° 03.415 (Google Maps).

On 16 January, a skirmish took place at Slingerfontein near Colesberg between 21 men of the New South Wales Lancers and a group of burghers led by Lieutenant P.C. van N. de Hart. Five of the Australians were killed in action and 13 were taken prisoner, but the rest managed to escape.[181]

P3.4.4 The gravestone of Sergeant-Major G.A. Griffin (32), 1st Australian Horse, killed in action on 16 January 1900.[182]
▶ British Garden of Remembrance, western side of Station Rd, near the northern limit of the town, Colesberg, Northern Cape.
◉ S30° 42.730, E25° 06.086 (Google Maps).

From the end of January, numerous units of the British forces in the Colesberg area were transferred to De Aar to join up with the vast force the British commanders in South Africa were assembling in preparation for an offensive on the western border of the Orange Free State. The Republican forces at Colesberg did not immediately realize that this was happening. From 5 February onwards, General Koos de la Rey continuously drove the British forces back towards Noupoort in the south. Both sides suffered light casualties in a series of engagements during this period.[183] On 9 February, the Republican forces suffered the loss of four burghers killed and nine wounded when the West Australian Mounted Infantry and Inniskilling Dragoons stubbornly defended a low hill for most of the day, before retiring in small groups after dark. The Imperial losses are not known, but included at least three Australians. The hill was subsequently called West Australian Hill.[184]

P3.4.5 Memorial on West Australian Hill commemorating these events.
▶ On farm land south of Colesberg, Northern Cape.
◉ GPS co-ordinates not available.

 P3.4.4
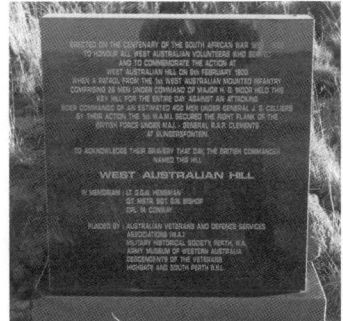 P3.4.5
 P3.4.6

---
179 Watt 2000, 48.
180 Breytenbach IV 1977, 44; Cloete 2010, 88; Pretorius 2010, 93.
181 Grobler 2004, 37; Cloete 2010, 91.
182 Watt 2000, 169.
183 Grobler 2004, 41; Cloete 2010, 100.
184 Cloete 2010, 102.

P3.4.6 The gravestone of William J. Lambie, war correspondent of the Melbourne "Age", killed in action south of Colesberg on 9 February 1900.[185]
▶ *British Garden of Remembrance, western side of Station Rd, near the northern limit of the town, Colesberg, Northern Cape.*
◉ *S30° 42.730, E25° 06.086 (Google Maps).*

On 12 February, the fighting around Colesberg flared up again when the Republican forces launched a determined assault on the British position on Keeromskop. This low hill was defended by units of the Worcester Regiment, who fought back valiantly, but were eventually forced to retire after suffering the loss of 37 men killed, 81 wounded and 19 taken prisoner. Republican losses were eight killed and 19 wounded. Keeromskop was subsequently called Worcester Hill.[186]

P3.4.7 Memorial on Worcester Hill commemorating Lieutenant-Colonel C. Coningham (48), Major A.K. Stubbs (32) and Captain B.H. Thomas (35),[187] as well as 19 non-commissioned officers and men of the 2nd Battalion Worcestershire Regiment who fell in this engagement on 12 February 1900 (see also CP11 on p. 133).
▶ *On farmland near Colesberg, Northern Cape.*
◉ *GPS co-ordinates not available.*

The Republican siege of the British garrison in Kuruman, which began on 11 November 1899, ended on 1 January 1900 when the British forces surrendered. This was the only successful siege attempted by the Republican forces. A total of three soldiers and one Cape Rebel were killed, and one burgher was wounded.[188]

P3.4.8 Gravestone of Private W. Ward (25), Cape Police, killed in defence of Kuruman on 31 December 1899.[189]
▶ *British Garden of Remembrance, West End Cemetery, corner of Green St & Reserve Rd, Kimberley, Northern Cape.*
◉ *S28° 44.078, E24° 44.170 (Google Maps).*

By mid-January 1900, General Buller in Natal resumed his attempt to break through the Republican defensive line north of the Thukela River and to relieve the besieged town of Ladysmith. This time he ordered his army, which by then consisted of about 30 000 men, to cross the river a few kilometres west of Colenso.[190] The Republican forces vigorously resisted this British advance. The first of a series of engagements these took place on 18 January on the farm Acton Holmes, about 11 km northwest of a prominent hill known as Spioenkop on the Upper Thukela River. Major H.W.G. Graham of the 5th (Royal Irish) Lancers ambushed 160 Boers under Field Cornet "Rooi" Daniël Opperman of Pretoria and Field Cornet N.J. Mentz of Heilbron. Mentz and at least three other Boers were killed, and 31 were wounded or taken prisoner.[191]

P3.4.7   P3.4.8   P3.4.9   P3.4.10

---

185 Watt 2000, 240.
186 Cloete 2010, 104.
187 Watt 2000, 83, 403 & 412.
188 Creswicke III ca 1902, 25-26; Grobler 2004, 16 & 32; Cloete 2010, 62, 65, 73, 80, 83 & 87.
189 Watt 2000, 437.
190 Grobler 2004, 31.
191 Breytenbach III 1973, 113-116; Pretorius 2010, 1.

Part 3 – The military history of the war: the first year (11 October 1899–10 October 1900)

P3.4.9 Gravestone of Field Cornet N.J. Mentz, killed in action on 18 January 1900.
▶ *On the wall of the Burgher Monument, Platrand, Ladysmith, KwaZulu-Natal.*
◙ *S28° 35.278, E29° 46.357.*

The British forces subsequently decided to occupy a hill known as Tabanyama, which was located on their preferred route to Ladysmith. However, this move was resisted by the Republican forces. After two days of heavy fighting, the British forces withdrew again, with at least 20 men killed and more than 200 wounded. The Republican forces also suffered casualties.[192]

Some of the British soldiers who fell in this battle were buried in the Rangeworthy military cemetery in the valley south of Tabanyama (see P7.4.6.1).
▶ *On the northern side of the gravel road to the Three Tree Lodge, about 5 km from the R616 between Bergville and Ladysmith, turn off about 15 km from Bergville, KwaZulu-Natal.*
◙ *S28° 39.042, E29° 28.097.*

The names of 20 burghers who were killed in action in the engagements on the Upper Thukela from 18 to 23 January 1900, as well as eight who died of other causes, are engraved in a roll of honour on the Burgher Monument at Platrand, Ladysmith, KwaZulu-Natal (see P3.2.3.19).
◙ *S28° 35.278, E29° 46.357.*

P3.4.10 Grave of W.H. Robbertse (33), killed in action at Tabanyama on 23 January 1900.
▶ *In the abandoned Robbertse family cemetery, on open ground, north-eastern corner of 3rd St & Romney Close, Chartwell A.H., Gauteng.*
◙ *S25° 59.419, E27° 58.493.*

The last battle of this eight-day long offensive occurred on the hill called Spioenkop on Wednesday 24 January. It was the biggest single battle of the whole war, and the British losses were severe. At Spioenkop, about 322 men were killed, 566 were wounded, and 300 were taken prisoner. The total Boer casualties are estimated at 68 killed and 140 wounded, of whom ten died of their wounds.[193]

There is a well-developed battlefield park on the summit of Spioenkop. The site offers a self-guided trail, with a brochure, among the graves, monuments and trenches. An entrance fee is payable. Open daily.
▶ *On P138 Eversholt, off the R616, KwaZulu-Natal.*
◙ *S28° 38.893, E29° 31.008.*

The memorials and graves in this battlefield park include the following:

P3.4.11 Gravestone: "In memory of unknown burger sentry killed on this spot 24th Jan 1900."

P3.4.11   P3.4.12   P3.4.13   P3.4.14

---

192 Breytenbach III 1973, 120-167; Cloete 2010, 93-94.
193 Breytenbach III 1973, 168-236; Cloete 2010, 94-96; Torlage 2014.

P3.4.12 The Burgher monument. Names of 106 burghers who fell in this battle and in clashes immediately preceding it are inscribed on this 5.5 m high memorial, unveiled in 1964.[194]

P3.4.13 British memorials along the main British trench (see also CP14 on p. 134).

P3.4.14 Location of the main British trench, where many men were buried where they fell.

P3.4.15 Imperial Light Horse memorial.

Some of the casualties of the Battle of Spioenkop were buried elsewhere:

P3.4.16 Grave of Major-General Sir Edward Woodgate (54), who was in command of the British troops that initially occupied the summit of Spioenkop. He was mortally wounded by shrapnel during the battle and died in the military hospital at Mooi River on 23 March 1900.[195]
▶ *St John's churchyard, next to the R622 to Greytown, on the southern side of the road, a few kilometres east of Mooi River, KwaZulu-Natal.*
◉ *S29° 12.633, E30° 01.241.*

P3.4.17 Grave of Private J.A.M. Fisher, Imperial Light Infantry, who was wounded in the Battle of Spioenkop and died in the military hospital at Mooi River on 22 February 1900.[196]
▶ *British Garden of Remembrance, 1st St, near 11th Ave, Bruntville, KwaZulu-Natal. South-east of Mooi River, turn southwards off the R622.*
◉ *S29° 13.044, E30° 00.736.*

P3.4.18 Grave of Lieutenant H.V. Lockwood (24), 2nd Scottish Rifles (Cameronians), wounded at Spioenkop on 24 January 1900, who died of his wounds in Durban on 25 February 1900.[197]
▶ *Ordnance Road Military Cemetery, in the small triangle between Ordnance Rd, Soldiers Way and Wyatt Rd, Durban, KwaZulu-Natal; entry from Wyatt Rd through the adjoining museum grounds.*
◉ *S29° 51.153, E31° 01.392.*

The names of 68 burghers who were killed in action in the Battle of Spioenkop, as well as ten who died of their wounds later, are engraved in a roll of honour on the Burgher Monument at Platrand, Ladysmith, KwaZulu-Natal (see P3.2.3.19).
◉ *S28° 35.278, E29° 46.357.*

In early February, the British forces made another attempt at crossing the Thukela River to relieve the besieged garrison in Ladysmith. However, Boer commandos at Vaalkrans north of the Thukela repulsed the British attack from

P3.4.15   P3.4.16   P3.4.17   P3.4.18

---

194   Bakkes 1989b, 234.
195   Watt 2000, 462.
196   Watt 2000, 137.
197   Watt 2000, 253.

Part 3 – The military history of the war: the first year (11 October 1899–10 October 1900)

5 to 7 February, and the British were forced to retreat. Boer losses amounted to 38 killed, 45 wounded and four missing. British losses were about 30 killed, 300 wounded and five missing.[198]

The names of 35 burghers who were killed in action in the Battle of Vaalkrans as well as four who died of other causes are engraved in a roll of honour on the Burgher Monument, Platrand, Ladysmith, KwaZulu-Natal (see P3.2.3.19).
◉ *S28° 35.278, E29° 46.357.*

P3.4.19 The British memorials and graves at Vaalkrans.
▶ *Next to the P182-2 gravel road, west of Ladysmith, KwaZulu-Natal.*
◉ *S28° 40.514, E29° 37.925.*

At the beginning of February 1900, the British forces on the western front attempted to trick General Piet Cronjé – who was still entrenched with the Republican forces at Magersfontein – by occupying Koedoesberg to the west, although they were actually planning to strike in the east. Cronjé was initially not convinced of this feint, but he nevertheless ordered General Christiaan de Wet to cover his western flank with 300 men. This resulted in the indecisive Battle of Koedoesberg from 5 to 8 February. British casualties were six killed, and a further eight men died of their wounds. As a result of the battle, the British eventually did succeed in convincing Cronjé to extend his flank to the west.[199]

P3.4.20 Gravestone of Lieutenant F.G. (Freddie) Tait (30), 2nd Black Watch, killed in action at Koedoesberg on 7 February 1900.[200] Tait was a former British amateur golf champion. He is honoured at the Freddie Tait Golf Museum at the Kimberley Golf Club, Kimberley, Northern Cape, which is the oldest golfing museum on the African continent and showcases artefacts from the very beginning of the sport in South Africa.[201]
▶ *West End Cemetery, corner of Green St & Reserve Rd, Kimberley, Northern Cape. This cemetery contains the gravestones of two other British officers killed in action in that battle and reinterred, namely Captain H.M. Blair (28), 2nd Battalion Seaforth Highlanders and Captain C. Eykyn (32), 42nd Royal Highlanders (Black Watch).[202]*
◉ *S28° 44.078, E24° 44.170 (Google Maps).*

3.5 The second British offensive, 11 February–12 March 1900

In December 1899, the Boers did not exploit the opportunity presented to them by the collapse of the British offensive to take the initiative themselves. Instead, they seemed to hold back, expecting the British to resume their offensive, which they soon did. British reinforcements poured into the country. In the aftermath of Black Week, Buller was replaced as supreme commander by the elderly but highly experienced Field-Marshal Lord F. Roberts. The equally capable and ruthless Field-Marshal Lord H.H. Kitchener was appointed as Roberts's Chief of Staff.[203]

P3.4.19

P3.4.20

---

198 Breytenbach III 1973, 237-330; Watt 1999b; Meijer 2000, 128-137; Pretorius 2010, 468-469.
199 Creswicke III ca 1902, 186-189; De Wet 1999, 46-49; Cloete 2010, 99-101.
200 Watt 2000, 407.
201 Freddie Tait Golf Museum s.a.
202 Watt 2000, 34 & 131.
203 Pakenham 1982, 244.

3.5.1 Western front

Roberts decided to launch a major offensive from the Cape Colony, rather than from Natal. From the end of January, he concentrated a massive force along the railway lines south and west of the Orange Free State, until he sent in his forces on 11 February. The Boers were caught off-guard by this renewed British offensive. In the west, General Piet Cronjé had felt secure behind his entrenchment at Magersfontein, and in Natal, General Louis Botha was confident that he could keep the British to the south of the Thukela River. However, Roberts easily outflanked Cronjé's men on the western front. On 12 February, General John French occupied both the south and the north bank of the Riet River at De Kiels Drift, from where he made deep inroads into the territory of the Orange Free State, confusing the Republican commanders.[204]

> *P3.5.1 Grave of Captain H.G. Majendie (34), Rifle Brigade, Second-in-Command of Roberts's Horse, who on 12 February 1900 died of wounds received at De Kiels Drift earlier the same day.[205]*
> ▶ *West End Cemetery, c/o Green St & Reserve Rd, Kimberley, Northern Cape.*
> ◉ *S28° 44.078, E24° 44.170 (Google Maps).*
> *The graves of other members of the Imperial forces who fell in this period and are buried in this cemetery include Private A. McGuire, 1st Battalion Gordon Highlanders, killed in action at Riet River on 15 February 1900.[206]*

A British force broke through the lines of a Republican force on 15 February by means of an old-fashioned cavalry charge, and relieved the besieged inhabitants of Kimberley (including Cecil John Rhodes). About 40 members of the British forces and 35 burghers were killed in action that day.[207]

> *The graves of Lieutenant A.E. Hesketh (25), 16th (Queen's) Lancers and of Lieutenant E.G. Carbutt (28), U Battery, Royal Horse Artillery, both killed in action on 15 February 1900[208](also see P7.4.5.17).*
> ▶ *Municipal cemetery, De Villiers St, Jacobsdal.*
> ◉ *S29° 08.091, E24° 46.510.*

In another engagement on 15 February, somewhat further to the south in the Orange Free State, General Christiaan de Wet managed to capture a very large British supply convoy at Waterval Drift on the Riet River. Both the British forces and the Republicans suffered casualties.[209]

> *P3.5.2 Grave of Private E.A. Dawson (24), City Imperial Volunteers. He was wounded on 15 February at Waterval Drift while serving with the Kimberley Relief Force, and succumbed to his wounds on 12 May 1900.[210]*
> ▶ *Anglo-Boer War Garden of Remembrance, Commonwealth War Graves section, Maitland Cemetery, Voortrekker Rd, Cape Town, Western Cape.*
> ◉ *S33° 55.022, E18° 32.280 (Google Maps).*

 P3.5.1  P3.5.2  P3.5.3

---

204 Grobler 2004, 41; Cloete 2010, 104.
205 Watt 2000, 262.
206 Watt 2000, 279.
207 Grobler 2004, 41; Cloete 2010, 106.
208 Watt 2000, 65 & 191.
209 De Wet 1999, 50-52; Cloete 2010, 105.
210 Watt 2000, 106.

Part 3 – The military history of the war: the first year (11 October 1899–10 October 1900)

On 16 February, the British forces caught up with Cronjé's large commando, which was hastily falling back towards Bloemfontein, at Klipkraal on the north bank of the Modder River. They immediately attacked the Boers, but were beaten back, suffering the loss of 11 men killed and 105 wounded. Seven were taken prisoner. The Boer casualties were eight men killed and 12 wounded.[211]

P3.5.3 Memorial stone plaque for 12 members of the 1st Battalion Oxfordshire Light Infantry killed in action in this engagement at Klip Drift.
▶ *Municipal cemetery, De Villiers St, Jacobsdal, Free State.*
◉ *S29° 08.091, E24° 46.510.*

Cronjé's laager moved further upstream along the Modder River to Paardeberg, where Kitchener launched a fierce attack on them on Sunday 18 February. The fighting lasted the whole day, with the burghers bravely defending their position and beating the soldiers back. The laager was, however, all but totally destroyed. The British forces suffered their highest casualties for a single day in this battle: 303 killed, 906 wounded and 61 men taken prisoner. The Republican losses amounted to about 70 killed and wounded.[212] Afterwards, the British forces besieged Cronjé's laager. A number of burgher commandos attempted to relieve Cronjé.

P3.5.4 The lone grave of Colonel Ormelie Campbell Hannay (51), who commanded the 1st Brigade Mounted Infantry. He was one of the first British soldiers killed in action that day.[213]
▶ *Hannay was buried where he fell, on the northern side of the gravel road numbered S383, Free State. Paardeberg is visible in the background.*
◉ *About 200 m north of S28° 56.490, E25° 08.853.*

P3.5.5 The Modder River in the area where Cronjé's laager was besieged.
▶ *Photograph taken from a spot near the Republican monument, which is signposted on the southern side of the S383, Free State.*
◉ *S28° 56.619, E25° 08.827.*

During the night of 18 to 19 February, the commander of the Free State forces, Chief Commandant I.S. Ferreira, was accidently shot by one of his own pickets when he went out after dark to inspect his sentries. General Christiaan de Wet subsequently took over the command of the Free State forces on this western front.[214]

P3.5.6 The monumental gravestone on the final grave of Ferreira. He was initially buried at Petrusburg in the Free State. In 1904 he was reinterred on his farm Destadesfontein, but in 1958 he was reburied here.[215]
▶ *Municipal cemetery, south-west of the c/o Piet Retief St & 6th Ave, Clocolan, Free State.*
◉ *S28° 55.289, E29° 33.682.*

P3.5.4   P3.5.5   P3.5.6

---

211 Pretorius 2010, 310.
212 Cloete 2000, 101-103; Lane 2001, 115-130; Judd & Surridge 2003, 165-167; Pretorius 2010, 311-313.
213 Jackson 1999, 88-89; Watt 2000, 177.
214 Meyer 1952, 8; Basson 1987, 277; Cloete 2000, 44; Grobler 2004, 44.
215 Van der Bank 1995, 16.

P3.5.7   P3.5.8   P3.5.9   P3.5.10

The British forces encircled Cronjé's laager at Paardeberg with 40 000 men and bombarded the laager with about 100 guns. Cronjé's men continued their valiant defence of their position for more than a week, while the burghers led by both De Wet and De la Rey attempted to come to their aid. However, the vastly superior numbers of the British eventually won the day. Cronjé surrendered to Roberts with 4 105 men on 27 February 1900. British losses in the period from 19 to 27 February 1900 at Paardeberg amounted to at least 1 400 officers and men, of whom at least 239 were killed, 1 095 were wounded and 68 were taken prisoner of war or went missing in action. Boer losses were at least 74 men killed and 195 wounded.[216]

P3.5.7 There is a small museum near the Paardeberg Battlefield, Free State, with exhibits on the battle and the surrender.
▶ At the old Paardeberg railway halt, on the northern side of the railway line.
◉ S28° 58.949, E25° 04.868.

P3.5.8 The diorama of the battle near the Republican Paardeberg Monument on the battlefield.
▶ Northern bank of the Modder River, between the river and the S383 gravel road, Free State.
◉ S28° 56.698, E25° 08.828.

P3.5.9 The Republican Paardeberg Monument containing the names of 136 burghers who were killed in action in defence of the laager, and were buried or reinterred there. It was erected by the War Graves Council in 1974 to commemorate the surrender and the place where it took place on 27 February 1900. A number of gravestones surround the monument.[217]
▶ Between the Modder River and the S383 gravel road, Free State.
◉ S28° 56.619, E25° 08.827.

P3.5.10 Some of the burghers who fell at Paardeberg were buried elsewhere.
▶ Field Cornet C.J. Wessels, who was killed in action on 23 February 1900, was buried in the municipal cemetery, Petrusburg, Free State.

P3.5.11   P3.5.12

216   Creswicke IV ca 1902, 62-79; Grobler 2004, 45.
217   Van der Bank 1995, 53-56.

Part 3 – The military history of the war: the first year (11 October 1899–10 October 1900)

◉ *About 50 m south of S29° 07.196, E25° 25.153.*

There are a number of memorials for and gravesites of British soldiers involved in the Battle of Paardeberg and the surrender of Cronjé:

P3.5.11 The British Garden of Remembrance with a memorial and graves at the battlesite.
▶ *Between the S383 gravel road and the Modder River, Free State (about one kilometre east of Hannay's grave).*
◉ *S28° 56.545, E25° 09.438.*

P3.5.12 The British Garden of Remembrance on the southern side of the Modder River.
▶ *Gruisbank, Free State, next to the S580, between the S115 and the N8.*
◉ *S28° 59.001, E25° 06.759.*

P3.5.13 British memorial on the southern side of the Modder River.
▶ *Also next to the S580, about 5.4 km north of the N8.*
◉ *S28° 57.671, E25° 08.402. (Google Maps)*

P3.5.14 The grave of Trooper E. Christian, Rimington's Guides, who was killed in action at Makows Drift on 28 February 1900.[218] The inscription on his gravestone states: "He died to save a comrade."
▶ *British Garden of Remembrance, municipal cemetery, Boshof, Free State, where a number of British soldiers who fell at Paardeberg were buried.*
◉ *South-eastern side of the town, near S28° 32.530, E25° 14.708.*

P3.5.15 The grave of Corporal George F. Collings, Yorkshire Regiment (previously awarded the Medal for Distinguished Conduct on New Zealand Hill on 15 January 1900), who was wounded at Paardeberg and died on 5 April 1900. He was the first person buried in the cemetery of the Imperial Yeomanry Hospital at Deelfontein.[219]
▶ *Imperial YeomanryWestern side of an unnamed road about 46 km southwest of De Aar, Northern Cape, on the western side of the railway line, a few hundred metres south of the old Deelfontein railway station.*
◉ *S30° 59.779, E23° 47.581.*

One of the Republican officers captured at Paardeberg was Commandant (later General) C.J. Spruyt of the Heidelberg Commando. This was before Cronjé's surrender. Spruyt managed to escape from the moving train that was taking him as prisoner to Cape Town near De Aar and walked back to the Boer forces at Colesberg.[220] Three other Boers who surrendered with Cronjé at Paardeberg, namely the brothers Petrus and Lewies Strydom and Jacobus Marais, also jumped off the train near Beaufort West and made their way to the Swartberg Mountains, where the inhabitants of the Gamkaskloof (The Hell) gave them sanctuary for more than a year. They were only re-captured in May 1901. Ten inhabitants of the Gamkaskloof were subsequently severely punished by a British military court in Prince Albert for helping the Boers.[221]

 P3.5.13
 P3.5.14
 P3.5.15

---
218 Watt 2000, 73.
219 Watt 2000, 82.
220 Blake 2015, 121-122.
221 Marincowitz 2014, 23-24.

▶ *To reach the Gamkaskloof by road one has to cross the Swartberg Mountain Pass via the R328. The turn-off to the Kloof is near the top.*
◉ *At S33° 20.371, E22° 02.310.*

Cronjé's surrender was disastrous for the Republics in more than one sense. They lost a sizeable percentage of their fighting men, and the surrender occurred on the 19th anniversary of the Battle of Majuba Hill. In this way, the British achieved their objective of avenging their ignominious defeat at Majuba in 1881.

3.5.2 Natal front

In the weeks before Cronjé's surrender at Paardeberg, many Boers were transferred from the Natal front to the western front. As a result, General Louis Botha's forces became so depleted that he eventually failed to prevent the overwhelming British forces opposing him from gaining the upper hand. From 16 to 27 February, a number of battles took place along the Thukela River below Colenso. The British refer to those encounters as the Battles of the Tugela Heights. On the very day of Cronjé's surrender to Roberts at Paardeberg, Buller broke through Botha's lines at Pieter's Hill in Natal. The next day, the British relieved the besieged Ladysmith garrison. Indeed, the Boer forces in Natal effectively collapsed at that time. However, the British victory came at a cost. The total British losses in all these battles were 300 officers and men killed, 1 850 wounded and 90 missing. Boer losses in the same period were at least 80 killed and 340 wounded.[222]

P3.5.16 Natal Naval Volunteers at Pieter's Hill, 26 February1900.
▶ *Relief sculpture on pedestal of Anglo-Boer War memorial, Francis Farewell Square, c/o Anton Lembede St & Dorothy Nyembe St, Durban, KwaZulu-Natal.*
◉ *S29° 51.525, E31° 01.514. (Google Maps)*

A roll of honour on the Burgher Monument, Platrand, Ladysmith, KwaZulu-Natal (see P3.2.3.19) commemorates 52 burghers who were killed in action in the battles of the Tugela Heights from 16 to 26 February, and 17 who died of their wounds or other causes. It also lists 40 burghers who were killed in action in the Battle of Pieter's Hill and 11 who died of their wounds.
◉ *S28° 35.278, E29° 46.357.*

There are a number of graves of British soldiers who fell in these battles, as well as British memorials commemorating the battles:

P3.5.17 Memorial garden at Onderbroekspruit.
▶ *On the western side of the road running parallel to the railway line between Colenso and Ladysmith, KwaZulu-Natal.*
◉ *S28° 42.066, E29° 49.446.*

P3.5.16

P3.5.17

---

222   Bakkes 1973, Chapters I-XIV; Pretorius 2010, 325-329; Gillings 2014.

Part 3 – The military history of the war: the first year (11 October 1899–10 October 1900)

P3.5.18 The grave of Sergeant J.D. (John) Chamberlain, 2nd East Surrey Regiment, killed in action on the Tugela Heights on 22 February 1900. It seems as if he was initially buried on the battlefield at Onderbroekspruit.[223]
▶ *Fort Napier military cemetery, Napier St, Napierville, Pietermaritzburg, KwaZulu-Natal. Phone Henry Davis at 0824737512 or 0825562485 about access to the cemetery.*
◉ *S29° 37.182, E30° 21.604.*

P3.5.19 Gravestone of Lance-Corporal H.W. Curtler, 2nd East Surrey Regiment, who died of wounds received in the battle on the Tugela Heights on 23 February 1900[224] while he was giving succour to a wounded comrade.
▶ *British Garden of Remembrance, 1st Street, near 11th Ave, Bruntville, KwaZulu-Natal. South-east of Mooi River, turn southwards off the R622.*
◉ *S29° 13.044, E30° 00.736.*

P3.5.20 The Somerset Light Infantry memorial.
▶ *On the eastern side of the road running parallel to the railway line between Colenso and Ladysmith, KwaZulu-Natal.*
◉ *S28° 41.849, E29° 49.582.*

There are a number of British graves and monuments, as well as the remains of Boer fortifications on the Thukela Heights, for example, the Connaught Rangers memorial at the base of Hart's Hill and British graves on Wynne's Hill.[225] These memorials are difficult to find, and some are in areas that are not easily accessible, so the use of knowledgeable local guides to find these sites is recommended.

P3.5.21 The memorial for General G. Barton's brigade on Pieter's Hill.
▶ *On a hill next to the P325, south-east of Ladysmith, KwaZulu-Natal (steep road to the top of hill).*
◉ *S28° 40.146, E29° 51.222.*

3.5.3 Southern and south-eastern fronts

Meanwhile, in the Eastern Cape, Major-General Brabant's unit, known as Brabant's Horse, attacked a Cape Rebel commando at Koffiefontein near Dordrecht on 16 February 1900. Seven Cape Colonial troops lost their lives in this encounter.[226]

The seven British soldiers are buried at Koffiefontein, where a neat stone wall was later built around their graves.[227]

On 12 February 1900, the Republican forces in the Colesberg area attacked the British forces at Keeromskop (subsequently called Worcester Hill by the soldiers). The Worcestershire Regiment, which was stationed there, put

P3.5.18

P3.5.19

P3.5.20

P3.5.21

---

223 Watt 2000, 70.
224 Watt 2000, 99.
225 Torlage & Watt 1999, 51-55; Von der Heyde 2012, 161-162; Gillings s.a., 47-49.
226 Amery III 1905, 489; Oosthuizen 1998, 22.
227 Oosthuizen 1998, 22.

up a spirited defence, but was ultimately forced to withdraw. British casualties amounted to 37 killed in action, 81 wounded and 19 taken prisoner. The Boers occupied the camp and captured a machine gun, but eight burghers were killed and 19 were wounded.[228]

> P3.5.22 The names of 17 members of the Worcestershire Regiment, plus one unknown soldier killed in action at Worcester Hill near Colesberg on 12 February 1900 (incorrectly indicated on the memorial as 13 February) are inscribed on this memorial.
> ▶ British Garden of Remembrance, western side of Station Rd, near the northern limit of the town, Colesberg, Northern Cape.
> ◙ S30° 42.730, E25° 06.086 (Google Maps).
> The graves of members of the Imperial forces who fell in this period and are buried in this Garden of Remembrance include
> - Lieutenant James Charles Roberts (27), First Victorian Mounted Rifles, who died on 12 February 1900 of wounds received the day before at Pink Hill (Rensburg).[229]
> - Lieutenant John William Powell, 1st South Australian Contingent, killed in action at Hobkirks Farm, on 12 February 1900 (see P1.15).
> - Major Francis Richard MacMullen (44), 2nd Wiltshire Regiment, killed in action near Colesberg on 14 February 1900.[230]
> - Trooper W.E. Smith, 1st SA Contingent, killed in action near Colesberg, on 22 February 1900.[231]
> - Captain Alexander F. Wallis (33), Duke of Wellington's (West Riding) Regiment, killed in action near Colesberg on 24 February 1900.[232]

The British forces around Colesberg were somewhat depleted by this time, since large numbers of soldiers had been diverted to the western front, so they retreated south, to Arundel. The Republican forces attacked the retreating British soldiers on 14 February, and 13 soldiers were killed or wounded, and 138 were taken prisoner. Two burghers were killed and four were wounded.[233] However, in the course of the next week, the balance of power on the Colesberg front changed dramatically in favour of the British forces. A number of developments contributed to this. Firstly, the size of the Republican force on this front was severely reduced by the fact that many burghers were transferred to the western Orange Free State to go to Cronjé's aid. Secondly, the British forces on the Colesberg front were strengthened and were ordered to go on the offensive. As a result, the burghers suddenly found themselves under severe pressure. Nevertheless, they managed to keep the British forces at bay in skirmishes south of Colesberg from 22 to 24 February.[234]

Towards the end of February, the Republican forces decided to withdraw from the Colesberg area and retreat into the Orange Free State. One of the last actions taken by the burghers before retiring across the Orange River was to dynamite the Norvalspont railway bridge on 3 March 1900.[235] The British repaired the bridge at a later stage, but at a cost.

> P3.5.23 Gravestone of Private Joseph H. Macdonald (32), No 4 Company, Railway Pioneer Regiment, originally from Los Angeles in the United States, who died on 14 May 1900 from injuries incurred whilst his regiment was repairing the bridge.[236]
> ▶ Municipal cemetery, Molteno, Eastern Cape.
> ◙ S31° 23.998, E26° 21.300.

To the southeast of Colesberg, in the Stormberg Mountains, Major-General Gatacre reoccupied Molteno. On 23 February, his troops engaged in a fierce skirmish with the Republican commando led by Cape Rebel Commandant

---

228 Breytenbach IV 1977, 154-156.
229 Watt 2000, 355.
230 Watt 2000, 260.
231 This is probably the Private W.E. Smith, 1 South Australia Mounted Rifles, killed in action at Arundel on 18 February and buried at Colesberg, who was mentioned by Watt (2000, 390).
232 Watt 2000, 434.
233 Breytenbach IV 1977, 159-160.
234 Grobler 2004, 47.
235 Celliers 1978, 79; Grobler ca 1937, 45; Cloete 2000, 114.
236 Watt 2000, 259.

Part 3 – The military history of the war: the first year (11 October 1899–10 October 1900)

Danie Schoeman on his own farm, Schoemanskop, near Stormberg junction. Gatacre's forces suffered casualties, amounting to at least 88 killed, wounded and missing, compared to the burghers' loss of three killed and seven wounded.[237]

P3.5.24 The graves of British officers and men of Montmorency's Scouts who fell at Schoemanskop on 23 February 1900. The damaged gravestone on the left is that of Lieutenant-Colonel F.H. Hoskier (35); the tall memorial gravestone next to it is that of Captain the Honourable R.H. de Montmorency (33), recipient of the Victoria Cross; the gravestone next to it that of Scout L.A. Maasdorp (23); and the gravestone fourth from the left is that of Corporal J. Weatherley.[238]
▶ *Municipal cemetery, Molteno, Eastern Cape.*
◉ *S31° 23.998, E26° 21.300.*

The grave of the burgher Hendrik Viljoen (30) who was killed in action at Schoemanskop is in the municipal cemetery, Bethulie, Free State.
▶ *On the outskirts of the town, directly north of Bovennoord St.*
◉ *S30° 29.561, E25° 58.279.*

On 3 to 5 March 1900, Major-General Brabant and his Colonial Division of 1 000 men attacked a Cape Rebel force of about 400 men commanded by Commandant Schoeman and Commandant Marthinus de Wet at Labuschagne's Nek, north of Dordrecht in the Eastern Cape. Commandant de Wet was covering the retreat northwards of the Free State forces who were at that time retreating from the southern front via Aliwal North. Even though the Cape Rebels were forced to withdraw after gaining the upper hand in the initial stages of the battle, they delayed Brabant long enough to ensure that he could not intervene in the general Free State retreat. Burgher losses were eight killed and 17 wounded, while the British losses were 14 or 15 killed and 29 wounded.[239]

P3.5.25 Grave of Sergeant P.D. Hunter, Frontier Mounted Rifles, killed in action at Labuschagne's Nek on 4 March 1900.[240] The British troops who fell in this engagement were initially buried on the battlefield, but were reinterred in Dordrecht. There is no memorial at Labuschagne's Nek.
▶ *British Garden of Remembrance, municipal cemetery, near Bekker St, Dordrecht, Eastern Cape.*
◉ *S31° 22.964, E27° 02.838.*

On 6 March, a British force of between 500 and 700 men with six field guns attacked a force of Cape Rebels under General Liebenberg on the farm Houwater, west of Britstown in the northern Karoo. The Rebels were initially under severe pressure, but they gained the initiative and forced the British soldiers to fall back all the way to Britstown. The British casualties were three killed, 14 wounded and seven taken prisoner, and on the Rebels' side two killed and three wounded.[241]

P3.5.22   P3.5.23   P3.5.24   P3.5.25

237 Creswicke IV ca 1902, 167-168; Cloete 2010, 113.
238 Watt 2000, 108, 203, 258 & 441.
239 Amery III 1905, 490-491; Oosthuizen 1998, 22; Pretorius 2010, 231.
240 Watt 2000, 209.
241 Breytenbach V 1983, 323-326; Grobler 2004, 59.

P3.5.26 The memorial gravestone of the burghers Johannes Senekal and Jacobus J. Naudé, who were killed in action at Houwater, as well as Christiaan Boonzaaier, a Cape Rebel from Calvinia, who drowned in the Brak River at Holgatsfontein around 15 September 1901.[242] Naudé was possibly also a Cape Rebel.[243]
▶ Far western side of the municipal cemetery, Britstown, Northern Cape.
◉ S30° 35.184, E23° 30.011.

3.5.4 British advance on Bloemfontein

After the Paardeberg disaster, the demoralized Boers in the Orange Free State could no longer halt the advance of the full force of much of the British army confronting them. On 7 March 1900, the British forces had a convincing victory over General Christiaan de Wet's Republican defenders at Poplar Grove, along the Modder River to the east of Paardeberg. However, Lord Roberts failed in his main objective of capturing De Wet's forces – they retreated, and most of the burghers lived to fight another day. Casualties in the battle were relatively low: an estimated eight were killed and 49 wounded on the British side, and on the Boer side, one man was killed and one wounded.[244]

P3.5.27 This monument next to the Modder River at Poplar Grove indicates where De Wet's burghers camped before the battle.[245]
▶ Next to the S319, between the S382 and the S141.
◉ S28° 54.544, E25° 21.859.

P3.5.28 Grave of Lieutenant David Johnstone Keswick (23), 12th Royal Lancers, killed in action at Poplar Grove on 7 March 1900.[246]
▶ British Garden of Remembrance, Paardeberg battlefield, between the S383 gravel road and the Modder River, Free State (about one kilometre east of Hannay's grave).
◉ S28° 56.545, E25° 09.438.

The Republican commandos retreated from Poplar Grove, but dug in again at Driefontein and Abrahamskraal in a final attempt to halt the British advance on Bloemfontein. On 10 March, Roberts deployed a massive force of 34 000 troops with 112 guns and 39 machine guns. Even though the combined forces of De Wet and De la Rey consisted of only about 1 500 burghers, they put up staunch resistance against the overwhelming British numbers. By dusk, however, the Boers ran low on ammunition, had been outflanked and were bombarded into conceding defeat. The casualties on the Boer side amounted to about 90 burghers, and on the British side to more than 420 men killed and wounded.[247]

The names of burghers who died in action appear on a roll of honour at the Armour Museum, Tempe military base, Bloemfontein, Free State.

 P3.5.26    P3.5.27    P3.5.28

---

242 Shearing & Shearing 2011a, 45.
243 Shearing & Shearing 2011b, 531.
244 Pretorius 2010, 341-343.
245 Van der Bank 2001, 11.
246 Watt 2000, 233.
247 Pretorius 2010, 130-132.

Part 3 – The military history of the war: the first year (11 October 1899–10 October 1900)

There is a Burgher monument containing 30 names of Republican casualties on the Driefontein battlefield, which is on private property west of Bloemfontein, Free State.[248]

The British Garden of Remembrance at Driefontein contains at least five marked graves, as well as a mass grave and a cairn commemorating members of the Welsh Regiment who fell in this battle.

3.6 The occupation of the Boer capitals, 13 March–5 June 1900

March 1900 was a month of crisis for the Boer Republics. They were unable to prevent Lord Robert's forces from occupying Bloemfontein on 13 March. The unofficial poet laureate of the British Empire, Rudyard Kipling, subsequently and with reference to Roberts, named the capital of the Orange Free State Bobsfontein.[249] On a more serious note numerous burghers subsequently decided that it would serve no purpose to prolong the war, since they did not think that the Boers would ever be able to defeat the British forces. These burghers deserted from the commandos in large numbers to return to their farms. The Republican presidents realised that they would have to intervene strongly if they hoped to continue the war. A few days after Bloemfontein fell, the most important military and civilian leaders of the two Republics held a joint meeting in the temporary Orange Free State capital, Kroonstad, to discuss future action. The meeting on 17 March decided that all was not lost, so plans were put into motion to implement guerrilla tactics.[250]

P3.6.1 The market building in Kroonstad where the meeting was held still exists today, but it is in a dilapidated condition. Steel gates were added between the iron pillars in 1960.[251]
▶ *C/o Market St & Murray St, Kroonstad, Free State.*
◎ *S27° 40.213, E27° 14.080.*

On 23 March 1900, there was a skirmish in the Karee area, to the north of Bloemfontein, between a British reconnaissance patrol and members of the Theron Scout Corps.[252]

P3.6.2 The grave of Lieutenant E.H. Lygon (23), Grenadier Guards, who was killed in action in this engagement on 23 March 1900, is in the Rooidam military cemetery.[253]
▶ *Frans Kleynhans Rd, western side of Bloemfontein, Free State*
◎ *S29° 03.814, E26° 10.437.*

The Commandant-General of the South African Republic, Piet Joubert, who had suffered from ill health ever since his fall from his horse in November 1899, died in Pretoria on Tuesday 27 March 1900, at the age of 69. Joubert was buried on his farm in the Volksrust district.[254] He was succeeded by Louis Botha (38).

P3.6.1 P3.6.2 P3.6.3

---

248 Van der Bank 2001, 13.
249 Pakenham 1982, 376.
250 Grobler 2004, 51; Cloete 2010, 124-125. According to Cloete, the meeting took place in Hurman's Hotel.
251 Richardson 2001, 181.
252 Cloete 2010, 126.
253 Van der Bank 2001, 53; Watt 2000, 257.
254 Grobler 2004, 53, 56.

P3.6.3 Joubert's mausoleum, in walking distance from his house on the farm Rustfontein.
▶ *Turnoff to the north from the R543, 26 km west of Volksrust, Mpumalanga.*
◉ *S27° 20.863, E29° 36.672.*

On 29 March, there was another engagement at Karee, about 25 km north of Bloemfontein, for possession of Tafelkop, a low hill that dominates the surrounding areas. After a long day of fighting, the British forces gained the ascendency, even though their casualties were much higher than those of the Boers. The British losses were 30 dead, 155 wounded and five missing; the Boer losses were three dead and 18 wounded.[255]

P3.6.4 Memorial to 20 officers, non-commissioned officers and men, 1st Battalion King's Own Scottish Borderers (KOSB), who were killed or died of wounds received in action at Karee on 29 March 1900.
▶ *British Garden of Remembrance, Karee, next to the R30 between Bloemfontein & Brandfort, Free State.*
◉ *GPS co-ordinates not available.*
This cemetery contains the graves of a number British soldiers who fell in this engagement, including Captain W.M. Marter (32), King's Dragoon Guards, and Captain A.C. Going and Lieutenant E.M. Young of the KOSB.[256]

P3.6.5 Grave of Commandant J. Kriegler, who was wounded at Karee and died of his wounds on 9 June 1900.[257]
▶ *Kloof Cemetery, on the banks of the Kloof Spruit, northern side of extension of Fenter St, Heidelberg, Gauteng.*
◉ *S26° 29.717, E28° 20.770.*

From the end of March 1900, General Christiaan de Wet emerged as an inspired military leader. On Saturday 31 March, he led about 1 600 Free State burghers against a British force of 1 800 men commanded by Brigadier General Robert Broadwood, who suffered a stinging defeat in the Battle of Sannaspos. British losses amounted to more than 150 men killed or wounded, and 420 taken prisoner, against Boer losses of 16 or 17 killed and wounded. More importantly, the Boers captured seven British field guns and 83 wagonloads of war supplies, including arms and ammunition.[258]

P3.6.6 The memorial on the battlesite, on both sides of the present main road (the N8) where it crosses the Koring Spruit between Bloemfontein and Thaba Nchu, Free State.
▶ *Signposted, next to the N8, on the southern side.*
◉ *S29° 09.304, E26° 31.909.*

P3.6.7 The graves of the British soldiers killed in action in this battle.
▶ *Small military cemetery near the old Sannaspos railway station building, southern side of the N8.*
◉ *S29° 09.575, E26° 32.782.*

P3.6.4   P3.6.5

P3.6.6

P3.6.7

---

255 Cloete 2010, 128-129; Grobler 2004, 54.
256 Watt 2000, 159, 267, 468.
257 Van der Westhuizen & Van der Westhuizen 2000, 170.
258 Hopkins 1963, 65-70; Pretorius 2010, 400-402.

Part 3 – The military history of the war: the first year (11 October 1899–10 October 1900)

P3.6.8 The grave of the Dutch military attaché, Lieutenant M.J. Nix, who died on 11 April 1900 of the wounds he sustained in this battle[259] is in the President Brand Cemetery.
▶ *Northern side of President St, west of corner with Church St, Bloemfontein, Free State.*
◙ *S29° 07.480, E26° 13.197.*

The Republican successes at Karee and especially at Sannaspos were more important than the Boers initially realised – De Wet destroyed pumping equipment at the waterworks which supplied Bloemfontein, which meant that the enormous British army then encamped in Bloemfontein was without fresh water for quite some time. This contributed to the development of a dysentery epidemic that eventually killed almost as many British soldiers as the number that died in battle.[260]

P3.6.9 The remains of the Republican waterworks at Sannaspos can still be seen.
▶ *Southern side of the N8, east of the battlefield, driving east, just before crossing the Modder River.*
◙ *S29° 09.742, E26° 34.226.*

P3.6.10 Large memorial in the President Brand Cemetery to commemorate 1 830 members of the British and Colonial forces who lost their lives in the war and whose remains rest in this cemetery.[261]
▶ *Northern side of President St, west of corner with Church St, Bloemfontein, Free State.*
◙ *S29° 07.480, E26° 13.197.*

On 3 to 4 April 1900, De Wet and his burghers defeated a British force of 500 men under Captain W.J. McWhinnie in the Battle of Mostert's Hoek, about 6 km north-east of Reddersburg in the southern Free State. The British losses were 11 men killed, 37 wounded and 459 taken prisoner. Boer losses were three dead and three wounded.[262]

P3.6.11 Memorial for Captain F.G. Casson (36) and Second Lieutenant C.R. Barclay (22), both 2nd Battalion 5th Fusiliers Mounted Infantry, killed in action near Reddersburg on 3 April 1900.[263] The names of eight non-commissioned officers and men killed in the same action are inscribed on the back of the monument.
▶ *Municipal cemetery, near Boven Kerk St, Edenburg, Free State.*
◙ *S29° 44.222, E25° 56.523.*

P3.6.12 Grave of Captain W.P. Dimsdale (30), Royal Irish Rifles, who was wounded at Mostert's Hoek on 3 April 1900, and succumbed to his wounds on 9 April 1900.[264]
▶ *Municipal cemetery, on the outskirts of the town, near Letta St, south of the corner with President Brand St, Reddersburg, Free State.*
◙ *S29° 39.463, E26° 10.210.*

P3.6.8   P3.6.9   P3.6.10   P3.6.11   P3.6.12

---

259   De Villiers II 2008, 162; Van der Bank 2001, 30
260   Pakenham 1982, 382; De Villiers II 2008b, 110.
261   Van der Bank 2001, 32.
262   De Wet 1999, 88-90; Grobler 2004, 56.
263   Watt 2000, 19 & 68.
264   Watt 2000, 112.

A Republican commando consisting of foreign volunteers commanded by the French adventurer, Colonel Georges-Henri De Villebois-Mareuil, engaged a British force commanded by Lord Methuen near Boshof in the western Free State on Thursday 5 April 1900 and were defeated. De Villebois-Mareuil and a number of the men who were with him died in the skirmish. He was buried at Boshof with full military honours by Methuen the next day.[265]

There is a memorial at the place where De Villebois-Mareuil fell in action on the farm Middelkuil, about 10 km south-east of Boshof, Free State.

P3.6.13-14 The grave of De Villebois-Mareuil and the six men with him and some unknown men who were killed in action on 5 April 1900.[266]
▶ Municipal cemetery, Boshof, Free State.
◉ South-eastern side of the town, near S28° 32.530, E25° 14.708.
The grave of Captain C.W. Boyle (47), Imperial Yeomanry, who was killed in action on 5 April 1901 in the engagement with De Villebois-Mareuil's commando, is also in this cemetery. He was the first Imperial Yeomanry officer to die in the war.[267]

There is a commemorative plaque for De Villebois-Mareuil attached to the Burgher Monument, Magersfontein (see P3.3.14).
▶ On the eastern side of an unnamed gravel road linking the S1320 and the S574, Northern Cape.
◉ S28° 57.201, E24° 44.071.

De Wet and his burghers attacked a British force commanded by Colonel E.H. Dalgety at Jammerberg's Drift near Wepener in the eastern Free State on 9 April 1900. They failed to rout Dalgety's men and subsequently besieged them for 16 days. The British forces held out successfully.[268]

P3.6.15 The British memorial on the battlefield, paying tribute to the members of the Colonial Division who lost their lives during the siege. A total of 33 names appear on the memorial, including those of Private H.H.P. (Hugo) de Burgh and Private P.E. (or P.L.) Horwood (26), both of the Cape Mounted Rifles,[269] whose graves are close to the memorial. There is also a Republican memorial.
▶ Robertson church and cemetery, Wepener, Free State.
◉ S29° 42.398, E26° 58.416 (courtesy of the Genealogical Society of South Africa).

On 23 to 24 April 1900, various skirmishes took place in the Leeukop-Roodekop area, about 30 km south-east of Bloemfontein, when British forces attempted to scatter the Republican commandos of General Manie Lemmer and Commandant Piet Fourie in that part of the Orange Free State. Both sides suffered casualties.[270]

Captain G.P. Brazier-Creagh (36), 9th Bengal Lancers, who was in command of Robert's Horse, was wounded at Kareefontein on 23 April and died on 27 April. He is buried in the Dewetsdorp military cemetery, together with Private W. MacDonald and Private H. Underwood of the 9th Lancers who were killed in action on 24 April 1900.[271] The officer commanding the 9th Lancers, Captain H.F.W. Stanley (37) of the 8th Hussars, died of his wounds on 28 April, and is buried in the President Brand cemetery, Bloemfontein.[272] Captain P.R. Denny of the Dragoon Guards, killed in action at Roodekop on 24 April, is also buried at Dewetsdorp military cemetery. He is commemorated by a bronze plaque in the Anglican Cathedral of St. Andrew and St. Michael in Bloemfontein.[273]

Boer commandos under General F.A. Grobler and Commandant F.J.W.J. Hattingh attempted, but failed, to block a British advance on Thaba Nchu on 25 April 1900. The British force was commanded by Lieutenant-General Sir Ian

---

265 Amery IV 1906, 212-214; Macnab 1975, 203-208; Van der Bank 1995, 12-13.
266 Van der Bank 1995, 12-13.
267 Watt 2000, 41.
268 De Wet 1999, 93-96; Grobler 2004, 57, 61.
269 Watt 2000, 107 & 203.
270 Cloete 2010, 139.
271 Watt 2000, 44, 259 & 426.
272 Watt 2000, 396.
273 Watt 2000, 110; Van der Bank 2001, 69.

Part 3 – The military history of the war: the first year (11 October 1899–10 October 1900)

Hamilton at Ysternek, near Israelspoort in the eastern Free State. British losses amounted to 27 men, including seven officers. Republican losses amounted to one burgher killed in action and one wounded.[274]

P3.6.16 Grave of Captain H.R. Gethin (37), Marshall's Horse, killed in action at Israelspoort, 25 April 1900.[275]
► British Garden of Remembrance, old town cemetery, southern side of Massyn St, Thaba Nchu, Free State.
◉ S29° 13.219, E26° 50.945.
This Garden of Remembrance contains the graves of a number of members of the Imperial forces who fell in this period, including

- Private J. Defoe (30), Royal Canadian Rifles, killed in action at Israelspoort on 25 April 1900.[276]
- Lieutenant Francis Geary (26), 2nd Battalion Hampshire Regiment, killed in action near Thaba Nchu on 27 April 1900.[277]
- Private T. Crabtree, A Squadron, 9th Lancers, who died on 30 April 1900 of wounds received two days before at Sprinkaansnek (see P4.3.21).[278]
- Lieutenant J.H. Parker, Kitchener's Horse, killed in action near Thaba Nchu on 28 April 1900. (He may have died on 1 May 1900 of wounds received in action at Hout Nek on 28 April 1900.[279])
- Private H. Cotton (23), Royal Canadian Rifles, killed in action at Jacobsrust, Thaba Mount, near Thaba Nchu on 30 April 1900.[280]
- Lance-Corporal J. Simpson, killed in action on 1 May 1900, and Private E. Chissel, killed in action on 30 April 1900, both at Jacobsrust near Thaba Mount and both of the 1st Battalion Gordon Highlanders (joint grave).[281]
- Captain E.G. Verschoyle (33), 2nd Battalion Grenadier Guards, who died on 6 May 1900 of wounds received in action at Thaba Nchu the previous day[282] (see CP12 on p. 133).

The grave of Private A. Jenkins, Prince Alfred's Guard, who was killed in action near Bethulie on 26 April (or 28 April, according to his grave marker) 1900, is in the municipal cemetery, Bethulie, Free State.[283]
► On the outskirts of the town, directly north of Bovennoord St.
◉ S30° 29.561, E25° 58.279.

On 29 April 1900, clashes between Republican and British forces occurred in the Thaba Nchu-Swartlapberg area east of Bloemfontein when Roberts got his forces in position to start his offensive against Pretoria. The next day, British mounted troops, most in a unit called Lumsdens Horse, engaged with burgher forces in the vicinity of Os Spruit, southeast of Karee, where both sides suffered limited casualties.[284]

 P3.6.13
 P3.6.14
 P3.6.15
 P3.6.16

---
274 Breytenbach V 1983, 315-316; Cloete 2000, 135.
275 Watt 2000, 154.
276 Watt 2000, 109.
277 Watt 2000, 153.
278 Watt 2000, 93.
279 Watt 2000, 322.
280 Watt 2000, 90.
281 Watt 2000, 73, 381.
282 Watt 2000, 429.
283 Watt 2000, 218.
284 Breytenbach V 1983, 395-396.

P3.6.17 Grave of Trooper H.C. Lumsden, Lumsdens Horse, killed in action at Os Spruit, near Glen (Spytfontein), 30 April 1900.[285]
▶ *British Garden of Remembrance, Karee, beside the R30 between Bloemfontein and Brandfort, Free State. The graves of Trooper A.F. Franks and of Trooper R.U. Case (24), both of Lumsdens Horse,*[286] *who fell in the same engagement, are also in this cemetery.*

Over the course of 30 April and 1 May, there was a major battle at Hout Nek (Tobaberg), where the wagon road between Thaba Nchu and Winburg crosses a low mountain. In this battle, General Philip Botha's burghers, who had two artillery pieces, assisted by the Russian Colonel E.J. Maximov and his International Legion of about 150 foreign volunteers, bravely resisted the advance of Lieutenant-General Hamilton's massive force of 5 500 men with about 24 field guns for more than 24 hours, before the British finally broke through. It seems that the foreign volunteers fought on their own for much of this battle, with the burghers looking on from a distance. The volunteers' casualties amounted to six killed, 28 (including Maximov) wounded and ten taken prisoner. At least two burghers were killed and three wounded. British casualties numbered 157.[287]

P3.6.18 J.J. du Plessis was killed in action on the first day of these engagements, on 29 April. He and two other burghers were reinterred in the municipal cemetery in Reddersburg, Free State, in 1906.
▶ *On the outskirts of the town, near Letta St, south of the corner with President Brand St.*
◉ *S29° 39.463, E26° 10.210.*

Lord Roberts's major offensive to the north, in which more than 25 000 British soldiers participated, began on 3 May 1900, with the British occupation of Brandfort. There was heavy fighting as the burgher commandos made futile attempts to block the British advance, but casualties were not heavy. On the Boer side, one burgher was killed, compared to six casualties on the British side.[288]

P3.6.19 The burgher who was killed was probably Johannes Hendrik van der Vijver, who was buried in the municipal cemetery at Chrissiesmeer. His gravestone in the cemetery states that he died in action at Brandfort on 3 May 1900.
▶ *Near the R542, western side of Chrissiesmeer, Mpumalanga.*
◉ *S26° 16.797, E30° 12.281.*

In a reception room at St Alban's Cathedral, Pretoria, there is a memorial plaque to members of the City of London Imperial Volunteers who died in active service in the war. The names of two soldiers killed in action at Brandfort on 3 May 1900, namely Sergeant D.P. Kingsford and Private M.W. Holland, are included on this plaque.[289]
▶ *Francis Baard St, between Paul Kruger St & Thabo Sehume St, Pretoria Central, Gauteng.*
◉ *S25° 44.970, E28° 11.373.*

Grave of Captain C.E. Rose (27), Royal Horse Guards, killed in action on the farm Welkom near Winburg, Free State, on 4 May 1900.[290]
▶ *On the farm Welkom.*
◉ *GPS co-ordinates not available.*

P3.6.20 Grave of Private J.G. Bainbridge, Northumberland & Durham Imperial Yeomanry, killed in action at Rooidam, 4 May 1900.[291]
▶ *British Garden of Remembrance, West End Cemetery, c/o Green St & Reserve Rd, Kimberley, Northern Cape.*
◉ *S28° 44.078, E24° 44.170 (Google Maps).*

---

285   Watt 2000, 257.
286   Watt 2000, 68, 145.
287   Davidson & Filatova 1995, 27-30; Grobler 2004, 64.
288   Breytenbach V 1983, 413-416, 424; Grobler 2004, 64.
289   Watt 2000, 199, 235.
290   Watt 2000, 360.
291   Watt 2000, 15.

Part 3 – The military history of the war: the first year (11 October 1899–10 October 1900)

The last session of the First Volksraad (People's Council) of the ZAR (Transvaal) was held on 7 May 1900.[292]

> *This meeting took place in the Council Chamber of the First Volksraad, in the Government Buildings, Church Square, Pretoria Central, Gauteng*[293] *(see P3.6.41).*

On 10 May, Roberts's forces defeated the Boers led by Commandant-General Louis Botha in the Battle of Zand River in the Orange Free State. The British casualties amounted to at least 115 men, of whom 23 were killed, nine died of wounds, 40 were wounded and 13 went missing. On the Boer side, at least ten burghers were killed and 69 were taken prisoner, of whom seven were wounded.[294]

> *P3.6.21 Grave of Captain C.K. Elworthy (34), Carabiniers (6th Dragoon Guards), killed in action at Zand River (Vredesverdrag, Virginia District) on 10 May 1900.*[295]
> ▶ *British Garden of Remembrance, western side of Noord Rd, Kroonstad, Free State.*
> *The graves of Captain L. Head (22), 1st Battalion, East Lancashire Regiment, and of Private G.W. (or F.G.W.) Floyd (22), Royal Canadian Regiment, who both fell at Zand River on 10 May 1900, is in the same Garden of Remembrance,*[296] *which also contains a memorial to six members of the Carabiniers, killed in action at Vredesverdrag, 10 May 1900.*
> ◉ *S27° 39.049, E27° 13.816.*

The Republican defeat in the Battle of Zand River resulted in the British occupation of the temporary Free State capital, Kroonstad, on 12 May.[297]

In Natal, British forces under General Buller pushed towards Newcastle after they had reoccupied Ladysmith at the end of February. The Boer forces resisted this advance, and on 13 May, a minor battle took place at Helpmekaar in the Biggarsberg Mountains. The Boer defenders were outflanked and were forced to retreat.[298]

> *The remains of the Boer fort on top of the hill and a British military cemetery behind the police station are the only reminders of this encounter.*

On 14 May, British forces reoccupied Newcastle, which remained in British hands until the end of the war. Troops were immediately stationed in Fort Amiel, which was built on a low hill on the outskirts of the town in 1876, and was also used by the British forces in the Anglo-Zulu War of 1879 and the Anglo-Transvaal War of 1880–1881.[299]

P3.6.17   P3.6.18   P3.6.19   P3.6.20   P3.6.21

---

292   Cloete 2010, 144.
293   Greyling 2000, 26.
294   Pretorius 2010, 225, 505-506.
295   Watt 2000, 128.
296   Watt 2000, 140 &187.
297   Creswicke V ca 1902, 106-107.
298   Amery IV 1906, 170-175; Meijer 2000, 144.
299   Eksteen 2008, 6.

P3.6.22 One of the older structures in Fort Amiel, with members of the present-day Dundee Diehards 'guarding' it. The watchtower was built after the British occupation in 1900. Buildings at the fort were used as a hospital during the war. Today, Fort Amiel is a museum, and the exhibits include material from the Anglo-Boer War.
▶ Fort Rd, south of junction with Amiel Rd, Newcastle, KwaZulu-Natal.
◉ S27° 44.758, E29° 55.278.

On 16 May, the Boers blew up the entrance to the Laings Nek Railway Tunnel in the hope of making this section of the railroad impassable. The tunnel was subsequently repaired and used by the British.[300]

P3.6.23 The old Laings Nek Tunnel is no longer a railway tunnel, but it still exists.
▶ Access via farm roads on the eastern side of the N11.
◉ S27° 27.483, E29° 52.408.

P3.6.24 The grave of an unknown gunner of the Transvaal State Artillery who was killed in action near Majuba Hill near Laings Nek in May 1900.
▶ At the foot of Majuba Hill; entry to the terrain from a gravel road west of the N11, signposted.
◉ S27° 27.969, E29° 50.402.

The British attempted to break through the Republican defence in Northern Natal with 360 men of Bethune's Mounted Infantry, led by Lieutenant-Colonel E.C. Bethune. This offensive failed on 20 May 1900. They attempted to make a surprise advance past Vryheid but a Boer commando under Commandant J.D. (Koot) Opperman defeated the invading task force at Scheepers Nek. One burgher was killed in this action. The British lost 31 men killed in action.[301]

P3.6.25 The British memorials and graves where the soldiers who fell were buried, about 1 km west of the battlefield at Scheepers Nek.
▶ Southwest of Vryheid, within viewing distance on the northern side of the R33/34, between the D303 and the P336, KwaZulu-Natal.
◉ S27° 51.132, E30° 39.984.

---
300 Grobler 2004, 68.
301 Torlage & Watt 1999, 8.

Part 3 – The military history of the war: the first year (11 October 1899–10 October 1900)

The British forces led by Lieutenant-General Sir Leslie Rundle occupied Senekal, east of Winburg in the Orange Free State, on 25 May 1900. Attempts by Republican commandos to halt their approach failed, but the British forces did suffer some casualties.[302]

> P3.6.26 Grave of Major H.S. Dalbiac (49), Imperial Yeomanry, killed in action on Senekal Koppie on 25 May 1900.[303] According to the rededication inscription on his gravestone, he was the officer who inspired the poem "The Jacket" by Rudyard Kipling.
> ▶ Municipal cemetery, Senekal.
> ◉ S28° 18.778, E27° 37.287.

Utrecht – at the time a prominent town in the ZAR (Transvaal) – was occupied by British forces on 30 May 1900. The Boers decided not to defend the town to ensure that it would not be bombarded by the British.

> P3.6.27 The Landdrost Office and Post and Telegraph Office where the Vierkleur (the flag of the ZAR) was lowered and a proclamation of General Buller was put up after the landdrost (magistrate) of Utrecht presented the town to Major-General Hildyard, who commanded the British forces.[304]
> ▶ 57 Voor St, between Van Rooyen & Loop St, Utrecht, KwaZulu-Natal.
> ◉ S27° 39.388, E30° 19.208.

> P3.6.28 The house of Hendrik Bosman, who was an attorney in Utrecht before the war but was serving in a Boer commando in mid-1900. The house was immediately occupied by the British forces as an officers' mess. Mrs Bosman and the Bosman children were eventually sent to the Merebank Concentration Camp in Durban.[305]
> ▶ 21 Voor St, between Klopper St & Koch St, Utrecht, KwaZulu-Natal.
> ◉ S27° 39.496, E30° 18.760.

> P3.6.29 The old parsonage in Utrecht, which is now a museum with exhibits on the Anglo-Boer War, especially from that area.
> ▶ Church St, Utrecht, KwaZulu-Natal.
> ◉ S27° 39.342, E30° 19.128.

General Chris Botha of the Republican forces in northern Natal met General Buller, commander of the British forces, in O'Neill's Cottage on the slopes of Majuba Hill for peace talks on 2 June 1900. The outcome was an armistice in the area from 2 to 5 June.[306]

> P3.6.30 O'Neill's Cottage. The same building was used in March 1881 for the peace talks that ended the Anglo-Transvaal War of 1880–1881.[307]

P3.6.28

P3.6.29

---

302 Amery IV 1906, 243; Grobler 2004, 72.
303 Watt 2000, 100.
304 Van der Westhuizen & Van der Westhuizen 2000, 22.
305 Van der Westhuizen & Van der Westhuizen 2000, 23.
306 Grobler 2004, 75.
307 Richardson 2001, 234-235.

▶ Exit from the N11 in the Laings Nek Mountain Pass, turn to the north; clearly signposted.
◉ S 27° 30.030, E 29° 51.388.

In the Orange Free State, the Republican forces achieved two significant victories at the end of May 1900. On 29 May, General A.I. de Villiers's approximately 400 Free State burghers were attacked by a British force consisting of about 4 000 men commanded by Lieutenant-General Rundle on the slopes of Biddulphsberg near Senekal. The burghers defended their positions valiantly. The British attackers were eventually forced to withdraw when a veld fire broke out and some of the wounded soldiers were burnt to death. The British losses amounted to 47 men killed, 130 wounded and eight missing. One burgher was killed and three were wounded, including General De Villiers himself, who died of his wounds a few days later.[308]

P3.6.31 There are a number of memorials, including this one for General De Villiers, on the slopes of the Biddulphsberg where the battle took place.
▶ *On private farmland near the S675, Libertas, between the S1226 and the S200 (ask at the farm house for directions), north-east of Senekal, Free State.*
◉ *S28° 16.234, E27° 46.375.*

The grave of Second Lieutenant A.H. (Alasdair) Murray (22), Grenadier Guards, who was wounded in the Battle of Biddulphsberg on 29 May 1900 and died of his wounds on 2 June 1900,[309] is in the municipal cemetery, Senekal.
◉ *S28° 18.778, E27° 37.287.*

At Fabersput [Faber's Well] in the northern Cape, the Cape Rebel commando of General P.J. (Piet) de Villiers attacked a British force commanded by Lieutenant-General Sir Charles Warren on 30 May 1900. After initial reverses, the British forces managed to drive off the attackers. Both sides suffered casualties. On the British side, 23 men were killed and 32 were wounded. The Rebels lost 38 killed and 50 wounded.[310] De Villiers and his Rebels never fully recovered from this setback, even though they remained active until the end of the war.

The battlesite is on private land a few kilometres south of Douglas in the Northern Cape.

P3.6.32 Some of the burghers were reburied at the Burgher Monument at Magersfontein. The inscription on the gravestone reads: "In Memory van den Burgers die Gesneuveld zijn op den 30st Mei 1900 te Fabers Puts [In memory of the burghers who were killed in action on 30 May 1900 at Fabersput]. J. vd Westhuisen, 21. W. Aggenbach, 32. G. Zwiegers, 23. P. Moller, 48. F. Tesbie. T. Brits, 22, C. De Beer, 21. Hoe zijn de helden gevallen in het midden van den strijd [How have the heroes fallen in the midst of the battle]. Opgericht door [Erected by] Mr C. Faber en [and] Miss Briedenhann." The names of these burghers also appear on the Burgher Memorial, Magersfontein (see P3.3.14). Van der Westhuizen, Zwiegers and Brits were Cape Rebels.[311]

P3.6.30

P3.6.31

P3.6.32

---

308 Meyer 1952, 14-15; Cloete 2000, 150-151; Pretorius 2010, 40-41.
309 Watt 2000, 303.
310 Amery IV 1906, 234-235.
311 Shearing & Shearing 2011a, 2011b, 2011c, 81, 815 & 978.

Part 3 – The military history of the war: the first year (11 October 1899–10 October 1900)

▶ *Eastern side of an unnamed road between the S1320 and the S574.*
◙ *S28° 57.201, E24° 44.071.*

P3.6.33 Memorial in honour of Lieutenant-Colonel W.A. Spence (Commanding Officer), Sergeant J.H. Orchard (43) and Private R. Chieveley, Duke of Edinburgh's Own Volunteer Rifles, killed in action at Fabersput on 30 May 1900.[312]
▶ *West End Cemetery, c/o Green St & Reserve Rd, Kimberley, Northern Cape.*
◙ *S28° 44.078, E24° 44.170 (Google Maps).*
There is also a memorial in honour of 12 members of the 8th Regiment Imperial Yeomanry, killed in action in the same engagement, in the West End Cemetery in Kimberley, as well as the gravestones of a number of British soldiers who fell at Fabersput and were reinterred there, including Private J.D.K. Bell (19), Imperial Yeomanry Paget's Horse, Private F.A. Hall-Hall (24), Imperial Yeomanry Paget's Horse, Bombardier W. Latimer (21), Royal Canadian Field Artillery, Sergeant-Major F.H. Newdigate (48), Cape Medical Volunteer Staff, Sergeant J.H. Orchard, Private D. Rew (24), Imperial Yeomanry, and Private C.T.P. Pochin, Imperial Yeomanry.[313]

On 27 May, the 13th Battalion Imperial Yeomanry, commanded by Lieutenant-Colonel B.E. (Basil) Spragge, arrived at Lindley in the Orange Free State after covering 144 km in three days, with rations for only two days. As they approached Lindley, they were fired upon by Boers. On 28 May, the plight of the Imperial Yeomanry worsened when Commandant Michael Prinsloo arrived with the Bethlehem Commando and surrounded their position from all sides. On the evening of 29 May, General Piet de Wet joined Prinsloo and the other Boers and took command of the operation. By then his force was about 2 000 strong, and they continuously fired on the Imperial Yeomanry with two field guns and rifles. Soon after midday on 31 May 1900, Spragge realised that his position was hopeless and surrendered with his whole force. The British casualties over the five days amounted to about 35 soldiers killed, 55 wounded and 464 taken prisoner. On the Boer side about 30 men were killed and 40 were wounded.[314]

P3.6.34 The British memorial on Yeomanry Hill on the outskirts of Lindley (top).
◙ *GPS co-ordinates not available.*

P3.6.35 Grave of Private G.J. Watson (22), Imperial Yeomanry, who died on 5 June 1900 of wounds received on his birthday, 31 May 1900, on Yeomanry Hill, Lindley.[315]
▶ *British Garden of Remembrance, municipal cemetery, Lindley, Free State (near the S192, between Diemont St and the S904).*
The other graves in this cemetery of soldiers who fell on Yeomanry Hill include those of Corporal T.K. Miller, Trooper Andrew Marshall Porter, a member of the Irish Bar, Trooper H.J. Robinson, Trooper John Smith and Private E.E. Wilmot-Chetwode (22).[316]
◙ *S27° 52.891, E27° 55.763.*

P3.6.33

P3.6.34

P3.6.35

---
312 Watt 2000, 72, 316 & 393.
313 Watt 2000, 28, 175, 242, 307, 316, 334 & 350.
314 Cloete 2000, 151-153; Pretorius 2010, 244-245.
315 Watt 2000, 440.
316 Watt 2000, 289, 357, 387, 456.

Meanwhile Roberts had resumed his offensive towards the Transvaal. Although the Boers blew up virtually all the major railway bridges, they could not halt the massive British force. Advance units of General French's forces crossed the Vaal River at Old Viljoen's Drift near present-day Parys on 24 May, with the main British force under Roberts himself following three days later. From 28 to 30 May, the Republican forces stubbornly resisted the British advance on Johannesburg in battles at Elandsfontein (Germiston), Klipriviersberg and Doornkop – the very site where L.S. Jameson and his raiders had surrendered four years and five months earlier. The losses of the Republican forces who opposed the British advance in these battles are not known. The British losses amounted to at least 28 killed and 134 wounded.[317]

> P3.6.36 The 21 members of the 1st Battalion of the Gordon Highlanders Regiment who were killed in action or died of wounds received in the Battle of Doornkop on 29 May are commemorated on this memorial in the New Roodepoort Cemetery.
> ▶ Bram Fischerville, Soweto, western side of Roodepoort Rd, near the corner with Van Onselen Rd; entry from Nana Street, memorial and graves about 150 m from the main entrance, towards the right.
> ◉ S26° 12.396, E27° 52.129.
>
> P3.6.37 The graves of two British officers who were killed in action on 29 May, Captain St John Meyrick (33), Gordon Highlanders – grave in the right foreground, and Lieutenant Hugh Wharton Fife (29), Duke of Cornwall's Light Infantry,[318] – grave left foreground, as well as other members of the British forces, some of whom fell in these encounters.
> ▶ Maraisburg Cemetery, Millward Rd, east of 6th Ave, Roodepoort, Gauteng.
> ◉ S26° 10.844, E27° 56.522.
>
> P3.6.38 Grave of Lieutenant M. Kortright (28), 3rd King's Own Hussars, who was wounded at Rietfontein Mine on 30 May 1900, and died of his wounds on 21 June 1900.[319]
> ▶ Braamfontein Cemetery, c/o Smit St & Graf St, Braamfontein, Johannesburg, Gauteng.
> ◉ S26° 11.669, E28° 01.442.

On 31 May, the British forces occupied Johannesburg – the heart of the gold mining industry.[320]

> P3.6.39 Memorial plaque at the place where the Johannesburg city authorities officially surrendered the city to the British forces.
> ▶ On Gandhi Square (then called Government Square) at Bus Terminus, in Main Rd, between Rissik St & Eloff St, Marshalltown, Johannesburg, Gauteng.
> ◉ Near S26° 12.393, E28° 02.607.

P3.6.36

P3.6.37

P3.6.38

---

317 Grobler 2004, 72.
318 Watt 2000, 136 & 287.
319 Watt 2000, 238.
320 Cloete 2010, 155.

Part 3 – The military history of the war: the first year (11 October 1899–10 October 1900)

The British forces did not linger after their occupation of Johannesburg and immediately resumed their march, heading for Pretoria. However, the Republican forces continued to hinder their advance. General Sarel du Toit and his burghers successfully halted General French's cavalry on the farm Kalkheuwel to the south-west of Pretoria on 3 June. In this engagement, one burgher was killed. The British lost three killed and six wounded.[321]

P3.6.40 Gravestone of Sergeant W. Belshaw, Corporal A. Blackman and Private A. Hall of the Carabiniers, killed in action at Kalkheuwel on 3 June 1900.[322]
▶ *British memorial garden at Rietfontein, Ifafi, near the Hartbeespoort Dam. On the western side of the R511 between Kleinste St & the R104 Kerk St, at the entrance to Birdwood Estate.*
◙ *Park outside the entrance, at S25° 44.760, E27° 54.535, and walk about 300 m north to the cemetery.*

Commandant-General Louis Botha considered defending Pretoria, but, as Roberts made it clear that he would not hesitate to bombard the city into submission, the Transvaal government decided against defending the capital. President Kruger left the city by train in good time – he went east, to Machadodorp, and then Waterval-Onder, where the Transvaal government was temporarily located.[323]

On 5 June 1900, the British occupied Pretoria and released virtually all the British officers and soldiers who were held there as prisoners of war by the Republican forces. The British occupation of Pretoria was publicly confirmed by the hoisting of the Union Jack in front of the Government Building (Ou Raadsaal) in Pretoria.[324]

P3.6.41 The Government Building still stands on the south-western corner of Church Square, Pretoria, Gauteng.
◙ *S25° 44.824, E28° 11.265.*

P3.6.42 Grave of Private J. Beardwood, 1ˢᵗ Battalion Scots Guards, who was wounded on 5 June 1900 in one of the engagements that accompanied the occupation of Pretoria and died of his wounds on 10 June 1900.[325]
▶ *Old Church Street West Cemetery, Pretoria, Gauteng. Entry from Es'kia Mphahlele St (previously D.F. Malan Dr), north of W.F. Nkomo Dr (previously Church St West).*
◙ *Near S 25°44.472, E 28°10.286.*

While the occupation of Johannesburg and Pretoria was in progress, skirmishes accompanied by casualties continued elsewhere in the Boer Republics.

P3.6.43 Grave of Lieutenant R.L.C. Hobson (24), Kings Royal Rifles, killed in action at Engelbrecht's Drift on the Vaal River near Vereeniging on 5 June 1900.[326]
▶ *British Garden of Remembrance, Maccauvlei Golf Course, Viljoensdrif, Free State, near the Club House. Entry from the R82 south of the bridge crossing the Vaal River into Vereeniging.*
◙ *S26°40.933, E 27°56.521*

P3.6.39

P3.6.40

P3.6.41

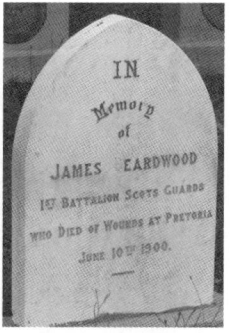
P3.6.42

---

321 Amery IV 1906, 155-156; Cloete 2010, 158.
322 Watt 2000, 28, 34 & 173.
323 Grobler 2004, 71.
324 Grobler 2004, 74.
325 Watt 2000, 25.
326 Watt 2000, 197.

After they had taken Pretoria, the British authorities took over numerous public and private buildings to use for their own purposes. Melrose House, the residence of George Heys, became the headquarters of Lord Roberts, the British Commander-in-Chief. The Staats Model School, which the Boers had used to accommodate British officers captured as prisoners of war, became a military hospital.

> P3.6.44 The Hollandia Hotel opposite the Pretoria railway station was promptly renamed Victoria Hotel by the British forces (the name is still in use), and it became a popular destination for Her Majesty's fighting men.[327]
> ▶ North-western c/o Paul Kruger St & Scheiding St.
> ◉ Near S25° 45.403, E28° 11.352.

The fall of Pretoria was another psychological defeat for the Boers. Again many burghers felt that it was time to end the war. There was no sign that any international pressure would be put on Britain to withdraw or stop the war. A Boer deputation visited numerous European heads of government, as well as the President of the United States of America. They were assured that virtually all European peoples and the Americans fully sympathised with them, but no help was forthcoming. Under these circumstances, many Boers, including high ranking officers, felt that the wise thing to do would be to accept a British victory, rather than keep on fighting and see their country devastated.[328]

These sentiments were rejected by those in power. Both President Kruger (who was temporarily living in a small house in a village called Waterval-Onder next to the Eastern Railway Line, east of the temporary Transvaal capital Machadodorp) and President Steyn felt that by giving up the struggle they would betray the sacrifices of those Boers who had laid down their lives for freedom. Botha, De Wet, De la Rey and the other senior commanders agreed with their presidents.[329]

> P3.6.45 Krugerhof, the small house where Kruger stayed in Waterval-Onder. It is currently a museum.
> ▶ Next to the N4, southern side of the road, Waterval-Onder, Mpumalanga.
> ◉ About 100 m south-east of S25° 38.775, E30° 23.033.

3.7 Persistent fighting, 6 June–10 October 1900

The Republican forces hit back two days after the British occupation of Pretoria. In the northern Orange Free State, General Christiaan de Wet split his burghers into three commandos that carried out simultaneous attacks on 7 June 1900, targeting sections of the main railway line. One commando occupied Vredefort Road Railway Station and took prisoner the soldiers guarding it. The second commando, under General C.C. (Stoffel) Froneman, attacked the British camp at the Renoster River railway bridge. The British casualties there were 36 men killed and 104 wounded. Another 486 officers and men surrendered.[330]

> P3.7.1 Some of the soldiers who fell were buried at this memorial on the northern side of the Renoster River railway bridge.

P3.6.43 P3.6.44 P3.6.45

327 Greyling 2000, 48-49.
328 Grobler 2004, 73.
329 Grobler 2004, 73.
330 De Wet 1999, 114-116.

Part 3 – The military history of the war: the first year (11 October 1899–10 October 1900)

▶ *Signposted on the R82 south of Koppies, Free State. Turn south on a gravel road east of the railway line. Drive south.*
◉ *S27° 15.717, E27° 32.795.*

On 7 June, De Wet himself attacked the British soldiers guarding Rooiwal Railway Station, which the British army had used as a supply depot. In the process he captured many tons of supplies. The Boers took away as much as they could carry, including wagonloads full of munitions which they buried in a dry river bed for future use. The rest of the supplies and a goods train at the station were blown up in the dead of night. It is said that this was the most spectacular fireworks display ever in the Orange Free State, and that the explosions could be heard 40 km away. The British casualties at Rooiwal were eight soldiers killed and 24 wounded. De Wet's total loss in the three-pronged operation was one burgher killed and four wounded.[331]

P3.7.2 The British soldiers killed in action at the Rooiwal Railway Station are buried in the military cemetery across the railway line from the station.
▶ *From the R82 south of Koppies, Free State, at Rooiwal Railway Station, turn west, cross the railway line, turn right immediately and follow the path next to the railway line to the cemetery on the right.*
◉ *S27° 17.966, E27° 31.296.*

P3.7.3 Grave of Lieutenant M.G. Blanchard, Royal Canadian Regiment, who on 15 June 1900 died of wounds received in action at Rooiwal Station on 7 June 1900.[332]
▶ *British Garden of Remembrance, western side of Noord Rd, Kroonstad, Free State.*
The grave of Second Lieutenant R.H. Hall, Sherwood Foresters, who was wounded in action at Renoster River on 7 June, died on 15 June 1900 at Honingspruit,[333] is also here.
◉ *S27° 39.049, E27° 13.816.*

On 8 June, the British forces commanded by General Buller in Natal managed to drive back the Republican forces who were defending Botha's Pass north of Newcastle and to enter the Orange Free State. The British forces suffered between 15 and 26 casualties in the process. Four burghers were wounded, of whom one, Nicolaas van Loggerenberg, died of his wounds.[334]

There are graves of three British soldiers killed in action at Botha's Pass. There are no memorials on the battlefield, but some of the trenches dug by participants in the battle on both sides can still be identified. Van Loggerenberg was buried in a trench, but the location of his grave is unknown.[335]

British forces hurriedly occupied large parts of the western Transvaal. This included towns such as Lichtenburg and Ventersdorp, both occupied on 7 June 1900, and Klerksdorp, where General A.P.J. Cronjé surrendered the town to

P3.7.1   P3.7.2   P3.7.3

331 Cloete 2000, 156; Grobler 2014, 188-189.
332 Watt 2000, 35.
333 Watt 2000, 174.
334 Cloete 2000, 157.
335 Torlage & Watt 1999, 8-10; Van der Westhuizen & Van der Westhuizen 2000, 38-40.

Captain H. Lambart after being tricked into believing that General Hunter was preparing to occupy the town with 20 000 British soldiers. However, Lambart's force consisted of only 33 men, with whom he marched into the town to accept its surrender on 8 June.[336]

> P3.7.4 The Railway Station at Klerksdorp, which was completed in 1897, featured prominently in the war after the town's occupation. Since it was at that time the western terminus of the so-called South Western Line, it was used extensively as a transit point for military personnel and war supplies. Thousands of women and children who were taken to the local concentration camp, or were relocated to other camps, as so vividly described by Alida Badenhorst in her book, Tant Alie of Transvaal,[337] passed through the entrance of this building in the last 18 months of the war.
> ▶ Near Margaretha Prinsloo St, between Delver St & Neser St.
> ◉ S26° 52.230, E26° 40.173.

Only a few days after occupying Pretoria, the British forces commanded by Roberts attacked the remnants of Commandant-General Louis Botha's commandos – about 4 000 burghers with about 30 artillery pieces – on 11 June 1900. The battlesite was Donkerhoek, which the British called Diamond Hill, located 25 km east of Pretoria, but the Boer front stretched from Kameelfontein north of the present Roodeplaat Dam in the north to Morskop, five kilometres south of Donkerhoek. Roberts himself commanded a force of 20 000 men and 83 artillery pieces in this battle. The Boers fought valiantly on the first day, but on 12 June, the British broke through Botha's defensive lines. The Boers fell back towards the east.[338]

> P3.7.5 There is a commemorative information plaque in a building with a thatched roof on the battlefield at Donkerhoek/Diamond Hill.
> ▶ Entry from the R515 (turn west a few kilometres south of the N4), then drive through the grounds of the Kleinfontein settlement.
> ◉ S25° 48.363, E28° 29.385.

> P3.7.6 The Boer memorial on the battlefield at Donkerhoek/Diamond Hill on the hillside above the information plaque.
> ▶ Same as P3.7.5.

> P3.7.7 There are a number of graves of British soldiers who were killed in action or died of wounds received in the Battle of Donkerhoek/Diamond Hill in the British Garden of Remembrance adjacent to the information plaque. These include the graves of Captain Charles James Kinahan Maguire (28) of the Royal Sussex Regiment, Lieutenant-Colonel D.S.W.O. Airlie, the Earl of Airlie (44), Major L.H.D. Fortescue (42), 17th Lancers, and Lieutenant William Rupert Marriott of the SW Mounted Rifles.[339]
> ▶ Same as P3.7.5.

P3.7.4

P3.7.5

P3.7.6

P3.7.7

---

336 Grobler 2004, 78.
337 E.g. Badenhorst 1923, 245-247.
338 Creswicke VI ca 1902, 12-19; Breytenbach VI 1996, 162-207; Pretorius 2010, 122-123.
339 Watt 2000, 3, 142 & 261. Marriott is not mentioned in Watt 2000.

Part 3 – The military history of the war: the first year (11 October 1899–10 October 1900)

The grave of Private B.W. Moodie (25), wounded in action at Diamond Hill on 11 June 1900, who died of his wounds on 16 June 1900, is in the Old Church Street West Cemetery, Pretoria, Gauteng.[340]
▶ *Entry from Es'kia Mphahlele St (previously D.F. Malan Dr), north of W.F. Nkomo Dr (previously Church St West).*
◉ *Near S25° 44.472, E28° 10.286.*

P3.7.8 Kameelfontein memorial which commemorates both British and Boer participants in the Battle of Donkerhoek.
▶ *In the Sable Hills Security Village – entrance from the Kameelfontein Road linking the R513 and the R573, Gauteng, north of where the Pienaar's River flows into the Roodeplaat Dam, western side of the road.*
◉ *Entrance at S25° 37.971, E28° 23.547 (Google Maps).*

On the same day as the commencement of the Battle of Donkerhoek, a skirmish took place at Alleman's Nek in the south eastern Free State, near Volksrust in present-day Mpumalanga, between the burghers of General Joachim Fourie and a British force commanded by Lord Dundonald. The burghers were eventually forced to retreat after sustaining 20 casualties, of which at least four were killed. The British losses amounted to 23 killed and 119 wounded.[341]

P3.7.9 The burghers' memorial for the Battle of Alleman's Nek.
▶ *Signposted. Near the junction of the R543 and the S782, west of Volksrust, Mpumalanga.*
◉ *S27° 23.977, E29° 41.541.*

P3.7.10 Memorial stone with the names of members of the 2nd Battalion Dorsetshire Regiment who lost their lives in the Battle of Alleman's Nek on 11 June 1900.
▶ *North of c/o Grens St & Kort St (visible on the western side of the R23 from the road, at the northern entrance of Volksrust, Mpumalanga).*
◉ *S27° 21.668, E29° 52.449.*

On 13 June 1900, Wakkerstroom in the southeast of the ZAR was occupied by a British force under General N.G. Lyttleton, who crossed Moolmanshoogte from the south. The *landdrost* (magistrate) handed over the keys of his office (today known as the Court House) to the British as a symbol of surrender before the British flag was raised.[342]

P3.7.11 The Court House.
▶ *Engelbrecht St, south-east of the corner with Van Riebeeck St, Wakkerstroom, Mpumalanga.*
◉ *S27° 21.247, E30° 08.644.*

In the meantime, there were frequent skirmishes between the invading British forces and burgher units, often resulting in casualties. On 14 June, a newly appointed Free State general, Reverend Paul Roux, attacked a British post at Sand River Bridge manned by 730 men under Colonel Capper, but was driven back.[343]

 P3.7.8  P3.7.9  P3.7.10

---

340   Watt 2000, 293.
341   Pretorius 2010, 8-9.
342   Van der Westhuizen & Van der Westhuizen 2000, 77.
343   Grobler 2004, 80.

P3.7.12 Grave of Major Louis I. Seymour (39), Railway Pioneer Regiment, a United States citizen, killed in action Sand River, near Virginia Siding, 14 June 1900.[344]
▶ *British Garden of Remembrance, western side of Noord Rd, Kroonstad, Free State. The graves of Lance-Corporal L.A. Matthew and Private T.B. Varker of the same regiment, who were killed in action in the same engagement, are also in that cemetery.[345]*
◉ *S27° 39.049, E27° 13.816.*

On 22 June, General De Wet again launched a three-pronged attack on British units guarding the railway line north of Kroonstad. It resulted in heavy fighting, especially at the Heuning Spruit Railway Halt, in which at least four British soldiers were killed and 25 wounded.[346] The extent of Republican casualties is not known.

P3.7.13 Grave of Major H.T. de C. Hobbs (43), West Yorkshire Regiment, killed in action at Honing (probably Heuning) Spruit, near Kroonvlei on 22 June 1900.[347]
▶ *British Garden of Remembrance, western side of Noord Rd, Kroonstad, Free State. The graves of Private R.J. Kerr (39) and Corporal J.F. Morden (26), both Royal Canadian Regiment, who were killed in action in the same engagement, are also in that cemetery.[348]*
◉ *S27° 39.049, E27° 13.816.*

On 23 June, British forces commanded by Sir Ian Hamilton occupied Heidelberg, a prominent town on the railway line between Standerton and Johannesburg. The occupation lasted up to the end of the war.[349]

P3.7.14 Stained glass window in the St Ninian's Anglican Church that commemorates the British occupation of Heidelberg.
▶ *C/o Marais St & Voortrekker St.*
◉ *S26° 29.801, E28° 21.280.*

On 25 June, General Boyes's brigade became involved in a skirmish with Republican forces near Ficksburg and suffered casualties.[350]

P3.7.15 Grave of Second Lieutenant G.L.D. Brancker (23) and Captain E.B. Grogan (35), both of the 1st Battalion South Staffordshire Regiment, killed in action near Ficksburg on 25 June 1900.[351]
▶ *Old town cemetery, Ficksburg, Free State. Entrance from Veld St, near corner with Piet Retief St.*
◉ *S28° 52.027, E27° 52.637.*

P3.7.11

P3.7.12

P3.7.13

---

344 Watt 2000, 374.
345 Watt 2000, 270 & 428.
346 Cloete 2010, 166-167.
347 Watt 2000, 197.
348 Watt 2000, 233 & 296.
349 Amery IV 1906, 300; Mangold 1988, 205 & 207 (footnotes 7 & 8).
350 Creswicke VII ca 1902, 39.
351 Watt 2000, 43 & 171.

Part 3 – The military history of the war: the first year (11 October 1899–10 October 1900)

On 30 June 1900, Major-General Clery's forces moved out of Standerton in a north-westerly direction with the objective of establishing communication with Heidelberg. By 2 July, his forces reached Greylingstad.[352] Their progress was accompanied by skirmishes with burgher forces which resulted in some casualties.

P3.7.16 Gravestone of Trooper Angus Jenkins, Strathconas Horse, killed in action at Witnek, near Waterval Railway Station, about half way between Standerton and Greylingstad, on 1 July 1900 (Canada Day). He was his regiment's first battle casualty.[353]
▶ *British Garden of Remembrance, new cemetery, Standerton, Mpumalanga. Entry from Walter Sisulu St.*
◉ *S26° 56.283, E29° 14.077.*

On 5 July, the Heidelberg Commando attacked a mounted Imperial force which included Canadians of Strathcona's Horse near Kraal Station. The fighting subsequently spread towards Mahemsfontein near Greylingstad in the southern Transvaal. Both sides suffered casualties. Sergeant A.H.L. Richardson was subsequently awarded the Victoria Cross for his gallant conduct in this engagement. Fighting resumed the next day, but no side could gain the ascendency.[354]

There are a number of memorials next to the Val Hotel (see P6.1.1 on p. 273) across the road from the railway station, including one for members of Strathconas Horse who fell in action. They were initially buried there but were reinterred in Standerton.[355]
▶ *The Val Hotel is on the eastern side of the R547, north of the railway line, Mpumalanga.*
◉ *S26° 47.794, E28° 56.093.*

From 6 to 7 July, Republican forces commanded by General Christiaan de Wet attempted to defend Bethlehem in the eastern Free State against a British onslaught led by Major-General R.A.P. Clements and Major-General A.H. Paget. Bethlehem was then the temporary capital of the Orange Free State. The defenders held out for more than a day, but were finally forced to fall back in a southerly direction into the Brandwater Basin. Fouriesburg was later proclaimed the new temporary capital, the last town to be declared a capital.[356]

P3.7.17 This memorial plaque attached to a rock in front of the Civic Centre in Bethlehem commemorates the Battle of Bethlehem.
▶ *20-22 Muller St, Bethlehem, Free State.*
◉ *GPS co-ordinates not available.*

P3.7.18 Captain J.B.S. Alderson (31), Royal Irish Regiment, died on 8 July 1900 of wounds received in action at Bethlehem on 7 July 1900.[357]
▶ *Old town cemetery, between Muller St & Boshoff St, near corner with Baxter St, Bethlehem, Free State.*

P3.7.14

P3.7.15

P3.7.16

---

352 Amery IV 1906, 400.
353 Watt 2000, 218.
354 Creswicke VI ca 1902, 195; Mangold 1988, 211-212; Uys 2000, 58; Cloete 2010, 171.
355 Watt 2000, 245 & 311.
356 Grobler 2004, 86.
357 Watt 2000, 3.

The grave of Corporal G. Cairns, 2ⁿᵈ Brabant's Horse, killed in action at Bethlehem on 8 July 1900 (according to his gravestone "fighting to assist a wounded comrade"), is in the same cemetery.[358]
◉ S28° 14.026, E28° 18.036.

Major-General E.T.H. Hutton set out to clear the countryside south-east of Pretoria of Boer commandos on 7 July. A section of his force commanded by Colonel Mahon was attacked by burghers under Commandant Piet Trichardt and Field Cornet A.J. Dercksen at Witkop, east of Bapsfontein. After suffering heavy casualties, Mahon was forced to retreat towards Tierpoort. Three burghers were killed and nine wounded. British casualties totalled about 50 men.[359]

P3.7.19 A memorial in the Braamfontein Cemetery pays tribute to ten members of the Imperial Light Horse Regiment killed in this engagement.
▶ C/o Smit St & Graf St, Braamfontein, Johannesburg, Gauteng.
◉ S26° 11.669, E28° 01.442.

On 11 July, General De la Rey's commando overran a British force of 240 men stationed at Silkaatsnek in the Magaliesberg Mountains, about 25 km west of Pretoria, capturing their two field guns in the process. British casualties amounted to 17 killed, 55 wounded and 189 (including the wounded) taken prisoner. Boer losses were seven killed and eight wounded.[360]

P3.7.20 Silkaatsnek in the Magaliesberg, North West, photographed from the north. There is no memorial at the Silkaatsnek battlefield.
▶ The R511 main road linking Brits to Schoemansville at the Hartbeespoort Dam crosses the Magaliesberg where the battlefield was.
◉ S25° 42.095, E27° 53.894.

P3.7.21 Memorial for 16 members of the 2ⁿᵈ Battalion, Lincolnshire Regiment, who were killed in action at Silkaatsnek. Most of the British casualties of the battle were reburied in the British memorial garden at Rietfontein. In addition, there is a memorial for Second Lieutenant T.D. Pilkington (24), 1ˢᵗ Royal Dragoons, who was killed in action at Silkaatsnek but was reinterred in the Brompton Cemetery in London.[361]
▶ On the western side of the R511 between Kleinste St and the R104 Kerk St, Ifafi, North West, at the entrance to Birdwood Estate. Park outside the entrance and walk about 300 m north to the cemetery.
◉ Park at S25° 44.760, E27° 54.535.

P3.7.22 The graves of three of the burghers killed in action in the battle, namely Adjutant C.F.F. Röth, P. Jacobs and Adjutant A.J.D. Mussmann.
▶ In a farm cemetery. Turn to the south off the R513, at Farm 16, a few kilometres east of the junction where the R513 turns off from the R511. There are also a memorial gravestone for the burghers C.J. Lee, H.C. Gerber, Momsen and one unknown man, all killed in action at Silkaatsnek on 11 July 1900.
◉ S25° 40.855, E27° 54.862.

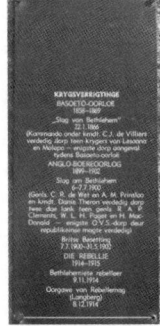
P3.7.17

P3.7.18

P3.7.19

P3.7.20

---

358   Watt 2000, 61.
359   Breytenbach VI 1996, 277-278.
360   Grobler 2004, 85.
361   Watt 2000, 333.

Part 3 – The military history of the war: the first year (11 October 1899–10 October 1900)

P3.7.23 The grave of Assistant Field Cornet C.J. Lee, killed in action at Silkaatsnek.
▶ *In a small cemetery on the farm of J.L. (Wannie) Scribante. Turn to the north off the R513, at Farm 19, a few kilometres east of the junction where the R513 turns off from the R511.*
◉ *S25° 40.447, E27° 55.147.*

On the same day, 11 July 1900, a skirmish between British forces commanded by Major-General H.L. Smith-Dorrien and a group of burghers commanded by General Sarel Oosthuizen (nicknamed Red Bull) took place at Dwarsvlei, north of Krugersdorp. The burghers managed to put their adversaries under tremendous pressure, but by dusk their attack faltered when Oosthuizen was seriously wounded. He died of his wounds about a month later.[362]

Oosthuizen was buried on the farm Zanddrift next to the Crocodile River, some distance north of Dwarsvlei. In 1904 he was reinterred in the Krugersdorp Cemetery, where he shares a grave with his brother, Corporal Izak Johannes Oosthuizen.

On 12 July, the Heidelberg Commando attacked General Clery's Imperial force of about 3 000 men at Mahemsfontein near Greylingstad, forcing them back into their camp after starting a veld fire. Both sides suffered casualties.[363]

P3.7.24 Gravestone of Private John Exon, Thornycroft's Mounted Infantry, who died of wounds received near Greylingstad on 12 July 1900.[364]
▶ *British Garden of Remembrance, new cemetery, Standerton, Mpumalanga. Entry from Walter Sisulu St.*
The graves of Private F. Norris and Corporal B.H. Lee of Strathconas Horse are also here.[365]
◉ *S26° 56.283, E29° 14.077.*

On 16 July 1900, General Ben Viljoen launched a determined attack with four Republican commandos on the Imperial forces of Major-General Hutton east and south-east of Pretoria (the Tierpoort, Rietvlei, Olifantsfontein area). Hutton's position soon became desperate, but he was saved when the approach of British reinforcements convinced the burghers to retire. The Imperial casualties included seven killed, 30 wounded and 24 taken prisoner. On the Boer side, five burghers were killed, 13 were wounded and two were taken prisoner.[366]

P3.7.25 Grave of Lieutenant H.L. Borden (22), 1st Battalion Canadian Mounted Rifles, killed in action at Rietvlei on 16 July 1900. He was the only son of Canadian Minister of Defence F.W. Borden.[367]
▶ *Braamfontein Cemetery, c/o Smit St & Graf St, Braamfontein, Johannesburg, Gauteng.*
The graves of Lieutenant J.E. Burch (26), Royal Canadian Dragoons, who fell in the same engagement, is also in this cemetery.[368]
◉ *S26° 11.669, E28° 01.442.*

P3.7.21   P3.7.22   P3.7.23   P3.7.24

362   Heath 1999, 43-44.
363   Mangold 1988, 216-218; Cloete 2010, 174.
364   Watt 2000, 131.
365   Watt 2000, 245 & 311.
366   Cloete 2010, 175; Breytenbach VI 1996, 280-281.
367   Watt 2000, 38; Amery IV 1906, 397; Cloete 2010, 175.
368   Watt 2000, 54.

British forces commanded by Lord Methuen and Major-General Smith-Dorrien forced General Manie Lemmer to abandon Olifant's Nek in the Magaliesberg south-east of Rustenburg on 21 July 1900. Despite the overwhelming size of the force advancing on them, Lemmer and his burghers managed to escape relatively unscathed.[369]

> P3.7.26 Grave of Lieutenant R.B. Wilson (26), 3rd Battalion Imperial Yeomanry, who was wounded in action at Olifant's Nek on 22 July 1900, and died of his wounds on 26 July 1900.[370]
> ▶ Old municipal cemetery, Rustenburg, North West. Entry from Nelson Mandela St, between Bosch St & Kock St.
> ◉ S25° 40.516, E27° 14.628.

On the same day, the Heidelberg Commando attacked a British camp at Vlakfontein (around where Balfour is today), near the Suikerboschrand River. After initial headway, they were eventually forced to retire. One burgher, Corporal J.A. Spruyt, was mortally wounded in this attack.[371]

> P3.7.27 Grave of Corporal J.A. Spruyt.
> ▶ Kloof Cemetery, on the banks of the Kloof Spruit, on the northern side of the extension of Fenter St, Heidelberg, Gauteng.
> ◉ S 26° 29.717, E 28° 20.770.

On Sunday 22 July 1900, General Manie Lemmer attacked 500 Australian Bushmen under Colonel Airey near the Selons River, between Rustenburg and Zeerust in the western Transvaal. The Australians were surrounded, their horses stampeded or were shot, and they suffered seven killed and 32 wounded. The fighting lasted an entire day before they were relieved by soldiers despatched from Rustenburg. The Boers referred to this engagement as the Battle of Rooipoeierspruit, but the British called it the Battle of Koster River or Selons River. During this engagement, British casualties were voluntarily tended to by a 19-year-old girl, Emily Charlotte Back.[372]

> P3.7.28 The Rooipoeierspruit Monument commemorates the burghers who fought in this battle. The monument was unveiled on 25 November 1938. The names of the four burghers killed in the battle, P.W. Venter, C. Malan, J. Viljoen and S. Drake, are engraved on the now vandalised monument.
> ▶ On a low hill south-east of the Moedwil Secondary School, on the southern side of the N4 toll road between Rustenburg and Swartruggens, North West.
> ◉ S25° 38.017, E26° 58.676.

> P3.7.29 Grave of Captain C.W. Robertson (30), 1st Regiment Australian Bushmen, killed in action on 22 July 1900 at Koster River.[373]
> ▶ Old municipal cemetery, Nelson Mandela St, between Kock St & Bosch St, Rustenburg, North West. The graves of the six Victoria Bushmen soldiers (Private J.I. McCartney, Lance-Corporal J. McClure, Private S.J. Oliver,

P3.7.25

P3.7.26

P3.7.27

---

369   Cloete 2010, 177.
370   According to Watt (2000, 458), Wilson was wounded at Olifant's Nek on 21 July 1900.
371   Cloete 2010, 177; Pretorius 2016, 115.
372   Amery IV 1906, 357; Cloete 2000, 172; Pretorius 2010, 241.
373   Watt 2000, 356.

Private H.O. Walford, Sergeant D.H. Pruden and Sergeant H.J. Goodman), killed in action at Koster River or died of wounds received there on 22 July 1900 are in the same cemetery.
◙ S25° 40.516, E27° 14.628.

P3.7.30 The memorial to commemorate Back. The inscription on this memorial reads: "This memorial was erected by the Houston family in loving memory of Emily Charlotte Back. Born 03-10-1880. Married to T.J. Houston 26-10-1903. Died 26-10-1960. In commemoration of her courage and bravery under fire, voluntarily tending the Australian casualties during the Battle of Koster River on 22 July 1900. Ps 27:3 Even if a whole army surrounds me I will not be afraid. 19 July 2003."
▶ *At the eastern edge of the grounds of the Moedwil Secondary School, near a family graveyard, about 100 m south of the N4 toll road between Rustenburg and Swartruggens, North West.*
◙ *S25° 37.888, E26° 58.557.*

The British forces resumed their offensive in the eastern Transvaal from the middle of July 1900. Conditions on the eastern Highveld were at times difficult for the soldiers to cope with, including spells of very cold weather, compared to what they were used to in other areas of South Africa.

P3.7.31 Grave of Second Lieutenant William Victor St. McLaren (23), Argyll & Sutherland Highlanders, who was born and bred in Heidelberg in the ZAR. He died on 26 July 1900 near Balmoral (according to Johanna van Warmelo, a former schoolmate) as a result of exposure during a snow storm.[374]
▶ *Kloof Cemetery, on the banks of the Kloof Spruit, on the northern side of the extension of Fenter St, Heidelberg, Gauteng.*
◙ *S26° 29.717, E28° 20.770.*

The British forces under General E.T.H. Hutton occupied Middelburg in the eastern Transvaal Mpumalanga, a town on the eastern railway line between Pretoria and Delagoa Bay (today Maputo), on 27 July 1900. The town remained in British hands until the end of the war.[375]

P3.7.32 The Dutch Reformed Church in Middelburg, built in 1890. After the British occupation, the Dutch Reformed community was allowed to use the building for services on Sunday mornings, but had to be off the premises by 11 am to make room for the British forces to have their own services.[376]
▶ *C/o Walter Sisulu St & Joubert St, Middelburg, Mpumalanga.*
◙ *S25° 45.726, E29° 27.407.*

Meanwhile, in July 1900, the bulk of the remaining Orange Free State forces were surrounded by the British in the Brandwater Basin, a mountainous area south of Bethlehem near the border with Basutoland. Intermittent fighting took place for control of the mountain passes which gave access to the Basin – fighting in which both sides suffered casualties.[377]

 P3.7.28
 P3.7.29
 P3.7.30
 P3.7.31

---

374 Brandt 2007, 56. According to Watt (2000, 281), McLaren died of syncope.
375 Cloete 2010, 179.
376 Van der Westhuizen & Van der Westhuizen 2000, 186.
377 Schoeman 2013, 36-43.

P3.7.33 Gravestone (left) of Trooper J.B. Bradfield (31) and Trooper C.T. Hancock (21), as well as the grave of Private M.L. Craigie (21) and Private E.A. Troup (22), all Imperial Yeomanry. All four were killed in action near Bethlehem on 13 July 1900.[378]
▶ *Old town cemetery, between Muller St & Boshoff St, near corner with Baxter St, Bethlehem, Free State.*
◉ *S28° 14.026, E28° 18.036.*

A number of Republican commandos, including that of General de Wet, managed to escape from the Brandwater Basin before the British forces sealed off the area. On 19 July, Brigadier General R.G. Broadwood and about 4 000 troops attempted to intercept De Wet's scouts, led by Captain Danie Theron, west of Petrus Steyn. A number of skirmishes resulted in the area of the Karoospruit, Palmietfontein and Tierbank. De Wet lost eight burghers, who were killed in action. On the British side, five soldiers were killed and 15 were wounded.[379]

P3.7.34 Memorial for Field Cornet S.J. Strydom, killed in action at Karoospruit on 19 July 1900.
▶ *On the farm Groenvlei, signposted about 10 km north-east of Lindley, on the northern side of the R707 to Petrus Steyn, Free State.*
◉ *GPS co-ordinates not available.*

Later the same day, Lieutenant Colonel M.O. Little of the 3rd Cavalry Brigade attacked De Wet's main convoy at Paardeplaats, near the Lindley/Kroonstad wagon road. The Boers managed to repulse the attackers until dusk, when the fighting ended. The Boers suffered five and the British about ten casualties.[380]

P3.7.35 Grave of Major H.G. Moor (29), West Australian Mounted Infantry, killed in action at Palmietfontein near Lindley on 19 July 1900.[381]
▶ *British Garden of Remembrance, municipal cemetery, near the S192, between Diemont St and the S904, Lindley, Free State.*
◉ *S27° 52.891, E27° 55.763.*

After crossing the main Kroonstad-Johannesburg railway line at Serfontein Siding on the evening of 21 July, De Wet and his commando reached the small village of Vredefort in the northern Orange Free State on 24 July, where they loaded five wagons with maize meal. However, a large British force arrived at the town as the Boers were leaving, and a heavy skirmish broke out in the Stinkhoutboom area. It resulted in the British capture of the wagons. Both sides suffered casualties.[382]

P3.7.36 Grave of Troopers J.H. Moore (25), A.W. Nicholas (20) and F.J. Tothill, all of the South Australia Imperial Bushmen, killed in action at Stinkhoutboom, 24 June 1900 (the date should be 24 July 1900).[383]
▶ *Municipal cemetery, Vredefort, Free State. Near the R59, between the S212 and the R59 1st Ave.*
◉ *S27° 00.019, E27° 21.826.*

 P3.7.32
 P3.7.33
 P3.7.34

---

378 Watt 2000, 42, 93, 176 & 422.
379 Pretorius 2001a, 50-57; Cloete 2000, 171.
380 Cloete 2010, 175; Grobler 2004, 87.
381 Watt 2000, 294.
382 Pretorius 2001a, 64-79.
383 Watt 2000, 295, 308 & 420.

Part 3 – The military history of the war: the first year (11 October 1899–10 October 1900)

P3.7.37 Grave and monument for nine burghers, of whom eight were killed in action, five on 22 July 1900 (the date should be 24 July 1900).
▶ *Same as P3.7.36.*

The British forces continued to consolidate their stranglehold in the eastern part of the Orange Free State around the Brandwater Basin, south of Bethlehem. Some of the Free State commandos put up stiff resistance, but extremely adverse weather conditions eroded their morale, especially after a heavy snowfall on 23 July. The British forces were gaining the upper hand, and managed systematically to tighten their cordon around the encircled Boer commandos in the Basin, but they too continuously suffered casualties.[384]

P3.7.38 Grave of Captain W. Gloster (37) and six other members of the Royal Irish Regiment, all killed in action at Slabberts Nek, near Bethlehem on 23 July 1900.[385]
▶ *Old town cemetery, between Muller St & Boshoff St, near the corner with Baxter St, Bethlehem, Free State.*
◉ *S28° 14.026, E28° 18.036.*
This cemetery also contains a plaque in memory of other British victims of fighting in the Brandwater Basin, namely Corporal G. Hogan, Royal Irish Regiment & Private W. Barron, Lovats Scouts, killed in action at Ararat on 26 July 1900; Corporal H. Jordan, Burmah Mounted Infantry, killed in action at Houtkop on 22 July 1900; Private C. Buck, Private E. Bennett and Private J. Mills, all of the 1ˢᵗ Royal Sussex Regiment, killed in action near Retief's Nek on 20 and 23 July 1900; and the grave of Captain E.Q. Robertson (32), 1ˢᵗ King's Own Scottish Borderers, killed in action at Stephansdraai, Wittebergen, near Bethlehem on 29 July 1900.[386]

By the end of July, the Republican officers in the Brandwater Basin, who were negatively influenced by the former Chief Commandant Marthinus Prinsloo, believed that the situation was hopeless. As a result, Prinsloo surrendered with 4 000 burghers on 30 July 1900. This was another crushing defeat – the Free State forces never recovered.[387]

P3.7.39 The memorial on Surrender Hill that commemorates this event.[388]
▶ *Next to the R711 between Clarens and Fouriesburg, Free State (signposted).*
◉ *S28° 36.567, E28° 23.148.*

De Wet and his commando, accompanied by President Steyn, made their way across the Vaal River into the Transvaal so that Steyn could discuss the war situation with President Kruger.[389] The members of this Free State commando were involved in a number of clashes with British forces participating in what became known as the 'First De Wet Hunt'.

There are no memorials commemorating the First De Wet Hunt. Specific places associated with De Wet's expedition include Tygerfontein, in what is today the North West section of the Vredefort Dome World

P3.7.35

P3.7.36

P3.7.37

P3.7.38

---

384   Amery IV 1906, 327-328; Cloete 2010, 176-179; Schoeman 2013, 42; Grobler 2014, 218.
385   Watt 2000, 158.
386   Watt 2000, 356.
387   Brink 1904, 83-91; Grobler 2004, 91; Schoeman 2013, 43-50.
388   Richardson 2001, 177.
389   Van Schoor 2009, 195.

ANGLO-BOER WAR Historical Guide to Memorials and Sites in South Africa

P3.7.39   P3.7.40   P3.7.41   P3.7.42

Heritage Site, and Olifant's Nek in the Magaliesberg in North West, and De Wet's escape route back across the Magaliesberg south of Wolhuterskop in North West.[390]

From 4 to 16 August 1900, General De la Rey and his burghers unsuccessfully besieged a British garrison at Brakfontein on the Eland's River (where Swartruggens is today) in the western Transvaal. A British force under Colonel Charles Hore consisting of about 200 Rhodesian Volunteers and 300 Australians bravely defended their position, especially on the first two days of the siege. The British casualties numbered 22 men killed and 58 wounded. By contrast, De la Rey lost only four men.[391]

▶ *There are a number of commemorative sites of this siege, in close proximity to each other on the western side of the municipal cemetery, which is on the northern side of the N4 toll road at the eastern entrance to Swartruggens, North West.*
◉ *S25° 38.965, E26° 42.432.*

P3.7.40 The memorial for Australian soldiers on the Eland's River battlefield.

P3.7.41 The memorial for Rhodesian soldiers on the Eland's River battlefield.

P3.7.42 The burgher memorial on the Eland's River battlefield.

P3.7.43 There is also a Garden of Remembrance for Imperial soldiers in the municipal cemetery of Swartruggens. Most of them fell in the Siege of Eland's River.

On 16 August, the same day on which De la Rey pulled out of the siege of Brakfontein, Commandant Potgieter and the Marico Commando occupied Zeerust, west of Brakfontein. A British force consisting of about 2 900 soldiers with 16 field guns, commanded by Lieutenant General Sir F. Carrington, attempted to disperse those burghers, but they were driven back by 600 Marico burghers under Commandant J.D.L. Botha and Commandant P.D. Swart at

P3.7.43   P3.7.44

390   Pretorius 2001a, 121-129 & 194.
391   Van den Bergh 1996, 74-80; Cloete 2010, 186.

Buffelshoek. Boer losses amounted to six burghers killed and ten (including Swart) wounded. British casualties are unknown.[392]

> P3.7.44 The gravestone of two of the burghers killed in action at Buffelshoek – Field Cornet Jan van Niekerk and Gert Snyman.
> ▶ Attached to the burgher memorial, c/o Hendrik Potgieter St & Forsman St, Zeerust, North West. These two burghers were reinterred here. The names of the six burghers who fell at Buffelshoek all appear on a granite plaque on this burgher monument.[393]
> ◉ S25° 32.501, E26° 04.540.

Fighting continued over a wide terrain and casualties continued to mount.

> P3.7.45 The British forces occupied Chrissiesmeer (Lake Chrissie) in the eastern Transvaal in mid-August 1900. They erected this corrugated iron building, which they had transported by ox wagon from Tempe in Bloemfontein, to serve as a recreation hall in the town.[394]

> P3.7.46 Grave of a burgher, J.B.M. van Reenen (21), killed in action on 14 August 1900. The circumstances surrounding his death could not be established.
> ▶ In the Golden Gate National Park, Free State, in a cemetery (signposted) about 100 m north of the R712 that runs through the park.
> ◉ S28° 30.205, E28° 35.466.

> P3.7.47 Memorial gravestone of Private F.W. Young (22) and of Private T.A. Brown (21), both of the 2nd Company, Imperial Yeomanry, both killed in action near Senekal in the Orange Free State on 20 August 1900.[395]
> ▶ Municipal cemetery, Senekal, Free State.
> ◉ S28° 18.778, E27° 37.287.

On 20 August, General J.G. Celliers and his burghers attacked a British patrol consisting mainly of Rhodesian troops who approached too close to President Steyn's escort near Waterval, north of Pretoria. One officer and four men of the Rhodesian Volunteer Regiment were killed in this engagement.[396]

> P3.7.48 Gravestone of Lieutenant-Colonel J.A. Spreckley (35), Southern Rhodesian Volunteers, killed in action near Hammanskraal on 20 August 1900.[397] There is a memorial for the four soldiers next to Spreckley's gravestone.
> ▶ British Garden of Remembrance near the Petronella railway station, north of Pretoria, next to the R101 (old

P3.7.45

P3.7.46

P3.7.47

---

392 Cloete 2010, 187.
393 Zeerust 1987.
394 Van der Westhuizen & Van der Westhuizen 2000, 111.
395 Watt 2000, 51 & 468.
396 Cloete 2010, 187.
397 Watt 2000, 394.

national road), on its western side, about 200 m north of the crossing with the Lusthof Road turning off to Vastfontein. The memorial garden is next to a Kanhym depot. There are pine trees behind the terrain.
◉ S25° 29.955, E28° 15.528.

The last major set-piece battle of the war took place in the eastern Transvaal, between Belfast and Machadodorp from 21 to 27 August 1900 – known to the Boers as the Battle of Bergendal. British sources refer to it as the Battle of Dalmanutha. Lord Roberts himself was in command of the British forces and Commandant-General Louis Botha led the Boer forces. After continuous fighting for seven days, the British broke the resistance of the 67 members of Commandant P.R. Oosthuizen's *Zuid-Afrikaansche Republiek Politie* (South African Republic Police), in the center of the Boer defensive line. A general retreat of Boer commandos followed. British and Boer losses during the seven-day battle as a whole have been estimated at about 385 and 78 respectively.[398]

P3.7.49 Members of the Zuid-Afrikaansche Republiek Politie and other burghers killed in action in the Battle of Bergendal are commemorated on the Burgher Monument on the battlefield (see P1.13).
▶ Signposted, clearly visible from the N4 national road between Belfast and Machadodorp, Mpumalanga, on the southern side of the road.
◉ S25° 44.072, E30° 06.198.

P3.7.50 The Rifle Brigade memorial at Bergendal commemorates the role of the unit specifically pitched in battle against the Zuid-Afrikaansche Republiek Politie.
▶ Same as P3.7.49.

P3.7.51 Grave of Captain A. Savory (22), 4th Hussars, killed in action on 23 August 1900, the third day of the battle of Bergendal, at Geluk Farm.[399]
▶ British Garden of Remembrance, Municipal cemetery, Machadodorp, Mpumalanga.
On the western side of the tarred road that connects the town to the N4 toll road, a few hundred metres south of the N4. The graves of Private F. Cole (20), Private A. McGrath (30), Private S. Slater (25) and Private J. Smith (23), all of the 1st Devonshire Regiment, all killed in action on 26 August 1900, the sixth day of the battle of Bergendal, are in the same cemetery.
◉ S25° 40.065, E30° 14.508.

P3.7.52 The names of 23 members of the 1st King's Liverpool Regiment and three other British soldiers killed in action on Geluk Farm on 23 August 1900 are on this monument in a small cemetery on that farm.
▶ About 500 m east of a gravel road linking the R33 between Belfast and Carolina and the Dalmanutha railway station, Mpumalanga. It is visible from the gravel road. The house of the farm owner, Willie Stols, is on the western side of this road.
◉ S25° 51.716, E30° 04.800.

While the Battle of Bergendal was raging in the eastern Transvaal, a section of General De la Rey's forces engaged

P3.7.48

P3.7.49

P3.7.50

P3.7.51

398 Pretorius 2010, 33-36.
399 Watt 2000, 369.

Part 3 – The military history of the war: the first year (11 October 1899–10 October 1900)

with a force of about 900 British soldiers at Kalkfontein, about 9 km from Zeerust in the western Transvaal. The result was inconclusive.[400]

> P3.7.53 Gravestone (damaged) of A.J.G. de la Rey (20), who on 28 August 1900 died of wounds received in action on 25 August.
> ▶ Municipal Cemetery, Lichtenburg, North West, near Christa St, between Lang St & Burgers St (entry from Thabo Mbeki St).
> ◉ S26° 08.461, E26° 09.228.

On 23 August 1900, Commandant (the former general) J.H. Olivier and his burghers managed to encircle Colonel H.M. Ridley's force of 300 Queenstown volunteers in a poplar grove on the farm Helpmekaar, about 16 km from Winburg in the Orange Free State. Kitchener was eventually forced to send more than 1 000 men as reinforcements before Ridley and his men could be freed after 48 hours. The British forces suffered more than 40 casualties. Four burghers were wounded.[401]

> P3.7.54 Grave of Private H.B. Brown (19), Queenstown Rifle Volunteers, killed in action at Helpmekaar near Winburg on 24 August 1900.[402]
> ▶ British Garden of Remembrance, c/o Jac Coetzer St & McLennan St, Winburg, Free State.
> ◉ S28° 31.158, E27° 00.411.

> P3.7.55 Grave of Sergeant Farrier R.P. Williams (20), Pembrokeshire Yeomanry, killed in action near Ventersburg, Orange Free State, on 25 August 1900.[403] He was probably among the soldiers who participated in the rescue of Ridley's Queenstown Volunteers.
> ▶ Old municipal cemetery, southern side of Eeufees St, between Smith St & Swart St, Ventersburg, Free State.
> ◉ S28° 04.861, E27° 08.085.

Olivier underestimated his foes on 27 August when he attacked the British garrison in Winburg, who had been forewarned about his plans. Olivier and his men were soon forced to flee and he became a prisoner of war. His future son-in-law, Pieter Kritzinger, was appointed as commandant in his place.[404]

> P3.7.56 Grave of Sergeant-Major A.E. Rütters, Brabant's Horse, killed in action at Winburg on 27 August 1900.[405]
> ▶ British Garden of Remembrance, c/o Jac Coetzer St & McLennan St, Winburg, Free State.
> ◉ S28° 31.158, E27° 00.411.

On 30 August 1900, General French's forces occupied both Waterval-Boven and Waterval-Onder on the Eastern Railway Line.[406] The British forces suffered some casualties in these operations.

P3.7.52   P3.7.53   P3.7.54   P3.7.55

400	Cloete 2010, 189
401	Cloete 2010, 188.
402	Watt 2000, 49.
403	Watt 2000, 454.
404	Cloete 2010, 190
405	Watt 2000, 365.
406	Cloete 2010, 191.

P3.7.57 Grave of Lieutenant J.L. Lawlor (26), Inniskilling Fusiliers, who was wounded on 30 August and died of his wounds on 31 August 1900.[407]
▶ *British Anglo-Boer War cemetery, about 100 m south of the N4, at the eastern end of Waterval-Onder, Mpumalanga.*
◉ *S25° 38.782, E30° 23.214.*

Also on 30 August, General Ben Viljoen released a large number of British prisoners of war – according to one source, nine officers and 1 697 men – from the camp at Nooitgedacht, about 20 km east of Waterval-Onder.[408]

The Nooitgedacht camp was near the Airlie Railway Station, where there is a small British Anglo-Boer War cemetery that contains the graves of members of the British forces who died in the Nooitgedacht prisoner-of-war camp.[409]

On 1 September, Commandant Piet Fourie became aware of the presence of a British outpost of little more than 100 British soldiers in Ladybrand in the eastern Free State. Early the next morning, he demanded the garrison's surrender, but the British commander refused to give up without a fight. The resulting battle became known as the "Siege of Ladybrand", which ended four days later with the arrival of a large British column.[410] The British garrison suffered slight casualties in this encounter. Boer casualties are not known.

P3.7.58 Grave of Private R.V. Cory, Imperial Yeomanry, who was wounded on active service at Leeuw River near Ladybrand on 4 September 1900, and died of his wounds on 5 September 1900.[411]
▶ *British Garden of Remembrance, old town cemetery, southern side of Massyn St, Thaba Nchu, Free State.*
◉ *S29° 13.219, E26° 50.945.*

Commandant Danie Theron accompanied General Christiaan de Wet throughout the First De Wet Hunt and on two occasions managed to capture British supply trains. From 12 August, he and his corps acted on their own in the western Witwatersrand area, harassing British troops and capturing a train on 31 August. Theron also used the opportunity to pay a visit to the grave of his late fiancée, Hannie Neethling, who had passed away in 1898. On 5 September 1900, while attempting to make contact with General Piet Liebenberg with the objective of launching an attack on the British forces under Major-General A. Fitzroy Hart, he became involved in a skirmish with a British military unit supported by artillery. He was killed by a lyddite shell during the engagement.[412]

P3.7.59 There are numerous sites associated with Theron. He spent part of his youth in this house.
▶ *21 Church St, Tulbagh, Western Cape.[413]*
◉ *S33° 17.170, E19° 08.310.*

P3.7.56

P3.7.57

P3.7.58

---

407 Watt 2000, 243.
408 Meijer 2000, 166-167.
409 Van der Westhuizen & Van der Westhuizen 2013, 259-260.
410 Amery V 1907, 6.
411 Watt 2000, 89.
412 Pretorius 2010, 454.
413 Fransen 2004, 370-371.

Part 3 – The military history of the war: the first year (11 October 1899–10 October 1900)

P3.7.60 A statue of Theron by Charl Engela, originally unveiled at the former Danie Theron Combat School in Kimberley in 1969.[414]
▶ *Fort Schanskop, Pretoria, Gauteng.*
◉ *S25° 46.628, E28° 11.035.*

P3.7.61 The 25 m high Theron memorial, unveiled in 1950, on the low hill where he was killed.[415]
▶ *Southern side of the N12 near Fochville, North West, 46.8 km from Potchefstroom. (Clearly visible from the N12).*
◉ *S26° 27.021, E27° 26.332.*

P3.7.62 Theron was buried by the British forces, reburied by his own companions three days later, and eventually re-buried a second time in 1903, next to his beloved Hannie Neethling.[416] *His grave is on the left, hers is fenced in on the right.*
▶ *Neethlingshof Cemetery, south-eastern c/o the intersection of the R82 (Old Vereeniging Rd) and the R550 (Kliprivier Rd), Eikenhof, Gauteng.*
◉ *S26°19.927; E27°59.112.*

In the eastern part of the Transvaal Republic, the Republican forces came under tremendous pressure from the British forces after the Battle of Bergendal, and decided to disperse. One group fell back towards the border of Mozambique, which was a Portuguese colony at the time. Since they wanted to ensure that their munitions would not fall into British hands, they destroyed most of the field guns and ammunition on the banks of the Crocodile River on 16 to 18 September 1900.[417]

P3.7.63 There is a memorial in the south of the Kruger National Park at the place where the munitions were blown up.
▶ *On the S25 gravel road (Crocodile River Rd), between Malelane and Crocodile Bridge.*
◉ *GPS co-ordinates not available.*

One of the four Long Tom guns was also destroyed – it is not clear exactly where, but it may have happened at Hectorspruit, east of Komatipoort, on 22 September 1900.[418] The British forces captured large amounts of Republican munitions in Komatipoort and destroyed whatever they could not use themselves in order to ensure that the Boers would not recapture the weapons. These dangerous operations had tragic results for a few soldiers.

P3.7.64 Memorial for two members of the 1st Battalion Gordon Highlanders, Lance Corporal J. McLachlan (or MacLachlan) and Private E.G. Parker, who were killed by an explosion while destroying ammunition on 30 September 1900.[419]

  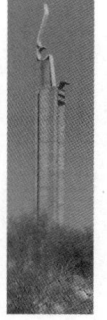 

P3.7.59   P3.7.60   P3.7.61   P3.7.62

---
414 Pretorius 1989a, 149.
415 Pretorius 1989a, 147-149.
416 Breytenbach 1949, 274; Spies 1972, 760.
417 Cloete 2010, 196.
418 Changuion 2001, 119.
419 Watt 2000, 260, 321.

▶ *British Garden of Remembrance, Henry Nettman St, between Redelinghuys St & Keurboom St, Barberton, Mpumalanga.*
◙ *S25° 45.970, E31° 03.284.*

A second group of Transvaal commandos fell back to the mountainous area to the east of Lydenburg, with British forces in hot pursuit. General Buller occupied Lydenburg on 7 September 1900 with 7 000 soldiers.[420]

P3.7.65 Grave memorial for Private P. Stewart (killed in action 8 September 1900), Private D.B Stuart (died of his wounds on 8 September 1900) and Sergeant W.F. Budgett (died of his wounds on 2 October 1900), all of the 2nd Battalion Gordon Highlanders Regiment.[421]
▶ *Old cemetery, western end of Buhrmann St, Lydenburg, Mpumalanga.*
◙ *Near S25° 05.188, E30° 26.747.*

The Boers at Lydenburg had two Long Tom guns which they dragged, with great difficulty, over the hilltops and through the valleys of the range called the Devil's Knuckles. These events were magnificently described by a burgher, Wilhelm Mangold, in his diary.[422]

P3.7.66 Replica of an original Long Tom gun, along with replicas of the gun's ammunition in a replica gun emplacement.[423]
▶ *Next to the Long Tom Pass (the R37 between Lydenburg and Sabie, Mpumalanga) at the point where the present road crosses the Devil's Knuckles. There is also a signposted Long Tom shell hole next to this scenic mountain pass.*
◙ *GPS co-ordinates not available.*

It became clear that President Kruger was too old to accompany the men in the field. His advisers and President Steyn persuaded him to withdraw to Europe in the hope of gaining assistance for the Boer Republics there. He reached the harbour of Lourenço Marques (later renamed Maputo) safely. There he embarked on a Dutch warship.[424] He received a hero's welcome in Europe, but no significant assistance. The European nations who supported the Boers could do nothing to assist the burghers by sending military aid, because Britain ruled the oceans with her mighty fleet.[425]

In the field, Steyn now became the main force behind the Boer resistance. After his visit to Kruger in Nelspruit, he made his way to Pilgrim's Rest. On his way there, on 26 September 1900 at the Mac-Mac Pass, Steyn met with General Gert Gravett, who urged him and his companions to hurry on to Pilgrim's Rest. Gravett subsequently held back the British forces of General Buller in a skirmish.[426]

The Mac-Mac Pass, on the road between Graskop and Sabie (the R532), about 14 km from Graskop, is still used today.

P3.7.63

P3.7.64

P3.7.65

P3.7.66

420 Van der Westhuizen & Van der Westhuizen 2000, 257.
421 Watt 2000, 53, 400 & 403.
422 Mangold 1988, 263-265; Grobler 2004, 96.
423 Swart 1989, 216-217.
424 Grobler 2004, 97.
425 Scholtz 1939, 115-135.
426 Cloete 2000, 190.

Part 3 – The military history of the war: the first year (11 October 1899–10 October 1900)

On 12 September, a skirmish took place at Manana, near Ottoshoop in the western Transvaal, between an Imperial unit and the burghers of Field Cornet Claassen. One Imperial officer was killed and one seriously wounded and taken prisoner.[427] Two weeks later, on 29 September, shots were exchanged between Boers and a unit of the Shropshire Imperial Yeomanry in the Rietpan area in the same district, with some casualties.

> *P3.7.67 Grave of Lieutenant R.J.L. White, 1st Regiment, Imperial Bushmen of New South Wales, killed in action 12 September 1900.[428]*
> ▶ *Municipal cemetery, Lichtenburg, North West, near Christa St, between Lang St & Burgers St (entry from Thabo Mbeki St).*
> ◉ *S26° 08.461, E26° 09.228.*
> *The grave of Lance-Corporal R.G. Partridge (20), Shropshire Imperial Yeomanry, who was wounded on 12 September in action at Putfontein (Rietpan?), near Lichtenburg, North West, but died of his injuries on 29 September 1900,[429] is also buried here.*

Shots were exchanged on 23 September between burghers and British soldiers near Belfast in the eastern ZAR.

> *P3.7.68 The gravestone of Trooper (or Private) D.M. (Donald) Spence, Royal Canadian Dragoons, killed in action at Boschpoort, near Belfast, eastern Transvaal, on 23 September 1900.[430]*
> ▶ *Old municipal cemetery, on an unnamed road between Spitskop St and Scheepers St (drive west), Belfast, Mpumalanga.*
> ◉ *S25° 41.694, E30° 01.663.*

On 24 September 1900, Commandant Frans van Aardt of Kroonstad was killed in action in a skirmish at Oliewenhoutfontein in the Orange Free State.[431]

> *P3.7.69 Grave of Commandant van Aardt and his wife. On the gravestone it is incorrectly stated that he was killed in action on 24 September 1901.*
> ▶ *British Garden of Remembrance, municipal cemetery, near the S192, between Diemont St and the S904, Lindley, Free State.*
> ◉ *S27° 52.891, E27° 55.763.*

On 29 September 1900, a skirmish took place near Modderfontein, west of Johannesburg, between the burghers of Commandant P. Steenkamp and a British force led by Colonel C.E. Bradley. Three members of the North Staffordshire Regiment were killed and another six wounded in this engagement.[432]

> *P3.7.70 Grave of Sergeant W.J. Woodburn (26), 2nd Battalion, Prince of Wales (North Stafford) Regiment, who on 30 September 1900 died of wounds received at Jockfontein, the day before.[433]*

 P3.7.67    P3.7.68    P3.7.69

427	Cloete 2010, 195.
428	Watt 2000, 448.
429	Watt 2000, 323.
430	Watt 2000, 393.
431	Cloete 2010, 198.
432	Cloete 2010, 200.
433	Watt 2000, 462.

▶ *Braamfontein Cemetery, c/o Smit St & Graf St, Braamfontein, Johannesburg, Gauteng.*
◉ *S26° 11.669, E28° 01.442.*

On 1 October, General Buller's forces reached Krugerspost in the eastern Transvaal, and occupied the village. In retaliation, the burgher forces shelled Buller's men with a Long Tom gun, inflicting casualties. British attempts to capture the Long Tom failed.[434]

P3.7.71 Grave of Second Lieutenant H.W. Cuming (23), Devonshire Regiment, killed in action at Krugerspost on 1 October 1900.[435]
▶ *Old cemetery, western end of Buhrmann St, Lydenburg, Mpumalanga.*
◉ *Near S25° 05.188, E30° 26.747.*

General De Wet's burghers captured a British military train at Wolwehoek, near Kroonstad in the Orange Free State on 1 October.[436]

P3.7.72 Grave of Trooper R.A. De Pentheny-O'Kelly (38), Lochs Horse, wounded in action at Wolverhoek (Wolwehoek, near Kroonstad) on 1 October 1900, died on 6 October 1900.[437]
▶ *British Garden of Remembrance, western side of Noord Rd, Kroonstad, Free State.*
◉ *S27° 39.049, E27° 13.816.*

P3.7.73 Grave of Trooper E.W. Harper, Driscolls Scouts, who died on 15 October 1900 in Lindley of wounds received in action at Doornkloof on 4 October.[438]
▶ *British Garden of Remembrance, municipal cemetery, Lindley, Free State (near the S192, between Diemont St and the S904).*
◉ *S27° 52.891, E27° 55.763.*

On 4 October 1900, Captain Henty of the 16th Middlesex Volunteers attacked a Republican force at Hammonesfontein, near Bultfontein in the Orange Free State. The skirmish lasted about three hours with a victory for the burghers. The British lost six men killed in action.[439]

P3.7.74 Grave of Lieutenant A.H. Thomas, Ceylon Mounted Infantry, killed in action at Hammonesfontein on 4 October 1900.[440]
▶ *Old town cemetery, Stofberg St, between Cilliers St & Dicken St, Bultfontein, Free State.*
◉ *S28° 17.221, E26° 08.989.*

 P3.7.70
 P3.7.71
 P3.7.72

---

434 Amery IV 1906, 480.
435 Watt 2000, 97.
436 Cloete 2010, 200.
437 Watt 2000, 314.
438 Watt 2000, 180.
439 Cloete 2010, 201.
440 Watt 2000, 412.

Part 3 – The military history of the war: the first year (11 October 1899–10 October 1900)

About 300 burghers attacked two railway repair parties on the Heidelberg-Standerton railway line near Vlakfontein on 9 October 1900. The engineers endured until they were rescued by a column under General Clery.[441]

In the British Garden of Remembrance in Standerton there is a white marble cross on the grave of Captain Archibold Dundonald Stewart (36) of the 1st Battery Rifle Brigade, killed in action on 9 October 1900 near Vlakfontein (Balfour). He was the eldest son of Major-General Robert Crosse Stewart.[442]
▶ *British Garden of Remembrance, new cemetery, Standerton, Mpumalanga; entry from Walter Sisulu St.*
◉ *S26° 56.283, E29° 14.077.*

The Orange Free State and the Transvaal were officially annexed as British colonies in May and September 1900 respectively.[443] Some commentators even pronounced then that the war was over. Thus Arthur Canon Doyle titled Chapter XXIX of his best-seller, *The Great Boer War*, "The end of the war".[444] It was certainly not the case. The Republican governments rejected the annexations and decided to keep on fighting in spite of the fact that more than 12 000 Boers were prisoners of war, were killed or wounded or had surrendered. The Republicans realised they would have to employ new tactics to keep the war going.

P3.7.73

P3.7.74

---

441 Amery V 1907, 52; Cloete 2000, 192.
442 Van der Westhuizen & Van der Westhuizen 2000, 137; Watt 2000, 399.
443 Amery VI 1909, 3-4.
444 Doyle 1900, 490-512.

Part 4

The guerrilla phase of the war (11 October 1900–31 May 1902)

The Republican commanders decided that their forces would break up into small mounted commandos and continue the war under the general direction of the Commandants-General. In accordance with their new tactics, the Boer forces would concentrate on attacking the British wherever and whenever they identified a weak spot in the enemy's defences. One of the burghers' specific aims was to disrupt railway communications as often as possible, since the British were still largely dependent on the railways for supplying the massive army.

4.1   The guerrilla war in the ZAR

Commandant-General Louis Botha and General Koos de la Rey were especially successful as commanders against the British forces in the guerrilla phase of the war in the ZAR. Both achieved memorable victories over British units, even though they also suffered defeats.

> *P4.1.1 This equestrian statue of Botha, by Coert Steynberg, portrays him as an Anglo-Boer War general. It was unveiled by his daughter, Mrs Helen de Waal, in 1946*[445] *(see P3.3.9).*
> ▶ *At the bottom end of the gardens of the Union Buildings, Stanza Bopape St, Arcadia, Pretoria, Gauteng.*
> ◉ *S25° 44.650, E28° 12.568.*
>
> *P4.1.2 Equestrian statue of De la Rey on his famous horse, Bokkie, by Hennie Potgieter, unveiled 1965.*[446]
> ▶ *Town square, near Coligny Rd between Scholtz St (R503) & Melville St (R505), Lichtenburg, North West.*
> ◉ *S26° 08.989, E26° 09.558.*
>
> *P4.1.3 Bust of De la Rey on his grave by sculptor Fanie Eloff.*[447]
> ▶ *Municipal cemetery, Lichtenburg, North West, near Christa St, between Lang St & Burgers St (entry from Thabo Mbeki St).*
> ◉ *S26° 08.461, E26° 09.228.*
>
> *P4.1.4 Bust of De la Rey, by sculptor Coert Steynberg.*[448]
> ▶ *Strijdom Square, adjacent to the municipal offices, Delareyville, North West. The town is named after him.*
> ◉ *S25° 45.752, E26° 68.581.*

P4.1.1

P4.1.2

P4.1.3

P4.1.4

---

445   Greyling 2000, 80-81; Brits 1989a, 198.
446   Pretorius 1989b, 158.
447   De Kamper & De Klerk 2011, 31.
448   Du Plessis 1968, 227.

Part 4 – The guerrilla phase of the war (11 October 1900–31 May 1902)

4.1.1 11 October–31 December 1900

On 12 October 1900, Republican forces fought a rear guard action against overwhelming odds at Witpoort in the Mapochsgronden in the eastern Transvaal. General Gert Gravett, who was standing next to one of the Transvaal State Artillery's last field guns, sustained a serious wound when he was hit by shrapnel. He later died at Roossenekal on 26 October, where he was buried under a tree.[449]

P4.1.1.1 Commemorative gravestone of General Gert Gravett.
▶ *Municipal cemetery, Primrose, Gauteng. Use the northern entrance from Cemetery Rd (about 100 m north of the main entrance), north of the intersection with Rietfontein Ave. The gravestone is about 100 m from the entrance on the northern side of the service road.*
◉ *S26° 11.719, E28° 08.722.*

On 13 October 1900, General Tobias Smuts's commando attacked a British unit on Geluk Farm, south of Belfast in the eastern Transvaal. British losses were nine men killed in action, and 29 wounded.[450]

The graves of Lieutenant F.H. Wylam, 8th Hussars, of Lieutenant P.A.T. Jones, Adjutant of the 8th Hussars, of Shoe Smith R. Sargeant, Royal Horse Artillery, and also the joint graves of Private F. Chubb and Private A. Langstone, 8th Hussars, and of Lance-Corporal C.J. Moore and Private Bagnall, 16th Lancers, who were all killed in action in this engagement,[451] are in the British cemetery at the Dalmanutha railway station (see P7.4.4.3).

The names of Privates W. Mears, 8th Hussars and B. Keegan, 14th Hussars, both killed in action in this engagement on 13 October 1900,[452] appear on a monument in a small cemetery on the farm Geluk, where it is incorrectly indicated that they died on 13 November 1900 (see P3.7.52).
▶ *About 500 m east of a gravel road linking the R33 between Belfast and Carolina and the Dalmanutha railway station, Mpumalanga. It is visible from the gravel road. The house of the farm owner, Willie Stols, is on the western side of this road.*
◉ *S25° 51.716, E30° 04.800.*

P4.1.1.2 The grave of Lieutenant A.W. Swanston (26), Inniskilling Dragoons. According to his gravestone, he was killed in action at Fevreden (it should be Tevreden), 16 October 1900, while endeavouring to save the life of Private J. Garlick. Three other soldiers fell in the same engagement.[453]
▶ *Municipal cemetery, Chrissiesmeer, Mpumalanga. Near the R542, western side of Chrissiesmeer.*
◉ *S26° 16.797, E30° 12.281.*

The State Artillery of the South African Republic (Transvaal) still had three of the famous Long Tom guns. One of these and its crew were in the Steenkampsberg Mountains, west of Lydenburg, and the second was

P4.1.1.1

P4.1.1.2

P4.1.1.3

---

449 Reitz 1931, 128; Van Zyl 1944, 169; Grobler 2004, 98.
450 Cloete 2010, 202.
451 Watt 2000, 14, 74, 224, 242, 294, 368, 466.
452 Watt 2000, 228, 285.
453 Watt 2000, 406.

in Pietersburg (today Polokwane) in the northern Transvaal. The third one was dragged from Ohrigstad in a northerly direction across the northern Drakensberg Mountains, using the old transport road (part of which later became the Abel Erasmus Pass – Route R36). It was subsequently taken across the Olifants River all the way to Leydsdorp and from there towards Haenertsburg. However, when its crew reached the Letaba River drift below the escarpment on 18 October, they decided to destroy the Long Tom, as well as the other artillery guns they had with them.[454]

> P4.1.1.3 The memorial on the south bank of the Letaba River, about 200 m downstream from the drift where the old transport road crossed the river and where the Long Tom was blown up.
> ▶ Next to the R528 (the Georges Valley Rd) between Tzaneen and Haenertsburg. Signposted.
> ◉ S23° 55.634, E 30° 02.559.

On 17 October, General Piet Liebenberg's commando surprised a patrol of 17 members of Marshall's Horse northeast of Potchefstroom in the western Transvaal. Seven soldiers fell in this engagement, four were wounded and the remainder were taken prisoner.[455]

> P4.1.1.4 Gravestone of Corporal George M. Addie (26), 19th Company (Lothian & Berwickshire) Imperial Yeomanry, killed in action at Frederikstad on 17 October 1900.[456]
> ▶ In the British Garden of Remembrance, Alexandra Cemetery, close to Olënpark, near Piet Bosman St, between James Moroka Drive & Kock St, Potchefstroom, North West, where he was reinterred.
> ◉ S26° 42.760, E27° 05.248.

> P4.1.1.5 Grave of Trooper L.G. Trollip (20), Marshall's Horse, who died on 6 November 1900 of wounds received in the engagement at Frederikstad on 18 October 1900.[457]
> ▶ Braamfontein Cemetery, c/o Smit St & Graf St, Braamfontein, Johannesburg, Gauteng.
> ◉ S26° 11.669, E28° 01.442.

> P4.1.1.6 Grave of Private T. Pearce (23), Prince Alfred's Guards, Mounted Infantry, killed in action at Van Wyksrust/Klip River Station on 20 October 1900.[458]
> ▶ British Garden of Remembrance, Maccauvlei Golf Course, Viljoensdrif, Free State, near the Club House. Entry from the R82, south of the bridge crossing the Vaal River into Vereeniging.
> ◉ S26°40.933, E 27°56.521.

From 20 to 25 October 1900, the famous Free State general Christiaan de Wet was involved in a battle with a British force commanded by Major-General Geoffrey Barton near the Frederikstad railway station in the valley of the Mooi River – about 20 km northeast of Potchefstroom in the western Transvaal. The outcome was, in the words of De Wet,

P4.1.1.4

P4.1.1.5

P4.1.1.6

---

454 Changuion 2001, 130-131; Rothmann 1976, 88-89.
455 Cloete 2010, 204.
456 Watt 2000, 2.
457 Watt 2000, 421.
458 Watt 2000, 326.

Part 4 – The guerrilla phase of the war (11 October 1900–31 May 1902)

"rather miserable" for the Republican forces. Their losses amounted to about 80 killed, wounded and taken prisoner. The British losses were 21 killed and 55 wounded.[459]

P4.1.1.7 The monument that commemorates 40 burghers who fell in the Battle of Frederikstad.
▶ *Turn off from the R501 between Carletonville and Potchefstroom in an easterly direction on the Klipdrif road. Cross the railway line, drive past the buildings on the left and then turn left to the old Frederikstad railway station buildings. The monument is in the sheep pasture in front of the old railway house, which now belongs to Thomas Jansen van Vuuren. The grave of the burgher Frederik Gerhardus Breytenbach (32), who was killed in action on 25 October 1900 in this battle, is next to the monument.*
◉ *S26° 30.547, E27° 08.988.*

On 2 November 1900, shots were exchanged at Lilliefontein, near Belfast in the eastern Transvaal, when a burgher commando attacked a large British force who were retiring to Belfast in the midst of an untimely blizzard. The British forces suffered 17 casualties – at least one Imperial officer and one soldier fell in this engagement. The officer was Captain T.W. Chalmers of the Canadian Mounted Rifles, who displayed conspicuous bravery when he rode back into the firing line to assist the heavily wounded Major Saunders. Chalmers secured Saunders's safety, but was himself mortally wounded.[460]

P4.1.1.8 Memorial to Private G. Smith, killed in action at Lilliefontein on 2 November 1900 and buried by the Boers.[461] Four other members of the 1st Battalion Gordon Highlanders Regiment are also honoured on this memorial.
▶ *Old cemetery, Belfast, Mpumalanga. (On an unnamed road between Spitskop St & Scheepers St (drive west). Captain Chalmers's grave is also in this cemetery.[462]*
◉ *S25° 41.694, E30° 01.663.*

P4.1.1.9 Grave markers of Trooper A. Wallis, Diamond Fields Horse, killed in action at Christiana on 7 November 1900[463] (left, bottom) and three other British soldiers who died of disease.
▶ *West End Cemetery, c/o Green St & Reserve Rd, Kimberley, Northern Cape.*
◉ *S28° 44.078, E24° 44.170 (Google Maps).*
This cemetery contains the graves of a number of Imperial soldiers who were killed in action or died of their wounds under unknown circumstances in the ZAR in this period. These include
- *Guide E.H.H. Devenish (21), Corps of Guides, who died on 30 November 1900 of wounds received at Rietvlei near Christiana.[464]*
- *Trooper (or Private) J. Hocking, Diamond Fields Horse, killed in action at Christiana on 31 December 1900. The grave marker of Trooper (or Private) G.G. Cox, Imperial Yeomanry, who died of disease at Christiana on 22 July 1901 is next to that of Hocking.[465]*

P4.1.1.7　　　　P4.1.1.8　　　　P4.1.1.9

459　Van den Bergh 1996, 89-93; De Wet 1999, 174-176; Pretorius 2010, 155-156.
460　Amery V 1907, 50-51; Cloete 2010, 208.
461　Watt (2000, 384) indicates that Smith was killed in action on 30 September 1900.
462　Watt (2000, 69) claims that Chalmers was a lieutenant.
463　Watt 2000, 434.
464　Watt 2000, 110.
465　Watt 2000, 92 & 197.

The Carolina Commando commanded by General Joachim Fourie and Commandant Hendrik Prinsloo attacked a British force consisting of 250 mounted soldiers, 1 000 footsoldiers and a battery of six guns commanded by Major-General Horace Smith-Dorrien at Witkloof near Carolina in the eastern Transvaal on 7 November 1900. The attack was warded off, and both Fourie and Prinsloo were killed in action.[466] This engagement is referred to as the Battle of Leliefontein in some sources.

> *P4.1.1.10 The Witkloof monument. Smith-Dorrien was so impressed by the courage that the burghers exhibited in this battle that he not only related the events to the London Times, but collected £213 (English pounds) in Britain for the erection of a monument in honour of Fourie and Prinsloo. He was present on 7 November 1927 when the monument was unveiled.[467]*
> ▶ *About 500 m west of the tarred road, the R33, between Carolina and Belfast, Mpumalanga, next to a farm road underneath a tree.*
> ◉ *S25° 57.001, E30° 00.830.*
>
> *Both were buried in the Carolina district, Fourie on the farm Welgevonden, and Prinsloo on own his farm Hawerfontein, in a small cemetery enclosed by a stone wall near the farmyard.*
>
> *P4.1.1.11 Painting of General Joachim Fourie on a wall of the Paul Kruger Hall.*
> ▶ *On the grounds of the Dutch Reformed Church in Church St, near Steyn St, between Breytenbach St and the R36, Carolina, Mpumalanga.*
> ◉ *S26° 04.204, E30° 06.768.*

On 19 November 1900, General Ben Viljoen and Commandant Chris Muller attacked the Balmoral and Wilge River Stations on the Eastern Railway Line east of Bronkhorstspruit. They captured an outlaying post near Balmoral, with the loss of 43 men to the British, but failed in their main objectives.[468]

> *P4.1.1.12 The Battle of Balmoral memorial.*
> ▶ *In front of the entrance to the concentration camp cemetery at Balmoral, Mpumalanga. (Take the Balmoral exit from the N4 between Bronkhorstspruit and Emalahleni. The cemetery is signposted, north of the N4 and on the western side of the road exiting from the N4.)*
> ◉ *S25° 52.050, E28° 58.040.*

A skirmish took place at Renosterkop, north of present-day Bronkhorstspruit, on 29 November 1900, between a British force commanded by Major-General Paget and the burghers of General Ben Viljoen and Commandant Chris Muller. Even though the burghers inflicted 83 casualties on the British and they lost only two burghers killed and 22 wounded, they abandoned their positions on the battlefield after dark that evening, and fell back to the northeast.[469]

P4.1.1.10

P4.1.1.11

P4.1.1.12

P4.1.1.13

---

466 Amery V 1907, 51; Van Zyl 1944, 171; Grobler 2004, 99; Cloete 2010, 209-210.
467 Van der Westhuizen & Van der Westhuizen 2000, 121.
468 Amery V 1907, 61.
469 Amery V 1907, 61-63; Van der Westhuizen & Van der Westhuizen 2000, 184-185.

Part 4 – The guerrilla phase of the war (11 October 1900–31 May 1902)

P4.1.1.13 There are no memorials on the battlefield, but the low hill is a well-known landmark.
▶ *Immediately to the east of the R25 between Bronkhorstspruit, Gauteng and Verena, Mpumalanga, about 8 km tot the north of the turnoff to Zusterstroom from the R25.*
◉ *S25° 35.947, E28° 56.815.*

P4.1.1.14 Memorial stone in honour of 23 officers and men from different units who died in this battle. The names of eight soldiers who died elsewhere also appear on the stone.
▶ *British Garden of Remembrance at Donkerhoek/Diamond Hill, Gauteng. There are a number of other memorials and gravestones for soldiers who fell at Renosterkop in this Garden of Remembrance. Entry from the R515 (turn west a few kilometres south of the N4), then drive through the grounds of the Kleinfontein settlement.*
◉ *S25° 48.363, E28° 29.385.*

Early in December 1900, General Koos de la Rey became aware of a convoy of 138 supply wagons, commanded by Colonel Woolridge-Gordon, heading from the east towards Rustenburg. He discussed the possibility of attacking the convoy with General Jan Smuts and Commandant F.J. Boshoff. They decided to attempt to capture the convoy when it passed through the Magaliesberg at Buffelspoort. The result was the Battle of Buffelspoort, which began in the early morning hours of 3 December and lasted most of the day. De la Rey's combined commandos captured all the wagons and 1 832 oxen. The British losses amounted to 18 killed, 46 wounded and 54 taken prisoner. On the Boer side, two burghers were killed and seven were wounded.[470]

P4.1.1.15 The marker indicates where the battle took place. British soldiers killed in action were buried in the Burgershoop Cemetery, Krugersdorp, Gauteng, but the burial place of the fallen burghers is unknown.
▶ *Next to the R104 Wonderkoppies, between the D1325 and the D153, east of the Buffelspoort Resort and Dam.*
◉ *S25° 45.797, E27° 30.262.*

General Manie Lemmer and his commando attacked a British convoy north of Lichtenburg in the western Transvaal on 8 December, but failed to capture the wagons. Both sides suffered casualties.[471]

P4.1.1.16 Grave of Lieutenant F. Arbuthnot, Imperial Yeomanry, was wounded in action at Lichtenburg on 7 December 1900,[472] probably against Lemmer's burghers, and died on 8 December.
▶ *Municipal cemetery, Lichtenburg, North West, near Christa St, between Lang St & Burgers St (entry from Thabo Mbeki St).*
◉ *S26° 08.461, E26° 09.228.*

On 9 December, General Manie Lemmer himself was killed in action in an engagement between his commando and the British troops of Lieutenant-Colonel C.G.C. Money at Wonderfontein, near Lichtenburg in western Transvaal. J.G. (Jan) Celliers was appointed as general in his place.[473]

P4.1.1.14

P4.1.1.15

P4.1.1.16

---

470   Van den Bergh, 1996, 98-102; Smuts 1999, 142-146; Grobler 2004, 102.
471   Lemmer 2000, 27-28.
472   Watt 2000, 9.
473   Lemmer 2000, 27-29 & 109-111; Gronum 1972, 65-66; Grobler 2004, 102.

P4.1.1.17 Lemmer was buried at Varkfontein, close to the present town of Coligny, North West. He is specifically commemorated at the Burgher Memorial in Delareyville, North West.
▶ *On Strydom Square, adjacent to the municipal offices.*
◉ *S25° 45.752, E26° 68.581.*

Earlier on in the war, on 18 September 1900, the Lancaster Regiment occupied Vryheid (in the present KwaZulu-Natal) on behalf of the British forces. They deployed about 900 soldiers on the hill north of the town, which they named Lancaster Hill, where the troops dug numerous trenches and built gun positions. A Boer commando attacked them at midnight on 11 December, but failed to dislodge the Lancaster Regiment, which suffered several losses, including Lieutenant-Colonel J.M. Gawne. Nine burghers were killed in action, and the Boers withdrew on 12 December.[474]

P4.1.1.18 The burghers and soldiers were buried in the Vryheid municipal cemetery. The soldiers' graves are in the British Garden of Remembrance in this cemetery.
▶ *Southern side of the town, Hoog St, between Landdrost St & Wes St, Vryheid, KwaZulu-Natal.*
◉ *S27° 46.887, E30° 47.952.*

P4.1.1.19 Memorial cairn to Gawne on Lancaster Hill. Remnants of British trenches and fortifications are still visible at North Gun Post, South Lancaster Point and South Gun Post on the same terrain.[475]
▶ *In the Vryheid Mountain Nature Reserve, signposted north of the town.*
◉ *GPS co-ordinates not available.*

Shots were also exchanged on 12 December between troopers of the Imperial Light Horse and burghers on the farms Zendelingspost and Vergenoeg, near Jacobsdal, a few kilometres south-west of Zeerust in the western Transvaal.

Grave of Trooper W.A.D. Laskie, C Squadron, Paget's Horse, Imperial Yeomanry, killed in action in the Zendelingspost/Vergenoeg area, near Jacobsdal/Zeerust on 12 December 1900.[476]
▶ *Cemetery, Carrington St, between Carney St & 1st Lane, Mahikeng, North West.*
◉ *S25° 51.448, E25° 38.202.*

One day later, on Thursday, 13 December, the Battle of Nooitgedacht was fought in the Magaliesberg. Major-General Ralph Clements was in command of a British force of 1 500 men in a camp at the southern foot of the mountain. Four companies of soldiers were stationed on the summit of the hill above the camp. General Koos de la Rey with 2 500 burghers, including the commandos of General Christiaan Beyers and General Jan Smuts, attacked the British force. Even though the burghers cleared the summit and forced the soldiers to abandon their camp, Clements managed to retreat with the bulk of his men. De la Rey had nevertheless achieved a significant victory. British casualties amounted to 332 men killed and wounded, and 306 taken prisoner. Boer losses were 17 men killed and 61 wounded.[477]

P4.1.1.17

P4.1.1.18

P4.1.1.19

---

474   Torlage & Watt 1999, 9.
475   Watt 2000, 153; Van der Westhuizen & Van der Westhuizen 2013, 7.
476   Watt 2000, 242.
477   Van den Bergh 1996, 103-112 & 176; Smuts 1999, 146-151; Pretorius 2010, 303-304.

Part 4 – The guerrilla phase of the war (11 October 1900–31 May 1902)

There is a memorial on the battlefield at Nooitgedacht, but this is on private land, so access to it is restricted.

P4.1.1.20 Memorial to 17 non-commissioned officers and men of the 2nd Battalion Northumberland Fusiliers, killed in action at Nooitgedacht on 13 December 1900.
▶ Burgershoop Cemetery, c/o Luipaard St & Halgryn St, Krugersdorp, Gauteng. The grave of Lieutenant A.J.C. Murdoch (24), Mounted Infantry Company 1st Battalion Cameron Highlanders, who was killed in action in the same battle, is also in this cemetery.
◉ S26° 06.095, E27° 45.612.

The graves of the Imperial soldiers and burghers who fell in this battle are spread over a number of cemeteries:

P4.1.1.21 Grave of Colour Sergeant C.W. Spencer, Northumberland Fusiliers, who died of wounds received at Nooitgedacht on 13 December 1900.[478]
▶ British Garden of Remembrance, Rietfontein, Ifafi, North West. On the western side of the R511 between Kleinste St & the R104 Kerk Street, at the entrance to Birdwood Estate.
◉ Park outside the entrance, at S25° 44.760, E27° 54.535, and walk about 300 m north to the cemetery.

P4.1.1.22 Grave of Lieutenant H.J.S. Stanton (22), Northumberland Fusiliers, who died on 30 December 1900 of wounds received in action at Nooitgedacht on 13 December 1900.[479]
▶ Old Church Street West Cemetery, Pretoria, Gauteng. Cemetery entrance from Es'kia Mphahlele St (previously D.F. Malan Dr), north of W.F. Nkomo Dr (previously Church St West).
◉ Near S 25° 44.472, E 28° 10.286.

P4.1.1.23 The memorial at Breedt's Nek to the burghers who were killed in action at Nooitgedacht and were buried in a cemetery there.
▶ About 100 m west of the D568, Maanhaarrand, at the foot of Breedt's Nek, on the southern side of the Magaliesberg, on a property known as Intaba Thulile Guest Farm, inside the gate, surrounded by a green palisade fence.
◉ S25° 52.704, E27° 26.773.

P4.1.1.24 Gravestone of Field Cornet F.E. van Zyl, killed in action at Nooitgedacht on 13 December 1900. His name also appears on the memorial at Breedt's Nek (see P4.1.1.23).
▶ On the grounds of the Nedbank Management Training Centre, on the northern side of the R374, to the east of its junction with the R540, north of Muldersdrift, Gauteng.

On 14 December, a burgher commando attacked a British convoy at Scheepers Nek, near Vryheid in the south-eastern Transvaal.

 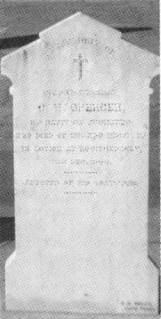   

P4.1.1.20   P4.1.1.21   P4.1.1.22   P4.1.1.23   P4.1.1.24

---

478   Watt 2000, 393.
479   Watt 2000, 396.

P4.1.1.25 The gravestone of Corporal Peter Comrie (52), Natal Carbineers, and Trooper George McKellar (20), Natal Carbineers, of the Volunteer Composite Regiment, killed in action on 14 December 1900 while opposing the attack on the convoy.[480]
▶ *British Garden of Remembrance, municipal cemetery, Vryheid, KwaZulu-Natal. On the southern side of the town, Hoog St, between Landdrost St & Wes St.*
◉ *S27° 46.887, E30° 47.952.*

Three days after the Battle of Nooitgedacht, on Sunday, 16 December 1900, the burghers under De la Rey and Beyers gathered on the slopes of the Magaliesberg to commemorate the Day of the Vow (also known as *Dingaan's Day*) and Paardekraal. The Reverend A.P. Kriel held a religious service, after which generals De la Rey, Beyers and Smuts each delivered an address. Afterwards everyone present brought forward a stone to erect a cairn to confirm his commitment to the spirit of the vows once made at Bloedrivier (Blood River). This event was held at Schimmelkop, Buffelsfontein, south of Noupoort.[481]

P4.1.1.26 In 1958, the stones were built into a memorial, called the Ebenhaezer Memorial, on private land near Boons, North West.
◉ *GPS co-ordinates not available.*

Commandant Fanie Buys and the Heidelberg Commando were attacked on 24 December 1900 by the 13th Hussars and the Rifle Brigade on Rietvlei Hills near Vlakfontein. The burghers fought back valiantly in a running battle that lasted until nightfall and forced the soldiers to retreat.[482] Two days later, Buys in turn attacked the British forces and overwhelmed a section of Lieutenant-Colonel Colville's column. Eleven British soldiers and three burghers were killed in these encounters.[483]

P4.1.1.27 The grave of Stefan Bronkhorst. On the gravestone it is indicated that he was killed in action at Modderbult, east of Grootvlei, on 24 December 1900. It was probably in this skirmish.
▶ *Kloof Cemetery, Heidelberg, Gauteng. On the banks of the Kloof Spruit, on the northern side of the extension of Fenter St.*
◉ *26° 29.717, E 28° 20.770.*

A white marble cross in the British Garden of Remembrance at Standerton commemorates the men of Colville's column that died in the engagements on 24 and 26 December 1900.
▶ *British Garden of Remembrance, new cemetery, Standerton, Mpumalanga. Entry from Walter Sisulu St.*
◉ *S26° 56.283, E29° 14.077.*

British forces occupied Utrecht, which was a district of the ZAR at that time, on 30 May 1900. The magistrate surrendered the town to Major-General Hildyard. On Christmas Day 1900, about 300 burghers of the Utrecht district, supported by a few foreign volunteers, attacked the Utrecht garrison. Since the British were forewarned,

 P4.1.1.25
 P4.1.1.26
 P4.1.1.27

480 Watt 2000, 83.
481 Celliers 1978, 181-182; Smuts 1999, 155-156; Cloete 2000, 207.
482 Cloete 2000, 208.
483 Cloete 2000, 209; Pretorius 2016, 164-165.

they repulsed the attack easily. Two Russian volunteers, Captain Petrov and Captain Duplov, and a Polish volunteer, Captain Leo Pokrowsky, were killed in this action.[484]

P4.1.1.28 Pokrowsky is commemorated on a plaque at the foot of the Burgher Memorial in front of the Dutch Reformed Church.
▶ *50 Church St, Utrecht, KwaZulu-Natal..*
◙ *S27° 39.293, E30° 19.211.*

On 29 December 1900, the combined commandos of General Ben Viljoen and Commandant Chris Muller attacked a British force at Helvetia, a link in the chain of British fortified positions that protected the road between Machadodorp and Lydenburg in the eastern Transvaal. Major S.L. Cotton was in command of the fortification. He was in charge of about 240 to 250 men and a 4.7 inch naval gun. The Boer attack, which began at 03:30 in the morning, took the British force completely by surprise. Cotton was severely wounded, and he surrendered after about 40 of his men had been killed and wounded. Two burghers were killed in action. Viljoen's men captured transport oxen, horses and mules, arms and ammunition, including the 4.7 inch gun, which they dubbed the Lady Roberts. State Secretary F.W. Reitz wrote a satirical poem, which was soon put to music and spread like wildfire through the Boer commandos and even reached the prisoner-of-war camps, about the capture of this gun.[485]

P4.1.1.29 British military cemetery on the battlefield at Helvetia. There is also a memorial plaque in this cemetery for the burghers who fell in this engagement.
▶ *In an opening between plantations on the eastern side of the R36, about 5 km north of the junction of the R36 and the N4, north of Machadodorp, Mpumalanga. The cemetery is south of a plantation road about 1 km east of the R36. The T-junction between the plantation road and the R36 is about 300 m north of the signposted turnoff from the R36 to Goedewil.*
◙ *S25° 34.844, E30° 18.210 (at cemetery).*

Also on 29 December 1900 the brothers Gert and Jack van den Heever of Commandant Fanie Buys's Heidelberg commando derailed a British goods train on the main line between Greylingstad and Standerton. The freight included a large store of whisky which was probably intended for British officers, but ended up being appreciated by the Boers. No casualties were suffered in this "Whisky Train" incident.[486]

P4.1.1.30 Memorial to the "Whisky Train".
▶ *Plaque attached to the side of a railway culvert between Val Station and Teakworth Siding, Mpumalanga.*
◙ *GPS co-ordinates not available.*

By the end of 1900, the British government was so confident that there would be no more fighting that Sir Alfred Milner was appointed High Commissioner of the Orange River Colony and the Transvaal Colony. By that time, the governments of both Republics were called "governments in the field". They had become fugitives in their own country.

P4.1.1.28

P4.1.1.29

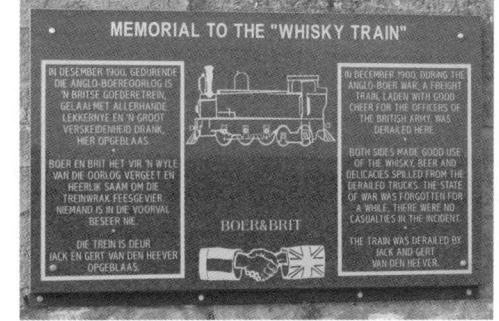
P4.1.1.30

---

484   Amery V 1907, 118; Kandyba-Foxcroft 1981, 236; Cloete 2010, 221.
485   Reitz 1910, 5-7; Pretorius 2010, 179-180.
486   Van den Heever 2001; Cloete 2010, 223.

4.1.2 ZAR January–June 1901

In the year 1901, skirmishes between Imperial soldiers and Republican burghers sporadically occurred across the territory of the ZAR (the Transvaal), and there were many casualties.

> *P4.1.2.1 Grave of Trooper D.S. Burgess, Imperial Light Horse, killed in action near Ventersdorp on 1 January 1901.*[487]
> ▶ *Municipal cemetery, near Grey St, between Kort St & Visser St, Ventersdorp, North West.*
> ◎ *S26° 19.042, E26° 49.126.*
> *This cemetery contains the graves of several Imperial soldiers who were killed in action or who died of wounds under unknown circumstances in the ZAR in this period. These include the grave of Trooper J.J. Bailey, Imperial Light Horse, killed in action at Elandsfontein, near Ventersdorp on 15 February 1901.*[488]

Less than three weeks after his success at the Battle of Nooitgedacht, General De la Rey was again victorious on 2 January 1901 in an engagement at Cyferfontein in the Western Transvaal, where he defeated a British force commanded by General James Babington.[489]

> *There is a memorial at Cyferfontein. The British soldiers who fell in this engagement were buried in the Burgershoop Cemetery in Krugersdorp in Gauteng.*

Three days later, on 5 January 1901, the Imperial Light Horse were caught in an ambush by burghers in the Naauwpoort area south of Rustenburg in the western Transvaal. When the burghers retreated again, Captain T. Yockney was shot by burghers who allegedly threw down their rifles in a gesture of surrender, but then caught up their weapons again. Three burghers involved in this incident were captured by British soldiers, and were executed the next day.[490]

> *P4.1.2.2 Memorial in memory of 23 members of the Imperial Light Horse, including Captain T. Yockney and Lieutenant A. Ormond, who fell at Naauwpoort Nek on 5 January 1901.*[491]
> ▶ *Burgershoop Cemetery, c/o Luipaard St & Halgryn St, Krugersdorp, Gauteng.*
> ◎ *S26° 06.095, E27° 45.612.*

During the night of 7 to 8 January 1901, the commandos under General Ben Viljoen launched a night attack on Belfast and on a number of British garrisons stationed on the Eastern Railway Line in the eastern part of the ZAR. Both sides suffered casualties.[492]

> *P4.1.2.3 Gravestone of Captain F.L. Fosbery (30), Royal Irish Regiment, killed in action on Monument Hill, Belfast, on 7 January 1901.*[493]

P4.1.2.1

P4.1.2.2

P4.1.2.3

---

487 Watt 2000, 55.
488 Watt 2000, 15.
489 Grobler 2004, 107.
490 Cloete 2010, 227.
491 Watt 2000, 317, 467.
492 Van der Westhuizen & Van der Westhuizen 2013, 235.
493 Watt 2000, 142.

Part 4 – The guerrilla phase of the war (11 October 1900–31 May 1902)

> ▶ *Old cemetery, Belfast, Mpumalanga, unnamed road between Spitskop St & Scheepers St (drive west).*
> ◉ *S25° 41.694, E30° 01.663.*
>
> *The names of three other soldiers killed in action on 8 January appear on a Gordon Highlanders memorial in the same cemetery.*
>
> *The grave of Private J. Bayston, 2nd Berkshire Regiment, who was killed in action on 8 January 1901,[494] is in the British cemetery at the Dalmanutha railway station (see P7.4.4.3).*
>
> *P4.1.2.4 Memorial (vandalised) in a small rural cemetery where four burghers who were killed in action in this engagement were buried by the Gordon Highlanders.[495]*
> ▶ *On the farm Wemmershuis, north of the R33 leading to Carolina, clearly visible from the road, about 1 km west of its junction with the N4, Mpumalanga.*
> ◉ *S25° 43.381, E30° 03.004.*

General Christiaan Beyers soon afterwards led his commando into the eastern Transvaal. As they passed south of Pretoria, they were so close to the capital that they could see Fort Klapperkop. On 12 January 1901, they crossed the railway line between the Kaalfontein Station and the Zuurfontein Station and became involved in skirmishes with the British troops on guard there.[496]

> *There is no physical structure that commemorates these skirmishes. Zuurfontein is in the area of what is now Kempton Park. Kaalfontein Station is next to the R21 highway, close to Esselenpark.*

On 16 January 1901, the Heidelberg Commando attacked Colonel Colville's British force of farm burners near the Bosmanspruit, east of Greylingstad, but there was insufficient reconnaissance and co-ordination. The attack was halted, and the burghers were forced to retreat after suffering some casualties.[497]

> *P4.1.2.5 Grave of Alfred Ueckermann, Heidelberg Commando, who was killed in action in this skirmish near Boesmankop on 16 January 1901.[498]*
> ▶ *Kloof Cemetery, on the banks of the Kloof Spruit, on the northern side of the extension of Fenter St, Heidelberg, Gauteng.*
> ◉ *S26° 29.717, E28° 20.770.*

On 17 January 1901, Commandant Fanie Trichard and Captain Jack Hindon captured two trains between Brugspruit and Balmoral.[499] This was the first of a number of successful attacks and raids on British trains in which Hindon was involved.

 P4.1.2.4  P4.1.2.5

---

494 Watt 2000, 25.
495 Van der Westhuizen & Van der Westhuizen 2013, 235.
496 Scholtz 1941, 53; Celliers 1978, 195.
497 Mangold 1988, 306-308; Cloete 2010, 229-230; Pretorius 2016, 183-185.
498 Van der Westhuizen & Van der Westhuizen 2000, 170.
499 Preller 1942a, 175-177; Trichard 1975, 182.

There is no memorial to commemorate these specific attacks. The present railway bridge near Brugspruit, between the Wakefield and Clewer Stations, where the trains were derailed and cargo was taken by the Boers, is at the northern end of Belvin Crescent, Clewer, Mpumalanga.
◉ *S25° 54.220, E29° 07.556.*

Small-scale clashes occurred regularly at numerous places in the ZAR.

P4.1.2.6 Gravestone of Private E.A. Wigmore (22), 2nd New Zealand Regiment, who was wounded at Balmoral, 23 January 1901, and died of his wounds on 27 January 1901.[500]
▶ *British Garden of Remembrance, Donkerhoek. Entry from the R515 (turn west a few kilometres south of the N4), then drive through the grounds of the Kleinfontein settlement.*
◉ *S25° 48.363, E28° 29.385.*

On 25 January 1901, Major-General Smith-Dorrien's forces engaged in heavy fighting with a large force of Republicans at Twyfelaar, between Wonderfontein and Carolina in the eastern ZAR. The burghers retreated after about five hours without suffering any casualties. On the British side, one officer was killed in action and 14 men were wounded.[501]

P4.1.2.7 Grave of Major W.R.D. Lloyd (40), 1st Suffolk Regiment, killed in action at Twyfelaar on 25 January 1901.[502]
▶ *British Garden of Remembrance, Municipal cemetery, near 16th St, Ermelo, Mpumalanga.*
◉ *S26° 30.402, E29° 58.760.*

On 27 January 1901, Major-General John French launched a major drive in the eastern Transvaal with five strong columns. They set out from a line stretching from Mooiplaas, which is to the east of Pretoria, to Springs on the Witwatersrand.[503] They met stiff resistance from Boer commandos.

P4.1.2.8 Gravestone of Sergeant D.B. Hammond (23) and of Sergeant D.J. McGregor (22) of the Canadian Scouts, both killed in action on 28 January 1901 at Vlakkraal, near Hatherley,[504] east of Pretoria.
▶ *British Garden of Remembrance, Donkerhoek. Entry from the R515 (turn west a few kilometres south of the N4), then drive through the grounds of the Kleinfontein settlement.*
◉ *S25° 48.363, E28° 29.385.*

On 29 January 1901, General Smuts and General Liebenberg and their burghers surrounded a British post at Modderfontein in the Gatsrand area, south of Krugersdorp. Their attack on 30 January was initially held back by the British, but at dawn on the 31 January, the British forces surrendered after 26 men were either killed or wounded. Two days later, a British force led by Brigadier General Cunningham attacked the Boers, who were still occupying the

P4.1.2.6   P4.1.2.7   P4.1.2.8

---

500   Watt 2000, 451.
501   Cloete 2010, 232.
502   Watt 2000, 252.
503   Amery V 1907, 159-161; Cloete 2010, 232.
504   According to Watt (2000, 176 & 278), they were killed in action on 27 January 1901.

Part 4 – The guerrilla phase of the war (11 October 1900–31 May 1902)

British camp at Modderfontein, but the burghers drove off the British attackers, who suffered about 40 casualties. Boer casualties are unknown.[505]

There is no memorial at the battlefield, in the Hillshaven area, where the R28 crosses low hills about two kilometres south of the N12.

P4.1.2.9 The gravestone of Lieutenant G.D. Green (29), Imperial Yeomanry, and of Civilian Surgeon W.L.M. Walker and three men of the South Wales Borderers who were killed in action at Modderfontein on 31 January 1901.[506]
▶ British Garden of Remembrance, Alexandra Cemetery, close to Olënpark, near Piet Bosman St, between James Moroka Dr & Kock St, Potchefstroom, North West, where they were reinterred. This Garden of Remembrance also contains the gravestone of Colour Sergeant W. Owens[507] and eight other non-commissiond officers, and men of the 2nd South Wales Borderers killed in action at Modderfontein on 2 February 1901.
◉ S26° 42.760, E27° 05.248.

On 2 February 1901, the Middelburg burghers, led by Field Cornet N.P. Gouws and Field Cornet W.J. Mouton, attacked the 18th Hussars of Lieutenant Colonel Campbell at Roodepoort/Bosmanpan, south of Middelburg in the eastern Transvaal. There were 18 British casualties.[508]

P4.1.2.10 Grave of Lieutenant C.F. Cawston (22), 18th Hussars, killed in action at Roodepoort on 2 February 1901.[509]
▶ British Garden of Remembrance, old municipal cemetery, entrance from Bhimy Damane St, Middelburg, Mpumalanga. The grave of Lieutenant R.E. Reade (21), King's Royal Rifles Corps (60th), who was wounded on 2 February 1901 at Roodepoort/Bosmanpan and died of wounds two days later,[510] is in the same British Garden of Remembrance.
◉ S25° 45.832, E29° 26.849.
This Garden of Remembrance contains the graves of a number of other Imperial soldiers who were killed in action or died of wounds under unknown circumstances in the ZAR in this period. These include the graves of
- *Lieutenant K.Z.P. Macauley (28), Loyal North Lancashire Regiment, wounded at Wonderfontein Station near Middelburg, Mpumalanga, on 28 January 1901, who died of his wounds on 30 January 1901.[511]*
- *Private J. Ellis, 85th Shropshire Light Infantry, killed in action near Wonderfontein on 10 March 1901.[512]*
- *Trooper Thomas Briscoe (40), Robert's Horse, killed in action near Wonderfontein Station on 19 March 1901.[513]*
- *Lieutenant A.E. Murphy (38), 5th Victorian Mounted Rifles, killed in action at Driefontein/Middelkraal, near Middelburg, Mpumalanga, on 29 May 1901.[514]*

P4.1.2.9

P4.1.2.10

---

505 Amery V 1907, 115; Van den Bergh 1996, 113-116 & 177; Cloete 2000, 219-220.
506 Watt 2000, 166 & 433.
507 Watt 2000, 319.
508 Cloete 2010, 234.
509 Watt 2000, 69.
510 Watt 2000, 346.
511 Watt 2000, 258.
512 Watt 2000, 127.
513 Watt 2000, 46.
514 Watt 2000, 302.

- Private H. Butler, The Carabiniers, killed in action at Middelkraal on 30 May 1901.[515]

P4.1.2.11 Grave of Sergeant J.A. Paterson (35), Canadian Scouts, killed in action at Schurwekop, near Wakkerstroom, on 4 February 1901.[516]
▶ British Garden of Remembrance, municipal cemetery, northern side of Kerk St, near corner with Scheiding St, Wakkerstroom, Mpumalanga.
◉ S27° 21.520, E30° 08.027.

The graves of several other members of the Imperial forces who also fell in action under unknown circumstances in this period are also in this cemetery. These include the graves of
- Major A.L. Howard, Howard's Scouts, killed in action on 7 February 1901.[517]
- Sergeant R.J. Northway, Canadian Scouts, killed in action at Rustplaats, about 16 km to the north-west of Piet Retief, on 16 February 1901.[518]
- Lieutenant F.J. Ryan (29), 6th New Zealand Regiment, killed in action at Gaoechoek (Paardeplaats) on 16 June 1901.[519]

On 6 February 1901, a force of about 2 000 burghers under General Louis Botha engaged in a pre-dawn attack near Chrissiesmeer in the eastern Transvaal on a British column of about 3 000 men led by Major-General Smith-Dorrien. Botha realised after about 45 minutes that the attack would fail and ordered his burghers to retreat. Boer casualties numbered about 30 burghers dead or wounded, and British casualties about 80.[520]

P4.1.2.12 Memorial to the burghers killed in action in the Battle of Chrissiesmeer near the battlefield.
▶ At the entrance of Chrissiesmeer, Mpumalanga, from Carolina, near c/o Mitchell St & Meyer St.
◉ S26° 16.733, E30° 12.639.

P4.1.2.13 The graves of British soldiers who fell in this battle.
▶ Municipal cemetery, near the R542, on the western side of Chrissiesmeer, Mpumalanga. There is also a memorial to the casualties of the 2nd West Yorkshire Regiment who fell in the same battle.
◉ S26° 16.797, E30° 12.281.

P4.1.2.14 The monumental gravestone to honour Field Cornets Dolf Spruyt, John Biccard and other burghers who fell in this battle.
▶ Municipal cemetery, near the R542, western side of Chrissiesmeer, Mpumalanga.
◉ S26° 16.797, E30° 12.281.

P4.1.2.11 P4.1.2.12 P4.1.2.13 P4.1.2.14

---

515 Watt 2000, 59.
516 According to Watt (2000, 324), Paterson was a Sergeant Major.
517 Watt 2000, 204.
518 Watt 2000, 311.
519 Watt 2000, 365.
520 Pretorius 2010, 86-87; Pretorius 2016, 190-192.

CP1 The Farewell 11-10-1899. Bronze statue by Danie de Jager in the garden of the War Museum of the Boer Republics, Bloemfontein, Free State (see also P2.1.5 on p. 26). [Photograph by Sonja Myburgh].

CP2 Talana. British graves on the grounds of the Talana Museum, Battlefield and Heritage Park in Dundee, KwaZulu-Natal (see pp. 33-34).

CP3 Magersfontein battlefield, seen from Magersfontein Ridge, Northern Cape, with a replica of a Krupp canon used by the Boers (see pp. 60-61).

CP4 Siege of Mafeking. British fort at Kanon Kopje, North West (see p. 41).

CP5 Siege of Ladysmith. Graves of British soldiers who fell defending Platrand, KwaZulu-Natal (see pp. 52-53).

CP6 Boer memorial, battle of Talana, Dundee, KwaZulu-Natal (see p. 33).

CP7 Scandinavian Corps memorial, Magersfontein, Northern Cape (see pp. 60-61).

CP8 Wauchope memorial near Matjiesfontein, Western Cape (see pp. 60-61). [Photograph by Hendri Havenga].

CP9 Platrand, KwaZulu-Natal. One of the symbolic hands of the Burgher Monument (see pp. 52-53).

CP10 Belmont, Free State. Republican memorial of the battle (see p. 56).

CP11 Worcester Hill monument near Colesberg, Northern Cape (see p. 66). [Photograph by A. van Dyk].

CP12 Grave of Captain E.G. Verschoyle, Thaba Nchu, Free State (see p. 83).

CP13 Boer memorial, battle of Kleinfontein, near Groot Marico, North West (see pp. 148-149).

ANGLO-BOER WAR   Historical Guide to Memorials and Sites in South Africa

CP14 Position of main British trench, Spioenkop, KwaZulu-Natal (see pp. 67-68).

CP15 Memorial plaque, Moordenaarspoort, near Dordrecht, Eastern Cape (see pp. 196-197).

CP16 British war graves, Klaarstroom, Western Cape (see p. 189).

CP17 Summit of Groenkop with Boer memorial in the distance, near Kestell, Free State (see p. 183).

CP18 Scheepers memorial near Arnot, Mpumalanga (see p. 202).

Part 4 – The guerrilla phase of the war (11 October 1900–31 May 1902)

P4.1.2.15 One of the burghers who was severely wounded in battle at Chrissiesmeer was Wilhelm Mangold of the Heidelberg Commando. His war diary, in which he recorded his experience of being wounded, was published long after the end of the war.[521] Mangold survived and lived another 21 years in Heidelberg, Gauteng.
▶ His grave is in the Kloof Cemetery, on the banks of the Kloof Spruit, on the northern side of the extension of Fenter St, Heidelberg, Gauteng.
◉ 26° 29.717, E 28° 20.770.

On 13 February 1901, Commandant Trichard and Captain H.F. Slegtkamp and their burghers captured a train – they called it the "Sugar Train" because of its cargo of sweets – near Brugspruit on the Eastern Railway Line.[522]

This was probably in the same area in which the raid on 17 January 1901 was launched. There is no memorial to commemorate this specific raid.

On 14 February 1901, Major-General Walter Kitchener commanded three columns consisting of altogether about 1 800 soldiers with nine guns in an attack from three sides (from Belfast, Lydenburg and Machadodorp) on General Ben Viljoen's camp on the farm Windhoek, to the west of Dullstroom. The venture failed and the British forces suffered about 15 casualties.[523]

P4.1.2.16 The gravestone of Captain J.E.T. Crichton (24), 1st Battalion Manchester Regiment, who succumbed on 14 February 1901 to the wounds he had received in action at Schwartzkopje near Belfast the day before.[524]
▶ Old cemetery, Belfast, Mpumalanga, on an unnamed road between Spitskop St & Scheepers St (drive west).
◉ S25° 41.694, E30° 01.663.

On 18 February 1901, a heavy skirmish took place around Hartbeesfontein in the western Transvaal. The outcome was indecisive and casualties were fairly even. The Boers, commanded by Generals Celliers, Du Toit and Liebenberg, suffered the loss of about 18 burghers killed and wounded, and 40 captured. Of Lord Methuen's British forces, 16 men were killed and 43 were wounded.[525]

P4.1.2.17 Grave of Lieutenant A.W. Hewett (25), Loyal North Lancashire Regiment, killed in action at Hartbeesfontein, 18 February 1901.[526]
▶ British Garden of Remembrance, municipal cemetery, Klerksdorp, North West, near Margaretha Prinsloo St, between O.R. Tambo St & Kadria St. The grave of Lieutenant W.H. Creak, Loyal North Lancashire Regiment, who was also killed in action at Hartbeesfontein, on 18 February 1901, is in the same cemetery.
◉ S26° 52.576, E26° 40.130.

P4.1.2.15 P4.1.2.16 P4.1.2.17

---

521 Mangold 1988, 324-334.
522 Trichard 1975, 183; Cloete 2000, 223.
523 Amery V 1907, 199; Cloete 2010, 238.
524 Watt 2000, 94.
525 Amery V 1907, 220-221; Cloete 2010, 239.
526 Watt 2000, 191.

This Garden of Remembrance contains the graves of several other Imperial soldiers who were killed in action or died of wounds under unknown circumstances in the Transvaal in this period, including the grave of Trooper F.H. Ogston, Imperial Light Horse, killed in action at Rietkuil (probably near Klerksdorp) on 17 April 1901.[527]

During the night of 2 to 3 March 1901, burghers of General de la Rey's commandos began attacking British-occupied Lichtenburg in the western Transvaal. By daybreak the next morning, it had turned into a full-scale battle for control of the town. It lasted the whole day, but after dark, De la Rey, realizing that victory was almost certainly impossible, withdrew his forces. Boer losses amounted to 14 killed and 38 wounded. On the British side, two officers and 16 men of other ranks were killed in this encounter.[528]

P4.1.2.18 Gravestone of Field Cornet Jan Blignaut, killed in action in the burghers' attack on Lichtenburg on 3 March 1901.
▶ On the wall of the burgher memorial, c/o Hendrik Potgieter St & Forsman St, Zeerust, North West, where Blignaut was reinterred. The gravestone of Wouter Kirstein, who died of wounds received in the same attack, is also on this memorial, where he too was reinterred.
◙ S25° 32.501, E26° 04.540.

P4.1.2.19 The memorial to 16 men of the 1st Northumberland Fusiliers, including the two officers, who fell in the Battle of Lichtenburg, in the town cemetery where they were buried on 4 March 1901. The grave of Driver John Beck (24), New Zealand Artillery, who on 24 March 1901 died of wounds received in action at Lichtenburg on 3 March,[529] is in the same cemetery.
▶ Near Christa St, between Lang St & Burgers St (entrance from Thabo Mbeki St), Lichtenburg, North West.
◙ S26° 08.461, E26° 09.228.

This cemetery contains the graves of a number of other Imperial soldiers who were killed in action or died of their wounds under unknown circumstances in the Transvaal in this period. These include the graves of Private B. Stapylton (30), Imperial Yeomanry, who died on 13 March 1901 of wounds received in action the previous day[530], Corporal J.J. Forrester (28), 68th Company, Paget's Horse, Imperial Yeomanry, and Trooper F.B. Nathan of the same unit, who fell in the same skirmish on 12 March 1901.[531]

As the autumn of 1901 approached, sporadic skirmishes between Republican commandos and British units continued to occur in the ZAR.

P4.1.2.20 Gravestone of the burgher P.C. Bronkhorst (17), killed in action on 11 March 1901.
▶ Old municipal cemetery, entrance from Bhimy Damane St, Middelburg, Mpumalanga.
◙ Near S25° 45.832, E29° 26.849.

P4.1.2.18   P4.1.2.19   P4.1.2.20

---

527 Watt 2000, 314.
528 Amery V 1907, 222-223; Van den Bergh 1996, 116 & 118.
529 Watt 2000, 26.
530 Watt (2000, 396) writes that his surname was Stapleton.
531 Watt 2000, 142 & 305.

Part 4 – The guerrilla phase of the war (11 October 1900–31 May 1902)

On 22 March, there was a skirmish north of Hartbeesfontein in the western Transvaal when General De la Rey's burghers attacked British scouts near Geduld. A unit of the Imperial Light Horse and burghers under the command of General Smuts also became involved, and a running battle developed. The British soldiers were under severe pressure, but managed to retreat to the safety of the town. The British lost seven men and the Boers four. Smuts himself received a light leg wound.[532]

> P4.1.2.21 The Imperial Light Horse memorial in honour of the two officers and four men of that regiment killed in action in this engagement.
> ▶ Municipal cemetery, eastern side of Deleklle Khoza St, Hartbeesfontein.
> ◙ S26° 45.679, E26° 25.530.

When British forces under General Plumer entered Pietersburg in the northern Transvaal (today called Polokwane, Limpopo) on 8 April 1901, their approach was resisted by a Dutch teacher in the town, Gerard Kooijker, who fired on the soldiers, killing two officers and a trooper. He was then attacked and killed himself.[533]

> P4.1.2.22 Kooijker's grave.
> ▶ Northern part of old municipal cemetery, Polokwane, Limpopo. Entry from Dahl St, across from the western end of Jorissen St.
> ◙ S23° 54.489, E29° 26.783.

The crews of the last two surviving Long Tom guns of the Transvaal State Artillery independently destroyed both, using dynamite, in April 1901 to ensure that they would not be captured by the British forces. On 16 April, the one Long Tom was blown up to the north of the Steenkampsberg, to the northwest of Lydenburg. Two weeks later, on 30 April, the last Long Tom was blown up on Feeskop, near Haenertsburg.[534]

> P4.1.2.23 The memorial which contains fragments of the last Long Tom blown up by the Boers in the northern Transvaal.
> ▶ Maré St, Haenertsburg, Limpopo.
> ◙ S23° 56.701, E29° 56.394.

> P4.1.2.24 The memorial at Feeskop where the last Long Tom gun was blown up.
> ▶ Signposted next to a gravel road that turns off to the north-west from the R71 between Haenertsburg and the Magoebaskloof Hotel, Limpopo.
> ◙ GPS co-ordinates not available.

Meanwhile, the burghers and Imperial soldiers were still sporadically exchanging shots in areas across the ZAR.

> P4.1.2.25 Grave of Sergeant F. Davidson (28), Canadian Scouts, killed in action at Nooitgedacht, near Klerksdorp on 11 April 1901.[535]

 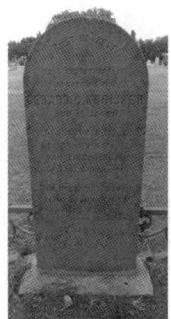  

P4.1.2.21   P4.1.2.22   P4.1.2.23   P4.1.2.24

---

532   Grobler 2004, 111.
533   Changuion 1986, 73; Grobler 2004, 114.
534   Changuion 2001, 136-139; Grobler 2004, 116.
535   Watt 2000, 103.

▶ British Garden of Remembrance, municipal cemetery, Klerksdorp, North West, near Margaretha Prinsloo St, between O.R. Tambo St & Kadria St.
◉ S26° 52.576, E26° 40.130.

The name of Trooper P. Linnie, South African Light Horse, who was killed in action on 28 April 1901 in a skirmish on Geluk Farm, Mpumalanga, appears on a monument in a small cemetery on that farm[536] (see P3.7.52).

A.B.W. van Niekerk, who was the principal of the Vrijheid School before the war, died on 28 April of wounds received in an engagement at Mahlabathini. It was reported that he shot 11 British soldiers, including an officer, before being wounded.[537]

P4.1.2.26 Van Niekerk and the 11 British soldiers were initially buried at Mahlabathini, but he were reinterred in the Vryheid municipal cemetery two years later.
▶ Southern side of Vryheid, KwaZulu-Natal, in Hoog St, between Landdrost St & Wes St.
◉ S27° 46.887, E30° 47.952.

In all parts of the ZAR, skirmishes between Boers and British soldiers continued throughout the winter months of 1901, and casualties mounted.

P4.1.2.27 Grave of Trooper E. Clark, Imperial Light Horse, killed in action at Palmietfontein on 9 May 1901.[538]
▶ In the British military cemetery about 2 km south-west of Coligny, south of the junction where the N14 to Delareyville turns off from the R503 to Lichtenburg, very close to the junction.
◉ S26° 19.607, E26° 17.443.

On 10 May 1901, Imperial units commanded by Colonel Ingouville-Williams engaged with Boers near Korannafontein (Ottosdal) in the western Transvaal. Six soldiers were killed in this engagement, nine were wounded and 12 taken prisoner. It is not known if the Boers suffered any casualties.[539]

P4.1.2.28 Grave of Lieutenant E.A. Lamb, 2nd New South Wales Mounted Rifles, killed in action at Korannafontein on 10 May 1901.[540]
▶ British Anglo-Boer War Garden of Remembrance, on the outskirts of Ottosdal, North West, near the D616, between the D855 & Visser St.
◉ S26° 48.271, E26° 00.773.

On 15 to 16 May 1901, Republican forces attacked Imperial troops at Grobbelaars Recht, near Carolina in the eastern Transvaal. An Imperial officer, Lieutenant F.W. Bell of the West Australian Mounted Infantry, was later awarded a Victoria Cross for bravery because he rushed to assist a severely wounded comrade under heavy fire. The Imperial forces suffered a number of casualties.[541]

P4.1.2.25   P4.1.2.26   P4.1.2.27   P4.1.2.28

---

536 Watt 2000, 250.
537 Van der Westhuizen & Van der Westhuizen 2000, 4.
538 Watt 2000, 75.
539 Cloete 2010, 259.
540 Watt 2000, 240.
541 Creswicke VII ca 1902, 213; Uys 2000, 86; Cloete 2010, 260.

Part 4 – The guerrilla phase of the war (11 October 1900–31 May 1902)

P4.1.2.29 Memorial stone of Sergeant F.F. Edwards and Privates J. Semple, F.T. Adams (or Adam), F. Page and B. Fisher, all of the West Australian Mounted Infantry, all killed in action at Brakpan (or Grobbelaars Recht) on 15 and 16 May 1901.[542]
▶ *British Garden of Remembrance, old municipal cemetery, entry from Bhimy Damane St, Middelburg, Mpumalanga. The gravestone of Lieutenant A.A. Forrest, from Perth, Western Australia, who was killed in action at Grobbelaars Recht on 15 May 1901, is also in this cemetery.*[543]
◉ *S25° 45.832, E29° 26.849.*

P4.1.2.30 Grave of Malcolm Clark (or Clarke), Army Intelligence Department, killed at Buffel's Hill on 18 May 1901.[544]
▶ *Northern part of old municipal cemetery, Polokwane, Limpopo. Entry from Dahl St, across from the western end of Jorissen St.*
◉ *S23° 54.489, E29° 26.783.*

On 23 May, General Liebenberg's commando of about 300 burghers attacked a British wagon convoy halfway between Potchefstroom and Ventersdorp. Both sides suffered casualties.[545]

P4.1.2.31 Grave of W.G. de Kock (19), a burgher killed in action at Kaalfontein on 23 May 1901.
▶ *In the British Garden of Remembrance, municipal cemetery, near Grey St, between Kort St & Visser St, Ventersdorp, North West.*
◉ *S26° 19.042, E26° 49.126.*

P4.1.2.32 Grave memorial to members of the 1st King's Liverpool Regiment who were killed in action in this period, namely Lance-Corporal C. (or D.W.) Cooper and Private T. Banks, who both died on 1 June 1901, and Privates F.G. Moxon and J.H. Brown, who both died on 28 May 1901.[546] *Private G.R. Gill of the same regiment, who died of enteric fever on 4 February 1902, is also listed on the memorial.*[547]
▶ *Old cemetery, western end of Buhrmann St, Lydenburg, Mpumalanga.*
◉ *Near S25° 05.188, E30° 26.747.*

On 29 May 1901, a battle took place at Vlakfontein, immediately north of the present town of Derby, North West, between Boer commandos led by General Jan Kemp and a British force commanded by Brigadier General H.G. Dixon. The Boers initially gained the upper hand, but were eventually driven off by a resolute British counter-attack. The British later alleged that the Boers had shot wounded soldiers. British losses amounted to at least 57 officers and men who were killed or died of wounds, another 115 who were wounded and eight who went missing. The Boer losses were at least seven men killed; two more burghers later died of their wounds.[548]

P4.1.2.29   P4.1.2.30   P4.1.2.31   P4.1.2.32

---

542   Watt 2000, 1, 124, 137, 319 & 373.
543   Watt 2000, 142.
544   Watt 2000, 77.
545   Creswicke VII ca 1902, 59-60.
546   Watt 2000, 18, 50, 87 & 300. According to Watt, they all died on 28 May 1901.
547   Watt 2000, 156.
548   Amery V 1907, 281-284; Kemp 1941, 391-404; Van den Bergh 1996, 122; Pretorius 2010, 478-479.

There is no battlefield memorial. The British soldiers who fell in this battle were originally buried in a military cemetery near Derby, but they were later reinterred in Krugersdorp.

P4.1.2.33 Memorial, "In Loving Memory of the Following Officers of the 7th Battalion Imperial Yeomanry, who were killed in action at Vlakfontein, on May 29th 1901. [Lt] Henry Alexander Campbell [38], son of Colonel John A. Campbell, Madras Staff Corps."[549] (There are other names on the sides).
▶ Burgershoop Cemetery, c/o Luipaard St & Halgryn St, Krugersdorp, Gauteng.
◉ S26° 06.095, E27° 45.612.

On 7 June 1901, a small group of scouts from Commandant Fanie Buys's commando engaged in a skirmish with a British unit at Rietfontein near Grootvlei in the southern Transvaal. One burgher was taken prisoner, but the British suffered seven casualties.[550]

P4.1.2.34 The grave of Lieutenant (Sir) Rose Price (21), 3rd Battalion, King's Royal Rifle Corps, killed in this action on 8 June 1901. It seems that he was initially buried at Leeuwspruit and then at Rietfontein, before finally being reinterred here.[551]
▶ British Garden of Remembrance, new cemetery, Standerton, Mpumalanga. Entry from Walter Sisulu St.
◉ S26° 56.283, E29° 14.077.

On the evening of 12 June 1901, a Boer commando of about 120 Middelburgers led by Commandant Chris Muller attacked a British force consisting of 350 Australians under Major Morris at Wilmansrust on the Middelburg-Ermelo wagon road in the eastern Transvaal. The Australians were caught by surprise and their camp was taken. The Boers captured two pom-poms, rifles, ammunition and other supplies. Five burghers were killed in this action.[552]

P4.1.2.35 The Wilmansrust battlefield (photographed from the north-east). The Australian camp was situated around a farmhouse, with trees in the centre of the camp. The Boers attacked from the east.
▶ South of Middelburg, Mpumalanga, about 700 m west of the R35, to the south of its intersection with the R542, around the ruins of an abandoned farmstead.
◉ S26° 08.864, E29° 27.177.

P4.1.2.36 A memorial for the five burghers killed in the Battle of Wilmansrust was erected where they were buried on the farm Kafferstad. This memorial was moved to Bethal in 1974, when the burghers were also reinterred.
▶ On the central town square, Bethal, Mpumalanga, Liebenberg Ave, between Vuyisile Mini St & Clerq St.
◉ S26° 27.333, E29° 27.756.

P4.1.2.37 Memorial with the names of 17 British soldiers killed in this battle.
▶ British Garden of Remembrance, old municipal cemetery, entry from Bhimy Damane St, Middelburg,

P4.1.2.33

P4.1.2.34

P4.1.2.35

---

549   Watt 2000, 63.
550   Van der Westhuizen & Van der Westhuizen 2000, 155.
551   Van der Westhuizen & Van der Westhuizen 2000, 137; Watt 2000, 339.
552   Grobler 2004, 118; Pretorius 2010, 494.

Part 4 – The guerrilla phase of the war (11 October 1900–31 May 1902)

Mpumalanga. The gravestone of Captain J.C. Watson, 9th Battery, Royal Field Artillery, killed in action at Wilmansrust on 12 June 1901, is also in the Garden of Remembrance.[553]
◉ *S25° 45.832, E29° 26.849.*

P4.1.2.38 Grave of Captain H.F. Scott, 3rd Royal Berkshire Regiment, commanding No 3 Company 11th Mounted Infantry, killed in action at Ruitspruit (Rietspruit?) near Houtkop, Vereeniging, on 14 June 1901.[554]
▶ *British Garden of Remembrance, Maccauvlei Golf Course, Viljoensdrif, Free State, near the Club House. Entry from the R82, south of the bridge crossing the Vaal River into Vereeniging.*
◉ *S26° 40.933, E 27° 56.521.*

4.1.3   ZAR July – December 1901

In addition to a number of noteworthy battles and skirmishes, British soldiers and Republican burghers occasionally exchanged shots throughout the second half of the year 1901 in all parts of the Transvaal. On 4 July 1901, the burghers of General C.F. Beyers captured a British troop train at Tobias Station, north of Naboomspruit in the northern ZAR, killing at least ten soldiers. Beyers and his men suffered no casualties.[555]

P4.1.3.1 Memorial for nine members of the 2nd Battalion Gordon Highlanders who were killed or died of wounds received near Naboomspruit on 4 July 1901.
▶ *Old municipal cemetery, northern part, Polokwane, Limpopo. Entry from Dahl St, across from the western end of Jorissen St.*
◉ *S23° 54.489, E29° 26.783.*

P4.1.3.2 Gravestone of Trooper W.S. McKenzie, Johannesburg Mounted Rifles, killed in action at Driefontein (Zondagsfontein) on 5 July 1901.[556]
▶ *Municipal cemetery, Primrose, Gauteng. Use the northern entrance from Cemetery Rd (about 100 m north of the main entrance), north of the intersection with Rietfontein Ave.*
◉ *S26° 11.719, E28° 08.722.*

P4.1.3.3 Grave of Lieutenant R. Anderson (27), Royal Engineers, who died on 11 July 1901 of wounds received in action at Zeekoegat on 10 July 1901.[557]
▶ *British Garden of Remembrance, old municipal cemetery, entrance from Bhimy Damane St, Middelburg, Mpumalanga.*
◉ *S25° 45.832, E29° 26.849.*
This Garden of Remembrance contains the grave of at least one other Imperial soldier killed in action under unknown circumstances in the ZAR in this period, namely Corporal John McCue, Mounted Infantry Company, Queen's Own Cameron Highlanders, killed on patrol near Strathrae on 11 December 1901.[558]

P4.1.2.36

P4.1.2.37   P4.1.2.38

P4.1.3.1

P4.1.3.2

---

553   Watt 2000, 440.
554   Watt 2000, 371.
555   Creswicke VII ca 1902, 116; Davitt 1902, 510.
556   Watt 2000, 281.
557   Watt 2000, 7.
558   Watt 2000, 275.

P4.1.3.4 Grave of Trooper Sergeant Major W. Chalmers, South African Constabulary, killed in action at Houtkop, near Vereeniging on 11 July 1901.[559]
▶ *British Garden of Remembrance, Maccauvlei Golf Course, Viljoensdrif, Free State, near the Club House. Entry from the R82, to the south of the bridge crossing the Vaal River into Vereeniging.*
◉ *S26°40.933, E 27°56.521.*

On 17 July, a skirmish took place between a section of the Imperial Yeomanry and General Jan Kemp's commando at Wildfontein, near Ventersdorp in the western Transvaal. At least one British officer, Lieutenant C.D. Kimber, son of the then Mayor of London, was killed in this engagement.[560]

P4.1.3.5 Grave of Lieutenant C.D. Kimber (38), Imperial Yeomanry, killed in action at Wildfontein whilst rescuing a comrade, on 17 July 1901.[561]
▶ *In the British military cemetery about 2 km to the south-west of Coligny, south of the junction where the N14 to Delareyville turns off from the R503 to Lichtenburg, very close to the junction.*
◉ *S26° 19.607, E26° 17.443.*
This Garden of Remembrance contains the grave of at least one other Imperial soldier who died under unknown circumstances in the ZAR in this period, namely Lieutenant C.G. Eyre, 10th Imperial Yeomanry, killed in action at Sterkfontein, on 15 or 16 November 1901.[562]

General C.J. Spruyt was mortally wounded on 20 July 1901 when he and his burghers crossed the railway line between the Val and Vlaklaagte (Holmdene) stations in the southern Transvaal. He died half an hour later.[563]

P4.1.3.6 Spruyt's gravestone in the Kloof cemetery, Heidelberg, Gauteng, where he was reinterred in 1903.
▶ *On the banks of the Kloof Spruit, on the northern side of the extension of Fenter St, Heidelberg, Gauteng.*
◉ *S26° 29.717, E28° 20.770.*

Field Cornet H.J. Kamfer's Heidelberg burghers attacked Major J.M. Vallentin's Heidelberg Volunteers at Braklaagte on 24 July 1901. At least three Volunteers were taken prisoner and shot by the Boers, since they were regarded as joiners[564] (see Section 5.7).

P4.1.3.7 Grave of Private J.E. Morrison, Heidelberg Volunteers, killed in action at Braklaagte on 24 July 1901. According to Watt, he was made a prisoner of war and shot.[565]
▶ *Kloof cemetery, on the banks of the Kloof Spruit, on the northern side of the extension of Fenter St, Heidelberg, Gauteng.*
◉ *S 26° 29.717, E 28° 20.770.*

P4.1.3.3 P4.1.3.4 P4.1.3.5 P4.1.3.6

---

559 Watt 2000, 69.
560 Cloete 2010, 279.
561 Watt 2000, 234.
562 Watt 2000, 131.
563 Van Zyl 1944, 329; Grobler 2004, 120; Pretorius 2016, 244.
564 Cloete 2010, 281.
565 Watt 2000, 298.

Part 4 – The guerrilla phase of the war (11 October 1900–31 May 1902)

On 6 August 1901, the burghers under General Ben Viljoen and the Lydenburg Commando under Commandant Piet Moll overpowered the garrison of Fort Mpisane, near Bosbokrand in the eastern Transvaal Lowveld. Most of the garrison belonged to the irregular British unit Steinaecker's Horse. Six burghers were killed in action and another six or seven died of wounds. On the British side, one officer, Captain Francis, was killed in action, as were a number of black support troops. Viljoen afterwards ordered the shooting of a number of armed black men who had participated in the fighting in support of the notorious Steinaecker's Horse.[566]

> *P4.1.3.8 The memorial to the Boers who died in the attack on Fort Mpisane.*
> ▶ *Old cemetery, western end of Buhrmann St, Lydenburg, Mpumalanga.*
> ◉ *Near S25° 05.188, E30° 26.747.*

On 10 August 1901, Captain Jack Hindon and his commando of 60 men, who were trained specifically to destroy railway lines used by the British forces, attacked and derailed a British supply train at Groenvlei on the Nylstroom-Naboomspruit railway line in the northern Transvaal. The ensuing fierce skirmish was disastrous for Hindon's burghers, who suffered heavy casualties and had to flee for their lives. On the British side, 15 soldiers and three black support troops were killed and about seven men were wounded.[567]

> *P4.1.3.9 The memorial for the burghers killed in this action is next to the present railway line, south of Mookgopong (formerly Naboomspruit), Limpopo, near the place where the derailment took place.*
> ▶ *Groenvlei, next to the D925 between the R519 and the D925. Turn off from the R101 (the old national road) between Modimolle and Mookgopong in an easterly direction, onto a gravel road at the road sign to Boekenhout Railway Station (this is the road to Nylsvlei). The road crosses the N1 via a bridge and then crosses the railway lines at Boekenhout Station. Turn left there and follow the road parallel to and on the eastern side of the railway line for 3.8 km in a northerly direction. Just before reaching the exit to Shumba's Rest on the right, there is a gate on the left (western) side of the road. Park there, walk through the gate and across the railway lines to the memorial, which is on the western side of the railway line.*
> ◉ *S24°36.525, E28°40.065.*

> *P4.1.3.10 Grave of the burgher Reinier Jansen van Vuuren, killed in action on 19 August 1901.*
> ▶ *Municipal cemetery, Modimolle, Limpopo. On the western side of Thabo Mbeki St (R101), which runs north-south through the town).*
> ◉ *S24° 42.161, E28° 24.164.*

On 31 August 1901, a Republican commando led by Captain Jack Hindon derailed a British train on the railway line between Waterval and Hammanskraal, north of Pretoria. It seems that dynamite was used. One officer, 13 soldiers, and three civilians lost their lives – at least some of them were shot by the Boers. The Boers also suffered several casualties.[568]

P4.1.3.7　　　　P4.1.3.8　　　　P4.1.3.9　　　　P4.1.3.10

566　Meijer 2000, 221-223; Van der Westhuizen & Van der Westhuizen 2000, 250-252.
567　Preller 1942a, 217-219; Cloete 2010, 285.
568　Creswicke VII ca 1902, 116; Grobler 2004, 121.

P4.1.3.11 The monument for nine soldiers killed in this incident in the cemetery of the former Waterval prisoner-of-war camp near the Petronella railway station.
▶ *North of Pretoria, Gauteng, next to the R101 (old national road) on its western side, about 200 m north of the intersection with Lusthof Rd, which turns off to Vastfontein. The memorial garden is next to a Kanhym depot; there are pine trees behind the terrain.*
◉ *S25° 29.955, E28° 15.528.*

P4.1.3.12 Grave of Lieutenant-Colonel C.F.S. (Seymour) Vandeleur (37), Irish Guards, killed in this action near Waterval on 31 August 1901.[569]
▶ *Old Church Street West Cemetery, Pretoria, Gauteng. Cemetery entrance from Es'kia Mphahlele St (previously D.F. Malan Dr), north of W.F. Nkomo Dr (previously Church St West). The grave of Civilian Conductor W. Birso (33), who died on 1 September 1901 of injuries received in same train derailment, is also in this cemetery.[570]*
◉ *Near S25° 44.465, E28° 10.283.*
This cemetery contains the grave of at least one other Imperial officer who was mortally wounded under unknown circumstances in the Transvaal in this period, namely Captain J.H.C. Ogilvy (27), 1st Battalion Gordon Highlanders, who died on 19 December 1901 of wounds received in action near Hebron the previous day.[571]

P4.1.3.13 Memorial stone of Trooper J.Q. Watson, a Canadian serving in the South African Constabulary, killed in action at Wolvefontein near Bronkhorstspruit on 12 September 1901.[572]
▶ *British Garden of Remembrance, Donkerhoek. Entry from the R515 (turn west a few kilometres south of the N4), then drive through the grounds of the Kleinfontein settlement.*
◉ *S25° 48.363, E28° 29.385.*
In this Garden of Remembrance, there is the grave of at least one other Imperial soldier killed in action under unknown circumstances in the Transvaal in this period, namely Sergeant J.E. Pemberton, Canadian Scouts, killed in action at Witnek, near Hatherley to the east of Pretoria on 27 October 1901.[573]

General Ben Viljoen set up his headquarters as Assistant Commandant-General for the north-eastern Transvaal at Pilgrim's Rest in September 1901. This mining village on the eastern escarpment had a population of about 200 at the outbreak of the war. At one stage, British forces occupied it, but they withdrew as the terrain was inaccessible, so the town remained in Boer hands until the end of the war.[574]

P4.1.3.14 The Royal Hotel, Main St, Uptown, Pilgrim's Rest, Mpumalanga, was already in operation at that time and was used as quarters by the Boers.
◉ *GPS co-ordinates not available.*

P4.1.3.11

P4.1.3.12

P4.1.3.13

569	Watt 2000, 428.
570	Watt 2000, 33
571	Watt 2000, 314.
572	Watt 2000, 440.
573	Watt 2000, 328.
574	Schultz 1999; Meijer 2000, 226-230.

Part 4 – The guerrilla phase of the war (11 October 1900–31 May 1902)

Commandos from the Transvaal sporadically operated in the districts of Utrecht and Vryheid to harass British forces in the south-eastern part of the Transvaal and thus to force the British military authorities to spread their forces. One such venture culminated in the Battle of Blood River Poort (called Bloedriviersport by the burghers) on 17 September 1901. Burghers led by Generals Louis Botha and J.D. Opperman defeated a British force commanded by Major H. de la P. Gough. The Boers captured the British field guns, large supplies of munitions, and about 210 horses.[575]

> P4.1.3.15 British memorials and graves of 21 Imperial soldiers on the Bloedriviersport battlefield.
> ▶ Signposted on a road that turns off from the R34 between Utrecht and Bloedrivier, KwaZulu-Natal, near the farm Spieshoek and a low hill, Aasvoëlkrans.
> ◙ S27° 46.941, E30° 32.151.

> P4.1.3.16 The four British officers killed in this battle were buried in the municipal cemetery in Vryheid. A large marble cross marks the grave of Major C.E. Dick (36), Royal Irish Fusiliers, who fell in this battle.[576]
> ▶ Southern side of the town, Hoog St, between Landdrost St & Wes St, Vryheid, KwaZulu-Natal.
> ◙ S27° 46.887, E30° 47.952.

> The grave of Andreas Theodorus Spies, a burgher who died on 5 November 1901 of wounds received at Blood River Poort, is in a cemetery on the farm Spieshoek in that area.[577]
> ◙ GPS co-ordinates not available.

> P4.1.3.17 Grave of Private G. Middlemist, Northumberland & Durham Imperial Yeomanry, who died of his wounds on 25 September 1901.[578] It is not known how and when he was wounded.
> ▶ Cemetery, Carrington St, between Carney St & 1st Lane, Mahikeng, North West.
> ◙ S25° 51.448, E25° 38.202.

On 30 September 1901, at daybreak, General de la Rey's commandos attacked a British force of about 930 men commanded by Colonel R.G. Kekewich in their camp on the farm Moedwil, about 700 m east of the Selon's River next to the road to Zeerust. It is uncertain how many Boers participated in the attack. The British managed to defend their positions successfully, but both sides suffered casualties. Of the British force, at least 61 officers and men were killed or died of wounds and 131 others were wounded. The burghers lost 11 men, including Commandant Tobias Boshoff, who were killed, 35 were wounded and ten were taken prisoner. One of these prisoners of war, a Dutch volunteer, Piet Schuil, who fought for the Boer forces, was accused by the British of firing on two soldiers after raising a white flag on his rifle. A military court found him guilty, and he was executed by a firing squad on 2 October 1901. The Boers alleged that three wounded burghers were murdered by soldiers after the battle.[579]

> P4.1.3.18 A section of the British cemetery next to the Moedwil battlefield.

P4.1.3.14

P4.1.3.15

P4.1.3.16

P4.1.3.17

---
575 Torlage & Watt 1999, 11; Cloete 2010, 297.
576 Watt 2000, 111.
577 Van der Westhuizen & Van der Westhuizen 2000, 12.
578 Watt 2000, 287.
579 Van den Bergh 1996, 126-130; Pretorius 2010, 288-290.

▶ In the open veld north of the N4 main road between Rustenburg and Swartruggens, entry from the N4 through the first farm gate to the east of the Selons river. Turn right immediately after going through the gate and drive in a north-easterly direction next to the fence for a few hundred metres, then turn 90 degrees left when reaching a fence and drive another about 300 metres along this fence. The fenced-in cemetery is then visible straight to the right. Phone the farm owner, Gert Nienaber, at 082-8086390 for access.
◉ S25° 38.085, E27° 01.993.

P4.1.3.19 Grave of Lieutenant H.N.C. Erskine-Flower (20), 1st Scottish Horse, who succumbed on 22 November 1901 to wounds received in the Battle of Moedwil on 30 September 1901.[580]
▶ Old municipal cemetery, Rustenburg, North West, Nelson Mandela St, between Kock St & Bosch St.
◉ S25° 40.516, E27° 14.628.

The burghers who died in action were buried on the farm Dwarsspruit, to the north of the battlefield. Phone the farm owner, Jan Haasbroek, at 082 8086390 for access.

P4.1.3.20 The grave of Bandsman L. Thurgood (19), 2nd Battalion Lincolnshire Regiment, died of wounds received whilst on sentry duty at Rietfontein on 8 October 1901.[581]
▶ British Garden of Remembrance at Rietfontein, Ifafi, North West. On the western side of the R511 between Kleinste St & Kerk St (R104), at the entrance to Birdwood Estate. Park outside the entrance and walk about 300 m north to the cemetery.
◉ S25° 44.760, E27° 54.535.
This Garden of Remembrance contains the grave of at least two other Imperial soldiers killed in action under unknown circumstances in the Transvaal in this period, Trooper G.A. Morris (21) & Trooper J.B. Jacques (20), D Troop, South African Constabulary, killed in action at Zoutpansdrift, 28 November 1901.[582]

P4.1.3.21 Grave of Private W. Harker, Imperial Yeomanry, killed in action at Sterkstroom on 22 October 1901.[583]
▶ Municipal cemetery, on the northern side of the N4 toll road at the eastern entrance of Swartruggens, North West.
◉ S25° 38.965, E26° 42.432.

The burghers of General De la Rey and General Kemp's commandos captured a large British convoy at Kleinfontein (Kemp referred to it as Driefontein) in the western Transvaal on 24 October 1901, but the British soldiers fought back bravely and managed to save most of the wagons, as well as the British artillery pieces. Boer casualties amounted to 20 dead and 31 wounded, including Field Cornet S.H. Oosthuizen (according to his gravestone, he was a Commandant), who died of his wounds. British losses amounted to 28 dead, 55 wounded, 15 wagons loaded with ammunition, and 300 horses and mules.[584]

 P4.1.3.18
 P4.1.3.19
 P4.1.3.20
 P4.1.3.21

---
580 Watt 2000, 129.
581 Watt 2000, 416.
582 Watt 2000, 215 & 297.
583 Watt 2000, 179.
584 Kemp 1941, 423-424; Van den Bergh 1996, 132-136; Grobler 2004, 125.

P4.1.3.22 The Boer memorial at Kleinfontein with the names of the fallen burghers (see also CP13 on p. 133).
▶ Signposted, next to the N4 toll road, on its southern side, about 6 km west of the small town of Groot Marico, North West.
◉ S25° 36.103, E26° 20.938.

P4.1.3.23 Gravestone of Commandant S.H. Oosthuizen, who died of wounds received at Kleinfontein on 23 October 1901.
▶ Attached to the burgher memorial, c/o Hendrik Potgieter St & Forsman St, Zeerust, North West. The gravestones of Matthys Kritzinger, Gerhardus Kritzinger and Burgher Godliep Malan, who was only 16 years old, are also attached to this memorial. They were reinterred here.
◉ S25° 32.501, E26° 04.540.

Private W. Christianson, 4th Railway Pioneer Regiment, who was killed in action at Groblaar's Kraal on 24 October 1901, is commemorated on a memorial in the British Garden of Remembrance in Standerton. According to Watt, he was taken prisoner and was shot by Boers.[585]
▶ British Garden of Remembrance, new cemetery, Standerton, Mpumalanga. Entrance from Walter Sisulu St.
◉ S26° 56.283, E29° 14.077.

An encounter between British units commanded by Lieutenant-Colonel George Benson and a Boer force under Commandant Hendrik Grobler and Commandant Willie Steyn of the Bethal and Middelburg Commandos took place at the farm Mooifontein near Bethal on 25 October 1901. Benson lost 17 men in this engagement.[586]

P4.1.3.24 Grave of Private/Lance-Corporal A. Dodd, Northumberland & Durham Imperial Yeomanry, killed in action at Lichtenburg on 29 October 1901.[587]
▶ Municipal cemetery, Lichtenburg, near Christa St, between Lang St & Burgers St (entry from Thabo Mbeki St).
◉ S26° 08.461, E26° 09.228.

On 30 October 1901, Commandant-General Louis Botha's combined commandos achieved a significant victory against an imposing British force commanded by Lieutenant-Colonel Benson in the Battle of Bakenlaagte. This engagement took place on the farm Nooitgedacht adjacent to Bakenlaagte and was the last major battle of the war in the eastern Transvaal. Benson, who was himself mortally wounded, lost about 77 men and another 161 were wounded. According to Botha, 52 Boers were killed and wounded.[588] For the Boers, this victory provided a much-needed psychological boost.

The Battle of Bakenlaagte took place on the western side of the R547, about halfway between Kinross and Kriel. There is no memorial at Bakenlaagte, but there are a number of memorial gravestones in the municipal cemetery in Primrose on the East Rand (Gauteng) for members of the British forces who were killed in this battle.

P4.1.3.22   P4.1.3.23   P4.1.3.24

---

585 Watt 2000, 73.
586 Pretorius 2010, 24.
587 Watt 2000, 114.
588 Scholtz 1974, 60-74; Pretorius 2010, 24-26.

▶ *Use the northern entrance from Cemetery Rd (about 100 m north of the main entrance), north of the intersection with Rietfontein Ave.*
◉ *S26° 11.719, E28° 08.722.*

P4.1.3.25 State of Victoria memorial containing 31 names. Other Bakenlaagte memorials and gravestones in the municipal cemetery in Primrose, Gauteng, include the following:
- *Grave of Captain T.H.E. Lloyd (30), 2nd Coldstream Guards.[589]*
- *Joint graves of Captain F.T. Thorold (28), Lieutenant E.V. Ingham Brooke (24) and Lieutenant R.E. Shepherd (26), Yorkshire Light Infantry.[590]*
- *Grave of Lieutenant J.M. Maclean (22), Royal Field Artillery.[591]*
- *Grave of Brevet Lieutenant-Colonel E. Guinness (41), Royal Field Artillery.[592]*
- *Grave of Brevet Major/Captain F.D. Murray (29), 42nd Royal Highlanders (Black Watch).[593]*
- *King's Royal Rifles Mounted Infantry memorial, containing six names. This memorial also commemorates Civilian Surgeon C.M. Robertson and Rifleman J. Egan, who were killed in action at Kafferstad, near Brugspruit in the eastern Transvaal, on 25 (or 27) October 1901.[594]*

P4.1.3.26 The gravestone of C.J. Combrinck (18), killed in action on 19 November 1901 in the western Transvaal.
▶ *At the Burgher Memorial, Strijdomplein, adjacent to the municipal offices, Delareyville, North West.*
◉ *S25° 45.752, E26° 68.581.*

On 20 November 1901, the Heidelbergers under Commandant Fanie Buys attacked a unit of the Railway Pioneers at Bothaskraal, between Greylingstad and Villiers in the southern Transvaal. The British suffered casualties, but Buys and eight of his men were taken prisoner when Colonel Rimington's cavalry arrived to support the Pioneers.[595]

P4.1.3.27 Memorial to six members of the Railway Pioneer Regiment who were killed in action or died of wounds received in the skirmish at Bothaskraal on 20 November 1901.
▶ *British Garden of Remembrance, new cemetery, Standerton, Mpumalanga. Entry from Walter Sisulu St.*
◉ *S26° 56.283, E29° 14.077.*

On 19 December 1901, General Chris Muller and Commandant Fanie Trichard ambushed Colonel C.W. Park at Elandspruit, near Dullstroom in the eastern Transvaal. The British suffered 37 casualties, and five burghers were killed and about 20 wounded.[596] The Boers referred to this encounter as the Battle of Ouhoutbossie.

P4.1.3.25   P4.1.3.26   P4.1.3.27   P4.1.3.28

---

589   Watt 2000, 252.
590   Watt 2000, 47, 377 & 416.
591   Watt 2000, 260.
592   Watt 2000, 171.
593   Watt 2000, 303.
594   Watt 2000, 125 & 356.
595   Amery V 1907, 419; Cloete 2010, 313.
596   Amery V 1907, 464; Cloete 2000, 285.

Part 4 – The guerrilla phase of the war (11 October 1900–31 May 1902)

P4.1.3.28 The British memorial and a few graves at Ouhoutbossie.
▶ *On the northern side of the R541 between Dullstroom and Lydenburg, Mpumalanga.*
◉ *S25° 18.555, E30° 12.985.*

The gravestone of Colour Sergeant T. Martin who was wounded in this engagement and died of his wounds on 1 January 1902,[597] is in the British Garden of Remembrance, municipal cemetery, Machadodorp, Mpumalanga.
▶ *Mpumalanga; on the western side of the tarred road connecting the town to the N4 toll road, a few hundred metres south of the N4.*
◉ *S25° 40.065, E30° 14.508.*

P4.1.3.29 The Republican memorial at Ouhoutbossie.
▶ *Southern side of the R541 between Dullstroom and Lydenburg, Mpumalanga. The burghers who were buried here after the battle were reinterred at the Burgher Monument at Bergendal in 1970.*
◉ *S25° 18.555, E30° 12.985.*

P4.1.3.30 The grave of Jacob Philippus Maré (Jnr), a burgher who was wounded at Ouhoutbossie, and died of his wounds on 11 February 1902. (See P7.2.2.3)
▶ *In the old municipal cemetery, Middelburg, Mpumalanga. Entry from Bhimy Damane St.*
◉ *S25° 45.832, E29° 26.849.*

P4.1.3.31 Grave of Burgher J.P. Swart, killed in action at Lake Banagher on 20 December 1901.
▶ *Municipal cemetery, Chrissiesmeer, Mpumalanga. Near the R542, on the western side of Chrissiesmeer.*
◉ *S26° 16.797, E30° 12.281.*

On 31 December 1901, the burghers of Commandant Joachim Prinsloo and Major J.F. Wolmarans engaged in a skirmish with Colonel Kipperley's Scots Greys near Bronkhorstspruit, who lost five men killed in action and 13 wounded; a further 23 were taken prisoner by the burghers.[598]

P4.1.3.32 Memorial (damaged) for six members of the Royal Scots Greys killed in action at Groenfontein, near Bronkhorstspruit, 1901-12-30 (this should be 1901-12-31): Lance-Corporal D. Fraser and Privates W. Humphreys, G. Bruce, J. Hastings, W. Gibson and P. Mitchell.[599]
▶ *British Garden of Remembrance, Donkerhoek. Entry from the R515 (turn west a few kilometres south of the N4), then drive through the grounds of the Kleinfontein settlement.*
◉ *S25° 48.363, E28° 29.385.*

Shots were also exchanged between Republican forces and a patrol of the South African Constabulary at Rooikop in the Potchefstroom area on the last day of 1901. This engagement resulted in at least three casualties.[600]

P4.1.3.29   P4.1.3.30   P4.1.3.31   P4.1.3.32

597 Watt 2000, 268.
598 Amery V 1907, 461; Preller 1938a, 10-11.
599 Watt 2000, 52, 146, 155, 184, 208 & 291.
600 Cloete 2010, 323.

P4.1.3.33 The gravestone of Trooper W.E. Walker, South African Constabulary, killed in action at Rooikop on 31 December 1901.[601]
▶ *British Garden of Remembrance, Alexandra cemetery, Potchefstroom, North West. Close to Olënpark, near Piet Bosman St, between James Moroka Dr & Kock St.*
The gravestone of Corporal H. Sloan, South African Constabulary, who died of wounds received at Rooikop on 31 December 1901, is in the same Garden of Remembrance.[602]
◉ *S26° 42.760, E27° 05.248.*

4.1.4 The controversial history of the Bushveldt Carbineers

The Bushveldt Carbineers was a unit of the British Army in South Africa established in February 1901. Its specific task was to crush Boer guerrilla activity in the northern Transvaal. A sizeable percentage of its officers and men were Australians. It was an effective force, but it engaged in activities which elicited outrage, and has attracted much controversy.[603]

The headquarters of the Bushveldt Carbineers was located at Fort Edward, a transportable steel fortress previously used by the Republican forces in fighting against the Venda (they called it Fort Hendrina, after Hendrina Joubert, the wife of Commandant-General Piet Joubert). Fort Edward was erected about 6 km to the south-west of the mission station and hospital at Elim.[604]

P4.1.4.1 Fort Hendrina (Fort Edward) today.
▶ *Erasmus St, to the west of the corner with Kruger St, Makhado (Louis Trichardt), Limpopo.*
◉ *S23° 02.565, E29° 54.510.*

The first incident in the controversial history of the Bushveldt Carbineers took place on 2 July 1901, when a patrol of this unit under command of Sergeant D.C. Oldham confronted and shot six civilian Boers, namely J.F. Vercuil (31), F.J.G. Potgieter (18), J.C. Greyling (25), J.J. Geyser (65), P.J. Geyser (12) and a man with the surname Van Heerden at Valdezia, about 20 km north-east of Fort Edward.[605]

P4.1.4.2 Gravestone of the six civilians shot at Valdezia on 2 July 1901 (left) and the monument in their honour unveiled in June 2010 by a Vercuil descendant, Dennis Eveleigh. The Dutch inscription on the gravestone describes them as South African heroes who died for their fatherland and freedom.
▶ *11.2 km east of the busy road crossing in the centre of Elim, on the Levubu road; turn left on the gravel road and drive through macadamia nut plantations for 2 km to the security gate of the Maclands Estate on the left (Tel. 015 556 7700, maclands@mweb.co.za). After about 1.5 km, the memorial is visible on the left about 50 m from the road, behind a high security fence. Ask permission at the gate to view the memorial and drive back on the inside of the farm about 500 m.*
◉ *S23° 06.549, E30° 09.072.*

P4.1.3.33

P4.1.4.1

P4.1.4.2

---

601 Watt 2000, 433.
602 Watt 2000, 383.
603 Pretorius 2010, 67; Leach 2012, xxviii-xxix.
604 Leach 2012, 5, 28-29.
605 Schulenburg 1981, 41 & 48; Leach 2012, 17-22.

Part 4 – The guerrilla phase of the war (11 October 1900–31 May 1902)

On 4 July 1901, Trooper B.J. van Buuren of the Bushveldt Carbineers, who witnessed the Valdezia incident and was afterwards seen talking to Boer women being escorted to the Pietersburg Concentration Camp, was shot near Fort Edward by a member of the Bushveldt Carbineers – allegedly by Lieutenant P.J. (Peter) Handcock.[606]

P4.1.4.3 Grave of Trooper Van Buuren (25).
▶ *At Fort Edward, signposted, about 50 m south of the tarred road between Elim and Bandelierkop, less than 6 km west of Elim, Limpopo, on the crest of a low hill.*
◉ *S23° 11.331, E30° 00.013.*

Captain P.F. (Percy) Hunt, the commanding officer of Fort Edward, and Sergeant F. Eland were killed in a night attack launched by the Bushveldt Carbineers on 6 August 1901. The Bushveldt Carbineers was supported by Lobedu warriors from nearby Modjadji in an attack on a group of Boers who were sleeping in the house of Commandant Herklaas Viljoen near Duiwelskloof (today called Modjadji's Kloof, Limpopo), south of Elim. Some of the Australian Bushveldt Carbineers officers, including Lieutenants Harry ("Breaker") Morant, Peter Handcock and G.R. Witton were enraged when they were informed of the mutilation of Hunt's body, allegedly by Boers, after he was killed. Their subsequent actions appear to have been motivated by a desire for vengeance.[607]

P4.1.4.4 Memorial at the site where Hunt's body was found. The ruins of the Viljoen house are in the background.
▶ *Turn off from the R36 north of Modjadjiskloof, before the turnoff to Ga-Kgapane, at a small farm signpost "AA 005, AA 006, CR 012" (at S23° 40.206, E30° 09.354). Drive 2 km on this farm road, passing a farmhouse. The memorial is at the ruins of the former Viljoen farmhouse.*
◉ *S 23° 39.433, E 30° 10.320.*

P4.1.4.5 Memorial of the Bushveldt Carbineers attack on 6 August 1901.
▶ *Next to R36 north of Modjadjiskloof, near the turnoff to Ga-Kgapane.*
◉ *S 23° 39.273, E 30° 10.231.*

P4.1.4.6 Captain Hunt's grave in the Medingen Mission cemetery.[608]
▶ *On an unnamed road turning out of the R578, behind the Mission church, visible from the road.*
◉ *S23° 38.251, E30° 14.397.*

P4.1.4.7 Sergeant Eland's grave.[609]
▶ *On the top of Ravenshill near the old Eland-Heckford houses, at the end of an unnamed road turning out of the R578, passing the Medingen Mission church and cemetery, then turning of the paved road to the left about 800 m from the church, driving uphill on a bad gravel road for about 3.5 km, where there is a gate that is usually locked. Walk for about 800 m to the old houses. The graves are behind the house on the left. Some of these houses can be rented for an overnight stay.*
◉ *S23° 36.555, E30° 15.338.*

P4.1.4.3   P4.1.4.4   P4.1.4.5   P4.1.4.6

---

606 Schulenburg 1981, 41-42, 48; Watt 2000, 427; Leach 2012, 22-23.
607 Schulenburg 1981, 42-43; Pretorius 2010, 68.
608 Watt 2000, 209.
609 Watt 2000, 126.

The next incident in the Bushveldt Carbineers history took place on 10 August 1901, at the Koedoes River near present-day Mooketsi in the northern Transvaal. A young Boer, Floris Visser (20), who was wounded in the Bushveldt Carbineers' attack on the Viljoen house on 6 August, was taken prisoner on 9 August by a Bushveldt Carbineers patrol under the command of Lieutenant Morant. He was shot, rather than taken to Fort Edward.[610] On 5 September, a small group of Boer women, children and an old man were attacked by a Bushveldt Carbineers patrol commanded by Lieutenant C.H.G. Hannam in the same area. Two Grobler boys, Jan Derk (14) and Jacobus Daniel (6), were killed, and their sister, Elizabeth Maria (9), was wounded in this incident.[611]

P4.1.4.8 The joint Visser-Grobler monument, which was unveiled in June 2010 by George Short, the present owner of the farm where the Grobler boys were shot.
▶ *On the eastern side of the R81 to Giyane, 96.5 km from Polokwane, just before crossing the Koedoes River at Jagtdrift (before the junction with the R578).*
◉ *S23° 29.961, E30° 12.569.*

More incidents in the notorious history of the Bushveldt Carbineers took place on 23 August 1901. Eight Boers, including four Dutch teachers, were being taken to the Fort on a wagon by an agent of the British Intelligence Department, but they were all shot by members of the Bushveldt Carbineers at Ballymore, close to Fort Edward. Three black wagon drivers were also shot.[612]

P4.1.4.9 The memorial for the eight burghers who were shot. The inscription reads: "On 23 August 1901, a party of 8 Burgers – 4 of whom were Dutch school teachers – were being escorted to Fort Edward as prisoners. They were met here by another BVC [Bushveldt Carbineers] patrol which included Ltns Breaker Morant, Handcock and Witton. Rev C.A.D. Heese and his Ndebele driver arrived and spoke to W.A. Vahrmeijer, principal of a school in Potgietersrust. Ltn Morant ordered Heese to leave or face arrest. The 8 men were then shot dead. They were: G.K. Westerhof, Baukens (Beauchamp?), W.A. Vahrmeijer, B. Wouters, C.P.J. Smit, Logenaar (Lochner?), J.J. du Preez, Pauskie (Paschke?). Three unnamed black attendants were chased by officers on horseback into Bristow's cattle kraal and also shot dead. Later that same day, Rev. Heese and his driver were both shot dead near Bandolierkop, presumably by Ltn P. Handcock."
▶ *On the farm currently owned by A.S. (Poog or Poek) Henning (Tel. 083 252 3857), 5 km west of Elim, Limpopo, on the Bandelierkop Road.*
◉ *S23° 10.528, E30° 01.250.*

Charles Bristow, the owner of the kraal where the three black men were shot, was also the owner of the Sweetwaters Hotel. Since this hotel was barely a kilometre from Fort Edward, its "Bushveld Saloon" was a favourite haunt of many members of the Bushveldt Carbineers. Captain 'Balula' Taylor of the British Army Intelligence Department and a close associate of the Bushveldt Carbineers even had his headquarters there.[613]

P4.1.4.7   P4.1.4.8   P4.1.4.9   P4.1.4.10

610   Schulenburg 1981, 43, 48; Leach 2012, 54-57.
611   Schulenburg 1981, 45-46; Leach 2012, 83-86.
612   Schulenburg 1981, 44, 48; Leach 2012, 61-72.
613   Leach 2012, 14.

P4.1.4.10 The Sweetwaters Hotel is no longer in operation. The buildings are still there, but currently they serve as servants' quarters.
▶ *In the valley to the west of the office on the farm owned by A.S. Henning.*
◙ *S23° 10.502, E30° 01.039.*

A German missionary, Rev. Heese and his Ndebele driver (whose name was not recorded) were travelling past the Vliegenpan area, south-west of Fort Edward, where they were confronted in the late afternoon of 23 August and shot, presumably by Lieutenant Handcock of the Bushveldt Carbineers.[614]

P4.1.4.11 The monument commemorating Heese at Vliegenpan south-west of Fort Edward.
▶ *On the southern side of the Elim Bandelierkop road (a few hundred metres away and not visible from the road), less than 5 km east of the N1.*
◙ *S23° 15.205, E 29° 52.150.*

On 7 September 1901, a Boer, Roelf van Staden, was on his way to the Sweetwaters Hotel with his sons Roelf (18) and Chris (12) to request permission to take the younger child, who had a severe fever, to the Elim Hospital for treatment. They were stopped by a patrol of the Bushveldt Carbineers, who ordered them to dig a grave and shot them. It seems that Trooper Botha (a 'joiner') actually requested permission to shoot the ailing youngster.[615] The Van Stadens were the last victims of the Bushveldt Carbineers.

P4.1.4.12 The old gravestone of the three Van Stadens and a memorial which Henning unveiled to the three victims on 26 June 2010.
▶ *Also on the farm of Poog Henning, in the plantation to the east of the Henning residence.*
◙ *S23° 10.582, E30° 01.333.*

P4.1.4.13 The monument and the memorial at Fort Edward that commemorate all the victims. These include the names of a number of victims for whom there are no specific memorials, including C.J. van den Berg, Njoba and Mattungen, who were all shot by Captain Taylor and a patrol.
▶ *At Fort Edward, signposted, about 50 m south of the tarred road between Elim and Bandelierkop, less than 6 km west of Elim, on the crest of a low hill.*
◙ *S23° 11.331, E30° 00.013.*

In October 1901, some non-commissioned officers and men of the Bushveldt Carbineers revealed a sequence of irregularities that led to the arrest and court martial of a number of members of the unit, including Lieutenants Morant, Handcock and Witton. The Bushveldt Carbineers was redesignated the Pietersburg Light Horse. On 27 February 1902, Morant and Handcock were executed by a British firing squad in Pretoria after being found guilty of murdering civilians as well as Boer combatants whom they had taken prisoner in the Spelonken region of the northern Transvaal. Witton was also found guilty of murder and sentenced to death, but Lord Kitchener commuted his sentence to penal servitude for life. He was released in August 1905.[616]

P4.1.4.11   P4.1.4.12   P4.1.4.13

---

614   Schulenburg 1981, 44-45& 49; Leach 2012, 73-82.
615   Schulenburg 1981, 46 & 49; Leach 2012, 87-90.
616   Witton 1907, 150, 236; Pretorius 2010, 68.

P4.1.4.14 Morant and Handcock were buried in the same grave.
▶ *Old Church Street West Cemetery, Pretoria, Gauteng. Entry from Es'kia Mphahlele St (previously D.F. Malan Dr), north of W.F. Nkomo Dr (previously Church St West).*
◙ *S 25°44.469, E 28°10.269.*

4.1.5 ZAR January–May 1902

A patrol of Colonel Kekewich's Imperial Yeomanry became involved in a skirmish with Boers at Holfontein in the western Transvaal on 2 January 1902, and one British officer was killed in action.[617]

P4.1.5.1 Grave of Lieutenant R.W. Woodhouse (19), 69th Company Imperial Yeomanry, killed in action at Holfontein on 2 January 1902.[618]
▶ *British Anglo-Boer War Garden of Remembrance, on the outskirts of Ottosdal, North West, near the D616 between the D855 & Visser St.*
◙ *S26° 48.271, E26° 00.773.*
This Garden of Remembrance contains the grave of at least one other Imperial soldier killed in action under unknown circumstances in the Transvaal in this period, namely Captain P.N. Field (32), 1st Scottish Horse, killed in action at Doornlaagte on 2 March 1902.[619]

On 4 January 1902, a commando of about 300 burghers commanded by General Koot Opperman trapped an advancing troop of mounted soldiers belonging to Brigadier General Plumer's column in an ambush at Bankkop, Onverwacht, east of Ermelo in the eastern Transvaal. The British losses amounted to 20 killed (including Major Vallentin of the Somerset Light Infantry), 45 wounded and 70 taken prisoner. Republican losses were minor, but included Opperman himself, who was regarded as one of Commandant-General Louis Botha's bravest officers.[620]

P4.1.5.2 Grave of Major John Maxmilien Vallentin (36), commander of the Victorian Bushmen.[621]
▶ *The British Garden of Remembrance in the municipal cemetery, near 16th St, Ermelo, Mpumalanga. There is a memorial for British soldiers who were killed in action at Onverwacht in the same cemetery, close to Vallentin's grave.*
◙ *S26° 30.402, E29° 58.760.*

P4.1.5.3 Memorial plaque for Vallentin (wall of the All Saints Anglican Church, Ladysmith).
▶ *Murchison St, north east of the corner with Princess St, Ladysmith, KwaZulu-Natal.*
◙ *S28° 33.840, E29° 46.649 (Google Maps).*

P4.1.5.4 There is also a memorial plaque for Vallentin inside St Ninian's Anglican Church in Heidelberg, Gauteng.

P4.1.4.14

P4.1.5.1

P4.1.5.2

---

617   Cloete 2010, 326.
618   Watt 2000, 462.
619   Watt 2000, 135.
620   Amery V 1907, 456-458; Cloete 2010, 292.
621   Watt 2000, 427.

Part 4 – The guerrilla phase of the war (11 October 1900–31 May 1902)

▶ *C/o Marais St & Voortrekker St.*
◉ *S26° 29.801, E28° 21.280.*

P4.1.5.5 General J.D. (Koot) Opperman's grave.
▶ *Municipal cemetery, Vryheid, KwaZulu-Natal (southern side of town, Hoog St, between Landdrost St & Wes St.*
◉ *S27° 46.887, E30° 47.952.*

P4.1.5.6 The grave of Burgher P.F. Smit, who was killed in action at Goedehoop on 19 January 1902.
▶ *Municipal cemetery, Chrissiesmeer, Mpumalanga (near the R542, on the western side of Chrissiesmeer).*
◉ *S26° 16.797, E30° 12.281.*

Soldiers of the Imperial Yeomanry commanded by Lieutenant-Colonel K. Chesney attacked General De la Rey's hospital at Treurfontein (near the present-day Coligny) in the western Transvaal on 21 January 1902. General Celliers and Commandant Jan Viljoen launched a counter-attack and drove the soldiers off. One burgher was killed in this engagement, but British losses amounted to 9 killed in action, 24 wounded and 41 captured.[622]

P4.1.5.7 Grave of Private R.W. Alderson (24), Imperial Yeomanry, killed in action at Treurfontein (Coligny) on 21 January 1902.[623]
▶ *In the British military cemetery about 2 km south-west of Coligny, south of the junction where the N14 to Delareyville turns off the R503 to Lichtenburg, very close to the junction.*
◉ *S26° 19.607, E26° 17.443.*
The grave of Sergeant G.H. Gordon, Bechuanaland Rifles, killed in action in that engagement at Treurfontein (Coligny) on 21 January 1902, is in the same cemetery. This cemetery also contains the grave of at least one other Imperial soldier killed in action under unknown circumstances in the Transvaal in this period, namely Private J. McDougall (or Macdougall), 1st Cameron Highlanders, killed on picket at Knoppenfontein on 12 April 1902.[624]

P4.1.5.8 The grave of Frederik C. Eloff, a burgher wounded at Zuurvlei in the Waterberg Mountains on 22 January 1902, who died the next day in Nylstroom.
▶ *Municipal cemetery, Modimolle (Nylstroom), Limpopo, on the western side of Thabo Mbeki St (R101), which runs north/south through the town.*
◉ *S24° 42.161, E28° 24.164.*

The Republican forces in the eastern Transvaal suffered a major setback on 25 January 1902 when their commander, General Ben Viljoen, was taken prisoner by the British in an ambush near Lydenburg.[625]

P4.1.5.3   P4.1.5.4   P4.1.5.5   P4.1.5.6   P4.1.5.7

---

622 Gronum 1974, 25.
623 Watt 2000, 3.
624 Watt 2000, 259.
625 Meijer 2000, 234.

P4.1.5.9 Memorial next to the Marambane Spruit where Viljoen was taken prisoner. His adjudant, Jacobus Nel, who was killed in this incident, is commemorated on the burgher memorial in the old cemetery in Lydenburg.[626]
▶ On the western side of the R37, about 6 km north of Lydenburg, Mpumalanga.
◉ S25° 03.150, E30° 25.822.

On the night of 4 February 1902, the Boers suffered a setback in the western Transvaal when more than a 100 burghers of the commando of Commandant Sarel Alberts, including Alberts himself, were taken prisoner by a British unit under Major H.P. Leader, who used joiners as scouts. Eight burghers were killed in action, and at least ten were wounded. British losses amounted to eight wounded. This engagement took place on the farm Gruisfontein, about 25 km to the east of Lichtenburg.[627]

P4.1.5.10 The memorial at Gruisfontein pays tribute to seven burghers who died in this battle: H.B. Kloppers, J.J. van der Schyff, G.J. Kruger, P.D. Bonthuizen, G. van Staden, A.J. Cronje and A. van Vuuren.
▶ Entrance to the farm Gruisfontein signposted on the D1241 (a gravel road) about 24 km east of Lichtenburg, North West, between the D138 and the D1242. The burgher monument is between Shed 7 & Shed 8 on an enormous poultry farm.
◉ S26° 09.886, E26° 22.941.

On 8 February, a patrol of about 130 members of the South African Constabulary was attacked by the burghers of General Coen Brits and Commandant Gert Claassen at Van Tondershoek, near Vlakfontein in the south-eastern Transvaal. At least eight members of the Constabulary were killed in action, and 35 were taken prisoner. Captain (Dr) A. Martin-Leake subsequently received the Victoria Cross for his gallant treatment of wounded soldiers while under fire.[628]

P4.1.5.11 Memorial to six members of the South African Constabulary killed in action at Van Tondershoek on 8 February 1902.
▶ British Garden of Remembrance, new cemetery, Standerton, Mpumalanga. Entry from Walter Sisulu St.
◉ S26° 56.283, E29° 14.077.

On 12 February 1902, about 250 burghers under Generals H.A. Alberts and J.N.H. Grobler managed to lure about 320 soldiers of the 28th Battalion Mounted Infantry, under the command of Major Dowell, into an ambush at Blesboklaagte, near Klip River Station, north of Vereeniging. Dowell himself was wounded and Lieutenant Howell was killed in action when he rushed to assist Dowell. British losses amounted to at least ten killed, 20 wounded and 50 taken prisoner. On the Boer side, five burghers were killed in action. The Boers fell back when an armoured train approached.[629]

Thirteen members of the 28th Battalion Mounted Infantry, who were killed in action or died of wounds, including Lieutenant E.G. Howell (23), Derbyshire Regiment,[630] are commemorated on a plaque in St Alban's Cathedral, Pretoria.

P4.1.5.8

P4.1.5.9

P4.1.5.10

P4.1.5.11

---

626   Van der Westhuizen & Van der Westhuizen 2000, 261.
627   Grobler 2004, 137.
628   Uys 2000, 101-102; Cloete 2010, 336.
629   Davitt 1902, 556-557; Cloete 2010, 337.
630   Watt 2000, 205.

Part 4 – The guerrilla phase of the war (11 October 1900–31 May 1902)

▶ *In a reception room at the Cathedral, Francis Baard St, between Paul Kruger St & Thabo Sehume St, Pretoria Central, Gauteng.*
◉ *S25° 44.970, E28° 11.373.*

Lieutenant Howell and four other members of the Derbyshire Regiment killed in action on 12 February 1902 are commemorated on the main British memorial at Maccauvlei.
▶ *British Garden of Remembrance, Maccauvlei Golf Course, Viljoensdrif, Free State, near the Club House. Entry from the R82 south of the bridge crossing the Vaal River into Vereeniging.*
◉ *S26°40.933, E 27°56.521.*

P4.1.5.12 Grave of Private B.A. Hebeler (31), 5th (Northumberland & Durham) Imperial Yeomanry, killed in action at Hartbeesfontein on 16 February 1902.[631]
▶ *British Garden of Remembrance, municipal cemetery, Klerksdorp, North West, near Margaretha Prinsloo St, between O.R. Tambo St & Kadria St.*
◉ *S26° 52.576, E26° 40.130.*

On 18 February 1902, Generals Alberts and Grobler again managed to ambush British troops, this time at Langzeekoeigat (Klippan), south of Nigel in the south-eastern Transvaal. A force of about 400 Scots Greys and Dragoon Guards commanded by Brigadier General Gilbert Hamilton were trapped when the Boers isolated two squadrons of the Scots Greys. British losses were ten soldiers wounded, of whom three died of wounds, and 47 were taken prisoner. According to British reports, ten burghers were killed in action.[632]

P4.1.5.13 Grave of Major C.W.M. Feilden (39), Royal Scots Greys, who died on 19 February 1902 of wounds received in action at Langzeekoeigat the previous day.[633]
▶ *Kloof cemetery, on the banks of the Kloof Spruit, on the northern side of the extension of Fenter St, Heidelberg, Gauteng. The graves of three other soldiers who were either killed in action or died of wounds received in the same engagement are also in this cemetery: Sergeant J. Glen, 2nd Dragoon Guards, Private D. Beatson of the same unit and Trooper G. Cruikshanks of the Royal Scots Greys.[634]*
◉ *S 26° 29.717, E 28° 20.770.*

P4.1.5.14 Grave of Lieutenant-Colonel R.W. Evans (49), Natal Volunteer Composite Regiment, killed in action at Langelegen, near Vryheid on 19 February 1902.[635]
▶ *West Street Cemetery, entrance from Theatre Lane between West St & Brook St, Durban, KwaZulu-Natal.*
◉ *S29° 51.517, E31° 00.841.*

General De la Rey, assisted by Generals Kemp, Liebenberg and Celliers and their burghers, achieved significant successes in the Transvaal in the early months of 1902. The first of these successes was at Ysterspruit (Yzerspruit),

P4.1.5.12   P4.1.5.13   P4.1.5.14

---

631 Watt 2000, 188.
632 Amery V 1907, 462; Cloete 2010, 339.
633 Watt 2000, 134.
634 Watt 2000, 158, 26 & 97.
635 Watt 2000, 130.

south-west of Klerksdorp, on 25 February 1902. They captured a whole British convoy, including two field guns and a pom-pom, numerous rifles and ammunition, 127 wagons and 1 500 mules, 400 oxen and 200 horses. The Boer casualties were 12 killed and 42 wounded. Of the British force led by Lieutenant-Colonel William Anderson, 53 men were killed, 130 were wounded and 241 were taken prisoner (but were released soon afterwards).[636]

P4.1.5.15 The Boer memorial on the battlefield.
▶ To reach the monument, turn to the south onto a gravel road from the N12 about 15 km west of Klerksdorp, North West (at a road sign to Dominionville, north of the N12). After about 12 km, turn left onto a gravel road and drive east. After 300 m, the road crosses the Ysterspruit. The monument is surrounded by thorn bushes about 40 m north of this gravel road, about 500 m east of the bridge across the Ysterspruit.
◉ S26° 59.875, E26° 29.260, at Ysterspruit Bridge (Google Maps).

P4.1.5.16 A memorial at Rietvlei was erected in 1935 for the burghers who fell at Yzerspruit and were originally buried there. The burghers were reinterred at the Burgher Monument in Delareyville in 1985, and the original memorial was removed. The current memorial was erected in 1986 on the spot where the 1935 memorial stood. The new memorial has been damaged.
▶ About 850 m south of the R507, linking Ottosdal and Hartbeesfontein. About 15 km east of Ottosdal, turn south on the gravel road to Witfontein (the same gravel road to the north goes to the Melliodora railway station). The cemetery and memorial are on the western side of the road. There are tall trees and a small gate to the cemetery next to the road.
◉ S26° 48.446, E26° 08.498.

There are a number of memorials for British soldiers who fell at Yzerspruit, as well as gravestones of soldiers who were either killed in action at Yzerspruit or died of wounds received there on 25 February 1902 in the British Anglo-Boer War Garden of Remembrance, municipal cemetery, Klerksdorp, North West, near Margaretha Prinsloo St, between O.R. Tambo St & Kadria St.
◉ S26° 52.576, E26° 40.130.
These memorials and gravestones include the following:
- A memorial to the memory of 16 members of the 5th (Northumberland & Durham) Imperial Yeomanry.
- A memorial in memory of 30 British soldiers of various units, killed in action at Yzerspruit on 25 February 1902, erected by the Guild of Loyal Women, Klerksdorp.
- A memorial for Captain F.R. Coates (25), Lieutenant H.G. Quin (20), Sergant Major W.G. McDonald and 29 non-commissioned officers and men, 1st Battalion 5th Fusiliers, killed in action at Yzerspruit [Elandslaagte] on 25 February 1902.[637] There is also a separate grave for Quin.
- Other gravestones in the cemetery include those of Private J.W. Swinburn, Northumberland & Durham Imperial Yeomanry, who died on 8 March 1902 of wounds received in action at Elandslaagte[638] [Yzerspruit]; Private J.W. Young, Northumberland & Durham Imperial Yeomanry, who died on 5 (or 8) March 1902 of

P4.1.5.15

P4.1.5.16

P4.1.5.17

---
636   Raath 2007, 459; Pretorius 2010, 503-504.
637   Watt 2000, 79, 276 & 343.
638   Watt 2000, 406.

wounds received in action at Elandslaagte[639] [Yzerspruit]; and Private T.C. Johnson, Northumberland & Durham Imperial Yeomanry, who died on 27 February 1902 of wounds[640] [probably also received in action at Yzerspruit on 25 February 1902].

De la Rey's burghers achieved a victory over British forces led by Lord Methuen at Tweebosch (the Boers referred to it as the battle of De Klipdrift) on 7 March 1902. This victory is regarded as the high point of successful Boer guerrilla tactics, as they charged on horseback and fired from the saddle. Methuen was marching his 1 300 men, with six field guns and a large convoy of wagons, towards Lichtenburg in the western Transvaal when De La Rey's 750 burghers, with two field guns and maxims that they had captured at Yzerspruit, attacked them from various directions. British resistance crumbled within two hours, after Methuen himself had been badly wounded. The Boer casualties numbered eight burghers killed and 26 wounded, some of whom died of their wounds. On the British side, 68 officers and men were killed, 121 were wounded and 859 taken prisoner. The Boers captured six field guns and ammunition, about 500 horses, 120 wagons loaded with supplies and other munitions. De la Rey released the wounded Methuen the next day in order to allow British army surgeons to take care of him. This resulted in their becoming lifelong friends.[641]

P4.1.5.17 The De Klipdrift/Tweebosch burgher memorial on the battlefield.[642] There is a mass grave of 13 burghers, of whom 12 were killed in action or died of wounds received at De Klipdrift/Tweebosch.
▶ *From Sannieshof, take the road to Ottosdal. Turn right (south) after 3.7 km to Rostrataville. Turn right again (west) after 1.9 km at the De Klipdrift sign. Go through farm gate and follow the farm road for 1 km. Turn right (north) at a clump of trees, which is approximately where Methuen was wounded. The memorials and graves are about 200 m to the north.*
◉ *S26° 34.317, E25° 46.887.*

P4.1.5.18 Grave of Lieutenant T.P.W. Nesham (21), Royal Field Artillery, killed in action at De Klipdrift/Tweebosch, 7 March 1902.[643]
▶ *British Anglo-Boer War Garden of Remembrance, on the outskirts of Ottosdal, North West, near the D616 between the D855 & Visser St.*
This cemetery also contains the graves of other soldiers who fell at De Klipdrift/Tweebosch, including Corporal T. (or P.) Wilmot, Northumberland & Durham Imperial Yeomanry, who died of his wounds; Privates H. Extine, L. Kriel, R. Martin and J. (or I.) Pretorius, Dennison's Scouts, killed in action; Private J.P. Slack, Northumberland & Durham Imperial Yeomanry, killed in action, and Private T. (or P.) Murphy, Northumberland & Durham Imperial Yeomanry, killed in action.[644]
◉ *S26° 48.271, E26° 00.773.*

P4.1.5.18   P4.1.5.19   P4.1.5.20

---

639   Watt 2000, 468.
640   Watt (2000, 221) inludes no Private T.C. Johnson or Johnstone in his roll of honour, but lists Private J. Johnstone, Northumberland Fusiliers, who died on 27 February1902 of wounds received at Elandslaagte two days before.
641   Scholtz 1979, 44-55; Raath 2007, 463-467; Pretorius 2010, 461-462.
642   Dreyer 2010, Chapters 1-8.
643   Watt 2000, 306.
644   Watt 2000, 131, 239, 268, 303, 339, 382 & 456.

From 13 March onwards, the Zoutpansberg Commando led by General Christiaan Beyers besieged the garrison of 55 men at Fort Edward, near Elim in the Spelonken area of the northern Transvaal. On 21 March, Colonel Denny attempted to rescue the besieged garrison, but the burghers counter-attacked vigorously and almost succeeded in capturing a British Armstrong field gun. Denny retreated to Dwars River, only to resume his offensive two days later. The Zoutpansberg Commando confronted the British force at Vliegenpan at a later stage, close to Fort Edward, and succeeded in driving them back. Denny subsequently abandoned the Fort Edward garrison to their fate.[645]

> 4.1.5.19 Vliegenpan battlefield memorial.
> ▶ On the southern side of the Elim-Bandelierkop road (a few hundred metres away, not visible from the road), less than 5 km east of the N1, Limpopo.
> ◉ S23° 15.205, E 29° 52.150.

> P4.1.5.20 Grave of Regimental Sergeant-Major T. Evans, Pietersburg Light Horse & Coldstream Guards, killed in action in the Battle of Vliegenpan at Spelonken on 23 March 1902.[646]
> ▶ Old municipal cemetery, Polokwane, Limpopo. Entry from Dahl St, across from the western end of Jorissen St.
> ◉ S23° 54.489, E29° 26.783.

Using Klerksdorp in the western Transvaal as their base, a British force of 16 000 men launched a massive drive on 24 March 1902. Their objective was to capture as many of De la Rey's burghers as possible. De la Rey himself eluded pursuit, but other commandos were forced to engage the British forces. Most of the Boers managed to escape the net after dark that evening. The extent of casualties on the two sides could not be established.[647]

> P4.1.5.21 Grave of Lieutenant M. Knowles (20), 1st Royal Dragoons, who died on 28 March 1902 of wounds received in action at Leeuwbosch, near Klerksdorp, four days previously, on 24 March.[648]
> ▶ British Garden of Remembrance, municipal cemetery, Klerksdorp, North West, near Margaretha Prinsloo St, between O.R. Tambo St & Kadria St.
> ◉ S26° 52.576, E26° 40.130.

On 30 March 1902, there was a railway accident that killed 43 people – including 36 members of the Hampshire Regiment – near Barberton in the eastern Transvaal.[649]

> P4.1.5.22 Memorial for the members of the Hampshire Regiment killed in the railway accident on 30 March 1902, and for other members of that regiment who died in the Barberton area during the war.
> ▶ British Garden of Remembrance, Henry Nettman St, between Redelinghuys St & Keurboom St, Barberton, Mpumalanga.
> ◉ S25° 45.970, E31° 03.284.

P4.1.5.21   P4.1.5.22   P4.1.5.23

---

645 Van Zyl 1944, 395; Scholtz 1949, 198; Cloete 2010, 346 & 348.
646 Watt 2000, 130.
647 Amery V 1907, 512-517; Cloete, 2010, 348-349.
648 Watt 2000, 238.
649 Cloete 2010, 350.

Part 4 – The guerrilla phase of the war (11 October 1900–31 May 1902)

Another engagement involving De la Rey's commandos occurred in the western Transvaal, at Boschbult on 31 March 1902. However, neither side could achieve a decisive victory; both lost men.[650]

P4.1.5.23 The monument on the Boschbult battlefield commemorating six burghers killed in action, namely I.J. Badenhorst, B. Deysel, J.H. Harmse, I.J. Naudé, W.H. Pretorius and P.G.W. Roets, as well as 27 British soldiers who lost their lives.
▶ *On the southern side of the R507 between Delareyville and Ottosdal, about 27 km from Ottosdal.*
◉ *S26° 47.781, E25° 44.305.*

P4.1.5.24 Memorial for Corporal F.S. McL. Howard, Canadian Mounted Rifles, who died on 27 April 1902 of wounds received at Boschbult on 31 March 1902.[651]
▶ *British Garden of Remembrance, municipal cemetery, Klerksdorp, North West, near Margaretha Prinsloo St, between O.R. Tambo St & Kadria St.*
There is also a memorial stone for Quartermaster-Sergeant G.G. Senior (34), 6th Dragoon Guards, killed in action at Boschbult on 31 March 1902.[652]
◉ *S26° 52.576, E26° 40.130.*

P4.1.5.25 Memorial in honour of eight soldiers of the 2nd Regiment Canadian Mounted Rifles who fell at Boschbult on 31 March 1902.
▶ *British Anglo-Boer War Garden of Remembrance, municipal cemetery on the outskirts of Ottosdal, North West, near the D616 between the D855 & Visser St. This Garden of Remembrance contains the graves of a number of Imperial soldiers who fell at Boschbult, including Captains R.R. Challenor (30) and G. de C. Le Marchant (22), both 1st Battalion Lancashire Fusiliers, killed in action; Second Lieutenant C.W.L. Churchill (18), 3rd Battalion Hampshire Regiment, who on 1 (or 2) April 1902 died of wounds received in action; Quartermaster-Sergeant G.G. [Smith-] Senior (34), 6th Dragoon Guards, killed in action; Private T.B. Day (24) and Corporal W.A. Knisley (26), both of the Canadian Mounted Rifles, killed in action; and Private D.H. Campbell, 2nd Regiment Canadian Mounted Rifles, who died of wounds received at Boschbult.[653]*
◉ *S26° 48.271, E26° 00.773.*

On 1 April 1902, a British force commanded by Colonel A.T. Lawley attempted a night raid on the commandos of Generals Piet Viljoen and J.J. Alberts at Boschman's Kop, south-east of Springs. The burghers were initially surprised, but launched a counter-attack in which the British forces lost 77 men. The burghers lost 33 men (most were wounded).[654]

P4.1.5.26 Memorial commemorating 23 men of the Queen's Bays (2nd Dragoon Guards) killed in action at Boschman's Kop on 1 April 1902.

 P4.1.5.24  P4.1.5.25  P4.1.5.26

---

650   Cloete 2010, 350-351.
651   Watt 2000, 204.
652   Watt 2000, 373.
653   Watt 2000, 63, 69, 74, 107, 238, 244 & 373.
654   Cloete 2010, 351.

▶ *British Garden of Remembrance, municipal cemetery, Primrose, Gauteng. Use the northern entrance from Cemetery Rd (about 100 m north of the main entrance), north of the intersection with Rietfontein Ave. The gravestone of Major J.C.A. Walker, Queen's Bays, who was killed in action at Boschman's Kop on 1 April 1902, is in the same cemetery.*
◉ *S26° 11.719, E28° 08.722.*
This cemetery also contains the graves of at least one Imperial soldier who, according to his gravestone, died in action under unknown circumstances in the Transvaal in this period: Private W.J. Leslie, Canadian Mounted Rifles, killed in action on 17 April 1902. According to Watt, he died of enteric disease.[655]

On 11 April, in the absence of General de la Rey, who was involved in preliminary peace talks (see Section 6), General Kemp attacked a very large British force commanded by Lieutenant-General Ian Hamilton at Roodewal in the western Transvaal. The Boer commandos were driven back by the British and suffered heavy casualties, including the brave Commandant Ferdinand Potgieter, who was leading a charge on the British position by Boers on horseback, firing from the saddle, when he was shot through the head barely 60 m from the enemy lines. Boer casualties were high: approximately 50 men were killed and more than a hundred were wounded and/or taken prisoner. British losses were about ten killed and 75 wounded. Roodewal was the last significant engagement of the war in the Transvaal.[656]

P4.1.5.27 *The mass grave of and memorial for the burghers who fell in the battle of Roodewal on 11 April 1902. The graves of both Commandant F.J. Potgieter of Wolmaransstad and Johannes Frederik Greyling (31), who was also killed in action in this battle, are in this same cemetery.*
▶ *On farm land, 6 km from the R507 between Ottosdal and Delareyville, about 17 km from Delareyville. Turn south on the gravel road to Migdol and drive past the old school on the left and a shop on the right. After 2.4 km turn left at the T-junction. After another 2.1 km, turn left on the Claudinia (Glaudina) road. Follow this road (the D1227) for 600 m (the road turns sharply to the right). Then turn left through a farm gate onto a farm road and follow this for 800 m. Again turn left to the memorial and graves, about 100 m from this point.*
◉ *S25° 50.034, E25° 39.298.*

P4.1.5.28 *Grave of Trooper H.A. (or H.M.) Mahood (22), No 2 Troop, South African Constabulary, who died on 13 April 1902 of wounds received in action at Roodewal on 11 April 1902.*[657]
▶ *In the British military cemetery about two km south-west of Coligny, south of the junction where the N14 to Delareyville turns off from the R503 to Lichtenburg, very close to the junction. There is a memorial for Trooper Mahood in the same cemetery, which also contains the graves of the following Imperial soldiers who fell at Roodewal, amongst others: Lieutenant R.A. Chaloner (22), Royal Inniskilling Fusiliers; Sergeant W. Murray, 1st Scottish Horse; Trooper (or Private) E.W. Parsons, Imperial Yeomanry; and Trooper (or Private) H.J. Ambridge, Imperial Yeomanry.*[658]
◉ *S26° 19.607, E26° 17.443.*

P4.1.5.27

P4.1.5.28

P4.1.5.29

---

655   Watt 2000, 248.
656   Pretorius 2010, 346, 394-395.
657   Watt 2000, 262.
658   Watt 2000, 6, 69, 304 & 323.

Part 4 – The guerrilla phase of the war (11 October 1900–31 May 1902)

On 12 April 1902, 15 soldiers from New Zealand were killed at Machavie, near Klerksdorp in the western Transvaal, when their troop train collided with a goods train and derailed.[659]

>P4.1.5.29 Memorial for the 15 members of the 8th New Zealand Contingent killed in the railway accident at Machavie on 12 April 1902.
>▶ British Garden of Remembrance, municipal cemetery, Klerksdorp, North West, near Margaretha Prinsloo St, between O.R. Tambo St & Kadria St.
>There is a separate memorial for Trooper (or Private) A.H. Macdonald, one of those unfortunate New Zealand soldiers, in the same cemetery.[660]
>◉ S26° 52.576, E26° 40.130.

A number of British soldiers, including an officer, were killed on 5 May 1902 in another railway accident involving an armoured train in Daspoort, on the northwestern side of the centre of Pretoria.

>P4.1.5.30 Memorial to non-commisisoned officers and men of the 2nd Battalion Royal Fusiliers killed in the Daspoort armoured train accident on 5 May 1902.
>▶ Old Church Street West Cemetery, Pretoria, Gauteng. Entry from Es'kia Mphahlele St (previously D.F. Malan Dr), north of W.F. Nkomo Dr (previously Church St West).
>◉ Near S 25°44.472, E 28°10.286.

Shots were exchanged between Boers and British soldiers in the western Transvaal until the very end of the war.

>P4.1.5.31 Grave markers of Private E. Conway, Royal West Kent's Mounted Infantry, who died on 22 April 1902 of wounds received in action near Bloemhof the day before, and Private J. Doyle, Lancashire Fusiliers, who died of disease on 7 March 1901.[661]
>▶ West End Cemetery, c/o Green St & Reserve Rd, Kimberley, Northern Cape.
>◉ S28° 44.078, E24° 44.170 (Google Maps).
>The grave of Sergeant H. Lawrence (25), A Division, South African Constabulary, killed in action at Leeuwfontein near Bloemhof on 29 April 1902[662] is in the same cemetery.

>P4.1.5.32 The gravestone of Canadian Trooper E.A. Woods, killed in action at Buffelsdoorn on 30 May 1902.[663]
>▶ British Garden of Remembrance, Alexandra Cemetery, North West, close to Olënpark, near Piet Bosman St, between James Moroka Dr & Kock St. The gravestone of another Canadian, Trooper P.L. Deveraux, South African Constabulary, who died on the last day of the war of wounds received at Buffelsdoorn on 30 May 1902,[664] is in the same Garden of Remembrance..
>◉ S26° 42.760, E27° 05.248.

P4.1.5.30

P4.1.5.31

P4.1.5.32

---

659 Cloete (2010, 356) states that 12 soldiers died.
660 Watt 2000, 258.
661 Watt 2000, 85 & 118.
662 Watt 2000, 243.
663 Watt 2000, 462.
664 Watt 2000, 110.

The last skirmish before the end of hostilities took place on the same day that the peace treaty was signed, on 31 May 1902, at Kalkkraal, near Klerksdorp in the western Transvaal. One soldier was killed and two were wounded in this engagement.[665]

> P4.1.5.33 Grave of Private J.R. Jackson, Northumberland & Durham Imperial Yeomanry, killed in action on 31 May 1902 at Kalkkraal.[666]
> ▶ British military cemetery, about 2 km south-west of Coligny, south of the junction where the N14 to Delareyville turns off from the R503 to Lichtenburg, very close to the junction.
> ◉ S26° 19.607, E26° 17.443.

4.2 The guerrilla war in Natal

> P4.2.1 Grave of P.J. Bergh, a burgher killed in action in April 1901. The circumstances of his death are not known. It is possible that he died of wounds in the British military hospital in Charlestown and that he was reinterred in Newcastle.[667]
> ▶ Near British Garden of Remembrance, municipal cemetery, Newcastle, KwaZulu-Natal. Entry from Hardwick St.
> ◉ S27° 45.369, E29° 56.616.

On 28 July 1901, there was a skirmish between a small British force and a Boer commando in the valley of the White Mfolozi River east of Fort Newdigate (an Anglo-Zulu War fortress). The burghers drove the soldiers steadily towards the west and almost captured a British field gun at Witklip, where the British lost a number of men killed in action, including Major C.B. Jervis-Edwards of the Hussars. Both the Boers and the British forces retired after sunset.[668]

> There is a stone cairn erected by the Boers on the field of action at Witklip. The six soldiers who were killed there were buried in the town cemetery in Nqutu. In the 1960s, they were exhumed and reinterred in Dundee.[669]

Approximately a week after Commandant-General Louis Botha's success against a British force at Bloedriviersepoort in the Vryheid district, he crossed the border into Natal with his forces. On 25 September 1901, he decided to attack two British outposts south of Babanango, namely Fort Itala and Fort Prospect. Both the attacks on 26 September were repulsed by the British defenders.[670]

> P4.2.2 The information board at Fort Prospect. The British soldiers who died in the attack on Itala are commemorated on a tall memorial on the battlefield. There are also a number of graves of British soldiers.
> At Fort Prospect, the only death was one soldier, Private C. (or G.) Duckworth, 1st South Lancashire Regiment, whose grave is in the plantation where the battle took place.[671]

P4.1.5.33

P4.2.1

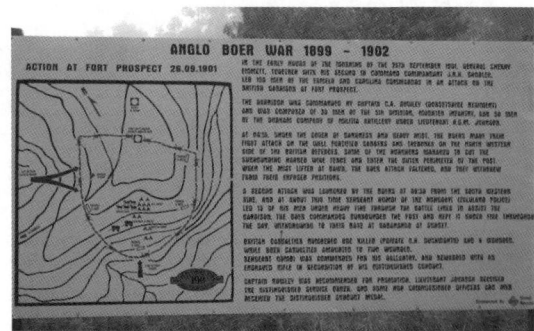
P4.2.2

---

665 Cloete 2010, 371.
666 According to Watt (2000, 215), Jackson's initials are R.J. and the engagement took place at Kaalkraal.
667 Van der Westhuizen & Van der Westhuizen 2000, 32.
668 Torlage & Watt 1999, 21.
669 Torlage & Watt 1999, 26-27; Watt 2000, 219.
670 Cloete 2010, 299.
671 Watt 2000, 119.

Part 4 – The guerrilla phase of the war (11 October 1900–31 May 1902)

▶ *From the T-junction where the Babanango road joins the road between Melmoth and Nkandla, travel about 4 km towards Nkandla. Take the turn-off onto a forestry road towards a watchtower on the right, a few hundred metres from the tarred road.*[672]

P4.2.3 The Boers wounded in this battle were treated in this house on the farm Gelykwater, which temporarily served as a hospital. The house was burned down by the British later in the war, but was rebuilt after the war.[673]
▶ *Near the road between Babanango and Nqutu, KwaZulu-Natal.*

P4.2.4 Memorial for the burghers who died in this battle.
▶ *In the family cemetery on the farm Gelykwater, near the road between Babanango and Nqutu, KwaZulu-Natal.*

P4.2.5 The graves of the burghers C.T. van Rooyen and P. Scholtz, who died in this battle.
▶ *In the family cemetery on the farm Gelykwater, near the road between Babanango and Nqutu, KwaZulu-Natal.*

The names of 23 burghers killed in action in the engagements at Itala are engraved on a roll of honour on the Burgher Monument at Platrand, near Ladysmith, KwaZulu-Natal (see P3.2.3.19).
◉ *S28° 35.278, E29° 46.357.*

4.3　The guerrilla war in the Orange Free State

The greatest leader of the guerrilla war in the Orange Free State was General Christiaan de Wet.

P4.3.1 Equestrian statue of De Wet, by Coert Steynberg, unveiled in 1954[674] *(see also CP23 on p. 299).*
▶ *On the grounds of the Fourth Raadsaal, south-eastern c/o President Brand St & Charles St, Bloemfontein, Free State.*
◉ *S29° 06.922, E26° 13.048.*

P4.3.2 Painting of De Wet in the Caledon Museum, showing him in action in the war.
▶ *The museum is in Douglas St, Smithfield, Free State.*
◉ *Less than 100 m south-east of S30° 12.604, E26° 31.930.*

P4.3.3 De Wet remained a prominent personality after the war and was highly respected, especially in the Orange Free State. This monument in Reddersburg commemorates him.
▶ *Next to Van Riebeeck St (the N6 national road), at corner with Boshoff St, Reddersburg, Free State.*
◉ *S29° 39.259, E26° 10.629.*

 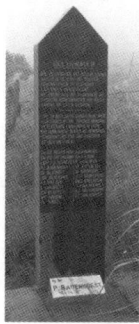  

P4.2.3　　　　P4.2.4　　　　P4.2.5　　　　P4.3.1

672　Van der Westhuizen & Van der Westhuizen 2000, 21.
673　Van der Westhuizen & Van der Westhuizen 2000, 15.
674　Van Schoor 1989a, 197.

P4.3.2

P4.3.3

P4.3.4

P4.3.4 De Wet, who died in 1922, was buried at the foot of the National Women's Monument.
▶ Monument Road, Bloemfontein, Free State.
◉ S29° 08.397, E26° 12.569.

As in the ZAR, there were several skirmishes in the territory of the Republic of the Orange Free State between Republican and British forces throughout the guerrilla period of the Anglo-Boer War. There were sporadic battles and other noteworthy engagements, which left behind a legacy of physical places of remembrance.

On the evening of 11 October 1900, a British unit commanded by Colonel Grove surprised the burghers of Field Cornet Koos de Wet, who were bivouacking at Moordpoortjie on Groenplaas, about 10 km east of Frankfort. Burgher losses were high: 11 burghers were killed, four were wounded and 17 were taken prisoner. British losses were three men killed.[675]

P4.3.5 Grave of burghers F.J. and P.M. Lotz, killed in action on 11 October 1900 at Moordpoortjie and reinterred in Frankfort 1987. The original gravestone was re-erected on the new grave.[676]
▶ Old town cemetery, Frankfort, Free State, next to the R34/26 on the eastern side of the town. The same cemetery contains a memorial gravestone for four burghers who were also killed in action at Moordpoortjie on 11 October 1900: Jurie Blom, Koos de Wet, Danie Cronjé and Piet Lourens.
◉ S27° 17.287, E28° 29.505.

P4.3.6 Grave of Lieutenant E.M. Hanbury (20), 3rd Battalion South Lancashire Regiment, killed in action at Gryskop, near Trompsburg in the southern Orange Free State, 13 October 1900. According to Watt, he belonged to the 2nd East Yorkshire Regiment.[677]
▶ Municipal cemetery, northern side of c/o Louw St & Van As St, Trompsburg, Free State.
◉ S30° 01.808, E25° 46.885.

P4.3.5

P4.3.6

P4.3.7

---

675 Cloete 2010, 202.
676 Van der Bank 1995, 33.
677 Watt 2000, 176.

Part 4 – The guerrilla phase of the war (11 October 1900–31 May 1902)

Republican forces under General J.B.M. Hertzog attacked the mining town of Jagersfontein in the south-western Orange Free State on 16 October 1900. The town was defended by a combination of troops and town guards, but a small group of burghers managed to reach the centre of town. They released all the prisoners from the goal and inflicted more than 20 casualties on the defenders.[678]

P4.3.7 Grave of Commandant P.J. Visser, killed in action in this assault on 16 October 1900.
▶ Municipal cemetery, Likkewaan St, Jagersfontein, Free State.
◉ S29° 45.633, E25° 26.268.

P4.3.8 Grave of Field Cornet C.C. Snyman, also killed in action on 16 October, near that of Visser. His grave is one of the few burgher graves with a British iron cross as marker. The burghers S. Spies and B.J. de Klerk, who were both killed in action at Paardeberg in February 1900, are also mentioned on the cross and are buried alongside Snyman.[679]
▶ Municipal cemetery, Likkewaan St, Jagersfontein, Free State.
◉ S29° 45.633, E25° 26.268.

P4.3.9 Grave of Private Fred(erick) G. Wallace (23), Jagersfontein Town Guard, killed in action on 16 October 1900.[680]
▶ Municipal cemetery, Likkewaan St, Jagersfontein, Free State.
◉ S29° 45.633, E25° 26.268.

P4.3.10 British monument commemorating the 12 members of the 2nd Battalion Seaforth Highlanders and two members of Jagersfontein Town Guard killed in action defending Jagersfontein on 16 October 1900 (the monument has been vandalised).
▶ Outskirts of Jagersfontein, on a low hill next to the R704 road leading to Fauresmith.
◉ S29° 45.523, E25° 25.284.

A Republican commando under the joint command of Commandants Gideon Scheepers and Willem Fouchee attempted to occupy Philippolis in the southern Orange Free State on 18 October 1900. The small British garrison successfully repulsed all the Boer attacks for six days, until British reinforcements arrived on 24 October and the burgher forces left the area.[681] The British forces subsequently introduced the scorched earth policy in this district by burning down numerous Boer farms and homesteads. The Dutch Reformed Church building was occupied by the troops and turned into a fortress. Almost the whole interior (including the organ) was destroyed. The parsonage was also set alight and the minister, Reverend Colin Fraser (President Steyn's father-in-law), was sent to the concentration camp in Norvalspont.[682]

P4.3.8

P4.3.9

P4.3.10

---

678 Cloete 2010, 203.
679 Van der Bank 1995, 45.
680 Watt 2000, 433.
681 Cloete 2010, 204-205.
682 Oosthuizen ca 2000, 30.

P4.3.11 The Dutch Reformed Church in Philippolis (repaired and enlarged after the war).
▶ Northern end of Voortrekker St, at the entrance of the town from Trompsburg, Free State.
◉ S30° 15.709, E25° 16.377.

P4.3.12 Grave of Driver W.A. Rodger (34) of Prince Alfred's Own (P.A.O.) Cape Artillery. His gravestone states that he was killed in action near Jacobsdal on 20 October 1900 while gallantly attending a wounded comrade, for which act he was posthumously awarded the Distinguished Conduct Medal, awarded for gallantry in the field by other ranks of the British Army.[683]
▶ Municipal cemetery, De Villiers St, Jacobsdal, Free State.
◉ S29° 08.091, E24° 46.510.

Very early on the morning of 25 October 1900, a Republican commando led by General J.B.M. Hertzog attacked the British forces occupying Jacobsdal in the western Orange Free State. The burghers advanced on the town along the bed of the Riet River and managed to reach the tented camp of the Cape Town Highlanders. In the fierce fighting that followed, 16 British soldiers were killed in action and 11 more were wounded. It is not known exactly what the Boer casualties were, but at least one burgher was killed while firing on the British forces from the cover of a stone wall. The Boers fled when reinforcements arrived for the British forces. The houses of inhabitants of Jacobsdal who had assisted the Boers were subsequently burned to the ground.[684]

P4.3.13 The burgher killed in the attack was Field Cornet Izak Daniel Bosman of Jacobsdal. The place where he fell, next to a stone wall near the centre of the town, is signposted.
▶ Sarel Cilliers St, between Piet Retief St & Rivier St, Jacobsdal, Free State.
◉ S29° 07.876, E24° 46.353.

P4.3.14 Bosman's tombstone.
▶ Municipal cemetery, De Villiers St, Jacobsdal, Free State.
A memorial tombstone for the soldiers of the Cape Town Highlanders killed in action during the engagement is also in this cemetery. The inscription reads: "Erected by the officers, non-commissioned officers and men of the Cape Town Highlanders to the memory of their comrades who fell at Jacobsdal on the 25th October, 1900. Sergeant H. Acres, Corporal J. Barlow, Bugler W.A. Clarke, P(rivate)s W. Dique, R. Smail and J. Pringle."
◉ S29° 08.091, E24° 46.510.

P4.3.15 Grave of Major J. Hanwell (38), Royal Field Artillery, killed in action near Ventersburg on 30 October 1900, in the old municipal cemetery, Ventersburg.[685]
▶ Old town cemetery, southern side of Eeufees St, between Smith St & Swart St, Ventersburg, Free State.
◉ S28° 04.861, E27° 08.085.

P4.3.11

P4.3.12

P4.3.13

P4.3.14

---

683   Watt 2000, 358.
684   Oosthuizen ca 2000, 17.
685   Watt 2000, 178.

P4.3.16 Graves of two members of the Northumberland & Durham Imperial Yeomanry, Private W. Jameson, who died of wounds, and Private J. Lynch, who was killed in action on 5 November 1900.[686]
▶ British Garden of Remembrance, western side of Noord Rd, Kroonstad, Free State.
◉ S27° 39.049, E27° 13.816.
The Kroonstad Garden of Remembrance contains a number of graves of Imperial soldiers who died under unknown circumstances in the Orange Free State in this period. These include the graves of
- Sergeant-Major Alfred Leo Whitfield (40), Kroonstad Scouts, killed in action near Kroonstad on 22 February 1901.[687]
- Private W. Davies, 1st Loyal Lancashire Regiment and Private W. Vick, 2nd Loyal Lancashire Regiment, both killed in action at Ventersburg Road on 1 March 1901.[688]
- Private P. Foster, Derbyshire Regiment, killed in action near Doorn River on 29 May 1901.[689]
- Trooper W. Finch, 85th Company Imperial Yeomanry, wounded in action at Dankbaarheid, Zand River (Doorn River) on 27 July 1901, "and afterwards shot", according to the inscription on his gravestone.[690]
- Private (or Rifleman) E. Hazlett, 60th Rifles (King's Royal Rifles), killed in action at Jas Kraal on 28 August 1901.[691]
- Captain D.E. Provis Wickham (44), Imperial Yeomanry (Rough Riders), killed in action at Mooifontein, Doorn River on 16 October 1901.[692]
- The graves of Lance-Corporal T. (or J.) O'Connor and of Second Lieutenant C.E.P. Wallis (22), both of the 2nd Royal Dublin Fusiliers, killed in action at Jas Kraal on 28 August 1901 are also here.[693]
- Memorial (vandalised) to Trooper D.S. Mowat (or Mowatt), Trooper H. Warn and Trooper J.T. Turnbull, all Imperial Yeomanry (Rough Riders), killed in action at Doorn River, near Richelieu/Palmietfontein, on 10 (or 16) October 1901.[694]

After the failure of the first hunt for De Wet, the British launched another series of intensive drives to capture this elusive Orange Free State commander. None of the attempts to drive De Wet back to the fences between the blockhouses succeeded. However, he had some narrow escapes – none more so than his escape at Doornkraal, near Bothaville in the north-western Orange Free State, when he and his burghers were surprised at daybreak on 6 November 1900 by a British force led by Colonel Philip Le Gallais. The Boer losses numbered 17 burghers killed and 114 taken prisoner, of whom 17 were wounded. The British casualties numbered 34, of whom some, including the valiant Le Gallais, were killed or died of wounds.[695]

P4.3.17 De Wet's escape at Doornkraal is commemorated on this memorial.

P4.3.15

P4.3.16

P4.3.17

---

686 Watt 2000, 216 & 257.
687 According to Watt (2000, 449), he died of his wounds.
688 Watt 2000, 104 & 429.
689 Watt 2000, 143.
690 Watt (2000, 136) writes that he was wounded and later shot while he was a prisoner of war.
691 Watt 2000, 187.
692 Watt 2000, 450.
693 Watt 2000, 313 & 434.
694 Watt 2000, 300, 423 & 437.
695 Amery V 1907, 15-21; Pieterse 1946, 127-129; De Wet 1999, 178-179; Pretorius 2010, 54.

▶ *4 km southwest of Bothaville, Free State, southern side of the R59 leading to Hoopstad.*
◙ *S27° 27.485, E26° 34.641 (Google Maps).*

P4.3.18 Grave of Colonel P.W.J. Le Gallais, 8th Hussars, commanding mounted troops of Lieutenant-General Sir Archibald Hunter's force, killed in action at Doornkraal on 6 November 1900.[696]
▶ *British Garden of Remembrance, old town cemetery, eastern side of the R30, between President St & Greyling St, Bothaville, Free State.*
This Garden of Remembrance also contains graves of other members of the British forces who fell in the engagement of 6 November 1900, including Captain F.J. Engelbach (33), "The Buffs" (Royal East Kent Regiment), Captain N.C. Welch (35), Hampshire Regiment, and Lieutenant W.A.G. Williams (27), 2nd Battalion South Wales Borderers.[697]
◙ *S27° 23.722, E26° 37.183.*

P4.3.19 Grave of Private J.G. Irvine, 2nd Battalion Seaforth Highlanders, killed in action at Nordhulp on 7 November 1900.[698]
▶ *Municipal cemetery, on the outskirts of the town, near Letta St, south of corner with President Brand St, Reddersburg, Free State.*
◙ *S29° 39.463, E26° 10.210.*

Despite De Wet's setback at Bothaville, his ability to outwit the British forces made him famous in Europe, where he was depicted as a hero in numerous newspapers. He continued to harass the British whenever he spotted an opportunity. On 16 November 1900, his burghers engaged with British troops near Thaba Nchu. The objective was to draw attention away from his main force of more than 1 500 burghers, who broke through the British blockhouse line at Sprinkaansnek later the same day.[699]

P4.3.20 Bedfordshire Regiment memorial in honour of Second Lieutenant L. Paxton (19), killed in action at Eden, near Thaba Nchu, 16 November 1900,[700] *as well as one non-commissioned officer and 16 men who were killed or died of disease at Thaba Nchu from September 1900 to April 1901.*
▶ *British Garden of Remembrance, old town cemetery, southern side of Massyn St, Thaba Nchu, Free State. Paxton's grave is also in this cemetery.*
◙ *S29° 13.219, E26° 50.945.*

P4.3.21 Sprinkaansnek (photo courtesy of A. van Dyk)
▶ *South of the N8, 13 m south-east of Thaba Nchu.*
◙ *S29° 17, E26° 57.*

P4.3.18

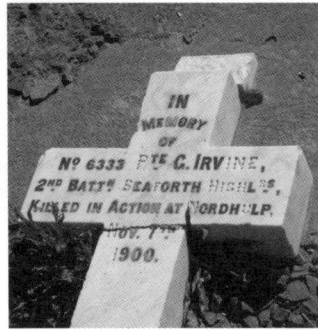
P4.3.19

P4.3.20

P4.3.21

---

696   Watt 2000, 244.
697   Watt 2000, 128, 443 & 455.
698   Watt 2000, 213.
699   De Wet 1999, 181-182; Cloete 2010, 211.
700   Watt 2000, 325.

P4.3.22 Grave Lieutenant A.M. Southey (28), 2nd Battalion Scots Guards, killed in action at Kranzfontein (Tigerskloof?), near Bethlehem on 22 November 1900.[701]
▶ *Old town cemetery, between Muller St & Boshoff St, near corner with Baxter St, Bethlehem, Free State.*
◉ *S28° 14.026, E28° 18.036.*

On 23 November 1900, General de Wet defeated the British forces occupying the Orange Free State town of Dewetsdorp, named after his father, but he was forced to abandon the town two days later.[702]

There is a British military cemetery on the north-eastern outskirts of Dewetsdorp (near S29° 34.619, E26° 40.136) and also a small British cemetery on Gloucester Hill on the north-western outskirts of Dewetsdorp (near S29° 34.968, E26° 39.521).[703]

P4.3.23 Grave of Sergeant A.E. Dearle (22), Imperial Yeomanry, who died on 1 December 1900 of wounds received in action on 30 November 1900 at Vrolykheid.[704]
▶ *Municipal cemetery, Piet Retief St, Ladybrand, Free State, at the entrance of the town from the R26.*
◉ *S29° 12.025, E27° 27.985.*

P4.3.24 Grave of a burgher, Joachim Potgieter, who died in January 1901 of wounds received in December 1900 near Rouxville in the south-eastern Orange Free State.
▶ *Directly behind the burgher monument on the grounds of the Dutch Reformed Church, Church St, Rouxville, Free State.*
◉ *Near S30° 24.995, E26° 50.088.*

The grave of a burgher, A.J. Coetzee, killed in action at Clocolan on 22 December 1900, is in the municipal cemetery in Reddersburg.
▶ *Municipal cemetery, on the outskirts of the town, near Letta St, south of the corner with President Brand St, Reddersburg, Free State.*
◉ *S29° 39.463, E26° 10.210. –*

P4.3.25 Grave of Lieutenant Basil Napier (21), Imperial Yeomanry, who died on 28 December 1900 of wounds received in action at Senekal the day before.[705]
▶ *Municipal cemetery, Senekal, Free State.*
◉ *S28° 18.778, E27° 37.287.*

There was a skirmish at Kromspruit on 3 January 1901, 25 km west of Reitz – about 60 burghers led by General Philip Botha attacked a patrol of 150 soldiers of the elite Commander-in-Chief's Bodyguard, commanded by Lieutenant-

P4.3.22   P4.3.23   P4.3.24   P4.3.25

701 Watt 2000, 392.
702 De Wet 1999, 182-186.
703 Oosthuizen ca 2000, 34.
704 Watt 2000, 108.
705 Watt 2000, 305.

Colonel D.T. Laing. Fierce fighting followed. Only one burgher fell, but British losses amounted to at least three officers and 21 men killed in action or died of wounds, and 20 men were wounded.[706]

Some of the British casualties were initially buried on the farm Frederiksdal, but they were reinterred in the British Garden of Remembrance in the old town cemetery in Reitz in the 1960s.[707] The names of 16 men of the Bodyguard who were killed in action or died of wounds appear on the main British memorial in that cemetery (see P7.4.5.27). Laing himself was buried at Heilbron, where his name is inscribed on the main British memorial, together with that of two other officers and four men who died in this engagement (see P7.4.5.16).

P4.3.26 Grave of Trooper S.W. Squire (37), volunteer in the Commander-in-Chief's bodyguard, who died on 24 February 1901 of enteric disease in Kroonstad Hospital after being severely wounded near Lindley on 3 January 1901.[708]
▶ British Garden of Remembrance, western side of Noord Rd, Kroonstad, Free State.
◉ S27° 39.049, E27° 13.816.

The British forces launched their Third Hunt (also called the "Great Hunt") for De Wet in the Orange Free State towards the end of January 1901. On 29 January Major-General C.E. Knox and Colonel T.D. Pilcher attacked De Wet's burghers at Tabaksberg and drove them south towards Verkeerdevlei, where they dug in and even launched a successful counter-attack after dark. The British casualties in this encounter numbered more than 40, compared to the burghers' four.[709]

P4.3.27 Grave of Lieutenant A.S. Way (24), 2nd Battalion Durham Light Infantry, killed in action at Tabaksberg on 29 January 1901.[710]
▶ Municipal cemetery, Brandfort, south-western c/o Marais St & Wes St.
◉ S28° 42.304, E26° 27.205.

De Wet subsequently made a second attempt to invade the Cape Colony. The British forces tried to block his advance, but he eventually managed to cross the Orange River into the Cape in February 1901, where several Cape Rebels joined his commandos. However, the Republicans were soon scattered by the pursuing British forces, and De Wet himself was forced to retreat to the Orange Free State again after suffering casualties. This invasion failed to produce significant results for the Republican cause in the short term.[711]

The mass grave of A.J. Roux, M.J.A. Slabbert, D.J.L. Hattingh and A.J. Snyman, who were killed in skirmishes between 13 and 27 February 1901 during this invasion, is in the municipal cemetery, Philipstown, Northern Cape. W.M. Wentworth, who was killed in action on 17 December 1900, is also commemorated on the tall gravestone, which serves as a memorial erected by the public of Philipstown for all the burghers who fell during the war (see P7.2.9.4).

P4.3.26

P4.3.27

P4.3.28

---

706   Amery V 1907, 131; Lourens & Lourens 2002, 39-42; Cloete 2010, 227.
707   Lourens & Lourens 2002, 42.
708   Watt 2000, 395.
709   Amery V 1907, 133; De Wet 1999, 205-206.
710   Watt (2000, 441) gives his date of death as 28 January 1901.
711   Amery V 1907, 138-152; De Wet 1999, 208-223.

Part 4 – The guerrilla phase of the war (11 October 1900–31 May 1902)

On 6 March 1901, one of the most able and respected generals of the Orange Free State, Philip Botha, was killed in a skirmish with British forces at Doornberg in the Ventersburg district. He was the elder brother of Commandant-General Louis Botha.[712]

P4.3.28 Grave of P.R. Botha on his farm in the Vrede district (photo courtesy of A. van Dyk).
◉ GPS co-ordinates not available.

P4.3.29 Grave of Trooper A.W.L. Wookey, 5th New Zealand Imperial Regiment, killed in action near Doornbult on 27 March 1901. According to Watt, he was killed by Boers while escaping.[713] The grave of Trooper T.H. Philpott (22), 5th New Zealand Imperial Regiment, killed in action near Kameelfontein on 28 March 1901,[714] is in the same British Garden of Remembrance.
▶ *Municipal Cemetery, Boshof, Free State.*
◉ *South-eastern side of the town, near S28° 32.530, E25° 14.708.*

P4.3.30 Cairn built on the farm Oudefontein in the southern Free State to commemorate two Cape Rebels, Ben Krüger and Jan Harm Coetzer. They drowned on 2 April 1901 on Oudefontein when their Cape Rebel commando, led by Commandant van Reenen, clashed with British forces.[715]
▶ *Northern end of Voortrekker St, Bethulie, Free State. The cairn was moved to this site when the Gariep Dam was built.*
◉ *Near S30° 29.599, E25° 58.519.*

P4.3.31 Grave of Lieutenant J.R. Key (22), 2nd East York Regiment (Mounted Infantry), who died on 4 April 1901 of wounds received in action near Thaba Nchu the previous day.[716]
▶ *British Garden of Remembrance, old town cemetery, southern side of Massyn St, Thaba Nchu, Free State.*
◉ *S29° 13.219, E26° 50.945.*

P4.3.32 Grave of Second Lieutenant A.R.A. Macdonald (20), 9th Lancers, killed in action at Vaalkop near Edenburg on 17 April 1901.[717]
▶ *Municipal cemetery, near Boven Kerk St, Edenburg, Free State.*
◉ *S29° 44.222, E25° 56.523.*

P4.3.33 Grave of Private S.F. Brown, Thorneycroft's Mounted Infantry, killed in action near Winburg on 24 April 1901.[718]
▶ *Municipal cemetery, Senekal, Free State.*
◉ *S28° 18.778, E27° 37.287.*

P4.3.29 P4.3.30 P4.3.31 P4.3.32

---

712 Amery V 1907, 234; Van Zyl 1944, 223.
713 Watt 2000, 463.
714 Watt 2000, 331.
715 Shearing & Shearing 2011a, 2011b, 2011c.
716 Watt 2000, 233.
717 Watt 2000, 258.
718 Watt 2000, 50.

P4.3.34 Grave of Private F.A.L. (or E.A.L.) Johnson, Imperial Yeomanry, killed in action at Villiersrust near Bethlehem on 24 April 1901.[719]
▶ *Old town cemetery, between Muller St & Boshoff St, near corner with Baxter St, Bethlehem, Free State.*
◉ *S28° 14.026, E28° 18.036.*

P4.3.35 Grave of Private Alfred S. Phillips, Thorneycroft's Mounted Infantry, who died on 26 April 1901 of wounds received in action near Winburg on 24 April 1901.[720]
▶ *British Garden of Remembrance, cemetery 1.3 km west of Voortrekker St, Winburg, Free State.*
◉ *S28° 31.134, E27° 00.003.*

P4.3.36 Grave of Quartermaster-Sergeant O.F. Schumann, South Australia Contingent, killed in action at Venterspruit (Tafelkop) near Frankfort on 6 May 1901.[721]
▶ *Old town cemetery, Frankfort, Free State, next to the R34/26, on the eastern side of the town.*
◉ *S27° 17.287, E28° 29.505.*

On 15 May 1901, Colonel W. Williams became involved in a skirmish on the farm Metz, in the Fauresmith District, which resulted in the death of two members of the South African Light Horse.[722]

P4.3.37 Grave of Second Lieutenant J. Alexander (20), South African Light Horse, killed in action at Metz Farm, 15 May 1901.[723]
▶ *Reichardt Park cemetery, south-west of the corner of Jacobs St & Fontein St, Fauresmith, Free State. This cemetery also contains the grave of Trooper Gibbons, South African Light Horse, who died on 15 May 1901 (probably also killed in action at Metz Farm).[724]*
◉ *S29° 45.093, E25° 18.763.*

On 17 May 1901, Republican forces managed to derail a British armoured train near the Amerika Siding in the Orange Free State.[725]

P4.3.38 Grave of Major E.K. Heath (38), 3rd Battalion South Lancashire Regiment, who was killed by the explosion of a mine near Amerika Siding, north-east of Kroonstad on 17 May 1901, while in command of an armoured train.[726]
▶ *British Garden of Remembrance, western side of Noord Rd, Kroonstad, Free State.*
◉ *S27° 39.049, E27° 13.816.*

P4.3.33

P4.3.34

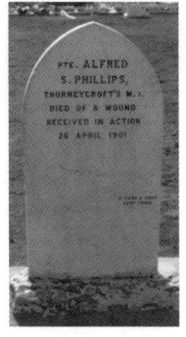
P4.3.35

P4.3.36

P4.3.37

719	Watt 2000, 220.
720	Watt 2000, 331.
721	Watt 2000, 370.
722	Cloete 2010, 260.
723	Watt 2000, 4.
724	Gibbons is not mentioned in Watt, 2000.
725	Cloete 2010, 260.
726	Watt 2000, 187.

Part 4 – The guerrilla phase of the war (11 October 1900–31 May 1902)

4.3.39 Gravestone of Lance-Corporal J. Mahood, 5th Battalion Royal Irish Rifles, who died of wounds received in action at Leeuwspruit on 17 May 1901.[727]
▶ *British Renoster River Memorial. Signposted on the R82 south of Koppies, Free State. Turn south and drive south along a gravel road to the east of the railway line.*
◉ *S27° 15.717, E27° 32.795.*

P4.3.40 Grave of Private R.A. Winn, 9th Lancers, killed in action at Ospoort, near Edenburg on 27 May 1901.[728]
▶ *Municipal cemetery, near Boven Kerk St, Edenburg, Free State.*
◉ *S29° 44.222, E25° 56.523.*

P4.3.41 Burgher grave, Jan David Ungerer, wounded at Soutpan on 1 June 1901, who died of his wounds at Bultfontein on 5 June 1901.
▶ *Old town cemetery, Stofberg St, between Cilliers St & Dicken St, Bultfontein, Free State.*
◉ *S28° 17.221, E26° 08.989.*

P4.3.42 Tombstone for an American who fought on the British side.[729] The inscription reads: "G.D. Toovey, Trooper D.F.H. late of Pattison, New Jersey, USA, killed in action at Blaauwbank, 3rd June 1901. Aged 22 years. R.I.P. Erected by his comrades."
▶ *British Garden of Remembrance, municipal cemetery, De Villiers St, Jacobsdal, Free State.*
◉ *S29° 08.091, E24° 46.510.*

P4.3.43 Grave of Captain (or Major) C.W. Hulse (40), 4th Regiment Imperial Yeomanry, killed in action at Braklaagte near Vrede on 4 June 1901.[730]
▶ *British Garden of Remembrance, municipal cemetery, Van Niekerk St, Vrede, Free State.*
◉ *S27° 25.665, E29° 10.124.*

On 6 June 1901, at Graspan near Reitz in the eastern Orange Free State, a British force of about 600 men captured a Boer women's laager, consisting of about 120 wagons and carts, and protected by about 100 elderly men. Reverend J.D. Kestell, who was at the laager at the time, was also taken captive. Upon hearing the news, General Christiaan de Wet immediately sent 200 burghers under General Piet Fourie and Commandant Davel to their aid. When the burghers attacked the British force, the British soldiers retired under cover of the wagons. In an engagement that lasted for more than four hours, the Boers managed to recapture the wagons and to free Kestell, but soon afterwards British reinforcements arrived, and the laager was retaken. The British forces suffered 26 killed and 25 wounded, and the burghers 17 killed and 20 wounded.[731]

 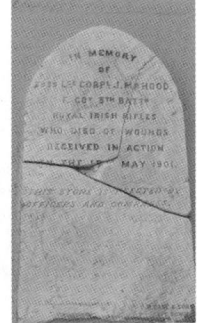    

P4.3.38   P4.3.39   P4.3.40   P4.3.41   P4.3.42   P4.3.43

---

727 Watt 2000, 262.
728 Watt 2000, 459.
729 Watt 2000, 419.
730 Watt 2000, 208.
731 Kestell ca 1903, 144-149; De Wet 1999, 233-235.

P4.3.44 Graspan Burgher Monument, erected by the Graspan Day of the Vow Committee.
▶ *Recently moved from the actual battlefield to the grounds of the Dutch Reformed Church, Church St, c/o Noord St, Reitz, Free State.*
◉ *S27° 48.255, E28° 25.803.*

P4.3.45 Graspan Burgher Monument. It contains the names of 16 burghers who fell in this battle.[732]
▶ *Old town cemetery, c/o Pan St & Zuider St, Reitz, Free State.*
◉ *S27° 47.782, E28° 26.007.*

4.3.46 Grave of Lieutenant C.P. Strong, Bedfordshire Regiment, killed in action at Graspan on 6 June 1901.[733]
▶ *British Garden of Remembrance, old town cemetery, c/o Pan St & Zuider St, Reitz, Free State. There are two memorials to British soldiers who fell in this battle in the same cemetery.*
◉ *S27° 47.782, E28° 26.007.*

The grave of the burgher J.J.H. Coetzee, killed in action at Ongelukskop on 16 June 1901, is in the municipal cemetery in Reddersburg – see gravestone of J.J. du Plessis, who died on 29 April 1900 (see P3.6.18).

P4.3.47 Grave of Lieutenant H.R. Hamilton, South African Constabulary, who died on 30 June 1901 of wounds received at Erasmushoop, near Petrusburg, the day before.[734]
▶ *Municipal cemetery, Petrusburg, Free State.*
◉ *About 50 m south of S29° 07.196, E25° 25.153.*

Nearly the whole Orange Free State government was captured at Reitz on 11 July 1901. President Steyn was fortunate - he managed to escape because he got warning of the attack, and was assisted by his *agterryer*, Ruiter[735] [see Section 5.1].

P4.3.48 Memorial to commemorate Steyn's escape.
▶ *C/o President C.R. Swart St & 1st Street, opposite the Post Office in Reitz, Free State.*
◉ *S27° 48.024, E28° 25.764.*

On 12 July, a number of Orange Free State burghers attacked an Imperial Yeomanry patrol at Braklaagte, about 14 km west of Vrede in the north-eastern Orange Free State. Some of the British soldiers fell in action, but others surrendered. As the burghers approached one of the wounded soldiers, the soldier grabbed his rifle and mortally wounded one of the Republican officers.[736]

P4.3.44

P4.3.45

P4.3.46

P4.3.47

P4.3.48

---

732 Van der Bank 1995, 60-61.
733 Watt 2000, 402.
734 Watt 2000, 176.
735 Labuschagne 1999, 79-86; Van Schoor 2009, 215-218.
736 Cloete 2010, 277.

P4.3.49 Grave of Captain Salomon Charles (Charlie) Botha (21), killed in action on 12 July 1901. He was a son of General P.R. Botha.
▶ *Next to the grave of General P.R. Botha on the General's farm in the Vrede district, Free State.*
◉ *GPS co-ordinates not available.*

P4.3.50 Grave of Hendrik C. Weideman (24), a burgher killed in action at Luckhoff on 15 July 1901.
▶ *Municipal cemetery, c/o Rabie St & Lombaard St, Luckhoff, Free State.*
◉ *S29° 44.969, E24° 46.945.*

The British military authorities executed a number of burghers whom they had taken prisoner and accused of having committed foul deeds, such as firing on soldiers under cover of a white flag, wearing British uniforms or using illegal types of bullets, such as dum-dum bullets.

P4.3.51 Grave of Gideon Christoffel Lourens (25), executed on 9 August 1901 by a British firing squad on the farm Maquatlingsnek. It could not be established what the accusations against him were. The names of 11 young burghers, or "penkoppe" as they were known, in his group also appear on the gravestone. Reinterred in Clocolan in 1976.
▶ *Municipal cemetery, south-west of the c/o Piet Retief St & 6th Ave, Clocolan, Free State.*
◉ *S28° 55.289, E29° 33.682.*

P4.3.52 Grave of Lieutenant R. Drysdale (25), 1st Battalion Royal Scots, killed in action at Slabberts Nek near Bethlehem on 31 August 1901.[737]
▶ *Old town cemetery, between Muller St & Boshoff St, near corner with Baxter St, Bethlehem, Free State.*
◉ *S28° 14.026, E28° 18.036.*

P4.3.53 Grave of Trooper G. Bremer, Imperial Light Horse, killed in action at Concordia near Bethlehem on 7 September 1901.[738]
▶ *Old town cemetery, between Muller St & Boshoff St, near corner with Baxter St, Bethlehem, Free State.*
◉ *S28° 14.026, E28° 18.036.*

P4.3.54 Grave of Corporal F. Connell, Imperial Light Horse, killed in action at Roodepoort near Bethlehem on 9 September 1901.[739]
▶ *Old town cemetery, between Muller St & Boshoff St, near corner with Baxter St, Bethlehem, Free State.*
◉ *S28° 14.026, E28° 18.036.*

On 19 September 1901, a force of 160 mounted infantry men and 30 men of the South African Constabulary were sent with two field guns from the Boesmanskop-Sannaspos blockhouse line to attack and take a Boer laager on the

P4.3.49

P4.3.50

P4.3.51

P4.3.52

P4.3.53

---

737   Watt 2000, 119.
738   Watt 2000, 44.
739   Watt 2000, 84.

farm Vlakfontein, 25 km south of Sannaspos. This British force was attacked by the burghers of General George Brand and Commandant J.R. Ackermann on the neighbouring farm Slangfontein and forced to surrender. The Boers captured the two guns and other war supplies. The British lost one officer and eight men killed, and the Boers lost one burgher killed.[740]

The name of H.A. Snyman, the burgher who was killed in action, appears on the burgher monument at the Gereformeerde Kerk in Reddersburg, Free State (see also P7.2.5.22).

The graves of Lieutenant F.M. Otter-Barry (25) and Sergeant A.E.G.N. Talbot, both of the Royal Horse Artillery, and the six soldiers who fell in this engagement at Vlakfontein.[741]
▶ *British military cemetery, north-eastern outskirts of Dewetsdorp, Free State.*
◉ *Near S29° 34.619, E26° 40.136.*

P4.3.55 Grave of Sergeant E. Thompson, South African Constabulary, who died on 25 September 1901 of wounds received in action at Oorlandspoort the day before.[742]
▶ *Municipal cemetery, Petrusburg, Free State.*
◉ *About 50 m south of S29° 07.196, E25° 25.153.*

On 28 September 1901, Colonel Lowry Cole and his men managed to surround a Boer commando near Wepener and to capture Commandant T.F.J. Dreyer and nine burghers.[743] In the fighting, at least one British officer fell.

P4.3.56 Gravestone of Lieutenant J.E. MacKay (22), King's Own Regiment, attached to 16th Battalion Mounted Infantry, killed in action at Rustmynziel near Wepener on 29 September 1901,[744] probably in this engagement.
▶ *Robertson Church and Cemetery, Wepener, Free State.*
◉ *S29° 42.398, E26° 58.416 (Courtesy of the Genealogical Society of South Africa).*

P4.3.57 Grave of Trooper M. O'Shea (22), Imperial Light Horse, killed in action at Tigers Kloof (Tygerkloof) near Bethlehem on 28 September 1901.[745]
▶ *Old town cemetery, between Muller St & Boshoff St, near corner with Baxter St, Bethlehem, Free State.*
◉ *S28° 14.026, E28° 18.036.*

P4.3.58 Grave of Sergeant R. Swaffield (28), 2nd Battalion Dorsetshire Regiment, killed in action at Karee on 3 October 1901.[746]
▶ *Municipal cemetery, south-western c/o Marais St & Wes St, Brandfort, Free State.*
◉ *S28° 42.304, E26° 27.205.*

P4.3.54   P4.3.55   P4.3.56   P4.3.57

---

740   Van der Bank 2001, 82.
741   Watt 2000, 318 & 407.
742   Watt 2000, 414.
743   Cloete 2010, 300.
744   Watt 2000, 259.
745   Watt 2000, 318.
746   Watt 2000, 405.

Part 4 – The guerrilla phase of the war (11 October 1900–31 May 1902)

P4.3.59 Grave of Trooper J.W. Townsend (45), Imperial Light Horse, killed in action at Nauwpoort Nek near Bethlehem on 7 October 1901.[747]
▶ *Old town cemetery, between Muller St & Boshoff St, near corner with Baxter St, Bethlehem, Free State.*
◉ *S28° 14.026, E28° 18.036.*

P4.3.60 Grave of Trooper H. Abercrombie (35), Imperial Light Horse, who died on 25 October 1901 of wounds received in action at Paardeplaatz, near Bethlehem.[748]
▶ *Old town cemetery, between Muller St & Boshoff St, near corner with Baxter St, Bethlehem, Free State.*
◉ *S28° 14.026, E28° 18.036.*

P4.3.61 Grave of Trooper C. Hooper, Imperial Light Horse, killed in action at Vischgat near Bethlehem on 11 November 1901.[749]
▶ *Old cemetery, between Muller St & Boshoff St, near corner with Baxter St, Bethlehem, Free State.*
◉ *S28° 14.026, E28° 18.036.*

P4.3.62 Grave of Lieutenant N.B. Fellowes (27), 2nd West India Regiment, attached to 16th Battalion Mounted Infantry, killed in action at Roodepoort near Wepener on 17 November 1901.[750]
▶ *Robertson church and cemetery, Wepener, Free State. The grave of Private J. Tierney, Manchester Regiment, killed in action in the same engagement, is also in this cemetery.[751]*
◉ *S29° 42.398, E26° 58.416 (Courtesy of the Genealogical Society of South Africa).*

P4.3.63 Burgher grave of Daniel Johannes Bloem, who died of wounds on 7 December 1901. It is not clear when Bloem was wounded.
▶ *Old town cemetery, Stofberg St, between Cilliers St & Dicken St, Bultfontein, Free State.*
◉ *S28° 17.221, E26° 08.989.*

One of the most respected Free State Republican officers, Commandant S.F. (Sarel) Haasbroek, was killed in a skirmish on the farm Bethal in the Senekal district on 16 December 1901.[752]

P4.3.64 Memorial for Commandant Haasbroek on the battlefield at Biddulphsberg.
▶ *On a farm near the S675, Libertas, northeast of Senekal, Free State, between the S1226 and the S200 (ask for directions at the farmhouse).*
◉ *S28° 16.234, E27° 46.375.*

Haasbroek was buried on his farm near Winburg.

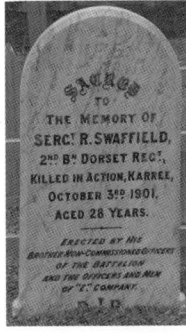
P4.3.58

P4.3.59

P4.3.60

P4.3.61

---

747 Watt 2000, 420.
748 Watt 2000, 1.
749 Watt 2000, 201.
750 Watt 2000, 134.
751 Watt 2000, 417.
752 Van Zyl 1944, 243; Haasbroek 1977, 373-374.

P4.3.62   P4.3.63   P4.3.64   P4.3.65   P4.3.66

P4.3.65 On the same day, 16 December 1901, Private Levi J. James of the Cape Town Highlanders was accidentally shot at Honeynestkloof near Jacobsdal.[753]
▶ *British Garden of Remembrance, municipal cemetery, De Villiers St, Jacobsdal, Free State.*
◉ *S29° 08.091, E24° 46.510.*

On 20 December 1901, General Wessel Wessels and his 300 burghers attacked a British force at Tafelkop near Frankfort. The burghers captured two field guns, but since all the artillery horses had been shot, they could not move the guns from the battlefield. Wessels eventually retreated when help arrived for the British forces. Republican casualties amounted to five burghers killed and 15 wounded. The British lost 33 killed and 45 wounded.[754]

P4.3.66 Grave of Captain C.L. Gaussen (32), 91st Imperial Yeomanry, killed in action at Tafelkop near Frankfort on 20 December 1901.[755]
▶ *British Garden of Remembrance, old town cemetery, Frankfort, Free State, next to the R34/26 on the eastern side of the town. The graves of Lieutenant W.J. Shand (23), Cameron Highlanders[756] and Trooper G.F. Melville, Damant's Horse,[757] who fell in the same engagement, are also in this garden of remembrance.*
◉ *S27° 17.287, E28° 29.505.*

P4.3.67 Grave of Captain R.M. Dowie (32), 3rd Battalion Suffolk Regiment Mounted Infantry, who died on 20 December 1901 of wounds received in action at Vredefort Rd near Kroonstad on 20 December 1901.[758]
▶ *British Garden of Remembrance, western side of Noord Rd, Kroonstad, Free State.*
◉ *S27° 39.049, E27° 13.816.*

P4.3.67   P4.3.68   P4.3.69   P4.3.70

---

753   Watt 2000, 216.
754   Amery V 1907, 424-427; Cloete 2010, 320.
755   Watt 2000, 152.
756   Watt 2000, 374.
757   Watt 2000, 286.
758   Watt 2000, 117.

Part 4 – The guerrilla phase of the war (11 October 1900–31 May 1902)

On Christmas Day 1901, De Wet achieved his last major success before the war ended. At daybreak, his approximately 500 burghers, including the Bethlehem commando under General Michael Prinsloo, attacked an isolated force of 470 men under Major F.A. Williams, stationed on the summit of Groenkop, a low hill near Bethlehem in the eastern Orange Free State. The soldiers did not expect anyone to climb the sharply rising western slope of the hill on which the camp was situated, so they were taken completely by surprise. Total confusion broke out among the defenders when Williams was killed. The British camp was in Boer hands before sunrise. Casualties on both sides were relatively high: 58 British soldiers killed and 84 wounded, on the Boer side, 14 killed and 30 wounded. The Boers captured a number of field guns, 500 horses and mules and vast quantities of supplies – items of great value to the burghers' continued war effort.[759]

P4.3.68 Boer memorial (vandalised) and P4.3.69 British memorial on the summit of Groenkop.
▶ *From Kestell, Free State, drive about 6.5 km west on the N5 (towards Bethlehem). Then turn north on a gravel road and drive 5 km to a farmhouse on the slope of the low hill west of this road. Request permission to visit the battlefield there. (See also CP17 on p. 135).*
◉ *S28° 14.189, E28° 39.500. (Google Maps).*

P4.3.70 Memorial erected by the officers and men of "B" Company 2nd Royal Irish Rifles, in memory of Private D. (or J.) Marshall, Sergeant G. Atkins and Private J. Nelis, killed in action at Vlaakplaat's (Vlakplaats) on 30 December 1901.[760]
▶ *British Garden of Remembrance, old town cemetery, southern side of Massyn St, Thaba Nchu, Free State.*
◉ *S29° 13.219, E26° 50.945.*

P4.3.71 Grave of Sergeant J.C. Hill (20), Thorneycroft's Mounted Infantry, who died on 21 January 1902 of wounds received in action at Witnek near Ficksburg the day before.[761]
▶ *Old town cemetery, Ficksburg, Free State. Entrance from Veld St, near corner with Piet Retief St.*
◉ *S28° 52.027, E27° 52.637.*

On 28 January 1902, General Charles Nieuwoudt and Commandant H.P.J. Pretorius launched a counter-attack on British forces pursuing them at Kalkfontein near Koffiefontein. Colonel L.E. Du Moulin and at least 10 soldiers were killed and six wounded. The Boers suffered no casualties.[762]

P4.3.72 Memorial for Colonel Du Moulin and soldiers of the Royal Sussex Regiment and British graves.[763]
▶ *Near the Kalkfontein Dam in the Riet River. Turn north from the tarred road between Koffiefontein and Fauresmith, Free State, about 21 km south-east of Koffiefontein, onto a gravel road leading north. The memorial is on the side of a low hill about 100 m west of this road.*
◉ *S29° 30.399, E25° 13.021.*

P4.3.71

P4.3.72   P4.3.73

---

759   Pretorius 2010, 170.
760   Watt 2000, 12, 266 & 306.
761   Watt 2000, 194.
762   Creswicke VII ca 1902, 182-183; Cloete 2010, 332.
763   Watt 2000, 119.

P4.3.73 Grave of Lieutenant B.H.E. Davies, 3rd Battalion Wiltshire Regiment, killed in action at Blesbokfontein near Lindley on 4 or 5 February 1902.[764]
▶ *British Garden of Remembrance, municipal cemetery, near the S192, between Diemont Street and the S904, Lindley, Free State.*
◉ *S27° 52.891, E27° 55.763.*

On 6 February 1902, Kitchener's "new model drive" was launched in the north-eastern Orange Free State in a desperate attempt to capture De Wet. A total of about 17 000 soldiers, supported by seven armoured trains, set their sights on cornering the Orange Free State forces against the blockhouse lines. However, De Wet slipped through the net on 7 February 1902. The British forces claimed to have killed, wounded or taken prisoner 286 Republicans, but some of those were boys and elderly men. It is not known how many were actually fighting burghers.[765]

P4.3.74 Grave of N.F. Bester, a burgher killed in action at Katkop on 7 February 1902.
▶ *Municipal cemetery, north of c/o Lang Markt St (the R57) & President St, Heilbron, Free State.*
◉ *S27° 16.756, E27° 58.174 (Google Maps).*

P4.3.75 Gravestone of Trooper J. Flanegan, Imperial Light Horse, who died on 8 April 1902 of wounds received in action at Katkop near Heilbron in the Orange Free State on 7 February 1902.[766] He was wounded in the attempt to capture De Wet.
▶ *British Garden of Remembrance, western side of Station Rd, near the northern limit of the town, Colesberg, Northern Cape.*
◉ *S30° 42.730, E25° 06.086 (Google Maps).*

On 13 February 1902, the "new model drive" against General De Wet resumed in the Orange Free State, with British units forming a line from Kroonstad in the north to Doornberg, south-east of Ventersburg, in the south, advancing eastwards towards Lindley in a solid phalanx.[767]

P4.3.76 Gravestone of Corporal W. Hobson and Privates J. Tranter, W. Moss, W. (or A.) Saunders and J. Tobin, all of the Worcestershire Regiment (17th Mounted Infantry), killed in action at Spytfontein near Doornberg on 14 February 1902.[768]
▶ *Grave on the farm Perseverance near Ventersburg, Free State.*
◉ *GPS co-ordinates not available.*

On 23 February 1902, General de Wet broke through a cordon of 30 000 British soldiers that had surrounded him and President Steyn, as well as a number of commandos, totalling about 1 000 burghers in the north-eastern Orange Free State by charging through a line of New Zealanders at Langverwacht (also known as Kalkkrans). Both De Wet

P4.3.74

P4.3.75

P4.3.76

P4.3.77

---

764 Watt 2000, 103.
765 Cloete 2010, 335-336.
766 Watt 2000, 138.
767 Cloete 2010, 337.
768 Watt (2000, 197, 299, 368, 418 & 420) writes that they were all killed in action on 8 February 1902.

and Steyn managed to escape unscathed, but in the process, they lost 400 burghers, who were taken prisoner by the British.[769]

P4.3.77 Monument for the New Zealanders who fell in this encounter on 23 February 1902. A total of 23 were killed in action and 49 were wounded.
▶ *At Kalkkrans, north of the Cornelis River, south of Bothasberg, about half way between Vrede and Warden, Free State.*
◉ *GPS co-ordinates not available.*

P4.3.78 Grave of Trooper J. Bekker, Farmers' Guard, a joiner who died of his wounds near Bloemfontein on 23 February 1902. The grave of Trooper J.L. Cremer (or Creamer), Farmers' Guard, a joiner who also died of his wounds on 23 February 1902, is also in this cemetery.[770]
▶ *Memoriam Cemetery, General Brand St, Bloemfontein, Free State.*
◉ *S29° 08.840, E26° 12.409.*

P4.3.79 Grave of Trooper W.A. Rathbone (23), South African Constabulary, who was wounded near Bothaville on 23 February 1902 and died of his wounds two days later.[771]
▶ *British Garden of Remembrance, eastern side of the R30, between President St & Greyling St, Bothaville, Free State.*
◉ *S27° 23.722, E26° 37.183.*

P4.3.80 Grave of the burghers Jan A. Jacobs (18) and George F. Pretorius (18), killed in action near Parys on 3 March 1902.
▶ *New municipal cemetery (where they were reinterred in 1987), near c/o Pistorius St & Carl Preller St, Parys, Free State.*
◉ *S26° 55.764, E27° 27.204.*

P4.3.81 Gravestone of Captain G.V. Clarke (28) and Sergeant E. Hoskins, both of the 87th Battery, Royal Field Artillery, killed in action on 8 April 1902 (probably at Uitvlucht) near Vrede.[772]
▶ *British Garden of Remembrance, municipal cemetery, Van Niekerk St, Vrede, Free State.*
◉ *S27° 25.665, E29° 10.124.*

General C.C.J. Badenhorst's Boshof-Hoopstad commando successfully attacked a British patrol at the Hartenbosch farms west of Bultfontein on 8 April 1902. The British casualties included at least one officer and one private killed, and 90 men taken prisoner.[773]

P4.3.78

P4.3.79

P4.3.80

P4.3.81

769   Scholtz 2003, 302-309; Cloete 2010, 340.
770   Watt 2000, 27 & 94.
771   Watt 2000, 345.
772   Watt 2000, 76 & 203.
773   Amery V 1907, 556; Cloete 2010, 353.

P4.3.82 Grave of Private T. Mooney, Thorneycroft's Mounted Infantry, killed in action at Hartenbosch on 8 April 1902.[774]
▶ *Old town cemetery, Stofberg St, between Cilliers St & Dicken St, Bultfontein, Free State.*
◉ *S28° 17.221, E26° 08.989.*

On 10 April 1902, at Vaalboschpan, about 60 km from Hoopstad in the north-western Orange Free State, Lieutenant H.L. Low of the Royal Irish Fusiliers met some men whom he regarded as comrades-in-arms, but who were actually Boers dressed in khaki. When he realised his mistake, he refused to surrender and was shot.

P4.3.83 Grave of Lieutenant H.L. Low (27), Royal Irish Rifles, killed in action on 10 March 1902 at Vaalboschpan, Hoopstad district.[775]
▶ *West End Cemetery, c/o Green St & Reserve Rd, Kimberley, Northern Cape.*
◉ *S28° 44.078, E24° 44.170 (Google Maps).*

On 20 April 1902, a Republican commando drew mounted British troops into an ambush at Moolman's Spruit, near Ficksburg. The British casualties amounted to six men killed in action, 19 wounded and six missing. The only Republican casualty was the *penkop* Charlie van Aardt.[776]

P4.3.84 Grave of Private O. (or C.O.) Thomas (23), Imperial Yeomanry, killed in action at Moolman's Spruit near Ficksburg on 20 April 1902.[777] In the background is a memorial to officers, non-commissioned officers and men of the Imperial Yeomanry who were killed in action or died of wounds received at Moolman's Spruit on 20 April 1902.
▶ *Old town cemetery, Ficksburg, Free State. Entrance from Veld St, near corner with Piet Retief St. The grave of Trooper N. Lloyd (20), Shropshire Imperial Yeomanry, killed in action in the same engagement on 20 April 1902, is also in this cemetery.[778]*
◉ *S28° 52.027, E27° 52.637.*

On the very same day, the 94th Mounted Infantry Regiment surprised a Republican commando at Schotland West, near Kroonstad. Ten burghers were killed in action, none surrendered. On the British side, one officer was killed in action.[779]

P4.3.85 Grave of Second Lieutenant G.N. Shea, 1st Royal Munster Fusiliers, 9th Mounted Infantry, killed in action at Schotland West on 20 April 1902.[780]
▶ *British Garden of Remembrance, western side of Noord Rd, Kroonstad, Free State.*
◉ *S27° 39.049, E27° 13.816.*

P4.3.82   P4.3.83   P4.3.84   P4.3.85

774   Watt 2000, 294.
775   Watt 2000, 256.
776   Cloete 2010, 359. There is a photograph of Van Aardt in Direko, Changuion & Jacobs 2003, 97.
777   Watt 2000, 412.
778   Watt 2000, 252.
779   Cloete, 2010, 359.
780   Watt 2000, 376.

Part 4 – The guerrilla phase of the war (11 October 1900–31 May 1902)

One of the last encounters in the Orange Free State took place on 10 May 1902, when Major-General Bruce Hamilton's forces attacked burghers near Bultfontein, with limited success.[781]

> P4.3.86 Grave of Private R. Maclean (24), Royal Scots, killed in action near Bultfontein on 10 May 1902.[782]
> ▶ Old town cemetery, Stofberg St, between Cilliers St & Dicken St, Bultfontein, Free State.
> ◉ S28° 17.221, E26° 08.989.

4.4 The guerrilla war in the Cape Colony

To relieve British pressure on the two Republics and to force Lord Kitchener (who succeeded Roberts as supreme commander in South Africa on 29 November 1900), to spread his forces over as wide an area as possible, a number of Republican commandos invaded the Cape Colony. As a result of the Boer incursions into the Cape Colony, the British authorities not only placed the whole Colony under martial law, but had to station military units throughout an area of the Cape Colony larger than the two Republics together. Furthermore, town guards were established in almost all towns in the Colony.[783]

> *Other than scattered graves and the remains or ruins of a few fortifications, there are almost no physical signs of the large British military presence today.*

General J.B.M. Hertzog led an invading commando over the Orange River on 15 December 1900. He was accompanied by Commandant George Brand (a son of the late President Jan Brand) and Commandant Charles Nieuwoudt. On 18 December, when crossing the railway line at Houtkraal north of De Aar, they exchanged shots with British soldiers travelling on an armoured train.[784]

> P4.4.1 Gravestone of Civilian Stoker Frederick Miles Adams (18), Cape Government Railways,[785] who died on "20 Dec 1900 from the effects of a gunshot wound received while working the armoured train at Hout Kraal".
> ▶ British Garden of Remembrance, De Aar, Northern Cape. On the northern side of town, next to the R48 to Philipstown, between the old cemetery and the railway line.
> ◉ S30° 38.718, E24° 00.971.

Hertzog and his commando made deep inroads into the Cape Colony, briefly occupying various towns, including Philipstown, Britstown, Calvinia, Vanrhynsdorp and Clanwilliam.[786]

> P4.4.2 Hertzog used the old Trutro police station in Vanrhynsdorp (parts of which were already built -in 1751) as his headquarters when his burghers occupied the town. Towards the end of 1901, the building was also used by General Smuts as his headquarters when the Boers re-occupied Vanrhynsdorp.
> ◉ Near S31° 36.496, E18° 44.220.

P4.3.86

P4.4.1

P4.4.2

---

781 Cloete 2010, 363.
782 Watt 2000, 281.
783 Scheepers Strydom 1943, 90, 124-131.
784 Neser 1988, 57; Cloete 2000, 207.
785 Watt 2000, 2.
786 Van Zyl 1944, 211; Van der Bank 2001, 29-30.

Early in January 1901, a detachment of 26 men under Commandant Nieuwoudt entered Lambert's Bay on the west coast of the Cape Colony. When they realized that a British warship, the *HMS Sybille*, was at anchor in the bay, they opened fire on her with their rifles. She returned fire with a few shells, but no casualties were suffered by either side.[787]

On 30 January 1901, there was a skirmish at the Brandewyns River east of the Pakhuis Pass across the Cederberg Mountains. After heavy fire from both sides, the British finally forced the Boers under Commandant Brand to retire towards Vanrhynsdorp. British casualties in this engagement were one officer killed and two men mortally wounded. Boer casualties reportedly amounted to three burghers.[788]

> P4.4.3 Grave of Lieutenant G.V.W. Clowes (20), 1st Battalion Gordon Highlanders, killed in action at the Brandewyns River on 30 January 1901.[789]
> ▶ Signposted next to the R364 about 40 km east of Clanwilliam, Western Cape.
> ◉ GPS co-ordinates not available.

Shots were sporadically exchanged between Boer and Brit throughout an ever-widening theatre of war in the Cape Colony. The details of many of these encounters are sketchy, but gravestones provide evidence of casualties suffered by the opposing parties.

> P4.4.4 Grave marker of Corporal R. Caton, 3rd Imperial Yeomanry, killed in action at Vryburg on 23 January 1901.[790]
> ▶ West End Cemetery, c/o Green St & Reserve Rd, Kimberley, Northern Cape.
> ◉ S28° 44.078, E24° 44.170 (Google Maps).
> This cemetery contains the graves of several Imperial soldiers who fell in action in the Cape Colony in this period. They include the graves of
> - Private W. McLean, 3rd Battalion Scottish Rifles, killed in action in Windsorton Road on 9 September 1901;[791] and
> - Trooper (or Private) A.A.B. Browne (18), Herbert Mounted Rifles, killed in action at Florasfontein near Douglas on 13 November 1901.[792]

In the eastern Swartberg area of the southern Karoo, there was fighting between burgher commandoes and British troops at the end of January 1901. The commando of Commandant Gideon Scheepers briefly occupied Uniondale on 20 January 1901 and Avontuur on 27 January.[793] The Acting Quartermaster Sergeant of the South African Light Horse, W.J. Langford, was killed in action at Uniondale on 27 January. On 29 January, Trooper A. Collins of the 71st Company Imperial Yeomanry (the sharpshooters) was killed in action in an engagement at Buffalo Klip in the Uniondale district. Two days later Trooper A.H. Jones of the same unit was killed in action near Meiringspoort.[794]

P4.4.3

P4.4.4

P4.4.5

---

787 Grobler 2004, 106.
788 Nel ca 2003, 79.
789 Watt 2000, 79.
790 Watt 2000, 68.
791 Watt 2000, 282.
792 Watt 2000, 51.
793 Cloete 2010, 230 & 232.
794 Watt 2000, 82, 222 & 241.

Part 4 – The guerrilla phase of the war (11 October 1900–31 May 1902)

P4.4.5 Troopers Collins and Jones are buried next to each other.
▶ *In the Anglican cemetery, De Waal St, Uniondale, Western Cape.*
Private A. Brassington, 10th Hussars, killed in action on 19 August 1901, is buried next to Jones.[795]
◉ *S33° 39.397, E23° 07.719 (Google Maps).*

On 2 February 1901, at least two more British soldiers were killed in action when Scheepers's commando clashed with a British patrol at Kredouw Pass in the passage (locally called "Die Gang") between Klaarstroom and Prince Albert. One burgher was seriously wounded and three were captured. When the soldiers returned to Prince Albert after driving the Boers back to Klaarstroom, the three prisoners were overwhelmed with gifts of shoes, clothes and food by local inhabitants who were well disposed towards them. The wounded burgher, Johannes Kleu, died later that day.[796]

P4.4.6 Graves of Lance-Corporal J. Boyd, Imperial Yeomanry, and Trooper S.K. Hirschford, Brabant's Horse, who were killed in action or died of wounds received in action on 2 February 1901[797] *(see also CP16 on p. 135).*
▶ *In the cemetery in the churchyard of the Anglican Church, Klaarstroom, Western Cape.*
◉ *S33° 19.801, E22° 32.076 (Google Maps).*

The homestead where Kleu died on the farm Remhoogte, next to the R407 in the Kredouw Pass, is still there, and so is his unmarked grave on the same farm.[798]

On 2 February 1901, Lord Methuen left Taung in the northern Cape Colony with a force of about 1 000 men of the Imperial Yeomanry, with the objective of proceeding to Klerksdorp in the ZAR. General Liebenberg's burghers continually harassed Methuen's soldiers, and engaged with them at Uitvalskop, Paardefontein and Leliefontein. At least one Imperial soldier fell in this skirmish.[799]

P4.4.7 Grave of Corporal C.W.B. Currie (28), South Australia Bushmen, killed in action at Uitvalskop near Vryburg on 2 February 1901.[800]
▶ *British Garden of Remembrance, municipal cemetery, Suid Str/South St, west of the corner with N18 Moffat St, southern side of town, Vryburg, North West.*
◉ *Near S26° 58.162, E24° 43.640 (Google Maps).*

P4.4.8 While they were briefly in possession of Calvinia, the Boers burned down the house of Jack van Dijk, who had earlier on, in their opinion, betrayed them. The house was rebuilt after the war.[801]
▶ *29 Water St, Calvinia, Northern Cape.*
◉ *S31° 28.543, E19° 46.383 (Google Maps).*

P4.4.6

P4.4.7

P4.4.8

---
795 Watt 2000, 43.
796 Marincowitz 2014, 11-13.
797 Watt 2000, 41 & 196.
798 Marincowitz 2014, 12.
799 Cloete 2010, 234.
800 Watt 2000, 99.
801 Fransen 2004, 535.

P4.4.9   P4.4.10   P4.4.11

P4.4.9 The Boers also had a photograph of themselves taken on the stairs of the Dutch Reformed Church.
▶ The photograph is in the Calvinia Museum, 44 Church St, Calvinia, Northern Cape.
◙ S31° 28.330, E19° 46.503 (Google Maps).

P4.4.10 The Dutch Reformed Church building, built in 1899-1900, is still used (above) as a church by the Dutch Reformed congregation.[802]
▶ c/o Dorp St & Hope St, Calvinia, Northern Cape.
◙ S31° 28.523, E19° 46.372 (Google Maps).

P4.4.11 Fraserburg in the Karoo was occupied by British forces for most of the second half of the war. According to local tradition, the British forces used the existing gunpowder magazine (built around 1870) on the outskirts of town for defensive purposes.[803]
▶ On the northern side of Fraserburg, Northern Cape, close to, but outside the town.
◙ GPS co-ordinates not available.

P4.4.12 There was no fighting in Fraserburg, but it is locally rumoured that the stone wall in town (of which only a small section, complete with a number of loopholes, still exists) was used for defensive purposes during the war.
▶ 15 Schalkwyk St, Fraserburg, Northern Cape.
◙ Near S31° 55.029, E21° 30.668 (Google Maps).

P4.4.13 Carnarvon was also occupied by British forces. A few Anglo-Boer War-related items are displayed in the Carnarvon Museum.
▶ Hanau St, west of corner with Grey St, Carnarvon, Northern Cape.
◙ S30° 58.175, E22° 07.767 (Google Maps).

P4.4.12   P4.4.13   P4.4.14

802   Fransen 2004, 535.
803   Fransen 2004, 543.

Part 4 – The guerrilla phase of the war (11 October 1900–31 May 1902)

P4.4.14 Hanover – bullet holes through a lamppost. Locals claim that these holes resulted from an exchange of gunfire between the town guard and a Boer commando during the war.
▶ *In front of the Hanover Museum, Viljoen St, Hanover, Northern Cape.*
◉ *S31° 03.922, E24° 26.460 (Google Maps).*

The British forces established a hospital and logistics depot in Noupoort, because the town already had a railway depot.

P4.4.15 The town museum, which was originally an Anglican church attended by British soldiers, contains eight wooden plaques with the names of members of the British forces who died in that area.
▶ *Shaw St, near corner with Voortrekker St, Noupoort, Northern Cape.*
◉ *S31° 10.689, E24° 57.180.*

P4.4.16 The municipal museum in Sterkstroom, Eastern Cape, displays exhibits on the war, especially on the British occupation of that town.
▶ *34 Van Zyl St, Sterkstroom, Eastern Cape.*
◉ *Near S31° 33.149, E26° 33.162 (Google Maps).*

P4.4.17 The Dutch Reformed Church building in Sutherland, Northern Cape, which was occupied for military purposes by the British forces during the war.[804]
▶ *C/o Piet Retief St (the R354) & Sarel Cilliers St (the R356), Sutherland.*
◉ *S32° 23.677, E20° 39.688.*

P4.4.18 Grave of Fredrik J. van Zyl (21), who was killed in action in a skirmish at Stellenboschvlei, Murraysburg, in 1901. The inscription on his gravestone reads: "He fought alongside burghers of the neighbouring states for freedom and justice."
▶ *Municipal cemetery, Richmond, Northern Cape.*
◉ *S31° 24.990, E23° 56.697.*

There was a skirmish between a burgher commando and British forces at Towerwaterpoort in the Willowmore district on 23 February 1901. At least two British soldiers fell in this engagement.

P4.4.19 Gravestone of Sergeant E. Liddiard, Imperial Yeomanry, and Sergeant R. Anderson, Brabant's Horse, both killed in action on 23 February 1901.[805]
▶ *Old section of the municipal cemetery, Willowmore, Eastern Cape.*
◉ *S33° 17.649, E23° 29.072.*

General Hertzog and his commando returned to the Orange Free State from the Cape Colony towards the end of February 1901. En route, they engaged in a skirmish between six of Hertzog's scouts and a section of Rimington's

P4.4.15

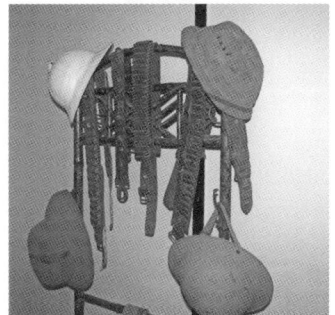
P4.4.16

P4.4.17

P4.4.18

804   Van Bart & Scholtz 2003, 111-112; Fransen 2004, 543.
805   Watt 2000, 7 & 249.

Guides on a low hill about 8 km south of Strydenburg in the Northern Cape. One British officer was fatally wounded, three burgher scouts were killed and the remaining three were taken prisoner.[806]

> P4.4.20 Grave of Captain T.W.P. Harvey (36), Rimington's Guides, who died on 1 March 1901 of wounds sustained in this action on 24 February 1901.[807]
> ▶ British Garden of Remembrance, De Aar, on the northern side of town, next to the R48 to Philipstown, between the old cemetery and the railway line.
> ◉ S30° 38.718, E24° 00.971.

On 18 May 1901, a member of the Willowmore District Mounted Troops, Corporal Ignatius Wilhelm Oosthuizen (19), was murdered in the Baviaanskloof by Cape Rebels who had deserted their commandos.[808]

> P4.4.21 Oosthuizen's grave.
> ▶ Old section of the municipal cemetery, Willowmore, Eastern Cape.
> ◉ S33° 17.649, E23° 29.072.

On 23 May 1901, the Kakamas Cape Rebel commando clashed with the British Border Scouts at N'Rougas, between Kakamas and Kenhardt. At least nine rebels were killed in action, several were wounded and two were taken prisoner.[809]

> P4.4.22 Memorial gravestone for eight burghers killed in action in the Battle of N'Rougas on 23 May 1901. Johannes Jacobs actually fell at Dreyersput. Hendrik Walton and Steenkamp were buried elsewhere.[810]
> ▶ Soetap cemetery, eastern side of Binne St, Kakamas, Northern Cape.
> ◉ Near S28° 46.917, E20° 37.583.

On 29 May 1901, there was a skirmish between the burghers led by Commandant Fouchee and British forces at Buffelsfontein, near Dordrecht in the Stormberg Mountains. At least one British soldier was killed in action in this engagement.[811]

> P4.4.23 The grave of Sergeant G.K. Jackson, Dordrecht Wodehouse Yeomanry, who fell at Buffelsfontein on 29 May 1901.[812]
> ▶ British Garden of Remembrance, municipal cemetery, near Bekker St, Dordrecht, Eastern Cape.
> ◉ S31° 22.964, E27° 02.838.

P4.4.19

P4.4.20

P4.4.21

P4.4.22

---

806 Amery V 1907, 147; Cloete 2010, 240-241.
807 Watt 2000, 183.
808 Watt 2000, 316.
809 Cloete 2010, 262.
810 According to Shearing and Shearing (2011b, 959), Walton's name was Willem.
811 Cloete 2010, 264.
812 Watt 2000, 214.

Part 4 – The guerrilla phase of the war (11 October 1900–31 May 1902)

On 1 June 1901, Commandant Gideon Scheepers's commando of about 100 men launched a surprise attack on Willowmore in the eastern Cape Colony. They initially met with some success, but the attack was repulsed through the staunch determination of the 263 defenders, including 100 men of the Willowmore Native Contingent. Scheepers lost one man, who was killed in action. The defenders lost six men and three were wounded.[813]

> P4.4.24 The grave of C.P. Marais (28), the member of Scheepers's commando, who died on 2 June 1901 of wounds received in the attack on Willowmore the previous day.
> ▶ Old section of the municipal cemetery, Willowmore, Eastern Cape.
> ◉ S33° 17.649, E23° 29.072.

On 2 June 1901, General P.J. de Villiers's commando of Cape Rebels clashed with British soldiers in the vicinity of the Border railway halt north of Kimberley. Casualties were suffered on both sides.[814]

> P4.4.25 Grave of Private L.D. Hardy (26), Cape Mounted Police, killed in action near Kimberley on 2 June 1901.[815]
> ▶ West End Cemetery, c/o Green St & Reserve Rd, Kimberley, Northern Cape.
> ◉ S28° 44.078, E24° 44.170 (Google Maps).

Also on 2 June 1901, Commandant Pieter Kritzinger's commando attacked Jamestown in the eastern Cape Colony. The local town guard had previously turned the hill overlooking the town into what they believed to be an impenetrable stronghold. However, on that cold winter night, Kritzinger's burghers easily overran the entrenchments and occupied the hamlet. The British re-occupied the town the next day, when reinforcements arrived from Aliwal North. One burgher and five British soldiers lost their lives in the engagement.[816]

> P4.4.26 Memorial for the four men of the Dordrecht District Volunteer Guard and (partly visible in the foreground) a memorial plaque for Lieutenant J.Q. Hogg of the Army Intelligence Department,[817] who were killed in action at Jamestown on 2 June 1901 or died of wounds received in action that day.
> ▶ Town cemetery, Jamestown, Eastern Cape.
> ◉ S31° 07.643, E26° 48.129.

Kritzinger's commando clashed with the Midland Mounted Rifles at Maraisburg (now Hofmeyr) in the eastern Karoo on 21 June 1901. The Imperial forces suffered casualties, including at least one officer killed in action and several soldiers taken prisoner.

> P4.4.27 The grave of Captain H.J.A. Spandaw, Midland Mounted Rifles, killed in action on 21 June 1901 at Mortimer, near Waterkloof, Eastern Cape.[818]

P4.4.23　　　　　P4.4.24　　　　　P4.4.25　　　　　P4.4.26

813　Diespecker 1993, n.p.; Cloete 2010, 265.
814　Raath 2007, 450; Cloete 2010, 265.
815　Watt 2000, 179.
816　Oosthuizen 1994, 148-149; Cloete 2010, 265.
817　Watt 2000, 198.
818　Watt 2000, 392.

▶ *Municipal cemetery, near c/o Dreary Lane and Stockenstrom St, Cradock, Eastern Cape.*
◉ *S32° 09.561, E25° 36.856.*

On 22 June 1901, Commandant Fouchee defeated the New England Mounted Rifles at Lyndale near Barkly East in the Stormberg Mountains in the eastern Cape Colony. Two of these Cape Volunteers fell in action and eight surrendered.[819]

P4.4.28 The grave of Lance-Corporal W.H. Ekron (26), Cape Police, who was killed in action at Lyndale on 22 June 1901.[820]
▶ *Municipal cemetery, Barkly East, Eastern Cape. To reach the cemetery, turn to the north on a gravel raod from White St, about midway between Jameson St & Powrie St. You will reach the old section after about 400 m.*
◉ *S30° 57.803, E27° 35.982.*

On 25 June 1901, the Boers attacked and briefly occupied Richmond in the central Karoo. One burgher and a number of defenders fell in this engagement.[821]

P4.4.29 The name of A.G. Erlank (24) from Utrecht (then in the ZAR), killed in action in this engagement, appears on this burgher monument.
▶ *Municipal cemetery, Richmond, Northern Cape.*
◉ *S31° 24.990, E23° 56.697.*

P4.4.30 Gravestone of James White (21) of the Richmond Town Guard, killed in action on 25 June 1901.[822]
▶ *Old Anglican Cemetery, southern side of Paul Street, Richmond, Northern Cape.*
◉ *S31° 25.028, E23° 56.739.*
The graves of Private Joseph Gibbs (37), Richmond Town Guard, and the following four members of the 4th North Stafford Regiment who were killed in action or died of wounds in this engagement are also in this cemetery: Privates William Gallimore, Joseph Smith and Alfred Lovatt, and Lance-Corporal Arthur Inskeep.[823]

The gravestone of Sergeant C.E. Leach (31), J Squadron, 1st Brabant's Horse, who died on 30 June 1901 of wounds received in action at Spytfontein near Hanover on 28 June 1901. No information on this engagement could be found.
▶ *Old cemetery, south side of N1, western exit of Hanover, Northern Cape.*
◉ *S31° 04.354, E24° 26.371.*

P4.4.27

P4.4.28

P4.4.29

P4.4.30

---

819 Cloete 2010, 271.
820 Watt 2000, 125.
821 Cloete (2010, 271) states that the attack was on 22 June.
822 Watt 2010, 448.
823 Watt 2000, 150, 154, 213, 255 & 387.

Part 4 – The guerrilla phase of the war (11 October 1900–31 May 1902)

On 29 July 1901, a skirmish took place between Boers and British forces at Winterhoek, near Indwe in the Stormberg Mountains. At least one British soldier was killed in this engagement.

P4.4.31 The grave of Private G.C. Thackwray (20), Dordrecht Volunteer Guard, killed in action at Winterhoek, 29 July 1901. The grave of his brother, Corporal S.K. Thackwray (20), who died in the war as the result of an accident, is next to that of G.C. Thackwray.[824] The surname is spelled Thackuray on the gravestone.
▶ British Garden of Remembrance, municipal cemetery, near Bekker St, Dordrecht, Eastern Cape.
◉ S31° 22.964, E27° 02.838.

The grave of Captain W.J.S. Rundle (25), Brabant's Horse & 6th Dragoon Guards (Carabiniers) who died of wounds received in action at Karree Bosch on 30 July 1901.[825] No information on this engagement could be found.
▶ Municipal cemetery, Bird St, Beaufort-West, Western Cape.
◉ S32° 21.474, E22° 35.149.

On 9 August 1901, Lieutenant-Colonel Scobell lost two of his men in a skirmish with the commandos of Commandant Hans Lötter and Commandant Jan Theron at Wolwevlei in the eastern Cape Colony.[826]

P4.4.32 Grave of Lieutenant S.R. Theobald (23), 9th Lancers, who died on 12 August 1901 of wounds received in action at Wolwevlei on 9 August 1901.[827]
▶ On a farm near Conway, Eastern Cape. Access and permission from farm owner, T.P. Vorster (083-4701186).
◉ GPS co-ordinates not available.

On 16 August 1901, a Boer commando and a British unit clashed at Misgund in the southern Karoo. At least two soldiers died in this engagement.

P4.4.33 Memorial plaque for Private W.F. Attwell, 10th Hussars, killed in action on 16 August 1901, and Private J.S. Ozzard of the same unit, who died on 12 September 1901 of wounds received in the engagement at Misgund.[828]
▶ In the Anglican cemetery, De Waal St, Uniondale, Western Cape.
◉ S33° 39.397, E23° 07.719 (Google Maps).

On 19 August 1901, the 10th Hussars launched an attack on Commandant Scheepers's commando of about 270 Republicans in the Langkloof near Avontuur. When Scheepers's men counter-attacked, the Hussars panicked and fled. Three Hussars were killed in action, 11 were wounded and 14 were taken prisoner. On Scheepers's side, Assistant Commandant Piet van der Merwe suffered a light wound.[829]

  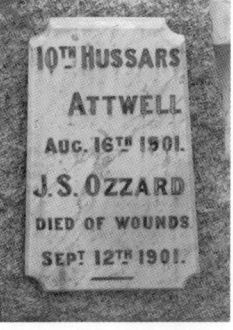 

P4.4.31　　　　　　　　P4.4.32　　　　　　　　P4.4.33　　　　　　　　P4.4.34

824　Watt 2000, 412.
825　Watt 2000, 363.
826　Cloete 2010, 285.
827　Watt 2000, 412.
828　Watt 2000, 13 & 319.
829　Smith 1946, 48-51; Cloete 2010, 288.

P4.4.34 Memorial plaque for Sergeant-Major W. Clarke (or Clark), Privates A. Brassington and W. Saunders, all 10th Hussars, killed in action on 19 August 1901.[830]
▶ *In the Anglican cemetery, De Waal St, Uniondale, Western Cape.*
◉ *S33° 39.397, E23° 07.719 (Google Maps) (see also P4.4.7).*

P4.4.35 Monument commemorating Scheepers's activities in this region.
▶ *On the western side of the R339 between Uniondale and Avontuur, Western Cape, about 2.2 km north of the R62.*
◉ *S33° 42.370, E23° 09.863 (Google Maps).*

On 24 August 1901, General P.J. de Villiers and Commandant Edwin Conroy attacked a British convoy at Rooikoppies, between Griquatown and Campbell in Griqualand West. Even though the burghers inflicted heavy casualties on the troops escorting the convoy, Conroy decided to break off the attack, as he did not believe his men should fight on the approaching Sabbath. This decision allowed most of the wagons to escape capture, and one burgher was wounded.[831]

P4.4.36 Grave plaque of Private A.B. Smyley (or Smyly), Imperial Yeomanry, who died on 22 November 1901 of wounds received at Rooikoppies near Griquatown on 24 August 1901.[832] The other soldiers commemorated on the plaque died of disease.
▶ *West End Cemetery, c/o Green St & Reserve Rd, Kimberley, Northern Cape.*
◉ *S28° 44.078, E24° 44.170 (Google Maps).*

General Jan Smuts (a former Transvaal state attorney who was later to become a future South African prime minister and world famous statesman) led a Republican invasion into the Cape Colony in the second half of 1901. His commando, which initially consisted of about 250 men, crossed the Orange River at Kiba's Drift near Herschel, south of Zastron and east of Aliwal North, on 4 September. They soon encountered the Herschel Native Police, who confronted them at the Wittenberg Mission Station, a few kilometres after they had crossed the drift. One burgher, J. Bodenstein (19) of Klerksdorp, was killed in action and three burghers were taken prisoner. The Police also suffered casualties.[833]

The Wittenberg Mission Station, where the famous author Olive Schreiner was born in 1855, still exists, but the original buildings have been rebuilt and enlarged. Bodenstein was reinterred in the town cemetery at Lady Grey in the Eastern Cape in 1906. His name appears on top on the Burgher Monument in that cemetery (see P7.2.7.5).

After the Wittenberg engagement, Smuts and his burghers rode deeper into the eastern Cape Colony. They were continuously attacked by British forces. On 6 September, on the farm Moordenaarspoort, north of Dordrecht, Smuts

P4.4.35   P4.4.36   P4.4.37

830   Watt 2000, 43 & 75. Watt does not mention Saunders.
831   Cloete 2010, 289.
832   Watt 2000, 391.
833   Stretton 2001, 18-22.

accompanied three of his officers on horseback to find a way through the mountains. They were riding up a narrow ravine when a British patrol, which had been observing their movements, fired on them at close range. One burgher, Captain Martiens Adendorff, was killed on the spot. His brother Willie and Jan Neethling were seriously wounded. Smuts managed to escape unscathed.[834]

> P4.4.37 Memorial plaque in a ravine on the farm Moordenaarspoort where the incident occurred.
> ▶ On the gravel road between Dordrecht and Rossouw, Eastern Cape. Turn off to the farmhouse of Daantjie Schoeman (dws@nokwi.co.za) (see also CP15 on p. 134).
> ◉ Farmhouse at S31° 14.095, E27° 11.487. Memorial plaque in the ravine at S31° 14.688, E27° 12.437.

> P4.4.38 Neethling died of his wounds and was buried in Dordrecht. Willie Adendorff, who also died of his wounds, and his brother Martiens are commemorated on a plaque on Neethling's grave.
> ▶ Municipal cemetery, near Bekker St, Dordrecht, Eastern Cape.
> ◉ S31° 22.964, E27° 02.838.

After ten days of a difficult advance, Smuts's commando surprised a squadron consisting of about 130 men of the 17th Lancers on the farm Modderfontein at the Elands River Poort on 17 September 1901. British losses amounted to 29 men killed and 41 wounded. Smuts's loss amounted to one man killed and six wounded. His men destroyed two field guns, which were of no use to them, but captured numerous horses and saddles, rifles and ammunition and large stores of provisions before retiring.[835]

> P4.4.39 The cemetery on the field of battle where the British soldiers were buried – officers in separate graves on the left, non-commissioned officers and ordinary soldiers in a mass grave on the right.
> ▶ British cemetery, Modderfontein. North of the R61 between Tarkastad and Cradock, Eastern Cape, east of the junction with the R401 to Hofmeyr, a gravel road turns off to Klein Mostertshoek. Follow the road for 10 km, passing the turnoff to Willie du Plessis's farmstead Modderfontein. Stop at a small gate on the left-hand side (western side of the road from where the cemetery is visible on a ridge). Walk through the gate to the cemetery.
> ◉ S31° 51.004, E26° 10.119 (at the gate).

Meanwhile, other skirmishes continued across the Cape Colony. The Free State commandant and alleged Cape Rebel J.C. (Hans) Lötter and his commando of 129 men found shelter from incessant rain in a house on the farm Bouwershoek between Graaff-Reinet and Cradock on the night of 4 September 1901. Lieutenant-Colonel Henry Scobell, commanding a unit consisting mainly of the 9th Lancers and Cape Mounted Riflemen, was informed of this and attacked them under cover of darkness. After heavy fighting, in which 14 burghers were killed and 46 were wounded, Lötter, who was wounded in the head, surrendered.[836]

> P4.4.40 Lieutenant-Colonel Henry Scobell achieved fame in the British ranks as a "guerrilla hunter". He survived the war and ended his military career as a major-general in the British Army. He was the last Officer Commanding of the Cape Colony District, 1909-1912.

P4.4.38   P4.4.39   P4.4.40

---

834 Stretton 2001, 26-31.
835 Pretorius 2010, 140-141.
836 Pretorius 2010, 249.

► *Scobell (1859-1912) is commemorated on a memorial plaque in St George's Cathedral, c/o Wale St & Queen Victoria St, Cape Town, Western Cape.*
◉ *S33° 55.461, E18° 25.139 (Google Maps).*

On 5 September 1901, a skirmish took place at Adamskraal near Ladismith in the Western Cape (not to be confused with Ladysmith in KwaZulu-Natal) in which at least one Imperial soldier was killed in action.

P4.4.41 The grave of Trooper G. Daniels (or Daniel) of the Prince of Wales Light Horse. He originally came from New Zealand.[837]
► *Cemetery, Towerkop Street, Ladismith, Western Cape.*
◉ *GPS co-ordinates not available.*

Very early on the morning of 10 September 1901, a British unit commanded by Colonel E.M.S. Crabbe surprised Commandant Piet van der Merwe's Republican commando on the farm Driefontein between Laingsburg and Ladismith, Western Cape (not to be confused with Ladysmith in KwaZulu-Natal). At least four burghers were killed – including the 19-year-old Van der Merwe, the youngest of all the Republican commandants. Another 29 burghers were wounded or taken prisoner. The British losses amounted to five men killed.[838]

P4.4.42 The grave of Van der Merwe, P. van Niekerk (20) and Sarel du Plessis (23), all Cape Rebels, is on the farm Vanzylsdamme, close to Driefontein, where they were reinterred after the war.[839]
► *On a secondary road about 25 kilometres west of Ladismith, Western Cape.*
◉ *Near S33° 28.773, E21° 02.138 (Google maps).*

P4.4.43 Memorial gravestone of Lieutenant J.F. Harper (24), Quarter-Master-Sergeant H.W. Vergette (19) and Trooper J.T. Eley (25), all of the 4th Imperial Yeomanry, who were killed in action at Driefontein on 10 September 1901.
► *Municipal cemetery, Laingsburg, Western Cape, where their remains were re-interred in 1905.*
◉ *GPS co-ordinates not available.*

The skirmish fought furthest south in the Anglo-Boer War took place on 12 September 1901, about 15 km south-south-east of Riversdale in the southern Cape Colony. In this engagement, Commandant Jan Theron's Boer commando clashed with the District Mounted Troops and Riversdale Town Guards of Lieutenant Smalberger and a unit of British troops under the command of Major Kavanagh. The Boers were positioned on the hills north-west, west, south-west and south-east of the valley. Two Boers, Field Cornet J.A. van Biljon of Kroonstad and R.C.H. Tiell of Johannesburg, were wounded and taken prisoner. The British troops suffered a number of casualties, but exact numbers are unknown.

P4.4.41

P4.4.42

P4.4.43

P4.4.44

---

837 Watt 2000, 101.
838 Smith 1946, 66-73; Cloete 2010, 294.
839 Coetzee 2003, 260-261.

Part 4 – The guerrilla phase of the war (11 October 1900–31 May 1902)

P4.4.44 Memorial at the site of the skirmish.
▶ *Next to the R305 that leads to Stilbaai, Western Cape, about 10 km south of the N2 national road south-east of Riversdale.*
◉ *S34° 13.130, E21° 21.374 (Google Maps).*

On 13 September 1901, Commandant Jan Theron's commando entered Heidelberg in the southern Cape Colony, about 30 km west of Riversdale. They soon became embroiled in a skirmish with the Heidelberg Town Guard and shots rang out in the streets of the town. At least one Cape Rebel who fought on the Republican side fell in this engagement.[840]

P4.4.45 This memorial commemorates all the casualties of the skirmish on 13 September 1901.
▶ *In front of the Dutch Reformed Church, c/o Fourie St & Van Riebeeck St (the R322), Heidelberg, Western Cape.*
◉ *S34° 15.405, E20° 57.511 (Google Maps).*

P4.4.46 The grave of Petrus Jacobus Bellingan, killed in action at Heidelberg on 13 September 1901.
▶ *Municipal cemetery, Uitenhage, Eastern Cape.*
◉ *GPS co-ordinates not available.*

The grave of Civil Constable Sam Colclough, Imperial Military Railways Police, killed in action at Agtertang on 14 September 1901.[841] No information on this engagement could be found.
▶ *British Garden of Remembrance, western side of Station Rd, near the northern limit of the town, Colesberg, Northern Cape.*
◉ *S30° 42.730, E25° 06.086 (Google Maps).*

A small party of Grenadier Guards attacked General Wynand Malan's commando at Visserskraal on the Noupoort/De Aar line near Hannover on 16 September 1901. However, they suffered a total defeat when the Boers led them into an ambush. One British officer and three men were killed and the rest surrendered.[842]

P4.4.47 Gravestone of Lieutenant M. Gurdon-Rebow (26), 3rd Battalion Grenadier Guards, killed in action in this engagement.[843]
▶ *British Garden of Remembrance, De Aar, on the northern side of town, next to the R48 to Philipstown, between the old cemetery and the railway line.*
◉ *S30° 38.718, E24° 00.971.*

On 17 September 1901, two British soldiers were killed in action in an encounter with a Boer commando near Oudtshoorn in the Little Karoo.

P4.4.45

P4.4.46

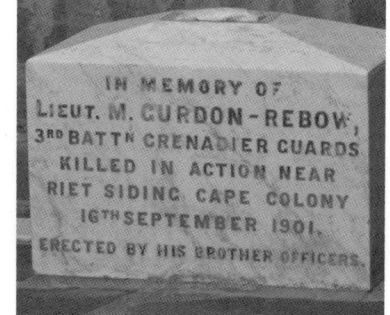
P4.4.47

P4.4.48

---

840 Cloete 2010, 295
841 Watt 2000, 81.
842 Amery V 1907, 389-390; Cloete 2000, 265.
843 Watt 2000, 172.

P4.4.48 Memorial plaque of Privates J. Phister and S. Stewart, members of the Uniondale District Mounted Troops, who fell in that engagement.[844]
▶ *In the Anglican cemetery, De Waal St, Uniondale, Western Cape.*
◉ *S33° 39.397, E23° 07.719 (Google Maps).*

P4.4.49 Grave of A.G. Dennison, Hannay's Scouts, who died on 18 September 1901 of wounds received in action the day before at Zoetlief, near Vryburg in the northern Cape.[845]
▶ *British Garden of Remembrance, municipal cemetery, Suid Str/South St, west of corner with N18 Moffat St, on the southern side of town, Vryburg, North West.*
◉ *Near S26° 58.162, E24° 43.640 (Google Maps).*

On 20 September 1901, 70 burghers of Kritzinger's commando surprised about 100 members of Lovat's Scouts under Lieutenant-Colonel Andrew Murray at Quaggafontein (Elandskloof) in the Herschel-Zastron area of the north-eastern Cape Colony. The Scouts suffered the loss of 20 men killed (including Murray) and 28 wounded before the rest surrendered. Kritzinger's burghers captured the British camp, as well as a 15-pounder Armstrong gun, two light guns and a number of horses.[846]

P4.4.50 Memorial for Lieutenant-Colonel A.D. Murray (37), his brother, Captain E.O. Murray (29) (left front) and other members of the British forces, including Captain R.T. Barrett and Sergeant J. Tetlow, both of Thorneycroft's Mounted Infantry, killed in action at Quaggafontein on 20 September 1901.[847]
▶ *British Garden of Remembrance, Junction Boulevard between Barkly St & King George St, Aliwal North, Eastern Cape.*
◉ *S30° 41.235, E26° 43.194.*

By the end of September 1901, Smuts and his commando had made their way into the Suurberg Mountains near Addo. On 3 October, three burghers, Arie van Onselen, Henry Rittenberg and Cornelius Vermaas, were killed in action when they were trapped by British soldiers on the slopes of the Brakkefontein Mountain.[848]

P4.4.51 Gravestone of Arie van Onselen and Henry Rittenberg.
▶ *Near Kariega Siding, north of the R75 between Uitenhage and Jansenville, Eastern Cape.*
◉ *Near S33° 26.145, E25° 16.182.*

P4.4.52 Grave of Cornelius Vermaas.
▶ *Uitenhage cemetery, Eastern Cape.*
◉ *GPS co-ordinates not available.*

P4.4.49   P4.4.50   P4.4.51   P4.4.52   P4.4.53

---

844   Watt 2000, 332 & 400.
845   Watt 2000, 110.
846   Amery V 1907, 387-388; Cloete 2010, 298.
847   Watt 2000, 21, 303 & 411.
848   Cloete (2010, 302) states they were executed after being captured by the British forces because they were wearing British khaki uniforms.

Part 4 – The guerrilla phase of the war (11 October 1900–31 May 1902)

Shots were exchanged between a Republican commando and British forces near Sterkstroom on 3 October 1901. One burgher, Field Cornet W.H.J. Pretorius, was killed in action in this engagement.

P4.4.53 The grave of Field Cornet Pretorius.
▶ *Municipal cemetery, on the outskirts Sterkstroom, next to the R344/397 to Molteno, Eastern Cape.*
◉ *S31° 33.202, E26° 32.759.*

At the beginning of October 1901, Commandant Gideon Scheepers and his commando criss-crossed the Little Karoo. On 1 October they left Calitzdorp in a south-westerly direction. They reached Buffelsfontein (near Vanwyksdorp), where they were involved in a skirmish with British troops the next day. In the days that followed, more skirmishes followed, and both sides suffered light casualties. Since Scheepers himself was so ill that he found it too painful to travel on horseback, he and his men left that area via the Anysberg and Little Swartberg Mountains on 8 October.[849]

P4.4.54 Memorial plaque and white concrete obelisk commemorating Scheepers's activities in this area.
▶ *On a rocky outcrop, on the western side of the R323, at the Miertjieskraal turn-off, about half way between Riversdale and Ladismith, Western Cape.*
◉ *S33° 49.039, E21° 08.614.*

Scheepers fell into British hands on 10 October 1901 on the farm Kopjeskraal, west of Prince Albert in the western Cape Colony, when he became ill and surrendered to obtain medical treatment.[850]

There is a memorial at the place where Scheepers fell in British hands.

One of the unfortunate results of the Republican invasions of the Cape Colony and the fact that many Cape Afrikaners joined the Republicans was ruthless British action against fighting burghers and any Cape Rebels whom the British took prisoner. [The treatment of Cape Rebels in general is discussed in Part 5.7]. A number were executed, either by hanging or by firing squad. Three Republican officers were also executed, the first two being Commandant J.C. (Hans) Lötter and his adjutant, P.J. Wolfaardt,.

P4.4.55 Lötter and Wolfaardt were executed at Middelburg, Eastern Cape, on 12 October 1901.[851] The so-called Chair Monument marks the spot where they were executed (see also CP26 on p. 300).
▶ *At Ouberg Koppie, next to the Richmond Road (R398) just outside Middelburg, Eastern Cape.*
◉ *S31° 29.650, E24° 59.433.*

P4.4.56 Lötter and Wolfaardt (together with Frederik A. Marais) are also commemorated on a monumental gravestone erected in 1908.
▶ *Municipal cemetery, Van Reenen St, Middelburg, Eastern Cape.*
◉ *S31° 30.004, E25° 01.131.*

P4.4.54   P4.4.55   P4.4.56   P4.4.57

---

849 Preller (ed.) 1938b, 71-73; Meintjes 1969b, 157 &158.
850 Preller (ed.) 1938b, 73-76; Marincowitz 2014, 30.
851 Cloete 2000, 271.

Commandant Gideon Scheepers was the best-known Republican officer executed by the British military authorities. After being captured on 10 October 1901, he was initially taken to the well-known railway station town Matjiesfontein, where he was treated in the British military hospital. He was then taken to Beaufort-West for further treatment. After his recovery, he was imprisoned, first in Middelburg in the eastern Cape Colony, and then in Graaff-Reinet, in the same area. At Graaff-Reinet, he was charged before a British military court on more than 30 counts of murder, arson, train-wrecking and the alleged ill-treatment of prisoners. He was sentenced to death and was executed on 18 January 1902.[852]

P4.4.57 The old prison in Graaff-Reinet, built in 1859/61, where Scheepers was imprisoned for the last weeks of his life.[853]
▶ *Eastern end of Middle St, northern side of the street near the river, Graaff-Reinet, Eastern Cape.*
◉ *S32° 15.184, E24° 32.471.*

P4.4.58 The memorial near Graaff-Reinet close to the spot where Scheepers was shot.[854]
▶ *2 km from Graaff-Reinet, opposite the Van Rhyneveldspas Dam, on the southern side of the R63 to Murraysburg, Eastern Cape.*
◉ *S32° 13.849, E24° 31.079.*

P4.4.59 Scheepers Memorial in the family cemetery on the farm Roodepoort, east of Middelburg, near Arnot, Mpumalanga. It was erected by supporters from all over South Africa and unveiled by his then 85-year-old mother on 20 January 1945 (see also CP18 on p. 136).
▶ *Leave the N4 at exit 153 between Middelburg and Belfast, Mpumalanga. Drive north towards the Arnot Railway Station. Turn right to Wonderfontein at the T-junction. Drive past the Mafube Mine. Turn left into a gravel road at the Arnot Station/Uitkyk exit. Turn left at a water tank decorated with Ndebele art, south of the railway line, and drive west along the railway line for a short distance before crossing it. Then drive back east again on the northern side of the railway line. After passing the railway station, the road turns in a northerly direction. Follow the road for a distance of 6.2 km after the crossing of the railway line. Then turn right (east) on another gravel road (the D1048). The road sign reads Wapadrand. Follow this road for 1.4 km before turning right again (south) onto a farm road. The sign there reads Oosthuizen (BNB1). Drive another 900 m, passing a farmhouse and kraals. The cemetery is on the left. It is surrounded by a stone wall, but the memorial is visible above the wall. Sophie and Geelbooi Sindane look after the cemetery and may arrive to request a donation.*
◉ *S25°44.390, E28° 48.669.*

Meanwhile Smuts and his commando in the course of October and November 1901 proceeded all the way from the eastern to the western Cape Colony where he eventually joined up with the commando of Commandant Manie Maritz. The latter had in the meanwhile undertaken one of the most successful Republican incursions into the western Cape Colony. On 10 October 1901, his men occupied Hopefield and destroyed the equipment in the telegraph office. Three days later they attacked and occupied Piketberg, capturing rifles and ammunition. On 15 October, they occupied

P4.4.58

P4.4.59

P4.4.60

852 Preller (ed.) 1938b, 73-112; Meintjes 1969b, 158-203; Pretorius 2010, 404-405.
853 Fransen 2004, 570.
854 Hattingh 1989a, 72-73.

Part 4 – The guerrilla phase of the war (11 October 1900–31 May 1902)

Moorreesburg. On the same day one of his patrols, consisting of Field Cornet Thys Boonzaaier and a few men from Hopefield, ventured all the way to Saldanha Bay on the west coast. While the burghers were looting the store at Hoedjies Bay and disrupting the transfer of cargo in the harbour, a British warship, the HMS Partridge, steamed into the bay. The burghers immediately opened fire from the shelter provided by the dunes, and the Partridge fired back. There seem to have been no casualties. However Maritz's attack on a British force at Vierentwintigriviere (Twenty-Four Rivers] the next day ended in failure and both sides suffered casualties. Maritz was forced to withdraw to the north.[855]

P4.4.60 Grave of Lieutenant Guy Falcon (24), Roberts' Horse, killed in action at Twenty-Four Rivers on 16 October 1901. According to Watt, he was treacherously shot.[856]
▶ *Anglo-Boer War Garden of Remembrance, Commonwealth War Graves section, Maitland cemetery, Voortrekker Rd, Cape Town, Western Cape.*
◙ *S33° 55.022, E18° 32.280 (Google Maps).*

In early November Maritz again ventured south, penetrating as far as the Mamre Mission Station, which is within sight of Table Mountain. The skirmish closest to Cape Town took place on 12 November 1901, a few kilometres north of Darling, when Maritz's burghers patrolled that area. One burgher was killed in action in the engagement.[857]

P4.4.61 The burgher who was killed was Field Cornet Casparus Hildebrand of Lichtenburg in the western Transvaal. In 1940, a memorial 13 m high was erected on his grave[858] (see also CP24 on p. 300).
▶ *From Darling, take the R315 going west to Yzerfontein, turn off on the unnamed gravel road to the north (Platteklip) just after leaving Darling and after passing the cemetery. Turn off from this gravel road to the right at S33° 19.484, E18° 22.417, drive further north and then west on farm roads for about 2 km to the monument.*
◙ *S33° 19.311, E18° 22.587.*

The grave of Private A. Skinner, Scotts Railway Guards, who died on 12 November 1901 at Taung of wounds received the same day at Pudimoe.[859] No information on this engagement could be found.
▶ *British Garden of Remembrance, municipal cemetery, Suid Str/South St, west of corner with N18 Moffat St, southern side of Vryburg, North West.*
◙ *Near S26° 58.162, E24° 43.640 (Google Maps).*

Five British soldiers were killed in action in running battles in the Floukraal-Rietvlei-Rietpoort area of the Aliwal North district.[860]

P4.4.62 Gravestone of Sergeant Alfred E. Spurling, Gorringe's Flying Column, killed in action at Rietpoort on 17 November 1901.[861]

P4.4.61

P4.4.62

P4.4.63

---

855 Smith 1946, 88-89; Fourie 1975, 95-97; Pretorius 2010, 299.
856 Watt 2000, 132.
857 Smith 1946, 91-92; Fourie 1975, 104; Kotzé 1989, 58.
858 Kotzé 1989, 58 &59.
859 Watt 2000, 382.
860 Cloete 2010, 312.
861 Watt 2000, 395.

▶ *British Garden of Remembrance, Junction Boulevard between Barkly St & King George St, Aliwal North, Eastern Cape.*
◉ *S30° 41.235, E26° 43.194.*

On 22 November 1901, a skirmish between Republicans and British forces took place in the Bamboesberg Mountains near Molteno in the Eastern Cape. A British officer was killed in action.

P4.4.63 Grave of Captain R.A. Blandy (31), Colonial Defence Force, killed in action in this engagement.[862]
▶ *Municipal cemetery, Molteno, Eastern Cape.*
◉ *S31° 23.998, E26° 21.300.*

A few days later, on 25 November 1901, a skirmish between Republicans and British forces took place at Oatlands, near Aberdeen in the Eastern Cape. At least one Cape Rebel on the Republican side was mortally wounded in this engagement.

P4.4.64 The grave of Gert Jacobus van der Watt, who died of wounds two days after the skirmish at Oatlands.
▶ *Municipal cemetery, western side of Aberdeen, Eastern Cape.*
◉ *S32° 28.735, E24° 03.564.*

Republicans and British forces again met on 27 November 1901 near Stormberg in the Eastern Cape. A British officer was killed in action.

P4.4.65 Grave of Second Lieutenant H.F. (or F.H.) Lyon (20) of the 3rd Battalion East Surrey Regiment, killed in action in this engagement.[863]
▶ *Municipal cemetery, Molteno, Eastern Cape.*
◉ *S31° 23.998, E26° 21.300.*

On 28 November 1901, the combined commandos of General Malan, Commandant Maritz, Commandant Lategan and Commandant Van Deventer attacked a British remount depot at Tontelboschkolk, south of Brandvlei in the western Karoo. The attack was repulsed by a combined force of 87 men of the Western Province Mounted Rifles and about 175 coloured soldiers of the Bushmanland Borderers, but the commandos captured about 300 horses. At least two of the attacking Cape Rebels and two men of the Western Province Mounted Rifles were killed in action.[864]

P4.4.66 The two Cape Rebels killed in action at Tontelboschkolk, J.J. van der Merwe and Jordaan, are commemorated on the Cape Rebel memorial in Calvinia.
▶ *Municipal cemetery, western side of Calvinia, Northern Cape.*
◉ *S31° 28.235, E19° 45.893.*

  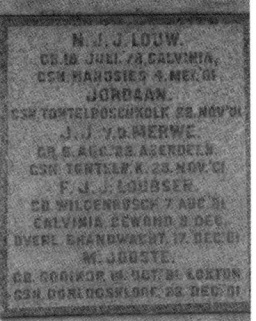 

P4.4.64   P4.4.65   P4.4.66   P4.4.67

---

862   Watt 2000, 35.
863   Watt 2000, 258.
864   Fourie 1975, 110-112; Neser 1988, 89 & footnote 257; Cloete 2010, 314-315.

Part 4 – The guerrilla phase of the war (11 October 1900–31 May 1902)

Smuts and his men arrived in the Calvinia-Nieuwoudtville area at about this time. His commando and those of Maritz and the other Boer officers who were active in this area joined forces soon afterwards.

Meanwhile on 29 November 1901, Boers and British soldiers clashed at Motkop in the Stormberg Mountains near Lady Grey in the eastern Cape Colony. At least one Boer was killed in this engagement.

P4.4.67 Photograph of J.A. Coetzee, a young burgher killed in action at Motkop on 29 November 1901, less than a month after his 16th birthday.
▶ *Barkly East museum, c/o White St & De Villiers St, Eastern Cape.*
◉ *S30° 57.998, E27° 35.645.*

On 15 December 1901, Kritzinger crossed the Orange River at Sand Drift for his third invasion of the Cape Colony. The next day, he and his commando were forced by the 5th Lancers to cross the De Aar-Noupoort blockhouse line in broad daylight near the Hanover Road Station. Kritzinger rushed back into the crossfire to rescue a lone wounded burgher, and he was seriously wounded. His men handed him to the British forces for medical treatment.[865] He recovered. He was subsequently accused of war atrocities, but was acquitted on all charges. He survived the war and lived to a ripe old age.

There are no specific sites to commemorate this incident.

On 30 December 1901 shots were exchanged between a Boer commando and a detachment of British troops near Tarkastad in the Eastern Cape. At least one burgher was killed in action.

P4.4.68 The grave of F.C.J. de Beer, killed in action on 30 December 1901.
▶ *Municipal cemetery, Craddock St, Tarkastad Eastern Cape (at the entrance of the town from Cradock/Hofmeyr).*
◉ *S32° 00.170, E26° 15.444.*

On 9 January 1902, a Boer commando exchanged shots with a detachment of British troops at Zwakfontein, near Dordrecht in the Stormberg Mountains. At least one British soldier was killed in action.

P4.4.69 The gravestone of Trooper E.H. Barrett (18), Midland Mounted Rifles, who fell at Zwakfontein on 9 January 1901.[866]
▶ *British Garden of Remembrance, municipal cemetery, near Bekker St, Dordrecht, Eastern Cape.*
◉ *S31° 22.964, E27° 02.838.*

On 13 January 1902, the Cape Rebel Commandant Conroy attacked a British convoy at Doornfontein, between Griquatown and Campbell in Griqualand West. Major R.E. Whitehead ordered a bayonet charge on Conroy's men. The soldiers charged gallantly, but were driven back and suffered casualties.[867]

P4.4.68   P4.4.69   P4.4.70

---

865 Cloete 2000, 283-284.
866 Watt 2000, 21.
867 Grobler 2004, 134.

P4.4.70 Grave of Major R.E. Whitehead (40), Royal Munster Fusiliers, killed in action at Doornfontein, near Griquatown, 13 January 1902.[868]
▶ West End Cemetery, c/o Green St & Reserve Rd, Kimberley, Northern Cape.
◉ S28° 44.078, E24° 44.170 (Google Maps).

On 17 to 18 January 1902, Commandant Ben Bouwer, who was active in the Clanwilliam-Olifants River area of the western Cape Colony, led a patrol to Doorn Bay on the west coast. On their arrival they spotted a British warship, probably the *HMS Monarch*, anchored about 1 500 m offshore. The burghers opened rifle fire on the ship, which fired back, before hauling anchor and sailing away.[869]

Doorn Bay, Western Cape
◉ S31° 48.956, E18° 14.111.

Shots were exchanged between a Boer commando and the Cradock Town Guard on 20 January 1902.

P4.4.71 The grave of Corporal W.H. Wych (32), Cape Colonial Force, killed in action in this engagement.[870]
▶ Municipal cemetery, near c/o Dreary Lane & Stockenstrom St, Cradock, Eastern Cape.
◉ S32° 09.561, E25° 36.856.

The gravestone of Lieutenant-Colonel A.L. Salmond, 3rd Derbyshire Regiment, who died on 4 August 1902 of wounds received in action on 31 January 1902.[871] No information could be found on this engagement.
▶ Imperial Yeomanry Hospital Cemetery, Deelfontein, Northern Cape (western side of an unnamed road about 46 km south-west of De Aar, western side of railway line, a few hundred metres south of the old railway station).
◉ S30° 59.779, E23° 47.581.

On 5 and 6 February 1902, the combined Republican commandos of Generals Jaap van Deventer and Jan Smuts attacked and defeated a British convoy on the farm Middelpos, between Sutherland and Calvinia. They captured a quantity of provisions and burned the rest. Three of the attackers were killed in this encounter. The British losses amounted to three officers and eight other ranks killed in action.[872]

P4.4.72 The Cape Rebels G.S. Loots, W. Grobbelaar and A. Weeber, killed in action in this encounter, are commemorated on the Cape Rebel monument in Calvinia, Northern Cape.
▶ Municipal cemetery, western side of Calvinia, Northern Cape.
◉ S31° 28.235, E19° 45.893.

P4.4.71

P4.4.72

P4.4.73   P4.4.74

868   Watt 2000, 449.
869   Pretorius 2010, 299.
870   Watt 2000, 466.
871   Watt 2000, 366.
872   Wessels 2002, 266-268; Cloete 2010, 335.

P4.4.73 The monument commemorating the British casualties of this engagement.
▶ *On the grounds of the hotel in Middelpos, next to the R354 gravel road linking Calvinia and Sutherland, Northern Cape.*
◉ *S31° 54.338, E20° 13.848.*

Also on 6 February 1902, at Uitspanningsfontein, between Fraserburg and Sutherland in the northern Cape Colony, General Wynand Malan and his burghers attacked and captured a British convoy. Some provisions were taken and the rest were destroyed. The British forces suffered 31 casualties, including Major H.W.G. Crofton.[873]

There is a British (Guards) memorial at the site of the engagement. Crofton was buried in Beaufort West, Western Cape.

On 18 February 1902, a Republican commando became involved in a skirmish with British soldiers on the farm Oorlogsfontein near Three Sisters, north of Beaufort-West. One burgher received a deadly wound, namely Commandant Hendrik Johannes (Henry) Hugo, 25, who had studied law in Britain and the Netherlands before the war. Despite his youth, Hugo often acted as a judge in military affairs before his death.[874]

P4.4.74 This memorial to Hugo was unveiled by General Wynand Malan in 1904.
▶ *On the farm Oorlogsfontein, near Wagenaarskraal, in the Northern Cape (about 20 km west-northwest of Tree Sisters Railway Station).*
◉ *GPS co-ordinates not available.*

P4.4.75 The Anglo-Boer War exhibition in the Victoria West Regional Museum contains information on Hugo.
▶ *47 Kerk Street, Victoria West, Northern Cape.*
◉ *GPS co-ordinates not available.*

On 24 February 1902, the Republican commandos in the Vanrhynsdorp area of the western Cape Colony united under General Smuts for an attack on the Cape Police at Windhoek, south of Vredendal. They succeeded in capturing the enemy positions as well as valuable supplies, but eight men were killed and at least ten wounded. The Cape Police lost one man killed and seven wounded.[875]

P4.4.76 Memorial for the burghers who fell at Windhoek on 24 February 1902.
▶ *Municipal cemetery, southern side of town, between the Troe Troe River and the camp ground, Vanrhynsdorp, Western Cape.*
◉ *S31° 36.789, E18° 44.101.*

P4.4.77 Gravestone of Private R. Osborne, 12th (Prince of Wales) Royal Lancers, who died on 1 March 1902 of wounds received in action at Geelbeksfontein on 27 February 1902.[876]

 P4.4.75 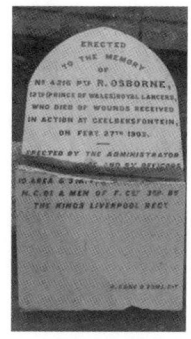 P4.4.76  P4.4.77   P4.4.78

---

873   Pieterse 1946, 315-326; Cloete 2010, 335.
874   Van Zyl 1944, 357; Pieterse 1946, 327-331; Cloete 2010, 338. Cloete states that Hugo was killed in action on 17 February 1902.
875   Grobler 2004, 138.
876   Watt 2000, 317.

▶ *Old Anglican Cemetery, southern side of Paul Street, Richmond, Northern Cape. This cemetery also contains the grave of Trooper D. Hardwick, Marshalls Horse, killed in action in the same action.*
◉ *S31° 25.028, E23° 56.739.*

On 18 March 1902, Colonel White attempted to break the cordon established by Bouwer and Maritz around Garies in the north-western Cape. One of his patrols became involved in a skirmish with the burghers of Commandant Steenkamp at Brandewynskop (Darter's Hill), south of Kamieskroon. The British patrol suffered a number of casualties and was forced to retreat to Garies.[877]

P4.4.78 Gravestone of Lieutenant Charles James Darter (31), Namaqualand Border Scouts, killed in action on 18 March 1902.[878]
▶ *About 15 km south of Kamieskroon, travelling on the N7 to Garies, on the top of a long rise, a large telephone mast is visible on the right, and there is a striking red rock in the veld on the left. Stop exactly between these two beacons. The grave is right there, next to a wild olive tree. One has to climb over the barbed wire fence to reach it.*
◉ *GPS co-ordinates not available.*

P4.4.79 Gravestone of Quartermaster-Sergeant H. Bidmead, Namaqualand Border Scouts. He was wounded in the engagement on 18 March and died of his wounds on 20 March 1902.[879]
▶ *Garies cemetery.*
◉ *GPS co-ordinates not available.*

On 23-24 March 1902 a British force consisting soldiers of Marshall's Horse and the Sutherland District Mounted Troops clashed with Commandant Japie Neser's commando at Renostervlei, a farm on the Old Coach Road between Sutherland and Fraserburg, at the western end of the Nuweveld Mountains. Nine soldiers were killed in this engagement. The Boers suffered no losses and captured the British camp, thus acquiring valuable war supplies.[880]

P4.4.80 The mass grave of the soldiers who fell at Renostervlei. One of them was F.P. Roux, an Afrikaner who came from the Boland. Watt writes that he was killed in action on 24 February, but all other sources indicate the date as 24 March.[881]
◉ *S32° 27.166, E21° 12.110.*

On 1 to 2 April the Republican forces in Namaqualand attacked and overwhelmed the defenders of the mining town Springbokfontein (today called Springbok). The commander of the defenders, Lieutenant R.J. Steward, was killed in this engagement.[882]

P4.4.79

P4.4.80

P4.4.81

---

877 Cloete 2010, 347.
878 Watt 2000, 102.
879 Watt 2000, 31.
880 Neser 1988, 97-100; Cloete 2010, 348-349.
881 Neser 1988, 98 footnote 286; Watt 2000, 361.
882 Cloete 2010, 351-352.

Part 4 – The guerrilla phase of the war (11 October 1900–31 May 1902)

P4.4.81 The grave of Private R.J. Stewart, Namaqualand Town Guard, and the volunteer Henri van Coevorden. Both were killed in action while defending Springbokfontein.[883]
▶ *Old military cemetery, Kleinzee Rd, on the western side of Springbok, Northern Cape.*
◎ *S29° 39.976, E17° 52.646.*

From 4 April to 4 May 1902, the Republican forces in Namaqualand besieged a strong British force in the mining town of Okiep. The besieged forces were protected by a circle of 15 blockhouses strategically positioned on *koppies* (low hills) around the town.[884]

P4.4.82 One of the koppies on which there was a blockhouse at the time of the siege.
▶ *Centre of Okiep.*
◎ *GPS co-ordinates not available.*

On 28 April 1902, a British column that had landed at Port Nolloth to rescue the besieged forces in Okiep failed in their first attempt, and four men were killed. They became involved in a skirmish with Boers under Commandant Jaap van Deventer near Steinkopf, but were forced to fall back to Klipfontein.[885]

P4.4.83 The graves of the four soldiers killed on 28 April 1902
▶ *In a small cemetery next to the R382 near Steinkopf, Northern Cape.*
◎ *GPS co-ordinates not available.*

The Republican siege of Okiep ended on 4 May 1902, with the arrival of a strong British relief column from Port Nolloth.[886]

P4.4.84 The grave of Private Samuel Richards, No 4 (Nababeep) Company Namaqualand Town Guard Brigade, killed in action in defence of Okiep on 12 April 1902.[887] *There are no memorials for either the defenders or the Republican forces involved in the siege of Okiep.*
▶ *Town cemetery, Okiep, Northern Cape.*
◎ *GPS co-ordinates not available.*

In the Cape Midlands and the eastern Cape Colony, small engagements continued throughout the final weeks of the war, resulting in occasional casualties.

The grave of Agent W. Budler, Army Intelligence Department, killed in action near Aliwal North on 21 April 1902.[888]
▶ *Town cemetery, at exit of town via De Beer St, Jamestown, Eastern Cape.*
◎ *S31° 07.643, E26° 48.129.*

P4.4.82

P4.4.83

P4.4.84

---
883 Watt 2000, 400 & 427. Watt does not mention Lieutenant R.J. Steward.
884 Cloete 2010, 352.
885 Grobler 2004, 142.
886 Cloete 2010, 362.
887 Watt 2000, 351.
888 Watt 2000, 54.

On 2 May 1902, a Boer commando and British forces exchanged shots at Tweefontein near Graaff-Reinet. One British officer was killed in this engagement.

> P4.4.85 Grave of Lieutenant R.H. Murray (33), Graaff-Reinet District Mounted Troops, killed in action at Tweefontein on 2 May 1902.[889] He was the youngest of the five sons of the late Rev. W. Murray of Worcester.
> ▶ Cradock Street Cemetery, Graaff-Reinet, Eastern Cape.
> ◉ GPS co-ordinates not available.

On 12 May 1902, shots were exchanged between Republican forces and members of the British forces at Dassiefontein, near Richmond in the Karoo. At least one British soldier was mortally wounded.

> P4.4.86 Iron cross on the grave of Trooper Smith, Imperial Yeomanry, and Lance-Corporal T. Bethell, 5th Lancers. Bethell was wounded at Dassiefontein on 12 May 1902, and died of his wounds on 13 May 1902.[890]
> ▶ Old Anglican Cemetery, southern side of Paul St, Richmond, Northern Cape.
> ◉ S31° 25.028, E23° 56.739.

On 18 May 1902, the recently appointed Commandant Carel van Heerden and his men, assisted by the commandos of General Wynand Malan and Commandant Willem Fouchee, attacked Aberdeen in the Cape Midlands and managed to capture more than 50 horses, which they desperately needed. However, the cost of the success was high, since Van Heerden himself (whose parents lived in Aberdeen), John Londt (whose wife and children lived in the town) and Josef Coetzee were killed in the attack.[891]

> P4.4.87 The granite obelisk and a cairn that indicate the approximate spot where Van Heerden fell.
> ▶ Southern side of the church square, Aberdeen, Eastern Cape.
> ◉ S32° 28.561, E24° 03.819.

> P4.4.88 Van Heerden's gravestone has the following inscription: "Aan Carel Petrus VAN HEERDEN in leven commandant der Boerenstrydmacht in den worstelstryd voor Vryheid en Recht 11 Oct. 1899–31 Mei 1902. Geboren te Groot Doornpan, dist. Prieska 5 Dec. 1875 en in de onmiddellyke nabyheid van het Godshuis gesneuveld te Aberdeen (K.K.) 18 Mei 1902." ["To Carel Petrus van Heerden, in life commandant of the Boer forces in the struggle for freedom and justice 11 October 1899–31 May 1902. Born at Groot Doornpan, Prieska district 5 December 1875 and killed in action very close to the House of God in Aberdeen (C.C.) 18 May 1902".]
> ▶ Municipal cemetery, western side of Aberdeen, Eastern Cape.
> ◉ S32° 28.735, E24° 03.564.

> P4.4.89 Londt's grave.
> ▶ Same as P4.4.88.

P4.4.85

P4.4.86

P4.4.87

---

889   Watt 2000, 304.
890   Watt 2000, 31. Smith's identity could not be established.
891   Van Zyl 1944, 363; Smith 1946, 159-166; Van Heerden 1946, 164-171.

Part 4 – The guerrilla phase of the war (11 October 1900–31 May 1902)

The last skirmish of the war in the Cape Colony took place on 3 June 1902, three days after the signing of the peace treaty on 31 May. At Groenberg, near Fraserburg, members of the Colonial Light Horse exchanged shots with a Republican commando. At least four of the British soldiers were killed in action.[892]

P4.4.90 Graves of Sergeant-Major T.R. Carter and Private A. Doveton, both of the Colonial Light Horse, killed in action on 3 June 1902.[893]
▶ *Municipal cemetery, Fraserburg, Northern Cape.*
◉ *S31° 55.039, E21° 31.113.*
An iron cross indicating the grave of Private J. Smith and Private A.A. Scott, both of the Colonial Light Horse, killed in action at Groenberg on 3 June 1902, is in the same cemetery. The name of Private W. Petersen of the Royal Army Medical Corps who died on 4 June 1902 also appears on the cross.[894]

P4.4.88　　　　　　　　　　　P4.4.89　　　　　　　　　　　P4.4.90

892　Neser 1988, 100; Cloete 2010, 371.
893　Watt 2000, 67 & 117.
894　Watt 2000, 330, 370 & 387.

Part 5

The war of attrition

5.1 Black South Africans and the war

When the war broke out in 1899, there seems to have been an unofficial agreement between the Boers and the British that it would be a "white man's war" and this was one of the reasons why the British did not make use of Indian troops in South Africa. However, the Anglo-Boer War turned out to be far from being strictly a "white man's war". Black people were affected right from the very start.[895] When the war broke out, there were nearly 100 000 black migrant workers on the Witwatersrand. Most of them immediately left the Transvaal, some voluntarily, and some under compulsion. They lost their incomes when the mines closed down, and found it difficult to survive without another means of subsistence in the areas where they came from.[896]

> P5.1.1 Memorial that commemorates, inter alia, the approximately 7 000 black miners who fled on foot from Johannesburg, passing Volksrust on their way to the British colony of Natal.
> ▶ On Voortrekker Square, at the municipal offices, c/o Laingsnek St & Joubert St, Volksrust, Mpumalanga.
> ◉ S27° 22.083, E29° 53.110.

Black workers in the Kimberley area were even less fortunate. It is estimated that the death rate during the siege was 48 per thousand for white people and 138 per thousand for members of other races. Most deaths were caused by disease and malnutrition.[897]

In Mafikeng the same situation prevailed, with hundreds of black people dying of starvation during the Boer siege of the town. Nevertheless, the vast majority of the black people provided valuable assistance to the British defenders of Mafeking, for example, by raiding cattle on farms in the vicinity of the besieged town and bringing the cattle into town, thus easing the increasingly acute shortage of food. One such raider was Mathakgong, who is described by Sol Plaatje as one of the unsung heroes of the siege.[898]

> P5.1.2 Tshidi Barolong memorial in honour of those who gave their lives during the Siege of Mafeking.
> ▶ Kgotla of the Barolong Boora Tshidi, Montshioa Stad, on an unnamed road between Prince of Wales Way & Doctor James Moroka Dr, Mahikeng, North West.
> ◉ S25° 52.552, E25° 37.791.

> P5.1.3 Memorial to Kgosi Besele I of the Barolong Boora Tshidi. The inscription reads: "He was commander in chief of Matsetse Regiment (Mophato) during the Siege of Mafikeng from 14 October 1899 to 17 May 1900."

P5.1.1

P5.1.2

P5.1.3

---

895   Warwick 1983.
896   Grobler 2004, 6.
897   Roberts 1984, 332.
898   Pretorius 2010, 270.

▶ *Kgotla of the Barolong Boora Tshidi, Montshioa Stad, on an unnamed road between Prince of Wales Way & Doctor James Moroka Dr, Mahikeng, North West.*
◉ *S25° 52.552, E25° 37.791.*

P5.1.4 Memorial plaque on the Wall of Fame at the Talana Museum, in remembrance of the Zulu people in the Mzinyathi region whose lives were affected by the war and who helped both the Boers and the British.
▶ *Talana Museum Battlefield and Heritage Park, Victoria St, between Hajee Jamal and the R33, Dundee, KwaZulu-Natal.*
◉ *S28° 09.346, E30° 15.617.*

P5.1.5 Exhibit on the involvement of black South Africans in the Anglo-Boer War, Klerksdorp Museum.
▶ *C/o Margaretha Prinsloo St & Lombaard St, Klerksdorp, North West.*
◉ *S56° 51.839, E26° 40.138.*

Black South Africans were indeed actively involved in the war from the very start. Many were used by both sides as servants and in non-combatant roles. Most of the wagon drivers and cooks on both sides were black. The British also used Indian stretcher-bearers. The most famous Indian to participate in the war in that role was Mohandas Gandhi, later the foremost Indian political leader of the 20th century. At the outbreak of the war, he assisted the British military authorities in Natal to form an Indian Ambulance Corps of 1 100 men, who served in the most important battles on the Natal front in removing wounded soldiers from the battlefield.[899]

P5.1.6 Exhibit on Indian stretcher bearers in the medical corps of the British army in South Africa, Siege Museum, Ladysmith.
▶ *Murchison Street, Ladysmith, KwaZulu-Natal.*
◉ *S28° 33.547, E29° 46.847 (Google Maps).*

P5.1.7 Indian stretcher bearers' memorial plaque on the Wall of Fame at the Talana Museum.
▶ *Talana Museum Battlefield and Heritage Park, Victoria St, between Hajee Jamal and the R33, Dundee, KwaZulu-Natal.*
◉ *S28° 09.346, E30° 15.617.*

As the war progressed, both sides, but especially the British, made extensive use of black scouts and even armed irregulars. The commandos of the Boer Republics involved black people to work on farms or to accompany the burghers as labourers. Some became guides, scouts and spies. Although it was against their official policy, the Boers certainly in some instances gave rifles to black men to help them fight the British. It is estimated that between 7 000 and 11 000 black people accompanied the Boer commandos during the war. The majority of those men were personal servants, who went on commando with their Boer employers. These men were generally referred to as *agterryers* [lit. those who rode behind].[900]

P5.1.4

P5.1.5

P5.1.6

P5.1.7

---

899   Tichmann 2002, 210-217; De Villiers I 2008a, 318-319; Pretorius 2010, 158.
900   Labuschagne 1999, 1 & 45-53.

P5.1.8 Statue of an agterryer holding ready a saddled horse (see also CP20 on p. 298).
▶ *In the gardens of the War Museum of the Boer Republics, Monument Rd, Bloemfontein, Free State.*
◉ *S29° 08.397, E26° 12.569.*

It is certain that at least 30 000 black people served the British forces. In some areas the Boers attacked the black people who assisted the British. In the western part of the ZAR, this developed into open warfare between the Boers and the Bakgatla of Kgosi Linchwe. In the early stages of the war, on 25 November 1899, a large number of Bakgatla warriors, led by Linchwe's half-brother Segale and supported by British artillery, attacked a Boer laager at Derdepoort, on the western border of the ZAR, north of Zeerust. A number of burghers and Bakgatla were killed in this engagement. The Bakgatla also attacked Derdepoort village about two kilometres from the laager, killing two white women. They forced 17 Boer women and children to go with them to Mochudi in Bechuanaland when they retreated,[901] although the women and children were soon released. In a revenge attack on 22 December 1899, Boer commandos destroyed three Bakgatla villages, resulting in casualties on both sides.[902]

P5.1.9 Memorial commemorating the Derdepoort events.
▶ *In front of the old Dutch Reformed Church building, Plein St, between Tuin St & Burger St, Rustenburg, North West.*
◉ *S25° 40.312, E27° 14.709.*

In addition to the two white woman who were killed at Derdepoort on 25 November 1899, at least 30 burghers were killed by black people in that area. These victims included J.H. Barnard, a member of the First Volksraad (People's Council) of the ZAR, as well as Marthinus Ras, manufacturer of the famous Ras canon of the Anglo-Transvaal War of 1880-1881.

P5.1.10 The tall monument commemorating 32 victims of Bakgatla attacks on burghers in the Derdepoort area in November 1899 and February 1900. The memorial stone on the right on the photograph specifically commemorates Ras, who was killed on 18 February 1900.
▶ *At Kaya se Put, North West.*
◉ *Near S24° 45.176, E26° 34.040 (Google maps).*

P5.1.11 The grave of Gert J. de Beer of Bethal, killed by black people at Saaihoek in November 1901.
▶ *Concentration camp cemetery, Balmoral, Mpumalanga. Exit from N4 between Bronkhorstspruit and Emalahleni at Balmoral, cemetery signposted, north of the N4 close to the highway.*
◉ *S25° 52.050, E28° 58.040.*

The grave of Gideon Jacobus Stephanus van Niekerk is on the farm Modderspruit, near Laersdrift in Mpumalanga. He was killed on 13 March 1902. Hostile black people under the command of Japhta cut his throat. This happened at Blaauwbank (also known as Maagschuur) in the presence of Van Niekerk's son and

P5.1.8   P5.1.9   P5.1.10   P5.1.11

901   Grobler 2004, 18.
902   Grobler 2004, 25; Pretorius 2010, 116-117.

British officers. He was initially buried at Renosterhoek, but was reinterred at Modderspruit in 1944. Captain Henri Slegtkamp made a speech at the reinterment ceremony.[903]

In the north-western Cape Colony, a number of local Afrikaner farmers in Namaqualand who were sympathetic towards the Republican cause but did not join the ranks of the Cape Rebels, formed a self-protection unit to guard their families and possessions against unruly members of a British unit called the Namaqualand Scouts. This unit consisted of Coloured volunteers led by British officers. On 2 May 1902, a patrol of Scouts ambushed a number of farmers at Bleskoppoort, east of Garies. J. Mostert was killed and A. Briers (17) was fatally wounded. The Scouts captured and brutally murdered two other farmers, namely Field Cornet G. Rossouw and S. Stone.[904]

P5.1.12 Grave monument of the four victims of the Bleskoppoort incident on 2 May 1902.
▶ Grounds of the Dutch Reformed Church, eastern side of the N7, Kamieskroon, Northern Cape.
◙ S30° 20.826, E17° 93.161.

The British also openly some armed black South Africans and sent them out against the Boers. These black groups became a major danger to the Boers, since they knew the land as well as the Boers did. The indigenous communities of Basutoland and Swaziland generally stayed out of the war, but in the south-east of the ZAR, the Zulu of the Vryheid district decided to join the British. On 6 May 1902, they attacked and killed 56 Boers hiding from the British forces at Holkrantz.[905]

P5.1.13 The memorial on the farm Bloemendal, where the Holkrantz incident took place.
▶ Signposted on the R33, north of Vryheid, KwaZulu-Natal.
◙ GPS co-ordinates not available.

P5.1.14 Memorial on the square in front of the Dutch Reformed Church in Vryheid that commemorates the victims of what the Boers denounced as the Holkrantz massacre. The names of the 56 burghers who lost their lives are listed on this monument, which was erected in 1905.[906]
▶ Kerkstraat, Vryheid, KwaZulu-Natal.
◙ S27° 46.066, E30° 47.533.

The names of the 56 burghers killed at Holkrantz on 6 May 1902, as well as ten burghers murdered elsewhere, are engraved on a roll of honour on the Burgher Monument at Platrand (see P3.2.3.19).
▶ Platrand, Ladysmith, KwaZulu-Natal.
◙ S28° 35.278, E29° 46.357.

Both the Republican and the British forces executed black people accused of providing assistance to the other side. Such incidents are mentioned in numerous accounts of the war,[907] but it is impossible to estimate the numbers of

P5.1.12   P5.1.13   P5.1.14   P5.1.15

---

903   Van der Westhuizen & Van der Westhuizen 2000, 200.
904   Nel ca 2003.
905   Warwick 1983, 90-93; Cloete 2010, 362.
906   Van der Westhuizen & Van der Westhuizen 2013, 2.
907   Grundlingh 1999, 217; Blake 2010, 67-71.

victims involved. There are no memorials for these victims, with one exception. In February 1901, the war produced a black martyr. Even before the occupation of Calvinia, a town in what is today the northern Cape Colony, by a Republican commando early in January 1901, a Coloured man named Abraham Esau had begun organising members of the local community into a fighting force. They failed to halt the Boer advance and did not resist the occupation of Calvinia. Esau was arrested, along with dozens of other locals, both Coloured and white. When he failed to give satisfactory answers to the Republicans when he was interrogated about his activities, he was given severe corporal punishment, and on 5 February 1901 he was shot in cold blood by a member of the commando.[908]

> P5.1.15 Esau's grave (see also CP21 on p. 298).
> ▶ A neglected cemetery on the southern side of the R355 on the outskirts of Calvinia, Northern Cape. A hospital on the northern side of the same road, east of the cemetery, has been named after Esau.
> ◉ GPS co-ordinates not available.

> P5.1.16 Memorial to Esau, sadly, it was vandalized at some time prior to December 2007, when this photograph was taken.
> ▶ Near Calvinia next to the main road to Sutherland (the R354), Northern Cape.
> ◉ GPS co-ordinates not available.

In January 1902, there was another incident in the north-western Cape, at the Leliefontein Methodist mission station in Namaqualand. General Manie Maritz of Smuts's Boer forces visited the station on 11 January to discuss the war with the local missionaries and then with the coloured population, of whom many were by then employed as scouts, despatch riders and wagoners by the British. Maritz warned them against cooperation with the British and threatened to punish them if they refused to cooperate with the Boers. However, Maritz and his small escort were attacked by the local community, and barely managed to escape with their lives. A day or two later, Maritz and his men retaliated, killing at least 30 local men and wounding many more, and laid waste to the whole area.[909]

> P5.1.17 The old mission church at Leliefontein, Northern Cape, where the incident took place.
> ◉ Near S30° 19.317, E18° 04.727.

> P5.1.18 The memorial plaque in the church with the names of the local victims of the Leliefontein incident.
> ◉ Near S30° 19.317, E18° 04.727.

Many black farm workers and *agterryers* remained loyal to the Boers throughout the war. An outstanding example is a Griqua, Jan Ruiter, President Steyn's *agterryer*, whose quick intervention assisted Steyn in escaping capture by a British military unit.[910]

> P5.1.19 Ruiter died long after the war, and was buried on Steyn's farm, Onze Rust, close to the graves of the Steyn family. The inscription on the gravestone reads: "Ruiter, geb [born] ±1866 – oorl [died] 1944. Agterryer van [of] President M.T. Steyn Anglo-Boereoorlog 1899-1902."

P5.1.16

P5.1.17

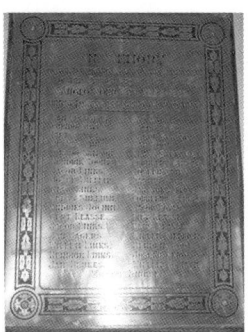
P5.1.18

---
908 Nasson 2003, 124-131.
909 Fourie 1975, 118-120; Pretorius 2010, 240-241.
910 Labuschagne 1999, 53 & 82-86; Pretorius 2010, 398.

▶ *Onze Rust is signposted on the N1 south of Bloemfontein, Free State.*
◉ *Near S29° 16.515, E26° 11.334.*

5.1.1 Concentration camps for the black civilian population

Many black South Africans found themselves in the same pitiful circumstances as the Boer women and children in the concentration camps. The black communities in the former Republics also became victims of the British scorched earth policy. In many cases, black domestic servants accompanied white families to the "white" concentration camps. However, separate concentration camps were established for black refugees, and the conditions there were the same as, or even worse than, those in white camps. About 110 000 black people were interned in a total of more than 60 camps erected for the black population. According to official British statistics more than 14 000 (perhaps as many as 21 000) black people died in those camps – most due to maltreatment.[911]

P5.1.20 The black concentration camps memorial at the site of the National Women's Monument. This memorial claims that there were 65 camps in which a total of 140 514 black South Africans were interned and that approximately 24 000 deaths occurred in those camps.
▶ *Monument Rd, Bloemfontein, Free State.*
◉ *S29° 08.397, E26° 12.569.*

Details on these camps, which were in most cases established close to railway sidings, are still sketchy. The following list indicates the location of 64 camps according to place names used in 1902:
- Transvaal Colony: Balmoral, Belfast, Heidelberg, Irene, Klerksdorp, Krugersdorp, Middelburg, Standerton, Vereeniging, Volksrust, Bantjes, Bezuidenhout's Valley, Boksburg, Brakpan, Bronkhorstspruit, Brugspruit, Elandshoek, Elandsrivier, Frederikstad, Greylingstad, Groot Olifants River, Koekemoer, Klipriviersberg, Klip River, Meyerton, Natalspruit, Nelspruit, Nigel, Olifantsfontein, Paardekop, Platrand, Rietfontein West, Springs, Van der Merwe Station, Witkop, Wilgerivier.
- Orange River Colony: Alleman, Amerika, Boschrand, Eensgevonden, Geneva, Harrismith, Heilbron, Holfontein, Honingspruit, Houtenbek, Koppies, Rooiwal, Rietspruit, Smaldeel, Serfontein, Thaba 'Nchu, Taaibosch, Vet River, Virginia, Ventersburg Road, Vredefort Road, Welgelegen, Winburg, Wolwehoek.
- Cape Colony and British Bechuanaland: Kimberley, Orange River, Taungs, Dryharts.[912]

P5.1.21 Black concentration camp memorial on the outskirts of Brandfort, at a site containing graves in what is believed to be a black concentration camp cemetery.
▶ *On the farm Louvain, near Brandfort, Free State.*
◉ *S28° 42.712, E26° 27.890.*

P5.1.19   P5.1.20   P5.1.21   P5.1.22

---

911   Kessler 2012, 244. Nasson (2013, 178 & 183), writes that even though little is known with absolute certainty, there seem to have been more than 80 camps in which over 120 000 black people were interned, and that the largest proportion of deaths occurred among the very young. Ongoing research is still revealing more about these camps.

912   SA History online. 2017. http://www.sahistory.org.za/topic/black-concentration-camps-during-anglo-boer-war-2-1900-1902.

P5.1.22 The graves of a number of people who died in the black concentration camp at Alleman Siding, north of Karee, Free State, can still be identified.
◎ *Near S28° 47.569, E26° 24.802.*

P5.1.23 Graves of people who may have died in a black concentration camp that can still be identified at Middelburg, Mpumalanga.
▶ *In Eastdene. Drive from the centre of Middelburg on the R555 Meyer St. Cross the Little Olifants River via Meyer Bridge and then turn to the right, up the hill, to the site (unmarked).*
◎ *S25° 45.527, E29° 28.869.*

P5.1.24 The War Museum of the Boer Republics exhibits a gravestone of a black concentration camp victim.
▶ *Monument Rd, Bloemfontein, Free State.*
◎ *S29° 08.397, E26° 12.569.*

P5.1.25 Memorial plaque for victims of the black and white concentration camps at Heidelberg, Gauteng.
▶ *Near the entrance of the municipal cemetery, on the outskirts of Heidelberg. Turn off the R42 leading to Nigel, immediately east of the N3.*
◎ *Near S26° 29.327, E28° 22.436.*

P5.1.26 Wall of remembrance for those who died in the black concentration camp in Klerksdorp, North West. This wall was built about 100 years after the war began in the area where the black camp cemetery was, to pay tribute to black people who died in the war. No signs of the cemetery are left. There are also no artefacts left of the camp, which was situated where the Ellaton suburb of Klerksdorp is today.
▶ *Municipal cemetery, Klerksdorp, North West, near Margaretha Prinsloo St, between O.R. Tambo St & Kadria St.*
◎ *S26° 52.576, E26° 40.130.*

There was a marker indicating the site of a concentration camp for black South Africans at Aliwal North, Eastern Cape, but it was recently destroyed by the local municipal authorities.

5.2 The scorched earth policy

By September 1900, Field Marshal Lord Roberts issued proclamations as British commander-in-chief stating that all the inhabitants of the Republics were henceforth British citizens. He threatened to burn down the homes of any Boers still fighting, to destroy their property and slaughter their livestock. When the Boers failed to surrender, Lord Roberts carried out his threats – the physical destruction of the Republics began.

Roberts's successor, Lord Kitchener, was adamant that he would crush Boer resistance once and for all. He decided to adopt stricter measures, albeit far more financially taxing on the Empire, in order to end the war as quickly as possible. The result was the introduction of the disgraceful scorched earth policy, later described by the leader of the opposition in the British parliament, Sir Henry Campbell-Bannerman, as "methods of barbarism". The British forces burnt down more than 30 000 farmhouses, destroyed whole towns, such as Lindley, Ventersburg, Reitz and

P5.1.23

P5.1.24

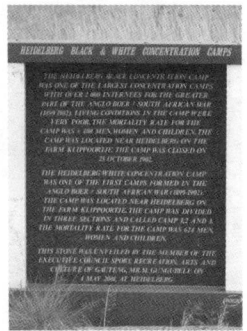
P5.1.25

P5.1.26

Bothaville in the Orange Free State and Ermelo in the Transvaal, removed or destroyed stock in the former Boer Republics, and forcibly removed the families of the Boers who were still fighting in the field from their farms. The objective was to ensure that the Boer commandos would get no aid from the civilian population. The result was one of the most controversial and horrific institutions created by the British during the Anglo-Boer War, namely the concentration camps.[913]

P5.2.1 Plaque showing a Boer farmhouse going up in flames in line with the British scorched earth policy.
▶ *On the Cape Anglo-Boer War memorial, Laborie Wine Estate, Paarl, Western Cape. Entrance at the western end of Taillefer St.*
◉ *S33° 45.961, E18° 57.529.*

P5.2.2 Plaque depicting the implementation of the scorched earth policy on a historical monument in front of the Dutch Reformed Church in Reitz.
▶ *Church St, c/o Noord St, Reitz, Free State.*
◉ *S27° 48.255, E28° 25.803.*

P5.2.3 Small model of the church in Lindley destroyed by the British. A new Dutch Reformed Church was erected in Lindley after the war. The scale model was built in the square of the new Dutch Reformed Church both to commemorate the effect of the scorched earth policy on that town and to commemorate burghers of the district who died in the war[914] (see also P7.2.5.20).
▶ *C/o Kerk St & Brand St, Lindley, Free State.*
◉ *S27° 52.864, E27° 55.223.*

P5.2.4 The bell of the Dutch Reformed Church in Frankfort, Free State – this was all that survived when the original church was burned down by the British forces in 1901. It is displayed on the grounds of the present church building, where the old church stood.
▶ *Brand St, between Baumann St & Beckwith St.*
◉ *S27° 16.378, E28° 29.665.*

P5.2.5 The bell of the Dutch Reformed Church in Ventersburg, Free State – this was all that survived when the original church was burned down by the British forces in 1901. It is displayed on the grounds of the present church building, where the old church stood.
▶ *Haker St, between Oranje St & Steyn St, Ventersburg, Free State.*
◉ *S28° 05.067, E27° 08.208.*

P5.2.6 The Dutch Reformed Church in Carolina in the eastern part of the ZAR was plundered by British troops after they occupied the town on 14 August 1900. The troops used it as a stable for their horses.[915] The building was extensively repaired after the war and a spire was added later.

P5.2.1   P5.2.2   P5.2.3

---

913   The most extensive source on the scorched earth policy is Spies 1977; also Pretorius 2001b.
914   Van der Bank 1995, 52-53.
915   Van der Westhuizen & Van der Westhuizen 2000, 117.

P5.2.4   P5.2.5   P5.2.6

▶ Kerk St, near Steyn St, between Breytenbach St and the R36, Carolina, Mpumalanga.
◉ S26° 04.204, E30° 06.768.

P5.2.7 The only house in Ermelo, in the eastern Transvaal, that was not destroyed by the British forces during the war. The only other building which the British left standing in Ermelo was the Dutch Reformed Church, at that stage a sandstone building, which they left badly damaged.[916] The church building was eventually demolished after the war when a new Dutch Reformed Church was built.
▶ De Jagerstraat 72, Ermelo, Mpumalanga.
◉ S26° 30.921, E29° 59.136.

P5.2.8 At Trichardtsfontein in the eastern Transvaal (now Trichardt, Mpumalanga), British forces burnt down the church of the local Hervormde (Reformed) congregation. The church bell was removed, probably by the Rhodesian Mounted Rifles, as it was recovered in 1903 in Bulawayo, Rhodesia (now Zimbabwe). It was brought back to Trichardt in 1904 and is today displayed in a special little building next to the church, which was rebuilt in 1906.[917]
▶ Prinsloo St, between Ruth First St & Rapportryer St, Trichardt, Mpumalanga.
◉ S26° 29.285, E29° 13.767.

Three Afrikaner monuments were desecrated by British troops during the Anglo-Boer War.

P5.2.9 The Covenant Monument on Monument Hill near Belfast in the eastern ZAR was erected in 1886. It was badly damaged by British soldiers, and rebuilt in 1905 by the local community after the war.[918]
▶ On an unnamed road immediately east of the R560, a few kilometres north of Belfast, Mpumalanga.
◉ S25° 40.466, E30° 04.182.

P5.2.7   P5.2.8   P5.2.9   P5.2.10

916   Van der Westhuizen & Van der Westhuizen 2000, 102.
917   Van der Westhuizen & Van der Westhuizen 2013, 144.
918   Van der Westhuizen & Van der Westhuizen 2000, 216.

P5.2.10 The language monument in Burgersdorp, Eastern Cape. This memorial was badly damaged and was removed by British troops during the war. It was discovered in King William's Town in 1939, and was re-erected in Burgersdorp.[919]
▶ *Between Jan Greyling St, Piet Retief St, Chase St & Church St.*
◉ *S 30° 59.632, E 26° 19.879.*

P5.2.11 The Paardekraal Monument in Krugersdorp, Gauteng. It was erected in 1890 above the cairn built by the burghers who attended the Paardekraal assembly in December 1880. At this assembly, they decided to declare independence after the British annexation of the ZAR in 1877. The Paardekraal decision led to the First Boer War of 1880-1881, which culminated in a Boer victory at Majuba on 27 February 1881 and the re-establishment of the ZAR. After their occupation of Krugerdorp in 1900, the British forces removed the stones from underneath the monument and dumped them in the Vaal River – it seems that they believed that the presence of the stones at the monument encouraged the burghers to keep fighting.[920]
▶ *From the R28 (Paardekraal Dr), turn east into Andries Pretorius St. The entrance to the monument is to the south, near the corner with Wolmarans Ave, Krugersdorp, Gauteng.*
◉ *S26° 05.613, E27° 46.792.*

5.3 Concentration camps for white civilians

One unforeseen result of the destruction was that the British had to make some provision for the now destitute civilian families of the Boers. The British response was to put all the homeless women, children and old men in refugee or concentration camps. By 1901, about 120 000 Boers, mostly women and children, had been taken to concentration camps. By the end of the war, a total of 50 concentration camps for whites had been established.[921]

In the camps, the women and children were initially horribly mistreated. Conditions in the camps were appalling: people lived in fly-ridden tents and slept on the bare ground. Many suffered from and died due to epidemics of typhoid and the measles, as well as malnourishment. By the time improvements were made, thousands of women and children had already died in the camps – by the end of the war, 27 000 had died, according to British statistics. The European press published graphic pictures portraying the suffering of Boer women and children in what they called "death camps".[922]

Indignation in Britain itself about the terrible conditions in the camps led to the formation of societies that attempted to alleviate these conditions. One Englishwoman who played an outstanding role in this regard was Emily Hobhouse, who became a heroine to many Afrikaners and holds special significance in Afrikaner war commemoration.[923]

P5.3.1 Emily Hobhouse memorial.
▶ *Voortrekker St, Philippolis, Free State.*
◉ *S30° 15.853, E25° 16.430.*

P5.2.11   P5.3.1   P5.3.2   P5.3.3

---
919 NALN 1989a, 74-75.
920 Oberholster 1972, 297-298; Van Zyl 1989, 144-146.
921 Grobler & Grobler 2013.
922 Pretorius 1998, 58-59.
923 Van Reenen (ed.) 1984; Balme 1994, 587-595.

P5.3.2 Emily Hobhouse memorial.[924]
▶ On the grounds of the Dutch Reformed Church, c/o Church St & 2nd St, Koppies, Free State.
◉ S27° 14.500, E27° 34.375.

These two memorials also commemorate the social work done by Hobhouse in South Africa after the war.

P5.3.3 Painting of Emily Hobhouse by Antoon van Welie, 1902.
▶ War Museum of the Boer Republics, Monument Rd, Bloemfontein, Free State.
◉ S29° 08.397, E26° 12.569.

The survivors of the concentration camps never forgot the terrible conditions in the camps, which aroused an immense bitterness against the British that lived on in people's memories long after the end of the war.

P5.3.4-7 The National Women's Monument (P5.3.4) was erected in 1913 to commemorate the suffering of women and children in the concentration camps. The obelisk has been cut from Kroonstad sandstone, and stands 36.5m tall. The centrepiece is a bronze by sculptor Anton van Wouw (who designed the whole monument, with the architect Frans Soff). The bronze shows a woman with a dying child on her lap and another woman standing next to her (P5.3.5). There are two side panels, one of a women and children on their way to a concentration camp (P5.3.6) and one portraying death in a concentration camp (P5.3.7).[925] Emily Hobhouse's ashes rest below the centrepiece.
▶ Monument Rd, Bloemfontein, Free State.
◉ S29° 08.397, E26° 12.569.

P5.3.8 Separate memorial stones stating the number of deaths in each white concentration camp.
▶ Along the paved walkway to the National Women's Monument, Monument Rd, Bloemfontein, Free State.
◉ S29° 08.397, E26° 12.569.

P5.3.9 The recently erected Garden of Remembrance on the grounds of the War Museum of the Boer Republics in Bloemfontein, Free State. The names of more than 35 000 black and white women and children who perished in the concentration camps are inscribed on granite panels attached to the walls of this memorial. (Photograph courtesy of the War Museum of the Boer Republics) (See also CP33 on p. 302).
▶ Monument Rd, Bloemfontein, Free State.
◉ S29° 08.397, E26° 12.569.

There were concentration camps not only in the two Boer Republics, but also in the Cape Colony and Natal. Using the present provincial borders of South Africa as a guideline, the following is a list of the 50 concentration camp sites for white civilians:

In Gauteng:
- Heidelberg
- Irene, south of Pretoria

P5.3.4

P5.3.5

P5.3.6

---

924   NALN 1989b, 124.
925   Van der Merwe s.a., 18-20; Van Zyl 2013, 211-225.

Part 5 – The war of attrition

P5.3.7

P5.3.8

- Johannesburg – Turffontein
- Krugersdorp
- Pretoria – Meintjieskop (for National Scouts)
- Pretoria – Van der Hovendrift (temporary)
- Vereeniging

In Mpumalanga:
- Balmoral
- Barberton
- Belfast
- Middelburg
- Standerton
- Volksrust

In Limpopo:
- Modimolle (Nylstroom Concentration Camp)
- Polokwane (Pietersburg Concentration Camp)

In North-West:
- Klerksdorp
- Mahikeng (Mafeking Concentration Camp)
- Potchefstroom
- Vryburg

In the Free State:
- Bethulie
- Bloemfontein
- Brandfort

P5.3.9

- Harrismith
- Heilbron
- Vredefort Road Concentration Camp (north of Koppies)
- Kromellenboog (temporary)
- Kroonstad
- Ladybrand (temporary)
- Springfontein
- Winburg

In KwaZulu-Natal:
- Colenso
- Dejagersdrift (temporary)
- Durban – Isipingo
- Durban – Jacobs
- Durban – Merebank
- Eshowe
- Howick
- Ladysmith
- Mooi River
- Pietermaritzburg
- Pinetown
- Wentworth

In the Northern Cape:
- Kimberley
- Orange River Station (near Hopetown)
- Norvalspont (near Colesberg)

In the Eastern Cape:
- Aliwal North
- East London
- Kabusi (Stutterheim)
- Port Elizabeth
- Uitenhage

There are memorials at most of the concentration camp sites, especially at the cemeteries where the men, women and children who died in the camps were buried. In addition, there are burial sites with gravestones that have survived in their original locations. Many gravestones have been moved to memorial walls or to places of safe-keeping. Not all the cemeteries survived, however, and in some cases those who died were reinterred in mass graves in or near the original cemetery sites. There are also a number of memorials in towns where there were concentration camps, and where there are no memorials at the original camp sites or cemeteries.

P5.3.1.1

P5.3.1.2

5.3.1 Gauteng

Heidelberg

P5.3.1.1 Concentration camp roll of honour in the Kloof cemetery.
▶ On the banks of the Kloof Spruit, northern side of extension of Fenter St, Heidelberg, Gauteng.
◙ S 26° 29.717, E 28° 20.770.

P5.3.1.2 Monument (erected in 1927) and graves at concentration camp cemetery, adjacent to the municipal cemetery.
▶ At the entrance gate of the municipal cemetery, on the eastern side of the N3 on the outskirts of Heidelberg, entrance signposted from the R42 to Nigel.
◙ S26° 29.063, E28° 22.243.

Irene

P5.3.1.3 Mass graves and, in the background, symbolic graves and a roll of honour. In addition, there are a number of memorials and also British war graves in this cemetery.
▶ Irene Concentration Camp Cemetery, Stopford Rd (signposted on Botha Ave).
◙ S29° 08.397, E26° 12.569.

Johannesburg – Turffontein

P5.3.1.4 Memorial and mass graves of the relocated concentration camp cemetery.
▶ Maluti St, between Magaliesberg St & Endymion St, Suideroord, Johannesburg, Gauteng.
◙ S25° 52.239, E28° 13.225.

Krugersdorp

P5.3.1.5 Memorial and graves in the concentration camp cemetery.
▶ Burgershoop cemetery, c/o Luipaard St & Halgryn St, Krugersdorp, Gauteng.
◙ S26° 06.095, E27° 45.612.

Pretoria – Meintjieskop

P5.3.1.6 All that is left of this camp is the corrugated iron cottage that served as an officer's mess for British officers who served at the camp. It is currently a restaurant.[926]
▶ C/o Parker St & Lys St, Rietondale, Pretoria, Gauteng.
◙ GPS co-ordinates not available.

P5.3.1.3

P5.3.1.4

---
926   Greyling 2000, 82-83.

P5.3.1.5 P5.3.1.6

Vereeniging

P5.3.1.7 Memorial and graves at the concentration camp cemetery.
▶ Old municipal cemetery, south of Beaconsfield Rd (near the showgrounds), Vereeniging, Gauteng.
◉ S26° 40.547, E27° 54.745.

5.3.2 Mpumalanga

Balmoral

P5.3.2.1 Memorial and graves at concentration camp cemetery.
▶ Take the Balmoral exit from the N4 between Bronkhorstspruit and Emalahleni, Mpumalanga. Drive north towards the R104. The concentration camp cemetery is signposted, west of this road, which links the N4 and the R104, a few hundred metres north of the N4.
◉ S25° 52.050, E28° 58.040.

Barberton

P5.3.2.2 Concentration camp memorial.
▶ Old town cemetery, c/o Duncan St & Gospel St, Barberton, Mpumalanga.
◉ S25° 46.683, E31° 02.828.
There is also an exhibit on the concentration camp in the Barberton Museum, but taking photographs is prohibited in this museum.
▶ 36 Pilgrim Street, Barberton, Mpumalanga.
◉ GPS co-ordinates not available.

Belfast

P5.3.2.3 Memorial, roll of honour and graves.

P5.3.1.7 P5.3.2.1 P5.3.2.2

P5.3.2.3   P5.3.2.4

▶ *Old town cemetery, on an unnamed road between Spitskop St & Scheepers St (drive west), Belfast, Mpumalanga.*
◉ *S25° 41.694, E30° 01.663.*

P5.3.2.4 *The Dutch Reformed Church Hall in Belfast which served as a school for children from the concentration camp (recently re-roofed).*[927]
▶ *Grounds of the Dutch Reformed Church, Du Plooy St, between Kerk St & Lizana Magagula St, Belfast, Mpumalanga.*
◉ *S25° 41.336, E30° 01.881.*

Middelburg

P5.3.2.5 *Memorials and graves in the concentration camp section, Mineralia cemetery.*
▶ *Oranje St, Middelburg, Mpumalanga.*
◉ *S25° 47.367, E29° 27.793.*

P5.3.2.6 *Concentration camp graves in old municipal cemetery.*
▶ *Entrance from Bhimy Damane St, Middelburg, Mpumalanga.*
◉ *S25° 45.832, E29° 26.849.*

P5.3.2.7 *Graves in Kanonkop cemetery.*
▶ *Karee Lane, across from the junction with Korhaan Lane, Kanonkop, Middelburg, Mpumalanga.*
◉ *S25° 44.667, E29° 28.104.*

Standerton

P5.3.2.8 *Concentration camp memorial and graves.*

P5.3.2.5   P5.3.2.6

---

927   Van der Westhuizen & Van der Westhuizen 2013, 230.

▶ *Old municipal cemetery, end of Prinses St, between Berg St & Schwikardt St, Standerton, Mpumalanga.*
◉ *S26° 56.999, E29° 15.044.*

P5.3.2.9-10 Memorial fountain donated by the Jewish major of Standerton in 1904 and 1905, C. Landau, to commemorate the women and children who died in the Standerton concentration camp and memorial for Mrs Magrietha Swart of Roodekrans whose eight children all died in the camp.
▶ *On the terrain where the camp was situated, on the banks of the Vaal River, near Handel St, between Berg St & Buiten St, Standerton, Mpumalanga.*
◉ *S26° 57.363, E29° 15.022.*

Volksrust

P5.3.2.11 Memorial, mass grave and roll of honour.
▶ *Voortrekker Square, at the municipal offices, c/o Laingsnek St & Joubert St, Volksrust, Mpumalanga.*
◉ *S27° 22.083, E29° 53.110.*

P5.3.2.12 Gravestones attached to memorial wall in old municipal cemetery, De Jager St, Volksrust, Mpumalanga.
◉ *S27° 21.880, E29° 53.679.*

5.3.3 Limpopo

Nylstroom Concentration Camp Cemetery

P5.3.3.1-2 Memorial in front of the old municipal cemetery and graves in the concentration camp cemetery section of the old municipal cemetery.
▶ *On the western side of Thabo Mbeki St (the R101, which runs from north to south through the town), south of the prominent white Dutch Reformed Church building, Modimolle, Limpopo.*
◉ *S24° 42.161, E28° 24.164.*

Pietersburg Concentration Camp cemetery

P5.3.3.3 The first memorial, with graves in the foreground.
▶ *Agaat St, Nirvana (Superbia – the industrial area), Polokwane, Limpopo.*
◉ *Entrance at S23° 54.568, E29° 26.254.*

See also both P1.18 on p. 21 and CP37 on p. 304, statue of emaciated concentration camp victim.

5.3.4 North-West

Klerksdorp

P5.3.4.1 Concentration camp graves, monument designed by architect Gerard Moerdijk and roll of honour with names of those who died in the camp (see also CP31 on p. 301).
▶ *Concentration camp section, municipal cemetery, Klerksdorp, North West, near Margaretha Prinsloo St, between O.R. Tambo St & Kadria St.*
◉ *S26° 52.576, E26° 40.130.*

There is a memorial plaque at Klerksdorp High School, which was established after the war on the site where the concentration camp stood.

See also P1.26, gravestone of Civilian Superintendent H.W. Howard (42), Superintendent Burgher Camp, Klerksdorp, who died on 29 December 1901.

Part 5 – The war of attrition

P5.3.2.7

P5.3.2.8

P5.3.2.9

P5.3.2.10

P5.3.2.11

P5.3.2.12

P5.3.3.1

P5.3.3.2

P5.3.3.3

P5.3.4.1

P5.3.4.2 P5.3.4.3

Mafeking Concentration Camp cemetery

P5.3.4.2 Memorial and graves in concentration camp cemetery.
▶ Next to the R49 to Vryburg, southern side of Mahikeng, North West.
◉ S25° 52.865, E25° 36.490.

See also P1.3 Statue of a Boer mother and child in the Mafeking Concentration Camp.

Potchefstroom

P5.3.4.3 Concentration Camp memorial (vandalized by 2010, when the photograph was taken).
▶ Alexandra cemetery, close to Olënpark, near Piet Bosman St, between James Moroka Dr & Kock St, Potchefstroom, North West.
◉ S26° 42.760, E27° 05.248.

P5.3.4.4-5 Memorial at Vyfhoek, site of concentration camp cemetery; roll of honour at Vyfhoek.
▶ C/o Burger St & Lanyon St, Potchefstroom, North West.
◉ S26° 42.477, E27° 06.787.

Vryburg

P5.3.4.6 Memorial and graves in Concentration Camp Cemetery.
▶ Hartbees St, near corner with Wildebees St, north-western side of Vryburg, North West.
◉ S26° 56.659, E24° 42.857.

5.3.5 Free State

Bethulie

P5.3.4.4 P5.3.4.5 P5.3.4.6

Part 5 – The war of attrition

P5.3.5.1

P5.3.5.2

P5.3.5.1 The relocated mass grave site and memorials. These include a cairn that consists of the stones of the original cairn that was built in June 1902 by inmates of the camp, as well as the statue of an angel which was originally unveiled in 1924. The sculptor was Mr Webster of Aliwal North.[928]
▶ *Signposted, on eastern side of Bethulie, Free State.*
◉ *S30° 29.089, E25° 59.954.*

Some of the structures at the old concentration camp cemetery site in Bethulie were not relocated. These include the solid but unfinished British memorial unveiled in 1919 – the only concentration camp memorial funded by the British government – as well as the tall memorial column that was unveiled in 1953 and of which the two side panels were moved to the new concentration camp memorial terrain.[929]

See also P1.19, gravestone of four-year-old Louis Hoffmann.

Bloemfontein

P5.3.5.2 The Bethulie concentration camp memorial in Bloemfontein.
▶ *Grounds of the War Museum of the Boer Republics, Monument Rd, Bloemfontein, Free State.*
◉ *S29° 08.397, E26° 12.569.*

P5.3.5.3 The Source of Inspiration, which symbolises the resurrection of the Afrikaner people [930] (and the Pond of Tears).
▶ *Entrance through a gate from Nelson Mandela St, at the building of the Bible Society, about 500 m east of the N1, Bloemfontein, Free State. Gate key at Bible Society office.*
◉ *S29° 05.362, E 26° 10.746.*

P5.3.5.3

P5.3.5.4

P5.3.5.5

---

928 Venter 2011, 162-163.
929 Venter 2011, 163-165.
930 Van der Bank 2001, 85-86;

P5.3.5.4 The concentration camp memorials erected in 1959 by the SA War Graves Council. The large memorial contains the names of 664 children under the age of 16 years who died in the Bloemfontein Concentration Camp. The two free-standing granite memorials contain the names of 106 and 105 "mothers and other victims above 16 years" respectively.[931]
▶ *President Brand Cemetery, northern side of President St, west of corner with Church St, Bloemfontein, Free State.*
◉ *S29° 07.480, E26° 13.197.*

P5.3.5.5 Memorials in the Memoriam Cemetery for the 1 976 victims of the Bloemfontein Concentration Camp, erected by the SA War Graves Council.[932]
▶ *Memoriam cemetery, General Brand St, Bloemfontein, Free State.*
◉ *S29° 08.840, E26° 12.409.*

Brandfort

P5.3.5.6 Memorial in front of the Dutch Reformed Church.
▶ *Voortrekker St, Brandfort, Free State.*
◉ *S28° 42.134, E26° 27.682.*

P5.3.5.7 Memorials and mass grave at the concentration camp cemetery site.
▶ *On the privately owned farm Louvain, near Brandfort, Free State.*
◉ *S28° 42.653, E26° 28.370.*

Harrismith

P5.3.5.8 Memorials and graves in the municipal cemetery.
▶ *North-east of c/o Laksman St & Greyling St, Harrismith, Free State.*
◉ *S28° 16.143, E29° 07.891.*

Heilbron

P5.3.5.9 Memorial and graves at the concentration camp cemetery.
▶ *Municipal cemetery, north of c/o Lang Markt St (the R57) and President St, Heilbron, Free State.*
◉ *S27° 16.756, E27° 58.174 (Google Maps).*

Vredefort Road Concentration Camp

P5.3.5.10 Memorial and graves at the concentration camp cemetery.

P5.3.5.6

P5.3.5.7

P5.3.5.8

---

931 Van der Bank 2001, 28-29.
932 Van der Bank 2001, 50.

Part 5 – The war of attrition

P5.3.5.9

P5.3.5.10

▶ On the farm Prospect. Drive 7.5 km north from Koppies on the R82, turn right (east) at the road sign on a gravel road; cross the railway line and then drive north parallel to the railway line for another 6 km.
◙ S27° 09.133, E27° 39.175.

Kroonstad

P5.3.5.11 Memorial and graves at the concentration camp cemetery.
▶ Western end of 10th Way, Kroonindustria, Kroonstad, Free State.
◙ S27° 40.329, E27° 12.410.

Springfontein

P5.3.5.12 Graves at concentration camp cemetery.
▶ Turn in an easterly direction into Emily Hobhouse St from Settlers St (the main street through Springfontein). Cross the railway line and after another 200 m, turn right (south). Follow the signs to the cemetery.
◙ S30° 16.586, E25° 42.793.

See also P1.20, cemetery entrance gate and graves of unbaptized children who died in the Springfontein concentration camp.

Winburg

P5.3.5.13 Memorial and graves at the concentration camp cemetery on the south-western edge of town.
▶ C/o Jac Coetzer St & McLennan St, Winburg, Free State.
◙ S28° 31.158, E27° 00.411.

P5.3.5.14 Graves and memorial wall at concentration camp cemetery 1.3 km west of c/o Jac Coetzer St & Voortrekker St, Winburg, Free State. This cemetery has been badly vandalised.

P5.3.5.11

P5.3.5.12

P5.3.5.13 — P5.3.5.14 — P5.3.6.1

▶ *Drive out of town in westerly direction on Jac Coetzer St.*
◉ *S28° 31.134, E27° 00.003.*

5.3.6 KwaZulu-Natal

Colenso

The graves and site of concentration camp cemetery have recently been rediscovered. The site has not yet been developed for visitors or tourism.

Durban

P5.3.6.1 Isipingo. Memorial at the site of the concentration camp cemetery.
▶ *Delahoo Lane, near corner with Sucrose Sykes Rd, Isipingo, Durban, KwaZulu-Natal (on the grounds of a church).*
◉ *Near S29° 59.308, E30° 55.478.*

P5.3.6.2 Jacobs. Memorial at the site of the concentration camp cemetery.
▶ *C/o Thorn Rd & Dudley St, Jacobs, Durban, KwaZulu-Natal.*
◉ *S29° 55.848, E30° 59.105.*

P5.3.6.3 Merebank memorial garden of remembrance. It contains a mosaic of a camp scene (above), a memorial, symbolic tents and mass graves.
▶ *Site of the concentration camp cemetery, in a corner of the Merewent Cemetery, surrounded by high brick walls, adjacent to the Muslim cemetery, on the south-eastern side of the M4 (Southern Freeway). Entry via Himalayas Rd, near the corner with Rawalpini Rd, Merebank, Durban, KwaZulu-Natal.*
◉ *S29° 57.060, E30° 57.747.*

P5.3.6.2 — P5.3.6.3 — P5.3.6.4

Part 5 – The war of attrition

Eshowe

The camp was at Fort Curtis, which no longer exists. There is a memorial plaque with the names of those who died in this camp, but its location could not be established.

Howick

P5.3.6.4 Memorial at the site of the concentration camp cemetery.
▶ Signposted, at a sports field, next to the R103 (Main Rd), south of the corner with Valley View Rd, Howick, KwaZulu-Natal.
◉ S29° 30.043, E30° 13.827.

Ladysmith

P5.3.6.5 Memorial plaque on the outer wall of the Platrand Burgher Monument.
▶ On Platrand, outside Ladysmith, KwaZulu-Natal (see P3.2.3.19).
◉ S28° 35.278, E29° 46.357.

Pietermaritzburg

P5.3.6.6 Old concentration camp memorial.
▶ In the Voortrekker Cemetery, on the south-western side of Chief Albert Luthuli St, across from the junction with Geere St, Pietermaritzburg, KwaZulu-Natal. The cemetery also contains a new concentration camp memorial and the mass grave of victims of the camp.
◉ S29° 36.425, E30° 23.064.

5.3.7 Northern Cape

Kimberley

P5.3.7.1 Memorial and mass grave where the remains of most victims were reinterred.
▶ Grounds of the Dutch Reformed Church, south-eastern corner of Schmidtsdrift Way & Black St, Newton, Kimberley, Northern Cape.
◉ S28° 44.670, E24° 45.518.

P5.3.7.2 Memorial and gravestones at the original site of the concentration camp graves.
▶ West End Cemetery, c/o Green St & Reserve Rd, Kimberley, Northern Cape.
◉ Near S28° 44.166, E24° 44.416.

P5.3.6.5

P5.3.6.6

P5.3.7.1

P5.3.7.2 P5.3.7.3 P5.3.7.4

Orange River Station (Doornbult Concentration Camp)

P5.3.7.3 Artefacts on the original site of the camp, and P5.3.7.4 Memorial and graves in the concentration camp cemetery.
► Signposted on the R369 between Hopetown and Orania, Northern Cape. Entry only possible via the farm of Rina Wiid, south of that road.
◉ S29° 39.967, E24° 09.756.

Norvalspont

P5.3.7.5 Memorial and mass graves in relocated concentration camp cemetery. There is also a roll of honour, with the names of the Norvalspont concentration camp victims in this cemetery, as well as original slate gravestones attached to the walls of the relocated cemetery. These are badly vandalised and have deteriorated beyond legibility, with one or two exceptions.
► Signposted on the R58 between Colesberg and Venterstad, a few kilometres east of Norvalspont, Northern Cape.
◉ S30° 38.695, E25° 27.263.

5.3.8 Eastern Cape

Aliwal North

P5.3.8.1 Memorial, including a symbolic grave, mass grave, roll of honour and original gravestones attached to a wall.
► On a site next to the N6 national road, southern entrance of Aliwal North, Eastern Cape (signposted).
◉ S30° 42.254, E26° 42.544.

P5.3.7.5 P5.3.8.1 P5.3.8.2

P5.3.8.3   P5.3.8.4   P5.3.8.5

Port Elizabeth

P5.3.8.2 Memorial (vandalized) in the North-End Cemetery, which also contains some concentration camp graves, including that of a nephew of General J.B.M. Hertzog, who died here in December 1900.
▶ *Paterson Rd, Port Elizabeth, Eastern Cape.*
◉ *Entrance at S33° 55.488, E25° 36.383; memorial near S33° 55.388, E25° 36.476.*

P5.3.8.3 Memorial in the area where the camp was located. It was unveiled in 1983.[933]
▶ *In the grounds of the Kemsley Park Sport Grounds adjacent to the Old Grey Sports Grounds. Entry from Lenox St, near corner with Mount Rd, Port Elizabeth, Eastern Cape.*
◉ *S33° 57.302, E25° 35.587.*

Uitenhage

P5.3.8.4-5 Old memorial on the site of concentration camp cemetery (left); new memorial on the site of the concentration camp cemetery (right).
▶ *Turn to the north from Verwoerd Dr, about 180 m east of the corner with Smuts Dr, Uitenhage, Eastern Cape.*
◉ *S33° 43.562, E25° 25.440.*

5.3.9 Other concentration camp places of remembrance

In addition to the National Women's Monument and to the separate memorials at each of the concentration camps, there are a number of public works of art that portray the suffering of the women and children in the concentration camps.

P5.3.9.1 Plaque illustrating the Bethulie Concentration Camp Cemetery.

P5.3.9.1   P5.3.9.2   P5.3.9.3

---
933   Hattingh 1989b, 264-265.

▶ On the Bethulie Concentration Camp memorial, grounds of the War Museum of the Boer Republics and the National Women's Monument, Monument Rd, Bloemfontein, Free State.
◉ S29° 08.397, E26° 12.569.

P5.3.9.2 Large stained glass window that portrays a scene in a concentration camp.
▶ Paul Kruger Hall, adjacent to the Dutch Reformed Church, Kerk St, near Steyn St, between Breytenbach St and the R36, Carolina, Mpumalanga.
◉ S26° 04.204, E30° 06.768.

P5.3.9.3 Bronze plaque in bas relief portraying women and children in a concentration camp, on the grave of Mrs Cornelia de Wet (wife of the famous general, Christiaan de Wet).
▶ Municipal cemetery, northern side of Dewetsdorp, Free State.
◉ S29° 34.635, E26° 39.798.

P5.3.9.4 Bronze plaque in bas relief portraying women and children in front of concentration camp tents.
▶ On the historical monument in front of the Dutch Reformed Church, Church St, c/o Noord St, Reitz, Free State.
◉ S27° 48.255, E28° 25.803.

P5.3.9.5 Plaque illustrating concentration camp victims.
▶ On the Cape Anglo-Boer War memorial, Laborie Wine Estate, Paarl, Western Cape. Entrance at the western end of Taillefer St.
◉ S33° 45.961, E18° 57.529.

P5.3.9.6 Memorial plaque on the pedestal of the Burgher Memorial.
▶ Upper end of Church Street, Cradock, Eastern Cape.
◉ S32° 10.177, E25° 37.063.

P5.3.9.7 Memorial plaque for women and children of the Jacobsdal area who died in concentration camps and also for men and boys from that area who died in prisoner-of-war camps during the war.
▶ Municipal cemetery, De Villiers St, Jacobsdal, Free State.
◉ S29° 08.091, E24° 46.510.

P5.3.9.8 Entrance gate of the Primary School Eenheid (Unity), Modimolle, Limpopo, which symbolically portrays new generations of Afrikaner people rising above the suffering of the concentration camps.
▶ Van Riebeeck St, Modimolle, Limpopo.
◉ S24° 42.437, E28° 24.619.

Concentration camp memorial plaques are also attached to several Burgher Monuments, for example, in Standerton (Mpumalanga), Ventersdorp (North West), Kroonstad (Free State) and Dundee (KwaZulu-Natal).

A number of museums display items related to the women and children's lives and deaths in the concentration camps.

P5.3.9.4

P5.3.9.5

P5.3.9.6

P5.3.9.7

 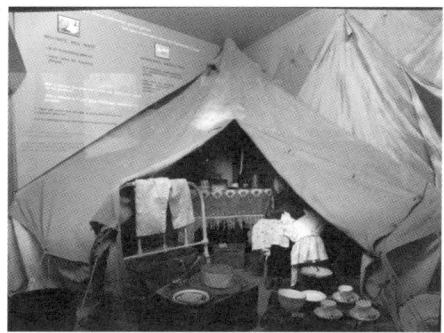 

P5.3.9.8 P5.3.9.9 P5.3.9.10

P5.3.9.9 The War Museum of the Boer Republics in Bloemfontein displays three paintings of concentration camp scenes, as well as a diorama of a concentration camp bell tent.
▶ Monument Rd, Bloemfontein, Free State.
◉ S29° 08.397, E26° 12.569.

P5.3.9.10 The S.P. Engelbrecht Museum displays a sketch of the layout of the Kimberley Concentration Camp made by one of the women forced to go into that camp.
▶ In the old church building on the grounds of the Hervormde Kerk, Wonderboompoort, 45 Eloff St, Eloffsdal, Pretoria. Phone Johann de Bruyn at 082 7333951 to arrange access.
◉ S25° 42.708, E28° 11.238.

The Wall of Names at Freedom Park in Pretoria, Gauteng, includes a section on the Anglo-Boer War that lists the majority of known concentration camp victims. The names are not alphabetically listed. The listing indicates the camp where each person died, and in some instances, the person's age and/or gender. The names of burghers who fell in the war are apparently randomly listed among the names of the women and children, with no further identification. This makes it impossible to make any sense of this list of names.

P5.3.9.11 The Anglo-Boer War (South African War) section of the Wall of Names at Freedom Park.
▶ Salvo Kop, south of the Pretoria Railway Station. Entrance from Kgosi Mampuru St, turning to the east into Skietpoort St (signposted), then south in Koch St.
◉ S25° 45.833, E28° 11.228 (at entrance).

There are a small number of memorial places for people involved in the administration of the concentration camps.

P5.3.9.12 Grave of Samuel Fairhurst, King's Liverpool Regiment, Principal of the Pietersburg Concentration Camp School, who died of enteric fever in 1902.[934]

P5.3.9.11 P5.3.9.12

---

934 Probably the S. Fairhurst of the Liverpool Regiment mentioned by Watt (2000, 132).

▶ *Northern part of the old municipal cemetery, Polokwane, Limpopo (entry from Dahl St, across from western end of Jorissen St).*
◉ *S23° 54.489, E29° 26.783.*

5.4 Boer women and children who eluded internment in the camps

Some Boer women avoided being sent to concentration camps by hiding in caves and mountains. One of the best known of the caves in which women found shelter for a long time was in Meiringskloof, near Fouriesburg in the Orange Free State.

Today it is in the Meiringskloof Nature Reserve.

Another example is Skuilkraal and Skuilkrans, in the Barnardskoppe.[935]

P5.4.1-2 Skuilkraal (left) and Skuilkrans (right).
▶ *On a farm belonging to Ludwig Ankiewicz in the Barnardskoppe, Mpumalanga, between Greylingstad & Villiers.*
◉ *S26° 53.676, E28° 39.244.*

Probably the best known of the Boer women who managed to elude capture and being sent to a concentration camp was Nonnie de la Rey, the wife of the famous general. She and her six youngest children, plus three servants, trekked through the western Transvaal for the last 19 months of the war, using a wagon and a four-wheeled cart. General De la Rey always seemed to know where they were and visited them whenever he could.[936]

P5.4.3 Nonnie de la Rey's gravestone seems to be the only memorial to her. She died 21 years after the end of the war, and was buried near her illustrious husband.
▶ *Municipal Cemetery, Lichtenburg, North West, near Christa St, between Lang St & Burgers St (entry from Thabo Mbeki St).*
◉ *S26° 08.461, E26° 09.228.*

A small number of women who managed to avoid being incarcerated in the camps nevertheless became victims of the war. Anna Susanna Sonnekus, an 18-year-old girl from the farm Klipkuil near Amalia in the present North-West province, was wounded in the back when a British patrol fired at her family one afternoon. She died a few hours later.

P5.4.4 Anna Sonnekus was buried in the family cemetery on Klipkuil, but was later reinterred in Amalia. In 1938, during the celebrations accompanying the Great Trek centenary, this memorial, featuring a statue of Sonnekus, was unveiled in Amalia.

P5.4.1

P5.4.2

P5.4.3

P5.4.4

---

935 Ankiewicz 2011, 88-90.
936 Pretorius 2010, 114; Rowan 2013, 80-87.

▶ *Old town cemetery, southern side of the town, west of Buite St, about 1.3 km from the R504, Amalia, North West.*
◉ *S27° 15.300, E25° 02.517 (courtesy of the Genealogical Society of South Africa).*

An interesting aspect of the war is that a large number of young boys eventually fought on the Republican side. They were called *penkoppe* (lit. "quill-heads" – a name given to young bullocks and rams that are starting to sprout horns). Some *penkoppe* earned great respect for their heroism – none more so than Japie Greyling, son of Commandant B.C. Greyling. On 2 March 1901, he refused to disclose the whereabouts of his father's commando to Colonel J.E.B. Seely of the Imperial Yeomanry. Even when he was stood against a wall on the Greyling farm and faced a firing squad that threatened to shoot him at point blank range if he kept refusing, he declared: "I will not say." In his report of the incident, Seely later expressed his admiration for Japie Greyling, who survived the war.[937]

P5.4.5 The Children's Monument contains memorial plaques that commemorate both Japie Greyling and other Boer boys who fought in the war.
▶ *On the grounds of the Oranje Girls School, 75 Aliwal Street, Bloemfontein, Free State.*
◉ *S29° 06.152, E26° 13.246.*

P5.4.6 The Japie Greyling memorial in Hoopstad.
▶ *On the grounds of the Dutch Reformed Church building, c/o Kerk St & Van Zyl St, Hoopstad, Free State.*
◉ *S27° 50.135, E25° 54.183.*

There is a Japie Greyling memorial at the Japie Greyling Primary School as well.[938]
▶ *C/o Blousysie St & Witkruisarend St, Daleside, Gauteng.*

5.5 The British blockhouse system

Between the major battles of the guerrilla phase, the burghers continued to harass the British forces, seizing supply wagons and blowing up railway culverts and bridges. The British forces attempted to counter these guerrilla tactics by constructing an extensive series of small fortresses called blockhouses. By the end of the war, the blockhouse lines stretched over thousands of kilometres, especially across the two Boer Republics. Blockhouses and fortifications were erected at numerous places all over the Cape Colony and Natal, as well as at strategic places, to safeguard bridges, railway lines and other installations. The blockhouse lines were intended to serve as "holding nets" in which the guerrilla commandos were to be trapped.

A blockhouse was usually a single free-standing roofed structure intended to serve as a fortification against attack by an enemy armed with rifles. It could not withstand artillery. There were two main types of blockhouses in South Africa, namely corrugated iron blockhouses (most built using a design by Major S.R. Rice of the Royal Engineers), and masonry blockhouses (mortared stonework and concrete structures, sometimes three levels in height). Both types were normally surrounded by trenches and coils of barbed wire. Blockhouses were often linked with barbed wire fences against which the British forces planned to drive the Republican commandos.

P5.4.5   P5.4.6

---

937   Pretorius 2010, 165-166.
938   Geyser 1989b, 132-133.

P5.5.1.1 P5.5.1.2 P5.5.1.3

Formal fortifications imply larger structures, sometimes not fully roofed, if roofed at all, often irregular in plan, built with dry, unmortared stonework. These forts were often built and manned by the local Town Guard on low hills close to the towns where they were stationed.

According to British military records, a total of about 7 500 corrugated iron and 440 masonry blockhouses were constructed in South Africa during the course of the war. It is not known how many fortifications were constructed.[939]

5.5.1 Blockhouses and fortifications in the ZAR

Blockhouses and fortifications built by the British forces in the ZAR that survived, or at least partly survived, include the following:

One on Meintjies Kop in Pretoria, Gauteng, called Johnson's Redoubt[940] (on what is today part of the presidential grounds).
One at Thaba Tshwane, also in Pretoria.

P5.5.1.1 Blockhouse known as Barton's Folly.[941]
▶ *On a low hill on the eastern side of the R563, about 150 m from and clearly visible from the R563, 3.5 km south of its junction with the R560, Hekpoort, Gauteng.*
◉ *S25° 55.045, E27° 37.169.*

P5.5.1.2 Blockhouse, Krugersdorp.[942]
▶ *On a square between Potgieter St, Sarel Oosthuizen St & Nicolaas Smit St, Monument, Krugersdorp, Gauteng.*
◉ *S26° 05.798, E27° 47.326.*

P5.5.1.4 P5.5.1.5 P5.5.1.6

---

939 Hattingh & Wessels, 1998; Tomlinson 2000, 340-352.
940 Greyling 2000, 90-91.
941 Oberholster 1972, 299; Richardson 2001, 203.
942 Richardson 2001, 203.

P5.5.1.3 Witkop blockhouse.
▶ *Eastern side of the R59 between Alberton and Vereeniging, Gauteng, at a petrol station near Daleside.*
◙ *S26° 28.093, E 28° 04.155.*

P5.5.1.4 Klerksdorp, North West, Rice-type blockhouse. This blockhouse is an exact replica of a similar blockhouse erected at the same place by the British forces towards the end of the war.
▶ *On Goudkoppie, overlooking the railway line, about 100 m directly south of the N12 (Joe Slovo Rd), west of the corner with Platan Ave.*
◙ *S26° 51.157, E26° 41.165.*

P5.5.1.5 Ruins of a masonary blockhouse, Kommando Nek in the Magaliesberg Mountains, west of the dam wall of the Hartbeespoort Dam.
▶ *Near the top where the R560 crosses the Magaliesberg Mountain, on the eastern side of the R560.*
◙ *About 50 m north of S25° 44.024, E27° 49.321.*

P5.5.1.6 Wood and corrugated-iron guard house in Barberton, Mpumalanga.
▶ *C/o Judge St & Lee St.*
◙ *S25° 47.441, E31° 03.401.*

P5.5.1.7 Rice-type blockhouse on the farm Roodedraai, Mpumalanga.
▶ *About 40 km west of Volksrust. It was moved there from its original location near Amersfoort.*
◙ *S27° 21.702, E29° 32.226.*

There is also a blockhouse called Fort Opperman on the farm Oppermanskraal, near the Sandspruit railway halt north of Volksrust, Mpumalanga. It was built of cement and is three storeys high.[943]

P5.5.1.8 Warmbaths blockhouse.
▶ *Paul Sauer Way, Bela-Bela, Limpopo (southern side of the railway line, south-west of the centre of the town).*
◙ *S24° 53.212, E28° 17.938.*

5.5.2 Blockhouses in the Orange Free State

A number of British blockhouses have survived in the former Republic of the Orange Free State. These include the following:

P5.5.2.1 The historic blockhouse at Jacobsdal was built by the British in 1901, using dolerite. During the Anglo-Boer War, it formed part of a line of similar blockhouses erected to protect the road link between the two railway lines that ran through Kimberley and Bloemfontein.[944]

P5.5.1.7   P5.5.1.8   P5.5.2.1

---
943 Van der Westhuizen & Van der Westhuizen 2013, 72.
944 Richardson 2001, 179; Oosthuizen ca 2000, 17.

P5.5.2.2　　　　　　　　　　　　P5.5.2.3　　　　　　　　　　　　P5.5.2.4

▶ C/o Kerk St & Willie Botha St, Jacobsdal, Free State.
◉ S29° 07.679, E24° 46.776.

P5.5.2.2 Rice-type blockhouse south of Springfontein.
▶ On the farm Prior Grange, on the hillside to the west of the N1 (clearly visible from the road). It was restored by the farm owner, Blackie de Swardt, in 1999.[945]
◉ S30° 20.645, E25° 41.685.

P5.5.2.3 Rice-type blockhouse.
▶ On the historic Steyn farm, Onze Rust (the blockhouse was moved there from Bethulie after the war). Onze Rust is signposted on the N1 south of Bloemfontein.
◉ Near S29° 16.515, E26° 11.334.

P5.5.2.4 Rice-type blockhouse. It originally stood where the Bloemfontein suburb Waverley developed later.[946]
▶ On the grounds of the War Museum of the Boer Republics, Monument Rd, Bloemfontein, Free State.
◉ S29° 08.397, E26° 12.569.

Other Anglo-Boer War blockhouses and fortifications in the Orange Free State which survived include the blockhouse at Harrismith.

5.5.3 Blockhouses and fortifications in the Cape Colony

The British military authorities constructed hundreds of blockhouses and fortifications at strategic points all over the Cape Colony. Several of these British blockhouses and fortifications have survived. Some are almost unscathed, others are partially in ruins. These edifices include the following:

P5.5.3.1　　　　　　　　　　　　P5.5.3.2　　　　　　　　　　　　P5.5.3.3

945　　Venter 2011, 71.
946　　Van der Bank 2001, 84.

Part 5 – The war of attrition

P5.5.3.4

P5.5.3.5

P5.5.3.6

P5.5.3.1 Fortification.
▶ Aties, near Vanrhynsdorp, Western Cape.
◙ GPS co-ordinates not available.

P5.5.3.2 Blockhouse.
▶ South of Tulbagh, Western Cape, next to the railway line.
◙ S33° 19.410, E19° 07.099.

P5.5.3.3-4 Two blockhouses. (See also CP25 on p. 300).
▶ Next to the R46, one on the eastern and one on the western side of the road and railway bridge where the railway line crosses the upper reaches of the Breede River, south of Wolseley, Western Cape.
◙ South-eastern blockhouse at S33° 26.940, E19° 12.406 (P5.5.3.3).
◙ North-western blockhouse at S33° 26.758, E19° 12.240 (P5.5.3.4).

P5.5.3.5 Blockhouse.
▶ Next to the railway line immediately north of Wellington, Western Cape, east of the R44 running between Wellington and Tulbagh.
◙ S33° 37.765, E18° 59.530.

P5.5.3.6 Blockhouse.
▶ Above the R62 tunnel through Kogmans Kloof, in the Langeberg Mountains between Ashton and Montagu, Western Cape.
◙ S33° 48.170, E20° 05.727.

P5.5.3.7 Blockhouse.
▶ On the hill south of and overlooking Uniondale, Western Cape. Exit the town via Kerk St to the south on a gravel road that winds its way to the top of the hill.
◙ S33° 39.591, E23° 07.990.

P5.5.3.7

P5.5.3.8

P5.5.3.9

P5.5.3.8 Blockhouse.
▶ On the southern side of the N1, 12 km east of Laingsburg, Western Cape, on the western side of the Geelbeks Bridge, between the road and the railway line.
◉ S33° 10.319, E20° 59.079.

P5.5.3.9 Blockhouse.
▶ In Beaufort West, on the western side of the main railway line, at the bridge at the western end of Gracia St, near the entrance to the Beaufort West Golf Club.
◉ S32° 20.724, E22° 34.647.

P5.5.3.10 Fortification.
▶ 2 km west of Williston, Northern Cape, near the R353.
◉ S31° 20.163, E20° 53.978.

P5.5.3.11 Rice-type blockhouse.
▶ On Koeëlkop, a prominent hill overlooking Carnarvon, Northern Cape.
◉ S30° 58.583, E22° 07.539 (at the gate at the foot of the hill).

P5.5.3.12 Stone blockhouse.
▶ Southeast of the railway bridge across the Modder River, on the river bank, at Ritchie, south of Kimberley, Northern Cape.
◉ S29° 02.352, E24° 37.551.

P5.5.3.13 Replica of a Rice-type blockhouse.
▶ Southwest of the railway bridge across the Modder River, close to the N12, at Ritchie, south of Kimberley, Northern Cape.
◉ S29° 02.352, E24° 37.551.

P5.5.3.14 Stone blockhouse.
▶ Western side of a railway bridge at Fortrug, on the gravel road between Victoria West and Merriman, Northern Cape.
◉ S31° 22.231, E23° 19.486.

P5.5.3.15 Stone blockhouse.
▶ Eastern side of a railway bridge to the north of Merriman, Northern Cape.
◉ S31° 12'25.034, E23° 37'23.903.

P5.5.3.16 Fortification.
▶ Next to the N1, Richmond, Northern Cape, between the N1 and the town, about 100 m to the west of the western end of Naudé St.
◉ Near S31° 24.694, E23° 56.761.

P5.5.3.17 Unique painted blockhouse.
▶ Hospital Hill, Noupoort, Northern Cape.
◉ S31° 10.518, E24° 56.886.

P5.5.3.18 Blockhouse site.
▶ A memorial next to the N9 north-east of Aberdeen, Eastern Cape, marks a low hill called Gordon's Kop, where there was a British blockhouse in the late stages of the war.
◉ S33° 48.170, E20° 05.727.

P5.5.3.19 Blockhouse.
▶ On a low hill next to the southern extension of Murray Street, on the southern side of Aliwal North, Eastern Cape.
◉ S32° 26.279, E24° 07.614.

Part 5 – The war of attrition

P5.5.3.10

P5.5.3.11

P5.5.3.12

P5.5.3.13

P5.5.3.14

P5.5.3.15

P5.5.3.16

P5.5.3.17

P5.5.3.18

P5.5.3.19

P5.5.3.20

P5.5.3.21

P5.5.3.20 Blockhouse
▶ *Beside the British Garden of Remembrance on Junction Boulevard, between Barkly St and King George St, on the eastern side of Aliwal North, Eastern Cape.*
◉ *S30° 41.235, E26° 43.194.*

P5.5.3.21 Blockhouse.
▶ *Northern side Burgersdorp, Eastern Cape, on a low hill west of the R58, where it enters the town from the north (from Aliwal North).*
◉ *S30° 59.381, E26° 19.934.*

P5.5.3.22 Blockhouse.
▶ *Western side of Burgersdorp, Eastern Cape, on a low hill north of the R58, where it enters the town from the west (from Venterstad).*
◉ *S30° 59.631, E26° 19.509.*

A number of other Anglo-Boer War blockhouses and fortifications of the former Cape Colony have survived. These include the following:
- *in the Western Cape, one at Knysna (in ruins); one on the northern bank of the Blood River near the Ketting railway halt (a poem by Rudyard Kipling, "Bridge Guard in the Karoo", refers to this blockhouse); one at the railway bridge at Leeu-Gamka and two next to the railway line at the Dwyka River bridge west of Prince Albert Road (Deneys Reitz refers to these two blockhouses in his famous memoir* Commando. A Boer Journal of the Boer War*) – all these blockhouses are in a derelict condition;*[947]
- *in the Northern Cape, one at Prieska, one at the Orange River Railway Station near Hopetown, and two at Kuruman, called the Denison and Brown Forts; and*
- *in the Eastern Cape, one at Jansenville, one at the Stormberg railway junction and two near Port Elizabeth.*

5.5.4 Blockhouses in Natal

There is still one blockhouse on the Upper Tugela River near Bergville. This blockhouse was built during the last part of the war. It served as a link in the Natal defence network against the incursions of Boer guerrilla commandos, and is the only known blockhouse of its kind in KwaZulu-Natal that has survived.[948]

5.6 Prisoners of war

5.6.1 Prisoner-of-war sites for British soldiers

The Republican forces took prisoner thousands of British soldiers in the course of the war. In the first stage of the war, these prisoners of war were all taken to Pretoria. The senior officers were held in the Staats Model School and

P5.5.3.22

P5.6.1.1

P5.6.1.2

P5.6.1.3

---

947 Marincowitz 2014, 41-42; Reitz 1931, 273.
948 Richardson 2001, 217.

the lower ranking officers, non-commissioned officers and privates were interned at the race track to the west of the city, where the Pretoria Show Grounds are today.

> *P5.6.1.1 The Staats Model School, completed in 1897.[949] It currently accommodates the Library of the Gauteng Department of Education and provides tours of the buildings to visitors.*
> ▶ *C/o Skinner St & Lilian Ngoyi St, Pretoria Central.*
> ◉ *S25° 45.012, E28° 11.598.*

Winston Churchill, then a young journalist, was taken prisoner by the Boers early in the war on the Natal front, and was held as a prisoner of war in the Staats Model School. He managed to escape on 12 December 1899, and fled on a coal train to Witbank in the then eastern Transvaal (today called Emalahleni, Mpumalanga). The fugitive was given shelter at the Clewer siding by John Howard, the manager of a coal mine. He resumed his flight on another train on 19 December, and managed to make his way to Lourenço Marques in Portuguese East Africa (today known as Maputo in Mozambique), where he arrived on 21 December. From there, he travelled by boat to Durban in Natal, where he received a hero's welcome.[950]

> *There are a number of Churchill-related sites and memorials:*
> - *A commemorative plaque was erected at the place where Churchill found a temporary safe haven near Witbank. This plaque was later moved to the Moth Hall in Witbank (today Emalahleni, Mpumalanga) to protect this artefact.*

> *P5.6.1.2 The commemorative plaque on the wall of the Central Post Office, Durban, where Churchill gave a public speech after his arrival on 23 December 1899.*
> ▶ *C/oDr Pixley Kaseme St & Dorothy Nyembe St, Durban, KwaZulu-Natal.*
> ◉ *S29° 51.479, E31° 01.506.*

The Staats Model School in Pretoria was only used as prisoner-of-war centre for British officers until March 1900. Early in 1900, the Transvaal authorities established two other prisoner-of-war camps – one at Pyramid, adjacent to the railway line north of Pretoria, and the other at Nooitgedacht, near Waterval-Onder in the eastern Transvaal lowveld.[951]

> *P5.6.1.3 The British Garden of Remembrance at the site of the Pyramid camp. It contains a memorial listing the names of 93 prisoners of war who died in this camp, as well as the names of British soldiers who were reinterred here from other cemeteries in the area around Petronella railway station.*
> ▶ *North of Pretoria, next to the R101 (old national road) on the western side, about 200 m north of the intersection with Lusthof Rd, which turns off to Vastfontein. The memorial garden is next to a Kanhym depot and there are pine trees behind the terrain.*
> ◉ *S25° 29.955, E28° 15.528.*

The Nooitgedacht camp was near the Airlie Railway Station, where there is a small British Anglo-Boer War cemetery that contains the graves of members of the British forces who died in the Nooitgedacht prisoner-of-war camp.[952]

After the British invasion of the Republics, the Boers no longer had any facilities for holding prisoners of war. They therefore released British soldiers whom they had taken prisoner after confiscating their weapons.

> *P5.6.1.4 Plaque in the lych-gate of the Fort Napier military cemetery, Pietermaritzburg, KwaZulu-Natal. The inscription reads: "To the Glory of God and in memory of those who died serving their country. This Lych Gate was begun by men of the Royal Engineers who were taken prisoner by the Boers on June 13th 1900 while repairing the railway line near Kroonstad. Refusing to be released on parole they were marched through the*

---

949   Oberholster 1972, 303-304; Jooste 1989, 192; Greyling 2000, 64-66; Richardson 2001, 208.
950   Churchill 1972, 265-304; Bossenbroek 2014, 170-195.
951   Grobler 2004, 27.
952   Van der Westhuizen & Van der Westhuizen 2013, 259-260.

Orange River Colony [the Orange Free State] for 21 days and were put over the Berg into Natal through Olivier's Hoek Pass eventually reaching Pietermaritzburg."
▶ Fort Napier military cemetery, Napier St, Napierville, Pietermaritzburg, KwaZulu-Natal. Contact Henry Davis at 082 473 7512 or phone 082 556 2485 to enquire about access to the cemetery.
◉ S29° 37.182, E30° 21.604.

5.6.2 Prisoner-of-war sites for Republican burghers

The British forces sent the Republican burghers whom they captured to prisoner-of-war camps in Bermuda, India, Ceylon (today Sri Lanka), and St Helena. Burghers who surrendered to the Portuguese authorities in Mozambique were sent to camps in Portugal. The sites associated with those prisoner-of-war camps outside South Africa fall beyond the scope of this publication, but there are still some memorials connected to these prisoners of war.

P5.6.2.1 This statue by Danie de Jager of two Boer prisoners-of-war on the deck of a ship – one an elderly burgher, the other a young penkop, stands in the garden of the War Museum of the Boer Republics. The names of burghers who died on their way to or in the camps overseas are listed on the pedestal of this memorial.[953]
▶ Monument Rd, Bloemfontein, Free State.
◉ S29° 08.397, E26° 12.569.

Republican prisoners of war were initially all sent to the Cape Colony, where they were held, amongst other places, in a camp at the Green Point Race Track[954] (approximately where the Cape Town Stadium is today). Some of those who died in captivity there were buried in the Fort Knokke cemetery, but in 1927 they were reinterred in the Maitland Cemetery.

P5.6.2.2 A memorial plaque for the Boer prisoners of war who died in captivity in this camp was recently unveiled at Fort Wynyard near the site of the former Green Point Race Track, now the Cape Town Stadium.
▶ Entrance at c/o Granger Bay Boulevard & Fort Wynyard St, Green Point, Cape Town, Western Cape.
◉ S33° 54.281, E18° 24.857.

P5.6.2.3 Memorial plaque for Republican prisoners of war who died in May and June 1900, and who were reinterred in the Maitland Cemetery.
▶ Anglo-Boer War Garden of Remembrance, Commonwealth War Graves section, Maitland Cemetery, Voortrekker Rd, Cape Town, Western Cape.
◉ S33° 55.022, E18° 32.280 (Google Maps).

P5.6.2.4 Memorial plaque for Boer prisoners of war who died in the Wynberg Hospital (1900-1902).
▶ St John's Cemetery, eastern side of Court Rd, north of the corner with Church St, Wynberg, Cape Town.
◉ S34° 00.216, E18° 27.999.

P5.6.1.4

P5.6.2.1

P5.6.2.2

P5.6.2.3

---

953 Van Schoor 1989c, 104-106.
954 Wessels 2010, 72-81.

Part 5 – The war of attrition

P5.6.2.4   P5.6.2.5   P5.6.2.6

Large numbers of Republican prisoners of war were held captive at Simonstown, some on land at the Bellevue Camp, others on board ships. A number of those burghers died during their captivity in this area.[955]

P5.6.2.5 Memorial in Simonstown for Republican prisoners of war buried there (see also CP28 on p. 301).
▶ *Old cemetery, northern side of Runciman Rd, south of the M4 (Queen's Rd), Simonstown, Western Cape.*
◉ *Entrance at S34° 11.770, E18° 26.559 (Google Maps).*

Numerous places in South Africa were used as transit camps for Boers taken prisoner during the war. In the Transvaal Republic, one such place was the Old Fort in Johannesburg *(see P2.4.2)*. Another was the prison in Klerksdorp. In Natal, one of those places was the Old Prison in Eshowe.

P5.6.2.6 The prison in Klerksdorp erected in 1891 (it is now a museum). Captured burghers were brought there before being sent in groups to more permanent prisoner-of-war camps.
▶ *C/o Margaretha Prinsloo St & Lombaard St, Klerksdorp, North West.*
◉ *S56° 51.839, E26° 40.138.*

P5.6.2.7 The Old Prison.
▶ *John Ross St, Eshowe, KwaZulu-Natal.*
◉ *S28° 54.128, E31° 27.960.*

The names of 69 burghers who died as prisoners of war in Natal are engraved on a roll of honour on the Burgher Monument at Platrand, near Ladysmith, KwaZulu-Natal (see P3.2.3.19).
◉ *S28° 35.278, E29° 46.357.*

P5.6.2.8 Grave of W. van de Merve (probably W. van der Merwe), a burgher taken prisoner by the British forces, who died as a prisoner of war on 2 April 1902.
▶ *British Garden of Remembrance, western side of Noord Rd, Kroonstad, Free State.*
◉ *S27° 39.049, E27° 13.816.*

P5.6.2.7   P5.6.2.8   P5.6.2.9

---

955   Wessels 2010, 62-71.

P5.6.2.10   P5.6.2.11

A small number of Republican prisoners of war were killed by their guards while attempting to escape or allegedly attempting to escape.

P5.6.2.9 The gravestone of Philip C. Cronjé (22), a burgher from Ficksburg (Orange Free State) who was a prisoner of war in Green Point, Cape Town. He was shot by a camp guard on the evening of 30 April 1900 while he and some friends were singing hymns by the light of a lamp near the camp fence.[956]
▶ *Anglo-Boer War Garden of Remembrance, Commonwealth War Graves section, Maitland Cemetery, Voortrekker Rd, Cape Town, Western Cape.*
◉ *S33° 55.022, E18° 32.280 (Google Maps).*

P5.6.2.10 The name of Henkie Bosch (16) is engraved on the tombstone of his father. Henkie was shot by guards when he attempted to escape from a prisoner of war camp in Bermuda, where he was then buried.[957]
▶ *Old Church Street West Cemetery, Pretoria, Gauteng, entry from Es'kia Mphahlele St (previously D.F. Malan Dr), north of W.F. Nkomo Dr (previously Church St West).*
◉ *Near S25° 44.472, E28° 10.286.*

P5.6.2.11 The gravestone of Charles Kestell, who was 17 years old when he died as a prisoner of war in Natal. He was one of the sons of the deeply revered Reverend J.D. Kestell[958] (see also P7.3.2.6-7).
▶ *Attached to the Burgher Monument at Platrand, Ladysmith, KwaZulu-Natal. The gravestone of Carel Visagie, who was 17 years old when he died as a prisoner of war in Natal, is also attached to this monument (see P3.2.3.19).*
◉ *S28° 35.278, E29° 46.357.*

P5.6.2.12 Burgher Petrus Pretorius died as a prisoner of war in the Princess Christian Hospital in Pinetown.
▶ *His name is at the bottom on the British Memorial in St John the Baptist Anglican Church, on the square between Church Lane, St Johns Ave & Payne St, Pinetown, KwaZulu-Natal.*
◉ *S29° 49.092, E30° 51.947.*

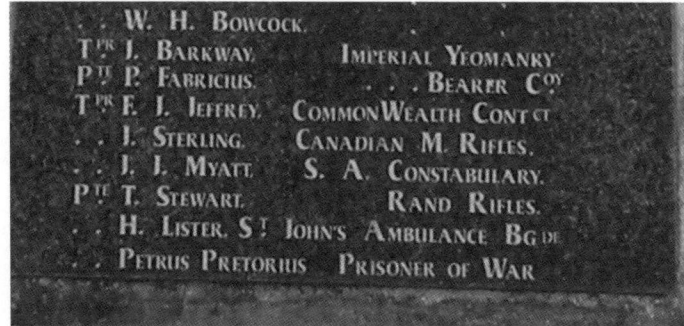 

P5.6.2.12   P5.6.2.13

---

956   Van Niekerk 1972, 62-63; Burger 1977, 109.
957   Blake 2015, 292-294.
958   Kestell ca 1903, dedication.

P5.6.2.13 Gravestone of J.H. de Lange (57). He was a prisoner of war on St Helena Island. Upon his return to South Africa, he died in Vryburg on his way back to his family and home.
▶ *Anglo-Boer War Concentration Camp Cemetery, Vryburg, North West, Hartbees St, near corner with Wildebees St (on the north-western side of the town).*
◉ *S26° 56.659, E24° 42.857.*

P5.6.2.14 A number of museums in South Africa exhibit items associated with the prisoners of war. These include objects made by burghers while they were imprisoned in these camps. An example is this wooden case made by C. Herselman while he was at Trichinopoly, India.
▶ *Exhibited in the S.P. Engelbrecht Museum, on the grounds of the Hervormde Kerk, Wonderboompoort, 45 Eloff St, Eloffsdal, Pretoria. Phone Johann de Bruyn at 082 7333951 to visit.*
◉ *S25° 42.708, E28° 11.238.*

5.7 The treatment of civilian opposition, perceived traitors and collaborators by both sides

5.7.1 A well-known civilian death

On 19 May 1901, the elderly former president of the ZAR, M.W. Pretorius (82), died of pneumonia in Potchefstroom, three days after being interrogated for two hours in cold night air outside his house by British officers.[959]

P5.7.1 Pretorius's monumental gravestone.
▶ *Alexandra Cemetery, close to Olënpark, near Piet Bosman St, between James Moroka Dr & Kock St, Potchefstroom, North West.*
◉ *S26° 42.760, E27° 05.248.*

5.7.2 Those accused of treason, collaboration with the enemy and committing foul deeds

In the course of the war, a number of civilians were accused by one or the other side of treason, of collaborating with the enemy or of committing foul deeds. Many of the accused were convicted and punished. Some were executed, sometimes publicly. For example, on 24 August 1900, the British executed Hans Cordua in Pretoria on charges of conspiring to kidnap Kitchener. Cornelis Broeksma, a Dutch citizen, was also executed in Johannesburg in 1901 on charges of spreading false reports of alleged British atrocities.[960]

P5.7.2 Cordua's grave in the Old Church Street West Cemetery, Pretoria, Gauteng. Cordua's name also appears on the Burgher Monument in this cemetery.
▶ *Entry from Es'kia Mphahlele St (previously D.F. Malan Dr), north of W.F. Nkomo Dr (previously Church St West).*
◉ *Near S25° 44.472, E28° 10.286.*

P5.6.2.14

P5.7.1

P5.7.2

P5.7.3

---

959 Grobler 2004, 116.
960 Brandt 2007, 58-59, 364, 366; Pretorius 2010, 107; Jooste & Webster 2002, 179-187.

P5.7.3 Broeksma's gravestone.
▶ *Near the Enoch Sontonga Memorial in the Braamfontein Cemetery, c/o of Smit St & Graf St, Braamfontein, Johannesburg, Gauteng.*
◉ *S26° 11.699, E28° 01.411.*

Some burghers signed an oath of neutrality and thereafter refrained from supporting the Republican struggle for freedom. They were called 'hendsoppers' and were considered traitors by the bitter-enders, who kept on fighting. Those hendsoppers who subsequently joined the British forces and fought against their former Republican comrades – the 'joiners' – were regarded in an even worse light. They were seen as the spiritual descendants of Judas Iscariot, who betrayed Jesus to the Pharisees in exchange for a handful of coins. Two Boer generals became joiners towards the end of the war, namely General Andries Cronjé (the brother of General Piet Cronjé, who surrendered at Paardeberg on 27 February 1900), and General Piet de Wet (brother of the famous General Christiaan de Wet). They were not captured by the Republican forces during the war, but nevertheless suffered an unwritten life-long sentence, as they were ostracized from Afrikaner society after the war until their deaths.[961]

P5.7.4 Grave of General Piet de Wet.
▶ *Municipal cemetery, near the S192, between Diemont St and the S904, Lindley, Free State.*
◉ *S27° 52.891, E27° 55.763.*

Commandant S.G. (Fanie) Vilonel, a lawyer from Senekal in the Orange Free State, also became a joiner around the middle of 1900. Soon afterwards he was taken prisoner by Republican forces and was put on trial in a special military court on a charge of treason. His sentence was five years imprisonment with hard labour. Since the Republican authorities had no prison building, Vilonel was placed under guard and moved about with the commandos. At the end of July 1900, he was in the Brandwater Basin with General Prinsloo, who used him as an intermediary to negotiate with the British forces about surrendering. All the burghers who eventually surrendered with Prinsloo were made prisoners of war, but Vilonel was set free. He was subsequently involved in the formation of the Orange River Colony Volunteers, a joiner unit.[962]

P5.7.5 Grave of S.G. Vilonel (1866-1918).
▶ *Municipal cemetery, Senekal, Free State.*
◉ *S28° 18.778, E27° 37.287.*

In the Winburg district of the Orange Free State, O.M. Bergh organized a number of hendsoppers and joiners as well as local black Africans into a corps which resorted under the overall command of a British officer. Bergh himself seems to have been given the rank of captain. He and his mixed corps carried out numerous attacks on Republican forces and individuals, burned down farm houses and molested Boer women and children.[963]

P5.7.4

P5.7.5

P5.7.6

---

961 Van Rensburg 1972, 192-194; Grundlingh 1999.
962 Grundlingh 1999, 307-314.
963 Grundlingh 1999, 216-217.

P5.7.6 Grave of O.M. (Oeloff) Bergh.
▶ *Municipal cemetery, east of the N1, between Pienaar St and Mmamahabane Rd, Ventersburg, Free State.*
◉ *S28° 05.076, E27° 08.760.*

Bergh's corps seems to have been responsible for the death of Jan Scott, a burgher of the Winburg district. It is alleged that they murdered him in cold blood in the course of carrying out a raid. Scott was buried on the farm Candy. The following words are inscribed on his gravestone: "*Gestorben door verraad*" [Died due to treason].[964]

The Republican forces executed several people found guilty of treason by military courts; for example, on 19 October 1900, the traitor Willie Robinson was executed north of Frederikstad in the western Transvaal after being sentenced to death by a Republican military tribunal. On 27 December 1900 two joiners, J.A.B. de Beer and P.C. de Bruyn, were executed on the farm Lapfontein, near Hartbeesfontein in the western Transvaal.[965] The same fate befell the joiners H.B. Massijn and J. Cross at Wolmaransstad on 18 October 1901, as well as at least four other joiners in the ZAR.[966] A number of joiners were executed in the Republic of the Orange Free State as well, including J.J. Morgendaal, T.D. Wasserman, H.J. de Bruyn and the brothers N.J. and J.B. Kotzee.[967]

The whereabouts of the graves of these men are unknown (see also P1.27 regarding the execution of G.B. Mousley).

In January 1901, the burghers arrested Meyer de Kock in the eastern Transvaal. He was a hendsopper from Belfast and a prominent member the local Peace Committee, and he attempted to persuade other burghers to surrender too. He was therefore accused of high treason. He was found guilty by a special military tribunal in Roossenekal and executed on 12 February in the Steenkampsberg Mountains.[968]

Meyer de Kock's grave is on the farm Windhoek, about 15 km west of Dullstroom, Mpumalanga, where he was executed.[969]
◉ *GPS co-ordinates not available.*

In January 1901, the Republican military tribunal in Wolmaransstad in the western Transvaal, a small town which was only occasionally occupied by the Imperial forces, sentenced eight men to death after finding them guilty of treason. Six of those men, namely J.P.D. Theunissen (48), his son C.J. Theunissen and his sons-in-law R. Machlachlan (29) and H.A. Ahrens (37), as well as the latter's brother W.F. Ahrens, and H.A. Matthysen were burghers of the ZAR. The seventh condemned man, G.F. Savage, was a citizen of the Orange Free State. R. Boyd (25), the eighth, was Scottish and a British citizen. General de la Rey and General Jan Smuts both confirmed six of the sentences, but C.J. Theunissen was pardoned and released, and W.F. Ahrens's sentence was changed to five years imprisonment with hard labour. Five of the men (J.P.D. Theunissen, Machlachlan, H.A. Ahrens, Boyd and Matthysen) were executed by a firing squad on 23 February 1901. It seems that both Savage and W.F. Ahrens were released in March 1901 by British forces when they occupied Wolmaransstad. Ahrens subsequently went to Natal, where he died of natural causes in October 1901. In 1903, Martha Machlachlan had the bodies of her husband, her father, her brother-in-law and Boyd reinterred in the Presbyterian Section of the cemetery in Klerksdorp. W.F. Ahrens was later reburied next to his brother.[970]

P5.7.7 The vandalised gravestones are, from right to left, those of Boyd, "killed at Wolmaransstad ... with his friends whom he tried to save", Machlachlan, Theunissen and the Ahrens brothers.
▶ *Municipal cemetery, Klerksdorp, North West, near Margaretha Prinsloo St, between O.R. Tambo St and Kadria St.*
◉ *S26° 52.576, E26° 40.130.*

---

964 Grundlingh 1999, 216.
965 Blake 2010, 130-138.
966 Blake 2010, 166-172; 176-189.
967 Blake 2010, 152-166; 190-201.
968 Blake 2010, 142-152; Pretorius 2010, 113.
969 Van der Westhuizen & Van der Westhuizen 2013, 226.
970 Blake 2010, 89-129.

In July 1901, a Republican military court convened on the farm Baltrasna, near Amersfoort in the south-eastern ZAR, to decide on the fate of eight alleged joiners who engaged in a skirmish with members of General Chris Botha's commando earlier that month. Five of the accused, namely the brothers Gert, Pieter, Okkert and Cornelius Brits and their brother-in-law Hendrik Koch, were sentenced to death after being found guilty of high treason. They were executed and buried on this farm. After the war, relatives erected gravestones for these men, containing messages condemning the actions of Botha and his officers.[971]

> *The original farmhouse on Baltrasna, where the accused were condemned, still exists.*
> ◉ *S26° 51.466, E30° 13.632.*[972]

In August 1901, two joiners were shot by a Republican firing squad after being sentenced by a military court in the south of the Heidelberg district in the ZAR.[973]

> *P5.7.8 Graves of Pieter Bouwer and Adolf van Emmenis.*
> ▶ *North of a gravel road between the N3 toll road and its junction with the R54, and Val in the east, Mpumalanga (on a farm).*
> ◉ *S26° 56.161, E28° 37.231.*

In the western Cape Colony, the Boers executed Lambert Colyn on 25 February 1902 near Vanrhynsdorp, after a duly constituted military court presided over by General Jan Smuts had found him guilty of spying for the British Army. Colyn had joined a Boer commando, but disappeared on the very night of a British attack.[974]

> *The house on the farm Windhoek, where Colyn was taken prisoner by members of Smuts's commando, still exists.*
> ◉ *S31° 45.044, E18° 39.606.*[975]

Another Boer who was accused of high treason by his own side was Hendrik Schoeman, a former general. He was acquitted, but was held in prison in Pietersburg (now Polokwane) for further proceedings. After the British occupation of Pietersburg in April 1901, the British released Schoeman and took him to Pretoria, where he was re-united with his family. On 26 May 1901, he was killed in his house when a supposedly spent bombshell which he was using as an ashtray exploded.[976]

> *P5.7.9 Schoeman's gravestone, which also commemorates his daughter, who was killed in the same explosion, and his wife, who died in 1940.*
> ▶ *Old Church Street West Cemetery, Pretoria, Gauteng, entry from Es'kia Mphahlele St (previously D.F. Malan Dr), north of W.F. Nkomo Dr (previously Church St West).*
> ◉ *Grave at S 25°44.473, E 28°10.359.*

P5.7.7

P5.7.8

P5.7.9

971 Blake 2010, 30-44.
972 Blake 2010, 280.
973 Blake 2010, 74-82; Ankiewicz 2011, 82-85.
974 Blake 2010, 230-238; Pretorius 2010, 95.
975 Blake 2010, 326.
976 Schoeman, J. 1950, 214-215; Blake 2010, 249-250.

In the Cape Colony, the British military forces executed a number of Cape Rebels and others who were accused of assisting the Republican cause or of having committed atrocities.

P5.7.10 Plaque illustrating the execution of a Cape Rebel by a British firing squad.
▶ *On the Cape Anglo-Boer War memorial, Laborie Wine Estate, Paarl, Western Cape. Entrance at the western end of Taillefer St.*
◙ *S33° 45.961, E18° 57.529.*

The Cape citizens who were executed by the British include the following (in chronological order):

- Hendrik van Heerden, a shopkeeper from the farm Sevenfontein in the Middelburg district in the Eastern Cape, was executed by a firing squad on 2 March 1901. His grave is next to a farm road opposite his house and shop. His name appears on the Burger Monument in Middelburg.[977]

    P5.7.11 Van Heerden's grave (see also CP27 on p. 300).
    ▶ *On the farm Sewefontein in the Middelburg district, Eastern Cape.*
    ◙ *GPS co-ordinates not available.*

- Charel (Karel) G.J. Nienaber, Jan P. Nienaber and Jan A. Nieuwoudt were sentenced to death by a military tribunal, executed and buried at De Aar on 19 March 1901. Their bodies were exhumed and reinterred in Hanover after the war on the initiative of Olive Schreiner and her husband S.C. Cronwright-Schreiner.[978]

    P5.7.12 Grave monument of the two Nienabers and Nieuwoudt.
    ▶ *Old Cemetery, southern side of N1, western exit to Hanover, Northern Cape.*
    ◙ *S31° 04.354, E24° 26.371.*

- Frederik A. Marais was executed in Middelburg on 10 July 1901.[979]

    Marais, Commandant Hans Lötter and P.J. Wolfaardt are commemorated on a memorial in the Middelburg municipal cemetery (see P4.4.56).

- Johannes Petrus Coetzee, a 16-year old boy from the farm Paardekraal in the Cradock district, joined a Boer commando, but was captured by British forces and sentenced to death by a British military court in Dordrecht. He was subsequently taken to Cradock, but was not informed about his fate. A gathering was held on the square next to the church on 12 July 1901, at which time the death sentence was read out. Coetzee was hanged the next day in the backyard of the local prison. A large number of "undesirables" were forced to witness the execution. He was buried at an unknown location along the banks of the Fish River.[980]

P5.7.10   P5.7.11   P5.7.12   P5.7.13

---

977 Jordaan 1917, 13-15; Jooste & Webster 2002, 30-32.
978 Schoeman, K. 1992, 142-144; Jordaan 1917, 16-31; Jooste & Webster 2002, 32-35.
979 Jordaan 1917, 33-37; Jooste & Webster 2002, 41-44.
980 Jooste & Webster 2002, 38-41.

P5.7.13 Coetzee's name is engraved on top on the burgher monument next to the church where his sentence was read out.
▶ Upper end of Church Street, Cradock, Eastern Cape.
◉ Near S32° 10.177, E25° 37.063.

- P.W. Klopper was hanged in Burgersdorp on 20 July 1901.[981]

P5.7.14 In Burgersdorp, Eastern Cape, there is still a stump of a tree where Cape Rebels were sentenced. It is now a monument. The inscription reads: "Blue gum tree, 90 years old. Largest tree in North Eastern Cape. Under this tree, the water scheme was opened in 1898. Burgher P. Klopper's death penalty was read out here in the Anglo-Boer War. Joint service held with the formation of the Union of South Africa. Commemorative plaque unveiled during the centenary ox wagon trek, Burgersdorp, 12 October 1938" (translated by the author).
▶ Town Square, between Jan Greyling St, Piet Retief St, Chase St and Church St, Burgersdorp, Eastern Cape.
◉ S 30° 59.632, E26° 19.879.

P5.7.15 The old jail (built in 1861) where Klopper was hanged.[982]
▶ Hopley St, at the northern entrance to Burgersdorp, Eastern Cape.
◉ S30° 59.460, E26° 19.976.

Klopper's name appears at the top of the burgher monument in the municipal cemetery, Burgersdorp (see P7.2.7.2).

- Cornelius Johannes Claassen (22), a farm worker from the Somerset East district, was hanged in Somerset East on 24 July 1901 after being sentenced to death by a British military court. His last resting place is not known.[983]

One of the exhibits in the Somerset East museum is a walking stick with his name carved upon it. The carving was done by a burgher interned in the Port Alfred camp.

- Hendrik Jacobs and Abraham Jooste, members of the Kakamas Cape Rebel Commando, were also executed on 24 July 1901. They were captured by the Border Scouts after the Battle of N'Rougas, where Jacobs was lightly wounded. A British military court in Kenhardt found them guilty of high treason and of being in possession of lead-tipped bullets, and it sentenced them to death. All the male inhabitants of Kenhardt were forced to witness their execution by firing squad. They were buried at an unknown location.[984]

P5.7.16 Memorial with the names of Jacobs and Jooste (photo courtesy of Martie du Toit, Genealogical Society of South Africa).
▶ Municipal cemetery, Kenhardt, Northern Cape.
◉ GPS co-ordinates not available.

P5.7.14　　　　　　　　　　　P5.7.15　　　　　　P5.7.16　　　　P5.7.17

981　Jordaan 1917, 43-51; Jooste & Webster 2002, 45-49.
982　Jooste & Webster 2002, 45-48.
983　Jooste & Webster 2002, 37-38.
984　Jordaan 1917, 57-60.

- Executed in Graaff-Reinet: P.J. Fourie, J. Van Rensburg and L.F.S. Pfeiffer on 19 August 1901, Daniel Olewagen and Ignatius Nel on 26 August 1901, Johannes Hermanus Roux on 7 October 1901, and J.F. Geldenhuys on 14 February 1902.[985]

  P5.7.17 This memorial in Graaff-Reinet commemorates Fourie, Van Rensburg, Pfeiffer, Olewagen, Nel, Roux, Geldenhuys and others executed by the British military authorities in that town. It was unveiled in 1908. It was erected on privately owned property donated by Jurie Laubscher, since both the town authorities and the council of the Dutch Reformed Church refused to allow the memorial on their grounds, probably fearing that the memorial would hamper post-war reconciliation between British and Afrikaners.[986]
  ▶ C/o Donkin St & Somerset St, Graaff-Reinet, Eastern Cape.
  ◙ S32° 15.199, E24° 31.667.

- The Cape Rebel John Alexander Baxter was found guilty of wearing parts of a British military uniform while fighting for the Republican cause. He was sentenced to death by a military court on October 1901. The sentence was carried out on the farm Government Marsh, Aberdeen, in the Eastern Cape.[987]

  P5.7.18 After the execution, Baxter was buried in the municipal cemetery at Aberdeen. On his gravestone he is described as "A hero of the Anglo-Boer War 1899-1902".
  ▶ Municipal cemetery, western side of Aberdeen, Eastern Cape.
  ◙ S32° 28.735, E24° 03.564.

- Those executed by the British in Tarkastad were Jacobus Schoeman, on 12 October 1901, P.W. van Heerden, on 13 November 1901, and Lieutenant Bester in December 1901.[988]

  P5.7.19 The grave of P.W. van Heerden. Few believed that he could have provided information on the whereabouts of the Republican commandos to anybody, since he suffered from bad eyesight.[989]
  ▶ Municipal cemetery, Craddock St, Tarkastad, Eastern Cape (at the entrance of the town from Cradock/Hofmeyr).
  ◙ S32° 00.170, E26° 15.444.

- The Cape Rebel Willie Louw was executed in Colesberg on 23 November 1901.[990]

  P5.7.20 Louw's name, as well as that of four other burghers or Cape Rebels who were executed in Colesberg appear on the Burgher memorial in that town.
  ▶ Station Rd, next to the British Garden of Remembrance, northern side of Colesberg, Eastern Cape, just south of and visible from the N1.
  ◙ S30° 42.700, E25° 06.114.

P5.7.18

P5.7.19

P5.7.20

---

985 Jordaan 1917, 63-79, 175-176; Jooste & Webster 2002, 50-61.
986 McNaughton s.a, 5.
987 Jordaan 1917, 105-108.
988 Jordaan 1917, 95-97, 143, 187-190.
989 Van Zyl 1944, 339.
990 Jordaan 1917, 131-139.

P5.7.21 P5.7.22

Louw's grave is in the family cemetery on the farm Eenzaamheid in that district.

- Arnold Renike (a Cape Rebel) and Louis Brink from the Mafeking district were publicly executed for murder at the Mafeking prison on 28 December 1901. Both men entered a plea stating that they had acted on the instructions of their commander, General Snyman.[991]

The Mafeking prison still stands but has been renovated beyond recognition.

- In Vryburg in the northern Cape Colony, four Cape Rebels – N.C. Rautenbach, J.G.W. Jansen and the brothers J. and H. Kuhn – were hanged in public near the prison after being found guilty of providing assistance to the Republican forces.[992]

P5.7.21 Front door of the Old Jail Museum with a granite plaque on the right which relates the fate of the Rebels (photo courtesy of the Genealogical Society of South Africa).
▶ *In the Leon Taljaard Game Reserve, on the western side of Vryburg, entry from the N14 leading to Kuruman.*
◉ *S26° 57.815, E24° 42.961.*

- Local tradition claims that C. Olivier, a young Cape Rebel who belonged to General Wynand Malan's commando, was shot in cold blood by two British soldiers on the farm Bulthoudersfontein, between Victoria West and Richmond in the Karoo. The inscription on his grave does not indicate the date of his death.[993]

P5.7.22 Grave of C. Olivier
▶ *On the farm Bulthoudersfontein, eastern side of the R63 southeast of Victoria West, 15.2 km north of the N1. The farm is currently owned by Louis Diederichs.*
◉ *S31° 38.319, E23° 19.538.*

P5.7.23 P5.7.24

---

991 Jordaan 1917, 145-146.
992 Jordaan 1917, 89-92 & 141.
993 Pieterse 1946, 229-230; Van Bart & Scholtz 2003, 257-258.

- In Dordrecht, Piet Bester, a Cape Rebel and former policeman, was captured by British forces on 18 November and summarily sentenced to death by a military tribunal in Dordrecht in the Eastern Cape. He was executed the next day.[994]

   P5.7.23 Memorial for four burghers reinterred in the municipal cemetery, including P. Bester.
   ▶ *Near Bekker St, Dordrecht, Eastern Cape.*
   ◙ *S31° 22.964, E27° 02.838.*

- In Aliwal-North in the Eastern Cape, a Republican officer, Lieutenant Izak Liebenberg (18), was hanged in the prison on 11 January 1902 after having been found guilty by a British military tribunal of murdering Lieutenant L.H. Nieumeyer. The latter was a joiner who became an officer in the Orange River Colony Police. It seems that Nieumeyer was shot after having been taken prisoner by Commandant Gideon Scheepers's commando but then attempted to escape on 23 November 1900. Liebenberg himself was taken prisoner by the British forces in July 1901 and taken to Aliwal-North where he was accused of the murder and found guilty.[995]

   Liebenberg's grave is in the family cemetery on the Farm Grootfontein, near Philippolis, Free State, where he was reinterred after the war. His name appears on the role of honour at the Aliwal-North Concentration Camp Monument[996] (see P5.3.8.1).

   P5.7.24 Nieumeyer's grave is in the British Garden of Remembrance, Aliwal North, Eastern Cape. The gravestone is in the front row, immediately left of the path leading to the Roll of Honour, on which his name appears as well.
   ▶ *Junction Boulevard between Barkly St & King George St.*
   ◙ *S30° 41.235, E26° 43.194.*

In addition to Cape Rebels and others who were executed, the British military authorities locked up numerous so-called undesirables in prisons or other places of safe-keeping for long periods during the war. Thus Professor J.L. Cachet of the Theological Seminary of the Reformed Church in Burgersdorp was locked up in the goal in that town, the same goal where the Cape Rebel P.W. Klopper was executed, because of Cachet's pro-Boer tendencies.

   P5.7.25 Memorial plaque on the wall of the old goal with information on Cachet's detention.
   ▶ *Hopley St, at the northern entrance of Burgersdorp, Eastern Cape.*

Reverend David Ross of the Dutch Reformed Church in Lady Grey, who had expressed a stern warning to his congregation against participation in the war on the Republican side, was nevertheless jailed for an extended period in Aliwal North on a charge of high treason. After his release, he never preached in English again, although he had often done so before the war.[997]

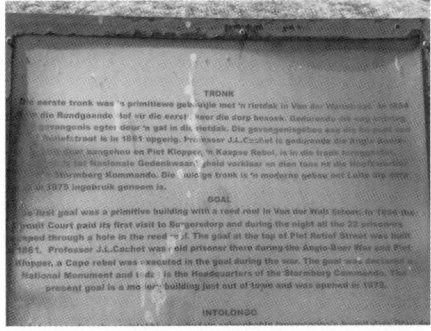   

P5.7.25   P5.7.26   P5.7.27   P5.7.28

---

994   Grobler 2004, 129.
995   Blake 2010, 209-211.
996   Blake 2010, 212.
997   Oosthuizen 1998, 51.

P5.7.26 The grave of Reverend David Ross and his wife Agnes.
▶ *Town cemetery, c/o Dwars St & Murray St, Lady Grey, Eastern Cape.*
◉ *S30° 42.556, E27° 12.663.*

A large number of Eastern Cape undesirables were "banned" (exiled) by the British military authorities to Port Alfred to isolate them from the remainder of the Cape population.[998]

P5.7.27 One of the Port Alfred undesirables, Casper Johan Lötter, died and was buried there.
▶ *Town cemetery, Port Alfred, Northern Cape.*

One of many to suffer under the British system of military imprisonment was Francois Malan, editor of the newspaper *Ons Land*. He was sentenced to one year in prison because his newspaper had published criticism of the conditions in the Howick Concentration Camp. He served his sentence in the Tokai Mansion, which was used as a reformatory at that time.[999] After the war, and from 1910, he became a member of the first cabinet of the Union of South Africa.

P5.7.28 Plaque illustrating a victim of British military imprisonment.
▶ *On the Cape Anglo-Boer War memorial, Laborie Wine Estate, Paarl, Western Cape. Entrance at the western end of Taillefer St.*
◉ *S33° 45.961, E18° 57.529.*

Natal Rebels

P5.7.29 Grave of P.J. de Wet (22). He came from the Newcastle District and died in prison in Pietermaritzburg on 10 November 1900. Reverend H.F. Schoon believed that De Wet died due to negligence – De Wet was already close to death when he arrived in Pietermaritzburg, either as a convicted rebel or as a person awaiting trial, but no doctor was called to treat him.[1000] His name is not listed on the Burgher Memorial at Platrand.
▶ *In the Voortrekker Cemetery, south-western side of Chief Albert Luthuli St, across from the junction with Geere St, Pietermaritzburg, KwaZulu-Natal.*
◉ *S29° 36.425, E30° 23.064.*

5.8 Medical support and the war

In addition to exhibits in the War Museum of the Boer Republics in Bloemfontein, Free State, the Cape Medical Museum contains excellent exhibits specifically on medical aspects of the Anglo-Boer War.[1001]
▶ *C/o Beach Rd & Portswood Rd, Green Point, Cape Town, Western Cape.*
◉ *S33° 54.312, E18° 25.085.*

P5.7.29

P5.8.1.1   P5.8.1.2

---

998   Radloff 1903, 91-96.
999   Preller 1968, 518; Oberholster 1972, 53.
1000 Wassermann 2004, 505.
1001 Van Bart & Scholtz 2003, 142-143.

5.8.1 Hospitals and ambulances

Republican medical services

> P5.8.1.1 The Rhode House Museum exhibits photographs of medical services in the Republics.
> ▶ Athlone Street, Mooi River, KwaZulu-Natal.
> ◉ S29° 12.548, E29° 59.760.

> P5.8.1.2 Ambulance wagon used by the Boer forces in the Battle of Stormberg, 10 December 1899.
> ▶ Exhibit in the town museum, Piet Retief St (the R58), north of corner with Chase St, Burgersdorp, Eastern Cape.
> ◉ S30° 59.554, E26° 19.898.

In addition to existing hospitals, such as the Volkshospitaal in Pretoria, the Republican military authorities were soon forced to use various public buildings such as the recently opened Staatsmeisjesschool (Government School for Girls) and churches for medical purposes as well.

The Volkshospitaal in Pretoria no longer exists, and the building has been demolished.

> P5.8.1.3 Staatsmeisjesschool. After occupying Pretoria in June 1900, the British forces also used this building as a hospital. After the war it finally became a school, and it still functions as one.[1002]
> ▶ Visagie St, between Sisulu St & Lilian Ngoyi St, Pretoria Central, Gauteng.
> ◉ S25° 45.113, E28° 11.680.

> P5.8.1.4 The Dutch Reformed Church in Jacobsdal, Free State. The original part of the church building (which has been extended and renovated since the war) was first used by the First German Red Cross Ambulance as a typhoid hospital. After their occupation of Jacobsdal in February 1900, the British forces also used this church building as a hospital.[1003]
> ▶ C/o Church St & Andries Pretorius St, Jacobsdal, Free State.
> ◉ S29° 07.731, E24° 46.460.

On the battlefield, the Republics used field ambulances. An unknown number of private houses, both in towns and on farms, were used as hospitals by the burgher forces, in most cases for brief periods only. One example is the following:

> P5.8.1.5 The house of Mrs Neethling, widow of Reverend Neethling of the Dutch Reformed Church, which she used during the war to nurse Boers.[1004]
> ▶ Church St, near corner with Van Rooyen St, Utrecht, KwaZulu-Natal.
> ◉ S27° 39.283, E30° 19.253.

P5.8.1.3 P5.8.1.4 P5.8.1.5

1002 Greyling 2000, 62.
1003 De Villiers 1998, 18-45.
1004 Van der Westhuizen & Van der Westhuizen 2013, 23.

British medical services

The British military forces in this war used both existing hospitals and turned existing buildings into hospitals. They also had a number of field hospitals, which consisted of temporary structures specifically erected to serve as hospitals. The following are among the many places of remembrance in connection with these hospitals in the Cape Colony:

> *P5.8.1.6 The Milner Hotel in Matjiesfontein was built in the early stages of the war. The town itself was headquarters to the British Cape Command for most of the war. Part of the hotel served as a convalescent hospital for British officers at the time when the sick Gideon Scheepers was there, before being taken away to be shot. The building's central turret was used as an armed lookout post.[1005]*
> ▶ *In the centre of Matjiesfontein.*
> ◉ *S33° 13.524, E20° 34.556.*

The Palace Barracks Hospital in Simonstown was used, amongst other things, by the British military medical service to nurse Republican prisoners of war who contracted enteric fever.[1006]

> *P5.8.1.7 Memorial for British soldiers who died at No 3 General Military Hospital at Rondebosch, Cape Town.*
> ▶ *Anglo-Boer War Garden of Remembrance, Commonwealth War Graves section, Maitland cemetery, Voortrekker Rd, Cape Town, Western Cape.*
> ◉ *S33° 55.022, E18° 32.280 (Google Maps).*

> *P5.8.1.8 Memorial for Presbyterian soldiers who died in the British military hospitals, Wynberg, Cape Town.*
> ▶ *Anglo-Boer War Garden of Remembrance, Commonwealth War Graves section, Maitland cemetery, Voortrekker Rd, Cape Town, Western Cape.*
> ◉ *S33° 55.022, E18° 32.280 (Google Maps).*

In Port Elizabeth, the Drill Hall was transformed into a military hospital with 50 beds, and in an emergency could provide 70 beds. There were two small isolation wards served by two civilian surgeons.[1007]

> *P5.8.1.9 The Drill Hall in Port Elizabeth.*
> ▶ *C/o Propect St & Daly St, Port Elizabeth Central, Eastern Cape.*
> ◉ *S33° 57.805, E25° 37.250.*

> *P5.8.1.10 The Rhenish mission church building in Carnarvon, built in 1858, was used as a hospital by the British forces.*
> ▶ *Union Square, Carnarvon, Northern Cape.*
> ◉ *S30° 57.981, E22° 07.719.*

> *P5.8.1.11 The original section of the Victoria Hospital, Mahikeng, North West, was built in 1899 to serve as hospital. It was named after Sister Victoria. It housed the wounded during the Siege of Mafeking. One of Winston Churchill's aunts, Lady Sarah Wilson (née Churchill), was a nurse here.[1008] Today it is a private hospital.*
> ▶ *Victoria Rd, between Warren St & Carrington St, Mahikeng, North West.*
> ◉ *S25° 51.595, E25° 38.500.*

> *P5.8.1.12 Nurses of Mercy Home, where the nurses of the Victoria Hospital were accommodated.*
> ▶ *Victoria Rd, next to the Victoria Hospital. Victoria Rd, between Warren St & Carrington St, Mahikeng, North West.*
> ◉ *S25° 51.595, E25° 38.500.*

1005 Westby-Nunn 2000, 87; Fransen 2004, 544.
1006 Van Bart & Scholtz 2003, 139.
1007 De Villiers I 2008a, 260.
1008 Westby-Nunn 2000, 156.

Part 5 – The war of attrition

P5.8.1.6

P5.8.1.7

P5.8.1.8

P5.8.1.9

P5.8.1.10

P5.8.1.11

P5.8.1.12

P5.8.1.13

P5.8.1.14

P5.8.1.15

P5.8.1.13 Building used as field hospital by the British forces.
▶ *South-eastern c/o Ryneveld and Darling streets, Hanover, Northern Cape.*
◉ *GPS co-ordinates not available.*

P5.8.1.14 Memorial. "Erected by the officers, n.c. officers and men of the Third Stationary Hospital, to the sacred memory of their comrades, who died from disease, contracted in the performance of their duty during the South African War."
▶ *Anglo-Boer War British Garden of Remembrance, De Aar, Northern Cape (on the northern side of town, next to the R48 to Philipstown, between the old cemetery and the railway line).*
◉ *S30° 38.718, E24° 00.971.*

P5.8.1.15 Imperial Yeomanry Hospital Memorial (see also CP19 on p. 297). A recent book claims that this field hospital was the largest surgical and convalescent facility of its kind ever used by the British Army.[1009] The inscription reads: "Sacred to the Memory of the Officers, NCO's and Men of the Imperial Yeomanry Hospital who died in the execution of their duty at Deelfontein." The following names appear on the Memorial: Dr R.T. Fitzhugh (27) (MB, London, Medical Officer Imperial Yeomanry Hospital), Surgeon Dresser Charles B. Sells (26), Sergeants C.E. Willmore (or Wilmore, St John's Ambulance), F. Phillips (47) & G. Vassie, Private J.V.L. Barrett (21, St John's Ambulance), Civilian Cook J. Harvey & Private G.M. Saunders (45).[1010]
▶ *Deelfontein cemetery, Northern Cape, on the western side of an unnamed road about 46 km southwest of De Aar, on the western side of the railway line, a few hundred metres south of the old railway station.*
◉ *S30° 59.779, E23° 47.581.*

P5.8.1.16 No 6 General Hospital, memorial for the "Nursing Sister and Men, Royal Army Medical Corps", who died during the war.
▶ *Gerrie Opperman St, Noupoort, Northern Cape.*
◉ *S31° 10.343, E24° 57.140.*

In Natal, the British authorities commandeered whatever facilities they could use as hospitals, or erected field hospitals.

P5.8.1.17 Victoria Hall, Maritzburg College, Pietermaritzburg, was used as a hospital for sick and wounded British soldiers.
▶ *College Rd, Pietermaritzburg, KwaZulu-Natal.*
◉ *S29° 36.995, E30° 22.873 (Google Maps).*

P5.8.1.18 Scale model of British military hospital in Mooi River.
▶ *Rhode House Museum, Athlone Street, Mooi River, KwaZulu-Natal. This museum exhibits photographs of that hospital as well.*
◉ *S29° 12.548, E29° 59.760.*

P5.8.1.16   P5.8.1.17   P5.8.1.18

1009   Willis, Van Dyk & De Villiers 2016, 12.
1010   Watt 2000, 21, 138, 183, 331, 368, 373, 428 & 456.

P5.8.1.19 P5.8.1.20 P5.8.1.21

P5.8.1.19 Granite pillar "In memory of the British officers and men who died in No 1 Stationary Hospital at Charlestown between August 1899 and July 1902 and now lie buried here at Newcastle".
▶ *Municipal cemetry, Hardwick St, Newcastle, KwaZulu-Natal.*
◉ *S27° 45.369 E29° 56.616.*

After their occupation of the Boer Republics, the British forces continued using a variety of facilities, including churches and school buildings, as hospitals. For example, in Bloemfontein in the Orange Free State, they took over the buildings of a well-known school, Grey College, as a military hospital.[1011]

P5.8.1.20 A building in Bloemfontein constructed in 1899, later to become the Elizabeth le Roux Hostel of the Oranje Meisies Skool, was used for the same purpose.[1012]
▶ *75 Aliwal Street, Bloemfontein, Free State.*
◉ *S29° 06.152, E26° 13.246.*

P5.8.1.21 The Fourth Raadsaal, where the Volksraad (People's Council) of the Republic of the Orange Free State held its meetings, was turned into a British hospital after their occupation of Bloemfontein[1013] (see also CP23 on p. 200).
▶ *South-eastern c/o President Brand St & Charles St, Bloemfontein, Free State.*
◉ *S29° 06.922, E26° 13.048.*

P5.8.1.22 The Dutch Reformed Church in Winburg. The cornerstone of this church was laid on 20 January 1899 by M.T. Steyn, President of the Orange Free State. During the war, the unfinished building was converted into a British hospital.[1014]
▶ *In front of the central Dutch Reformed Church, Church Square, c/o Nico van der Merwe St & Wilcocks St, Winburg, Free State.*
◉ *S28° 31.115, E27° 00.700.*

P5.8.1.22 P5.8.1.23 P5.8.1.24

1011 De Villiers I 2008a, 290.
1012 Richardson 2001, 171; Van der Bank 2001, 22.
1013 NALN 1989d, 86; De Villiers I 2008a, 290.
1014 Richardson 2001, 188-189.

In the ZAR (the Transvaal), after their occupation of Pretoria, the British forces used a number of well-known buildings as hospitals. This included the Staatsmeisjesschool building (*P5.8.1.3*), the Staats Model School building (*P5.6.1.1*), a private residence called Merton Keep (*currently the headquarters of the French Embassy in Pretoria*) and the then still not completed Palace of Justice building in the city centre.[1015]

P5.8.1.23 Palace of Justice.
▶ *North-western corner, Church Square, Pretoria, Gauteng.*
◉ *S25° 44.747, E28° 11.256.*

P5.8.1.24 The Dutch Reformed Church in Rustenburg (western Transvaal) had been completed but not yet inaugurated when the war broke out. The Republican forces used the building as a hospital early in the war. The British forces also used it as a hospital after their occupation of the town.[1016]
▶ *Plein St, between Tuin St & Burger St, Rustenburg, North West.*
◉ *S25° 40.312, E27° 14.709.*

P5.8.1.25 The Dutch Reformed Church, Klerksdorp, North West, was inaugurated in October 1898. It was used as a hospital by the British army during the war.
▶ *C/o R30 Anderson St & Bram Fischer St, Klerksdorp, North West.*
◉ *S26° 51.998, E26° 39.964.*

5.8.2 Medical personnel who died in battles/skirmishes or of wounds

P5.8.2.1 Memorial to all medical personnel who served during the war.
▶ *Municipal cemetery, De Villiers St, Jacobsdal, Free State.*
◉ *S29° 08.091, E24° 46.510.*

Republican medical personnel casualties

The best known Republican medical officer killed in action was Captain (Dr) J.O. Höhls, Chief of Medical Services of the Transvaal State Artillery.

P5.8.2.2 He was buried with full military honours in the German section of the Old Cemetery, Church Street West, Pretoria.
▶ *Old Church Street West Cemetery, Pretoria, Gauteng, entry from Es'kia Mphahlele St (previously D.F. Malan Dr), north of W.F. Nkomo Dr (previously Church St West).*
◉ *Grave at S25° 44.473, E28° 10.359.*

P5.8.1.25

P5.8.2.1

P5.8.2.2

1015 Greyling 2000, 22, 62, 66, 81.
1016 Richardson 2001, 269; De Villiers I 2008, 625.

Part 5 – The war of attrition

British medical personnel casualties

Major E.W. Gray (37), Royal Army Medical Corps, died on 31 October 1899 of wounds received in action at Lombard's Kop the previous day.[1017]

> P5.8.2.3 The gravestone of Major Gray.
> ▶ Municipal cemetery, southern side of Cemetery Road, between Illings St & Mandela St, Ladysmith, KwaZulu-Natal.
> ◉ S28° 33.322, E29° 47.687.

Grave of Sergeant-Major F.H. Newdigate (48) of the Cape Medical Volunteer Staff, killed in action at Fabersput in Griqualand West in a battle against Cape Rebels on 30 May 1900.[1018] His wife had the following engraved on his tombstone: "Killed by rebels here … while on ambulance duty…".

> P5.8.2.4 Newdigate's grave.
> ▶ In the West End Cemetery, c/o Green St & Reserve Rd, Kimberley, Northern Cape. There is also a memorial in this cemetery on which his name is listed (see also P3.6.42).
> ◉ S28° 44.078, E24° 44.170 (Google Maps).

Surgeon-Lieutenant Herbert A. Palmer (27), 5th Victorian Contingent, was killed in action at Wilmansrust in the eastern Transvaal on 12 June 1901.[1019]

> P5.8.2.5 Palmer's gravestone
> ▶ British Garden of Remembrance, old municipal cemetery, entry from Bhimy Damane St, Middelburg, Mpumalanga.
> ◉ S25° 45.832, E29° 26.849.

5.8.3 Medical personnel who died of disease

Republican medical personnel who died of disease

> P5.8.3.1 Grave of Mrs Louise Laridon (née van Houten) (1850-1900), a member of the Belgian-German Ambulance which arrived in Pretoria via Lourenço Marques in January 1900 to serve the Boers. She was from a prominent Belgian family. A dedicated and respected nurse, during the Boer retreat from Bloemfontein, she worked in a typhoid hospital in Kroonstad. She contracted the disease herself and died on 10 May 1900 near Lindley, and was buried there. Several dignitaries were present at her funeral.[1020]
> ▶ Municipal cemetery, near the S192, between Diemont St and the S904, Lindley, Free State.
> ◉ S27° 52.891, E27° 55.763.

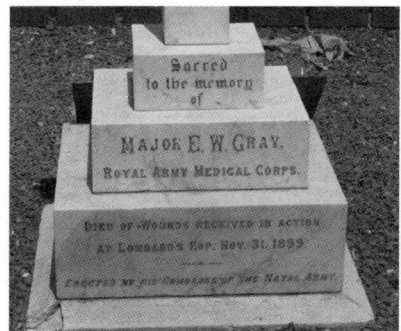
P5.8.2.3

P5.8.2.4

P5.8.2.5

P5.8.3.1

1017 Watt 2000, 165.
1018 Watt 2000, 307.
1019 Watt 2000, 320.
1020 De Villiers I 2008a, 532.

P5.8.3.2

P5.8.3.3

P5.8.3.4

British medical personnel who died of disease

P5.8.3.2 Grave of Sister Superintendent Margaret Cassilis Rose (31), Army Nursing Service, who died in Durban on 3 January 1900.[1021] She was the Sister Superintendent on board the hospital ship Lismore Castle.
▶ West Street Cemetery, entry from Theatre Lane between West St & Brook St, Durban, KwaZulu-Natal.
◉ S29° 51.517, E31° 00.841.

P5.8.3.3 Grave of Nursing Sister Eleanor O'Brien, who died at Ladysmith on 29 December 1899.[1022]
▶ Municipal cemetery, on the southern side of Cemetery Rd, between Illings St & Mandela St, Ladysmith, KwaZulu-Natal.
◉ S28° 33.322, E29° 47.687.

P5.8.3.4 Graves of Dr R.T. Fitzhugh, Medical Officer in the Imperial Yeomanry Hospital, who died of enteric fever on 15 June 1900, Major T.A.P. Marsh (44), Royal Army Medical Corps, who died on 22 May 1900 of enteric fever contracted whilst in command of the De Aar Military Hospital, and Second Lieutenant B.E. Cummings (21), Royal Artillery, who died of enteric fever on 9 May 1900.[1023]
▶ Deelfontein cemetery, Northern Cape, western side of an unnamed road about 46 km southwest of De Aar, on the western side of the railway line, a few hundred metres south of the old railway station. Fitzhugh is also mentioned on the Imperial Yeomanry Hospital Memorial, in the same cemetery (also see P5.8.1.15).
◉ S30° 59.779, E23° 47.581.

P5.8.3.5 Grave of Major Surgeon Quinten R. Veitch (43), Cape Medical Staff Corps, who died of disease on 2 February 1902.[1024]
▶ Anglo-Boer War Garden of Remembrance, Commonwealth War Graves section, Maitland Cemetery, Voortrekker Rd, Cape Town, Western Cape.
◉ S33° 55.022, E18° 32.280 (Google Maps).

P5.8.3.5

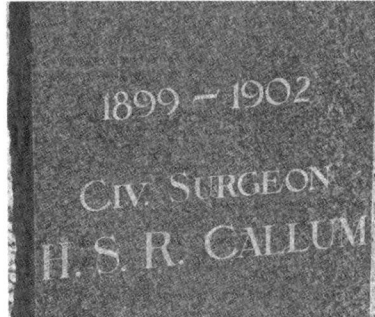
P5.8.3.6

P5.8.3.7

1021   Watt 2000, 360.
1022   Watt 2000, 312.
1023   Watt 2000, 98, 138 & 266.
1024   Watt 2000, 429.

P5.8.3.6 Grave of Civilian Surgeon H.S.R. Callum, drowned at Sannaspos on 14 April 1902.[1025]
▶ *British battlefield cemetery, Sannaspos, Free State.*
◉ *S29° 09.568, E26° 32.783 (Google Maps).*

P5.8.3.7 Gravestones (from left to right) of Surgeon Herbert Davies (26), Surgeon Tom Jones (52) and Nursing Sister Florence Louise Sage (32), all of the Welsh Hospital, who all died of disease in Springfontein in June 1900 and were buried there.[1026] This was before the concentration camp was established.
▶ *Concentration camp cemetery. Turn in an easterly direction into Emily Hobhouse St from Settlers St (the main road through Springfontein). Cross the railway line and turn right (south) after another 200 m. Follow the signs to the cemetery.*
◉ *S30° 16.586, E25° 42.793.*

P5.8.3.8 Grave of Trooper F.W. Owles (26), Royal Army Medical Corps, 23rd Field Hospital, who died of disease at Bethlehem on 27 November 1900.[1027]
▶ *Old town cemetery, between Muller St & Boshoff St, near corner with Baxter St, Bethlehem, Free State.*
◉ *S28° 14.026, E28° 18.036.*

P5.8.3.9 Grave of Nursing Sister A.M. (Maud) Webster, Army Nursing Service (a colonial volunteer), who died of disease at Kroonstad on 3 June 1901.[1028]
▶ *British Garden of Remembrance, western side of Noord Rd, Kroonstad, Free State.*
◉ *S27° 39.049, E27° 13.816.*

P5.8.3.10 Graves of Lady Superintendant Marian A. Lloyd, Army Nursing Service Reserve, who died of disease on 17 December 1901; Nursing Sister Ethel Beatrice Lloyd, Army Nursing Service Reserve, who died of disease on 24 April 1901; Nursing Sister E. O'Neill (39), Army Nursing Service Reserve, who died of disease at the Imperial Yeomanry Hospital in Pretoria on 12 March 1901; and of two officers who died of enteric disease..[1029]
▶ *Old Church Street West Cemetery, Pretoria, Gauteng, entry from Es'kia Mphahlele St (previously D.F. Malan Dr), north of W.F. Nkomo Dr (previously Church St West).*
◉ *Near S25° 44.477, E28° 10.283.*

5.8.4 Medical personnel who survived the war, but for whom there are memorial sites

Republican memorials

At the time of the Great Trek Centenary in 1938, a memorial was erected for Mrs H.E.C. Armstrong, the organiser of the voluntary nursing service for inmates of the Irene Concentration Camp provided by ladies from Pretoria.[1030]

P5.8.3.8

P5.8.3.9

P5.8.3.10

1025 Watt 2000,
1026 Watt 2000, 104, 224 & 366.
1027 Watt 2000, 319.
1028 Watt 2000, 442.
1029 Watt 2000, 252 & 316.
1030 Pienaar 1977, 31; Armstrong 1980.

There is a memorial for Armstrong and the other voluntary nurses.
▶ *At the southern end of the Irene Concentration Camp Cemetery, Stopford Rd, signposted from Botha Rd, Irene, Gauteng.*
◉ *Near S25° 44.477, E28° 10.283.*

Voluntary medical services to inmates of the concentration camps were also provided by numerous other individuals all over South Africa.

The small house of House of Dr Hoexter, who treated camp victims in Aliwal North, still stands.
▶ *7 Levy Street, Aliwal North, Eastern Cape.*
◉ *Near S30° 41.876, E26° 42.681.*

P5.8.4.1 *Memorial plaque for Dr Hoexter at the Concentration Camp Memorial.*
▶ *Site next to the N6 national road at the southern entry to Aliwal North, Eastern Cape (signposted).*
◉ *S30° 42.254, E26° 42.544.*

P5.8.4.2 *Gravestone of Dr Otto Karl Heinrich Krause and his wife, who provided assistance to the camp inmates in Bloemfontein.*[1031]
▶ *Memoriam cemetery, General Brand St, Bloemfontein, Free State.*
◉ *S29° 08.840, E26° 12.409.*

The grave of Dr Carel Menning (1864-1949), who assisted the Boers as an ambulance doctor, is in the old part of the municipal cemetery in Lydenburg.
▶ *Western end of Buhrmann St, Lydenburg, Mpumalanga.*
◉ *Near S25° 05.188, E30° 26.747.*

British memorials

P5.8.4.3 *Grave of Nursing Sister H.A. Cruickshank (35), Army Nursing Service Reserve, who died at the Irene Concentration Camp on 3 (or 5) July 1902.*[1032]
▶ *At the southern end of the Irene Concentration Camp Cemetery, Stopford Rd, signposted from Botha Rd, Irene, Gauteng.*
◉ *Near S25° 44.477, E28° 10.283.*

P5.8.4.4 *Nursing Sister M.F. Patterson, Army Nursing Service Reserve, died at Barberton on 5 February 1903.*[1033]
▶ *British Garden of Remembrance, Henry Nettman St, between Redelinghuys St & Keurboom St, Barberton, Mpumalanga.*
◉ *S25° 45.970, E31° 03.284.*

P5.8.4.1   P5.8.4.2   P5.8.4.3   P5.8.4.4

1031   Van der Bank 2001, 51.
1032   Watt 2000, 97.
1033   Watt 2000, 324.

Part 6

Peace

6.1 Preliminary meetings

As the war progressed, there were sporadic talks about ending the war. On 28 February 1901, Commandant-General Louis Botha of the ZAR met the British Commander-in-Chief in South Africa, Lord Kitchener, in Middelburg in the eastern Transvaal (today Mpumalanga), for discussions which bore no immediate fruit, but at which the basis for the eventual Vereeniging Peace Treaty was laid.[1034]

> There is no memorial to indicate the exact location where these negotiations took place. The approximate site is in the central business district, where numerous shops and businesses can be found today.

An important meeting between members of the governments of the ZAR (the Transvaal) and the Orange Free State was held in a farmhouse (subsequently destroyed by British soldiers) near the site of the present hotel at Val Station in the southern Transvaal, from 19 to 21 June 1901. The meeting was attended by then Acting President S.W. (Schalk) Burger, State Secretary F.W. Reitz, Commandant-General Louis Botha, General Koos de la Rey and General Jan Smuts of the ZAR, as well as President M.T. Steyn, General Christiaan de Wet and General J.B.M. Hertzog of the Orange Free State. The meeting decided to continue the war.[1035]

> P6.1.1 The old hotel has been renovated and is now a guest house which contains exhibits on the war. The basic structure of the house remains unchanged.
> ▶ Next to the Val Railway Station, Mpumalanga, on the main railway line between Standerton and Heidelberg, on the northern side.
> ◉ S26° 47.794, E28° 56.093.

Peace negotiations between the Boers and the British began in March 1902. A preliminary meeting of Boer commanders was held at Klerksdorp in April 1902 to discuss the prospect of laying down arms.[1036]

> P6.1.2 Memorial where the first negotiations took place (the memorial plate has been stolen). The inscription (translated) reads: "Memorial erected to commemorate the First Peace Negotiations which were held in Klerksdorp. Unveiled on 31.8.1968 by H.Ex. Min. A. Hertzog."
> ▶ Grounds of Unie Primary School, Voortrekker Rd, Oudorp, between Joe Slovo St & Unie St, Klerksdorp, North West.
> ◉ S26° 51.891, E26° 39.096.

P6.1.1

P6.1.2

P6.1.3

1034 Grobler 2004, 109.
1035 Grobler 2004, 118.
1036 Grobler 2004, 141.

P6.1.3 The exhibit in the Klerksdorp Museum on this preliminary meeting. It includes the table and chairs used by the delegates during the discussions.
▶ *C/o Margaretha Prinsloo St & Lombaard St, Klerksdorp, North West.*
◉ *S56° 51.839, E26° 40.138.*

The Republican governments reached an agreement with the British military authorities, in terms of which leading Boer officers would be allowed to hold meetings with commandos that were still fighting, to enable them to elect delegates to a peace conference to be held at Vereeniging on the Vaal River in the second half of May. In accordance with this agreement, numerous meetings were held, including on the banks of the Egode River outside Paulpietersburg in the south-eastern ZAR (now in KwaZulu-Natal) where Commandant-General Botha met the Utrecht Commando.[1037]

P6.1.4 The town council of Paulpietersburg attached plaques to two huge rocks on the Egode River bank in 1935 to commemorate that meeting. There are two commemorative plaques – one rock bears an inscription in Afrikaans, and the other rock an inscription in English. The latter reads: "Honour our Heroes. These stones mark the spot where General Louis Botha in April 1902 met the Utrecht Commando to elect delegates to the Peace Conference at Vere[e]niging. Paulpietersburg Local Board 1935."
▶ *On the outskirts of Paulpietersburg, KwaZulu-Natal, next to the P45 to Luneburg.*
◉ *S27° 25.493, E30° 48.396.*

6.2 Vereeniging and Melrose House

In May 1902, a meeting of 60 representatives of various commandos took place at Vereeniging to discuss the issue of the peace negotiations. By that time, the Orange Free State's president, President Steyn, was desperately ill. The delegates met in a large tent on 15 May for the first time, and elected General C.F. Beyers as chairman of the peace conference.[1038]

P6.2.1 The Beyers monument in Modimolle, Limpopo, commemorates his role as Assistant Commandant-General for the northern Transvaal in the guerrilla phase of the war.
▶ *On the western side of Thabo Mbeki St (the R101, which runs north-south through Modimolle), at the entrance of the concentration camp cemetery.*
◉ *S24° 42.161, E28° 24.164.*

When the possibility of negotiating a peace was discussed, it quickly became clear that a number of delegates, including General Christiaan de Wet, wanted to continue fighting. Others, including Generals Botha and De la Rey, argued that a combination of factors threatened the continued existence of the Boer nation, and that this made negotiating for peace essential. Eventually the decision was taken to appoint a committee to negotiate with British representatives about terms under which the war could be terminated.[1039]

P6.1.4

P6.2.1

P6.2.2

1037 Van der Westhuizen & Van der Westhuizen 2013, 93.
1038 Grobler 2004, 145.
1039 Grobler 2004, 146.

P6.2.2 The memorial in Vereeniging, Gauteng, on the site where the Republican delegates discussed the possibility of peace.
▶ *On the southern side of the R42, Barrage Rd, between the R59 on the western side and Lewis Ave on the eastern side. It is on the grounds of Vereeniging Refractories, next to a cricket field. Entry is strictly controlled. Phone Louise le Roux at 016-4506160 or 082-4441252 to gain access.*
◉ *S26°41.569, E 27°54.922.*

The Republican committee, which did not include President Steyn, proceeded by train to Pretoria. They met with Lords Kitchener and Milner, who represented the British government, to negotiate at Melrose House, the British military headquarters in Pretoria. The meeting resulted in a draft peace treaty which contained the conditions under which Britain would end the war, including the loss of the Republics' independence. The British government demanded that the Boers accept the treaty before the end of May.

When the delegates returned to Vereeniging, they discussed the proceedings with Steyn, whose health had deteriorated further. Since Steyn believed that his oath of office made it impossible for him to negotiate ending his Republic's independence, he resigned from office after appointing General Christiaan de Wet acting president.[1040] Only at this point was De Wet persuaded that it was in the best interest of the Boers to accept the peace conditions. On Saturday, 31 May 1902, the Republican delegates at Vereeniging decided by a majority of 54 to six votes to accept the treaty. The Anglo-Boer War finally ended about an hour before midnight on that same day, when representatives of the Republics and of the British Government signed the Treaty of Vereeniging at Melrose House in Pretoria.[1041]

P6.2.3 Melrose House museum, where the table at which the peace treaty was signed is on display.[1042]
▶ *Southern side of Jacob Maré St, between Andries St and Van der Walt St. Entry from the back, via Scheiding St, between Lilian Ngoyi St & Andries St.*
◉ *S 25°45.388, E 28°11.556.*

P6.2.4 The peace memorial in Vereeniging, Gauteng, by Coert Steynberg.[1043]
▶ *On a square surrounded by a palisade fence next to the City Hall, entrance to parking lot from Joubert St, at the corner with Market Ave. Phone Mary at 013-4503024 to gain access to the memorial.*

6.3 The reasons for which the Boers surrendered

P6.3.1 The surrender memorial at Soetwater, near Calvinia, Northern Cape.[1044]
▶ *On the farm Oorlogsfontein, 30 km west of Calvinia next to the R27 leading to Nieuwoudtville.*
◉ *GPS co-ordinates not available.*

P6.2.3   P6.2.4   P6.3.1

1040   Van Schoor 2009, 279-283.
1041   Grobler 2004, 146.
1042   Picton-Seymour 1989, 168-169.
1043   Brits 1989b, 130-131.
1044   Kapp 1989b, 261.

There were several reasons why the Boers were prepared to discuss ways of ending the war by the approach of winter in 1902.

The first reason was the fact that their numbers were dwindling, less due to war casualties, than to the growing number of burghers who surrendered to the British to become either prisoners of war, or to join the British forces against their own people.

Secondly, the Republican leaders were concerned about the increasing numbers of black South Africans entering the war on the British side. In some rural areas, local black groups harassed and harmed Boer families that still lived on their farms.

Another development that directly contributed to the decision of the Boers to surrender in May 1902 was the scorched earth policy followed by the British military authorities in the Republics. By the end of the war, the British themselves conceded that they had destroyed 30 000 homes.

A final factor that contributed to the Boer decision to end the war was the precarious situation in which thousands of women and children, both those in the concentration camps and those adrift on the veldt, found themselves. The Boer delegates themselves explained in a formal statement that they could not reasonably expect to ensure their independence by prolonging the war; under the prevailing circumstances, it was not justifiable to carry on fighting; and carrying on could result in their destruction and that of their descendants at a social and material level.[1045]

P6.3.2 The bittereinder statue by Danie de Jager in the garden of the War Museum of the Boer Republics portrays a burgher on the back of his over-worked horse, with abandoned rifles strewn around the base of the statue as a sign of surrender.[1046] (The name bittereinder refers to burghers who fought up to the "bitter end" of the war.)
▶ *Monument Rd., Bloemfontein, Free State.*
◉ *S29° 08.397, E26° 12.569.*

The ten clauses of the Treaty of Vereeniging can be summarised as follows:
- The burghers of the two former Republics had to lay down arms and acknowledge the British king as their sovereign.
- The burghers who surrendered would not be deprived of their liberty and their property.
- Assistance would be given for the repatriation of all burghers, both prisoners of war and those in concentration camps, back to their homes. Stock and implements would be provided so that the people could re-establish themselves on their farms.
- Legal proceedings would not be instituted against burghers for acts of war.
- An amount of £3 million would be set aside to compensate people for losses suffered as a result of war.
- The Dutch language would be taught in public schools where the parents of the children desired it, and would be used in courts of law when necessary for the better administration of justice.
- The burghers would be allowed to own licensed firearms for their protection.
- Civilian government would replace military rule as soon as possible and representative bodies would be introduced.

P6.3.2

P6.3.3

P6.3.4

1045   Kestell & Van Velden 1909, 210.
1046   Van Schoor 1989c, 107.

- The whole issue of franchise for black people in the former Republics would be dealt with after the introduction of self-government.
- No special tax would be levied in the two former Republics to defray the cost of the war.[1047]

One of the agreements made at this time between the Republican representatives and the British negotiators was that Field Cornet Salmon van As could be prosecuted by the British authorities for a war crime which he was supposed to have committed, namely the shooting of Lieutenant Miers. Van As was indeed prosecuted by a British military court, found guilty, sentenced to death and executed by firing squad on 23 June 1902 in the courtyard of the goal in Heidelberg, Transvaal.[1048]

P6.3.3 Grave of Lieutenant R.H.M.C. Miers (25), 2nd Battalion Somersetshire Light Infantry, Captain in the South African Constabulary, who was shot at Riviersdraai, near Heidelberg, on 25 September 1901. It was alleged that Miers was shot by Van As when Miers attempted to convince Van As to surrender.[1049]
▶ *Kloof cemetery, on the banks of the Kloof Spruit, northern side of extension of Fenter St, Heidelberg, Gauteng.*
◙ *S26° 29.717, E28° 20.770.*

P6.3.4 The goal building is still standing and the place where Van As was executed can be viewed.
▶ *On the north-western side of Jordaan St, near north-western end of Ueckerman St, Heidelberg, Gauteng.*
◙ *S 26° 29.815, E 28° 21.174.*

P6.3.5 Grave of Field Cornet Salmon van As.
▶ *Kloof cemetery, on the banks of the Kloof Spruit, on the northern side of the extension of Fenter St, Heidelberg, Gauteng. He was reinterred here after being initially buried in the veld by the British.[1050]*
◙ *S 26° 29.717, E 28° 20.770.*

One result of the outcome of the war and the Boer surrender was that President Paul Kruger refused to return to South Africa. He remained in exile in Europe and settled in Clarens, Switzerland, where he died in 1904, aged 79.

P6.3.6 There is one famous statue in South Africa portraying Kruger in exile. It was created by French sculptor J.P. Achard.[1051]
▶ *In front of the old City Hall, Plein St, between Tuin St & Burger St, Rustenburg, North West.*
◙ *S25° 40.312, E27° 14.709.*

P6.3.5   P6.3.6

1047   Grobler 2004, 146.
1048   Van der Westhuizen & Van der Westhuizen 2000, 164.
1049   Watt 2000, 287; Cloete 2010, 299.
1050   Van der Westhuizen & Van der Westhuizen 2000, 165.
1051   Krüger 1968, 475.

Part 7

The legacy of the war

The Anglo-Boer War was an event of major significance in South African history. The most important short-term results of the war were that
- the two Boer republics ceased to exist;
- British supremacy was firmly established in southern Africa;
- a small minority of burghers who refused to accept the loss of Boer independence and to recognise the British king as their sovereign emigrated to Angola, Kenya and Argentina in an attempt to live free from British rule; and
- the outcome of the war contributed greatly to the unification of South Africa under the British flag in 1910.

About 22 000 British soldiers lost their lives in this war – a third more than the Boer casualties. The majority of deaths on both sides were the result of disease, rather than enemy bullets. For Britain, it was the biggest and most costly war since the wars against Napoleon, which ended with Waterloo in 1815.

For the Boer people, the war was a demographic disaster, since the deaths of the more than 30 000 women and children represented a loss of about ten per cent of the white population in the Boer Republics in the long term. In the short run, the legacy of the war was economic deprivation for the Boer people. The destruction which accompanied the British scorched earth policy had the long-term result of impoverishing a large percentage of all the peoples of the former Republics. Psychologically, the war also had long-term negative effects. The concentration camps generated deep-seated hatred in the heart of many Boers for the hendsoppers and joiners – an issue which divided even families for generations to come. It also generated hatred for the British, a hatred so overwhelming that many Afrikaners subsequently supported any country that opposed the British, including Nazi Germany in the Second World War. The anti-British feeling also contributed to the resurgence of Afrikaner nationalism throughout South Africa soon after 1902.

Even though black South Africans also suffered the long-term negative economic impact of the war, an even more unfortunate effect of the war was that it contributed to enmity from many Afrikaners towards fellow black South Africans.[1052] The exclusion of black South Africans from accessing political rights in terms of the peace treaty was to shape race relations in South Africa for most of the 20th century.

A glaring gap in the legacy of the Anglo-Boer War for tourism is that there are not sufficient memorials to commemorate the participation in and impact of the war on black South Africans. This should be addressed as a matter of urgency.

7.1 The "age of the generals"

The prominence of Republican generals and other senior Republican officers in Afrikaner society in the first half century after the war was so striking that a South African historian has dubbed this era the "age of the generals".[1053]

P7.1.1

P7.1.2

P7.1.3

1052   Grobler 2002.
1053   Krüger 1961.

Part 7 – The legacy of the war

Numerous sites commemorate Anglo-Boer War Republican generals and their prominent role in South Africa in this era. Commandant-General Louis Botha, the first and only Prime Minister of the Transvaal Colony after the British government granted self-government to the former ZAR in 1906, was initially the most prominent.

P7.1.1 The memorial indicating Botha's birthplace.
▶ *Anton Menn Dr, Sevenoaks, between Dr Wessels St and the R33, south of Greytown, KwaZulu-Natal.*
◉ *S29° 05.527, E30° 36.436.*

In 1910, after the unification of the four British self-governing colonies in South Africa, Botha became the first Prime Minister of the Union of South Africa. He died at the age of 57 in 1919.

P7.1.2 Statue of Botha as Prime Minister of South Africa.[1054]
▶ *Botha Gardens, c/o Berea St and the R102 (Julius Nyerere St), Durban, KwaZulu-Natal.*
◉ *S29° 51.638, E31° 00.576.*

P7.1.3 There is also a statue of Botha as Prime Minister, unveiled in 1931.
▶ *Stalplein, c/o Plein St & Roeland St, Cape Town, Western Cape.*
◉ *S33° 55.670, E18° 25.163.*

P7.1.4 Botha's grave is in the Rebecca Street cemetery, Pretoria-West.
▶ *Entrance at c/o Rebecca St and Staatartillerie Rd, Philip Nel Park, Pretoria, Gauteng.*
◉ *About 80 m north of the cemetery office, near S25° 44.316, E28° 09.181.*

Botha was succeeded as Prime Minister of the Union of South Africa by his close friend and political ally, General Jan Smuts, who served in that capacity for a total of 14 years (from 1919 to 1924 and 1939 to 1948).

P7.1.5 There are numerous sites in South Africa where Smuts is commemorated. This includes this statue in Durban, KwaZulu-Natal, which portrays him as a world statesman. Scenes from Smuts's illustrious career are portrayed in bass relief sculpture on the pedestal of the statue. The inscription on the pedestal reads: "In honour of Field Marshal the Right Honourable Jan Christiaan Smuts (1870-1950). Soldier, Statesman, Philosopher, Architect of the Union of South Africa and the British Commonwealth of Nations. A great son of South Africa who was shared by this country with the whole world."
▶ *Francis Farewell Square, c/o Anton Lembede St & Dorothy Nyembe St, Durban, KwaZulu-Natal.*
◉ *S29° 51.525, E31° 01.514 (Google Maps).*

P7.1.6 This statue of Smuts by British sculptor Sydney Harpley, unveiled in 1964, attracted much controversy.[1055]
▶ *Company Gardens, Cape Town, Western Cape, in front of the National Art Gallery.*
◉ *S33° 55.709, E18° 24.986.*

P7.1.4

P7.1.5

P7.1.6

1054 Van Tonder ca 1974, 11.
1055 Grobler 2012, 26.

P7.1.7 Statue of Smuts by Ivan Mitford-Barberton, unveiled in reaction to Harpley's statue in 1974.[1056]
▶ *Top of Adderley St, at the entrance of the Company Gardens, Cape Town, Western Cape.*
◉ *S33° 55.504, E18° 25.206.*

There is also a memorial statue of Smuts in the Gardens of the Union Buildings, Pretoria,[1057] but it is in a restricted area, and is not accessible to the public.
◉ *Near S25° 44.406, E28° 12.573.*

P7.1.8 Smuts House Museum.
▶ *Jan Smuts Ave, about 1.4 km south of the M31 (Nellmapius Dr), where it is signposted.*
◉ *Near S25° 53.314, E28° 13.924.*

The third Republican Anglo-Boer War general who became Prime Minister of South Africa was James Barry Munnik Hertzog. He held this position for 15 years, from 1924 to 1939.

P7.1.9-10 There are no statues of Hertzog representing him as an Anglo-Boer War general. However, there are two large statues of him as Prime Minister.[1058]
▶ *Northern side of Charles St, across from the Fourth Raadsaal, Bloemfontein, Free State (P7.1.9).*
◉ *S29° 06.899, E26° 13.096.*
▶ *In the gardens of the Union Buildings, Arcadia, Pretoria, Gauteng (P7.1.10).*
◉ *Near S25° 44.542, E28° 12.762.*

P7.1.11 Hertzog died in 1942. His grave is on the farm Waterval (north of Emalahleni), Mpumalanga.
▶ *Western side of the R544 linking Emalahleni and Verena, south of the junction of that road with a local gravel road that turns west to Zusterstroom.*
◉ *S25° 35.205, E29° 06.196.*

7.2 Burgher monuments

Even though the Boers were beaten, numerous war heroes emerged, especially Generals De Wet and De la Rey. Several books and poems have been written about them and other Boer heroes. Statues and monuments to commemorate all those who died for the Boer cause have been erected all over South Africa. These include the following:

P7.1.7

P7.1.8 P7.1.9

P7.1.10

1056 Kapp 1989a, 30-31.
1057 Kapp 1989a, 30.
1058 Van Tonder ca 1974, 13; Geyser 1989a, 108.

7.2.1 Gauteng

Boksburg

P7.2.1.1 Burgher Monument. Commemorates General Gert Gravett and numerous other officers and burghers of the East Rand commandos who died during the war.
▶ *Grounds of the old Dutch Reformed Church, c/o Voortrekker St & Gracht St, Boksburg, Gauteng.*
◉ *S26° 13.231, E28° 15.276.*

Heidelberg

P7.2.1.2 Memorial plaque above the entrance of the Primary School Volksskool ("People's School"). The inscription reads (translated): "To the glorious memory of those of the Heidelberg District who died in the war of 1899-1902, namely 90 burghers killed in action, 624 men, women and children who died in the camps, 153 who died at home or in the veld, [a total of] 867 sacrifices for freedom, fatherland and people." There are also plaques containing the names of the burghers who fell in the war on both sides of the entrance.[1059]
▶ *C/o Voortrekker St & Begeman St, Heidelberg, Gauteng.*
◉ *S 26° 29.861, E 28° 21.407.*

P7.2.1.3 Burgher Monument, erected in January 1938.[1060]
▶ *Kloof Cemetery, on the banks of the Kloof Spruit, northern side of extension of Fenter St, Heidelberg, Gauteng.*
◉ *S 26° 29.717; E 28° 20.770.*

Johannesburg

P7.2.1.4 "Oudstryders-monument" (Veterans' Memorial)
▶ *On low hill directly north of the c/o 2nd St & Hull St, Vrededorp, Johannesburg, Gauteng (close to the Hervormde Church building).*
◉ *S26° 11.525, E28° 01.118.*

Pretoria

P7.2.1.5 Burgher Monument, Old Church Street West Cemetery, Pretoria, with names of burghers who died in the war (killed in action, died of wounds or disease, or executed) and were buried in this cemetery.
▶ *Entry from Es'kia Mphahlele St (previously D.F. Malan Dr), north of W.F. Nkomo Dr (previously Church St West).*
◉ *Near S 25°44.473, E 28°10.323.*

P7.1.11

P7.2.1.1

P7.2.1.2

1059 Van der Westhuizen & Van der Westhuizen 2000, 176.
1060 Van der Westhuizen & Van der Westhuizen 2000, 169.

P7.2.1.3   P7.2.1.4   P7.2.1.5   P7.2.1.6

P7.2.1.6 Memorial plaque for Dutch citizens and former Dutch citizens who gave their lives for the Boer Republics in the war. Erected by the Nederlandsch Zuid-Afrikaansche Vereeniging (Dutch-South African Society). One of the names on the plaque is that of C.V. (Cor) van Gogh, the youngest brother of the famous painter Vincent van Gogh. Cor van Gogh was buried in an unmarked grave at Brandfort, Free State.[1061]
▶ *In the outer wall of the Nederduitsch Hervormde Church building, western side of Du Toit St, between Madiba St and Stanza Bopape St (previously named Church St), Pretoria, Gauteng.*
◉ *S25° 44.701, E28° 11.862.*

7.2.2 North West

Delareyville

P7.2.2.1 Burgher Monument.
▶ *Strijdomplein, adjacent to the municipal offices, Delareyville, North West.*
◉ *S25° 45.752, E26° 68.581.*

Lichtenburg

P7.2.2.2 Burgher Monument, vandalised.
▶ *Municipal offices, near Coligny Rd between R503 Scholtz St & R505 Melville St, Lichtenburg, North West.*
◉ *S26° 08.989, E26° 09.558.*

Potchefstroom

P7.2.2.3 Memorial unveiled in 1906 for the five theology students of the seminary of the Gereformeerde Church who died in action during the war, namely Commandants Karel Dawid Coetzee and Calman Efraim Lion-Cachet, and Jacob Philippus Maré, Johannes Abram Venter and Jan Christoffel Kruger.

P7.2.2.1   P7.2.2.2   P7.2.2.3   P7.2.2.4

1061   Nienaber & Le Roux 1983, 9; Van der Bank 1995, 7-8, 2001, 42.

Part 7 – The legacy of the war

▶ At the Gereformeerde Church, Potchefstroom North, north-western c/o Thabo Mbeki St & Borcherds St, Cachet, Potchefstroom, North West.
◉ S26° 41.608, E27° 05.845.

Rustenburg

P7.2.2.4 Burgher Monument listing Hermann Müller, Abraham Absalom de Villiers, Sarel Francois Malan and two unknown burghers reinterred there during the Great Trek centenary in 1938.
▶ Old municipal cemetery, Rustenburg, North West. Entry from Nelson Mandela St, between Bosch St & Kock St.
◉ S25° 40.516, E27° 14.628.

P7.2.2.5 Burgher memorial erected in 1999 as part of the Anglo-Boer War centenary celebrations. It also commemorates women and children who died as a result of the war.
▶ In front of the new church building of the Hervormde Church, on the eastern side of the R24 linking Rustenburg and Krugersdorp, 2.3 km south of the N4.
◉ S25° 43.344, E27° 15.652.

Ventersdorp

P7.2.2.6 Burgher Memorial that commemorates 26 burghers of that area who fell in the war. One plaque on the memorial pays tribute to the men, women and children in the concentration camps and elsewhere who paid with their lives "for freedom and justice".
▶ C/o Visser St & Jacob Wilken St, Ventersdorp, North West.
◉ S26° 18.871, E26° 49.429.

Zeerust

P7.2.2.7. Burgher Memorial and mass grave containing the remains of reinterred burghers, as well as original gravestones and rolls of honour containing the names of 93 burghers of the Marico and surrounding areas who fell in the war.[1062]
▶ In a memorial garden, c/o Hendrik Potgieter St & Forsman St, Zeerust, North West.
◉ S25° 32.501, E26° 04.540.

7.2.3 Limpopo

Modimolle

P7.2.3.1 Memorial grave of six burghers who died in the war and who were reinterred in the municipal cemetery in 1985.

P7.2.2.5

P7.2.2.6

P7.2.2.7

1062 Zeerust 1987.

 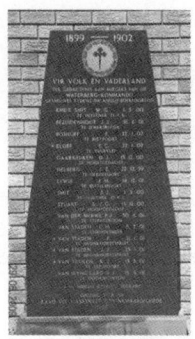  

P7.2.3.1   P7.2.3.2   P7.2.3.3   P7.2.3.4

▶ On the western side of Thabo Mbeki St (the R101), south of the prominent white Dutch Reformed Church building, Modimolle, Limpopo Province.
◉ S24° 42.161, E28° 24.164.

P7.2.3.2 Memorial plaque with the names of burghers of the Waterberg Commando who were killed in action in the war, on the wall of the Nylstroom Concentration Camp Cemetery.
▶ On the western side of Thabo Mbeki St (the R101), south of the prominent white Dutch Reformed Church building, Modimolle, Limpopo Province.
◉ S24° 42.161, E28° 24.164.

Modjadji's Kloof

P7.2.3.3 Burgher Monument
▶ In front of the municipal offices, next to the R36 (Botha St), the main street of Modjadji's Kloof (previously Duiwelskloof), Limpopo Province.
◉ S23°41.707, E30°08.659.

P7.2.3.4 Mass grave where 16 burghers were reinterred.
▶ Grounds of the Dutch Reformed Church, top of Pearl St, Modjadji's Kloof, Limpopo Province.
◉ S23°41.710, E30°08.103.

7.2.4 Mpumalanga

Amersfoort

P7.2.4.1 Burgher Monument, Amersfoort, Mpumalanga. The names of 16 burghers who died during the war are listed on the monument, which was unveiled in 1913.[1063]

P7.2.4.1   P7.2.4.2   P7.2.4.3   P7.2.4.4

1063   Van der Westhuizen & Van der Westhuizen 2013, 99-100.

Part 7 – The legacy of the war

▶ *Square in the centre of the town, near c/o Plein St & Sybrandt van Niekerk St.*
◉ *S27° 00.457, E29° 52.178.*

Belfast

P7.2.4.2 Burgher Monument, Belfast, Mpumalanga, showing the names of 78 burghers from the district who lost their lives in the war.[1064]
▶ *Grounds of the Belfast Rusoord (Old Age Home), Coetzee St.*
◉ *S25° 41.478, E30° 01.929.*

Bergendal (Dalmanutha)

See P1.13.

Bethal

P7.2.4.3 Burgher Monument, Bethal, Mpumalanga. Unveiled in 1974, this memorial contains a mass grave and displays a list of the names of burghers who died in action in that part of the eastern Transvaal and were reinterred.
▶ *Central town square, Liebenberg Ave, between Vuyisile Mini St & Clerq St.*
◉ *S26° 27.333, E29° 27.756.*

Carolina

P7.2.4.4 Burgher Monument, vandalized. The names of 44 burghers who died on active service are listed on the monument.[1065]
▶ *C/o Church St & Steyn St, north-western corner of the grounds of the Dutch Reformed Church, Carolina, Mpumalanga.*
◉ *S26° 04.163, E30° 06.745.*

Dullstroom

P7.2.4.5 Burgher Monument.
▶ *Memorial garden, eastern side of Lion St (the R540), between Hugenoten St & Beelaerts van Blokland St, Dullstroom, Mpumalanga.*
◉ *S25° 25.135, E30° 06.387.*

P7.2.4.5

P7.2.4.6

P7.2.4.7

P7.2.4.8

1064 Van der Westhuizen & Van der Westhuizen 2013, 231.
1065 Van der Westhuizen & Van der Westhuizen 2013, 131.

Ermelo

P7.2.4.6 Burgher Monument (unveiled by General Jan Smuts, 1935) for 77 burghers.[1066]
▶ In front of the Dutch Reformed Church, Joubert St, between Jan van Riebeeck St & Kerk St, Ermelo, Mpumalanga.
◉ S26° 31.263, E29° 59.062.

Lydenburg

P7.2.4.7 Burgher Monument.
▶ Grounds of the Dutch Reformed Church, Kerk St, between Kantoor St & Lange St, Lydenburg, Mpumalanga.
◉ S25° 05.478, E30° 27.111.

Middelburg

P7.2.4.8 Burgher Monument, erected in 1938. The names of 107 burghers of Middelburg and the surrounding district who lost their lives in the war are listed.[1067]
▶ Rooth Square, southern side of the Dutch Reformed Church, Joubert St, Middelburg, Mpumalanga.
◉ S25° 45.753, E29° 27.408.

Morgenzon

P7.2.4.9 Burgher Monument.
▶ Grounds of the Dutch Reformed Church, Kleynhans St, between Martha St & De Jager St, Morgenzon, Mpumalanga.
◉ S26° 44.112, E29° 37.054.

Roodebank

P7.2.4.10 Memorial to burghers, women and children who died in the war. Six names of burghers who were killed in action in that area appear on the memorial.
▶ Day of the Vow terrain, Roodebank, on farm land between the R50 & the R547, about 7.5 km south of the junction, Mpumalanga.
◉ S26° 37.760, E29° 01.116.

Standerton

P7.2.4.11 Burgher Monument, vandalised.

P7.2.4.9

P7.2.4.10

P7.2.4.11

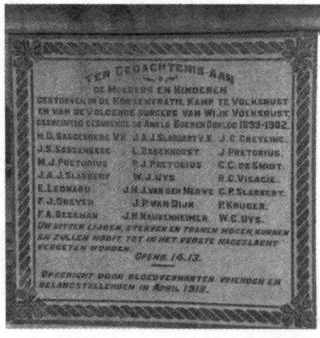
P7.2.4.12

1066   Van der Westhuizen & Van der Westhuizen 2013, 114.
1067   Van der Westhuizen & Van der Westhuizen 2013, 201.

Volksrust

P7.2.4.12 The concentration camp memorial in the centre of town is also a burgher memorial. The names of 21 burghers of the Ward Volksrust killed in action in the war are inscribed on the pedestal.
▶ *Municipal offices, Voortrekker Square, c/o Laingsnek St & Joubert St, Volksrust, Mpumalanga.*
◉ *S27° 22.083, E29° 53.110.*

Wakkerstroom

P7.2.4.13 Burgher Monument, vandalised. It contains the names of 73 burghers of the Wakkerstroom Commando who died during the war.[1068]
▶ *Grounds of the Dutch Reformed Church, western side of Van Riebeeck St (the R543), Wakkerstroom, Mpumalanga.*
◉ *S27° 21.242, E30° 08.554.*

7.2.5 Free State

Bethlehem

P7.2.5.1 Memorial plaque in the entrance hall of the Dutch Reformed Church containing the names of 51 burghers of that congregation who fell in the war. It was unveiled by General A.M. Prinsloo on 11 June 1904.[1069]
▶ *Church St, near corner with Murray St.*
◉ *S28° 14.062, E28° 18.657.*

Bethulie

Memorial in the form of a white marble gravestone containing the names of 11 Bethulie burghers killed in action in the war. Unveiled by General J.B.M. Hertzog on 20 January 1906.[1070]
▶ *Municipal cemetery, northern side of Boven Noord St.*
◉ *S30° 29.530, E25° 58.290.*

P7.2.4.13

P7.2.5.1

P7.2.5.2

1068 Van der Westhuizen & Van der Westhuizen 2013, 84.
1069 Van der Bank 1995, 4-6.
1070 Van der Bank 1995, 6.

Bloemfontein

Marble plaque in the entrance hall of the Twin Tower Church, in commemoration of 78 Dutch and former Dutch people who were killed in action fighting on the side of the Republics in the war. Erected in May 1909 by the Nederlandsch Zuid-Afrikaansche Vereeniging (NZAV – Dutch South African Society),[1071] identical to P7.2.1.6 in Pretoria, Gauteng.
▶ Charles St, east of corner with Wes Burger St.
◉ S29° 06.957, E26° 13.333.

P7.2.5.2 Memorial at the War Museum of the Boer Republics, erected in 2012 to commemorate all the burghers who died on commando (see also CP34 on p. 302).
▶ Monument Rd, Bloemfontein, Free State.
◉ S29° 08.397, E26° 12.569.

Boshof

P7.2.5.3 Burgher Monument, unveiled on 29 June 1907, commemorating 60 burghers led by General C. Badenhorst who were killed in action in the western part of the Orange Free State.[1072]
▶ Grounds of the Dutch Reformed Church, c/o Kerk St & Mark St.
◉ S28° 32.361, E25° 14.243.

Bothaville

P7.2.5.4 Burgher Monument. It consists of an equestrian statue of white marble imported from Italy. The granite pedestal has four panels containing the names of 67 burghers who "made the biggest sacrifice on the altar of freedom". Unveiled by General J.B.M. Hertzog on 13 April 1938[1073] (see also CP30 on p. 301).
▶ In front of Dutch Reformed Church, c/o Van der Lingen St & President St, Bothaville, Free State.
◉ S27° 23.580, E26° 36.906.

Dewetsdorp

P7.2.5.5 Burgher Monument, unveiled in 1906 by President M.T. Steyn. Its marble panels contain the names of 23 burghers of that congregation killed in action, and those of 13 burghers from elsewhere killed in action in that area.[1074]
▶ Grounds of the Dutch Reformed Church, in front of the church hall, c/o Kerk St & Carroll St, Dewetsdorp, Free State.
◉ S29° 35.104, E26° 39.685.

P7.2.5.3   P7.2.5.4   P7.2.5.5   P7.2.5.6

1071 Van der Bank 1995, 7-9.
1072 Van der Bank 1995, 9-11.
1073 Nienaber & Le Roux 1983, 15; Van der Bank 1995, 13-15.
1074 Van der Bank 1995, 17-19.

Edenburg

P7.2.5.6 Burgher Monument. It was unveiled in 1908 by the Colonial Treasurer of the Orange River Colony, Dr A.E.W. Ramsbottom, and lists the names of 11 burghers killed in action.[1075]
▶ Next to the R717 through town, near Brand St, opposite the Dutch Reformed Church, Edenburg, Free State.
◉ S29° 44.166, E25° 56.227.

Fauresmith

P7.2.5.7 Burgher Monument. The original monument was unveiled in 1906, when several burghers from Fauresmith who fell in the war were also reinterred. The monument commemorates 70 burghers who "gave their lives in the war against England" (both burghers from the district who died elsewhere, and burghers from elsewhere who died near Fauresmith). It also commemorates six "unknown burghers". The monument was rebuilt and unveiled again in 1931 by Minister N.C. Havenga, who hailed from the district and was himself a bittereinder.[1076]
▶ Reichardt Park Cemetery, south-west of c/o Jacobs St & Fontein St, Fauresmith, Free State.
◉ S29° 45.093, E25° 18.763.

Ficksburg

P7.2.5.8 Marble plaque containing the names of 68 burghers from the district who died in the war, including 28 who died as prisoners of war. It was unveiled on 15 December 1934.[1077]
▶ Entrance hall of the Dutch Reformed Church, Voortrekker St, Ficksburg, Free State.
◉ S28° 52.420, E27° 52.660.

Fouriesburg

P7.2.5.9 Burgher Monument erected in 1917. In addition to a panel with the names of the 20 burghers of that area who died on active duty in the war, there is also a panel with the names of 11 burghers who died as prisoners of war, one with the names of 15 women and one with the names of the 53 children of the district who died in concentration camps.[1078]
▶ In front of the Dutch Reformed Church, c/o Kerk St & Reitz St, Fouriesburg, Free State.
◉ S28° 37.310, E28° 12.413.

Frankfort

Marble plaque containing the names of burghers from the district who died in the war in the entrance hall of the Dutch Reformed Church.[1079]

P7.2.5.7   P7.2.5.8   P7.2.5.9   P7.2.5.10

1075   Van der Bank 1995, 21-22.
1076   Van der Bank 1995, 23-25.
1077   Van der Bank 1995, 25-28.
1078   Van der Bank 1995, 28-31.
1079   Van der Bank 1995, 31-32.

▶ *Brand St, between Baumann St & Beckwith St, Frankfort, Free State.*
◉ *S27° 16.378, E28° 29.665.*

Groenvlei

P7.2.5.10 Burgher Monument for burghers who died in Anglo-Boer War and were reinterred there in 1958.
▶ *On the farm Groenvlei, signposted about 10 km north-east of Lindley, on the northern side of the R707 to Petrus Steyn, Free State.*
◉ *GPS co-ordinates not available.*

Harrismith

P7.2.5.11 Burgher Monument, unveiled in 1930 by Reverend J.D. Kestell. It commemorates 77 burghers of the Harrismith Commando who "sacrificed their lives for the freedom of their country and people".[1080]
▶ *In front of the Dutch Reformed Church, c/o Piet Retief St & Warden St, Harrismith, Free State.*
◉ *S28° 16.289, E29° 07.578.*

P7.2.5.12 Burgher Monument commemorating burghers of the Harrismith Commando who "fought and suffered for their freedom" in the Anglo-Boer War, and mothers and children who died in the Harrismith Concentration Camp and elsewhere in the war. It was unveiled on 8 November 1938.[1081]
▶ *In Deborah Retief Park, near c/o Warden St & Bester St, Harrismith, Free State.*
◉ *S28° 16.196, E29° 07.489.*

P7.2.5.13 Burgher Monument of polished granite, erected by the National Monuments Council in 1987. The 45 names engraved on the monument commemorate burghers and three nurses of the Harrismith Commando who died during the Anglo-Boer War and were reinterred there in 1938.[1082]
▶ *Municipal cemetery, north-east of c/o Laksman St & Greyling St, Harrismith, Free State.*
◉ *S28° 16.143, E29° 07.891.*

Heilbron

P7.2.5.14 Burgher Monument unveiled in 1924. The names of 81 burghers who died "in the struggle for the big ideal of freedom" are engraved on the monument. A total of 787 women and children (probably from that district) who died in the concentration camps are also commemorated.[1083]
▶ *In front of the Dutch Reformed Church, c/o Lang Markt St & Church St, Heilbron, Free State.*
◉ *S27° 17.008, E27° 58.253.*

P7.2.5.11   P7.2.5.12   P7.2.5.13   P7.2.5.14   P7.2.5.15

1080 Van der Bank 1995, 37-39.
1081 Kapp 1989b, 261; Van der Bank 1995, 35-36.
1082 Van der Bank 1995, 39-41.
1083 Van Tonder ca 1974, 12; Van der Bank 1995, 41-43.

Hoopstad

P7.2.5.15 Burgher Monument.
▶ Memorial plaque in front of the Dutch Reformed Church, Church St, Hoopstad, Free State.
◉ S27° 50.138, E25° 54.196.

Jacobsdal

P7.2.5.16 Burgher Monument. The names of 22 burghers plus that of Commandant D.S. Lubbe on a separate panel [see P7.3.2.24] appear on the monument.[1084]
▶ In front of the Dutch Reformed Church, c/o Andries Pretorius St & Church St, Jacobsdal, Free State.
◉ S29° 07.731, E24° 46.459.

Jagersfontein

P7.2.5.17 Burgher Monument. It commemorates seven burghers who died on active service.[1085]
▶ Municipal cemetery, Likkewaan St, Jagersfontein, Free State.
◉ S29° 45.633, E25° 26.268.

Kroonstad

P7.2.5.18 Burgher Monument, unveiled on 2 July 1910 by President M.T. Steyn. It commemorates 126 burghers of the Kroonstad Commando who died on active service and whose names are engaved on the monument, and the 1 400 women and children who perished in the Kroonstad Concentration Camp.[1086]
▶ In front of the Dutch Reformed Church, Cross St, Kroonstad, Free State.
◉ S27° 40.033, E27° 14.061.

Ladybrand

P7.2.5.19 Burgher Memorial – commemorative plaque attached to a rock (see also P7.3.1.1).
▶ On the grounds of the Dutch Reformed Church, c/o Piet Retief St & Erasmus St.
◉ S29° 11.744, E27° 27.505.

Lindley

P7.2.5.20 Burgher Monument. The names of 39 burghers are listed on the three doors of this replica of the local church building destroyed by British forces during the war[1087] (see also P5.2.3).

P7.2.5.16   P7.2.5.17   P7.2.5.18   P7.2.5.19   P7.2.5.20

1084   Van der Bank 1995, 43-45; Oosthuizen ca 2000, 15, 17.
1085   Van der Bank 1995, 45-46.
1086   Van der Bank 1995, 46-49.
1087   Van der Bank 1995, 52-53.

▶ On the grounds of the Dutch Reformed Church, c/o Kerk St & Brand St, Lindley, Free State.
◎ S27° 52.864, E27° 55.223.

Parys

P7.2.5.21 Commemorative plaque on the historical monument on the grounds of the Dutch Reformed Church.
▶ C/o Maré St & Hefer St, Parys, Free State.
◎ S26° 54.036, E27° 27.358.

Reddersburg

P7.2.5.22 Burgher Monument, unveiled on 25 July 1906, listing 22 burghers who fell in the war.[1088]
▶ In front of the Gereformeerde Church, c/o Kerk St & Letta St, Reddersburg, Free State.
◎ S29° 39.183, E26° 10.330.

P7.2.5.23 Commemorative gravestone for burghers and a two-year-old girl killed in the war.
▶ Municipal cemetery, on the outskirts of the town, near Letta St.
◎ S29° 39.463, E26° 10.210.

Reitz

P7.2.5.24 Commemorative marble plaque containing names of 45 burghers from Reitz and the surrounding district who fell in the war, attached to the historical monument in front of the Dutch Reformed Church.[1089]
▶ C/o Church St & Noord St, Reitz, Free State.
◎ S27° 48.255, E28° 25.803.

Rouxville

P7.2.5.25 Burgher Monument, unveiled by General C.C. Froneman on 16 December 1906, and listing 17 burghers from Rouxville and one from the Transvaal who fell in the war.[1090]
▶ In front of the Dutch Reformed Church, c/o Roux St & Church St, Rouxville, Free State.
◎ S30° 24.995, E26° 50.088.

Senekal

P7.2.5.26 Burgher Monument, unveiled by President M.T. Steyn in 1909, showing the names of 61 burghers from Senekal who died on active service during the war.[1091]

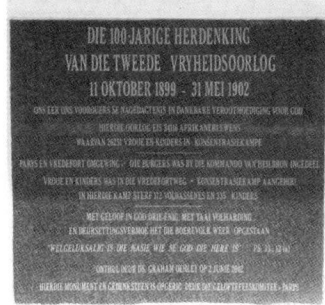
P7.2.5.21

P7.2.5.22

P7.2.5.23

P7.2.5.24

P7.2.5.25

1088   Van der Bank 1995, 57-58.
1089   Van der Bank 1995, 58-60.
1090   Van der Bank 1995, 62-63.
1091   Van der Bank 1995, 63-66.

▶ In front of the Dutch Reformed Church, c/o Noorder St & Malan St, Senekal, Free State.
◉ S28° 19.341, E27° 37.322.

Smithfield

P7.2.5.27 Burgher Monument, listing the names of 22 burghers and one woman who died on active service during the war.[1092]
▶ In front of the Dutch Reformed Church, c/o Voortrekker St & Kerk St, Smithfield, Free State.
◉ S30° 12.642, E26° 31.867.

Ventersburg

P7.2.5.28 Obelisk for Commandant Simon Begemann and four other burghers.[1093]
▶ New municipal cemetery, east of the N1, between Pienaar St & Mmamahabane Rd, Ventersburg, Free State.
◉ S28° 05.076, E27° 08.760.

Verkeerdevlei

P7.2.5.29 Burgher Monument, unveiled on 6 April 1931, and listing the names of 30 burghers who died on active service during the war.[1094]
▶ In front of the Dutch Reformed Church, c/o Louis Wessels St & Kerk St, Verkeerdevlei, Free State.
◉ S28° 50.015, E26° 46.696.

Vrede

P7.2.5.30 Burgher Monument, unveiled by President M.T. Steyn on 10 December 1910. It was transferred to its present position and provided with a granite pedestal during the Great Trek Centenary in 1938. It lists 69 burghers of Vrede who died on active service during the war.[1095]
▶ In front of the Dutch Reformed Church, Church Square, between Van der Lingen St & Voortrekker St, Vrede, Free State.
◉ S27° 25.599, E29° 09.852.

Wepener

Burgher monument, unveiled on 11 November 1905 by (amongst others) General J.B.M. Hertzog and General P.H. Kritzinger. It contains the names of 11 burghers who died in the war.[1096]

P7.2.5.26 P7.2.5.27 P7.2.5.28 P7.2.5.29 P7.2.5.30

1092 Van der Bank 1995, 66-67.
1093 Van der Bank 1995, 68-69.
1094 Van der Bank 1995, 69-71.
1095 Van der Bank 1995, 71-73.
1096 Van der Bank 1995, 73-74.

▶ *In the municipal cemetery.*
◉ *GPS co-ordinates not available.*

Winburg

P7.2.5.31 Burgher Monument, unveiled on 23 February 1909 by President M.T. Steyn.[1097]
▶ *In front of the central Dutch Reformed Church, Church Square, c/o Nico van der Merwe St & Wilcocks St, Winburg, Free State.*
◉ *S28° 31.115, E27° 00.700.*

P7.2.5.32 Framed roll of honour with the names of 137 burghers who died in the war.[1098]
▶ *In the entrance hall of the Dutch Reformed Church, Winburg, Free State.*
◉ *S28° 31.115, E27° 00.700.*

Zastron

P7.2.5.33 Burgher Monument, unveiled on 17 March 1906 by General P.H. Kritzinger, and showing the names of 10 burghers who died in the war.[1099]
▶ *In front of the Dutch Reformed Church, Zastron, Free State.*
◉ *GPS co-ordinates not available.*

7.2.6 KwaZulu-Natal

Ladysmith

P7.2.6.1 Burgher Monument in the municipal cemetery, commemorating 25 burghers who were originally buried there, but were reinterred at the Platrand Burgher Monument in 1979.
▶ *Southern side of Cemetery Rd, between Illings St & Mandela St, Ladysmith, KwaZulu-Natal.*
◉ *S28° 33.322, E29° 47.687.*

Burgher Monument on Platrand, Ladysmith—see also P3.2.3.19.

Utrecht

P7.2.6.2 Burgher Monument.
▶ *In front of the Dutch Reformed Church, 50 Church St, Utrecht, KwaZulu-Natal.*
◉ *S27° 39.293, E30° 19.211.*

P7.2.5.31   P7.2.5.32   P7.2.5.33   P7.2.6.1   P7.2.6.2

1097   Van der Bank 1995, 75.
1098   Van der Bank 1995, 76-79.
1099   Van der Bank 1995, 79-80.

Vryheid

P7.2.6.3 Burgher Monument. The names of 81 burghers from Vryheid and burghers from elsewhere who died in the Vryheid district in the war are listed on the monument.[1100]
▶ *Grounds of the Dutch Reformed Church, Church St, Vryheid, KwaZulu-Natal.*
◉ *S27° 46.066, E30° 47.533.*

P7.2.6.4 Burgher Monument.
▶ *Municipal cemetery, southern side of the town, Hoog St, between Landdrost St & Wes St, Vryheid, KwaZulu-Natal.*
◉ *S27° 46.887, E30° 47.952.*

7.2.7 Eastern Cape

Burgersdorp

P7.2.7.1 Burgher Monument, made of local sandstone in 1933.
▶ *On the town square, between Jan Greyling St, Piet Retief St, Chase St & Church St, Burgersdorp, Eastern Cape.*
◉ *S30° 59.632, E26° 19.879.*

P7.2.7.2 Burgher Monument that commemorates P. Klopper, who was hanged by the British forces, as well as 12 men who, according to the inscription, were killed in action at the Stormberg railway junction in December 1900 (this should be 1899).
▶ *In the municipal cemetery, Burgersdorp, Eastern Cape.*
◉ *S30° 59.803, E26° 20.044.*

Cradock

P7.2.7.3 Burgher Monument.
▶ *At the Dutch Reformed Church, upper end of Church St, Cradock, Eastern Cape.*
◉ *Near S32° 10.177, E25° 37.063.*

Dordrecht

P7.2.7.4 Burgher Monument.
▶ *In front of the Dutch Reformed Church, Grey St, Dordrecht, Eastern Cape.*
◉ *S31° 22.352, E27° 02.907.*

P7.2.6.3 P7.2.6.4 P7.2.7.1 P7.2.7.2 P7.2.7.3

1100 Van der Westhuizen & Van der Westhuizen 2013, 1-2.

Lady Grey

P7.2.7.5 Burgher Monument.
▶ *In the municipal cemetery, north-western c/o Murray St & Dwars St, Lady Grey, Eastern Cape.*
◉ *S30° 42.558, E27° 12.659.*

Middelburg

P7.2.7.6 Burgher Monument erected in 1929 to honour the memory of 29 burgers who fell near Middelburg.
▶ *In front of the municipal offices, Meintjies St, Middelburg, Eastern Cape.*
◉ *S31° 29.757, E25° 00.329.*

7.2.8 Western Cape

Paarl

P7.2.8.1 Cape Anglo-Boer War memorial.
▶ *On the Laborie Wine Estate, Paarl, Western Cape. Entrance at the western end of Taillefer St.*
◉ *S33° 45.961, E18° 57.529.*

7.2.9 Northern Cape

Calvinia

P7.2.9.1 Burgher Monument. This monument commemorates Cape Rebels who supported the Republican cause.
▶ *In the municipal cemetery, western side of Calvinia, Northern Cape.*
◉ *S31° 28.235, E19° 45.893.*

Colesberg

P7.2.9.2 Burgher Monument. The names of 46 burghers who fell in that area during the war as well as five executed by the British forces (see also P5.7.20) appear on the monument.
▶ *Station Rd, next to the British Garden of Remembrance, northern side of Colesberg, Eastern Cape, just south of and visible from the N1.*
◉ *S30° 42.700, E25° 06.114.*

Kamieskroon

P7.2.9.3 Burgher Monument. The inscription (translated) reads: "Died for Afrikaners in Namaqualand. Field Cornet M. Boonzaaier, A.C. Koch, L. Hesselman, A. Nel, J. van der Merwe and J.J. van Zyl".

P7.2.7.4 P7.2.7.5 P7.2.7.6 P7.2.8.1 P7.2.9.1

CP19 Cemetery of the Imperial Yeomanry Hospital, Deelfontein, Northern Cape (see p. 266).

CP20 Agterryer. Bronze statue in the garden of the War Museum of the Boer Republics, Bloemfontein, Free State (see pp. 213-214).

CP21 The grave of Abraham Esau, Calvinia, Northern Cape (see p. 216).

CP22 Horse Memorial, Port Elizabeth, Eastern Cape (see p. 29).

CP23 Statue of Christiaan de Wet in front of the Fourth Raadsaal, Bloemfontein, Free State (see pp. 167 and 267).

ANGLO-BOER WAR Historical Guide to Memorials and Sites in South Africa

CP24 Hildebrand memorial near Darling, Western Cape (see p. 203).

CP25 British blockhouse at railway bridge near Wolseley, Western Cape (see Section 5.5, pp. 241-248).

CP26 The Chair Monument, where Lötter and Wolfaardt were executed, Middelburg, Eastern Cape (see p. 201).

CP27 The grave of Hendrik van Heerden, Sevenfontein, near Middelburg, Eastern Cape (see p. 257).

CP28 Memorial for Republican prisoners of war buried in the Seaforth Cemetery, Simonstown, Western Cape (see p. 251).

CP29 British Garden of Remembrance, Volksrust, Mpumalanga (see p 324).

CP30 Burgher Monument, Bothaville, Free State (see p. 288).

CP31 Concentration camp memorial and graves, Klerksdorp, North West (see p. 228) [Photograph by Marelize Swanepoel].

TELL ENGLAND, YE WHO PASS THIS MONUMENT,
WE, WHO DIED SERVING HER, REST HERE CONTENT.

CP32 Inscription on Imperial Light Horse Memorial, Mareetsane, North West (see pp. 17).

CP 33 Roll of honour of the victims of the Concentration Camps, War Museum of the Boer Republics, Bloemfontein, Free State (see pp. 222, 223).

CP34 Roll of honour, burghers who died in the war, War Museum of the Boer Republics, Bloemfontein, Free State (see pp. 287, 288).

CP35 British Garden of Remembrance, Fort Napier military cemetery, Pietermaritzburg, KwaZulu-Natal (see p. 337).

CP36 British Anglo Boer War memorial, Maitland Cemetery, Cape Town, Western Cape (see p. 346).

CP37 Statue of a young victim of the war staring across the rows of graves in the Pietersburg Concentration Camp Cemetery, Polokwane, Limpopo (see p. 21). [This statue was stolen in 2015 and has not been recovered].

▶ *On the grounds of the Dutch Reformed Church, De Waal St, Kamieskroon, Northern Cape.*
◙ *S30° 12.497, E17° 55.884.*

Philipstown

P7.2.9.4 Memorial erected by the public of Philipstown for all the burghers who fell during the war. It also serves as the gravestone on the mass grave of five burghers killed in action.
▶ *Municipal cemetery, Philipstown, Northern Cape.*
◙ *S30° 26.023, E24° 28.534.*

Richmond

P7.2.9.5 Burgher Monument.
▶ *Municipal cemetery, Market St, Richmond, Northern Cape.*
◙ *S31° 24.990, E23° 56.697.*

7.3 Other Boer commemorative places

In addition to burgher monuments, several other types of Boer memorials were created and erected after the war. In addition, numerous existing places associated with the war in some way have been recognized as war sites.

7.3.1 Historical buildings closely associated with the war

At least two orphanages were opened by the Boers after the war to accommodate children left destitute by the concentration camps. One of these was erected in Ladybrand in the Free State and was aptly named the Memorial Orphanage. The other, in Johannesburg, was named after one of the seven ministers of religion who served the Boer commandos throughout the war, Abraham Kriel.

P7.3.1.1 Cornerstone of the first orphanage in Ladybrand, laid by General J.B.M. Hertzog on 30 July 1904. The inscription confirms that the orphanage was built to commemorate Ladybrand's war victims. A framed roll of honour in the entrance hall contains the names of 64 burghers from Ladybrand who died on active duty.[1101]
▶ *1 Collins St, Ladybrand, Free State.*
◙ *S29° 12.221, E27° 27.527.*

Some of the concentration camp orphans were taken to the Cape Colony, where they were accommodated in school hostels. In Lang Street, Riebeeck-Wes in the Western Cape, a building currently called Dennehof was built in 1903 on the initiative of the headmaster of the local school to accommodate Boer orphans.[1102]

P7.2.9.2

P7.2.9.3

P7.2.9.4

P7.2.9.5

P7.3.1.1

1101 Van der Bank 1995, 49-52.
1102 Van Bart & Scholtz 2003, 100.

P7.3.1.2   P7.3.1.3

P7.3.1.2 The hall of a primary school, the Volksskool in Heidelberg in Gauteng, built in 1907, commemorates the 90 burghers from that district who were killed in action or died of wounds, as well as the 624 local men, women and children who died in concentration camps, and 153 others who died at home or in the veld as a result of the impact of the war.[1103]
▶ *C/o of Voortrekker St & Begeman St, Heidelberg, Gauteng.*
◉ *S26° 29.861, E28° 21.407.*

P7.3.1.3 During the war years, the house which is now the Koopmans De Wet House Museum in Cape Town was owned by Mrs Marie Koopmans-De Wet. She did all in her power to avert the war. Later, she campaigned strongly against the concentration camp system, and used her house as a depot from which hundreds of crates filled with food, medicine and clothing were sent to the suffering women and children in the camps in various parts of South Africa.[1104]
▶ *35 Strand St, Cape Town, Western Cape.*
◉ *S33° 55.249, E18° 25.285.*

P7.3.1.4 This is the cottage in which Olive Schreiner is said to have lived with her husband throughout the war, or perhaps after the war.[1105] Schreiner was a staunch opponent of the war and she campaigned against what she considered brutal tactics employed by the British military authorities, especially in the Cape Colony.
▶ *Cottage behind Olive Schreiner House, c/o Grace St & Nuwe St, Hanover, Northern Cape.*
◉ *S31° 03.899, E24° 26.585.*

7.3.2 Sites associated with participants in the war

Other places of remembrance of the war include sites associated with specific participants who either played leading roles, or are especially remembered for what they did in the war, but who died after the peace treaty was signed at Vereeniging.

P7.3.1.4   P7.3.2.1

1103 Van Tonder ca 1974, 94-95; Richardson 2001, 192.
1104 Cronjé 1989a, 26.
1105 Schoeman, K. 1992, 192.

The Republican presidents

P7.3.2.1 Kruger House Museum. President Kruger owned this house, which was built for him in 1883-1884. It was one of the first houses in Pretoria which had a telephone and electric lighting installed before 1899. His wife, Gezina, née Du Plessis, died in the house on 20 July 1901. It was subsequently used by the British military police department.[1106]
▶ Northern side of W.F. Nkomo St (previously Church St), about 670 m west of Church Square, Pretoria, Gauteng.
◙ S25° 44.810, E28° 10.883.

P7.3.2.2 The grave of President Paul Kruger (1825-1904) of the ZAR.
▶ Old Church Street West Cemetery, Pretoria, Gauteng, near the south-eastern corner of the cemetery. Entry from Es'kia Mphahlele St (previously D.F. Malan Dr), north of W.F. Nkomo Dr (previously Church St West).
◙ Near S25°44.484, E28°10.358.

A number of other places associated with President Kruger have not yet been mentioned in this book:

- Statue of Kruger in Krugersdorp, Gauteng.
▶ Begin St, near corner with the R28.
◙ S26° 05.506, E27° 46.701.

- Kruger's house on his farm Boekenhoutfontein, North West.
▶ Western side of the R565 between Rustenburg & Sun City, North West. Signposted.
◙ Gate at S25° 32.828, E27° 07.679.

- Busts of Kruger, inter alia at the Kruger Gate of the Kruger National Park, Mpumalanga (◙ S23° 54.720, E29° 27.105), and on the Civic Square in Polokwane, Limpopo (◙ S23° 54.720, E29° 27.105).

P7.3.2.3 The Presidency, Bloemfontein, Free State. It served as the official residence of both Presidents M.T. Steyn and of his predecessor as president of the Orange Free State, namely F.W. Reitz, who was the state secretary of the ZAR for the duration of the war. It was taken over by the British authorities after their occupation of Bloemfontein in March 1900.
▶ President Brand St, near corner with St George's St.
◙ S29° 07.185, E26° 12.937.

P7.3.2.4 President Steyn's house on his farm Onze Rust.[1107]
▶ Onze Rust is still in the Steyn family. It is signposted on the N1 south of Bloemfontein, Free State.
◙ Near S29° 16.515, E26° 11.334.

P7.3.2.2

P7.3.2.3

P7.3.2.4

1106 Oberholster 1972, 300-301; Cronjé 1989bc, 190; Greyling 2000, 31-32; Richardson 2001, 210.
1107 NALN 1989c, 92.

P7.3.2.5 Grave of President M.T. Steyn (1857–1916) of the Orange Free State and of his wife Rachel Isabella, née Fraser.
▶ *At the foot of the National Women's Monument, Monument Rd, Bloemfontein, Free State.*
◎ *S29° 08.397, E26° 12.569.*

Several other places are associated with President Steyn but have not been mentioned in this book before:

- The house where Steyn was born in Winburg in the Free State.
- Busts of Steyn, inter alia at the War Museum of the Boer Republics and in the Old Presidency Museum, Bloemfontein, Free State.

Ministers of religion

A number of ministers who accompanied the commandos into the field served throughout the war or became prisoners of war with the men in their congregations. They have been commemorated for their service and contribution to the Republican cause in various ways.

P7.3.2.6 Bust of Reverend J.D. Kestell, the Kerkman (Church Man) of the Free State, sculpted by Laurika Postma.
▶ *War Museum of the Boer Republics, Monument Rd, Bloemfontein, Free State.*
◎ *S29° 08.397, E26° 12.569.*

P7.3.2.7 Kestell's burial site. He survived the war and continued to play a leading role in church and community matters, especially in the Orange Free State, for four decades after the war. In recognition of his dedication, a town in the eastern Free State was named after him. Furthermore, he was buried at the foot of the National Women's Monument.
▶ *Monument Rd, Bloemfontein, Free State.*
◎ *S29° 08.397, E26° 12.569.*

P7.3.2.8 The role played by Reverend J.M. Louw of Boksburg as "Volksman" is commemorated on his gravestone.
▶ *Grounds of the Dutch Reformed Church, c/o Voortrekker St & Gracht St, Boksburg, Gauteng.*
◎ *S26° 13.231, E28° 15.276.*

P7.3.2.9 Reverend A.P. Burger (1853-1937) of Middelburg in the eastern Transvaal accompanied the Middelburg Commando as its pastor and advisor, but in a strictly non-combatant role. He was captured on 20 February 1902 and was sent to a prisoner-of-war camp in India.[1108]
▶ *Burger's gravestone, old municipal cemetery. Entry from Bhimy Damane St, Middelburg, Mpumalanga.*
◎ *S25° 45.832, E29° 26.849.*

P7.3.2.5   P7.3.2.6   P7.3.2.7

1108   Burger 1936, Chapters II-XX; Van der Westhuizen & Van der Westhuizen 2000, 186.

P7.3.2.8　　　　　　　　　　P7.3.2.9　　　　　　　　　　P7.3.2.10

Reverend General Paul Roux's grave is in the cemetery in Bird St, in a town named after him – Paul Roux, Free State.

P7.3.2.10 Grave of Reverend M.J. Goddefroy, who in the first phase of the war accompanied the Pretoria Commando as their pastor and later served the burghers of General Beyers in the same capacity until June 1901, when he was captured by the British. He was sent to India as a prisoner of war.[1109]
▶ *Old Church Street West Cemetery, Pretoria, Gauteng, entry from Es'kia Mphahlele St (previously D.F. Malan Dr), north of W.F. Nkomo Dr (previously Church St West).*
◙ *Grave near S 25°44.776, E 28°10.553.*

Republican generals

Several burial sites of Republican generals (in addition to the graves already included in this book) can still be found.

P7.3.2.11 Memorial gravestone for Assistant Chief Commandant C.C.J. Badenhorst of the Western Free State (1872-1911).
▶ *Municipal cemetery, Boshof, Free State.*
◙ *South-eastern side of the town, near S28° 32.530, E25° 14.708.*

P7.3.2.12 The grave of Free State General George Alfred Brand (1875-1922), who continued to fight throughout the war and was present at the Vereeniging peace negotiations.
▶ *Brand was buried next to his father, President Jan Brand, the fourth president of the Orange Free State (b. 1823, president 1864-1888), in the President Brand Cemetery on the northern side of President St, west of the corner with Kerk St, Bloemfontein, Free State.*
◙ *S29° 07.480, E26° 13.197.*

P7.3.2.11　　　　　P7.3.2.12　　　　　P7.3.2.13　　　　　P7.3.2.14

1109　Botha 1981, 146-148.

P7.3.2.13 Grave of General Jan Crowther.
▶ *Municipal cemetery, Piet Retief St, at the entrance of the town from the R26, Ladybrand, Free State.*
◉ *S29° 12.025, E27° 27.985.*

P7.3.2.14 Grave of General Pieter Kritzinger.
▶ *Municipal cemetery, near c/o Dreary Lane & Stockenstrom St, Cradock, Eastern Cape.*
◉ *S32° 09.610, E25° 36.854.*

P7.3.2.15 General J.H. Olivier, the Republican commander in the Battle of Stormberg (10 December 1899), was taken prisoner in August 1900 and sent to Ceylon (now Sri Lanka). His offer to become a joiner was turned down by Kitchener. He died in 1930.[1110]
▶ *Municipal cemetery, Volksrust, Mpumalanga.*
◉ *S27° 21.880, E29° 53.679.*

P7.3.2.16 General Antonie Michael Prinsloo of the Bethlehem Commando remained in the veld until the end of the war. This memorial marks the spot where he was shot by an alleged madman in 1930.[1111] *(A site visit in August 2012 revealed that the memorial had been vandalised. The signpost has been removed).*
▶ *Eastern side of Lomond St, near corner with Church St, Bethlehem, Free State.*
◉ *S28° 13.345, E28° 18.823.*

P7.3.2.17 The grave of H.W. Lategan (1856-1914), a Cape Rebel who became a Republican general.
▶ *Old cemetery, Church St, Colesberg, Northern Cape.*
◉ *S30° 42.988, E25° 06.026.*

P7.3.2.18 The grave of General P.J. de Villiers (1853-1944).
▶ *Municipal cemetery, Petrusburg, Free State.*
◉ *South of S29° 07.196, E25° 25.153.*

P7.3.2.19 The monumental gravestone of the Transvaal General Lukas Meyer in Vryheid, KwaZulu-Natal, where there is also a Lukas Meyer museum.
▶ *Municipal cemetery, southern side of the town, Hoog St, between Landdrost St & Wes St in Vryheid, KwaZulu-Natal.*
◉ *S27° 46.887, E30° 47.952.*

P7.3.2.20 Grave of General P.A. Cronjé and his wife, H.A. Cronjé.
▶ *Jan Boomplaas Historical Cemetery, western side of the R30 linking Klerksdorp and Ventersdorp, North West.*
◉ *S26° 32.940, E26° 38.023.*

P7.3.2.15

P7.3.2.16

P7.3.2.17

1110 Uys 1968, 628; Grundlingh 1999, 205.
1111 Nienaber & Le Roux 1983, 4.

Part 7 – The legacy of the war

P7.3.2.18   P7.3.2.19   P7.3.2.20   P7.3.2.21

P7.3.2.21 Grave of General J.L. (Jaap) van Deventer.
▶ Rebecca Street Cemetery, Pretoria-West, entrance at c/o Rebecca St & Staatsartillerie Rd, Philip Nel Park, Pretoria, Gauteng.
◙ Near S25° 44.277, E28° 09.167.

P7.3.2.22 Grave of General S.G. (Manie) Maritz.[1112]
▶ Rebecca St Cemetery, Pretoria-West, entrance at c/o Rebecca St & Staatsartillerie Rd, Philip Nel Park, Pretoria, Gauteng.
◙ Near S25° 44.150, E28° 09.000.

Other Republican officers and officials

P7.3.2.23 Grave of N.C. Havenga (1882–1957). He came from Fauresmith, fought throughout the war, and served as General J.B.M. Hertzog's secretary-adjutant. He was wounded thrice. Later, he served for many years as South Africa's Minister of Finance.[1113]
▶ Reichardt Park Cemetery, south-west of c/o Jacobs St & Fontein St, Fauresmith, Free State.
◙ S29° 45.093, E25° 18.763.

P7.3.2.24 Memorial plaque for Commandant D.S. Lubbe, who led the Jacobsdal Commando in numerous encounters early on in the war.
▶ Attached to the burgher monument in front of the Dutch Reformed Church, Church St, Jacobsdal, Free State.
◙ S29° 07.731, E24° 46.459.

P7.3.2.25 Grave of Lieutenant-Colonel Alexander Ross (1854-1943), a bittereinder Free State commandant.
▶ Old town cemetery, Frankfort, Free State, next to the R34/26 on the eastern side of town.
◙ S27° 17.287, E28° 29.505.

P7.3.2.22   P7.3.2.23   P7.3.2.24   P7.3.2.25

1112   Du Plessis 1989, 200-201.
1113   Brits 1981, 227-234.

P7.3.2.26 Grave of Major J.L. (Lood) Pretorius, famous Boer artillerist. At the start of the Battle of Talana on 20 October 1899 one of the field guns of his battery hit the British camp with the very first shot that was fired. The excited reaction of one of the burghers was to shout out "Skote Petoors". According to tradition that was the origin of this Afrikaans exclamation of delight when somebody hits a challenging target.[1114]
▶ Old Church Street West Cemetery, Pretoria, Gauteng, entry from Es'kia Mphahlele St (previously D.F. Malan Dr), north of W.F. Nkomo Dr (previously Church St West).
◉ Grave near S25° 44.776, E28° 10.553.

The grave of Commandant Willem Fouchee, a bittereinder who was especially active in the eastern Cape, is in a cemetery on the farm Nooitgedacht near Swartruggens, North West. A memorial gravestone was unveiled on the grave in 1977.[1115]

The grave of Commandant "Rooi" Jozua Joubert of the Wakkerstroom Commando, a bittereinder who was wounded twice during the war, but only passed away in 1919, is on the farm Bergvliet, a few kilometres south of Amersfoort, Mpumalanga.[1116]

The grave of Commandant S.B. (Fanie) Buys of the Heidelberg Commando, who was wounded and taken prisoner in November 1901, and passed away in 1917, is in his family's cemetery on the farm Leeuspruit in the Grootvlei area, Mpumalanga.[1117]

P7.3.2.27 Grave of Commandant Ben Bouwer. He ended his post-war military career as a Brigadier General in the Union Defence Force.
▶ Anglo-Boer War Garden of Remembrance, Commonwealth War Graves section, Maitland Cemetery, Voortrekker Rd, Cape Town, Western Cape.
◉ S33° 55.022, E18° 32.280 (Google Maps).

P7.3.2.28-29 Grave of Captain Oliver John (Jack) Hindon (1874–1919), who achieved fame as an intrepid fighter and who derailed a number of British military trains (P7.3.2.28) and grave of the famous Boer scout Henri Slegtkamp, who fought till the end of the war and only passed away in 1951 (P7.3.2.29).
▶ Old municipal cemetery; entry from Bhimy Damane St, Middelburg, Mpumalanga.
◉ S25° 45.832, E29° 26.849.

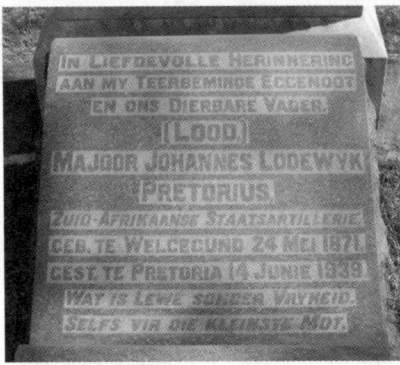
P7.3.2.26

P7.3.2.27

P7.3.2.28

1114 Brits 1977, 710.
1115 Van Bart & Scholtz 2003, 104-105.
1116 Van der Westhuizen & Van der Westhuizen 2013, 102.
1117 Van der Westhuizen & Van der Westhuizen 2013, 164.

P7.3.2.29   P7.3.2.30   P7.3.2.31

P7.3.2.30 Grave of Captain A.F. von Dalwig, ZAR State Artillery, who was seriously wounded at Dalmanutha on 27 August 1900, recovered, but died in Pretoria on 18 February 1911.
▶ Old Church Street West Cemetery, Pretoria, Gauteng, entry from Es'kia Mphahlele St (previously D.F. Malan Dr), north of W.F. Nkomo Dr (previously Church St West).
◉ Near S25° 44.473, E28° 10.323.

P7.3.2.31 Grave of T.A.H. Dönges, Field Cornet of the Heidelberg Commando. After the war he became headmaster of the Heidelberg Volksskool (People's School). He died in 1951.[1118]
▶ Kloof Cemetery, on the banks of the Kloof Spruit, northern side of extension of Fenter St, Heidelberg, Gauteng.
◉ S26° 29.717, E28° 20.770.

The grave of a French nobleman who fought on the Republican side, Robert de Kersauson de Pennendreff, is in Franschhoek in the Western Cape.

A unique individual

N.P.J.J. van Rensburg of the western Transvaal was a well-known figure. He is especially associated with General Koos de la Rey. It was widely believed that he had the power to foresee the future, and that he sporadically had visions which made it possible for him to predict what would happen. It is said that De la Rey attached great value to "Siener" (Seer) van Rensburg's visions.[1119]

P7.3.2.32 Portrait of N.P.J.J. (Siener) van Rensburg.
▶ Ampie Bosman Museum, at the municipal offices, Lichtenburg, North West, near Coligny Rd between R503 Scholtz St & R505 Melville St.
◉ S26° 08.989, E26° 09.558.

P7.3.2.32   P7.3.2.33   P7.3.2.34

1118   Van der Westhuizen & Van der Westhuizen 2000, 172.
1119   Pretorius 1981, 749-750.

Writers and artists

The war has been kept alive in the historical memory of many Afrikaners through the works of authors of war narratives, fiction and poetry, including some who participated in the war themselves. For example, nationalist historian Gustav Preller served in the Republican ranks until he was taken prisoner early in 1902. He was sent to a prisoner-of-war camp in India. Jan F.E. Celliers, the author of an outstanding war diary,[1120] as well as numerous moving poems on the war and its victims, was a *bittereinder*. Two other famous Afrikaans poets who wrote on the war, Eugene N. Marais and C. Louis Leipoldt, did not participate in combat themselves.

> *P7.3.2.33 Gustav Preller's gravestone.*
> ▶ *Farm cemetery at Pelindaba, North West.*
> ◉ *GPS co-ordinates not available.*
>
> *P7.3.2.34 Jan F.E. Celliers lived in Pretoria most of his life. There is a bust of Celliers at the Primary School Jan Celliers in Greenside, Johannesburg.*
> ▶ *Gravestone for Celliers and his wife close to the Heroes Acre, Old Church Street West cemetery, Pretoria, Gauteng. Entry from Es'kia Mphahlele St (previously D.F. Malan Dr), north of W.F. Nkomo Dr (previously Church St West).*
> ◉ *Grave near S25° 44.806, E28° 10.547.*
>
> *P7.3.2.35 Eugene N. Marais (1871-1936).*
> ▶ *Gravestone next to that of Celliers in the Old Church Street West Cemetery, Pretoria, Gauteng. Entry from Es'kia Mphahlele St (previously D.F. Malan Dr), north of W.F. Nkomo Dr (previously Church St West).*
> ◉ *Grave near S25° 44.806, E28° 10.547.*
>
> *P7.3.2.36 Burial site, C. Louis Leipoldt.*
> ▶ *Signposted next to the R364 in the Pakhuis Pass, in the Cederberg Mountains, about 17 km east of Clanwilliam, Western Cape.*
> ◉ *GPS co-ordinates not available.*

F.W. Reitz, President Steyn's predecessor as head of state of the Orange Free State, served as secretary of state of the ZAR for the duration of the war and signed the Vereeniging Peace Treaty in that capacity. He is also remembered for numerous poems that he wrote about and during the war, especially those in which he ridiculed the British military authorities, for example, in the well-known poem "Lady Roberts".

> *P7.3.2.37 Statue of Reitz as president of the Orange Free State.*
> ▶ *Gardens of the old Government Buildings, President Brand St, western side of the junction with Maitland St, Bloemfontein, Free State.*
> ◉ *S29° 06.979, E26° 12.997.*
> *Reitz's grave is in the Maitland Cemetery, Cape Town, Western Cape.*

P7.3.2.35   P7.3.2.36   P7.3.2.37   P7.3.2.38   P7.3.2.39

1120   Celliers 1978.

The war was also kept alive in Afrikaner memory by the folk song "Sarie Marais". The song was based on an American folk song "Ellie Rhee", but was given completely new words in Afrikaans. The Afrikaans origins are not clear. An inscription on the grave of Jacobus Petrus Toerien, who wrote under the pseudonym of Jepete, claims that he was responsible for the free translation of "Ellie Rhee" into "Sarie Marais".[1121]

> P7.3.2.38 Grave of J.P. Toerien (Jepete).
> ▶ Old municipal cemetery; entry from Bhimy Damane St, Middelburg, Mpumalanga.
> ◎ S25° 45.832, E29° 26.849.

The most outstanding artist to portray the war was sculptor Anton van Wouw, best known in this context for creating the centre-piece of the National Women's Monument in Bloemfontein.[1122]

> P7.3.2.39 Van Wouw was 82 years old when he died in 1945. He was buried in the Rebecca Street Cemetery, Pretoria-West.
> ▶ Entrance c/o Rebecca St & Staatsartillerie Rd, Philip Nel Park, Pretoria, Gauteng.
> ◎ Near S25° 44.082, E28° 09.014.

7.4 British memorials and gardens of remembrance

Memorials and gardens of remembrance to commemorate the role of British soldiers have been erected all over South Africa. Furthermore, there are graves of British soldiers in cemeteries across the country. These include the following that have not been mentioned earlier in this book:

7.4.1 Gauteng

Donkerhoek (Diamond Hill)

> P7.4.1.1 British Garden of Remembrance. It contains the graves of 110 Imperial soldiers, of whom 87 were killed in action or died of wounds in the Battle of Donkerhoek (see Part 3.7) or in other battles in this area.[1123]
> ▶ Entry from the R515 (turn west a few kilometres south of the N4), then drive through the grounds of the Kleinfontein settlement.
> ◎ S25° 48.363, E28° 29.385.

Heidelberg

> P7.4.1.2 British Garden of Remembrance. It contains the graves of 144 Imperial soldiers, of whom 28 were killed in action or died of wounds.[1124]

P7.4.1.1　　　　　　　　　　P7.4.1.2　　　　　　　　　　P7.4.1.3

1121　Van der Westhuizen & Van der Westhuizen 2000, 190.
1122　Duffey 2008, 162-166.
1123　Watt 2000, 470.
1124　Watt 2000, 470.

►*Kloof Cemetery, on the banks of the Kloof Spruit, on the northern side of the extension of Fenter St., Heidelberg, Gauteng.*
◉ *S26° 29.717, E28° 20.770.*

P7.4.1.3 St Ninian's Anglican Church contains commemorative plaques of the war (see P3.7.14 & P4.1.5.4)
►*C/o Marais St & Voortrekker St, Heidelberg, Gauteng.*
◉ *S26° 29.801, E28° 21.280.*

Johannesburg

The Anglo-Boer War Memorial (formerly Rand Regiments War Memorial – see P1.15.

P7.4.1.4 British Garden of Remembrance in the Braamfontein Cemetery. In addition to several memorials, it contains the graves of 509 Imperial soldiers, of whom 84 were killed in action or died of their wounds.[1125]
►*C/o Smit St & Graf St., Johannesburg, Gauteng.*
◉ *S26° 11.669, E28° 01.442.*

The Maraisburg Cemetery contains 11 Imperial war graves and a memorial (the New South Wales Memorial Cross) and several Australian graves. Six of these soldiers died in action or of their wounds.[1126]
►*Millward Rd, east of 6th Ave, Roodepoort, Gauteng.*
◉ *S26° 10.844, E27° 56.522.*

P7.4.1.5 Scottish Horse War Memorial.
►*On a low hill on the northern side of Highland Rd, between Katoomba & Good Hope Street (east of Jeppe Boys High).*
◉ *S26° 12.042, E28° 05.109.*

The Indian Army Memorial, Steyn St, south of intersection with Urania St, Observatory, Johannesburg. Walker writes: "This memorial was erected towards the end of 1902, on the highest point in Johannesburg; Observatory Ridge. It honours Hindus, Sikhs, Christians, Muslims and Zoroastrians, members of the Indian Army that lost their lives in the Anglo-Boer War. Sadly the years and vandals have taken their toll on the monument and in the late 1980s some of the marble tablets were smashed."[1127] The memorial is in a fenced-off area that is not easily accessible.

Krugersdorp

P7.4.1.6 The Burgershoop Cemetery contains 363 Imperial war graves. Of these soldiers 244 were killed in action or died of wounds.[1128] The centrepiece is this British memorial, "In proud remembrance of British

P7.4.1.4   P7.4.1.5   P7.4.1.6   P7.4.1.7

1125 Watt 2000, 471.
1126 Watt 2000, 471.
1127 Walker s.a.(b). See also Itzkin 2000, 63-68.
1128 Watt 2000, 471.

Part 7 – The legacy of the war

soldiers who died during the South African War 1899-1902 originally buried at Nooitgedacht, Cyferfontein, Quaggafontein and Vlakfontein and who are now buried here with their comrades at Krugersdorp."
▶ Burgershoop Cemetery, c/o Luipaard St & Halgryn St, Krugersdorp, Gauteng.
◉ S26° 06.095, E27° 45.612.

Pretoria

The St Alban's Anglican Cathedral in Francis Baard St contains a number of memorials for members of the British forces who died in the war. That includes an altar cross for Prince Christian Victor, a memorial plaque for the City of London Imperial Volunteers and also one for soldiers of the 28th Battalion killed in the war.
▶ In a reception room at the Cathedral, Francis Baard St, between Paul Kruger St & Thabo Sehume St, Pretoria Central, Gauteng.
◉ S25° 44.970, E28° 11.373.

P7.4.1.7 The Old Church Street West Cemetery in Pretoria contains contains the graves of 1185 Imperial soldiers, of whom 70 were killed in action or died of wounds,[1129] as well as a number of memorials. In addition to the many graves already mentioned, the gravestone (above) of Brevet Major Prince Christian Victor of Schleswig-Holstein (33), King's Royal Rifles, commemorates this soldier, who died of enteric disease in Pretoria on 20 October 1900. He was one of Queen Victoria's grandsons.
▶ Entry from Es'kia Mphahlele St (previously D.F. Malan Dr), north of W.F. Nkomo Dr (previously Church St West), Pretoria, Gauteng.
◉ Near S 25°44.472, E 28°10.286.

The military cemetery in Thaba Tshwane, Pretoria, contains the graves of 139 Imperial soldiers.[1130]

P7.4.1.8 Memorial plaque paying tribute to 79 members of Bethune's Mounted Infantry (a Johannesburg regiment) who lost their lives during the war.
▶ At Fort Schanskop on the grounds of the Voortrekker Monument, Eeufees Rd, Pretoria, Gauteng.
◉ S25° 46.628, E28° 11.035.

Petronella

British Garden of Remembrance (see P5.6.1.3).

Primrose

P7.4.1.9 British Garden of Remembrance. It contains a number of memorials, as well as the graves of 544 Imperial soldiers, of whom 181 were killed in action or died of their wounds.[1131]

P7.4.1.8   P7.4.1.9   P7.4.2.1

1129   Watt 2000, 472.
1130   Watt 2000, 472.
1131   Watt 2000, 470.

▶ Municipal cemetery, Primrose, Gauteng. Use the northern entrance from Cemetery Rd (about 100 m north of the main entrance), north of the intersection with Rietfontein Ave.
◉ S26° 11.719, E28° 08.722.

7.4.2 North-West

Coligny

P7.4.2.1 British military cemetery. It contains the graves of 34 Imperial soldiers, of whom 31 were killed in action or died of their wounds.[1132]
▶ About 2 km south-west of Coligny, south of the junction where the N14 to Delareyville turns off the R503 to Lichtenburg, very close to the junction.
◉ S26° 19.607, E26° 17.443.

Groot Marico

The British Garden of Remembrance contains 18 graves of Imperial soldiers who were all killed in action or died of their wounds.[1133]

Ifafi

P7.4.2.2 The British Garden of Remembrance at Rietfontein. It contains the graves of 123 Imperial soldiers, of whom 79 were killed in action or died of their wounds.[1134]
▶ On the western side of the R511 between Kleinste St and the R104 (Kerk St), at the entrance to Birdwood Estate (near the Hartbeespoort Dam). Park outside the entrance and walk about 300 m north to the cemetery, Ifafi, North West.
◉ S25° 44.760, E27° 54.535.

Klerksdorp

P7.4.2.3 British Garden of Remembrance. It contains the graves of 218 Imperial soldiers, of whom 104 were killed in action or died of their wounds.[1135]
▶ Municipal cemetery, near Margaretha Prinsloo St, between O.R. Tambo St & Kadria St, Klerksdorp, North West.
◉ S26° 52.576, E26° 40.130.

P7.4.2.2

P7.4.2.3

P7.4.2.4

1132 Watt 2000, 469.
1133 Watt 2000, 470.
1134 Watt 2000, 470.
1135 Watt 2000, 471.

Lichtenburg

P7.4.2.4 British Garden of Remembrance. In addition to individual graves and memorials already included in this guide, there is a memorial to members of Paget's Horse, Imperial Yeomanry, killed in action in various engagements around Lichtenburg. A total of 101 Imperial soldiers, of whom 38 were killed in action or died of wounds, were buried here.[1136]
▶ Municipal cemetery, Lichtenburg, North West, near Christa St, between Lang St and Burgers St (entry from Thabo Mbeki St).
◉ S26° 08.461, E26° 09.228.

Mahikeng

P7.4.2.5 Part of the British Garden of Remembrance. It contains the graves of 229 Imperial soldiers, of whom 103 were killed in action or died of their wounds.[1137]
▶ Cemetery, Carrington St, between Carney St & 1st Lane, Mahikeng, North West.
◉ S25° 51.448, E25° 38.202.

Ottosdal

P7.4.2.6 British Garden of Remembrance. It contains the graves of 117 Imperial soldiers, of whom 113 were killed in action or died of their wounds.[1138] The large granite memorial in the centre states that it was erected "[i]n proud remembrance of British soldiers originally buried at Boschpan, Brakspruit, De Klip Drift and Korannafontein, who now lie buried here at Ottosdal."
▶ On the outskirts of town, near the D616, between the D855 and Visser St, Ottosdal, North West.
◉ S26° 48.271, E26° 00.773.

Potchefstroom

P7.4.2.7 British Garden of Remembrance. It contains the graves of 243 Imperial soldiers, of whom 105 were killed in action or died of their wounds.[1139]
▶ Alexandra cemetery, close to Olënpark, near Piet Bosman St, between James Moroka Dr and Kock St, Potchefstroom, North West.
◉ S26° 42.760, E27° 05.248.

The Military Base cemetery in Potchefstroom contains the graves of 104 Imperial soldiers.[1140]

P7.4.2.5

P7.4.2.6

P7.4.2.7

1136 Watt 2000, 471.
1137 Watt 2000, 471.
1138 Watt 2000, 472.
1139 Watt 2000, 472.
1140 Watt 2000, 472.

Rustenburg

P7.4.2.8 The old municipal cemetery contains the graves of 76 Imperial soldiers, of whom 25 were killed in action or died of their wounds.[1141]
▶ Entry from Nelson Mandela St, between Kock St & Bosch St, Rustenburg, North West.
◉ S25° 40.516, E27° 14.628.

Ventersdorp

P7.4.2.9 British Garden of Remembrance. It contains the graves of 42 Imperial soldiers, of whom 13 were killed in action or died of their wounds.[1142]
▶ Municipal cemetery, near Grey St, between Kort & Visser St, Ventersdorp, North West.
◉ S26° 19.042, E26° 49.126.

Vryburg

P7.4.2.10 British Garden of Remembrance. It contains the graves of 115 Imperial soldiers, of whom 33 were killed in action or died of their wounds,[1143] as well as this memorial, "[i]n proud remembrance of British soldiers previously buried at Brussels Siding, Geluk, Schweizer-Reneke, Taung, Vryburg Old Cemetery, Wolmaransstad, now interred here at Vryburg".
▶ Vryburg Municipal cemetery, Suid Str/South St, west of corner with N18 Moffat St, southern side of town, Vryburg, North West.
◉ Near S26° 58.162, E24° 43.640 (Google Maps).

Zeerust

There is a British Garden of Remembrance. It contains the graves of 110 Imperial soldiers, of whom 76 were killed in action or died of their wounds.[1144]

7.4.3 Limpopo

P7.4.3.1 Polokwane: British Garden of Remembrance, which contains the graves of 123 Imperial soldiers, of whom 57 were killed in action or died of their wounds,[1145] as well as this memorial for British soldiers who died on active service in the northern Transvaal.
▶ Old Pietersburg (Polokwane) municipal cemetery, northern part, entry from Dahl St, across from the western end of Jorissen St., Polokwane, Limpopo.
◉ S23° 54.489, E29° 26.783.

P7.4.2.8

P7.4.2.9

P7.4.2.10

1141 Watt 2000, 472.
1142 Watt 2000, 473.
1143 Watt 2000, 473.
1144 Watt 2000, 473.
1145 Watt 2000, 472.

7.4.4 Mpumalanga

Badfontein

The British military cemetery contains the graves of 18 Imperial soldiers, of whom 12 were killed in action or died of their wounds.[1146]
▶ On the eastern side of the R36 between Lydenburg and Machadodorp, Mpumalanga.
◉ GPS co-ordinates not available.

Barberton

P7.4.4.1 British Garden of Remembrance, erected by South African War Graves Board in 1976. A total of 130 Imperial soldiers, of whom 10 were killed in action or died of their wounds, were reinterred here from cemeteries in Nelspruit, Barberton, Komatipoort, Hectorspruit, Kaapmuiden and Alkmaar.[1147]
▶ Henry Nettman St, between Redelinghuys St and Keurboom St, Barberton, Mpumalanga.
◉ S25° 45.970, E31° 03.284.

Belfast

P7.4.4.2 British Garden of Remembrance. It contains the graves of 47 Imperial soldiers, of whom 40 were killed in action or died of their wounds.[1148]
▶ Old municipal cemetery, on an unnamed road between Spitskop St and Scheepers St (drive west), Belfast, Mpumalanga.
◉ S25° 41.694, E30° 01.663.

Chrissiesmeer

The municipal cemetery contains the graves of 37 Imperial soldiers killed in action or who died of their wounds.[1149]
▶ Near the R542, western side of Chrissiesmeer, Mpumalanga.
◉ S26° 16.797, E30° 12.281.

Dalmanutha

P7.4.4.3 British military cemetery. It contains the graves of 10 Imperial soldiers, of whom eight were killed in action or died of their wounds.[1150]

P7.4.3.1

P7.4.4.1

P7.4.4.2

1146 Watt 2000, 469. Van der Westhuizen and Van der Westhuizen (2000, 269) claim that 17 soldiers are buried there.
1147 Watt 2000, 469; Van der Westhuizen & Van der Westhuizen 2000, 244.
1148 Watt 2000, 469; Van der Westhuizen & Van der Westhuizen 2000, 215.
1149 Watt 2000, 471.
1150 Watt 2000, 469.

► Less than 100 m directly south of the Dalmanutha Station, north of an unnamed gravel road.
◉ S25° 45.384, E30° 10.192.

Dullstroom

There is a British Garden of Remembrance at the foot of Suikerboskop, on its eastern side, below a British Anglo-Boer War fort. It contains the graves of 14 Imperial soldiers, who were all killed in action or died of their wounds.[1151]
◉ GPS co-ordinates not available.

Emalahleni (Witbank)

P7.4.4.4 Two British war graves. In 1990, there were still six iron crosses. The soldiers buried here probably died in a British military hospital located nearby.[1152]
► Near the Witbank Dam at Naauwpoort, turn north from the R544 (to Bethal) a few kilometres south of Emalahleni.
◉ S25° 57.009, E29° 16.257.

Ermelo

P7.4.4.5 Ermelo: British Garden of Remembrance with memorials for and the graves of 131 Imperial soldiers, of whom 65 were killed in action or died of their wounds in this area during the war.[1153]
► Municipal cemetery, near 16th St, Ermelo, Mpumalanga.
◉ S26° 30.402, E29° 58.760.

Kaapsche Hoop

P7.4.4.6 Three British Anglo-Boer War graves in the town cemetery.[1154]
► Directly east of the town. Surrounded on all sides by trees, about 140 m east of the main road.
◉ S25° 35.392, E30° 45.707.

Lydenburg

P7.4.4.7 British Garden of Remembrance with memorials for and the graves 88 Imperial soldiers, of whom 30 were killed in action or died of their wounds.[1155]

P7.4.4.3

P7.4.4.4

P7.4.4.5

1151   Watt 2000, 470; Van der Westhuizen & Van der Westhuizen 2000, 207.
1152   Van der Westhuizen & Van der Westhuizen 2000, 181.
1153   Watt 2000, 470; Van der Westhuizen & Van der Westhuizen 2000, 104-105.
1154   Van der Westhuizen & Van der Westhuizen 2000, 240; Watt 2000, 471.
1155   Watt 2000, 471.

P7.4.4.6　　　　　　　　　　P7.4.4.7　　　　　　　　　　P7.4.4.8

▶ Old municipal cemetery, at the western end of Buhrmann St, Lydenburg, Mpumalanga.
◉ Near S25° 05.188, E30° 26.747.

Machadodorp

P7.4.4.8 British Garden of Remembrance. It contains the graves of 111 Imperial soldiers, of whom 48 were killed in action or died of their wounds.[1156]
▶ Municipal cemetery, Machadodorp, Mpumalanga. On the western side of the tarred road that connects the town to the N4 toll road, a few hundred metres south of the N4.
◉ S25° 40.065, E30° 14.508.

Middelburg

P7.4.4.9 Garden of Remembrance and memorial. It contains the graves of 503 Imperial soldiers, of whom 109 were killed in action or died of their wounds.[1157]
▶ Old municipal cemetery, entry from Bhimy Damane St, Middelburg, Mpumalanga.
◉ S25° 45.832, E29° 26.849.

Standerton

P7.4.4.10 Garden of Remembrance. It contains the graves of 549 Imperial soldiers, of whom 105 were killed in action or died of their wounds.[1158] There are also memorials.
▶ British military cemetery, at the new municipal cemetery, entry from Walter Sisulu St., Standerton, Mpumalanga.
◉ S26° 56.283, E29° 14.077.

P7.4.4.9　　　　　　　　　　P7.4.4.10　　　　　　　　　　P7.4.4.11

1156　Watt 2000, 471.
1157　Watt 2000, 471.
1158　Watt 2000, 472.

Volksrust

P7.4.4.11 Garden of Remembrance. It contains the graves of 78 Imperial soldiers, of whom 55 were killed in action or died of their wounds. Five unknown soldiers were also reinterred here[1159] (see also CP29 on p. 301).
▶ North of c/o Grens St & Kort St (visible from the R23, on the western side of that road, where it enters the town from the north), Volksrust, Mpumalanga.
◉ S27° 21.668, E29° 52.449.

Wakkerstroom

P7.4.4.12 The British Garden of remembrance contains memorials to, and the graves of 115 Imperial soldiers, of whom 33 were killed in action or died of their wounds.[1160]
▶ British Garden of Remembrance, municipal cemetery, northern side of Kerk St, near corner with Scheiding St, Wakkerstroom, Mpumalanga.
◉ S27° 21.520, E30° 08.027.

Waterval-Onder

P7.4.4.13 There was a British military hospital, close to the railway station.[1161] The cemetery contains the graves of 41 Imperial soldiers, of whom three were killed in action or died of their wounds.[1162]
▶ About 100 m south of the N4, at the eastern end of Waterval-Onder, Mpumalanga.
◉ S25° 38.782, E30° 23.214.

7.4.5 Free State

Bethlehem

P7.4.5.1 British Garden of Remembrance. It contains the graves of 172 Imperial soldiers, of whom 84 were killed in action or died of their wounds.[1163]
▶ Old town cemetery, between Muller St & Boshoff St, near corner with Baxter St, Bethlehem, Free State.
◉ S28° 14.026, E28° 18.036.

Bethulie

P7.4.5.2 British Garden of Remembrance. It contains the graves of 22 Imperial soldiers, of whom eight were killed in action or died of their wounds.

P7.4.4.12

P7.4.4.13

P7.4.5.1

1159 Watt 2000, 473.
1160 Watt 2000, 473.
1161 Van der Westhuizen & Van der Westhuizen 2000, 237.
1162 Watt 2000, 473.
1163 Watt 2000, 469.

Part 7 – The legacy of the war

P7.4.5.2   P7.4.5.3   P7.4.5.4

► In the municipal cemetery, northern side of Boven Noord St, Bethulie, Free State.
◉ S30° 29.530, E25° 58.290.

Bloemfontein

P7.4.5.3 The President Brand Cemetery contains the graves of 1731 Imperial soldiers, of whom 42 were killed in action or died of their wounds, and 1648 died of disease.[1164] In addition, it contains numerous regimental memorials, including a memorial for members of the Telegraph Division, Royal Engineers, who died on active service in the Orange Free State and the Cape Colony in the war.
► Northern side of President St, west of corner with Kerk St., Bloemfontein, Free State.
◉ S29° 07.480, E26° 13.197.

P7.4.5.4 Seaforth Highlanders Memorial. Erected by their comrades of the 2nd Battalion Seaforth Highlanders Ross-Shire Buffs, the Duke of Albany's, in memory of ten officers and 122 non-commissioned officers and men who died of disease or accidents in South Africa from 1899 to 1902.[1165]
► In King's Park, next to Kingsway, Bloemfontein, Free State.
◉ S29° 06.913, E26° 12.304.

There is also a Canadian Memorial in King's Park, erected by the Imperial Order Daughters of the Empire in Canada in proud and grateful memory of those Canadians who gave their lives for the Empire in the South African War 1899-1902.[1166]

P7.4.5.5 Waverley Road Memorial. In October 1901, the Bloemfontein City Council decided to close the President Brand Cemetery and to establish a new cemetery between Naval Hill and Signal Hill. This cemetery was in active use until 1908. A total of 228 Imperial soldiers, of whom ten were killed in action or died of their

P7.4.5.5   P7.4.5.6   P7.4.5.7

1164   Watt 2000, 469.
1165   Nienaber & Le Roux 1983, 9; Van der Bank 2001, 57.
1166   Nienaber & Le Roux 1983, 9; Van der Bank 2001, 58.

wounds, were buried here. In 1950, the gravestones in the Waverley Road Cemetery were removed. The terrain was transformed into a Garden of Remembrance, with a sarcophagus containing the names of soldiers and family members who were buried there.[1167]
▶ Northern side of Waverley Road, between Whites St & Josef Henning St, Bloemfontein, Free State.
◉ S29° 05.356, E26° 13.608.

P7.4.5.6 Memorial plaque for 16th Battalion Mounted Infantry.
▶ Cathedral of St Andrew and St Michael, southern side of St George's St, at corner with Gordon St, Bloemfontein, Free State.
◉ S29° 07.253, E26° 13.174.

Boshof

P7.4.5.7 British Garden of Remembrance. It contains the graves of 120 Imperial soldiers, of whom 22 were killed in action or died of their wounds.[1168]
▶ Municipal cemetery, Boshof, Free State.
◉ South-eastern side of the town, near S28° 32.530, E25° 14.708.

Bothaville

P7.4.5.8 British Garden of Remembrance. It contains the graves of 28 Imperial soldiers, of whom 17 were killed in action or died of their wounds.[1169]
▶ Old municipal cemetery, eastern side of the R30, between President St & Greyling St, Bothaville, Free State.
◉ S27° 23.722, E26° 37.183.

Brandfort

P7.4.5.9 British Garden of Remembrance. It contains the graves of 31 Imperial soldiers, of whom eight were killed in action or died of their wounds.[1170]
▶ In municipal cemetery, south-western c/o Marais St & Wes St, Brandfort, Free State.
◉ S28° 42.304, E26° 27.205.

Dewetsdorp

The British military cemetery on the north-eastern outskirts of Dewetsdorp (near S29° 34.619, E26° 40.136) contains the graves of 58 Imperial soldiers, of whom 32 were killed in action or died of their wounds. In

P7.4.5.8

P7.4.5.9

1167 Van der Bank 2001, 52; Watt 2000, 469.
1168 Watt 2000, 469.
1169 Watt 2000, 469.
1170 Watt 2000, 469.

P7.4.5.10   P7.4.5.11

addition, there are seven graves of soldiers killed in action on Gloucester Kop on the north-western outskirts of Dewetsdorp.[1171]
◙ Near S29° 34.968, E26° 39.521.

Edenburg

P7.4.5.10 British Garden of Remembrance in the municipal cemetery. It contains the graves of 47 Imperial soldiers, of whom 32 were killed in action or died of their wounds.[1172]
▶ Near Boven Kerk St, Edenburg, Free State.
◙ S29° 44.222, E25° 56.523.

Fauresmith

P7.4.5.11 British Garden of Remembrance. According to Watt, it contains the graves of 15 Imperial soldiers, of whom 13 were killed in action or died of their wounds. Oosthuizen lists 18 Imperial soldiers who were buried here.[1173]
▶ Reichardt Park cemetery, south-west of c/o Jacobs St & Fontein St, Fauresmith, Free State.
◙ S29° 45.093, E25° 18.763.

Ficksburg

P7.4.5.12 The old town cemetery contains the graves of 69 Imperial soldiers, of whom 17 were killed in action or died of their wounds.[1174]
▶ Entry from Veld St, near corner with Piet Retief St, Fickburg, Free State.
◙ S28° 52.027, E27° 52.637.

P7.4.5.12   P7.4.5.13

1171   Watt 2000, 470.
1172   Watt 2000, 470.
1173   Oosthuizen ca 2000, 23; Watt 2000, 470.
1174   Watt 2000, 470.

P7.4.5.14   P7.4.5.15   P7.4.5.16

Frankfort

P7.4.5.13 British Garden of Remembrance. It contains the graves of 98 Imperial soldiers, of whom 55 were killed in action or died of their wounds.[1175]
▶ Old town cemetery, next to the R34/26 on the eastern side of town, Frankfort, Free State.
◉ S27° 17.287, E28° 29.505.

Harrismith

P7.4.5.14 British Garden of Remembrance. It contains the graves of 437 Imperial soldiers, of whom 111 were killed in action or died of their wounds.[1176]
▶ Municipal cemetery, north-east of c/o Laksman St & Greyling St, Harrismith, Free State.
◉ S28° 16.143, E29° 07.891.

P7.4.5.15 Memorial that commemorates British soldiers who died in the war.
▶ In front of the town hall, Warden St, south-east of corner with Bester St, Harrismith, Free State.
◉ S28° 16.188, E29° 07.478.

Heilbron

P7.4.5.16 Memorial in British Garden of Remembrance. It commemorates the British soldiers who died in the war in that area and is surrounded by the graves of 306 Imperial soldiers, of whom 57 were killed in action or died of their wounds.[1177]
▶ Municipal cemetery, north of c/o Lang Markt St (the R57) & President St, Heilbron, Free State.
◉ S27° 16.756, E27° 58.174 (Google Maps).

P7.4.5.17   P7.4.5.18

1175   Watt 2000, 470.
1176   Watt 2000, 470.
1177   Watt 2000, 470.

Jacobsdal

P7.4.5.17 Garden of Remembrance with numerous British war graves and a memorial erected by the War Graves Council in 1968.[1178] The graves in the foreground are those of Lieutenant E.G. Carbutt, Royal Horse Artillery, and Lieutenant A.E. Hesketh, Lancers, killed in action at Roodewal on 15 February 1900.[1179]
▶ Municipal cemetery, De Villiersstraat, Jacobsdal, Free State.
◉ S29° 08.091, E24° 46.510.

Jagersfontein

P7.4.5.18 British Garden of Remembrance. It contains the graves of 31 Imperial soldiers, of whom 19 were killed in action or died of their wounds.[1180]
▶ Municipal cemetery, Likkewaan St., Jagersfontein, Free State.
◉ S29° 45.633, E25° 26.268.

Karee

P7.4.5.19 British Garden of Remembrance. It contains the graves of 70 Imperial soldiers, of whom 44 were killed in action or died of their wounds.[1181]
◉ GPS co-ordinates not available.

Koffiefontein

There is a memorial in the town cemetery that commemorates British soldiers who died in the war.
◉ GPS co-ordinates not available.

Kroonstad

P7.4.5.20 Memorial, and in the background, the entrance to the large British Garden of Remembrance. It contains the graves of 977 Imperial soldiers, of whom 143 were killed in action or died of their wounds.[1182]
▶ Western side of North St, Kroonstad, Free State.
◉ S27° 39.049, E27° 13.816.

P7.4.5.21 Garden of Remembrance. It contains the graves of 40 Imperial soldiers, of whom four were killed in action or died of their wounds.[1183]

P7.4.5.19

P7.4.5.20

P7.4.5.21

1178 Oosthuizen ca 2000, 17.
1179 Watt 2000, 65, 191.
1180 Watt 2000, 471.
1181 Watt 2000, 471.
1182 Watt 2000, 471.
1183 Watt 2000, 471.

▶ C/o Turner St, Beyers St & Marais St, Kroonstad, Free State.
◉ S27° 39.088, E27° 14.306.

Ladybrand

P7.4.5.22 Memorial to British soldiers who died on duty in the Anglo-Boer War, especially those of the Black Watch. It also commemorates the coronation of King Edward VII.
▶ Collins St, Ladybrand, Free State.
◉ S29° 12.044, E27° 27.177.

The municipal cemetery in Ladybrand contains 39 Imperial war graves, of which four are those of men killed in action or who died of their wounds.[1184]

Lindley

P7.4.5.23 British Garden of Remembrance. It contains the graves of 125 Imperial soldiers, of whom 64 were killed in action or died of their wounds.[1185]
▶ Municipal cemetery, near the S192, between Diemont St and the S904, Lindley, Free State.
◉ S27° 52.891, E27° 55.763.

Luckhoff

British soldiers were buried there during the war, but their gravestones have either disappeared or are no longer legible.

Petrusburg

P7.4.5.24 British war memorial in the municipal cemetery, which contains the graves of 28 Imperial soldiers, of whom seven were killed in action or died of their wounds.[1186]
▶ Municipal cemetery, Petrusburg, Free State.
◉ About 50 m south of S29° 07.196, E25° 25.153.

Philippolis

P7.4.5.25 British Garden of Remembrance. It contains the graves of 17 Imperial soldiers, of whom 11 were killed in action or died of their wounds.[1187]

P7.4.5.22   P7.4.5.23   P7.4.5.24   P7.4.5.25

1184   Watt 2000, 471.
1185   Watt 2000, 471.
1186   Watt 2000, 472.
1187   Watt 2000, 472.

Part 7 – The legacy of the war

▶ Municipal cemetery, Dwars St, at the south-western end of town, Philippolis, Free State.
◉ S30° 16.131, E25° 16.238.

Reddersburg

P7.4.5.26 British war graves.
▶ Municipal cemetery, on the outskirts of the town, near Letta St, Reddersburg, Free State.
◉ S29° 39.463, E26° 10.210.

Reitz

P7.4.5.27 British Garden of Remembrance. It contains the graves of 61 Imperial soldiers, of whom 47 were killed in action or died of their wounds.[1188]
▶ Old town cemetery, c/o Pan St & Zuider St, Reitz, Free State.
◉ S27° 47.782, E28° 26.007.

Senekal

P7.4.5.28 British memorial of polished granite with names of soldiers who died on active service in that area, as well as the graves of 109 Imperial soldiers, of whom 72 were killed in action or died of their wounds.[1189]
▶ Municipal cemetery, Senekal, Free State.
◉ S28° 18.778, E27° 37.287.

Smithfield

P7.4.5.29 Graves of 20 Imperial soldiers – 11 were killed in action or died of their wounds.[1190]
▶ Municipal cemetery, western end of President Hofman St, Smithfield, Free State.
◉ S30° 12.569, E26° 31.652.

Springfontein

P7.4.5.30 There are graves of 299 Imperial soldiers, of whom 16 were killed in action or died of their wounds,[1191] in this cemetery where concentration camp victims were also buried.
▶ Turn in an easterly direction into Emily Hobhouse St from Settlers St (the main street through Springfontein). Cross the railway line and turn right (south) after another 200 m. Follow the signs to the cemetery.
◉ S30° 16.586, E25° 42.793.

P7.4.5.26

P7.4.5.27

P7.4.5.28

1188 Watt 2000, 472.
1189 Watt 2000, 472.
1190 Watt 2000, 472.
1191 Watt 2000, 472.

P7.4.5.29   P7.4.5.30   P7.4.5.31

Thaba Nchu

P7.4.5.31 British Garden of Remembrance. It contains the graves of 123 Imperial soldiers, of whom 42 were killed in action or died of their wounds.[1192]
▶ Old town cemetery, southern side of Massyn St, Thaba Nchu, Free State.
◉ S29° 13.219, E26° 50.945.

Trompsburg

P7.4.5.32 British military graves.
▶ Municipal cemetery, northern side of c/o Louw St & Van As St, Trompsburg, Free State.
◉ S30° 01.808, E25° 46.885.

Viljoensdrif

P7.4.5.33 British Garden of Remembrance and Memorial. It contains the graves of 72 Imperial soldiers, of whom 41 were killed in action or died of their wounds.[1193]
▶ British Garden of Remembrance, Maccauvlei Golf Course, Viljoensdrif, Free State, near the Club House. Entry from the R82 south of the bridge crossing the Vaal River into Vereeniging.
◉ S26°40.933, E 27°56.521.

Vrede

P7.4.5.34 British Garden of Remembrance. It contains the graves of 112 Imperial soldiers, of whom 60 were killed in action or died of their wounds,[1194] as well as this memorial of polished granite.

P7.4.5.32   P7.4.5.33   P7.4.5.34

1192 Watt 2000, 472.
1193 Watt 2000, 471.
1194 Watt 2000, 473.

Part 7 – The legacy of the war

P7.4.5.35

P7.4.5.36

▶ Municipal cemetery, Van Niekerk St, Vrede, Free State.
◉ S27° 25.665, E29° 10.124.

Vredefort

P7.4.5.35 The municipal cemetery contains the graves of 11 Imperial soldiers, of whom seven were killed in action or died of their wounds.[1195]
▶ Near the R59, between the S212 and 1st Ave (the R59), Vredefort, Free State.
◉ S27° 00.019, E27° 21.826.

Wepener

The municipal cemetery contains the graves of 13 Imperial soldiers, of whom six were killed in action or died of their wounds.[1196]

Winburg

P7.4.5.36 British Garden of Remembrance and war graves. It contains the graves of 76 Imperial soldiers, of whom 14 were killed in action or died of their wounds.[1197]
▶ C/o Jac Coetzer St & McLennan St, Winburg, Free State.
◉ S28° 31.158, E27° 00.411.

P7.4.5.37 Entrance to the badly vandalized British military cemetery outside the town. Memorial plaque with roll of honour visible in the background on the right. It contains the graves of 185 Imperial soldiers, of whom 13 were killed in action or died of their wounds.[1198]

P7.4.5.37

P7.4.6.1

1195   Watt 2000, 473.
1196   Watt 2000, 473.
1197   Watt 2000, 473.
1198   Watt 2000, 473.

▶ *1.3 km from Voortrekker St, Winburg, Free State.*
◉ *S28° 31.134, E27° 00.003.*

7.4.6 KwaZulu-Natal

Bergville district

P7.4.6.1 The Rangeworthy military cemetery contains the graves of 80 Imperial soldiers, of whom 79 were killed in action or died of their wounds.[1199]
▶ *On the northern side of the gravel road to the Three Tree Lodge, about 5 km from the R616 between Bergville and Ladysmith; turn-off about 15 km from Bergville, KwaZulu-Natal.*
◉ *S28° 39.042, E29° 28.097.*

Colenso

P7.4.6.2 There are three large British military cemeteries in the Colenso area, at Ambleside, at Chieveley and at Clouston. Together, they contain 387 graves of Imperial soldiers, of whom 260 were killed in action or died of their wounds.[1200] The photograph is of graves in Clouston.
▶ *Clouston Cemetery is next to R74, a few km south of Colenso, KwaZulu-Natal.*
◉ *S28° 46.748, E29° 48.596.*

Dundee

There are British war graves/memorials on the grounds of the Talana Museum, the St James Churchyard, Betania and the municipal cemetery in Talana. A total of 134 Imperial soldiers, of whom 80 were killed in action or died of their wounds, were buried here.[1201]

Durban

P7.4.6.3 Memorial to commemorate soldiers from that area who served in the British forces. Scenes from the war are depicted in bass relief on the four sides of the pedestal of this memorial.
▶ *Francis Farewell Square, c/o Anton Lembede St & Dorothy Nyembe St, Durban, KwaZulu-Natal.*
◉ *S29° 51.525, E31° 01.514 (Google Maps).*

P7.4.6.4 Ordnance Road Military Cemetery. Graves of 78 British soldiers who died on active service in the Anglo-Boer War.[1202] The graves in the foreground date from earlier encounters.

P7.4.6.2

P7.4.6.3

P7.4.6.4

1199 Watt 2000, 472.
1200 Watt 2000, 469.
1201 Watt 2000, 470.
1202 Watt 2000, 470.

▶ *In a small triangle between Ordnance Road, Soldiers' Way and Wyatt Rd; entry from Wyatt Rd through the adjoining museum grounds.*
◎ *S29° 51.153, E31° 01.392.*

P7.4.6.5 West Street Cemetery. The grave of a British soldier of the Imperial Light Horse who was wounded at Wagon Hill, Ladysmith, on 6 January 1900, and died of his wounds in Durban on 28 March 1900. His name is no longer legible. The 22 Imperial Anglo-Boer War graves in this large cemetery are spread among other graves, and some gravestones have been damaged.[1203]
▶ *Entry from Theatre Lane between West St & Brook St, Durban, KwaZulu-Natal.*
◎ *S29° 51.517, E31° 00.841.*

Elandslaagte

P7.4.6.6 The Battleridge Cemetery on the battlefield. A total of 43 Imperial soldiers who all died in action in the Battle of Elandslaagte on 21 October 1899 were buried here.[1204]
▶ *On the southern side of the D771, east of the Elandslaagte Railway Station, KwaZulu-Natal, about 40 m from the entrance to a game ranch.*
◎ *S28° 25.463, E29° 58.949 (Google Maps).*

Estcourt

P7.4.6.7 Garden of Remembrance. Commemorates 150 British soldiers who died in the Anglo-Boer War in this area, including 15 who were killed in action or died of their wounds.[1205]
▶ *Alexandra St, between Paterson St & Alfred St, Estcourt, KwaZulu-Natal.*
◎ *S29° 00.391, E29° 52.858.*

Howick

P7.4.6.8 Memorial to British soldiers buried at the Howick military cemetery. It contains the graves of 66 Imperial soldiers, of whom one was killed in action or died of his wounds.[1206]
▶ *Signposted, at a sports field, next to the R103 (Main Rd), south of the corner with Valley View Rd, Howick, KwaZulu-Natal.*
◎ *S29° 30.043, E30° 13.827.*

P7.4.6.5

P7.4.6.6

P7.4.6.7

1203 Watt 2000, 470.
1204 Watt 2000, 470.
1205 Watt 2000, 470.
1206 Watt 2000, 470.

P7.4.6.8 P7.4.6.9 P7.4.6.10

Kokstad

P7.4.6.9 The inscription on this tall memorial reads: "Erected in memory of Cape Mounted Riflemen & Volunteers from East Griqualand who fell in the South African War 1899-1902."
▶ In front of the Town Hall, Main St, Kokstad, KwaZulu-Natal.
◉ S30° 32.870, E29° 25.461.

Ladysmith

P7.4.6.10 British Garden of Remembrance. It contains the graves of 472 Imperial soldiers, of whom 119 were killed in action or died of their wounds.[1207]
▶ Municipal cemetery, on the southern side of Cemetery Rd, between Illings St & Mandela St, Ladysmith, KwaZulu-Natal.
◉ S28° 33.322, E29° 47.687. This cemetery contains numerous British war memorials and dozens of graves of British soldiers who died on active service in the war.

P7.4.6.11 Memorial for members of the 18th Hussars who were killed in action or died of disease during the war.
▶ In front of the All Saints Anglican Church, Murchison St, north east of corner with Princess St, Ladysmith, KwaZulu-Natal.
◉ S28° 33.840, E29° 46.649 (Google Maps).

P7.4.6.12 Intombi Garden of Remembrance and Cemetery. Contains the graves of 658 British soldiers, of whom 42 were killed in action or died of their wounds.[1208]
▶ Between the Klip River and the railway line, 7.2 km south of the Ladysmith Siege Museum, near the L1298, Ladysmith, KwaZulu-Natal.
◉ S28° 35.748, E29° 49.313.

P7.4.6.11 P7.4.6.12 P7.4.6.13

1207 Watt 2000, 471.
1208 Watt 2000, 471.

Mooi River

P7.4.6.13 Garden of Remembrance and military cemetery. It contains the graves of 303 Imperial soldiers, of whom 45 were killed in action or died of their wounds.[1209]
▶ 1st St, Bruntville, near 11th Ave, Mooi River, KwaZulu-Natal.
◉ S 29° 13.044, E 30° 00.736.

P7.4.6.14 St John's churchyard. It contains the graves of three Imperial soldiers, one of whom was killed in action or died of his wounds.[1210]
▶ Next to the R622 to Greytown, on the southern side of the road, near Bruntville, KwaZulu-Natal.
◉ S 29° 12.633, E 30° 01.241.

Newcastle

P7.4.6.15 The municipal cemetery contains British Anglo-Boer War memorials and 419 graves of Imperial soldiers who died between May 1900 and March 1903. This includes reinterments from Ngagane and 167 from Charlestown.[1211]
▶ Entry from Hardwick St, Newcastle, KwaZulu-Natal.
◉ S27° 45.369, E29° 56.616.

Newcastle area

P7.4.6.16 British military cemetery at Schuinshoogte (Ingogo). It contains graves of British soldiers of both the Anglo-Transvaal War of 1880-1881 and the Anglo-Boer War of 1899-1902. The dates given on the latter graves are wrong, because there are no records of British soldiers active close to that area on those dates.[1212]
▶ Next to the P279, between the P186 and the D98, KwaZulu-Natal.
◉ S 27° 36.954, E 29° 52.661.

Pietermaritzburg

P7.4.6.17 Anglo-Boer War memorial.
▶ C/o Chief Albert Luthuli St & Church St, Pietermaritzburg, KwaZulu-Natal.
◉ S29° 36.104, E30° 22.741.

P7.4.6.18 British Garden of Remembrance in the Fort Napier military cemetery, which contains the graves of 478 Imperial soldiers, of whom 52 were killed in action or died of their wounds[1213] (see also CP35 on p. 303).

P7.4.6.14

P7.4.6.15

P7.4.6.16

1209   Watt 2000, 471.
1210   Watt 2000, 471.
1211   Torlage & Watt 1999, 5.
1212   Van der Westhuizen & Van der Westhuizen 2000, 36.
1213   Watt 2000, 472.

P7.4.6.17 P7.4.6.18 P7.4.6.19

▶ Napier St, Napierville, Pietermaritzburg, KwaZulu-Natal. Phone Henry Davis at 082 473 7512 or phone 082 556 2485 about access to the cemetery.
◉ S29° 37.182, E30° 21.604.

Pinetown

P7.4.6.19 Memorial "To the Glory of God and in Memory of … Officers and Men who died at the Princess Christian hospital during the Boer War 1899-1902 and are interred in this plot".
▶ Grounds of St John the Baptist Anglican Church, on the square between Church Lane, St John's Ave and Payne St, Pinetown, KwaZulu-Natal. This cemetery contains the graves of 40 Imperial soldiers.[1214]
◉ S29° 49.092, E30° 51.947.

Utrecht

P7.4.6.20 British Garden of Remembrance containing 11 Anglo-Boer War graves in the old municipal cemetery.[1215]
▶ Voor St extension, at the eastern end of town, Utrecht, KwaZulu-Natal.
◉ S27° 39.267, E30° 19.654.

Vryheid

P7.4.6.21 The municipal cemetery contains the graves of and memorials to 81 Imperial soldiers, of whom 31 were killed in action or died of their wounds.[1216]
▶ Southern side of the town, Hoog St, between Landdrost St & Wes St, Vryheid, KwaZulu-Natal.
◉ S27° 46.887, E30° 47.952.

P7.4.6.20 P7.4.6.21

1214   Watt 2000, 472.
1215   According to Watt (2000, 472), during the Anglo-Boer War, 12 soldiers were buried here.
1216   Watt 2000, 473.

7.4.7 Eastern Cape

Aberdeen

P7.4.7.1 British Garden of Remembrance. It contains the graves of 23 Imperial soldiers, of whom 18 were killed in action or died of their wounds.[1217]
▶ *Municipal cemetery, western side of Aberdeen, Eastern Cape.*
◉ *S32° 28.735, E24° 03.564.*

Aliwal North

British Garden of Remembrance. It contains the graves of 122 Imperial soldiers, of whom 52 were killed in action or died of their wounds[1218] (see also P5.7.24).
▶ *Junction Boulevard between Barkly St & King George St, Aliwal North, Eastern Cape.*
◉ *S30° 41.235, E26° 43.194.*

Barkly East

P7.4.7.2 British memorial. There are also graves of seven or eight Imperial soldiers in the municipal cemetery.[1219]
▶ *Molteno St, near c/o Graham St, Barkly East, Eastern Cape .*
◉ *S30° 58.064, E27° 35.594.*

Burgersdorp

P7.4.7.3 British Garden of Remembrance. It contains the graves of 38 Imperial soldiers, of whom two were killed in action or died of their wounds.[1220]
▶ *Municipal cemetery, Burgersdorp, Eastern Cape.*
◉ *S30° 59.803, E26° 20.044.*

Cradock

P7.4.7.4 British Garden of Remembrance. It contains the graves of 66 Imperial soldiers, of whom 31 were killed in action or died of their wounds.[1221]
▶ *Municipal cemetery, near c/o Dreary Lane & Stockenstrom St, Cradock, Eastern Cape.*
◉ *S32° 09.561, E25° 36.856.*

P7.4.7.1

P7.4.7.2

P7.4.7.3

1217 Watt 2000, 469.
1218 Watt 2000, 469.
1219 Oosthuizen 1998, 24; Watt 2000, 469.
1220 Watt 2000, 469.
1221 Watt 2000, 469.

P7.4.7.4   P7.4.7.5   P7.4.7.6

Dordrecht

P7.4.7.5 British Garden of Remembrance. It contains the graves of 40 Imperial soldiers, of whom 27 were killed in action or died of their wounds.[1222]
▶ Municipal cemetery, near Bekker St, Dordrecht, Eastern Cape.
◉ S31° 22.964, E27° 02.838.

East London

P7.4.7.6 Equestrian monument in front of City Hall. Unveiled in 1908 by General E.Y. Brabant. The East Bank cemetery in East London contains the graves of 53 Imperial soldiers, of whom two died in action or of their wounds.[1223]
▶ C/o Oxford St & Buxton St, East London, Eastern Cape.
◉ S33° 00.885, E27° 54.241.

Graaff-Reinet

P7.4.7.7 Memorial in the St James Cemetery to British soldiers who died during the war. This cemetery contains graves of 18 Imperial soldiers, three of whom were killed in action or died of their wounds.[1224]
▶ Donkin St, south of corner with Park St, Graaff-Reinet, Eastern Cape.
◉ S32° 14.978, E24° 31.566.

Grahamstown

P7.4.7.8 The Winged Figure of Peace graces the memorial to "the Men of Albany" who lost their lives in the Anglo-Boer War of 1899-1902. The sculpture is by Stanley Nicholson Babb, and Rudyard Kipling specially wrote the inscription.[1225]

P7.4.7.7   P7.4.7.8   P7.4.7.9

1222   Watt 2000, 470.
1223   Watt 2000, 470.
1224   Watt 2000, 470.
1225   Albany Anglo-Boer War Memorial s.a.

▶ On the traffic island in High St, at the corner with Bathurst St, Grahamstown, Eastern Cape.
◉ S33° 18.562, E26° 31.702.

Jamestown

There are a number of British war graves in the municipal cemetery, Jamestown, Eastern Cape.
◉ S31° 07.643, E26° 48.129.

Middelburg

The municipal cemetery contains the graves of 40 Imperial soldiers, of whom six died in action or of their wounds.[1226]
▶ Van Reenen St., Middelburg, Eastern Cape.
◉ S31° 30.004, E25° 01.131

Port Elizabeth

P7.4.7.9 Prince Alfred's Guard Memorial.
▶ In St George's Park, enclosed by Park Dr, Rink St & Western Rd, Port Elizabeth, Eastern Cape.
◉ S33° 57.833, E25° 36.372.

The large South End Cemetery, situated south of Victoria Park Dr & Mitchell St, contains the graves of 15 Imperial soldiers, four of whom were killed in action or died of their wounds.[1227]
◉ S33° 58.522, E25° 37.390.

Queenstown

The municipal cemetery contains the graves of 41 Imperial soldiers, three of whom were killed in action or died of their wounds.[1228]
◉ GPS co-ordinates not available.

Sterkstroom

P7.4.7.10 British Garden of Remembrance. It contains the graves of 59 Imperial soldiers, only one of whom was killed in action or died of his wounds.[1229]
▶ Municipal cemetery, next to the R344/397, Sterkstroom, Eastern Cape.
◉ S31° 33.202, E26° 32.759.

P7.4.7.10

P7.4.7.11

P7.4.7.12

1226   Watt 2000, 471.
1227   Watt 2000, 472.
1228   Watt 2000, 472.
1229   Watt 2000, 472.

Uitenhage

P7.4.7.11 British memorial in front of the Town Hall, c/o Market St & Rich St. It was unveiled in 1904 and lists Uitenhage citizens who died in the Anglo-Boer War. The features of the life-size soldier were reportedly copied from that of an actual soldier in King William's Town.
◉ S33° 46.148, E25° 24.032.

Willowmore

P7.4.7.12 Old section of the municipal cemetery, graves of four Imperial soldiers.[1230]
◉ S33° 17.649, E23° 29.072.

7.4.8 Northern Cape

Britstown

P7.4.8.1 British Garden of Remembrance. It contains the graves of 15 Imperial soldiers, four of whom were killed in action or died of their wounds.[1231]
▶ West End Cemetery, Victoria Street, Britstown, Northern Cape.
◉ S30° 35.184, E23° 30.011.

Carnarvon

P7.4.8.2 British Garden of Remembrance. It contains the graves of 22 Imperial soldiers.[1232]
▶ Municipal cemetery, on the outskirts of the town a few hundred metres from the road to Williston, Carnavon, Northern Cape.
◉ S30° 57.901, E22° 07.242.

Colesberg

P7.4.8.3 British Garden of Remembrance. It contains the graves of 282 Imperial soldiers, of whom 141 were killed in action or died of wounds.[1233]
▶ Western side of Station Rd, near the northern limit of the town, Colesberg, Northern Cape.
◉ S30° 42.730, E25° 06.086 (Google Maps).

P7.4.8.1   P7.4.8.2   P7.4.8.3

1230 Watt 2000, 473.
1231 Watt 2000, 469.
1232 Watt 2000, 469.
1233 Watt 2000, 469.

Part 7 – The legacy of the war

P7.4.8.4　　　　　　　　　　　P7.4.8.5　　　　　　　　　　　P7.4.8.6

De Aar

P7.4.8.4 British Garden of Remembrance in the badly vandalized section of the municipal cemetery. It contains the graves of 193 Imperial soldiers, of whom 14 were killed in action or died of their wounds.[1234]
▶ *On the northern side of town, next to the R48 to Philipstown, between old cemetery and railway line, De Aar, Northern Cape.*
◉ *S30° 38.718, E24° 00.971.*

Deelfontein

P7.4.8.5 British Garden of Remembrance near the site of the Imperial Yeomanry Hospital. It contains the graves of 131 Imperial soldiers, of whom ten were killed in action or died of their wounds.[1235]
▶ *Western side of an unnamed road about 46 km southwest of De Aar, on the western side of the railway line, a few hundred metres south of the old railway station, Deelfontein, Northern Cape.*
◉ *S30° 59.779, E23° 47.581.*

Fraserburg

P7.4.8.6 British Garden of Remembrance in the municipal cemetery. It contains the graves of 10 Imperial soldiers, of whom five were killed in action or died of their wounds.[1236]
◉ *S31° 55.039, E21° 31.113.*

Kimberley

P7.4.8.7 Imperial war graves in the Gladstone cemetery. It contains the graves of 151 Imperial soldiers, of whom 20 were killed in action or died of their wounds.[1237]

P7.4.8.7　　　　　　　　P7.4.8.8　　　　　　　　P7.4.8.9　　　　　　　　P7.4.8.10

1234　Watt 2000, 469.
1235　Watt 2000, 470.
1236　Watt 2000, 470.
1237　Watt 2000, 471.

▶ Eastern side of Kenilworth Rd, opposite junction with Gulab Ave (immediately to the north of the De Beers Stadium), Kimberley, Northern Cape.
◉ S28° 43.357, E24° 46.601 (Google Maps).

P7.4.8.8 British war graves in the Kenilworth cemetery.
▶ Kenilworth Cemetery, eastern side of Tienie Louw St, Kimindustria, Kimberley, Northern Cape.
◉ S28° 41.909, E24° 47.481 (Google Maps).

P7.4.8.9 West End Cemetery. The memorial is surrounded by 1 224 war graves, of which 578 belong to men who were killed in action or died of their wounds,[1238] in a vast British Garden of Remembrance: "In proud remembrance of British soldiers who were killed in action or who died as a result of service during the South African War at places enumerated on this monument and who now lie buried here at Kimberley." The places enumerated are Belmont, Enslin (Graspan), Modder River, Magersfontein, Barkly West, Bloemhof, Campbell, Christiana, Danielskuil, Dordrecht Farm, Douglas, Fabersput, Griquatown, Honeynest Kloof, Hopetown, Koekama, Koodoosberg Drift, Kuruman, Mayeng Reserve, Motlhoeng, Orange River Station, Postmasburg, Rooidam, Schmidtsdrif, Warrenton, Windsorton and Witpan.
▶ C/o Green St & Reserve Rd, Kimberley, Northern Cape.
◉ S28° 44.078, E24° 44.170 (Google Maps).

Noupoort

P7.4.8.10 British Garden of Remembrance. It contains the graves of 280 Imperial soldiers, of whom five were killed in action or died of their wounds.[1239]
▶ Municipal cemetery, Gerrie Opperman St, Noupoort, Northern Cape.
◉ S31° 10.343, E24° 57.140.

Petrusville

There are five graves of Imperial soldiers in the municipal cemetery, of whom two were killed in action or died of their wounds.[1240]
▶ Graeven St, north of corner with De Beer St, Petrusville, Northern Cape.
◉ S30° 04.647, E24° 39.613.

Prieska

The British Garden of Remembrance in the Prieska Old Cemetery contains a memorial to nine soldiers who died of wounds or disease at that town.[1241]

P7.4.8.11

P7.4.8.12

P7.4.8.13

1238 Watt 2000, 471.
1239 Watt 2000, 472.
1240 Watt 2000, 472.
1241 According to Watt (2000, 472) 12 British soldiers were buried there.

▶ On the outskirts of Prieska, on the south-eastern side.
◉ S29° 40.030, E22° 45.270.

Richmond

P7.4.8.11 British Garden of Remembrance. It contains the graves of 21 Imperial soldiers, of whom 16 were killed in action or died of their wounds.[1242]
▶ Old Anglican Cemetery, southern side of Paul Street, Richmond, Northern Cape.
◉ S31° 25.028, E23° 56.739.

Sutherland

P7.4.8.12 British Garden of Remembrance. It contains the graves of 11 Imperial soldiers, of whom three were killed in action or died of their wounds.[1243]
◉ S32° 39.926, E20° 65.824.

Victoria West

P7.4.8.13 British war graves.
▶ Anglican cemetery, eastern side of N12 just after entering town, Victoria West, Northern Cape.
◉ S31° 24.141, E23° 07.060.

Hutchinson, near Victoria West

P7.4.8.14 Grave of Private Maurice O'Leary, Thorneycroft's Mounted Infantry, who was killed by lightning on 17 February 1901,[1244] and two other British war graves in an abandoned cemetery.
▶ 13 km southeast of Victoria West on the Richmond road, the R63. Signage and graves are west of the railway line, but the road to the graves runs east of the railway line, turning in a northerly direction off the R63, Hutchinson, Northern Cape.
◉ S31° 29.463, E23° 11.507.

Williston

P7.4.8.15 Iron cross on the grave of the only four British soldiers buried here.[1245]
▶ Municipal cemetery, Williston, Northern Cape.
◉ Gate at S31° 20.569, E20° 55.421.

P7.4.8.14   P7.4.8.15   P7.4.9.1

1242   Watt 2000, 472.
1243   Watt 2000, 472.
1244   Watt 2000, 315.
1245   Watt 2000, 473.

P7.4.9.2
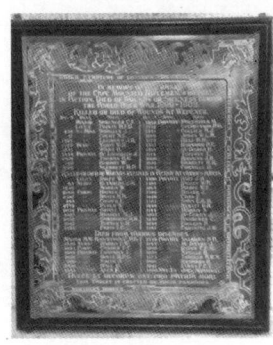
P7.4.9.3

P7.4.9.4

7.4.9 Western Cape

Beaufort-West

P7.4.9.1 British Garden of Remembrance. It contains the graves of 25 Imperial soldiers, of whom seven were killed in action or died of their wounds.[1246]
▶ Municipal cemetery, Bird St, Beaufort-West, Western Cape.
◉ S32° 21.474, E22° 35.149.

Cape Town

P7.4.9.2 Anglo-Boer War Memorial. Erected in 1908 in line with King Edward VII's statue. Consists of the seated figure of Hope and a very alert-looking volunteer.
▶ Grand Parade, across the road from the Old Drill Hall, Darling St, Cape Town, Western Cape.
◉ S33° 55.537, E18° 25.495 (Google Maps).

P7.4.9.3 Commemorative plaque for the Cape Mounted Riflemen who were killed in action, or died of their wounds or of disease in the war.
▶ St George's Cathedral, c/o Wale St & Queen Victoria St, Cape Town, Western Cape.
◉ S33° 55.461, E18° 25.139 (Google Maps).

P7.4.9.4 Anglo-Boer War Garden of Remembrance (see also CP36 on p. 303).
▶ Commonwealth War Graves section, Maitland Cemetery, Voortrekker Rd, Cape Town, Western Cape. It contains the graves of 542 members of the British forces who passed away during the war.[1247]
◉ S33° 55.022, E18° 32.280 (Google Maps).

P7.4.9.5

P7.4.9.6

P7.4.9.7

1246 Watt 2000, 469.
1247 Watt 2000, 469.

Part 7 – The legacy of the war

P7.4.9.5 Wynberg Memorial for and graves of 248 members of the British forces who passed away during the war, of whom more than half died in the military hospital in Wynberg.[1248]
▶ St John's cemetery, eastern side of Court Rd, north of corner with Church St, Wynberg, Cape Town.
◉ S34° 00.210, E18° 28.000.

Clanwilliam

P7.4.9.6 Cemetery with graves of 24 British Anglo-Boer War soldiers, of whom 12 were killed in action or died of their wounds.[1249]
▶ Grounds of the Anglican Church, c/o Visser St & Mark St, Clanwilliam, Western Cape.
◉ S32° 10.840, E18° 53.579.

Mossel Bay

P7.4.9.7 Old cemetery, containing four Anglo-Boer War-related graves.[1250]
▶ C/o Bland St & Beach St, Mossel Bay, Western Cape.
◉ S34° 10.874, E22° 09.194.

Piketberg

P7.4.9.8 Old cemetery containing two British Anglo-Boer War graves.[1251]
▶ Die Trek Rd, Piketberg, Western Cape.
◉ S32° 54.544, E18° 45.348.

Simonstown

P7.4.9.9 Old Burying Ground. It contains the graves and memorial plaques of 56 Imperial soldiers who died during the war.[1252]
▶ Northern side of Runciman Rd, south of the M4 (Queen's Rd), Simonstown, Western Cape.
◉ Entrance at S34° 11.770, E18° 26.559 (Google Maps).

Uniondale

P7.4.9.10 British memorial and war graves. It contains the graves of nine Imperial soldiers who were all killed in action or died of their wounds.[1253]

P7.4.9.8

P7.4.9.9

P7.4.9.10

1248   Watt 2000, 469.
1249   Watt 2000, 469.
1250   Watt 2000, 471.
1251   Watt 2000, 472.
1252   Watt 2000, 472.
1253   Watt 2000, 472.

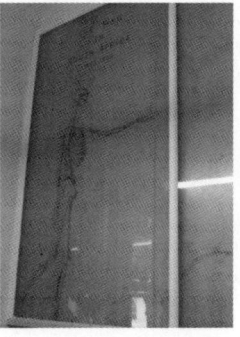

P7.4.9.11   P7.4.10.1   P7.4.10.2

▶ *In the Anglican cemetery, De Waal St, Uniondale, Western Cape.*
◉ *S33° 39.397, E23° 07.719 (Google Maps).*

Vanrhynsdorp

P7.4.9.11 British Garden of Remembrance. It contains the graves of 542 Imperial soldiers, of whom 36 were killed in action or died of their wounds.[1254]
▶ *Municipal cemetery, southern side of town, between the Troe Troe River and the campground, Vanrhynsdorp, Western Cape.*
◉ *S31° 36.789, E18° 44.101.*

7.4.10 British graffiti

British soldiers in a number of places marked their presence by either laying out their regimental badges or other identification on hillsides, using whitewashed stones, or by graffiti on cliffs or rocks. The following are examples:

In Gauteng:

P7.4.10.1 Portrayal of the nature of the war in South Africa, by British officers who were prisoners of war, on the wall of a room in the Staats Model School in Pretoria, where they were held captive. The British officers also painted a map of Natal indicating war-related sites on the wall next to the skeleton.
▶ *C/o Skinner St & Lilian Ngoyi St, Pretoria Central, Gauteng.*
◉ *S25° 45.012, E28° 11.598.*

P7.4.10.3   P7.4.10.4   P7.4.10.5

1254   Watt 2000, 473.

In Mpumalanga:

P7.4.10.2 A knot symbolising the Staffordshire Regiment.[1255]
▶ *On a hillside on the eastern side of Wakkerstroom, Mpumalanga – photograph taken from centre of town.*

In North West:

P7.4.10.3 Rock on Goudkoppie, Klerksdorp, where an Australian soldier left his mark. There are other rocks with war graffiti on the same low hill.
▶ *Goudkoppie, Klerksdorp, North West.*
◉ *S26° 51.267, E26° 41.113.*

In the Free State:

P7.4.10.4-5 Harrismith: The Regimental Badges of respectively the 42nd Black Watch of the Royal Highlanders, the Manchester Regiment and the South Staffordshire Regiment are laid out on the hills around the town.[1256] *(Both photographs were taken from the town.)*

P7.4.10.6 Bloemfontein: The White Horse Stone. This memorial was laid out during the Anglo-Boer War by the garrison of the Wiltshire Regiment stationed at Naval Hill.[1257]
▶ *Eastern slope of Naval Hill, viewed from Andries Pretorius St.*

In KwaZulu-Natal:

P7.4.10.7 Ladysmith: British graffiti.
▶ *On a large rock in the low hill above the central part of the town.*

P7.4.10.8 Ladysmith, Platrand (Wagon Hill): British graffiti on a large rock on the battlefield.
◉ *S28° 35.458 E29° 45.575.*

In the Northern Cape:

P7.4.10.9 Deelfontein, on a hillside on the north-western side of the cemetery: The words IYH, indicating the location of the Imperial Yeomanry field hospital.
▶ *Western side of an unnamed road about 46 km south-west of De Aar, on the western side of the railway line, a few hundred metres south of the old railway station.*
◉ *Near S30° 59.779, E23° 47.581.*

P7.4.10.6

P7.4.10.7

P7.4.10.8

1255 Oosthuizen ca 2000, 77.
1256 Richardson 2001, 177.
1257 Richardson 2001, 177; Van der Bank 2001, 17.

P7.4.10.10 Garies: British graffiti on the 'Letterklip' (Letter stone), which consists of a number of huge stones.
▶ *On a low hill west of the town, about 2 km from the northern end of the main street of the town.*
◉ *S30° 55.551, E17° 97.619.*

P7.4.10.11 Sutherland: British graffiti on wooden panels in the Dutch Reformed Church, which was occupied for military purposes by the British forces for the latter part of the war.
▶ *C/o Piet Retief St (the R354) & Sarel Cilliers St (the R356), Northern Cape.*
◉ *S32° 23.677, E20° 39.688.*

P7.4.10.9   P7.4.10.10   P7.4.10.11

Sources

Albany Anglo-Boer War Memorial, Grahamstown, Eastern Cape. s.a. http://www.artefacts.co.za/main/Buildings/bldgframes.php?bldgid=10571, accessed 13 February 2015.

Amery, L.S. (ed.), I. 1900. *The Times history of the war in South Africa, 1899-1902, Vol I*. London: Sampson, Low, Marston and Company.

Amery, L.S. (ed.), II. 1902. *The Times history of the war in South Africa, 1899-1902. Vol II*. London: Sampson, Low, Marston and Company.

Amery, L.S. (ed.), III. 1905. *The Times history of the war in South Africa, 1899-1902, Vol III*. London: Sampson, Low, Marston and Company.

Amery, L.S. (ed.), IV. 1906. *The Times history of the war in South Africa, 1899-1902, Vol IV*. London: Sampson, Low, Marston and Company.

Amery, L.S. (ed.), V. 1907. *The Times history of the war in South Africa, 1899-1902, Vol V*. London: Sampson, Low, Marston and Company.

Amery, L.S. (ed.), VI. 1909. *The Times history of the war in South Africa, 1899-1902, Vol VI*. London: Sampson, Low, Marston and Company.

Ankiewicz, L. 2011. *Vanaf die Suikerbosrante tot by die Vaalrivier. Dié deel van die Ommidraai Kronkelroete*. Derde uitgawe. s.l.: Die Skrywer.

Armstrong, H.E.C. 1980. *Camp diary of Henrietta E.C. Armstrong: Experiences of a Boer nurse in the Irene concentration camp, 6 April – 11 October 1901*. Edited and annotated by T. van Rensburg. Pretoria: Human Sciences Research Council.

Badenhorst, A. 1923. *Tant' Alie of Transvaal. Her Diary 1880-1902. Translated from the Taal by Emily Hobhouse*. London: Allen & Unwin.

Bakkes, C.M. 1973. *Die Britse Deurbraak aan die Benede-Tugela op Majubadag 1900*. (Sentrale Dokumentasiediens, Suid-Afrikaanse Weermag, Publikasie Nr. 3). Pretoria: Staatsdrukker.

Bakkes, C.M. 1989a. Burgergedenkteken op die Platrand – Ladysmith. In Swart, M.J. (et al., reds.), *Afrikanerbakens*. Johannesburg: Federasie van Afrikaanse Kultuurvereniginge, pp. 231-233.

Bakkes, C.M. 1989b. Spioenkop – Ladysmith. In Swart, M.J. (et al., reds.), *Afrikanerbakens*. Johannesburg: Federasie van Afrikaanse Kultuurvereniginge, pp. 234-235.

Balme, J.H. 1994. *To love one's enemies. The work and life of Emily Hobhouse compiled from letters and writings, newspaper cuttings and official documents*. Cobble Hill, British Columbia: Hobhouse Trust.

Basson, J.L. 1987. Ferreira, Ignatius Stephanus. In Beyers, C.J. (hoofred.). *Suid-Afrikaanse Biografiese Woodeboek Deel V*. Pretoria: Raad vir Geesteswetenskaplike Navorsing, pp. 276-277.

Blake, A. 2010. *Boereverraaier. Teregstellings tydens die Anglo-Boereoorlog*. Kaapstad: Tafelberg.

Blake, A. 2015. *Ontsnap! Boerekrygsgevangenes se strewe na vryheid*. Kaapstad: Tafelberg.

Bossenbroek, M. 2014. *Die Boereoorlog*. Translated from Dutch into Afrikaans by Anne-Marie Mischke. Johannesburg: Jacana.

Botha, J.P. 1967. *Die beleg van Mafeking*. Ungepubliseerde D.Litt et Phil tesis, Unisa, Pretoria.

Botha, S.J. 1981. *Ds Marié Joseph Goddefroy – 1848-1920. Sy lewe en betekenis*. Pretoria: HAUM.

Bourquin, S.B. & Torlage, G. 2014. *The Battle of Colenso 15 December 1899*. Pinetown: 30° South Publishers.

Brandt, J. 2007. *The war diary of Johanna Brandt*. Edited and annotated by Jackie Grobler. Pretoria: Protea Book House.

Breytenbach, J.H. (ed.). 1949. *Gedenkalbum van die Tweede Vryheidsoorlog*. Cape Town: Nasionale Pers.

Breytenbach, J.H. 1954. *Die geskiedenis van die Krugerstandbeeld*. Pretoria: Krugergenootskap.

Breytenbach, J.H. I. 1969. *Die geskiedenis van die Tweede Vryheidsoorlog in Suid-Afrika, 1899-1902, Deel I. Die Boere-offensief Okt – Nov 1899*. Pretoria: Staatsdrukker.

Breytenbach, J.H. II. 1971. *Die geskiedenis van die Tweede Vryheidsoorlog in Suid-Afrika, 1899-1902, Deel II. Die eerste Britse offensief Nov – Des 1899*. Pretoria: Staatsdrukker.

Breytenbach, J.H. III. 1973. *Die geskiedenis van die Tweede Vryheidsoorlog in Suid-Afrika, 1899-1902, Deel III. Die stryd in Natal Jan – Feb 1900*. Pretoria: Staatsdrukker.

Breytenbach, J.H. IV. 1977. *Die geskiedenis van die Tweede Vryheidsoorlog in Suid-Afrika, 1899-1902, Deel IV. Die Boereterugtog uit Kaapland*. Pretoria: Staatsdrukker.

Breytenbach, J.H. V. 1983. *Die geskiedenis van die Tweede Vryheidsoorlog in Suid-Afrika, 1899-1902, Deel V. Die Britse opmars tot in Pretoria*. Pretoria: Staatsdrukker.

Breytenbach, J.H. VI. 1996. *Die geskiedenis van die Tweede Vryheidsoorlog in Suid-Afrika, 1899-1902, Deel VI. Die beleg van Mafeking tot met die slag van Bergendal*. Pretoria: Staatsdrukker.

Brink, J.N. 1904. *Recollections of a Boer prisoner-of-war at Ceylon*. Amsterdam & Cape Town: Hollandsch-Afrikaansche Uitgevers-Maatschappij.

Brits, J.P. 1977. Pretorius, Johannes Lodewicus (Lood), *in* Krüger, D.W. & Beyers, C.J. (hoofreds), *Suid-Afrikaanse Biografiese Woordeboek Deel III*. Pretoria: Raad vir Geesteswetenskaplike Navorsing, pp. 710-711.

Brits, J.P. 1981. Havenga, Nicolaas Christiaan, *in* Beyers, C.J. (hoofred), *Suid-Afrikaanse Biografiese Woordeboek Deel IV*. Pretoria: Raad vir Geesteswetenskaplike Navorsing, pp. 227-234.

Brits, J.P. 1989a. Louis Botha – Pretoria. In Swart, M.J. (et al., reds.), *Afrikanerbakens*. Johannesburg: Federasie van Afrikaanse Kultuurvereniginge, p. 198.

Brits, J.P. 1989b. Vredesmonument – Vereeniging. In Swart, M.J. (et al., reds.), *Afrikanerbakens*. Johannesburg: Federasie van Afrikaanse Kultuurvereniginge, pp. 130-131.

Burger, A.P. 1936. *Worsteljare. Herinneringe van ds A.P. Burger, Veldprediker by die Republikeinse Magte tydens die Tweede Vryheidsoorlog*. Verwerk deur A.J.V. Burger. Kaapstad: Nasionale Pers.

Burger, S.J. 1977. *Oorlogsjoernaal van S.J. Burger 1899-1902*. Redaksie en annotasies deur T. Van Rensburg. Pretoria: Raad vir Geesteswetenskaplike Navorsing.

Casey, E.S. 1987. *Remembering. A Phenomenological Study*. Bloomington & Indianapolis, IN: Indiana University Press.

Celliers, J.F.E. 1978. *Oorlogsdagboek van Jan F.E. Celliers 1899-1902*. Redaksie en annotasies deur A.G. Oberholster. Pretoria: Raad vir Geesteswetenskaplike Navorsing.

Changuion, L. 1986. *Pietersburg. Die eerste eeu 1886-1986*. Pretoria: Stadsraad van Pietersburg.

Changuion, L. 2001. *Silence of the guns. The history of the Long Toms of the Anglo-Boer War*. Pretoria: Protea Book House.

Christopher, B. & Christopher, E. 1982. *All Saints – Ladysmith. Church of the Province of Southern Africa*. Ladysmith: Tugela Press.

Churchill, W.S. 1972. *My Early Life. A Roving Commission*. London and Glasgow: Collins.

Cloete, P.G. 2000. *The Anglo-Boer War: a chronology*. Pretoria: J.P. van der Walt.

Cloete, P.G. 2010. *Die Anglo-Boereoorlog: 'n chronologie*. Klerksdorp: P.G. Cloete.

Coetzee, N. 2003. Boeregraf bewaar op Vanzylsdamme in Klein Karoo. In Van Bart, M. & Scholtz, L. 2003. *Vir vryheid en vir reg. Anglo-Boereoorlog gedenkboek*. Kaapstad: Tafelberg.

Craw, B. 1972. *A Diary of the Siege of Ladysmith*. Ladysmith: Ladysmith Historical Society, reprint.

Creswicke, L. I ca 1902. *South Africa and the Transvaal War. Vol I – From the foundation of the Cape Colony to the Boer ultimatum of 9th Oct. 1899*. Edinburgh: T.C. & E.C. Jack et al.

Creswicke, L. II ca 1902. *South Africa and the Transvaal War. Vol II – From the commencement of the war to the Battle of Colenso, 15th Dec. 1899*. Edinburgh: T.C. & E.C. Jack et al.

Creswicke, L. III ca 1902. *South Africa and the Transvaal War. Vol III – From the Battle of Colenso, 15th Dec. 1899, to Lord Roberts's advance into the Free State, 12th Feb. 1900*. Edinburgh: T.C. & E.C. Jack et al.

Creswicke, L. IV ca 1902. *South Africa and the Transvaal War. Vol IV – From Lord Roberts' entry into the Free State to the Battle of Karree*. Edinburgh: T.C. & E.C. Jack et al.

Creswicke, L. V ca 1902. *South Africa and the Transvaal War. Vol V – From the Disaster at Koorn Spruit to Lord Roberts's entry into Pretoria*. Edinburgh: T.C. & E.C. Jack et al.

Creswicke, L. VI ca 1902. *South Africa and the Transvaal War. Vol VI – From the occupation of Pretoria to Mr Kruger's departure from South Africa, with a condensed account of the guerilla war to March 1901*. Edinburgh: T.C. & E.C. Jack et al.

Creswicke, L. VII ca 1902. *South Africa and the Transvaal War. Vol VII – The Guerilla War* [etc]. Edinburgh: T.C. & E.C. Jack et al.

Cronjé, B. 1989a. Koopmans-De Wet-Huis, Kaapstad. In Swart, M.J. (et al., reds.). 1989. *Afrikanerbakens*. Johannesburg: Federasie van Afrikaanse Kultuurvereniginge, pp. 26-27.

Cronjé, B. 1989b. Magersfontein – naby Kimberley. In Swart, M.J. (et al., reds.). 1989. *Afrikanerbakens*. Johannesburg: Federasie van Afrikaanse Kultuurvereniginge, p. 77.

Cronjé, B. 1989c. Die Krugerhuismuseum, Pretoria. In Swart, M.J. (et al., reds.). 1989. *Afrikanerbakens*. Johannesburg: Federasie van Afrikaanse Kultuurvereniginge, pp. 190-191.

D'Assonville, V.E. (red.) 2001. *Totius se Oorlogsdagboek*. Tweede uitgawe. Weltevredenpark: Marnix.

Davidson, A. & Filatova, I. 1995. The Russian Boer General. *Historia*, 40(2), Nov, 20-38.

Davitt, M. 1902. *The Boer fight for freedom*. New York, NY & London: Funk & Wagnalls.

De Kamper, G. & De Klerk, C. 2011. *Sculptured. The complete works of Fanie Eloff*. Pretoria: University of Pretoria.

De Villiers, J.C. 1998. *Vier maande in Jacobsdal (21 November – 16 Maart 1900). 'n Geneeskundige chronologie van 'n Vrystaatse dorp*. Bloemfontein: Oorlogsmuseum van die Boererepublieke.

De Villiers, J.C. I. 2008a. *Healers, helpers and hospitals, Volume I*. Pretoria: Protea Book House.

De Villiers, J.C. II. 2008b. *Healers, helpers and hospitals, Volume II*. Pretoria: Protea Book House.

De Wet, C.R. 1999. *Die stryd tussen Boer en Brit. Die herinneringe van die Boere-Generaal C.R. de Wet*. In Afrikaans vertaal met verklaring deur M.C.E. van Schoor. Kaapstad: Tafelberg.

Diespecker, D. 1993. The attack on Willowmore, 1 June 1901. *Military History Journal (Journal of the South African Military History Society)*, 9(4), December.

Sources

Direko, W.I., Changuion, L. & Jacobs, F. 2003. *Suffering of war. A photographic portrayal of the suffering in the Anglo-Boer War emphasising the universal elements of all wars.* Bloemfontein: Kraal Publishers for the War Museum of the Boer Republics.

Doyle, A.C. 1900. *The Great Boer War.* Sixth Impression. London: Smith, Elder, & Co.

Dreyer, H.C. 2010. *Die De Klipdrift Monument, Sannieshof.* Sannieshof: Die Skrywer.

Duffey, A.E. 2008. *Anton van Wouw: the smaller works.* Pretoria: Protea Book House.

Du Pisani, J.A. 1999. Oorsake van die Anglo-Boereoorlog: is ons al nader aan 'n antwoord?. *Tydskrif vir Geesteswetenskappe* (Spesiale uitgawe), 39(3 & 4), September & Desember, pp. 205-215.

Du Plessis, J.G. 1989. Manie Maritz, Pretoria. In Swart, M.J. (et al., reds.), *Afrikanerbakens*. Johannesburg: Federasie van Afrikaanse Kultuurverenigine, pp. 200-201.

Du Plessis, J.S. 1968. De la Rey, Jacobus Hercules, in De Kock, W.J. (hoofred.). 1968. *Suid-Afrikaanse Biografiese Woordeboek, Deel I.* Kaapstad: Tafelberg, vir die Raad vir Geesteswetenskaplike Navorsing, pp. 223-227.

Durbach, R. 1988. *Kipling's South Africa.* Diep River: Chameleon Press.

Eksteen, L. 2008. *Newcastle during the Anglo-Boer War.* Newcastle: Fort Amiel Museum.

Flower-Smith, M. & Yorke, E. 2000. *Mafeking: the story of a siege.* South Africa: Covos-Day; St Albans: Verulam.

Fourie, L.M. 1975. *Die militêre loopbaan van Manie Maritz tot aan die einde van die Anlgo-Boereoorlog.* Potchefstroom: MA-verhandeling, Potchefstroomse Universiteit vir Christelike Hoër Onderwys.

Fransen, H. 2004. *A guide to the old buildings of the Cape.* Johannesburg & Cape Town: Jonathan Ball.

Freddie Tait Golf Museum. s.a. *https://www.sa-venues.com/things-to-do/northerncape/freddie-tait-golf-museum/*, accessed 9 September 2017.

Gardner, B. 1966. *Mafeking, a Victorian legend.* London: Cassell.

Geyser, O. 1989a. J.B.M. Hertzog, Bloemfontein. In Swart, M.J. (et al., reds), *Afrikanerbakens*. Johannesburg: Federasie van Afrikaanse Kultuurverenigine, pp. 108-109.

Geyser, O. 1989b. Japie Greylingmonument, Daleside. In Swart, M.J. (et al., reds), *Afrikanerbakens*. Johannesburg: Federasie van Afrikaanse Kultuurverenigine, pp. 132-133.

Gillings, K. 2014. *The Relief of Ladysmith. Breakthrough at Thukela Heights 13-28 February 1900.* Pinetown: 30° South Publishers.

Gillings, K. s.a. *Battles of KwaZulu-Natal. A pictorial souvenir of the Battles of KwaZulu-Natal 1818-1906.* Durban: Art Publishers.

Greig, D.E. 1970. *Herbert Baker in South Africa.* Cape Town: Purnell.

Greyling, P. 2000. *Pretoria en die Anglo-Boereoorlog. 'n Gids tot geboue, terreine, grafte en monumente / Pretoria and the Anglo-Boer War. A guide to buildings, terrains, graves and monuments.* Pretoria: Protea Boekhuis.

Grobler, J. 2002. Haat, vrees, afsku – Boerevroue se houding teenoor swartmense soos weerspieël in dagboeke tydens die Anglo-Boereoorlog, 1899 – 1902, en die nalatenskap daarvan. *Journal for Contemporary History* (Bloemfontein), 27(2), May, 31-44.

Grobler, J. 2006. Memories of a lost cause. Comparing the commemoration of the Civil War in the American South and the Anglo-Boer War in South Africa. *Historia*, 51(2), November, 199-226.

Grobler, J. 2012. *Monumentale Erfenis. 'n Gids tot 50 Afrikaner-gedenktekens.* Pretoria: Kontak-Uitgewers.

Grobler J. & Grobler, M. 2013. *Women's camp journal. The concentration camps of the Anglo-Boer War.* Pretoria: Heroloda Wordworx.

Grobler, J. 2014. *Oorlog-Beeld. Nuusblad oor die stryd tussen Boer en Brit.* Johannesburg & Kaapstad: Jonathan Ball.

Grobler, J.E.H. 2004. *The war reporter. The Anglo-Boer War through the eyes of the burghers.* Johannesburg & Cape Town: Jonathan Ball.

Grobler, M.J. ca 1937. *Met die Vrystaters onder die Wapen. Generaal Prinsloo en die Bethlehem-Kommando.* Bloemfontein: Nasionale Pers.

Gronum, M.A. 1972. *Die Engelse Oorlog 1899-1902. Die gevegsmetodes waarmee die Boere-republieke verower is.* Kaapstad & Johannesburg: Tafelberg.

Gronum, M.A. 1974. *Die Bittereinders 1901-1902.* Kaapstad & Johannesburg: Tafelberg.

Grundlingh, A. 1999. *Die "Hendsoppers" en "Joiners". Die rasionaal en verskynsel van verraad.* Tweede uitgawe. Pretoria: Protea Boekhuis.

Haasbroek, D.J.P. 1977. Haasbroek, Sarel François. In Krüger, D.W. & Beyers, C.J. (Editors-in-chief), *Dictionary of South African Biography III.* Cape Town: Tafelberg, for the Human Sciences Research Council, pp. 363-364.

Hall, D. 1999. *Halt! Action Front! With Colonel Long at Colenso.* Weltevreden Park: Covos-Day.

Harris, D. 1931. *Pioneer, soldier and politician: summarised memoirs of Colonel Sir David Harris.* London: Low, Marston & Co.

Hattingh, J.L. 1989a. Gideon Scheepers – Graaff-Reinet. In Swart, M.J. (et al., reds.), *Afrikanerbakens*. Johannesburg: Federasie van Afrikaanse Kultuurverenigine, pp. 72-73.

Hattingh, J.L. 1989b. Konsentrasiekampe. In Swart, M.J. (et al., reds.), *Afrikanerbakens*. Johannesburg: Federasie van Afrikaanse Kultuurverenigine, pp. 262-265.

Hattingh, J. & A. Wessels. 1998. *Britse fortifikasies in die Anglo-Boereoorlog (1899-1902)*. Bloemfontein: War Museum.
Heath, I. 1999. *Die Rooi Bul van Krugersdorp. Veggeneraal S.F. Oosthuizen*. Centurion: Isak Heath.
Holt, E. 1958. *The Boer War*. London: Putnam.
Hopkins, H.C. 1963. *Maar één soos hy. Die lewe van kommandant C.A. van Niekerk met 'n voorwoord deur P.A. Weber*. Kaapstad: Tafelberg.
Hutchinson, J. 2009. Warfare and the sacralisation of nations: the meanings, rituals and politics of national remembrance. *Millenium – Journal of International Studies*, 38(2), 1-17.
Itzkin, E. 2000. *Gandhi's Johannesburg. Birthplace of Satyagraha*. Johannesburg: Witwatersrand University Press in association with Museum Africa.
Jackson, T. 1999. *The Boer War*. London: Channel 4 Books.
Jooste, G. & Webster, R. 2002. *Innocent blood*. Cape Town: Spearhead.
Jooste, G.J. 1989. Die Staatsmodelschool Pretoria. In Swart, M.J. (et al., reds.), *Afrikanerbakens*. Johannesburg: Federasie van Afrikaanse Kultuurvereniginge, pp. 192-193.
Jordaan, G. 1917. *Hoe zij stierven. Mededelingen aangaande het einde dergenen, aan wie gedurende de oorlog 1899-1902, in de Kaap-kolonie het doodvonnis voltrokken is*. Tweede druk. Kaapstad: HAUM.
Judd, D. & Surridge, K. 2003. *The Boer War*. London: John Murray.
Kandyba-Foxcroft, E. 1981. *Russia and the Anglo-Boer War 1899-1902*. Roodepoort: Cum.
Kapp, P.H. 1989a. J.C. Smuts. In Swart, M.J. (et al., reds.), *Afrikanerbakens*. Johannesburg: Federasie van Afrikaanse Kultuurvereniginge, p. 30.
Kapp, P.H. 1989b. Burgergedenktekens. In Swart, M.J. (et al., reds.), *Afrikanerbakens*. Johannesburg: Federasie van Afrikaanse Kultuurvereniginge, pp. 259-261.
Kemp, J.C.G. 1941. *Vir vryheid en vir reg*. Kaapstad: Nasionale Pers.
Kessler, S. 2012. *The Black Concentration Camps of the Anglo-Boer War 1899-1902*. Bloemfontein: War Museum of the Boer Republics.
Kestell, J.D. ca 1903. *Met de Boeren-Commando's. Mijne Ervaringen als Veldprediker*. Amsterdam: Höveker & Wormser.
Kestell, J.D. & Van Velden, D.E. 1909. *De vredesonderhandelingen tusschen de regeering der twee Zuid-Afrikaansche Republieken en de vertegenwoordigers der Britsche regeering welke uitliepen op den Vrede, op 31 Mei 1902 te Vereeniging gesloten*. Pretoria, Amsterdam: De Bussy.
King, A. 1998. *Memorials of the Great War in Britain: the symbolism and politics of remembrance*. Oxford & New York, NY: Berg.
Kotzé, J.S. 1989. Hildebrandmonument – Darling. In Swart, M.J. (et al., reds), *Afrikanerbakens*. Johannesburg: Federasie van Afrikaanse Kultuurvereniginge, pp. 58-59.
Krüger, D.W. 1961. *The age of the generals. A short political history of the Union of South Africa, 1910-1948*. Johannesburg: Dagbreek Book Store.
Krüger, D.W. 1968. Kruger, Stephanus Johannes Paulus, in De Kock, W.J. (Ed-in-chief), *Dictionary of South African Biography I*. Cape Town: Nasionale boekhandel (for the National Council of Social Research), pp. 444-455.
Labuschagne, P. 1999. *Ghostriders of the Anglo-Boer War (1899-1902). The role and contribution of the Agterryers*. Pretoria: University of South Africa.
Lane, J. 2001. *The War Diary of Burgher Jack Lane, 1899-1900*. Edited by William Lane. Van Riebeeck Society Publications, Second Series, 32.
Leach, C. 2012. *The legend of Breaker Morant is dead and buried. A South African version of the Bushveldt Carbineers in the Zoutpansberg May 1901 – April 1902*. Louis Trichardt: Charles Leach.
Lemmer, G. 2000. *Lemmers in die Anglo-Boereoorlog*. Outjo: I.G. Lemmer.
Lombard, W.A. 1989. Berg-en-Dalmonument. In Swart, M.J. (et al., reds), *Afrikanerbakens*. Johannesburg: Federasie van Afrikaanse Kultuurvereniginge, pp. 222-223.
Lourens, J. & Lourens, J.A.J. 2002. *Te na aan ons hart: aspekte van die Anglo-Boeroorlog in die Reitz-omgewing*. Reitz: The authors.
Macdonald, D. 1900. *How we kept the flag flying. The story of the siege of Ladysmith*. London, New York & Melbourne: Ward, Lock & Co. (reprinted by Covos Books, Roodepoort, 1999).
Macnab, R. 1975. *The French Colonel. Villebois-Mareuil and the International Brigade with the Boers*. Cape Town: Oxford University Press.
Malan, A.F. 1989. Piet Joubert – Pretoria. In Swart, M.J. (et al., reds.), *Afrikanerbakens*. Johannesburg: Federasie van Afrikaanse Kultuurvereniginge, p. 188.
Mangold, W. 1988. *Vir vaderland, vryheid en eer. Oorlogsherinneringe van Wilhelm Mangold 1899-1902*. Geredigeer en geannoteer deur T. van Rensburg. Pretoria: Raad vir Geesteswetenskaplike Navorsing.
Marincowitz, H. 2014. *Prince Albert and the Anglo-Boer War 1899-1902*. Third Print. Prince Albert: Fransie Pienaar Museum.

Sources

McFadden, P. 1999a. *The Battle of Talana 20 October 1899*. Randburg: Ravan.

McFadden, P. 1999b. *The Battle of Elandslaagte 21 October 1899*. Randburg: Ravan.

McNaughton, A. s.a. *When ants get angry! The importance of Graaff-Reinet in the Anglo-Boer War.* Graaff-Reinet: privately published.

Meijer, J.W. 2000. *Generaal Ben Viljoen 1868 – 1917*. Pretoria: Protea Boekhuis.

Meintjes, J. 1969a. *Stormberg, a lost opportunity. The Anglo-Boer War in the North-Eastern Cape Colony, 1899-1902*. Cape Town: Nasionale Boekhandel.

Meintjes, J. 1969b. *Sword in the sand. The life and death of Gideon Scheepers*. Cape Town: Tafelberg.

Meintjes, J. 1971. *The Commandant-General. The life and times of Petrus Jacobus Joubert of the South African Republic 1831-1900*. Cape Town & Johannesburg: Tafelberg.

Meyer, I.A. 1952. *Die Ervarings van 'n Veldkornet in die Engelse Oorlog 1899-1902*. Ladybrand: The authors.

Mouton, J.A. 1957. Genl. Piet Joubert in die Transvaalse Geskiedenis. In *Archives Year Book for South African History* 20:I. Parow: Cape Times Limited, for the Government Printer.

NALN. 1989a. Taalmonument, Burgersdorp. In Swart, M.J. (et al., reds.), *Afrikanerbakens.* Johannesburg: Federasie van Afrikaanse Kultuurvereniginge, pp. 74-75.

NALN. 1989b. Emily Hobhouse, Koppies. In Swart, M.J. (et al., reds.), *Afrikanerbakens.* Johannesburg: Federasie van Afrikaanse Kultuurvereniginge, pp. 124-125.

NALN. 1989c. Onze Rust, Bloemfontein. In Swart, M.J. (et al., reds.), *Afrikanerbakens.* Johannesburg: Federasie van Afrikaanse Kultuurvereniginge, pp. 92-93.

NALN. 1989d. Raadsaal, Bloemfontein. In Swart, M.J. (et al., reds.), *Afrikanerbakens.* Johannesburg: Federasie van Afrikaanse Kultuurvereniginge, pp. 86-87.

Nasson, B. 2003. *Abraham Esau's War: A Black South African War in the Cape, 1899- 1902.* West Nyack, NY: Cambridge University Press.

Nasson, B. 2013. Black people and the camps. In Nasson, B. & Grundlingh, A. (eds). 2013. *The War at Home. Women and families in the Anglo-Boer War.* Cape Town: Tafelberg, 169-193.

Nasson, B. & Grundlingh, A. (eds). 2013. *The War at Home. Women and families in the Anglo-Boer War.* Cape Town: Tafelberg.

National Museum of Military History, http://www.ditsong.org.za/militaryhistory_exhibits.htm, accessed 17 January 2015.

Nel, E. ca 2003. *Die Kaapse rebelle van die Hantam-Karoo [tydens die] Anglo-Boereoorlog 1899-1902*. Pretoria: Bienedell.

Neser, J.P. 1988. Die oorlogsherinneringe van Kommandant Jacob Petrus Neser. Geredigeer en geannoteer deur A. Wessels. *Christiaan de Wet-Annale 7,* Maart.

Nienaber, P.J. & Le Roux, C.J.P. 1983. *Vrystaat-fokus. Monumente en gedenktekens van die Oranje-Vrystaat.* Foto's: Etienne Botha. Roodepoort: Cum.

Oberholster, J.J. 1972. *The historical monuments of South Africa.* Cape Town: National Monuments Council.

Oosthuizen, A.V. 1994. *Rebelle van die Stormberge.* Pretoria: Van der Walt.

Oosthuizen, A.V. (compiler). 1998. *A Guide to the battlefields, graves and monuments of the Anglo-Boer War in the North Eastern Cape / 'n Gids na die slagvelde, grafte en monumente van die Anglo-Boereoorlog in Noordoos-Kaapland.* Bloemfontein: Vriende van die Oorlogsmuseum / Friends of the War Museum.

Oosthuizen, A.V. ca 2000. *Anglo-Boereoorlog gids vir die Suid-Vrystaat / Anglo Boer War Guide for the Southern Free State.* Bloemfontein: Vriende van die Oorlogsmuseum / Friends of the War Museum.

Oosthuizen, J. 1942. Die eerste slag van die Tweede Vryheidsoorlog – Kraaipan. *Historiese Studies,* 3(3), 68-86.

Pakenham, T. 1982. *The Boer War.* London & Sydney: Macdonald.

Picton-Seymour, D. 1989. *Historical buildings in South Africa.* Cape Town: Struikhof.

Pienaar, T.C. 1977. Armstrong, Henriette Ester Carolina. In Krüger, D.W. & Beyers, C.J. (hoofreds), *Suid-Afrikaanse Biografiese Woordeboek Deel III.* Pretoria: Raad vir Geesteswetenskaplike Navorsing, p. 31.

Pieterse, H.J.C. 1946. *Oorlogsavonture van genl. Wynand Malan.* Kaapstad: Nasionale Pers, tweede druk.

Plaatjie, S. 1973. *The Boer War Diary of Sol T. Plaatje.* Edited by J. Comaroff. Johannesburg: Macmillan.

Ploeger, J. (with H.J. Botha). 1968. *Die fortifikasie van Pretoria. Fort Klapperkop – gister en vandag.* Pretoria: Staatsdrukker.

Ploeger, J. 1972. Coster, Hermanus (Herman) Jacob. In De Kock, W.J. & Krüger, D.W. (hoofreds). 1972. *Suid-Afrikaanse Biografiese Woordeboek Deel II.* Kaapstad & Johannesburg: Tafelberg, pp. 148-149.

Porter, A.N. 1980. *The origins of the South African War. Joseph Chamberlain and the diplomacy of imperialism 1895-99.* Manchester: Manchester University Press.

Preller, G.S. 1938a. *Ons parool. Dae uit die dagboek van 'n krygsgevangene.* Kaapstad, Bloemfontein en Port Elizabeth: Nasionale Pers.

Preller, G.S. (ed). 1938b. *Scheepers se dagboek en die stryd in Kaapland (1 Okt. 1901 – 18 Jan. 1902).* Kaapstad, Bloemfontein en Port Elizabeth: Nasionale Pers.

Preller, G.S. 1942a. *Kaptein Hindon. Oorlogsavonture van 'n Baasverkenner.* Kaapstad: Nasionale Pers, derde druk.

Preller, G.S. 1942b. *Talana: die driegeneraalslag by Dundee met lewensskets van genl. Daniël Erasmus.* Cape Town: .
Preller, J.F. 1968. Malan, Francois Stephanus. In De Kock, W.J. (Ed-in-chief). 1968. *Dictionary of South African Biography* I. Cape Town: Nasionale boekhandel (for the National Council of Social Research), pp. 495-499.
Pretorius, F. 1989a. Danie Theron – Gatsrand. In Swart, M.J. (et al., reds.), *Afrikanerbakens.* Johannesburg: Federasie van Afrikaanse Kultuurvereniginge, pp. 147-149.
Pretorius, F. 1989b. J.H. de la Rey – Lichtenburg. In Swart, M.J. (et al., reds.), *Afrikanerbakens.* Johannesburg: Federasie van Afrikaanse Kultuurvereniginge, p. 158.
Pretorius, F. 1998. *The Anglo-Boer War 1899-1902.* Cape Town: Struik.
Pretorius, F. 2001a. *The Great Escape of the Boer Pimpernel Christiaan de Wet. The making of a legend.* Pietermaritzburg: University of Natal Press.
Pretorius, F. (red.). 2001b. *Verskroeide Aarde.* Kaapstad: Human & Rousseau.
Pretorius, F. 2010. *The A to Z of the Anglo-Boer War.* Lanham: Scarecrow Press.
Pretorius, Z.L. 1981. Van Rensburg, Nicolaas Pieter Johannes Jansen. In C.J. Beyers (hoofred.), *Suid-Afrikaanse Biografiese Woordeboek Deel IV.* Pretoria: Raad vir Geesteswetenskaplike Navorsing, pp. 749-750.
Pretorius, W.J. 2016. *"Perre toe". Wekroep aan Heidelbergkommando tot aksie. Oorlogsdagboeke van Marthinus Jacobus (Ouboet) Viljoen, 16 Januarie 1900 – 5 Junie 1902.* Met inleiding, verwerking, teksversorging en geskiedkundige aantekeninge deur Willem J. Pretorius. Pretoria: Zeroplus.
Raath, A.W.G. 2007. *De la Rey. 'n Stryd vir Vryheid.* Brandfort: Kraal.
Radloff, C.H. 1903. *Gevangenisstemmen. Toespraken en preeken gehouden in die gevangenis te Graaff Reinet in de maanden Maart, April en mei van 1901 door den gevangene C.H. Radloof, predikant van Pearston.* Amsterdam & Kaapstad: Hollandsch-Afrikaannsche Uitgevers-Maatschappij.
Reitz, D. 1931. *Commando. A Boer journal of the Boer War.* London: Faber & Faber, second edition.
Reitz, F.W. 1910. *Oorlogs en andere Gedichten.* Potchefstroom: Uitgave van "Het Westen"-Drukkerij.
Richardson, D. 2001. *Historic sites of South Africa.* Cape Town: Struik.
Roberts, B. 1984. *Kimberley, turbulent city.* Cape Town: David Philip, second impression.
Ross, E. 1980. *Edward Ross: Diary of the siege of Mafeking, October 1899 to May 1900.* Edited by B.P. Willan. Cape Town: Van Riebeeck Society Publications, Second Series, 11.
Rothmann, F.L. 1976. *Oorlogsdagboek van 'n Transvaalse burger te velde 1900-1901.* Met inleiding en aantekeninge deur MER. Tweede uitgawe. Kaapstad: Tafelberg.
Rowan, Z. 2013. In the veld with Nonnie de la Rey. In Nasson, B. & Grundlingh, A. (eds), *The War at Home. Women and families in the Anglo-Boer War.* Cape Town: Tafelberg, pp. 73-91.
SA History online. 2017. Black concentration camps, http://www.sahistory.org.za/topic/black-concentration-camps-during-anglo-boer-war-2-1900-1902, accessed 1 August 2017.
Scheepers Strydom, C.J. 1943. *Kaapland en die Tweede Vryheidsoorlog.* Kaapstad: Nasionale Pers, tweede druk.
Schoeman, C. 2013. *Vegter en balling. Boereoorlog-ervarings van Veldkornet Charles von Maltitz.* Kaapstad: Tafelberg.
Schoeman, J. 1950. *Generaal Hendrik Schoeman – was hy 'n verraaier?* Pretoria: The author.
Schoeman, J.M. 1972. Kock (Kok), Johannes Hermanus Michiel. In De Kock, W.J. & Krüger, D.W. (hoofreds). 1972. *Suid-Afrikaanse Biografiese Woordeboek Deel II.* Kaapstad & Johannesburg: Tafelberg, pp. 378-379.
Schoeman, K. 1992. *Only an anguish to live here: Olive Schreiner and the Anglo-Boer War 1899-1902.* Cape Town: Human & Rousseau.
Scholtz, G.D. 1939. *Europa en die Tweede Vryheidsoorlog 1899-1902.* Johannesburg & Pretoria: Voortrekkerpers.
Scholtz, G.D. 1941. *Generaal Christiaan Frederik Beyers 1869-1914.* Johannesburg: Voortrekkerpers.
Scholtz, G.D. 1949. Genl. Christiaan Beyers en die Stryd in die Noorde. In Breytenbach, J.H. (red.). 1949. *Gedenkalbum van die Tweede Vryheidsoorlog.* Cape Town: Nasionale Pers, pp. 191-199.
Scholtz, L. 1974. Die Slag van Bakenlaagte, 30 Oktober 1901. *Historia* 19(1), Mei, 60-74.
Scholtz, L. 1979. Die Slag van Tweebosch, 7 Maart 1902. *Historia* 24(2), September, 44-55.
Scholtz, L. 2003. *Generaal Christiaan de Wet as veldheer.* Pretoria: Protea Boekhuis.
Schulenburg, C.A.R. 1981. "Die 'Bushveldt Carbineers': 'n Greep uit die Anglo-Boereoorlog", *Historia* 26(1), Mei, 37-58.
Schultz, J.O. 1999. *Pilgrim's Rest and the Anglo-Boer War.* Pilgrim's Rest: The Pilgrim's Rest Museum Research Departement.
Shearing, T. & Shearing, D. 2011a. *The rebel record, Vols 1: A – H.* Mossel Bay: T. & D. Shearing.
Shearing, T. & Shearing, D. 2011b. *The rebel record, Vol 2: H – S.* Mossel Bay: T. & D. Shearing.
Shearing, T. & Shearing, D. 2011c. *The Rebel Record, Vol 3: S – Y.* Mossel Bay: T. & D. Shearing.
Smith, I. 1996. *The origins of the South African War, 1899 – 1902.* London & New York: Longman.
Smith, J.A. 1946. *Ek Rebelleer.* Kaapstad: Nasionale Pers.
Smuts, J. 1999. *Memoirs of the Boer War.* Edited by G. Nattrass & S.B. Spies. Paperback edition. Johannesburg: Jonathan Ball.

Sources

Spies, S.B. 1972. Theron, Daniel Johannes Stephanus. In De Kock, W.J. & Krüger, D.W. (Editors-in-chief), *Dictionary of South African Biography* II. Cape Town: Tafelberg for the Human Sciences Research Council, pp. 737-739.

Spies, S.B. 1977. *Methods of Barbarism? Roberts and Kitchener and civilians in the Boer Republics, January 1900 – May 1902.* Cape Town, Pretoria: Human & Rousseau.

Stafleu, A. 1985. *Die beleg van Mafeking. Dagboek van Abraham Stafleu.* Geredigeer deur A.P. Smit & L. Maré. Pretoria: Raad vir Geesteswetenskaplike Navorsing.

Stretton, S. 2001. *Smuts in the Stormberg.* Dordrecht: Anderson Museum.

Swart, M.J. 1989. Long Tom-gedenkteken – Sabie. In Swart, M.J. (et al., reds.). 1989. *Afrikanerbakens.* Johannesburg: Federasie van Afrikaanse Kultuurvereniginge.

Tichmann, P. 2002. The Indian Ambulance Corps. In Wassermann, J. & Kearney, B. (eds), *A warrior's gateway. Durban and the Anglo-Boer War 1899-1902.* Pretoria: Protea Book House.

Tomlinson, R. 2000. British Blockhouses and British Forts. In Westby-Nunn, T. (ed.), *A tourist guide to the Anglo Boer War 1899-1902.* Simon's Town: Westby-Nunn.

Torlage, G. & Watt, S. 1999. *A guide to the Anglo-Boer War Sites of KwaZulu-Natal.* Randburg: Ravan.

Torlage, G. 2014. *The Battle of Spioenkop 23-24 January 1900.* Pinetown: 30° South.

Trichard, S.P.E. 1975. *Geschiedenis werken en streven van S.P.E. Trichard, Luitenant Kolonel der vroegere Staats-artillerie ZAR door hemzelve beschreven.* Edited and annotated by O.J.O Ferreira. Pretoria: Human Sciences Research Council.

Uys, C.J. 1968. Olivier, Jan Hendrik. In De Kock, W.J. (hoofred.), *Suid-Afrikaanse Biografiese Woordeboek Deel I.* Pretoria: Raad vir Geesteswetenskaplike Navorsing, pp. 628-629.

Uys, I. 2000. *Victoria Crosses of the Anglo-Boer War.* Knysna: Fortress.

Van Bart, M. & Scholtz, L. 2003. *Vir vryheid en vir reg. Anglo-Boereoorlog gedenkboek.* Kaapstad: Tafelberg.

Van den Bergh, G. 1996. *24 veldslae en slagvelde van die Noordwes Provinsie.* Potchefstroom: The author.

Van den Heever, J.G. 2001. *Op Kommando onder Kommandant Buys.* Pretoria: Bienendal.

Van der Bank, D.A. 1995. *Burgermonumente van die Anglo-Boereoorlog in die Oranje-Vrystaat.* Bloemfontein: Nasionale Museum.

Van der Bank, D.A. 2001. *Slagvelde, gedenktekens en grafte van die Anglo-Boereoorlog in Bloemfontein en omgewing / Battlefields, monuments and graves of the Anglo-Boer War in Bloemfontein and vicinity.* Bloemfontein: Nasionale Museum, in opdrag van die Vriende van die Oorlogsmuseum.

Van der Merwe, N.J. s.a. *Die Nasionale Vrouemonument.* Bloemfontein.

Van der Westhuizen, G. & Van der Westhuizen, E. 2000. *Gids tot die Anglo-Boereoorlog in die Oos-Transvaal / Guide to the Anglo Boer War in the Eastern Transvaal.* Greylingstad: The authors.

Van der Westhuizen, G. & Van der Westhuizen, E. 2013. *Gids tot die Anglo-Boereoorlog in die Oos-Transvaal / Guide to the Anglo Boer War in the Eastern Transvaal.* Revised ed. Volksrust: The authors.

Van Dyk, J.H. 1977. Eloff, Sarel Johannes. In Krüger, D.W. & Beyers, C.J. (Editors-in-chief), *Dictionary of South African Biography* III. Cape Town: Tafelberg for the Human Sciences Research Council, pp. 277-278.

Van Heerden, A.J. 1946. Kommandant Carl Petrus van Heerden. Sy karakter soos blyk uit vertellinge van sy strydmakkers. *Historiese Studies,* 7(4), Desember, 164-171.

Van Niekerk, H.H. 1972. Dagboek. Geredigeer en geannoteer deur M.C.E. van Schoor. *Christiaan de Wet-Annale 1,* Oktober.

Van Reenen, R. (ed.). 1984. *Emily Hobhouse Boer War letters.* Cape Town, Pretoria: Human & Rousseau.

Van Rensburg, A.P.J. 1972. De Wet, Pieter Daniël. In De Kock, W.J. & Krüger, D.W. (Editors-in-chief), *Dictionary of South African Biography* II. Cape Town: Tafelberg for the Human Sciences Research Council, pp. 192-194.

Van Schoor, M.C.E. 1989a. C.R. de Wet, Bloemfontein. In Swart, M.J. (et al., reds.), *Afrikanerbakens.* Johannesburg: Federasie van Afrikaanse Kultuurvereniginge, pp. 97-99.

Van Schoor, M.C.E. 1989b. M.T. Steyn, Bloemfontein. In Swart, M.J. (et al., reds.), *Afrikanerbakens.* Johannesburg: Federasie van Afrikaanse Kultuurvereniginge, pp. 95-96.

Van Schoor, M.C.E. 1989c. Beeldgroep by Vrouemonument, Bloemfontein. In Swart, M.J. (et al., reds.), *Afrikanerbakens.* Johannesburg: Federasie van Afrikaanse Kultuurvereniginge, pp. 104-107.

Van Schoor, M.C.E. 2009. *Marthinus Theunis Steyn – regsman, staatsman en volksman.* Pretoria: Protea Boekhuis.

Van Tonder, J.J. ca 1974. *Fotobeeld van 300 monumente, standbeelde en gedenktekens.* Krugersdorp: The author.

Van Vollenhoven, A. 1995. *Die militêre fortifikasies van Pretoria 1880-1902.* Pretoria.

Van Wijk, J. 1989. Ierse monument – Johannesburg. In Swart, M.J. (et al., reds.), *Afrikanerbakens.* Johannesburg: Federasie van Afrikaanse Kultuurvereniginge, p. 138.

Van Zyl, J. 2013. The Women's Monument: Planning, design and inauguration. In Nasson, B. & Grundlingh, A. (eds), *The War at Home. Women and families in the Anglo-Boer War.* Cape Town: Tafelberg, pp. 211-225.

Van Zyl, M.C. 1989. Paardekraal – Krugersdorp. In Swart, M.J. (et al., reds.), *Afrikanerbakens.* Johannesburg: Federasie van Afrikaanse Kultuurvereniginge, pp. 144-146.

Van Zyl, P.H.S. 1944. *Die helde-album. Verhaal en foto's van aanvoerders en helde uit ons vryheidstryd.* Johannesburg: Afrikaanse Pers Boekhandel.

Venter, T. 2011. *Bethulie en die Anglo-Boereoorlog.* Bethulie: The author.

Von der Heyde, N. 2012. Field guide to Irish involvement in the siege and relief of Ladysmith, 1899 to 1900. In McCracken, D.P. (ed.), *Essays and source material on Southern African-Irish History.* (Southern-African-Irish Studies Vol 4, Series 2, No 1). Durban: The Ireland and Southern African Project, pp. 145-175.

Von der Heyde, N. 2013. *Field guide to the Battlefields of South Africa.* Cape Town: Struik Travel & Heritage.

Walker, D.R. s.a.(a). The Anglo-Boer War Memorial at the Museum of Military History. http://www.allatsea.co.za/cems/anglomemorial.htm, accessed 19 August 2009.

Walker, D.R. s.a.(b). The Indian Army Memorial on Observatory Ridge, http://www.allatsea.co.za/cems/indianmemorial.htm, accessed 19 August 2009.

Warwick, P. 1983. *Black people and the South African War, 1899-1902.* Cambridge: Cambridge University Press.

Wassermann, J.M. 2004. The Natal Afrikaner and the Anglo-Boer War. Unpublished DPhil Thesis, University of Pretoria.

Watt, S. 1999a. *The Siege of Ladysmith 2 November 1889 – 28 February 1900.* Randburg: Ravan.

Watt, S. 1999b. *The Battle of Vaalkrans 5-7 February 1900.* Randburg: Ravan.

Watt, S. 2000. *In Memoriam. Roll of Honour Imperial Forces Anglo-Boer War 1899-1902.* Pietermaritzburg: University of Natal Press.

Watt, S. 2014. *The Battle of Modder Spruit & Tchrengula. The fight for Ladysmith 30 October 1899.* Pinetown: 30° Degrees South.

Wessels, E. 2002. *Veldslae Anglo-Boereoorlog 1899-1902.* Pretoria: Lapa.

Wessels, E. 2010. *Bannelinge in die vreemde. Die krygsgevangenes van die Anglo-boereoorlog 1899-1902.* Centurion: Kraal.

Westby-Nunn, T. (ed.). 2000. *A tourist guide to the Anglo Boer War 1899-1902.* Simon's Town: Westby-Nunn Publishers.

Willis, R., Van Dyk, A. & De Villiers, J.C. 2016. *Yeomen of the Karoo. The Story of the Imperial Yeomanry Hospital at Deelfontein.* Brandfort: Firefly.

Witton, G.R. 1907. *Scapegoats of the Empire. The Story of the Bushveldt Carbineers.* Second edition. Melbourne: Paterson.

Zeerust. 1987. *Onthulling van die Burgergedenkgraf Zeerust.* [Printed programme of the unveiling of the burgher memorial – in the author's personal collection].

Index

of persons mentioned in the text and of selected places, sites, battles and skirmishes

Abercrombie, H. – 181
Aberdeen, Eastern Cape – 204, 210, 246, 259, 339
Abrahamskraal (see Driefontein)
Achrad, J.P. – 277
Ackermann, J.R. – 180
Acres, H. – 170
Adam (or Adams), F.T. – 141
Adams, F.M. – 187
Addie, G.M. – 116
Adendorff, M. – 197
Adendorff, W. – 197
Aggenbach, W. – 88
Agtertang – 13, 39, 199
Ahrens, H.A. – 255
Ahrens, W.F. – 255
Airey, Colonel – 100
Airlie, D.S.W.O. (Earl of Airlie) – 94
Alberts, S. – 158
Alberts, H.A. – 158, 159
Alberts, J.J. – 163
Alderson, J.B.S. – 97
Alderson, R.W. – 157
Alexander, J. – 176
Alexander McGregor Memorial Museum, Kimberley – 45
Alexandra Cemetery, Potchefstroom – 116, 127, 152, 165, 230, 253, 319
Aliwal North Concentration Camp – 236
All Saints Anglican Church, Ladysmith – 48, 156, 336
Alleman's Nek – 95
Ambleside Cemetery – 63, 334
Ambridge, H.J. – 164
Anderson, R., Lieutenant – 143
Anderson, R., Sergeant – 191
Anderson, W. – 160
Anglican Cathedral of St Andrew and St Michael, Bloemfontein – 82, 324
Arbuthnot, F. – 119
Archibald, Duke/Earl of Ava – 53, 55
Armstrong, H.E.C. – 271
Atkins, G. – 183
Attwell, W.F. – 195
Babb, S.N. – 340
Babington, J. – 124
Back, E.C. – 100, 101
Badenhorst, A. – 23, 94
Badenhorst, C.C.J. – 185, 288, 309
Badenhorst, I.J. – 163
Baden-Powell, Colonel – 40, 42, 43
Badfontein British military cemetery, Mpumalanga – 321
Bagnall, Private – 115
Bailey, H. – 53
Bailey, J.J. – 124
Bainbridge, J.G. – 84
Bakenlaagte, Battle of – 149-150
Baker, H. – 45, 47
Baldowes, W. – 53
Balmoral Concentration Camp – 214, 226
Balmoral, action at – 118
Banks, T. – 141

Barberton British Garden of Remembrance – 109-110, 162, 272, 321
Barberton Concentration Camp – 226
Barclay, C.R. – 81
Barkly East, Eastern Cape – 194, 205, 339
Barlow, J. – 170
Barnard, J.H. – 214
Barrett, E.H. – 205
Barrett, J.V.L. – 266
Barrett, R.T. – 200
Barron, W. – 103
Barton, G. – 75, 116
Baxter. J.A. – 259
Bayston, J. – 125
Baukens (Beauchamp?) – 154
Beardwood, J. – 91
Beatson, D. – 159
Beaufort West, Western Cape – 56, 73, 195, 202, 207, 246, 346
Beck, J. – 138
Begemann, S. – 293
Bekker, J. – 185
Belfast Concentration Camp – 18, 226-227
Belfast, old municipal cemetery – 111, 117, 125, 137, 226-227, 321
Bell, F.W. – 140
Bell, J.D.K. – 89
Bellingan, P.J. – 199
Belmont, Battle of – 56, 133
Belshaw, W. – 91
Bennett, E. – 103
Benson, G. – 149
Bergendal, Battle of – 106
Bergendal Burgher Monument – 18
Bergh, O.M. – 254, 255
Bergh, P.J. – 166
Besele I, Kgosi – 212
Bester, Lieutenant – 259
Bester, N.F. – 184
Bester, P. – 261
Bethell, T. – 210
Bethlehem British Garden of Remembrance – 97-98, 102, 103, 173, 176, 179, 180, 181, 271, 324
Bethulie Concentration Camp – 17, 21, 231, 237
Bethulie old town cemetery – 77, 83, 287, 324-325
Bethune, E.C. – 86
Beyers, C.F. – 120, 122, 125, 143, 162, 274, 309
Biccard, J. – 128
Biddulphsberg – 88
Bidmead, H. – 208
Birso, W. – 146
Blackman, A. – 91
Blair, H.M. – 69
Blanchard, M.G. – 93
Bland, W. – 53
Blandy, R.Y. – 204
Blignaut, J. – 138
Bloem, D.J. – 181
Bloedriviersport, Battle of – 147

Bloemfontein Concentration Camp – 231-232
Bloemfontein, Fourth Raadsaal – 267, 299
Bloemfontein, War Museum of the Boer Republics – 14, 15, 16, 19, 26, 30, 31, 129, 214, 218, 222, 231, 238, 239, 244, 250, 262, 276, 288, 298, 302, 308
Blom, J. – 168
Blundell, W.A.H. – 56
Bodenstein, J. – 196
Bonthuizen, P.D. – 158
Boonzaaier, C. – 78
Boonzaaier, M. – 296
Boonzaaier, T. – 202
Borden, F.W. – 99
Borden, H.L.- 99
Bosch, H. – 252
Boschbult – 163
Boshof old town cemetery – 57, 73, 82, 175, 309, 326
Boshoff, F.J. – 119
Boshoff, J.N. – 34
Boshoff, T. – 147
Bosman, H. – 87
Bosman, I.D. – 170
Botha, C. (Chris) – 87, 256
Botha, J.D.L. – 104
Botha, L. (Louis) – 37, 38,59, 61, 62, 70, 74, 79, 85, 91, 92, 94, 106, 114, 128, 147, 149, 156, 166, 175, 273, 274, 278, 279
Botha, N.J. – 46
Botha, P.R. (Philip) – 84, 173, 175, 179
Botha, P.J. – 46
Botha, S.C. (Charles) – 179
Botha, Trooper – 155
Botha's Pass – 93
Bothaville British Garden of Remembrance – 172, 185, 326
Bothaville Burgher Monument – 288, 301
Bouwer, B. – 206, 208, 312
Bouwer, P. – 17, 256
Boyd, J. – 189
Boyd, R. – 255
Boyes, General – 96
Boyle, C.W. – 82
Braamfontein Cemetery – 90, 98, 99, 112, 116, 254, 316
Brabant, A.E. – 49
Brabant, Y.E. – 49, 75, 77, 340
Bradfield, J.B. – 102
Bradley, C.E. – 111
Bradshaw, W.E.J. – 62
Brancker, G.L.D. – 96
Brand, G.A. – 180, 187, 188, 309
Brandfort Concentration Camp – 232
Brandfort old town cemetery – 174, 180, 282, 326
Bradshaw, W.E.J. – 62
Brandwater Basin – 97, 101, 102, 103, 254
Brassey, P.F. – 47
Brassington, A. – 189, 196
Brazier-Creagh, G.P. – 82
Bremer, G. – 179

359

Breytenbach, F.G. – 117
Briedenhann, Miss – 88
Briers, A. – 215
Brine, R.W.M. – 56
Brink, L. – 260
Briscoe, T. – 127
Bristow, C. – 154
British South African Police Fort (Warren's Fort) - 42
Brits, C. – 256
Brits, G. – 256
Brits, O. – 256
Brits, P. – 256
Brits, T. – 88
Britstown, Northern Cape – 77-78, 187,
Broadwood, R. – 80, 102
Broeksma, C. – 253, 254
Bronkhorst, P.C. – 138
Bronkhorst, S. – 122
Brown, A.W. – 65
Brown, F. – 42
Brown, H.B. – 107
Brown, J.H. – 141
Brown, S. – 37
Brown, S.F. – 75
Brown, T.A. – 105
Browne, A.A.B. – 188
Bruce, G. – 151
Bruce, L.M. – 19
Brynbella (see Willow Grange)
Buck, C. – 103
Budgett, W.F. – 110
Budler, W. – 209
Buffelspoort, Battle of – 119
Buller, R. – 58, 62, 63, 66, 69, 74, 85, 87, 93, 110, 112
Burch, J.E. – 99
Burger, A.P. – 308
Burger, S.W. (Schalk) – 52, 273
Burgershoop Cemetery, Krugersdorp – 119, 121, 124, 142, 316, 317
Burgess, D.S. – 124
Butler, H. – 128
Buys, S.B. (Fanie) – 122, 123, 142, 150, 312
Buxton, W. – 51
Cachet, J.L. – 261
Cairns, G. – 98
Callum, H.S.R. – 271
Calvinia, Northern Cape – 187, 189-190, 204, 205, 206, 216, 275, 296, 298
Campbell, D.H. – 163
Campbell, H.A. – 142
Campbell, J.A. – 142
Campbell, Lieutenant Colonel – 127
Campbell-Bannerman, H. – 218
Capper, Colonel – 95
Carbutt, E.G. – 70, 329
Carnarvon, Northern Cape – 190, 246, 264, 342
Carrington, F. – 104
Carter, T.R. – 211
Case, R.U. – 84
Casson, F.G. – 81
Caton, R. – 188
Cawston, C.F. – 127
Celliers, J.F.E. – 314

Celliers, J.G. (Jan) – 105, 119, 137, 157, 159
Challenor, R.R. – 163
Chalmers, F.W. – 117
Chalmers, W. – 144
Chaloner, R.A. – 164
Chamberlain, J.D. – 75
Chesney, K. – 157
Chieveley – 38
Chieveley, R. – 89
Chissel, E. – 83
Chrissiesmeer, Battle of – 128, 137
Chrissiesmeer municipal cemetery – 84, 115, 128, 137, 151, 157, 321
Christian, E. – 73
Christianson, W. – 149
Christian Victor, Prince – 317
Chubb, F. – 115
Churchill, C.W.L. – 163,
Churchill, W.S. – 15, 38, 249, 264,
Church Square, Pretoria – 26, 85, 91, 268
Claassen, C.J. – 258
Claassen, Field Cornet – 111
Claassen, G. – 158
Clanwilliam, Western Cape – 187, 188, 206, 314, 347
Clapham, W.M.J. – 37
Clark, E. – 140
Clark (or Clarke), M. – 141
Clarke, G.V – 185
Clarke, J.R. – 61
Clarke, W.A. – 170
Clarke (or Clark), W. – 196
Cleaver, W. – 37
Clements, R.A.P. – 97, 120
Clery, General – 97, 99, 113
Clouston Memorial Garden – 63, 334
Clowes, G.V.W. – 188
Coates, F.R. – 160
Coetzee, A.J. – 173
Coetzee, J.A. – 205
Coetzee, J.J.H. – 178
Coetzee, Josef – 210
Coetzee, J.P – 257, 258
Coetzee, K.D. – 282
Coetzer, J.H. – 175
Colclough, S. – 199
Cole, F. – 106
Cole, L. – 180
Colenso, Battle of – 62-63
Colenso Concentration Camp – 224, 234
Colesberg Boer graves memorials – 259-260, 296, 310
Colesberg British Garden of Remembrance – 20, 59, 64, 65, 66, 76, 342
Colesberg, Worcester Hill – 66, 133
Coleskop (Coles Hill), near Colesberg – 65
Coligny British military cemetery – 140, 144, 157, 164, 166, 318
Collings, G.F. – 73
Collins, A. – 188, 189
Colville, A.E. – 37
Colyn, L. – 256
Colville, Colonel – 122, 125
Combrinck, C.J. – 150
Comrie, P. – 122
Coningham, C. – 66

Connell, F. – 179
Conroy, E. – 196, 205
Conway, E. – 165
Cooper, C. (or D.W.) – 141
Cordua, H. – 253
Cory, R.V. – 108
Coster, H.J. – 36
Cotton, H. – 83
Cotton, S.L. – 123
Cowie, W.R. – 61
Cox, G.G. – 117
Cox, T. – 53
Crabbe, E.M.S. – 198
Crabtree, T. – 83
Craigie, M.L. – 102
Creak, W.H. – 137
Cremer (or Creamer), J.L. – 185
Crewe, F.H. – 42
Crichton, J.E.T. – 137
Crofton, H.W.G. – 207
Cronjé, A.J. – 158,
Cronjé, A.P.J. (Andries) – 93, 254
Cronjé, D. – 168
Cronjé, H.A. – 310
Cronjé, P.A. (Piet) – 40, 69, 70, 71, 72, 73, 74, 76, 254, 310
Cronjé, P.C. – 252
Cronwright-Schreiner, S.C. – 257
Cross, J. – 255
Crowther, J. – 310
Cruickshank, , H.A. – 272
Cruikshanks, G. – 159
Cuming, H.W. – 112
Cummings, B.E. – 270
Cunningham, G.G. – 126
Currie, C.W.B. – 189
Curtler, H.W. – 75
Dalbiac, H.S. – 87
Dalgety, E.H. – 82
Dall, J. – 42
Dalmanutha, Battle of (see Bergendal)
Dalmanutha British military cemetery – 115, 125, 321-322
Dalzel, A.F. – 52
Daniel (or Daniels), G. – 198
Darter, C.J. – 208
Davel, Commandant – 177
Davidson, F. – 139
Davies, B.H.E. – 184
Davies, H. – 271
Davies, W. – 171
Dawson, E.A. – 70
Day, T.B. – 163
De Aar, Northern Cape – 56, 65, 73, 187, 192, 199, 205, 257, 266, 270, 343
Dearle, A.E. – 173
De Beer, J.A.B. – 255
De Beer, C. – 88
De Beer, F.C.J. – 205
De Beer, G.J. – 214
De Bruyn, H.J. – 255
De Bruyn, P.C. – 255
De Burgh, H.H.P. – 82
De Hart, P.C. van N. – 65
Deelfontein (Imperial Yeomanry Hospital) – 73, 206, 266, 270, 297, 343, 349

Index

Defoe, J. – 83
De Hart, P.C. van N. – 65
De Jager, C.J. – 54
De Jager, D. – 26, 250, 276
De Kersauson de Pennendreff – 313
De Klerk, B.J. – 169
De Kock, J. – 53
De Kock, M. – 255
De Kock, W.G. – 141
De Lange, J.H. – 253
De la Rey, A. – 58
De la Rey, A.J.G. – 107
De la Rey, Nonnie – 140
De la Rey, J.H. (Koos) – 17, 32, 44, 46, 57, 58, 60, 65, 72, 78, 92, 98, 104, 106, 114, 119, 120, 122, 124, 138, 139, 147, 148, 157, 159, 161, 162, 163, 164, 240, 255, 273, 274, 280
De Montmorency, R.H. – 77
Dennison, A.G. – 200
Denniss, G.B.B. – 53
Denny, Colonel – 162
Denny, P.R. – 82
De Penthenny-O'Kelly, R.A. – 112
Dercksen, A.J. – 98
Devenish, E.H.H. – 117
Deveraux, P.L. – 165
De Villebois-Mareuil, G.H. – 82
De Villiers, A.A. – 283
De Villiers, A.I. – 88
De Villiers, C.J. – 32, 52
De Villiers, D.T. – 51
De Villiers, P.J. (Piet) – 88, 193, 196, 310
De Villiers, T. – 51
De Wet, C.R. (Christiaan) – 14, 37, 69, 70, 71, 72, 78, 80, 81, 92, 93, 96, 97, 102, 103, 104, 108, 116, 167, 168, 171, 172, 173, 174, 177, 183, 184, 238, 254, 273, 274, 275, 280, 299
De Wet, Cornelia – 238,
De Wet, J.M. – 60
De Wet, Koos – 168
De Wet, M. – 77
De Wet, P. (Piet) – 64, 89, 254
De Wet, P.J. – 262
Dewetsdorp British military cemetery – 82, 173, 180, 326-327
Deysel, B. – 163
Diamond Hill (see Donkerhoek)
Dick, C.E. – 147
Dick-Cunyngham, W.H. – 54
Digby-Jones, R.J.T. – 53
Dimsdale, W.P. – 81
Dique, W. – 170
Dixon, H.G. – 141
Dodd, A. – 149
Dönges, T.A.H. – 313
Donkerhoek (Diamond Hill), British Garden of Remembrance – 94, 119, 126, 146, 151, 315
Donkerhoek (Diamond Hill), Battle of – 94-95
Doornbult (Orange River Station) Concentration Camp – 17, 236
Dordrecht, Eastern Cape – 75, 77, 134, 192, 195, 196-197, 205, 257, 261, 295, 340
Doveton, A. – 211

Doveton, D.E. – 55
Dowell, Major – 158
Dowie, R.M. – 182
Doyle, A.C. – 113
Doyle, J. – 165
Drake, S. – 100
Dreyer, T.F.J. – 180
Driefontein (Abrahamskraal) – 78-79
Dronfield – 46, 47
Drysdale, R. – 179
Duckworth, C. (or G.) – 166
Du Moulin, L.E. – 183
Dundonald, Lord – 95
Du Plessis, J.J. – 84, 178
Du Plessis, S. – 198
Duplov, Captain – 123
Du Preez, J.J. – 154
Durban, Isipingo Concentration Camp – 234
Durban, Jacobs Concentration Camp – 234
Durban, Merebank Concentration Camp – 17, 87, 234
Du Toit, S. – 91, 137
Dwarsvlei – 99
Eager, E.B. – 56
Eager, H.A. – 60
Earle, S. – 58
Edenburg British Garden of Remembrance – 81, 175, 177, 327
Edward VII, King – 330, 346
Edwards, F.F. – 141
Egan, J. – 150
Eksteen, J.P. – 42
Eland, F. – 153
Elandslaagte – 34-36
Eley, J.T. – 198
Elim – 14, 152, 153, 154, 155, 162
Elliot, T. – 51
Ellis, J. – 127
Eloff, F. – 114
Eloff, F.C. – 157
Eloff, S. – 42, 43
Elworthy, C.K. – 85
Engela, C. – 109
Engelbach, F.J. – 172
Enslin (see Graspan)
Erlank, A.G. – 194
Ermelo British Garden of Remembrance – 126, 156, 322
Erskine-Flower, H.N.C. – 148
Esau, A. – 17, 216, 298
Eshowe Concentration Camp – 235
Estcourt, KwaZulu-Natal – 38, 335
Evans, R.W. – 159
Evans, T. – 162
Exon, J. – 99
Extine, H. – 161
Eykyn, C. – 69
Eyre, C.G. – 144
Faber, C. – 88
Fabersput (Faber's Well) – 88, 89, 269, 344
Fairhurst, S. – 239
Falcon, G. – 203
Fauresmith Reichardt Park cemetery – 176, 289, 311, 327
Feilden, C.W.M. – 159

Fellowes, N.B. – 181
Fergusson, G.C.D. – 51
Ferreira, I.S. – 71
Ficksburg old town cemetery – 23, 96, 183, 186, 327
Field, P.N. – 156
Fife, H.W. – 90
Finch, W. – 171
Fisher, B. – 141
Fisher, J.A.M. – 68
Fitzhugh, R.T. – 266, 270
Fitzpatrick, G.J. – 38
Fitzpatrick, P. – 38
Floyd, G.W. (or F.G.W.) – 85
Fly Kraal cairn, Ladysmith – 48
Flygare, Johannes – 60
Forrest, A.A. – 141
Forrester, J.J. – 138
Fort Amiel – 19, 85, 86,
Fort Brown – 248
Fort Daspoortrand – 30
Fort Denison – 248
Fort Edward (Fort Hendrina) – 14, 152, 153, 154, 155, 162
Fort Itala – 166
Fort Klapperkop – 30, 125,
Fort Knokke – 250
Fort Mpisane – 145
Fort Napier military cemetery – 75, 249, 250, 303, 337
Fort Newdigate – 166
Fort Opperman – 243
Fort Prospect – 166
Fort Schanskop – 28, 30, 109, 317
Fort Wonderboompoort – 30
Fort Wynyard – 250
Fortescue, L.H.D. – 94,
Fortrug – 246
Fosbery, F.L. – 124
Foster, P. – 171
Fouchee, W. – 169, 192, 194, 210, 312
Fourie, L.H. (Lourens) – 62
Fourie, J. (Joachim) – 95, 118
Fourie, P. (Piet) – 82, 108, 177
Fourie, P.J. – 259
Francis, Captain – 145
Francis, D. – 41
Francis, W. – 41
Frankfort old town cemetery – 168, 176, 182, 311, 328
Frankish, W. – 42
Franks, A.F. – 84
Fraser, C. – 169
Fraser, D. – 151
Fraserburg, Northern Cape – 190, 207, 208, 211, 343
Frederikstad, Battle of – 116-117
French, J. – 34, 64, 70, 90, 91, 107, 126
Froneman, C.C. (Stoffel) – 92, 292
Fryer, F.L. – 56
Gallimore, W. – 194
Game Tree Hill Fort (see Platboomfort)
Gamkaskloof (The Hell) – 73-74
Gandhi, M. – 213
Garies, Northern Cape – 208, 350
Garlick, J. – 115

Gatacre, W. – 58, 59, 63, 76, 77
Gates, T.St.W.L. – 44
Gaussen, C.L. – 182
Gawne, J.M. – 320
Geary, F. – 83
Geldenhuys, J.F. – 259
Gerber, H.C. – 98
Gethin, H.R. – 83
Geyser, J.J. – 152
Geyser, P.J. – 152
Gibbons, Trooper – 176
Gibbs, J. – 194
Gibson, W. – 151
Gill G.R. – 141
Glen, J. – 159
Gloster, W. – 103
Goddefroy, M.J. – 309
Goffe, E. – 46
Going, A.C. – 80
Goodman, H.J. – 101
Gordon, G.H. – 157
Gough, B. – 39
Gough, H. De la P. – 147
Gouws, N.P. – 127
Government Buildings (Ou Raadsaal), Pretoria – 85, 91
Graaff-Reinet, Eastern Cape – 202, 210, 259, 340
Graham, H.W.G. – 66
Graspan (Enslin, Rooilaagte), Battle of – 57
Gravett, G. – 110, 115, 281
Gray, E.W. – 269
Green, G.D. – 127
Greyling, B.C – 241
Greyling, Japie – 241
Greyling, J.C. – 152
Greyling, J.F. – 164
Griffin, G.A. – 65
Grobbelaar, W. – 206
Grobler, E.M. – 154
Grobler, F.A. - 82
Grobler, G. – dedidacation page
Grobler, H. – 149
Grobler, H. (born Van Zyl) – dedication page
Grobler, Jan Derk & Jacobus Daniel – 154
Grobler, J.A.P. – 35
Grobler, J.N.H. – 158, 159
Groenewald, M.C. – 57
Groenkop, Battle of – 135, 183
Grogan, E.B. – 96
Grove, Colonel – 168
Guinness, E. – 150
Gurdon-Rebow, M. – 199
Haasbroek, S.F. – 181
Hall, A. – 91
Hall, R.H. – 93
Hall-Hall, F.A. – 89
Hamilton, B. – 187
Hamilton, G. – 159
Hamilton, H.R. – 178
Hamilton, I. – 82, 84, 96, 164
Hammond, D.B. – 126
Hanbury, E.M. – 168
Hancock, C.T. – 102
Handcock, P.J. – 153, 154, 155, 156
Hannam, C.H.G. – 154

Hanney, O.C. – 71
Hanover, Northern Cape – 191, 194, 205, 257, 266, 306
Hanwell, J. – 170
Hardy, L.D. – 193
Hardwick, D. – 208
Harker, W. – 148
Harmse, J.H. – 163
Harper, E.W. – 112
Harper, J.F. – 198
Harpley, S. – 279
Harris, D. – 45
Harrismith Concentration Camp – 232
Harrismith municipal cemetery – 16, 290, 328
Hart, A.F. – 108
Harvey, C.B. – 64
Harvey, J. – 266
Harvey, T.W.P. – 192
Hastings, J. – 151
Hattingh, F.J.W.J. – 82
Hattingh, J.D.L. – 174
Havenga, N.C. (Klasie) – 60, 289, 311
Hazlerigg, A. – 43
Hazlett, E. – 171
Head, L. – 85
Heath, E.K. – 176
Hebeler, B.A. – 159
Heese, C.A.D. – 154, 155
Heidelberg Concentration Camp – 225
Heilbron Concentration Camp – 232
Heilbron municipal cemetery – 174, 184, 328
Helvetia, action at – 123
Henty, Captain – 112
Herselman, C. – 253
Hertzog, A. – 273,
Hertzog, J.B.M. – 16, 169, 170, 187, 191, 237, 273, 287, 293, 305, 311
Hesketh, A.E. – 70, 329
Hesselman, L. – 296
Hewett, A.W. – 137
Heys, G. – 92
Hildebrand, C. – 203, 300
Hildyard, H.J.T. – 87, 122
Hill, J.C. – 183
Hindon, O.J. (Jack) – 125, 145, 312
Hirschford, S.K. – 189
Hobbs, H.T. de C. – 96
Hobhouse, E. – 221, 222
Hobson, R.L.C. – 91
Hobson, W. – 184
Hocking, J. – 117
Hoexter, G. – 272
Hoffmann, L. – 21, 231
Hogan, G. – 103
Hogg, J.Q. – 193
Höhls, J.O. – 268
Holkrantz – 215
Holland, M.W. – 84
Hollandia Hotel (see Victoria Hotel)
Hooper, C. – 181
Hore, C. – 104
Horwood, P.E. (or P.L.) – 82
Hoskier, F.H. – 77
Hoskins, E. – 185
Houwater – 77-78

Howard, A.L. – 128
Howard, F.S. McL. – 163
Howard, H.W. – 23, 228
Howard, J. – 249
Howell, E.G. – 158, 159
Howick British memorial – 335
Howick Concentration Camp – 235, 262
Hugo, H.J. (Henry) – 207
Hulse, C.W. – 177
Humphreys, W. – 151
Hunt, E. – 53
Hunt, P.F. – 153
Hunter, A. – 50, 94, 172
Hunter, P.D. – 77
Hutton, E.T.H. – 98, 99, 101
Ingham Brooke, E.V. – 150
Ingouville-Williams, Colonel – 140
Inskeep, A. – 194
Intombi Cemetery, Ladysmith – 49, 55, 336
Irene Concentration Camp – 17, 19, 225, 271-272
Irvine, J.G. – 172
Itala and Prospect, action at – 166-167
Jackson, C. – 53
Jackson, G.K. – 192
Jackson, J.R. – 166
Jacobs, G.G. – 53
Jacobs, H. – 258
Jacobs, Johannes – 192
Jacobs, J.A. – 185
Jacobs, P. – 98
Jacobsdal municipal cemetery – 26, 70, 71, 170, 177, 182, 238, 268, 329
Jacques, J.B. – 148
Jagersfontein municipal cemetery – 169, 291, 329
James, L.J. – 182
Jameson, L.S. – 90
Jameson, W. – 171
Jamestown, Eastern Cape – 193, 209, 341
Jammerberg's Drift – 82
Jansen, J.G.W. – 260
Jansen van Vuuren, R. – 145
Japhta – 214
Jenkins, A. – 83
Jenkins, Anus – 97
Jervis-Edwards, J.B. – 166
Johannesburg Fort – 30
Johnson, F. – 33
Johnson, F.A.L. (or E.A.L.) – 176
Johnson, T.C. – 161
Johnson, W.M. – 64
Jones, A.H. – 188, 189
Jones, P.A.T. – 115
Jones, T. – 271
Jooste, A. – 258
Jordaan, a Cape rebel – 204
Jordan, H. – 103
Joubert, H. – 28, 152
Joubert, J. – 312
Joubert, P.J. (Piet) – 28, 30, 32, 38, 47, 59, 79, 80, 152
Kameelfontein memorial – 95
Kamfer, H.J. – 144
Kamieskroon, Northern Cape – 208, 215, 296
Karee – 79, 80, 81, 83, 84, 218, 329

Index

Kavanagh, Major – 198
Keegan,, B. – 115
Keith-Falconer, C.E. – 40
Keith-Falconer, V.F.A. – 40
Kekewich, R.G. – 45, 46, 147, 156
Kemp, J. (Jan) – 141, 144, 148, 159, 164
Kerr, R.J. – 96
Keswick, D.J. – 78
Kestell, C. – 252
Kestell, J.D. – 52, 177, 252, 290, 308
Key, J.R. – 175
Kimber, C.D. – 144
Kimberley Concentration Camp – 235
Kimberley, Gladstone Cemetery – 47, 343
Kimberley, Kenilworth Cemetery – 47, 344
Kimberley, Siege of – 45-47
Kimberley, West End Cemetery – 22-23, 40, 46, 47, 56, 57, 58, 61, 62, 66, 69, 70, 84, 89, 117, 165, 186, 188, 193, 196, 206, 235, 269, 344
Kingsford, D.P. – 84
Kipling, R. – 15, 79, 87, 248, 340
Kipperley, Colonel – 151
Kirstein, W. – 138
Kitchener, H.H. – 69, 71, 107, 155, 184, 187, 218, 253, 273, 275, 310,
Kitchener, W. – 137
Klaarstroom, Western Cape – 135, 189
Kleinfontein, Battle of – 133, 148-149
Klerksdorp cemetery, British Garden of Remebrance – 23, 137-138, 139-140, 159, 160-161, 162, 163, 165, 218, 255, 318
Klerksdorp Concentration Camp – 23, 94, 228, 301
Klerksdorp Museum – 213, 251, 274
Klerksdorp peace memorial – 273
Klerksdorp Railway Station – 94,
Kleu, J. – 189
Klipriviersberg – 90
Kloof Cemetery, Heidelberg, Gauteng – 36, 54, 80, 100, 101, 122, 125, 137, 144, 159, 225, 277, 281, 313, 315-316
Klopper, P.W. – 258
Kloppers, H.B. – 158
Knapp, J.C. – 49
Knisley, W.A. – 163
Knowles, M. – 162
Knox, C.E. – 174
Koch, A.C. – 296
Koch, H. – 256
Kock, J.H.M. (Jan) – 34
Koedoesberg, Battle of – 69
Kooijker, G. – 139
Koopmans-De Wet, M. – 306
Kortright, M. – 90
Kotzee, J.B. – 255
Kotzee, N.J. – 255
Kraaipan – 32
Krause, O.K.H. (Dr and Mrs) – 272
Kriegler, J. – 80
Kriel, A.P. – 122, 305
Kriel, L. – 161
Kritzinger, G. – 149
Kritzinger, M. – 149
Kritzinger, P.H. – 107, 193, 200, 205, 293, 294, 310

Kroonstad British Garden of Remembrance, Noord Rd – 85, 96, 112, 171, 174, 176, 182, 186, 251, 271, 329
Kroonstad British Garden of Remembrance, Turner St – 329-330
Kroonstad Concentration Camp – 233
Krüger, B. – 175
Kruger, G. (née Du Plessis) – 307
Kruger, G.J. – 158
Kruger, J.C. – 282
Kruger, S.J.P. (Paul) – 25, 26, 27, 29, 42, 91, 92, 103, 110, 277, 307
Krugerhof Museum – 92
Krugersdorp Concentration Camp – 225
Kuhn, H. – 260
Kuhn, J. – 260
Labram, G. – 46, 47
Ladybrand Concentration Camp – 224
Lady Roberts (British gun, poem) – 123, 314
Ladysmith, Siege of – 47-55
Ladysmith Concentration Camp – 53, 224, 235
Ladysmith British Garden of Remembrance, municipal cemetery – 14, 21, 22, 37, 49, 50, 51, 52, 53, 54, 55, 269, 270, 336
Ladysmith Lyre, The – 49
Lagenaar (Lochner?) – 154
Laing, D.T. – 174
Laings Nek Railway Tunnel – 86
Lamb, E.A. – 140
Lambart, H. – 94
Lambie, W.J. – 66
Lambton, A.F. – 61
Landau, C. – 228
Langford, W.J. – 188
Langstone, A. – 115
Laridon, L. – 269
Laskie, W.A.D. – 120
Lategan, H.W. – 204, 310
Latimer, W. – 89
Laubscher, J. – 259
Lawler, J.L. – 108
Lawley, A.T. – 163
Lawrence, H. – 165
Leach, C.E. – 194
Leader, H.P. – 158
Lee, B.H. – 99
Lee, C.J. – 98, 99
Le Gallais, P.W.J. – 171, 172
Leipoldt, C.L. – 314
Le Marchant, G. de C. – 163
Lemmer, H.R. (Manie) – 82, 100, 119, 120
Lemmer, P.J. – 44
Leslie, W.J. – 164
Lichtenburg municipal cemetery – 44, 107, 111, 114, 119, 138, 149, 240, 319
Liddiard, E. – 191
Liebenberg, I. – 261
Liebenberg, P.J. (Piet) – 43, 77, 108, 116, 126, 137, 141, 159, 189
Linchwe, Kosi – 214
Lindley municipal cemetery – 89, 102, 111, 112, 184, 254, 269, 330
Linnie, P. – 140
Lion-Cachet, C.E. – 282
Little, M.O. – 102

Lloyd, E.B. - 271
Lloyd, M.A. – 271
Lloyd, N. – 186
Lloyd, T.H.E. – 150
Lloyd, W.R.D. – 126
Lockwood, H.V. – 68
Londt, J. – 210
Long Tom guns – 30, 31, 41, 47, 50, 52, 109, 110, 112, 115-116, 139
Loots, G.S. – 206
Lötter, C J. – 262
Lötter, J.C. (Hans) – 195, 197, 201, 257
Lotz, F.J. – 168
Lotz, P.M. – 168
Lourens, G.C – 179
Lourens, P. – 168
Louw, J.M. – 308
Louw, W. – 259, 260
Lovatt, A. – 194
Low, H.L. – 186
Lubbe, D.S. – 291, 311
Lumsden, H.C. – 84
Lutyens, E. – 20
Lydenburg, old town cemetery – 110, 112, 141, 145, 272, 322-323
Lygon, E.H. – 79
Lynch, J. – 171
Lynn, H. – 47
Lynn, T. – 56
Lyon, H.F. (or F.H.) – 204
Lyttleton, N.G. – 95
Maasdorp, L.A. – 77
Macauley, K.Z.P. – 127
Maccauvlei Garden of Remembrance – 91, 116, 143, 144, 159, 332
MacDougall, J.T. – 37
Macdonald, A.H. – 165
Macdonald, A.R.A. – 175
Macdonald, J.H. – 76
MacDonald, W. – 82
Machlachlan, M. – 255
Machlachlan, R. – 255
MacKay, J.E. – 180
Maclean, J.M. – 150
Maclean, R. – 187
MacMullen, F.R. – 76
Machadodorp British Garden of Remembrance – 106, 151, 323
MacMullen, F.R. – 76
Mafeking Concentration Camp – dedication page, 14, 223, 230
Mafeking (Mahikeng), Kanon Kopje – 41, 131
Mafeking, Siege of – 40-45
Magersfontein battlefield and battle – 15, 18, 60, 61, 130, 132
Maguire, C.J.K. – 94
Mahemsfontein – 97, 99,
Mahikeng British Garden of Remembrance – 41, 42, 43, 44, 45, 120, 147, 319
Mahikeng Museum – 45
Mahon, B.T. – 44, 98,
Mahood, H.A. (or H.M.) – 164,
Mahood, J. – 177
Maitland Cemetery, Cape Town – 22, 63, 70, 203, 250, 252, 264, 270, 303, 312, 314, 346
Majendie, H.G. – 70

Majuba Hill – 27, 28, 74, 86, 221
Malan, B.G. – 149
Malan, C. – 100
Malan, F.S. – 262
Malan, S.F. – 283
Malan, W. – 199, 204, 207, 210, 260
Mance, A.W. – 55
Mangold, W. – 110, 137
Marais, C.P. – 193
Marais, E.N. – 314
Marais, F.A. – 201, 257
Marais, J. – 73
Maraisburg Cemetery – 90, 316
Maratiwa House – 40
Maré, J.P. – 151, 282
Mareetsane, North West, Imperial Light Horse Memorial – 17, 43, 301, 302
Maritz, S.G. (Manie) – 202, 203, 204, 205, 208, 311
Maritzburg College – 22, 266
Marriott, W.R. – 94
Marsh, T.A.P. – 270
Marshall, D. (or J.) – 183
Marsham, D.H. – 41
Marter, W.M. – 80
Martin, R. – 161
Martin, T. – 151
Martin-Leake, A. – 158
Masonic Lodge, Mahikeng – 43
Massijn, H.B. – 255
Mathakgong, cattle raider - 212
Matjiesfontein – 56, 61, 132, 202, 264
Matthew, L.A. – 96
Matthysen, H.A. – 255
Mattungen – 155
Maximov, E.J. – 84
McCartney, J.I. – 100
McClure, J. – 100
McCue, J. – 143
McDonald, W.G. – 160
McDougall (or Macdougall), J. – 157
McGrath, A. – 106
McGregor, D.J. – 126
McGuire, A. – 70
McKellar, G. – 122
McKenzie, W.S. – 143
McLaclan (or MacLachlan), J. – 109
McLaren, W.V.S. – 101
McLean, W. – 188
McWhinnie, W.J. – 81
McLaren, W.V.St. – 101
Mears, W. – 115
Melrose House – 92, 275
Melville, G.F. – 182
Memoriam Cemetery, Bloemfontein – 185, 232, 272
Menning, C. – 272
Mentz, N.J. – 66, 67
Menzies, A. – 53
Methuen, Lord – 55, 56, 57, 58, 60, 63, 82, 100, 137, 161, 189
Metcalfe, C. – 50
Meyer, L. – 33, 310
Meyrick, St John – 90
Middelburg, Eastern Cape, Chair Monument – 201, 300

Middelburg, Eastern Cape, municipal cemetery,– 201, 257, 341
Middelburg, Mpumalanga, Concentration Camp – 15, 24, 227
Middelburg, Mpumalanga, Kanonkop cemetery – 227
Middelburg, Mpumalanga, old municipal cemetery – 127, 138, 141, 142, 143, 151, 227, 269, 308, 312, 315, 323
Middlemist, G. – 147
Miers, R.H.M.C. – 277
Millen, E. – 22
Miller, T.K. – 89
Mills, J. – 103
Mills, S. – 55
Milne, W. – 61
Milne-Miller, R.M. – 51
Milner, A. – 25, 26, 123, 275
Mineralia Cemetery, Middelburg, Mpumalanga – 24, 227
Mitchell, P. – 151
Mitford-Barberton, I. – 280
Modder River (*Twee Riviere* – Two Rivers), Battle of – 57-58
Modder Spruit and Nicholson's Nek, Battle of – 37
Moedwil, Battle of – 147-148
Moerdijk, G. – 35, 228
Molema, S. – 40
Moll, P. – 145
Moller, P. – 88
Momsen, a burgher – 99
Money, C.G.C – 119
Moodie, B.W. – 95
Mooi River, KwaZulu-Natal – 31, 68, 75, 263, 266, 337
Mooney, T. – 186
Moor, H.G. – 102
Moore, C.J. – 115
Moore, J.H. – 102
Morant, H. (Breaker) – 14, 153, 154, 155, 156
Morden, J.F. – 96
Morgendaal, J.J. – 255
Morris, G.A. – 148
Morris, Major – 142
Morrison, J.E. – 144
Moss, W. – 184
Mostert, J. – 215
Mount Nelson Hotel – 15
Mournful Monday – 37
Mousley, G.B. – 23, 255
Mouton, W.J. – 127
Mowat (or Mowatt), D.S. – 171
Moxon, F.G. – 141
Muir, T. – 46
Muller, C. – 118, 123, 142, 150
Müller, H. – 283
Murdoch, A.J.C. – 121
Murphy, A.E. – 127
Murphy, T. (or P.) – 161
Murray, A. D. (Andrew) – 200
Murray, A.H. – 88
Murray, E.O. – 200
Murray, F.D. – 150
Murray, R.H. – 210

Murray, W. – 164
Murray, W. (Reverend) – 210
Mussmann, A.J.D. – 98
National Women's Monument, Bloemfontein – 20, 168, 217, 222, 237, 238, 308, 315
Napier, B. – 173
Naudé, I.J. – 163
Naudé, J.J. – 78
Neethling, H. (Hannie) – 108, 109
Neethling, J. – 197
Neethling, Reverend & Mrs – 263
Nel, A. – 296
Nel, I.W. – 259
Nel, J. – 158
Nelis, J. – 183
Neser, J. – 208
Nesham, T.P.W. – 161
Newcastle municipal cemetery – 166, 267, 337
Newdigate, F.H. – 89, 269
New Roodepoort Cemetery, Gauteng – 90
Nicholas, A.W. – 102
Nicol, R.G. – 50
Niemeyer, J. – 51
Nienaber, C.G.J. (Karel) – 257
Nienaber, J.P. – 257
Nienhuis, H. – 54
Nieumeyer, L.H. – 261
Nieuwoudt, C. – 183, 187, 188
Nieuwoudt, J.A. – 257
Nix, M.J. – 81
Njoba – 155
Nooitgedacht, Battle of – 120-121
Norris, F. – 99
Northcott, H.P. – 58
Northway, R.J. – 128
Norvalspont Concentration Camp – 169, 236
Noupoort British Garden of Remembrance – 344
Noupoort Museum – 191
Nylstroom Concentration Camp, Modimolle – 157, 228, 284
O'Brien, E. – 270
O'Connor, T. (or J.) – 171
Ogilvy, J.H.C. – 146
Ogston, F.H. – 138
Okiep, Northern Cape – 209
Old Church Street West Cemetery, Pretoria – 36, 51, 54, 55, 91, 95, 121, 146, 156, 165, 252, 253, 256, 268, 271, 281, 307, 309, 312, 313, 314, 317
Oldham, D.C. – 152
O'Leary, M. – 345
Olewagen, D. – 259
Oliver, S.J. – 100
Olivier, C. – 260
Olivier, J.H. – 39, 59, 107, 310
O'Neill, E. – 271
O'Neill's Cottage – 87
Oosthuizen, I.J. – 99
Oosthuizen, I.W. – 192
Oosthuizen, O. – 40
Oosthuizen, P.R. – 106
Oosthuizen, S. (Sarel) – 99
Oosthuizen, S.H. – 148, 149
Opperman, J.D. (Koot) – 86, 147, 156

Index

Opperman, "Rooi" Daniël – 66
Orchard, J.H. – 89
Ormond, A. – 124
Ordnance Road Military Cemetery, Durban – 68, 334
Osborne, R. – 207
O'Shea, M. – 180
Otter-Barry, F.M. – 180
Ottosdal British Garden of Remembrance – 140, 156, 161, 163, 319
Oudstryders (Veterans') Memorial, Cottesloe, Johannesburg – 18, 281
Owles, F.W. – 271
Owens, W. – 127
Ozzard, J.S. – 195
Paardeberg, Battle of – 71-74
Page, F. – 141
Paget, A.H. – 97, 118
Palmer, H.A. – 269
Park, C.W. – 150
Parker, E.G. – 109
Parker, J.H. – 83
Parsons, E.W. – 164
Partridge, R.G. – 111
Paterson, J.A. – 128
Patterson, M.F. – 272
Patterson, R. – 51
Pauskie (Paschke?) – 154
Paxton, L. – 172
Pearce, T. – 116
Pemberton, J.E. – 146
Penn-Symons, W. – 16, 33
Petersen, W. – 211
Petronella British Garden of Remembrance – 105-106, 146, 249, 317
Petrov, Captain – 123
Petrusville, Northern Cape – 344
Pfeiffer, L.F.S. – 259
Philipstown – 174, 187, 305
Phillips, A.S. – 176
Phillips, F. – 266
Philpott, T.H. – 175
Phister, J. – 200
Pietermaritzburg Concentration Camp – 235
Pietersburg Concentration Camp – 21, 153, 228, 239, 304
Pieter's Hill, near Ladysmith – 74-75
Piketberg, Western Cape – 202, 347
Pilcher, T.D. – 174
Pilkington, T.D. – 98
Pinetown, KwaZulu-Natal – 252, 338,
Plaatje, S. – 40, 212
Platboomfort (Game Tree Hill Fort) – 41
Platrand Burgher Monument – 18, 33, 34, 35, 36, 38, 53, 62, 67, 68, 69, 74, 132, 167, 215, 235, 251, 252, 262, 294
Platrand (Wagon Hill), action at – 52-55
Plumer, H.C.O. – 42, 44, 139, 156
Pochin, C.T.P. – 89
Pokrowsky, L. – 123
Polokwane municipal cemetery – 139, 141, 143, 162, 239-240, 320
Poplar Grove, Battle of – 78
Port Elizabeth Concentration Camp – 237
Port Elizabeth, Horse memorial – 19, 29, 299
Porter, A.M. – 89

Postma, L. – 308
Potchefstroom Concentration Camp – 230
Potgieter, Commandant – 104
Potgieter, F.J. (Ferdinand) – 164
Potgieter, F.J.G. – 152
Potgieter, J. – 173
Potgieter, H. – 114
Powell, J.W. – 20, 76
Preller, G. – 314
President Brand Cemetery, Bloemfontein – 81, 82, 232, 309, 325
Pretoria Meintjieskop Concentration Camp – 225
Pretoria, Victoria Hotel (Hollandia Hotel) – 92
Pretorius, G.F. – 185
Pretorius, H.P.J. – 183
Pretorius, J. (or I.) – 161
Pretorius, J.L. (Lood) – 312
Pretorius, M.W. – 253
Pretorius, P. – 252
Pretorius, W.H. – 163
Pretorius, W.H.J. – 201
Primrose municipal cemetery – 115, 143, 149-150, 163-164, 317-318
Pringle, J. – 170
Prinsloo, A.M. (Michael) – 89, 183, 287, 310
Prinsloo, Jacobus – 56, 57
Prinsloo, Joachim – 151
Prinsloo, Marthinus. – 32, 52, 103, 254
Pruden, D.H. – 101
Queenstown municipal cemetery – 341
Queenstown Museum – 60
Quin, H.G. – 160
Raath, A.W. – 53
Ramsbottom, A.E.W. – 289
Rangeworthy military cemetery – 67, 334
Ras, M. – 214
Rathbone, W.A. – 185
Rautenbach, N.C. – 260
Reade, R.E. – 127
Rebecca Street Cemetery, Pretoria – 279, 311, 315
Reddersburg municipal cemetery – 81, 84, 172, 173, 178, 331
Reitz, D. – 248
Reitz, F.W. – 123, 273, 307, 314
Reitz old town cemetery – 174, 177-178, 331
Renike, A. – 260
Renosterkop, Battle of – 118-119
Rew, D. – 89
Rhode House Museum, Mooi River, KwaZulu-Natal – 31, 263, 266
Rhodes, C.J. – 45, 47, 70
Rice, S.R. – 241
Richards, S. – 209
Richardson, A.H.L. – 97
Richmond, Northern Cape – 191, 194, 208, 210, 246, 305, 345
Ridley, H.M. – 107
Rietfontein (Ifafi) Garden of Remembrance, Northwest – 91, 98, 121, 148, 318
Rimington, Colonel – 150
Rittenberg, H. – 200
Robbertse, W.H. – 67
Roberts, F.H.S. (Freddy) – 63

Roberts, F.S., Lord – 17, 63, 69, 70, 72, 74, 78, 79, 83, 84, 85, 90, 91, 92, 94, 106, 187, 218
Roberts, J.C. – 76
Robertson, C.M. – 150
Robertson, C.W. – 100
Robertson, E.Q. – 103
Robinson, H.J. – 89
Robinson, J.A.W. – 57
Robinson, W. – 255
Rodger, W.A. – 170
Roe, H.V. – 53
Roets, P.G.W. – 163
Roodewal, action at – 164
Rooiwal – 93
Rooidam military cemetery, Bloemfontein – 79
Rooipoeierspruit (Koster River) – 100
Rooiwal Railway Station – 93
Roos, F.J. – 54
Roos, J. (Jo) – 21
Rose, C.E. – 84
Rose, M.C. – 170
Rose Price, Lieutenant – 142
Ross, A. – 311
Ross, D. – 261, 262
Ross, W. – 59
Rossouw, G. – 215
Röth, C.F.F. – 98
Roux, A.J. – 174
Roux, F.P. – 208
Roux, J.H. – 259
Roux, P. – 95, 309
Ruiter, J. – 178, 216
Rundle, L. – 87, 88
Rundle, W.J.S. – 195
Rustenburg old municipal cemetery – 100, 148, 283, 320
Rütters, A.E. – 107
Ryan, F.J. – 128
Sage, F.L. – 271
Salisbury, Lord – 29
Salmond, A.L. – 206
Sanford, H.C. – 41
Sannaspos – 80-81
Sargeant, R. – 115
Saunders, G.M. – 266
Saunders, Major – 117
Saunders, W. – 196
Saunders, W. (or A.) – 184
Savage, G.F. – 255
Savory, A. – 106
Scheepers, G. – 136, 169, 188, 189, 193, 195, 196, 201, 202, 261, 264
Scheepers Nek – 86
Schoeman, D. – 77
Schoeman, H. – 256
Schoeman, J. – 259
Scholtz, P. – 167
Schoon, H.F. – 262
Schreiner, O. – 196, 257, 306,
Schuil, P. – 147
Schultz, J. – 56
Schumann, O.F. – 176
Scobell, H. – 195, 197, 198
Scott, A.A. – 211

Scott, H.F. – 143
Scott, J. – 255
Scott-Chisholme, J.J. – 34, 35
Seely, J.E.B. – 241
Segale, brother of Kgosi Linchwe – 214
Sells, C.B. – 266
Semple, J. – 141
Senekal, J. – 78
Senekal municipal cemetery – 87, 88, 105, 173, 175, 331
Senior, G.G. – 163
Seymour, L.I. – 96
Shand, W.J. – 182
Shea, G.N. – 186
Shepherd, R.E. – 150
Silkaatsnek – 98-99
Simmonds, W. – 53
Simonstown, Western Cape – 251, 264, 301, 347
Simpson, J. – 83
Skinner, A. – 203
Slabbert, M.J.A. – 174
Slack, J.P. – 161
Slater, S. – 106
Slegtkamp, H.F. (Henri) – 137, 215, 312
Sloan, H. – 152
Smail, R. – 170
Smalberger, Lieutenant – 198
Smit, C.P.J. – 154
Smit, P.F. – 157
Smith, G. – 117
Smith, J. – 89, 106, 194, 211
Smith, Trooper – 210
Smith, W.E. – 76
Smith, W.S. – 21, 22
Smith-Dorrien, H.L. – 99, 100, 118, 126, 128
Smithfield Caledon Museum – 167
Smithfield municipal cemetery – 331
Smith-Senior, G.G. – 163
Smuts, J.C. (Jan) – 18, 119, 120, 122, 126, 139, 196, 197, 200, 202, 205, 206, 207, 216, 255, 256, 273, 279, 280, 286
Smuts, T. – 115
Smyley (or Smyly), A.B. – 196
Snyman, A.J. – 174
Snyman, C.C. – 169
Snyman, G. – 105
Snyman, H.A. – 180
Snyman, Kootjie – 42, 260
Soff, F. – 222
Sonnekus, A.S. – 240
South African National Museum of Military History, Johannesburg – 16, 20
Southey, A.M. – 173
Spandaw, H.J.A. – 193
Spanier, H. – 51
Spence, D.M. – 111
Spence, W.A. – 89
Spencer, C.W. – 121
Spies, A.T. – 147
Spies, S. – 169
Spioenkop, Battle of – 67-68, 134
Spragge, B.E. – 89
Spreckley, J.A. – 105
Springfontein Concentration Camp cemetery – 17, 21, 233, 271, 331

Spruyt, C.J. – 73, 144
Spruyt, D. – 128
Spruyt, J.A. – 100
Spurling, A.E. – 203
Squire, S.W. – 174
Staats Model School, Pretoria – 92, 248-249, 268, 348
Standerton British Garden of Remembrance – 97, 99, 113, 122, 142, 149, 150, 158
Standerton Concentration Camp – 227-228, 238
Stanley, H.F.W. – 82
Stanton, H.J.S. – 121
Stapylton (or Stapleton), B. – 138
Stark, A.C. – 49
Sterkstroom municipal cemetery – 60, 341
Sterkstroom Museum – 60
Steyn, M.T. – 25, 92, 103, 105, 110, 169, 178, 184, 185, 216, 273, 274, 275, 288, 291, 292, 293, 294, 307, 308, 314
Steyn, R.I. (née Fraser) – 308
Steyn, W. – 149
Steynberg, C. – 114, 167, 275
Steenkamp, Commandant – 208
Steenkamp, Cape rebel – 192
Steenkamp, P. – 111
Steevens, G. – 49
Steward, R.J. – 208
Stewart, A.D. – 113
Stewart, P. – 110
Stewart, R.C. – 113
Stewart, R.J. – 209
Stewart, S. – 200
St Alban's Anglican Cathedral, Pretoria – 84, 158, 317
St George's Cathedral, Cape Town – 26, 198, 346
St John's Anglican Church, Mahikeng – 45
St Ninian's Anglican Church, Heidelberg, Gauteng – 96, 156, 316
Stone, S. – 215
Stopford, H.S. – 58
Stormberg, Battle of – 59-60
Strong, C.P. – 178
Strydom, L. – 73
Strydom, P. – 73
Strydom, S.J. – 102
Stuart, D.B. – 110
Stubbs, A.K. – 66
Suffolk Hill (see Graskop)
Surprise Hill (see Vaalkop)
Sutherland, Northern Cape – 191, 206-207, 345, 350
Sutton, J. – 47
Swaffield, R. – 180
Swanston, A.W. – 115
Swart, J.P. – 151
Swart, M. (Mrs) – 228
Swart, P.D. – 104, 105
Swinburn, J.W. – 160
Tait, F.G. (Freddy) – 69
Talana, Battle of – 33, 34, 130, 132
Talana Museum, Dundee, KwaZulu-Natal – 33, 213, 334
Talbot, A.E.G.N. – 180
Talbot, F. – 63

Taylor, B. (Captain) – 154, 155
Tesbie, F. – 88
Tetlow, J. – 200
Thaba Nchu British Garden of Remembrance – 83, 108, 172, 175, 183, 332
Thackwray, G.C. – 195
Thackwray, S.K. – 195
Theobald, S.R. – 17, 195
Theron, D. (Danie) – 102, 108, 109
Theron, J. – 195, 198, 199
Theunissen, C.J. – 255
Theunissen, J.P.D. – 255
Thomas, A.H. – 112
Thomas, B.H. – 66
Thomas, O. (or C.O.) – 186
Thompson, E. – 180
Thornycroft, H. – 45
Thorold, F.T. – 150
Thurgood, L. – 148
Tiell, R.C.H. – 198
Tierney, J. – 181
Timlin, W.T. – 45
Tobin, J. – 184
Toerien, J.P. (Jepete) – 315
Toovey, G.D. – 177
Tothill, F.J. – 102
Townsend, J.W. – 181
Tranter, J. – 184
Trichard, S.P.E, (Fanie) – 125, 137, 150,
Trichardt, P. (Piet) – 98
Trollip, L.G. – 116
Troup, E.A. – 102
Tugela Heights – 13, 74, 75
Turffontein Concentration Camp, Johannesburg – 17, 225
Turnbull, J.T. – 171
Tweebosch (De Klipdrift), Battle of – 161
Tygerfontein – 103
Ueckermann, A. – 125
Uitenhage, Eastern Cape – 199, 200, 237, 342
Uitenhage Concentration Camp – 237
Underwood, H. – 82
Ungerer, J.D. – 177
Uniondale, Western Cape – 188-189, 195-196, 200, 245, 347
Utrecht British Garden of Remembrance – 338
Utrecht Museum – 28, 87
Uys, P.L. – 34
Vaalkop (Surprise Hill) – 50-51
Vaalkrans, Battle of – 68-69
Vahrmeijer, W.A. – 154
Vallentin, J.M. – 144
Van Aardt, C. – 186
Van Aardt, F. – 111
Van As, S. – 277
Van Biljon, J.A. – 198
Van Buuren, B.J. – 153
Van Coevorden, H. – 209
Vandeleur, C.F.S. – 146
Van den Berg, C.J. – 155
Van den Heever, G. – 123
Van den Heever, J. – 123
Van der Merwe, J. – 296

Index

Van der Merwe, J.J. – 204
Van der Merwe, N.F. – 58
Van der Merwe, P. – 195, 198
Van der Merwe, S.W. – 58
Van der Merwe, W. – 251
Van der Schyff, J.J. – 158
Van der Vijver, J.H. – 84
Van der Watt, G.J. – 204
Van der Westhuisen, J. – 88
Van Deventer, J.L. (Jaap) – 204, 206, 209, 311
Van Dijk, J. – 189
Van Emmenis, A. - 17, 256
Van Gogh, C.V. – 282
Van Heerden, a burgher – 152
Van Heerden, C.P. – 210
Van Heerden, H. – 257, 300
Van Heerden, P.W. – 259
Van Loggerenberg, N. – 93
Van Niekerk, A.B.W. – 140
Van Niekerk, G.J.S. – 214
Van Niekerk, J. – 105
Van Niekerk, P. – 198
Van Onselen, A. – 200
Van Reenen, Commandant – 175
Van Reenen, J.B.M. – 105
Van Rensburg, J. – 259
Van Rensburg, N.P.J.J. (Siener) – 313
Vanrhynsdorp – 187-188, 207, 245, 256, 348
Van Rooyen, C.T. – 167
Van Rooyen, I.S. – 60
Van Staden, C. – 155
Van Staden, G. – 158
Van Staden, R. – 155
Van Tonder, J.C. – 60
Van Vuuren, A. – 158
Van Warmelo, J. – 101
Van Welie, A. - 222
Van Wijk, J. – 28
Van Wouw, A. – 14, 16, 26, 222, 315
Van Zyl, F.E. – 121
Van Zyl, F.J. – 191
Van Zyl, J.J. – 296
Varker, T.B. – 96
Vassie, G. – 266
Veitch, Q.R. – 270
Venter, J.A. – 282
Venter, P.W. – 100
Ventersburg, Free State, town cemeteries – 107, 170, 255, 293
Ventersdorp, North West, municipal cemetery – 124, 141, 320
Vercuil, J.F – 152
Vereeniging Concentration Camp – 226
Vergette, H.W. – 198
Vermaas, C. – 200
Vernon, R.J. – 41
Verschoyle, E.G. – 83, 133
Vick, W. – 171
Victoria West, Northern Cape – 207, 246, 345

Viljoen, B. (Ben) – 99, 108, 118, 123, 124, 137, 145, 146, 157, 158
Viljoen, Hendrik – 77
Viljoen, Herklaas – 153, 154
Viljoen, J. – 100
Viljoen, Jan (Commandant) – 157
Viljoen, Piet – 163
Vilonel, S.G. – 254
Visser, F. – 154
Visser, P.J. – 169
Vlakfontein, Battle of – 141-142
Volksrust British Garden of Remembrance – 95, 324
Volksrust Concentration Camp – 228
Von Dalwig, A.F. – 313
Von Zeppelin, H. – 36
Voortrekker Cemetery, Pietermaritzburg – 235, 262
Vrede municipal cemetery – 177, 185, 332-333
Vredefort Road Concentration Camp – 17, 232-233
Vredefort municipal cemetery – 102, 333
Vryburg Concentration Camp – 230, 253
Vryburg municipal cemetery – 189, 200, 203, 320
Vryheid municipal cemetery – 120, 122, 140, 147, 157, 295, 310, 338
Wagner, F.W. – 54
Wagon Hill (see Platrand)
Wakkerstroom municipal cemetery – 128, 324
Walford, H.O. – 101
Walker, J.C.A. – 164
Walker, W.E. – 152
Walker, W.L.M. – 127
Wallace, F.G. – 169
Wallis, A. – 117
Wallis, A.F. – 76
Wallis, C.E.P. – 171
Walton, H. (or W.) – 192
Ward, W. – 66
Warn, H. – 171
Warren, C. – 88
Warren's Fort (see British South African Police Fort)
Wasserman, T.D. – 255
Waterval-Onder British war cemetery – 108, 324
Watson, A.J. – 64
Watson, G.J. – 89
Watson, J.C. – 143
Watson, J.Q. – 146
Wauchope, A. – 60, 61, 62, 132
Way, A.S. – 174
Weatherley, J. – 77
Webster, A.M. – 271
Webster, sculptor – 231
Weeber, A. – 206
Weideman, H.C. – 179

Welch, N.C. – 172
Wentink, D.E. – 25
Wentworth, W.M. – 174
Wessels, C.J. – 72
Wessels, H.N.W. – 53
Wessel, W. – 182
West, A.V. – 64
Westerhof, G.K. – 154
White, Colonel – 208
White, G. – 36, 37, 47, 48
White, J. – 194
White, R.J.L. – 111
Whitehead, R.E. – 205, 206
Whitfield, A.L. – 171
Wickham, D.E.P. – 171
Wigmore, E.A. – 126
Wilford, E.P. – 37
Wilkins, W. – 57
Wilmore (or Willmore), C.E. – 266
Williams, F.A. – 183
Williams, R.P. – 107
Williams, W., Colonel – 176
Williams, W.A.G. – 172
Williston, Northern Cape – 246, 345
Willow Grange (Brynbella) – 38-39
Willowmore, Eastern Cape – 191, 192, 193, 342
Wilmansrust – 142-143
Wilmot, T (or P.) – 161
Wilmot-Chetwode, E.E. – 89
Wilson, Lady Sarah – 43, 264
Wilson, R.B. – 100
Winburg cemeteries – 17, 107, 176, 333
Winburg Concentration Camp – 233-234
Winn, R.A. – 177
Witton, G.R. – 153, 154, 155
Wolfaardt, P.J. – 201, 257
Wolmarans, J.F. – 151
Wolseley, Western Cape – 245, 300
Wood, C.C. – 40
Woodburn, W.J. – 111
Woodgate, E. – 68
Woodhouse, R.W. – 156
Woods, E.A. – 165
Wookey, A.W.L. – 175
Woolrifge-Gordon, Colonel – 119
Wouters, B. – 154
Wych, W.H. – 206
Wylam, F.H. – 115
Yockney, T. – 124
Yeomanry Hill, Lindley – 89
Young, E.M. – 80
Young, F.W. – 105
Young, J.W. – 160
Yzerspruit, Battle of – 159-161
Zeerust burgher memorial – 40, 42, 100, 105, 138, 149, 283
Zwiegers, G. – 88